BECOMING A TEACHER OF YOUNG CHILDREN

BECOMING A

Margaret Z. Lay
SYRACUSE UNIVERSITY

John E. Dopyera
CUMBERLAND HILL ASSOCIATES

Illustrated by Martha Perske

D.C. HEATH AND COMPANY
Lexington, Massachusetts   Toronto

TEACHER OF YOUNG CHILDREN

Cover illustration by Martha Perske

International Standard Book Number: 0-669-99796-X

Library of Congress Catalog Card Number: 76-14635

TO
John's Daughters
    BARBARA, SUZANNE, AND CAROLINE

and Our Parents
    DARELL AND BERDENA LAY
    JOHN AND ELIZABETH DOPYERA

PREFACE

Our intent in this book is to provide students with organizing concepts and materials that will enable them to assume considerable responsibility for their own preparation for teaching. We suspect that unless the student is aware of and, to some extent, in command of the preparation process, our efforts as teacher educators to change behavior, attitudes, and skills will have at best only a temporary impact. It seems important that students have, from the beginning of their preparation, a comprehensive view of what is necessary to become a teacher. By proposing to the reader that the effective teacher has four attributes—*commitment, sensitivity, resourcefulness,* and *organizational abilities*—and by demonstrating how one can immediately begin to develop these qualities, we hope to make the teacher preparation task comprehensible enough so as not to be overwhelming.

Findings on child growth and development, educational methods, and prototypic programs have been related to the development of these four teaching attributes. By so doing, we feel there is greater likelihood that this information will be retained and used than if the same information were presented as independent topics with less explicitly drawn relationships to what a teacher actually does.

We generally concur with the adage that "teachers teach as they were taught, not as they were taught to teach." Therefore, throughout the text we attempt to model the principles that we value and that we wish to have emulated by teachers in their work with children. These include (1) active involvement in using, reacting to, or extending the information presented, (2) personalization of learning activities by responding to topics on the basis of one's own experiences, (3) assessment of the benefit of specific learning activities by comparing responses before and after the activity, (4) provision of options that allow learners to choose the most appropriate form of involvement for themselves and that allow instructors to better understand the points of view of individual students.

The materials in the text are equally appropriate for use in either a competency-based teacher education program or a more conventional course-based program. Assessment, either by the readers themselves or by others who wish to evaluate their progress or status, is therefore an integral part of the text. We believe that the development of measurable competence need not be equated with uniformity or depersonalization of instruction or evaluation. We seek to demonstrate that objectives that permit very individualistic and creative performance may be precisely assessed and thus may serve in meeting competence criteria, as well as the more convergent objectives typically equated with competency-based teacher education. Although the book is arranged to be used within a continuous course format, segments of it might also be used independently in programs with a different overall rationale and sequencing schema.

The organization of this book differs in several respects from typical early childhood textbooks and from the format of many teacher preparation programs. We believe that commitment and sensitivity are two qualities essential for effective and satisfying teaching and that they can be taught. Although most books and programs recognize that these are valuable qualities to possess, their actual development is often left to chance. We begin the book by challenging the students to assess their commitment to teaching and to consider what will be required of them. The next section presents the need for teachers to be sensitive to their students and gives specific activities for developing the quality of sensitivity.

We then concentrate on the development of teaching resourcefulness—the repertoire for providing instruction and other facilitative experiences—prior to familiarizing students with the program organizations within which such skills are applied. We believe that if we can first develop students' abilities to provide appropriate instruction for a given child or group of children under any circumstances (for example, in a living room or at a picnic), they will be in a far stronger position to apply those skills in a classroom situation.

The section on resourcefulness is organized around representative situations within which broad aspects of development can be fostered, rather than according to the traditional "methods" categories such as language arts, reading, science, mathematics. Although subject-matter classifications are convenient, we favor more activity-specific classifications for the initial development of a teaching repertoire. The resourcefulness section does not lack in methods for subject-matter teaching even though its organization is different, more comprehensive, and therefore more generalizable.

We believe that the qualities of commitment, sensitivity, and resourcefulness are critical to effective teaching within any of the many contrasting kinds of programs provided for young children. These qualities are equally valuable for teachers using different program models (such as behaviorist, developmental, or diagnostic-prescriptive). Naturally, we have our own view regarding the kind of program organization that will most benefit the greatest number of children. In the section on program organization, however, our preferred program alternatives are not promoted or presented in any greater detail than other programing options.

For greatest benefit to be derived from the text, it will be useful for students to exchange ideas with their peers—to compare others' responses and experiences with their own so that they may gain additional ideas and perspectives. In the Introduction we suggest ways in which readers might independently arrange these interchanges. In addition, each chapter of the book includes Response Sections, which, in our experience, have served well as the stimuli for both small-group interactions (four or five students) and subsequent sharing among a total class group.

Our own substantial experiences as teacher educators have made us acutely aware of many of the problems instructors face in preparing students for a teaching career. We hope that this text will help solve some of them.

Acknowledgments

Many friends and associates contributed to this book. A major contributor is Martha Perske. Her sensitive drawings serve to enhance and extend the messages of the text. We are also indebted to our friends and colleagues for their willingness to let us use photographs they supplied.

Grateful appreciation is expressed to those who read our manuscript in its early stages. We especially value the extensive reviews of Dr. Linda Lamme of the University of Florida and Dr. Martha Abbott of Georgia State University.

We express sincere appreciation as well to those who contributed indirectly through what we have learned from them and used in our writing. In this group are Lyman C. Hunt, Jr., Ira J. Gordon, and many others among our respective colleagues and students at Pennsylvania State University, Antioch College (especially the Antioch Experimental Elementary School), Florida Division of Mental Retardation, Connecticut State Department of Education, and Syracuse University. The Skytop "Responsive Care" group at Syracuse University deserves special mention—Betty Robinson, Norma Schlessinger, Phyllis Reicher, Bette Tryon, Barbara Clark, Dorothy Middleton, Dorothy Shave, Eileen Sorrentino, Beatrice Cook, Tom Miller, Margaret McDivitt, Lois Betsey, Jeff Hummel, Jane Strauss, Joyce Parker, Ursula Moeller, Joan Richert, David Zakem, Jefflyn Weed, Donna Kaufmann, and all our other responsive teacher/caregivers. In conclusion, we lovingly note the contribution of our families and close friends, who kept us at our writing tasks by their persistent inquiries as to when we would be finally "finished!"

CONTENTS

INTRODUCTION   xv

Section One / **Commitment**   3

1. THE NATURE OF THE COMMITMENT   5
   Overview
   Decision-making
   Some Background Information on Teaching
   Pros and Cons of Becoming a Teacher of Young Children
   Summary

2. DECIDING WHETHER TEACHING IS FOR YOU   31
   Overview
   Three Beginning Teachers
   Commitment: The Differing Experiences of Kay,
       June, and Nancy
   Assessing Your Own Commitment
   Comparing Your Orientation with That of Kay,
       June, and Nancy
   Considering the Tasks of Teaching
   Assessing Your Feelings About Your Experiences
       with Young Children
   Summary

Section Two / **Sensitivity**   55

3. WAYS OF VIEWING THE CHILD   57
   Overview
   The Effects of Professional Training on Sensitivity
   Contrasting Views of the Child: Three Major
       Orientations
   Some Basic Principles of Child Development
   Becoming a Skilled Observer of Children
   Alternative Formats for Recording Observations
   Making Observations of Individual Children
   Summary

4. INCREASING SENSITIVITY TO CHILDREN'S PHYSICAL
   CHARACTERISTICS AND MOTOR BEHAVIOR   85
   Overview

Motor Behavior and Physical Characteristics of
Infants and Toddlers
Motor Behavior and Physical Characteristics of
Children Ages Three Through Seven
Observing Motor Behavior and Physical Characteristics
of Individual Children
Transition into Resourcefulness Section
Summary

5. INCREASING SENSITIVITY TO CHILDREN'S AFFECTIVE
AND SOCIAL BEHAVIOR   117
Overview
Affective Development
Social Development
Observing Affective and Social Behavior in Individual
Children
Transition into Resourcefulness Section
Summary

6. INCREASING SENSITIVITY TO CHILDREN'S COGNITIVE
AND INTELLECTUAL BEHAVIOR   145
Overview
Cognitive and Intellectual Development Prior to
Age Three
Cognitive and Intellectual Development from Ages Three
through Seven
Observing Cognitive and Intellectual Behavior in
Individual Children
Transition into Resourcefulness Section
Summary

7. ASSESSMENTS OF INDIVIDUAL CHILDREN   185
Overview
Integrating and Summarizing Observations
Obtaining Information from Other Sources
Planning for the Whole Child
Summary

Section Three / **Resourcefulness**   215

8. RESOURCEFULNESS WITH MANIPULATIVE MATERIALS   217
Overview
Your Resourcefulness and Children's Development
Further Extensions and Applications
Summary

9. RESOURCEFULNESS WITH ANIMALS   245
Overview

Your Resourcefulness and Children's Development
Further Extensions and Applications
Summary

10. RESOURCEFULNESS WITH CHILDREN'S LITERATURE   273
Overview
Your Resourcefulness and Children's Development
Further Extensions and Applications
Summary

11. RESOURCEFULNESS WITH CHILDREN'S PRETEND PLAY   299
Overview
Your Resourcefulness and Children's Development
Further Extensions and Applications
Summary

12. RESOURCEFULNESS IN HELPING CHILDREN SHARE
IDEAS AND EXPERIENCES   319
Overview
Your Resourcefulness and Children's Development
Further Extensions and Applications
Summary

13. GUIDELINES FOR RESOURCEFUL TEACHING   343
Overview
Mental Sets to Enhance Your Resourcefulness
Applications of Resourcefulness to Prepared Curricula
    and Instructional Packages
Applications of Resourcefulness in Varied Settings
Summary

Section Four / **Organizational Abilities**   361

14. CONTRASTING PROGRAM MODELS   363
Overview
The Environmentalist View of Programs
The Maturationist View of Programs
The Interactionist View of Programs
The Prevalence of Eclectic Practice
Summary

15. ANALYSIS OF PROGRAM DECISIONS   401
Overview
Decisions about the Organization of Time
Decisions about Facilities: Space, Equipment,
    and Materials
Decisions about Ground Rules

Decisions about Relationships with Families
Summary

16. YOUR OWN PROGRAM DECISIONS   431
Overview
Describing a Setting and Context for Teaching
Making Your Program Decisions
Summary

EPILOGUE   453

APPENDIXES
    1. Outline for Portfolio   460
    2. Resource Organizations   461
    3. Periodicals   463
    4. Publishers' Addresses   464
    5. Equipment and Materials   466
    6. Sources for Equipment and Materials   469
    7. Guidelines for Job-Hunting   470

REFERENCES   473

GLOSSARY   479

INDEX   487

INTRODUCTION

The teaching of children from ages three through seven, the age span considered in this book, is challenging and sometimes difficult; it is also almost invariably rewarding for those who carefully select and prepare for this career. Whether the teacher of young children works with a kindergarten or primary class in a public school or in a nursery-school or child-care setting, the responsibilities are the same—to provide circumstances that support the development and learning of each child. The central objective of *Becoming a Teacher of Young Children* is to help you understand what you must do if you wish to prepare for this important professional role.

Personal and active involvement

This is a book that, if taken seriously at all, will put demands on you. We fully expect you to become personally and actively involved in reacting to these materials. You will constantly be asked to reflect, research, list, try out, choose, examine, and reexamine. Why? Because we know that only through your own conscious and persistent efforts can you become an effective teacher of young children. We think we can help you by guiding your efforts, but the prime focus of our writing will be on you, and only secondarily on education and the teaching profession.

This book is organized around the four qualities we believe you will need if you are to become a competent teacher of young children. These qualities are *commitment, sensitivity, resourcefulness,* and *organizational ability.* A major section of the text is devoted to each.

Commitment

To make a *commitment* to being a teacher is to personally take on the responsibility for developing your abilities to help children grow and learn. From commitment will come the motivation and the energy to work hard at becoming more sensitive, more resourceful, and better organized, all of which are essential aspects of effective teaching. We believe that your own commitment to teaching can only be derived from realistic knowledge of yourself, of your own proclivities and needs, as well as realistic knowledge of what you will be encountering in the teaching role. Section One is intended to help you gain these perspectives.

Sensitivity

Sensitivity to children's development and behavior is quite obviously a necessary quality in an effective teacher. Only if a teacher can accurately assess what children feel, need, can do, and are learning to do is there any assurance that what is provided in the program will be appropriate for them. The function of Section Two is (1) to diagnose your existing ability to observe and diagnose children's feelings, concerns, interests, abilities, and strivings; (2) to provide you with greater awareness of how your own unresolved needs and interests may unknowingly influence and distort your current views of children; (3) to increase your sensitivity to children by increasing your awareness of how various theorists and researchers view child behavior and development; (4) to assist you in summarizing and integrating the observations you make of individual children; (5) to begin the difficult process of translating sensitivity into appropriate learning experiences for children. The constant interplay between sensitivity and teaching resourcefulness will be emphasized in both Section Two and Section Three.

Resourcefulness

In Section Three you will be helped to appraise and strengthen your repertoire for teaching *resourcefulness*. To better understand the concept of **repertoire,** which is central to our thinking about teaching, consider the analogy of cooking. Given some basic ingredients, such as salt, flour, soy sauce, onions, potatoes, carrots, lemon, honey, butter, eggs, apples, and ground beef, what is your cooking repertoire? How many different dishes could you prepare? What would you be able to provide for a diabetic's lunch? For an infant? Whether your current repertoire for cooking is broad or narrow, there is no doubt that you could extend that repertoire through conscious effort should you care to do so.

To complete the analogy, consider your own resourcefulness in regard to teaching. Given a set of tin cans, some sand, some water, and a set of small plastic cars of various shapes and colors, what is your teaching repertoire? What learning experiences could you provide for a group of children with these materials? For an angry nonverbal child? For a child who is reading a bit and is just learning to spell? For a child who has only recently become interested in learning ordinal position names—first, second, third, etc.? For a child who lacks self-confidence? How might you use these materials to accomplish different goals for any one child, such as learning the concepts of roundness or roughness or trying something unfamiliar? An appropriate provision for children's diverse needs and abilities is dependent upon the teacher's resourcefulness repertoire.

It is our hypothesis that the teacher who develops a repertoire for providing varied instruction and other facilitative experiences while using commonly available materials such as sand and water will be equipped to provide for children's learning regardless of circumstances. Therefore, in the section on resourcefulness, we first help you to assess your existing teaching repertoire using common materials and typically recurring social situations, and we then assist you in expanding your repertoire. We expect that you will find as you go along that you are, indeed, becoming more resourceful. The need for a broad and varied repertoire, that allows you to provide for quite diverse individual needs is constantly demonstrated and emphasized throughout the section.

Organizational ability

Section Four focuses on your *organizational ability*. Having responsibility for a classroom is sometimes likened to running a three-ring circus. Just as there are probably many ways to run a circus, so there are many alternatives for organizing programs for young children. There are many different ways of organizing time schedules, arranging classroom space and usage patterns within that space, and establishing and maintaining ground rules for children's behavior. We describe the organizational features of various well-known types of early childhood programs and show how these arrangements are related to the particular programer's philosophy and objectives. What is most important for you, however, will be learning to select, implement, and evaluate your own organizational plan. The importance of explicitness in describing your organizational plan and its rationale, especially as your plan contrasts with other alternatives, is emphasized in this section.

The following three procedures are recommended as a means of maximizing the benefits you derive from the text.

Discussion/action group 1. Identify other persons who are interested in participating with you in a **discussion/action group.** You will find it useful to exchange impressions of the text materials and to share your individual experiences and outside reading.

At several points in each chapter, you will find Response Sections, which invite you to consider a particular point or engage in further activity related to the preceding material. You will find this much more meaningful if you and others in your discussion/action group mutually share and explore your efforts and responses.

Field experience with children 2. Make arrangements to have experiences with young children in which you both observe and interact with them. If you are currently enrolled in a college teacher-preparation program, you may have such **field experiences** arranged for you. If not, you should make your own arrangements for contact with children who are three through seven years of age. The following are possible ways to obtain this kind of experience:

a. Volunteer your services to assist teachers in nursery school, day care, kindergarten, or primary grades. Keep your commitments within a range, so that you can be dependable given other commitments.
b. Arrange to baby-sit for children of varying ages.
c. Volunteer to assist the persons responsible for church school classes.
d. Volunteer to assist with the child-care arrangements often provided by organizations during special events.
e. Volunteer to assist the librarians in the children's section in a public library.

Can you think of others? Perhaps one of the first tasks for your discussion/action group might be to assist each other in finding ways to increase your fieldwork contacts.

Portfolio 3. Develop a **portfolio** of materials related to your professional growth. Such a portfolio could contain your own writings done in response to suggestions in the text; collections of related news clippings, articles, and references; activity suggestions; directories of resources; and catalogs. By developing a usable system for collecting, storing, and retrieving relevant materials, you will find that many of your professional efforts will be facilitated. For suggestions in classifying these materials, turn to Appendix 1.

The process of becoming a competent teacher is continuous and will not be completed in the course of using this textbook or in the course of the current teacher-preparation program in which you might be enrolled. Nor will it be completed when you have "graduated" and are employed as a teacher. You will see major progress made if you are willing to commit yourself and to follow the guidelines offered in this text. These learning experiences will serve as an excellent practical base for your continued professional development. As authors, we have a vested interest in helping you become a successful and effective teacher, but it is really *your* task.

BECOMING
A TEACHER OF
YOUNG
CHILDREN

SECTION
ONE
COMMITMENT

To have a commitment to teaching young children means to be thoroughly and realistically convinced that it is something with which you wish to be personally identified. Most of us make only a limited number of firm commitments in our lives—perhaps to a person we care deeply about, to a religious conviction, to a way of life, to a political ideology, to a benevolent cause. One's profession, especially if it is to be teaching, warrants a commitment of nearly this magnitude. This section is intended to help you consider whether you wish to be thus identified with and committed to an early childhood teaching career. It further helps you assess the extent to which you have or are willing to develop such a commitment and the implications for you should you try to become a teacher of young children without sufficient commitment.

Chapter 1 provides a range of information on the teaching profession. We first discuss the profound effects of occupational choice on the potential for making an impact with one's life. The crucial nature of this decision and the need to view it as one of the most significant you will ever make are emphasized. General descriptions of various aspects of teaching young children follow, such as certification requirements, teaching duties, types of positions, and the job market. We also attempt to convey in some detail the hassles and rewards that are encountered in this occupation. The total thrust of this chapter is to provide more realistic perspectives than you may currently hold on what is involved in becoming a teacher of young children.

Chapter 2 focuses on providing a further sense of reality of what it might mean to you personally to become a teacher. Three case studies of beginning teachers provide some insights into the characteristics that lead to success versus those that lead to frustration, disappointment, and failure. Differing levels of commitment, sensitivity, resourcefulness, and organizational skill are illustrated in these case studies and in the comparisons that follow. A variety of questions and tasks requiring your personal response are included to provide insights about the extent to which your own interest in teaching is based on a realistic appraisal or is distorted by wishful thinking.

It is not the intent of this section to convince you to become a teacher of young children. In fact, after learning what such a career entails and after examining your own attitudes more closely, you may feel that it is not right for you. However, if your motivation remains high after reading and deliberating on the contents of this section, we anticipate that you will have a deeper, firmer, and more realistic commitment than you currently hold. This commitment should then serve as a motivating and sustaining force as you continue with your preparation for teaching.

CHAPTER 1
The Nature
of the
Commitment

Overview

Decision-making

Some Background Information on Teaching
THE FIELD
CERTIFICATION
COMPARISONS WITH OTHER PROFESSIONS
THE CHANGED MILIEU
PREKINDERGARTEN, KINDERGARTEN, AND PRIMARY LEVELS
OTHER FEATURES OF TEACHING AS A PROFESSION

Pros and Cons of Becoming a Teacher of Young Children
THE NEED VERSUS THE DIFFICULTY
CREATIVE OPPORTUNITY VERSUS CRITICISM
CLASSROOM FREEDOM VERSUS SITUATIONAL RESTRAINT
SHARING WITH CHILDREN VERSUS ADULT ISOLATION
SELF-DEVELOPMENT

Summary

PREASSESSMENT

When you have completed this chapter you should be able to describe and compare the following:

1. *implications of occupational choice for your life.*
2. *prekindergarten, kindergarten, and primary teaching.*
3. *roles of early childhood professionals as they relate to other professional roles.*
4. *early childhood education prior to the 1960s, during the 1960s, and at present.*
5. *alternative approaches to preparing for teaching and becoming certified.*
6. *advantages and disadvantages of teaching young children generally, and for you personally.*

Before beginning to read this chapter, take enough time to write what you already know about each of the above topics.

Save what you write for rereading, comparison, and elaboration after you have studied and discussed these materials.

Overview

This chapter has three objectives. The first is to emphasize the importance of decision-making in your life, especially in the critical choice of profession. The second is to provide background on the teaching field, certification, the current teaching milieu, the age-level divisions within early education, and other similar information. The third is to discuss the advantages and disadvantages of becoming a teacher of young children.

Decision-making

The evolving conception of humankind

Each of our lives is an expression about what human beings are and can become. What you personally choose to be and do as you live your daily life is the means by which you make a contribution to the evolving conception of humankind. You are constantly engaged in making decisions about how you will spend your time, with whom, and about how you will describe what you have done. In so doing, you have already made a strong personal commentary about what human life is and can be.

Most of the choices you have made, however, probably have not seemed like choices. You probably have done what others around you were doing without much thought about its ultimate value. Even though we constantly face choices, we seldom ponder alternatives apart from what is expected of us. All of us typically make our choices from such a narrow range of alternatives that there seems to be little reason to weigh one against another. Perhaps the human condition would improve dramatically if our daily decision-making became considered rather than habitual and unthinking.

Certainly there is reason for strong deliberation before deciding on something as crucial as an occupational commitment. Some of the more important statements that you make with your life will be related to your chosen work. Many of the further choices available to you will be, to a large extent, dependent upon restrictions and expectations imposed by the particular kind of work you do.

RESPONSE SECTION

We have taken the position that you express your values and beliefs concerning humankind and human capabilities by the daily decisions you make, especially in your choice of occupation. Do you agree with this? Whether you agree or not, keep the idea in mind as you think about the following:

1. Why are you considering teaching as a career? Try to make a list of your reasons. Consider whether the personal rewards that you anticipate from teaching young children reflect what you believe to be your values. What are these values?
2. What other occupations have you considered? Which of your values would most likely be fulfilled in teaching and which in those other occupations?
3. Try to visualize the way you would like your life to be ten years from now; twenty years from now. What is the likelihood that becoming a teacher will allow you to have the kind of life you want to have?
4. How do you think you will change and develop as you become a teacher of young children? Will these changes be in accord with your life goals?

In your choice of occupation you will be making a major decision about what your future life will be. What kind of statement can you make with your life if you become a teacher of young children? Are the possibilities within teaching supportive of your life goals and your idealized self-image? Will your hours and days as a teacher allow you to be the kind of person you want to be?

The commitment to become a teacher should be considered carefully. Teaching is not something in which one can be lightly engaged. Perhaps you could be a secretary or a pilot or an insurance salesperson and make only partial use of your abilities and interests while on the job, reserving major *A total personal* portions of yourself for nonwork pursuits. This is far less possible in teach-
commitment ing. Teaching requires much more of a total personal commitment, of which you will become increasingly aware as you read through the two chapters in this section.

Some Background Information on Teaching

This is a rather selective presentation of background information but is in keeping with our goal of focusing on *how you can become a teacher* rather than talking *about* education. If, after reading what is presented, you feel the need for more basic information of this type, be sure to consult the Additional Reading section at the end of the chapter.

THE FIELD

The education of our nation's children requires a vast number of professionals. Nearly 1.2 million persons are employed in teaching children from kindergarten through sixth grade. Large numbers of others work in programs providing care and educational experiences for those younger than school age. According to analyses of data collected in 1972, over 4.5 million children, ages three through five (45 percent of the total population in this age span), were enrolled in some type of program—prekindergarten, kindergarten, or first grade (Standard Education Almanac, 1975). The proportion of children in programs prior to first grade has increased dramatically within the last decade with, of course, concomitant increases in the number of early educators employed.

A field for both men Elementary teaching continues to be the largest field of professional em-
and women ployment for women, and the number of men in this field has been rapidly increasing in recent years as well. Teaching the young is becoming a viable occupational choice for both men and women.

CERTIFICATION

There have been continuing efforts by state governments to set formal teacher **certification** requirements to ensure adequate educational experiences for the young. All states require that teachers in public schools be certified by their departments of education as being qualified to teach. Many

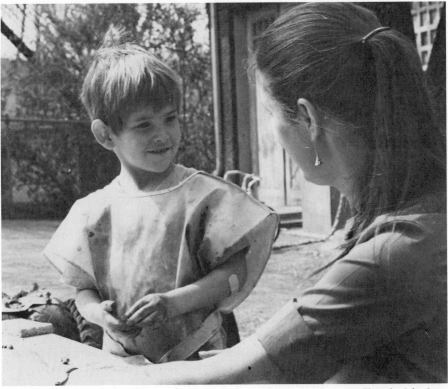

Photo by John James.

states require certification for teachers in private and parochial schools as well. Program administrators increasingly view certification as desirable for prekindergarten teaching.

Certification through state-approved bachelor degree programs

Certification in recent years has typically been issued only to those persons having at least four years of approved college preparation. The four-year programs have consisted of approximately one-fourth time in professional study, with the remaining time in liberal arts. Some study of human behavior and learning is usually required. Twelve states require that teachers complete a fifth year of study or a master's degree within a certain number of years after receiving an initial provisional certificate, and some individual school systems have even more stringent certification requirements than those set by the state. In nearly all states certification is issued by the State Department of Education on the basis of transcripts of credits and recommendations from approved colleges and universities. Certification is issued to applicants from other states only if prescribed programs have been completed at accredited colleges and if the coursework meets the specific requirements of that state.

In addition to the many four-year college programs that prepare students to meet state certification requirements, there are increasing numbers of two-year programs which also prepare personnel for work in early education.

Noncertification two-year associate degree programs

While graduates of these two-year programs do receive an **associate degree** from their institution, indicating specialized training, they are not certified by the state as qualified for professional responsibility in public schools. Persons with associate degrees, however, do take very responsible roles in many nonpublic nursery and child-care settings and work as paraprofessionals in public school programs. Often they work under the supervision of others who hold bachelor degrees and/or state certification.

The competency-based CDA credential

A new category of credentialed professionals in the field of early childhood education/child development are called **Child Development Associates,** or CDAs. These are persons who have been assessed and found competent to assume responsibilities for three- to five-year-olds in a group setting and to work with parents. Some teaching experience and formal or informal education or training is required. Participation in workshops, seminars, and in-service programs may be considered sufficient training, and completion of a college program is not required.

COMPETENCY-BASED TEACHER EDUCATION

In a statement designed to stimulate debate about competency-based teacher education (CBTE), John G. G. Merrow II (1975) reviewed current efforts and raised concerns (such as the lack of evidence that the competencies that are becoming the focus of the CBTE programs will actually make differences for children in classrooms). His commentary includes the following descriptions.

> If it works, CBTE could mean that future teachers will be told what teaching skills (competencies) they will need to be successful in the classroom, and they will study until they can demonstrate the required competencies. (p. 2)
>
> Defining CBTE is not hard; what is difficult is determining who is doing what to whom, and whether the activity resembles that described in the definitions, one of which begins as follows: "A revolution is shaking teacher education in America—not a gradual, comfortable, deliberate development, but drastic upheaval and sudden climactic change."
>
> After the rhetoric, the definition that emerges boils down to:
> 1. "Competencies" mean knowledge, skills and behaviors that the teacher (or would-be teacher) must have.
> 2. Competencies are based on what teachers actually do in the classroom.
> 3. Criteria for determining competence are explicit and public.
> 4. Performance is the major source of evidence of competence.
> 5. Rate of progress through the program is determined by demonstrated competency (not time, semester hours or some other standard). (pp. 13–14)

The potential CDA must take primary responsibility for the day-to-day activities of a group of children. A person desiring to be a master teacher, a center director, or a curriculum specialist, however, needs competencies beyond those considered sufficient for a CDA.

The U.S. Government's Office of Child Development (OCD) funded the CDA Consortium, composed of forty-two organizations whose members are directly involved in some phase of early education or child development. This consortium developed the performance-based system for assessing competency and a system for awarding the CDA credentials. The first few credentials were awarded in July 1975, the first time teaching credentials had been awarded under a federally sponsored plan rather than through state certification programs.

The move to competency-based state certification

At the present time many states are also moving rapidly away from requirements for any specific numbers or types of courses and perhaps ultimately away from requiring a college degree for teaching certification. Instead, a candidate would be required to demonstrate competence in particular specified areas via examination and/or actual classroom performance. The criteria for judging competence are currently under development by state education departments, colleges and universities, and professional teacher organizations.

COMPARISONS WITH OTHER PROFESSIONS

Teaching, like medicine and law, has been classified as a profession, since entry into the field requires professional training, state licensing, and even differential training for different roles and levels. As in other professional fields, professional organizations provide members with information, monitor the quality of programs, lobby for legislation, and attempt in various ways to advance the profession's goals and status. A list of these organizations is included in the appendixes.

A teacher's clients are seen in groups

However, in some significant respects, teaching is simply not comparable to other professions. There is, for example, a difference between clients. In the typical situation, the clients of the early educator are small children who are seldom seen individually in the normal course of work. The task of the teacher is to work with groups, not individuals. All efforts to **individualize** instruction for any single child must be done while simultaneously maintaining attention to group concerns. This is quite a different matter than seeing one client at a time, as is typical in other professions.

Another interesting difference is the lack of long-term continuity with clients. A group of children and their parents are typically served intensively for a year or two and then are not contacted again as the group moves on to other teachers.

The parents, who might well be considered the real clients, do not typically initiate contact with a particular teacher to perform services for their child. They often have little opportunity to determine who will teach their children. Moreover, parents are usually unavailable for consultation while the teacher is performing professional functions, as opposed to most other professionals. The responsibility of the teacher for children covers a much broader scope than that of other professionals. Even though there is often little opportunity for direct parental contact, the teacher is legally expected to serve *in loco parentis*, that is, to stand in the relation of parent and guardian to pupils, to regulate their conduct while under school supervision, and to take measures necessary for the pupils' safety, health, and welfare.

Responsibility to the community

The teacher has societal responsibilities that may sometimes influence his or her actions more heavily than the needs of the particular clients being served. What is done in a classroom is of significance to the broader community, and consequently the demands upon the teacher from community representatives (such as the board of education, administrators, and pressure groups) are sometimes far more influential than the needs and wishes of the children's parents, who are the direct recipients. This responsibility to the public appears to influence the performance of teachers, especially public school teachers, far more than it does the performance of social workers, nurses, doctors, psychologists, and other professionals.

THE CHANGED MILIEU

Prior to the sixties

Within the past fifteen years there have been marked changes in the field of early childhood education. Before the 1960s, programs for preschool children were uncommon and consisted primarily of nursery schools for upper-middle-class and university families. While there were some child-care centers, many dating back to depression and wartime days, these focused primarily on attending to children's physical needs and safety and were not considered to be of educational significance. Trained teachers in those years did not typically seek employment in such centers. Kindergarten programs were typically available only in urban areas. Although there were marked differences in the quality and quantity of materials and equipment available in classrooms across the country, the methods employed in teaching in the primary grades did not vary to any significant degree. Prior to the 1960s, education for young children was much more homogeneous than at present.

A turning point

The **Head Start** legislation of 1965 was inaugurated within a milieu of professional interest and societal concern. The need was obvious, since many children from low-income families had been shown repeatedly to lack school readiness and to lag in academic achievement after admission. It was hoped that an even start could be provided through special federally funded programs that would break down the "vicious cycles" of poverty.

The extensive efforts in the summer of 1965 reached over one-half million children with comprehensive medical, social, nutritional, and educational programs. Americans in all walks of life consequently became aware that handicaps resulting from either meager or different home experiences leave many children ill prepared for school. The Head Start programs intended to prepare youngsters for successful participation in the American way of life, for which school entrance traditionally marked the critical beginning point.

COMPENSATORY EDUCATION

In the 1960s there emerged a rationale for **compensatory education**, efforts to provide in organized programs the experiences that "disadvantaged" children were thought not to receive in their homes and neighborhoods. Benjamin Bloom's (1964) study of environmental effects suggested that half of the variation seen in later intelligence is evident already by age four, and that loss of development in one period could not be fully recovered in another period. J. McVicker Hunt's (1961) analysis of research and theory also concluded that deficits in functioning follow early lacks and, conversely, that benefits can be expected from early enrichment. Several experimental **intervention** projects seemed to lend credence to these views, since they reported that special programs for young "disadvantaged" children produced gains on cognitive measures. Theory and research converged to support the view of early education as compensation for environmental deficiencies.

With the initiation of Head Start and the development of other programs designed to provide low-income children with early educational opportunities, the public became aware of the general value of early education, and programs for middle- and upper-income children also became more popular. Although at midcentury kindergarten programs were not common, by 1975 fourteen states had mandated kindergarten programs and forty-six had provided some form of aid, mostly through state education funds (Education Commission of the States, 1975).

The number of opportunities for work in early childhood education grew rapidly throughout this period. In many parts of the country, the teaching of young children emerged as a professional specialization distinct from elementary teaching. However, even now there is little consensus from one location to another about such basic issues as the span of years that "early childhood" encompasses. In some states this specialization refers to preschools only; in others it includes preschools and kindergarten; in still others, the span for which the early childhood teacher is trained includes the primary grades, at least through second grade.

The current diversity in early childhood

In some university training programs, early childhood education includes preparation for work with infants and toddlers either directly or through their parents. The women's movement, combined with a new concern for early intellectual development, has resulted in growing interest in quality child-care programs in which professional teachers, as well as *paraprofessionals,* provide sound programing for children at early ages. In some areas, the teaching roles in child-care programs still do not require professional training, while in others the trend is toward requiring that most personnel have degree qualifications. At present, being a teacher of young children can mean quite different things, depending upon the setting.

This acceleration of activity in the early childhood education field has resulted in a renewed interest in finding answers to age-old questions of how

TYPES OF SPONSORSHIP FOR EARLY CHILDHOOD PROGRAMS

Private nonprofit	Church groups, Community Chest, etc.
Private profit	Owner-run, franchises
Private (service to personnel)	Universities, business firms, hospitals, industries, etc.
Pubic (federal)	Head Start, parent-child centers, Title IV-A of Social Security Act
Public (state)	California early childhood programs, New York State prekindergarten programs
Public (local)	Public school programs
Parent cooperatives and play centers	Neighborhood or community groups governed and maintained by the parents of children being served

Note: A given program can have multiple sources of funding and/or sponsorship.

A proliferation of different programs children should be educated and reared. Professionals with markedly different views have put forth their ideas, and quite different programs have resulted from these views. These programs vary in many dimensions, including goal orientation and degree of structure. Among the differing goal orientations are emphases on academic, cognitive, or socio-emotional development. Differences in the degree of **structure** refers to the amount of sequencing and organization of children's activities and the predictability or prescheduling of children's behavior. Programs such as Behavior Analysis, DISTAR, Montessori, and Cognitive Curriculum present wide variation in these and other dimensions (see Section Four).

TYPES OF PROGRAM SETTINGS

Nursery school Program provided for children ages two, three, and/or four; typically a half-day program (two to three hours); the term "nursery school" traditionally refers to private or parent cooperative programs rather than to publicly supported programs

Prekindergarten Program generally restricted to children under age five for the year or years prior to entrance to kindergarten

Kindergarten Program generally restricted to children under age six for the year prior to entrance into first grade

Preprimary Program generally restricted to children under the age of six or seven for the years prior to entrance into first grade; may encompass what is typically identified as prekindergarten and kindergarten

Primary   Program generally restricted to children ages six, seven, and eight in grades (or equivalents thereof) one, two, and three

Child-care centers (or day-care centers)   Programs of four or more hours in duration; may accommodate varying ages, from infants through elementary school age (after-school care)

Family day care   Child care provided for a small group of children in the home of the caregiver who may or may not have had training for the role; may accommodate varying ages, from infants through school age (after-school care)

Head Start   Program (under federal support) for "disadvantaged" children prior to entrance in regular public school programs; may be half-day or full day; involves comprehensive services including nutritional and medical care; anticipates parental involvement

Parent-child center   Programs (under federal support) providing health, education, and social services for impoverished parents and their infants and toddlers

Back yard groups/mobile preschools   Programs for small groups of neighborhood prekindergarten children conducted in the home of one of the children; may be coordinated by a professional and implemented by paraprofessionals and/or mothers

Home programs (home visitor)   Programs for the direct instruction of a child and/or the parent (to benefit the child); professional (classroom teacher or other) or trained paraprofessional makes regular home visits; implemented at range of ages, either in connection with or separately from an in-class program

Hospital schools   Program within hospital settings; may involve group attendance in a "classroom" or "playroom" and/or one-to-one teaching of children in their quarters

Laboratory/demonstration schools   Programs within training and/or research settings such as universities, colleges, and institutes

---

Federally sponsored programs such as **Project Follow Through** have attempted to help Head Start "graduates" sustain any advantage gained by their preschool experience. As the new program models developed for Head Start and Follow Through have become generally known, some of their features have been adopted by individual teachers and by entire education centers and systems, although often in modified form. As a result, there is now far greater diversity in the field than in years past, both at the prekindergarten and primary levels.

With the increased activity in early education, there has been a corresponding expansion in the variety of roles an early educator can consider filling, such as teacher, head teacher, program director, curriculum specialist, parent educator, program evaluator, or training specialist.

Teacher   Person having primary program responsibility for a group of children; may share responsibility with other teachers

Head teacher   Person who, in addition to having primary program responsibility for a group of children, is responsible for the supervision of other workers, professional and/or paraprofessional aides, and volunteers

Paraprofessional aide   Person serving as a teacher who lacks professional certification or degree and who is supervised by professional personnel

Cooks, Drivers, Custodians, Secretaries   Persons who serve specialized role in offering services, and whose frequent interactions with children have educational implications

Program director   Administrator of a program, which may consist of several class groups or only one group; responsible for staff supervision, purchasing, budgeting, hiring, public relations, etc.

Curriculum specialist   Professional educator who plans and develops materials and activities appropriate for specific educational goals

Parent educational specialist   Person who has responsibility for developing and/or conducting programs for parents that will benefit the children (including home visitations to train parents to work with their own children)

Program evaluator   Educator or psychologist with advanced training in measurement whose task it is to determine whether a program is meeting specified objectives

Training specialist   Person responsible for developing or improving skills of personnel working with children; may involve inservice training or specialized training programs in colleges, institutes, etc.

Note: A single individual often fills multiple roles.

In the past, persons entering teaching sometimes did so because of the abundance of jobs throughout the country and, for women, the ease of job reentry after child rearing. However, the teaching job market has changed markedly and the availability of jobs cannot be assumed. Despite the increased number of preschool programs, there is currently an oversupply of teachers relative to the number of jobs, and this condition is likely to continue.

Enrollments in the 1980s are expected to fall below the 1970 levels due to declining birth rates. The number of persons qualified for teaching may far exceed the number of openings if patterns of entry and reentry to the profession continue in line with past trends. Even now, fully qualified professional teachers in some parts of the country are forced to take lower-paying jobs as paraprofessional aides if they wish to be involved in teaching.

As a result, those who are now preparing to teach must increasingly assume a very different orientation than did their predecessors. It is now essential that the decision to become a teacher be based on far more than a desire for job security.

Competence is essential in today's job market

If you wish to become a teacher, you must be prepared to demonstrate your level of teaching mastery, and you will need to take very seriously the preparation for that task. Where yesterday's graduates only had to know "about" teaching and to have had some experience as an apprentice or "student" teacher, you must now try to ready yourself as a competent teacher. You will find it impossible to reach this higher level of readiness without a considerable commitment and expenditure of time and energy. With insufficient knowledge, it is impossible to make a commitment of any depth, so it is important for you at this point to gain as complete and realistic a picture of teaching as possible.

PREKINDERGARTEN, KINDERGARTEN, AND PRIMARY LEVELS

While the jobs of teaching prekindergarten in either a nursery school or a child care setting and teaching kindergarten or a primary grade have much in common, there are some marked differences.

The prekindergarten teacher

Prekindergarten teachers usually work in conjunction with another adult in teaching the same group of three- and four-year-old children, with typically fifteen to twenty children per group. Often the relationship between these two adults is hierarchical, with one taking the professional position as

Photo by permission of Bernice Wright Cooperative Nursery School.

head teacher and the other taking the "paraprofessional" role typically designated as teacher **aide.** Prekindergarten teaching positions are more likely to be part-time than are kindergarten and primary teaching positions. Prekindergarten teachers employed in private settings tend to receive lower pay and fewer benefits than those employed in public institutions. Increasingly, during the 1960s, prekindergarten education, especially for those children considered to be **disadvantaged,** has been supported by federal, state, and local funding. As public awareness of the value of early education has heightened, the status, salaries, and benefits for teachers at this age level have improved and, in a few instances, now match those of kindergarten and elementary teachers.

Programs for prekindergarten children vary greatly. The daily schedule of most programs falls within either the very brief nursery school span of two and one-half to three hours for five days or fewer per week, or within the extended day (eight hours or more) of child-care programs.

The kindergarten teacher

In most public schools the **kindergarten** teacher has sole responsibility for two groups of five- to six-year-old children. The groups typically range in size from fifteen to thirty-five, one set attending in the morning and another in the afternoon. Some school systems have recently arranged a full-day schedule for kindergarten children identical to the schedule of children in elementary school.

The primary teacher

The **primary** teacher, like the kindergarten teacher, typically has sole responsibility for children in a self-contained classroom. While "special" teachers of art, music, and health may be available to teach or assist at certain time periods during the week, the availability of aides in the kindergarten or primary classroom is not common. The class size in the primary grades typically ranges from fifteen to thirty-five or more, with an average of around twenty-five.

The primary classroom typically includes children at a single grade level—first, second, or third grade. In recent years, **multiage** and **nongraded** classrooms have become more common. In multiage classes children at ages six, seven, or eight (or some other age combination) may be placed together without regard to their academic progress, with the expectation that instruction be geared to their diverse levels via individualized instruction or **flexible grouping.** In some nongraded classrooms, however, children of mixed ages may be placed together on the basis of their similar **achievement levels** in academic work. In other situations, primary-age children may have a departmentalized program in which they are taught by different teachers for each of several academic areas. In what is called **flexible scheduling,** a large group of children may receive instruction individually, in small subgroups, or as a total group at different points in the program day, from any one or several of a team of teachers jointly responsible for their progress.

OTHER FEATURES OF TEACHING AS A PROFESSION

Long hours are typical

All teachers, whether prekindergarten, kindergarten, or primary, spend many hours each week in professional effort beyond their direct work with children. Additional time is spent planning, preparing materials, maintaining the classroom setting, keeping records, preparing reports, and attending staff and other professional meetings. The mean number of hours per week spent on duties by elementary teachers was reported to be forty-six in one assessment of teacher status (NEA, 1972).

While the teacher's workday is intense and not nearly as short as the in-class time would seem to suggest, there are compensating features. Employment in classroom teaching has typically been somewhat less affected by adverse economic conditions than many other occupations. While a scarcity of money can result in a reduction of supportive personnel and material resources, the total number of classroom teachers fluctuates very little as a result of changes in the economy. Fluctuations in population affect the employment picture far more radically than economic factors.

Salaries are increasingly adequate
Employment in public schools has typically been for only nine or ten months duration at an annual salary that, while modest, has become increasingly adequate. The average salary for a public school teacher, for example, as compiled from a survey of 885 selected school districts during 1974–1975, was $11,121 (Newsfront, Education U.S.A., 1975). The mean beginning salary for a bachelor's degree was $8300, and for a master's, $9338. Salaries in child-care positions are typically lower than those in public school. For example, at a Rochester, New York conference, it was determined that of the fifty child-care workers in attendance, half earned less than $8000, although 64 percent had college degrees (Myer, 1975).

In some school districts a year-round calendar now requires a longer period of service each year. The liberal sprinkling of holidays, however, provides occasional reprieves from constant service and thereby boosts the morale of teaching staffs. In addition, **tenure** provisions protect those teachers who have served a probationary period from arbitrary dismissal, and pension and sick leave plans have become increasingly adequate due to the efforts of professional organizations.

RESPONSE SECTION

We have briefly described teaching as a profession in early childhood education, including some of the major changes that have occurred during the past several years. There can be great differences among school systems and private early childhood teaching programs, from state to state, and even within the same state. We are concerned that you become aware of the nature and status of employment opportunities and of certification requirements and procedures in the locations where you might wish to teach.

1. Select three states where you might wish to become employed. Write to their state certification divisions, requesting their current certification requirements for teaching children ages three to eight and any

projected changes in these requirements. Address your inquiry to:

> State Certification Officer
> State Department of Education
> (State Capitol), State

2. Select three different locales (in the same state or in different states) where you might wish to teach. Contact the school district in these locations, requesting the following types of information regarding prekindergarten, kindergarten, and primary grades:

size of classroom groups
pupil-teacher ratios
per-child expenditure
hours for daily sessions
yearly calendar
salary for beginning teacher with bachelor's degree
maximum salary for classroom teaching with a master's degree
provision for sick leave
tenure provisions
additional benefits

Direct these inquiries to:

> Personnel Division
> (City or Town or Area) School District
> (City), (State)

3. Select three or more specific early childhood centers that are not under the supervision of the public school district. Request information from these centers similar to that suggested under (2) above. To obtain a listing of such centers, consult the yellow pages in a telephone directory. Look under *Schools, Nurseries, Day Nurseries.*

Your task will be easier, of course, if you coordinate efforts with others who are interested in obtaining information for the same areas. Perhaps you can obtain this kind of information in a more direct manner through personal contacts. It is important to get some sense of the variations among areas in which you have a direct personal interest.

Pros and Cons of Becoming a Teacher of Young Children

In this part of the chapter we try to give you the "inside" view of what it is like to be a teacher of young children. We think you need to be aware of both the good side and the bad side, and we hope this discussion will help you to be more realistic.

THE NEED VERSUS THE DIFFICULTY

"The need is so great but the task is so difficult"

A major reason for becoming a teacher is the opportunity to be engaged in work that is socially relevant and personally satisfying. There are few, if any, major social problems that cannot in some way be addressed in early education settings. Teachers have little reason to question whether the work they do is important or whether they can make significant contributions to the lives of others. Adults who serve as teachers of young children become second only to parents and siblings in their impact upon the child. What a teacher does or does not do in the classroom can be influential years and even decades later, not just for the children in the classroom but also for those that they in turn will influence. We have never known of a teacher who doubted the crucial nature of his or her job. The needs of children for instruction, attention, and caring are obvious.

There are many persons, however, who eventually leave teaching because of the conflict between meeting their own personal needs and adequately caring for the children. There is just no way that a teacher can realistically meet all the needs of all the children typically congregated in a "classroom." One third-year teacher put it this way:

> When I started teaching—WOW! That first year was something else. Just the management of everything was so difficult that I thought I was really doing well if I just made it through the day with the kids and the equipment physically intact and if I had kept myself from becoming psychologically undone in the process. A lot of it was just a matter of getting my feet on the ground and my head together. But what continues to bug me, even after three years of experience, and I know it is true of the teachers who've taught twenty years also, is the hopeless feeling at the end of each day as I think about the individual children in my classroom who desperately needed and could really have benefited if I had given them more time and attention. If I concentrate on those kids the next day, it's just another set of kids I then neglect. I just can't do it. It's impossible to help them all as much as I feel they should be helped.

Would you have difficulty living with this feeling of never being able to do all that you felt should be done for the children you teach? Of course, this is not a problem unique to teaching. Other professionals face the same dilemma. Physicians, for example, often end the day knowing that while they have helped many patients to some extent and some patients a great deal, many others needed more attention, more time, and more information than they were able to give. To continue to engage in medical practice, it is necessary for a physician to live with the constant knowledge of what is not being done that should be done. The social worker also encounters the seemingly endless needs of clients, and the same pressures face many other groups, both professional and nonprofessional.

Can you be satisfied with doing your best, knowing that your best is inadequate to the need? In teaching, the frustration of never doing "enough" can be balanced by the satisfaction of knowing that what has been done was well worth doing. Not all occupations offer this level of reward.

CREATIVE OPPORTUNITY VERSUS CRITICISM

"There's opportunity for inventiveness but everyone's an expert"

Teaching continues to be more of an art than a science, despite an increasing accumulation of knowledge about classroom cause and effect. Across the next decade, new knowledge will gradually be introduced into teaching practice. So much of teaching, however, is simply a matter of opinion, a personal judgment, that it is impossible to make many very definitive statements about what constitutes a good teacher or the most effective way to teach. This open-ended state of affairs has both its advantages and disadvantages.

The main advantage is the amount of latitude that an individual teacher or a school system has in determining teaching methods. In the same city, at the same age level, it is often possible to find quite opposite arrangements in such basic matters as criteria for grouping children or standards for promotion. Even within a single school building it is not unusual to find teachers who disagree on issues of how reading should be taught, means of discipline, how to evaluate children's progress, and other important matters. While there are convincing rationales for quite diverse views of how children should be educated and cared for, there is little solid evidence to justify any one particular view.

This creates a situation that prevents educators from saying, "This way has been demonstrated to be superior." The closest legitimate statement typically is, "Other ways have not been demonstrated to be superior to the way I favor." This of course leaves most issues within the realm of personal preference, and thus allows you to experiment, to invent, and to fashion for yourself a style of teaching that is distinctly your own. The lack of consensus on crucial issues gives you plenty of opportunity to be creative as you become involved in seeking answers, solving problems, and inventing new procedures.

The problem with this open-ended state of affairs is that in the absence of a professionally accepted body of facts and operating procedures, anyone on the street can legitimately prescribe how schools should be run, how subjects should be taught, and how teachers and students should behave. Since there is no firm science of teaching, it is difficult to find grounds on which to persuade laypersons that they do not know as much about teaching as the certified teacher. After all, they went to school many years and were exposed to various teaching styles.

We have all seen teachers at work for approximately 10,000 hours by the time we are seniors in high school. Quite often laypersons have the opportunity to read as much up-to-date opinion on education in the popular press as the teacher has access to in the professional journals. Given such exposure, it is inevitable that many will claim to know how schools should be run. Is this not true of you, for example? Do you not have a number of opinions on education based on your own experiences as a student?

During the process of training the teacher becomes aware that there are many legitimate ways to reach the same goals and that all of the methods have drawbacks in certain situations and with certain children. In knowing this, the teacher is better prepared to exercise professional judgment regarding which method to use in any given situation. The layperson is less aware of the vast array of alternatives and consequently is more apt to think dogmatically. The result is that teachers, more than professionals such as electricians, druggists, physicians, and computer programers, are confronted by people with partial but insufficient knowledge who tell them how their job should be done.

If you are to become a teacher you must learn how to clearly and confidently state and defend your teaching goals and methods and demonstrate progress in meeting these goals. Otherwise you will be vulnerable to the self-proclaimed experts you will encounter, each of whom "knows" other superior ways of doing your job. You should be forewarned, however, that the teaching profession will give you many more opportunities to feel creative and innovative than opportunities to feel secure and protected by the knowledge that any particular teaching practice is the *best* way.

CLASSROOM FREEDOM VERSUS SITUATIONAL CONSTRAINT

Teachers traditionally have had almost no control over some very significant aspects of their teaching, while maintaining almost total control over other aspects. The individual teacher often has little control over the number of children assigned to the classroom group, the composition of those groups, the equipment available, the scheduling of the program year, the length of the program day, and many other similar matters. They may be assigned a particular curriculum or be told to use a given set of commercial materials that largely prescribes their teaching activity. However, even during their first year, teachers are often left almost entirely to their own devices in matters of classroom instruction and management. There may be little help, counsel, or interest from others in the school about the teaching process.

"In some areas there's no teacher authority; in others, total responsibility"

The input of supervisors to individual teachers is often quite minimal. The administrators of public and private schools (and the directors of child-care centers) have quite a different set of responsibilities than the teacher. Whereas the teacher is primarily concerned with child management and instruction, administrators must focus on such noninstructional matters as public relations, ordering and distribution of supplies, scheduling of space, transportation, management of food operations, and other similar concerns. The opportunities for teacher-administrator discussion regarding issues of basic philosophy, objectives, or program structure are typically very limited.

Once they have been certified and employed, teachers are given an amazing amount of leeway to operate their classrooms as they wish, within the givens of number, mix, hours, general curriculum guides, physical space, and equipment. Unless their operation in some way violates the administrator's general perception of what should be happening, they normally operate without interference. One superintendent of a small school system flatly tells new teachers:

> I don't care what you do in your classroom. You use the methods you want. Of course, if I walk by your room and see something happening that I don't understand, I'll stop and ask you about it and you had better have an objective in mind that I can understand. If you don't, I'll tell you to get things back in line. But until then you can do things the way you think best.

Teachers may find themselves reporting to superiors who have quite different views of how classrooms should be conducted and who, because of their administrative burden, lack the time and motivation to explore the significance of these differences. Conversely, many teachers do have ample opportunity to discuss their views and concerns about education with interested administrators.

If you become a teacher, you should not assume that you will have close direction and assistance from the administrators to whom you report. You should prepare yourself to proceed quite independently. It may also be important that you not be "undone" by criticism—either by immediately giving in or by becoming defensive or antagonistic—but rather be able to justify your actions. To do this requires that you carefully cultivate your own competence and confidence.

SHARING WITH CHILDREN VERSUS ADULT ISOLATION

Teachers of young children are likely to find some of their greatest rewards in sharing the freshness with which these children experience the world. "Innocence" or "simplicity of heart," while stereotyped terms, do reflect the honest wonder and delight with which children respond to phenomena such as snow falling, snails crawling, rhythmic speech patterns, or spring sunshine. Being a teacher of the young serves to keep one more in touch with the possibilities for sensory experiencing than do most other occupations.

It is continuously intriguing to participate with children in their struggles to manipulate the physical environment, to use language, and to try to make sense out of what they are encountering. Every teacher has anecdotes about how their pupils have figured and wondered and speculated about the things and ideas they encounter. One of the authors, for example, especially remembers the wise conclusion of Ken, age seven, upon hearing his classmates trying to top each other with the magnitude of their own ages, the ages of their siblings, and the ages of their parents. Ken quipped, "Being older than other people is good, isn't it, until you start getting gray hair and then it isn't so good."

Or the puzzlement of Gordon, age six, in struggling through a passage in an abridged version of *The Three Billy Goats' Gruff* in which the text reads, "The first billy goat said, 'I want to go over the bridge. I want to eat the good green grass. I want to get fat." Gordon finished the passage saying, "You

Photo by John James.

know, I knew that word *fat* 'cause it's just *at* with *f* on it first. But you know what I don't know? Why does the goat want to get fat? That gives you heart stroke. My uncle *died* of heart stroke because he was too fat." Why, indeed? What a boost for the adult, who long ago ceased to wonder about the why of those three billy goats trip-trapping over the bridge or the nature of the troll underneath, to experience it all over again with the freshness of the child encountering it for the first time.

"There are many joys in teaching but it's a lonely job"

Although there are many positive aspects of sharing one's workdays with children, the lack of opportunity for adult contact can be a problem for some teachers. Most prekindergarten programs have at least two adults per group of children, but this is more the exception than the rule for the kindergarten and primary grades. The problem with children as social companions is that while you can share and delight in their perspectives, there is no way they can share in most of yours. Yet your pupils are constantly there, in your charge, whether you feel like being with them or not. Once the school day is under way, there is little chance for a teacher to have a "time out." The complaint of many teachers of young children, especially beginners, is, "I never even have a chance to go to the bathroom."

Thus, in contemplating teaching as a career, it is important that you first consider to what extent your morale requires adult interaction and, second,

to what extent you are likely to provide yourself with necessary supportive relationships outside the work milieu.

Quite realistically, if you are the type of person who derives your greatest satisfactions from the exploration of new adult relationships, you should be aware that in teaching you may find fewer opportunities for this enjoyment than in many other professions. Despite shifts in the proportion of males entering teaching, the school environment continues to be an especially poor choice for young women seeking men with whom they might develop primary relationships. Conversely, it can be a great place for young men to locate caring and idealistic young women. The nursery, kindergarten, and elementary school world still tends, despite some reversal of the trends, to be primarily populated with children and women. In short, if you are capable of satisfying your personal needs for adult society outside the work situation, you will have a better chance of enjoying the children's world of the classroom than if your off-work hours are socially isolated.

SELF-DEVELOPMENT

Every act of self-improvement is an act toward improved teaching. A very exciting aspect of teaching is knowing that development of oneself as a person goes hand in hand with development of oneself as a teacher. Skills of organization, communication, breadth of knowledge, sensitivity, all of which are helpful in one's daily life, become especially important in teaching. Every teacher who helps children helps them according to his or her own strengths. Teaching is far more than the application of techniques. The teacher's personal qualities make teaching either thin and mean or rich and meaningful for the children. It is difficult to think of any area of personal development that would not somehow improve teaching.

Arthur Combs describes the teaching process as using "self as instrument." He and his associates at the University of Florida point out that in teaching, as in other "helping" professions such as nursing, counseling, and social work, "instantaneous responses" to unique situations are constantly required. The interchange between teacher and child is different at every moment and the teacher must continuously react to each child in terms of the particular question, idea, or concern then being expressed. If teachers are to act instantaneously in a way that will benefit children's growth and learning, they must themselves be healthy, aware, and secure. They have an obligation and an opportunity to employ themselves fully in their work. In teaching, more than in most occupations, there is the possibility for uniting avocation and vocation.

RESPONSE SECTION

The advantages and disadvantages of early childhood education as a profession have been described in this portion of the chapter. Please do not take our word for all of this. The following questions are presented so that you can draw your own conclusions based upon your own experience and perspectives.

1. Compare our views with those of persons currently engaged in teaching young children. Arrange to talk with at least three practicing teachers regarding their experiences. Try to obtain the following information and contrast what you hear with what we have been presenting.

    a. Do you feel that your work as a teacher is important? How do you think it compares with other professions in making an important contribution to the lives of others and to the betterment of society?

    b. In teaching do you typically feel satisfied that you have done as much as possible for the children you teach? Or do you find yourself worrying about whether you should do something more or do things differently?

    c. Do you feel that you have opportunities to be creative as a teacher? Or is what you do quite prescribed and repetitive? Do you have a chance to try out new ideas and new techniques?

d. Do you feel that there is generally agreement among the teachers you work with about how to teach? Or are there many differences of opinion?

e. Do you find that other people—friends, acquaintances, strangers—try to tell you how to teach and how schools should be run? Do you think this happens to teachers more than to people in other professions?

f. Can you generally decide how you will run your classroom? Or are you told how to do things?

g. How much supervision do you have? What kind of supervision?

h. Does someone evaluate your teaching? How is that done?

i. How much contact do you have with other teachers in your school on a typical day? With adults other than teachers? Who are these adults—men or women, older or younger than yourself?

j. What are some of the things that are most enjoyable for you in working with children?

k. What personal characteristics do you feel are important for success in teaching? What kind of self-development would you think a prospective teacher might attempt?

2. Considering what we have presented and what you have heard in interviews, try to answer the following three questions.

a. What are the advantages/disadvantages that are significant to you personally? List these.

b. To what extent does the sum of the advantages outweigh the disadvantages (or vice versa) for you personally?

c. In what ways are your values reflected in your responses to the above?

Summary

All of us make statements with the choices we make in our own lives about what humans are and can become. Some of the more potent statements are often made through one's work. The decision about occupation, especially if that occupation is to be teaching, is a critical one with far-reaching consequences.

The field of teaching offers excellent career opportunities for both men and women, even though teaching positions are not now as plentiful as in years past. Those considering teaching need to be aware that there will be competition for jobs and that the preparation process will be far more demanding than in the past. A more advanced state of readiness as a beginning teacher is now necessary. Commitment is essential. Despite the scarcity of jobs, there are opportunities for well-qualified applicants in early education in a great variety of roles and settings.

Certification requirements are set by states for work in public schools. These vary from state to state and are currently being shifted in many locales from course requirements to competency-based or performance requirements. Associate degrees for work with young children are awarded in two-year college programs and by the federally sponsored Child Development Associate Consortium program.

The pros and cons of teaching could be summarized by the following:

"The need is so great but the task is so difficult."
"There's opportunity for inventiveness but everyone's an expert."
"In some areas there's no teacher authority and in others, total responsibility."
"There are joys in teaching but it's a lonely job."
"It matters who you are as a person."

REASSESSMENT

Reread what you wrote for the preassessment as you began this chapter, comparing this with your current understandings. Now write on these topics again and incorporate your new insights and knowledge. Continue to update as you prepare for teaching. Save your materials for your portfolio.

Additional Reading

Men as Teachers Kendall, E. We have men on the staff. *Young Children,* 1974, 29, 358–62.

Lee, P. C. Male and female teachers in elementary schools: An ecological analysis. *Teachers College Record,* 1973, 75, 79–98.

Lee, P. C., and Wolinsky, A. L. Male teachers of young children: A preliminary empirical study. *Young Children,* 1973, 28, 342-52.

Milgram, J. I., and Sciarra, D. J. Male preschool teachers: The realities of acceptance. *The Educational Forum,* 1974, 38, 245–7.

Seifert, K. The best men for child care work. *Child Care Quarterly,* 1975, 4, 188–93.

Vairo, P. D. Wanted, 20,000 male first grade teachers. *Education,* 1969, 89, 222–4.

Certification Woellner, E. H. *Requirements for certification for elementary schools, secondary schools, junior colleges.* 37th ed., 1972–1973. Chicago: University of Chicago Press, 1972.

Child Development Associate Credentials The federal government, child care and the Child Development Associate: A dissenting view. *Child Care Quarterly,* 1973, 2, 136–41.

Klein, J. A new professional for the child care field: The Child Development Associate. *Child Care Quarterly,* 1973, 2, 56–60.

Klein, J., and Williams, C. R. The development of the Child Development Associates (CDA) program. *Young Children,* 1973, 28, 139–45.

Current Information about the CDA credential can be obtained from

The CDA Consortium
7315 Wisconsin Avenue
Suite 601E
Washington, D.C. 20014

Project Head Start Frost, J.L., Ed. *Revisiting early childhood education: Readings.* New York: Holt, Rinehart and Winston, 1973. See Part 6, pp. 398–421.

Osborn, K. Project Head Start: An assessment. *Educational Leadership*, 1965, 23, 99–101.

Smith, M., and Bissell, J. Report analysis: The impact of Head Start. *Harvard Educational Review*, 1970, 40, 51–104.

Willmon, B. Parent participation as a factor in the effectiveness of Head Start programs. *Journal of Educational Research*, 1969, 62, 406–10.

Zigler, E. Project Head Start: Success or failure? *Learning*, 1973, 1, 43–47.

Classroom Alternatives Anderson, R. H. The nongraded school: An overview. *The National Elementary Principal*, 1967, 47, 4–10.

Goodlad, J., and Anderson, R. H. *The nongraded elementary school.* New York: Harcourt Brace Jovanovich, 1959.

Hawkes, T. Grouping. In D. W. Allen and E. Seifman, Eds. *The teacher's handbook.* Glenview, Ill.: Scott, Foresman, 1971.

Lambert, P. Team teaching for the elementary school. *Educational Leadership*, 1960, 18, 85–88, 128.

Tillman, R. Self-contained classroom: Where do we stand? *Educational Leadership*, 1960, 18, 82–84.

Teaching as a Career Beyer, E. *Teaching young children.* New York: Pegasus, 1968.

Broudy, H. S. *The real world of the public schools.* New York: Harcourt Brace Jovanovich, 1972.

Richey, R. W. *Preparing for a career in education: Challenges, changes, issues.* New York: McGraw-Hill, 1974.

Sarason, S. B. *The culture of the school and the problem of change.* Boston: Allyn and Bacon, 1971.

CHAPTER 2
Deciding Whether Teaching Is for You

Martha

Overview

Three Beginning Teachers
  KAY FIELDS
  JUNE BROOKS
  NANCY WOODS

Commitment: The Differing Experiences of Kay, June, and Nancy

Assessing Your Own Commitment

Comparing Your Orientation with That of Kay, June, and Nancy

Considering the Tasks of Teaching

Assessing Your Feelings About Your Experiences with Young Children

Summary

PREASSESSMENT

When you have completed this chapter you should be able to describe and compare the following:

1. *experiences that beginning teachers of young children might have.*
2. *factors associated with effective and satisfying teaching.*
3. *actual tasks involved in teaching young children and your feelings about them.*
4. *experiences you have had with young children and your feelings about these.*
5. *ways of determining the extent to which you are personally committed to becoming a teacher of young children.*

Before beginning to read this chapter, take enough time to write what you already know about each of the above topics.

Save what you write for rereading, comparison, and elaboration after you have studied and discussed these materials.

Overview

Our concern in this chapter is to help you determine the extent to which you are both willing and able to make a commitment to undertake the extensive training and preparation required in becoming a teacher of young children. We recognize that such a commitment is to some extent dependent on your knowledge of what you are getting into and that much of that knowledge is not available without direct involvement. While we have suggested in the preface ways in which you can have informal experiences with children if formal ones are not available within a training program, we recognize that you must begin your preparation and commitment without much background information or direct experience with children.

Consequently, we attempt to provide information in this section which, while vicarious, should be useful in creating more of a "reality base" than you may currently have. Obviously, the better you understand both yourself and the teaching profession, the more you will benefit from your training and avoid the waste and frustration of discovering too late that you are a misplaced person.

In this chapter, then, we present three accounts of beginning teachers. These case studies are fairly typical of the motivations, attitudes, and skills we have seen in teacher trainees who have worked with us over the past several years. The major characteristics that we feel are associated with professional effectiveness and personal feelings of success are reflected in these examples. After presenting these three case studies, we will review several teacher characteristics, using them to make explicit comparisons between the three beginning teachers. Also, as part of this discussion, we will present a series of self-assessment tasks to help you determine your own commitment to becoming a teacher of young children.

Three Beginning Teachers

Following are the accounts of three people who obtained their first teaching jobs in the same school district and were assigned to the same school building. Their experiences in teaching, however, were quite different. The first two found that they had made poor choices in selecting teaching as a profession. Both remained in teaching only briefly and had a very painful time, as did the children they taught. The third seemed to find considerable satisfaction in teaching and is continuing with a successful career. Note which of the three you most strongly identify with. Which behaviors and experiences would you predict for yourself should you become a teacher?

KAY FIELDS

Little career interest

Kay Fields grew up in a wealthy suburban area. She is attractive, dresses fashionably, and is socially sophisticated. She had little career interest until, after two years in the college of liberal studies in the large university she attended, she decided to enter a teacher preparation program so that she could work while her fiancé continued his medical studies. During her training program she did well in both her coursework and in her student teaching, but she showed little interest in nonrequired learning. She tended to talk with her fiancé and friends, not about what she was learning, but about the expectations of her professors, often complaining that they were either unreasonable, "Mickey Mouse," or unclear. She never seemed to think of herself as someone preparing for a professional career but only as someone confronted with immediate demands. Each requirement was completed and dismissed as summarily as possible.

Avoidance of "tough" tasks

In student teaching Kay maneuvered to get "easy" assignments in suburban schools, in the middle grades, and with very competent supervising teachers. The classrooms operated well; Kay followed the teachers' patterns and received a successful rating in each of the two situations to which she was assigned. She sought only those teaching tasks in which she anticipated success, and avoided the more challenging ones. For example, she suggested to her supervisor that she do a science teaching unit since she had already planned one as part of a previous course requirement. She busied herself with the preparation of the science materials during the mathematics period because she felt insecure in mathematics instruction. She failed to take advantage of opportunities for observing other teachers in the building, to attend teachers' meetings or inservice training sessions, or to become familiar with the extensive holdings of the district's curriculum resource center.

Kay and her fiancé were married shortly after her graduation, and they moved into an urban apartment complex near the university medical center. She applied for and received an appointment to teach first grade in a city school close by. The school was populated by a mix of children from university families (students and professors) and low-income black families who had recently moved into the district from the poorer ghetto areas. She was awarded the position on the basis of the interview, in which her poise and tactful amiability had pleased the interviewer, the school principal. Knowing little about first grade itself, the assistant superintendent who did the formal hiring based his choice on the premise that young children should have attractive and pleasant young teachers. He could visualize Kay's friendly smile greeting the youngsters as they arrived at school each day. And her record appeared adequate. Besides, she made a good case for her need to support her husband as he continued his medical studies.

Kay spent little time in preparation during the summer; instead she waited to see what the policy of the school would be. As it turned out, little of the program was prescribed, although a set of basal reading materials and mathematics workbooks were available. Kay lamented to husband and friends that the school was very disorganized and provided "absolutely no guidance."

Simply not prepared   This was the prelude to what turned out to be a nightmare for Kay, for the children and their parents, and, ultimately, for the school administration. Kay was simply not prepared, having avoided the difficulties of working with young children as an undergraduate. And she had never sought any experiences with children outside the formal training settings. The pressures on her from the first day were intense and unyielding. She found that the children's behavior—talking, running, teasing, laughing, chasing—violated her expectations, yet she lacked the skills for redirecting them into acceptable channels. She therefore began to alternately cajole, bribe, and threaten the children. She frequently overregulated them (for example, not allowing access to the lavatory although the facilities were in the room), but at other times provided insufficient supervision (for example, sending children on errands in the building, a confusing and unfamiliar structure). She found that classroom control was best maintained through large group instruction and avoided small groups and individualized teaching. She justified this by calling what she did "review" for the most advanced and "readiness training" for the least advanced. When some of the children did not meet her demands for sitting still and for correctly responding, she called them "baby."

Limited repertoire of teaching strategies

Lacking a sufficient repertoire of teaching skills and techniques, Kay repeatedly and unsuccessfully tried to use the few strategies at her command. Nothing in her previous experience had prepared her for admitting her inadequacies and seeking help, so she continued on with her frantic but unsuccessful efforts to control the children. She attributed her failure to the excessively difficult children she had in the classroom. Her anger at the children, usually carefully controlled behind a professional smile, would break out unpredictably behind the the closed doors of her classroom.

The children's reactions were varied. Some of them, although very enthusiastic about school as kindergartners, became disenchanted, sometimes even crying and asking to go home. Many of the children tried desperately to please her, bringing flowers, pictures, and cookies, and showing great concern about being "good" and "grown-up." Most of the children followed Miss Field's example and verbally criticized Charlie, the child she frequently pointed out as doing "bad" things. Other children delighted in following Charlie's lead and, with this peer encouragement, Charlie's antics and belligerency grew. Overall, the children's energies and attention were more involved with either placating or defying their teacher than in learning of any kind.

When parents came in to talk with Miss Fields, they were greeted by a very controlled, courteous, and smiling young woman, who assured them that all was going well and that their own child in particular was performing admirably—unlike "some of the other children." "Sometimes" she reminded them, "children exaggerate when they report school happenings at home." Even Charlie's mother was given this message. Requests to visit, however, were met with evasions and delays. When parents went to the principal with their concerns, they were told what a fine young woman Miss Fields was, how she was always friendly and cooperative, and how difficult it was to achieve proper discipline now that the "unruly element" was there. The principal admitted to little knowledge of how Miss Fields was handling her classroom or how she approached the teaching, and promised to look into the situation and make sure that things were in order.

This tale of Kay Fields' teaching could continue on to its unsuccessful conclusion, but the major points have already been made. A personable young woman with little commitment to becoming a competent teacher, and therefore with inadequate preparation, failed miserably in establishing a

Preoccupied with classroom control

teaching program for her children. She became preoccupied with classroom control rather than instruction. She had developed little sensitivity to children's developmental levels; her repertoire for providing instruction to children of varied interests and backgrounds was inadequate; and she had no workable plan for organizing her program. Although her pleasing manner and willingness to meet the specific objectives set for her were sufficient to obtain certification, she was quite lacking in a personal commitment to teaching.

JUNE BROOKS

Socially concerned

June Brooks is a very intelligent young woman who excelled in her studies at the urban high school she attended. She has had a very active interest in social issues ever since childhood, showing indignation at the plight of the poor and the powerless and participating in various neighborhood social movements near the urban university she attended. She was involved, with some of her more socially concerned friends, in helping a group of mothers arrange a child-care exchange, thereby reducing their feelings of entrapment and helplessness. It was during this involvement that she became interested in the possibilities of teaching.

June remembered with continuing discomfort the strictness and the requirements she had encountered from her own teachers as a youngster. When she discovered that some of the children she got to know from the child-care exchange were doing poorly in school and professed to hate it, she made arrangements to visit their classes to determine why. Reporting her observations to friends, she said, "It's just like my school was. The teachers

Strong reactions to oppression

never smile, the kids have to walk through the halls in lines and ask permission to talk, and the lessons are a bore. There's nothing interesting there, no wonder the kids hate it." It was the next semester that she, as a junior, elected to enter the teacher preparation program. She had little interest in the economic side of a teaching career. Her major motivation was to help children through teaching.

June began avidly to read books that were recommended by some of the people she knew who had started a "free" school. She found that the writings of A. S. Neill, John Holt, Edgar Friedenberg, Jonathan Kozol, James Herndon, and other critics were all very exciting. The idea that her role in teaching would be to free children from oppression was especially appealing. She had experienced a strict upbringing as a younger child in a large family. She described her parents as "cold," "uncaring," and "preoccupied with making money," and she was determined that her own life would be different. Her own personal growth she felt, had been greatly supported by the warmth and concern of friends in her cooperative housing situation, and this

Teaching as an opportunity to love, nurture, and free children

experience had helped her to see other ways of living that seemed more appealing than those she had previously encountered. In choosing teaching she saw an opportunity to provide love, nurturance, and freedom for children.

In her teacher preparation courses June eagerly read all the materials she could find on "open" education. Giving children more opportunities to choose their own involvements and greater access to concrete materials made a great deal of sense to her. She became especially interested in encouraging children's creative expression through dramatic activities, music, writing, and art. However, much of what she encountered in her courses and in her student teaching was incompatible with her own philosophy, and she often found herself countering her instructor's admonitions concerning classroom organization and management. She articulated the virtues of an educational system free from the oppressive influences of established curricula, textbooks, and discipline practices. Whenever possible, she took courses from those professors who were most vocal in criticizing traditional schooling. She was pleased to find that virtually all of her professors believed that children would benefit from a greater variety of experiences, learning materials, and optional activities than are typically provided in most school situations.

During her student teaching experiences June received mixed ratings. She was seen as hard working, dedicated, and inventive. She received recognition and praise for managing to "reach" certain children with whom the regular classroom teacher had been unsuccessful, but whenever she took total responsibility for the classroom, confusion and antagonisms developed between children and were seldom resolved. The supervising teacher tended to attribute this to June's lack of experience, although June described it as the natural result of giving the children more freedom than the supervising teacher allowed. The real problem, she said, was the restrictiveness of the regular program. She skillfully defended her practices to her university supervisor, and, in view of her very creative and able efforts with individual children, she was given an excellent overall rating.

Problems in group management

June's sincere interest in helping children and the knowledge of the low-income groups within the community that she had derived from her previous volunteer work both helped her obtain a teaching job in the university area. She was thus able to continue living in the cooperative house where she lived as an undergraduate and to maintain her previous social base. During the summer she helped in a voter registration drive in the area, so she had the opportunity to get acquainted with her prospective second-grade pupils. She visited the homes of many of the pupils she had been assigned and learned a great deal about their individual living situations, their interests, and their strengths and weaknesses. When September came, she was eagerly awaiting her opportunity "to make a difference" in the lives of these children she had come to know.

June firmly believed that by creating an environment in which she, as an adult, demonstrated concern and respect for each child, the children would soon learn to respect each other and the need for imposing direct behavioral control would thereby be reduced. She was not surprised to find that initially the children bickered with each other, were destructive of materials, and seemed only briefly interested in the many activities she made available to them. "After all," she told her friends at the co-op, "they've never had this kind of freedom and opportunity before." Even as the daily number of interpersonal hassles and her own work load of cleanup and repreparation of materials increased, June remained optimistic. She spent a great deal of time in personal confrontation with individual children regarding their behavior, being careful to let them know that she was not rejecting them as individuals, only their specific behavior. For example, she would say, "I don't like it

Hassles and destructiveness

when you throw clay on the floor, Jimmy," or "Bobby doesn't want you to break his toy, Brenda." For many of the children this kind of personal confrontation resulted in a heightened awareness of their own and others' feelings and in an increased capacity for emotional expression.

As the weeks went by, however, there was no decrease in these kinds of behaviors and only sporadic increases in productive learning experiences for most of the children. Many of them began to tell both June and their parents that they wished she would teach them something, as their first-grade teacher had. The poorer children lamented that they were not learning anything. The middle-class children complained that it was too noisy in the class, and that they would like Miss Brooks to start acting more like a teacher. When June countered to both the children and their parents that it would be far better for them to take responsibility for their own learning, and that although she was eager to help them she would not force them to work, some of the children simply continued to "goof around." Others asked for math and reading books and, in the absence of other instructional activities, plodded methodically through these materials in a most unimaginative way. June continued trying to stimulate more productive learning through the introduction of such fascinating equipment as balance scales, printing equipment, tapes and tape recorder, and personal notebooks, but found that her efforts were typically interrupted by the teasing, destructiveness, and tattling of noninvolved children.

Energies to defending practices   In addition to the energy drain of trying to maintain a calm, caring attitude in the midst of these daily frustrations, June also found that she had to expend increasing energy defending her practices to parents, the principal, other teachers, and even the custodian! The noise, the clutter, the "disrespect" of the students, which spilled over from June's classroom to hallways and playground, were annoying to many people. As the pressures on her increased, June found herself sometimes feeling and reacting with annoyance to behaviors that were not what she wished them to be. When she did let her anger show, she justified it to herself as an honest expression of feelings. She still saw no justification, however, for setting up ground rules for behavior and enforcing them, as other teachers did. This would have been quite contrary to her deeply held philosophy of education. She continued to hope that the children would eventually choose to behave in desirable ways through their own volition.

Although June's concerns for children were admirable, and although she had a great deal going for her in terms of personal attributes, her demise as a teacher of young children was predictable. By the Christmas recess June had concluded that teaching was not for her and that if the children were to be given the freedom to learn as she felt they should be, it would best be done in some alternative to the public school.

NANCY WOODS

Nancy Woods is a young woman of varied interests—photography, cooking, history, archaeology, singing, sculpting, hiking, reading, languages, sewing, and gardening. She likes working with others and feels confident in leadership roles. As a student her energy level was sufficient to maintain a busy social schedule, involvement in a variety of extracurricular activities, and a good academic record. She was an assistant leader in a neighborhood girls' club while a teenager and worked during her vacations at a variety of jobs, such as postal helper and museum assistant.

When Nancy entered college she was considering a career in public communication, stemming from her photographic interests. During her sophomore year, however, she became acquainted with an able young teacher, Emily, during participation in a political campaign. Emily talked about her teaching career in a way that intrigued Nancy, so she visited Emily's classroom on several occasions and found that she thoroughly enjoyed being there. She was surprised to find the teaching role quite different from her recollection of her own school years. She was delighted at the prospect of earning one's living in such an enjoyable way and, after a period of deliberation, decided to transfer into a teacher preparation program as a junior.

Nancy recognized that, although she was well accepted by the children in Emily's classroom and interacted with them easily, she lacked the kinds of skills, ideas, and awarenesses that Emily constantly exhibited in her teaching. She therefore entered her teacher training coursework firmly committed to picking up all the useful ideas, techniques, and knowledge that she could. Whenever a course turned out to be less helpful than she had hoped, she supplemented it with an independent effort, talking with other people about the topics. She found her friend Emily very helpful, as were a retired teacher who lived next door, the parents of certain schoolchildren she knew, and a school board member she had become acquainted with through her parents. She frequently talked with them about their views on controversial and practical issues she was trying to resolve for herself. She also read professional books and journals on a variety of educational topics, whether or not they were assigned for courses. She set up a filing system for the ideas and insights she encountered. As her collection grew, she weeded out the less-valuable items and became more selective in her new entries.

With her customary energy level Nancy continued her active participation in campus events, attending lectures, films, and exhibits, and even sponsoring a drama improvisation series. Although it was not required for her coursework, Nancy often used Emily's class to try out ideas and activities that she was studying. Some of the things she tried were very successful and enjoyable, while, as might be expected, others flopped. She learned a great deal about the need for preparedness, and, since Emily talked with her as a friend rather than a supervisor, Nancy willingly divulged her insecurities and asked for advice.

When Nancy reached the point of student teaching, therefore, she felt quite competent in the role of teacher. She asked for a challenging assignment that would ensure continued professional growth even though it would be difficult. Her only experience had been in classrooms like Emily's, populated with very privileged middle-class children. Nancy therefore asked for an inner-city assignment with children who experience other types of difficulties in their daily lives and who reflect some of these difficulties in their school behavior and in their learning.

Even though Nancy's assignment in student teaching was to a classroom considered very "difficult," she worked hard until she was able to manage the total classroom group while sensitively providing for individual children's needs. Because she managed well in that situation, she was given permission to seek additional enriching experiences within that school and elsewhere in the district. She became a dedicated observer, learning from both the skilled and the "lousy" teachers she encountered. In the words of her university supervisor, "She seems to view herself as a teacher already. Although interested in our help, she isn't waiting for us to transform her into a teacher. She realizes that it is she, not we, who will benefit or suffer from her level of preparedness, and consequently she is more concerned with her own self-appraisal than with our appraisal of her."

Nancy often described to her friend Emily the experiences she had in the teaching role. For example, on one occasion, she related the following:

Wow, did I ever learn something today. Jeffrey was just transferred into our class from another school. His mother seemed really anxious about whether he would do well in this new class and quite reluctant to leave him. Jeffrey, also, seemed quite edgy, really quite hyperactive. He was constantly scanning the children and me but also moving about touching materials during the activity time. He never really got involved in using anything; he just sidled about, watching.

When all of the children came together for sharing time at the end of the morning, Jeffrey continued to walk about, a little faster and a little jerkier than before, sort of giggling nervously. I said, "You can sit down here by Fred." At that he said, "No" with a giggle and started moving around a table with a sort of sideways step as though he were trying to elude capture. Of course, by this time the children were watching him in amazement. I really didn't know what to think and, really without thinking, said more sharply than I probably should have, "Jeffrey, you sit down right here." I guess I was really feeling my authority as teacher being threatened. Well, anyway, as soon as I said that, he got even wilder in his behavior, jumped up on the table and danced around there. Although his actions were clearly defiant, or so I felt, I was struck by the nervous sound of his laughter and the way he was drooling—you know, really drooling!

I suddenly realized that this kind of defiant behavior might be even more unusual and upsetting for him personally than it was for me. So, on an impulse, I totally flipped my reactions and stopped talking to Jeffrey at all and instead turned to the other children and said as softly as I could, "You know I've been watching Jeffrey this morning during the work period. And you know what, Jeffrey spent the whole time looking over the possibilities of things to do here. He really noticed everything.

And whenever he is ready he's going to be really well set to try out lots of things."

I noticed that Jeffrey had climbed down from the table and had come quite close and was standing still to hear what I was saying about him. So I continued, "Jeffrey is really doing very well in getting to know about this classroom." Jeffrey was by this time standing quite still and the nervous giggling and drooling had totally stopped. I turned to him and said, "We're really glad that you are here with us, Jeffrey. You are really doing well here. I think we're going to like you a lot, Jeffrey." As I said these things, he finally smiled and sat down quietly. Now what do you make of all that?

Needless to say, Nancy gained many insights from Emily and other associates as she related her teaching experiences in this manner. She seemed to feel as secure in relating her failures as her successes, seeking alternative views that might prove more successful in the future.

A well-organized program with many options for children

It was easy for Nancy to receive a teaching appointment in the school district close to the university where she had done her student teaching, since she had demonstrated that she was able, cooperative, and committed. As she had been working for over two years to prepare herself for teaching, she had few quandaries as a new teacher about how to organize the classroom or about the kind of relationship she would have with the children. She also knew, based on her investigations, how her own teaching style differed from other teachers' and the reasons why she operated one way versus another.

Her experience enabled her to predict accurately what responses were likely to be elicited from children, given certain classroom conditions and her own behavior. She felt no qualms about taking an active role in developing expectations with the children about what they could and could not do within the classroom setting. On the other hand, she felt no personal need to overcontrol the children. She had learned from experience the advantage of providing a number of options as long as it was possible to keep them manageable. She exuded confidence and enthusiasm and it was contagious—others had confidence in her. The teaching task was therefore easier for her than for most novice teachers, and she was able to maintain many of her outside interests. She shared many of these interests—ecology, guitar playing, photography—with the children, thus enriching their lives. Nancy enjoyed teaching and the children benefited in having her as a teacher.

Commitment: The Differing Experiences of Kay, June, and Nancy

Lack of commitment based on realistic expectations

Thus far, we have presented a personal and detailed account of what teaching was like from the perspectives of three beginning teachers. To us these accounts reflect the relevance of the four major teacher characteristics with which this book is concerned—commitment, sensitivity, resourcefulness, and organizational skills. They quite clearly illustrate some of the negative consequences that stem from a lack of initial commitment based on a realistic orientation to the profession and its training demands.

We do not mean to imply that commitment is an either/or phenomenon. We do not think it makes sense to talk about those who are and are not committed to becoming teacher. That is, commitment is a characteristic that varies in degree both between and within people. We have also cited the need for commitment to be based on reality. Just as commitment is not an either/or phenomenon, neither is reality, at least in relation to a topic such as the teaching profession. For example, Kay selected only a limited aspect of the total reality of teaching as the basis for her commitment—those factors associated with social and economic position and authority. Teachers *do* hold a position that is generally respected in the community, they *are* paid in a manner that is increasingly commensurate with training and work performed, and they *do* have legal and interpersonal authority vested in them. But Kay lacked a realistic understanding of what would be involved in preparing herself to become an effective teacher. She also lacked a realistic view of her own needs and the extent to which they could be met in teaching. These orientation deficiencies were in large part responsibile for her frustration, disappointment, and lack of success in the teaching role.

Position and authority are associated with teaching

June, on the other hand, selected and distorted reality in quite the opposite direction. Whereas Kay emphasized authority and position, June rejected these concerns in order to focus on the freedom of individual children. She did not understand that some degree of rules and organization are a necessary backdrop for freedom, and that an essential requirement for teaching is the active management of groups of children. She ignored opportunities for learning how to structure (arrange, organize, and maintain) a classroom. Some of that information would have been quite compatible with her concern for developing children's sense of freedom and choice.

Rules and organization are necessary

It appears that her own personal resentment of all forms of structure for herself blinded her to the fact that all programs have some conscious or unconscious structure, even the one she eventually provided in her own classroom. Her personal rejection of anything she perceived as structure was so dominant that she let it drive her from teaching rather than reconsidering her stance. Had she reconsidered, she may well have become an excellent teacher, one who derived great satisfaction from allowing her children increasing freedom of choice based upon carefully arranged options. She was

---

TEACHER CHARACTERISTICS AND CHILDREN'S GROWTH

Enthusiasm was cited as one of the few teacher characteristics found to be related to children's growth by Rosenshine and Furst (1973) in a review of over fifty studies of the relationship between teacher behavior and measures of pupil growth. Among other variables reported to yield significant and/or consistent results were clarity, variability or flexibility, task-oriented or businesslike behavior, and criticism of pupils. The latter was found to be negatively related to pupil growth.

---

committed to becoming sensitive and resourceful, but not to developing organizational abilities. This distortion of the realities of teaching did her in!

Nancy did not appear to distort any of the essential aspects of the teaching role, her preparation for it, her view of herself, or her personal goals in becoming a teacher. Her broad interests, her enthusiasm, her appetite for new experiences that took her into Emily's classroom, all seemed to serve her well in reaching a very realistic commitment to and preparation for teaching.

This discussion of the realities of teaching in no way implies that current educational structures are necessarily what should be or must be. On the contrary, new and changed realities are constantly brought about through the efforts of classroom teachers who are dissatisfied with the status quo. The problem for those who wish to change traditional educational practices, as was June's goal, is not with their idealism but with their means for successfully implementing and demonstrating alternative practices. Those individuals who possess the broadest repertoires of concepts and skills are the ones who have greatest success in bringing about change. Mastery of, or at least familiarity, with, existing practice is necessary in order to establish a comparative base against which to compare and measure new, alternative practices.

Mastery of existing practice often necessary·prior to initiating change

RESPONSE SECTION

You have just read accounts of three beginning teachers who had different orientations and who fared quite differently in their classroom work. The three, Kay, June, and Nancy, differed in many respects. It will be useful for you to make a list of the major points of difference you noted. Some possible examples could be difference in energy level and difference in willingness to learn from various sources. What else?

Once you have prepared your list, we suggest that you summarize for yourself your own orientation regarding each of the items. In the interest of honesty, try to think whether there is any evidence that either supports or contests the statements you are making about yourself.

Further consider your own orientation by completing the following sentence stems:

1. I am considering a teaching career primarily because ———
2. In preparation for teaching, both in my coursework and my extracurricular experiences, I plan to ———
3. When I consider my own current level of knowledge in such academic areas as the sciences, literature, history, etc., I assume ———
4. My expectations in regard to work and compensation are ———
5. I believe that success in teaching is primarily a matter of ———
6. At the present time, in regard to my interests and skills, I ———
7. When I hear a teacher discussing troublesome discipline problems, I assume ———

Assessing Your Own Commitment

Commitment is a complex issue that poses difficulties for decision-making. We believe, however, that by considering certain questions and issues in a serious, honest manner, you can derive helpful perspectives on such questions as, "How much commitment is required for success as a teacher of young children?" and "How committed am I?" In the next several pages we will explore these questions and issues.

Comparing Your Orientation with That of Kay, June, and Nancy

Through the following task we seek to ensure that you further consider several explicit points of contrast between the three beginning teachers, Kay, June, and Nancy, and between them and yourself.

For each of the following sentence stems, the same ones that were included in the response section, we have proposed three possible endings, each of which reflects the orientation of one of the three teachers on the issue in question. Try to determine which of the three, if any, are similar to your own perspective. If none are, consider *why* you hold the perspective you do and what its implications might be.

1. I am considering a teaching career primarily because
   a. I have no other career interests at present.
   b. I want to give children the freedom I wish I had had as a child.
   c. I enjoy helping others learn something that I already know.
2. In preparing for teaching, I plan to
   a. do what is required of me in a way that will be seen as commendable by my supervisors.
   b. set my own goals as much as possible and try to avoid courses/ experiences that are not in tune with my philosophy and approach.
   c. gain as broad and varied a set of exposures and challenges as possible.
3. When I consider my own current level of knowledge in such academic areas as the sciences, literature, history, etc., I
   a. hope it is nearly sufficient for certification without further study.
   b. feel confident it is adequate since I intend to help children learn and not directly teach subject matter anyway.
   c. intend to continue expanding the breadth and depth of my knowledge.
4. In my occupation I hope to
   a. work a reasonable amount for a reasonable wage.
   b. throw myself into doing something worthwhile regardless of pay.
   c. work hard but have sufficient time and resources (pay) to pursue other activities and interests as well.
5. I believe that success in teaching is primarily a matter of
   a. keeping control of the classroom situation.
   b. being supportive of children's activity, whatever direction it takes.
   c. continuously providing experiences that absorb the children in learning within a well-planned and predictable environment.

6. At the present time, in regard to interests and skills, I
   a. have few that I can share with others.
   b. have many, but seldom share them with others.
   c. have many that I often enjoy sharing with others.
7 When I hear teachers discussing troublesome discipline problems, I assume
   a. they are referring to the handling of children with special emotional problems.
   b. that they are too authoritarian and, thereby, have created the problems.
   c. they might benefit from improved skills in classroom organization and management.

As you have undoubtedly realized, the (a) responses in each of the seven items reflect Kay's orientation, while (b) and (c) respectively represent June's and Nancy's. While none of these items, taken singly or even in combination, can be considered as valid indicators of success or satisfaction in teaching, your responses should provide you with some insights into your motivation for teaching and the focus of your orientation.

Photo by permission of Syracuse University
Early Childhood Education Center.

In his book *Life in Classrooms,* Philip Jackson (1968) comments, as follows, on the "busyness" of classroom life:

> Anyone who has ever taught knows that the classroom is a busy place, even though it may not always appear so to the casual visitor. Indeed, recent data have proved surprising even to experienced teachers. For example, we have found in one study of elementary classrooms that the teacher engages in as many as 1000 interpersonal interchanges per day. An attempt to catalogue the interchanges among students or the physical movement of class members would doubtlessly add to the general impression that most classrooms, though seemingly placid when glimpsed through the window in the hall door, are more like the proverbial beehive of activity. (p. 11)

Considering the Tasks of Teaching

Let us next explore your perceptions of what it will be like to teach young children on a daily basis. When you imagine yourself teaching, what do you see yourself doing? This is a three-part task:

1. Before referring to Table 2.1, list all the things you can visualize yourself doing as a teacher of young children. Take no more than ten minutes to make your list.

2. Now that you have made your list, look at Table 2.1, which lists many activities we have observed teachers of young children engaging in frequently. Compare your list with what is presented in the table. How would you characterize the differences?

3. With the items from your list and those from the table, do a self-survey to determine how you feel about the tasks associated with the teaching role. For each item, rate as follows:

   ++ really enjoy doing this
    + feel comfortable doing this
    0 uncertain
    − feel uncomfortable doing this (possibly due to inexperience)
   −− would certainly not enjoy doing this

As you consider your ratings for each item, what is your overall impression? If you were to be regularly engaged in these tasks, would you find it satisfying? Are there a sufficient number of tasks that you believe would be satisfying to compensate for those you feel negative toward?

Table 2.1 Tasks of Teachers of Young Children

The Tasks	Your Rating
Plan for following days, weeks, etc. (objectives, activities and materials, time allotments, procedures, setting arrangements, etc.)	
Maintain accurate attendance records for all children	
Maintain basic supplies in readiness for children's use	
Prepare materials for expressive activities (mix paints, prepare clay, etc.)	
Prepare equipment for use (take from storage, place in appropriate location)	
Prepare and/or select instructional materials (posters, flannel board, work sheets, etc.)	
Collect scrap materials from home and community to supplement those provided from commercial suppliers	
Interact with children (listen, ask questions, explain, give directions, discuss, relate personal experiences) individually and in groups	
Grant or deny children's requests	
Set and enforce standards for children's behavior	
Initiate and direct children's transitions from one location and/or type of activity to another	
Monitor (and sometimes intercede) in children's interactions or conflicts	
Observe and keep records on children's behavior and progress	
Conduct group sharing sessions (oral and/or visual sharing of experiences, expressive products, work efforts, etc.)	
Conduct group lessons (plan, set objectives, select materials and activities, involve children, evaluate, etc.)	
Conduct music activities (singing, dancing, movement, use of instruments, listening, etc.)	
Involve children in mathematical activities (counting, comparing group sizes, ordering according to number or other dimensions, etc.)	
Involve children in activities or lessons that develop reading concepts or skills (function of written language, the correspondence between written words and spoken words, between spoken sounds and letters, etc.)	
Print (manuscript printing) (directions, announcements, reminders, notes, etc.) on paper and chalkboard, on posters	
Show children how to correctly form and space letters and numerals	
Involve children in science activities (observing, inferring, experimenting, etc. with a variety of materials)	
Keep majority of children constructively occupied while working with an individual child or a small group	
Supervise and/or conduct playground activities	
Arrange and conduct field trips to other locations	
Supervise children's toileting	
Serve and supervise snacks and/or lunches	
Help children in dressing (zippers, ties, boots)	
Take care of ill or injured children (vomiting, crying, drowsy, bleeding, etc.) until parents or medical personnel are available	
Maintain physical orderliness in classroom, replacing equipment and teaching materials after use	
Take care of or supervise care of classroom pets and plants	
Arrange displays on walls, tables, bulletin boards	
Create and maintain activity centers for particular purposes (planting and observing growth, printing, developing motor coordination, etc.)	
Communicate with parents via home visits, conferences, notes, etc.	
Work with other teachers to coordinate efforts and make joint program decisions	
Discuss and/or defend your teaching practices with supervisory personnel and fellow teachers	

Prescott, Jones, and Kritchevsky (1967) studied fifty day-care centers in Los Angeles County and, among other findings, reported on teachers' involvements. Over three-quarters of all teacher behavior was directed to individual children, even though the observations were made in group settings. About half of their interactions were spent in guidance and encouragement and far less (7 percent) in restricting children's behavior. One-fifth of the teachers' time was spent in noncommunicative activities—observing, preparing materials, etc. These data provide a useful overview of teachers' efforts within day-care settings.

Assessing Your Feelings About Your Experiences with Young Children

The following series of questions will be useful for you only in relation to your first-hand experiences. If you have already had extensive opportunity to be with young children, consider these past contacts. If not, delay consideration of these questions until after you have had some actual encounters.

You should not, at this point, be particularly concerned with your success or lack of success in planning and managing experiences for children but should concentrate instead on how you feel about whatever happens. Our questions ask, not about whether things went well or smoothly, but about your own reactions and feelings. You may find it more useful to answer in terms of separate specific experiences you have had rather than trying to respond in a general way.

- When you have responsibility for children do you find that the time passes relatively quickly and enjoyably, or do you find yourself wishing to terminate the responsibility?
- When you have responsibility for children do you try to anticipate how they will respond to different experiences, conditions, or environments, or do you simply wait until things happen without trying to predict their reactions?
- When you are with children does your interaction include giving help, talking seriously, and giving information, or do you only engage in giving directions, teasing, and/or horseplay?
- When you are with children do you find that your voice and your facial and bodily expressions are typical of the way you are when you are with people your own age, or do you behave differently? How are you the same? How are you different?
- When you have responsibility for young children do you feel comfortable in insisting that they do some things that they prefer not to do, or do you refrain from giving any directives?

- When children ignore you or behave toward you in hostile ways are you able to "keep your cool" and continue on with a positive approach, or do you find yourself feeling hurt or angry and responding in kind?
- When you are with a group of children do you note how individual children react differently to you and to the situation and do you find that you vary your responses to the children accordingly, or do you find that you behave toward all the children in rather similar ways?

While your past reactions to young children may not be indicative of how you will react in the future, these reactions are the best data you currently have as to your own proclivities. In the following paragraphs we would like to consider with you the possible implications for one type of reaction versus another.

If you feel uncomfortable in the presence of children and are relieved when contact can be terminated, there is good reason to expect that you will not enjoy teaching as a profession. Strangely, many persons seem to assume that being a teacher of children will be very different from relating to children in the role of a relative, neighbor, or friend. While it is true that the classroom

Photo by John James.

structure prescribes certain role relationships that are less prevalent in other situations, your feelings about your interactions with children typically will not differ markedly in the classroom from your current, less formal relationships.

Visualizing and planning in advance

If foresight is one of the talents you have not developed, you might balk at the constant need in teaching to have materials and ideas in readiness. Advance preparation, both through physical arrangements and through planning, is very crucial to teaching, and a person whose preferred style is to react spontaneously may find some other career more rewarding.

If your current behavior with children only includes such activities as holding and fondling, teasing and playing, and directing or bossing, you should further test yourself to find out whether you will also enjoy an instructional relationship. Try to assess to what extent you are able to take the child's point of view and give appropriate help and information. If you continue to find yourself predominantly giving physical affection, teasing, or directing, you might well question whether you will have the inclination or the ability to take the teaching role. Although such behaviors are engaged in by teachers, they are not sufficient to facilitate children's learning.

The naturalness of your interactions with children

If your behaviors when with children are very different from your normal behavior, you should ask yourself whether your adoption of the teaching role is going to be uncomfortable. To some extent, being a teacher will always involve some role playing, that is, it will require some behaviors that are unique to the teaching role. The crucial question is how different these role behaviors are from those you emit when you are feeling most comfortable. If

Photo by permission of Bernice Wright
Cooperative Nursery School.

you become committed to playing a role that feels unnatural and undesirable, even though you may learn to do it very well, the chance for satisfaction is limited. Is your "natural" style of interaction one that makes it easy for you to relate to children, or do you find it necessary to slow down or speed up your reaction time, your rate of talking, or your level of enthusiasm and intensity?

The authoritative role

If you feel personally uncomfortable taking on the decision-making responsibility for children in given situations, you may have difficulty accepting the authoritative side of teaching. If you, like June in the prior part of this chapter, deeply feel a need to let all other persons, even young children, behave in an unrestricted fashion, you will probably experience considerable discomfort in assuming teaching responsibilities. While overregulation of children's behavior has undesirable consequences for development and learning, a lack of regulation is likely to have disruptive effects.

If you have the idea that you wish to become a teacher of young children because you think they are affectionate and loving (that is, for your own needs), you are in for some surprises. Just as children are very open in their expression of warm feelings, so are they open in their expression of indifferent or hostile feelings. You will find that while you will receive love and approval in good measure, you will also receive less than positive feelings on occasion. Only a secure person who receives warmth and support outside the classroom typically has the equilibrium to continue caring for children who quite naturally fluctuate between happy and hostile attitudes. It is important that a teacher not be so personally dependent on children's positive regard that hostility is taken as a personal affront or loss, with resultant rejection of the child. Rather, the child needs assistance from a stable adult in more acceptably expressing the concerns that generate hostile feelings.

Awareness of individual variation between children

If you have, at this point, little awareness of how different children, even of the same age, vary in their abilities, attitudes, and interests, you may need more experience before making a firm commitment to teaching as a career. Without this knowledge, you probably have unrealistic views of what teaching involves. For example, you may expect that a good teacher should be able to design lessons or arrange experiences that will be equally appropriate for all children of a given age. However, despite the kind of instruction given, there will be increasing differences among children as they progress in age in both the rate at which they learn and the means by which they learn. Any group of three-year-olds will have a wide range of ability to use language, to care for their own personal needs, to understand and follow directions, to use equipment, or to interact with each other. The amount of variation will be even greater in a group of five-year-olds, greater yet in a group of seven-year-olds.

We are predicting that you will be more likely to find teaching a satisfying occupational choice if, in your informal contacts with children, you (1) find that the time seems to pass quickly and enjoyably; (2) have a tendency to anticipate how children will respond to different experiences, conditions, and environments; (3) include giving help, talking seriously, and giving information in your interactions with children; (4) behave in ways that are

You have been presented with three self-assessment tasks: (1) a comparison of your orientation with that of Kay, June, and Nancy; (2) a consideration of your awareness of and reaction to the tasks of teaching; (3) an assessment of your feelings about your experiences with young children.

At this point, we suggest that you summarize for yourself your conclusions regarding the following:

1. What additional experiences or information do you feel you still need before you can determine whether you wish to make a commitment to a teaching career and become fully engaged in the tasks of preparation? How will you obtain these?

2. What is your present stance on becoming a teacher of young children? What evidence have you acquired to date that leads you to believe that your commitment is sufficient and is based on a realistic appraisal of your self, of what will be involved in preparation, and of what teaching will entail?

not particularly atypical of your daily behavior; (5) feel comfortable in imposing restrictions on children's behavior where these seem necessary; (6) maintain your positive approaches and feelings despite children's negativisim; (7) note how individual children differ from each other and react to them accordingly.

Summary

There are varied reasons for becoming a teacher of young children. Motives can range from the desire for economic security, to social approval and respect from the community, to interest in bringing about significant social change. Whatever the motivation, the commitment to teaching should be based on a realistic knowledge of oneself, the requirements for training, and the demands of the profession—if it is to lead to personal satisfaction and professional success.

In Chapter 1 basic information was offered on the nature of the teaching profession. In this chapter, the contrasting experiences of beginning teachers have been presented and analyzed, and you have been presented with a set of tasks intended to give you a more complete and realistic appraisal of your own motivations and perceptions. It is our hope that you will soon reach the point of decision regarding a teaching career. Should you decide positively, we hope that your motivation and commitment have been strengthened and that you are ready to put forth a maximum effort to become a very special and important person—a teacher.

Reread what you wrote for the preassessment as you began this chapter, comparing this with your current understandings. Now write on these topics again and incorporate your new insights and knowledge. Continue to update as you prepare for teaching. Save your materials for your portfolio.

Additional Reading

Almy, M. *The early childhood educator at work.* New York: McGraw-Hill, 1975.

Ashton-Warner, S. *Teacher.* New York: Simon and Schuster, 1965.

Cohen, M., Ed. *A lap to sit on—and much more: Reprints from "Childhood Education."* Washington, D.C.: Association for Childhood Education International, 1971.

Hymes, J. L. *Early childhood education: An introduction to the profession.* Washington, D.C.: National Association for the Education of Young Children, 1975.

Katz, L. G. *Teacher-child relationships in day care centers.* ERIC Document Reproduction Service No. ED 046 494. 1972.

Yardley, A. *The teacher of young children.* New York: Citation, 1973.

SECTION TWO
SENSITIVITY

Teachers of young children need to understand many aspects of children's behavior and development, what they can and cannot do at any given time. They need to infer from a child's behavior how that child is viewing the world, what his or her concerns and needs are. In order to do this accurately teachers must be able to differentiate between their own personal wants and concerns and those of the child. Only then can a teacher take actions that will benefit the child.

Accordingly, the three major emphases in this section are:

1. Your own continuing quest for self-knowledge or self-awareness and the conditions that influence your behavior.
2. The development of your understanding of children's physical development and motor behavior; affective and social behavior; cognitive and intellectual behavior.
3. The development of your ability to study individual children as a basis for both your own teaching and for effective communication with parents, colleagues, and others about the children.

Chapter 3 examines your current sensitivity to young children, ways of enhancing that sensitivity, and its relevance for you as a teacher. Three general ways of viewing human growth, development, and functioning are presented, each one representing the rational foundation for an approach to early education. You may wish to compare your own beliefs with each of these perspectives and to compare each with the others. The reciprocal influence of theory and personal sensitivity will become obvious as you consider the focus of particular theorists as they look at children.

The remaining chapters in Section Two concentrate on behavior, growth, development, and learning in three major areas. Chapter 4 is concerned with physical characteristics and motor behavior; Chapter 5 with affective and social behavior; Chapter 6 with cognitive and intellectual development. Each of these chapters provides both theoretical perspectives and suggestions for observing and studying young children. Implications for teaching are introduced as a prelude to further exploration in the third section of the book.

Chapter 7 is concerned with compiling, organizing, and using information about a given child in order to plan appropriate learning experiences and to communicate with parents, colleagues, and other professionals.

CHAPTER 3
Ways of Viewing the Child

PERSKE

Overview

The Effects of Professional Training on Sensitivity

Contrasting Views of the Child: Three Major Orientations
ENVIRONMENTALIST ORIENTATION
MATURATIONIST ORIENTATION
INTERACTIONIST ORIENTATION

Some Basic Principles of Child Development

Becoming a Skilled Observer of Children
IDENTIFYING FACTORS THAT LIMIT SENSITIVITY
SORTING OUT "YOU" FROM WHAT YOU VIEW
RECOGNIZING THE INFLUENCE OF CONTEXT ON BEHAVIOR

Alternative Formats for Recording Observations
DESCRIPTIVE NARRATIVE
CATEGORY SYSTEMS

Making Observations of Individual Children

Summary

PREASSESSMENT

When you have completed this chapter you should be able to describe and compare the following:

1. effects of professional training on sensitivity.
2. professional perspectives on how humans develop and learn.
3. basic principles of child development.
4. factors that distort observations, even for sensitive professionals.
5. levels of interpreting observational data.
6. methods of recording observations of children.

Before beginning to read this chapter, take enough time to write what you already know about each of the above topics.

Save what you write for rereading, comparison, and elaboration after you have studied and discussed these materials.

Overview

This introductory chapter on sensitivity has several objectives. First, it explores the relationship between professional training and experience and the development of a higher level of teaching sensitivity. Next, it explores some of the major ways in which children are viewed by professional psychologists and educators. In the latter portion of the chapter the focus is on developing your own skill as an observer of children. You will be helped to (1) identify factors that limit your sensitivity, (2) understand how you tend to distort what you see, and (3) recognize the influence of context on your own and children's behavior. Alternative formats and procedures for observing individual children will then be presented.

The Effects of Professional Training on Sensitivity

Sensitivities vary according to experience

We all know, if we stop to reflect, that different people are sensitive to different things depending on what their particular experiences have been. As an example, consider three friends, Barbara, Suzanne, and Caroline, all of whom grew up in the same small town and attended the same college as undergraduates. Barbara subsequently became a geologist, working with the U. S. Geological Survey; Caroline's advanced training was in meteorology, which led to employment with the U. S. Weather Service; Suzanne became a botanist with the Conservation Department. During a recent summer their vacations happened to coincide and, for the first time since college, they found themselves together again in their hometown. They decided that it would be fun to revisit an area where they had spent many enjoyable hours as teenagers.

Changed perceptions

As they walked and talked about old times and what had happened to them since, they discovered that their intervening experiences had changed their perceptions of the area around them. Barbara pointed it out first as she began to comment on the particular rock formations. She drew their attention to the huge cracks in a rock at the edge of a cliff. "In those days," she said, "this was merely an interesting bunch of rocks, but now I see it as a glacial waterfall dumping millions of gallons of melted ice and gouging out that deep pool at the bottom, what is now the lake."

As she concluded, Barbara commented, "I've changed much more rapidly than the geological phenomena I study. Certainly my capacity for perceiving the geological world has changed markedly. It is probably a thousand times more acute than it used to be. Now, when I look at rocks, I know what kinds they are, where they come from, what uses they have, what they probably looked like ten thousand years ago, and what they'll probably look like ten thousand years from now. I'd say I've changed quite a bit in what I see and understand since the last time I walked out here."

A STORY ABOUT DIFFERING SENSITIVITIES

The following story, cited by Alphenfels (1964), illustrates the differing sensitivities developed in persons with different experiences.

> A backwoodsman, walking along Fifth Avenue one day, suddenly stopped his New Yorker friend and said, "I hear a cricket."
>
> "You couldn't possibly hear a cricket in all the traffic on Fifth Avenue."
>
> "Oh, yes, I can," replied the woodsman, "and I'll show you how."
>
> He took a dime from his pocket, held it out and let it drop. The moment that dime hit the pavement everyone within fifty yards turned around to see if it was his dime that had fallen. Few of us would have heard the cricket, but most of us would have heard the dime, for our ears are tuned to hear dimes. (p. 168)

Suzanne and Caroline were quietly laughing to themselves, obviously thinking about how they too had changed. As they continued their walk each one took turns describing her own perception of the physical environment. It soon became obvious that their perceptions were far more specialized and divergent today than they were ten years earlier. At the conclusion of their stroll, Suzanne summed things up by saying, "Fascinating, isn't it, how our perceptions of things have changed?"

The foregoing illustrates how occupational training and experience influence a person's sensitivity. An important part of becoming a trained professional is the development of refined sensitivities within a given field. Having once developed such professional sensitivity, a person can never again perceive the world as he or she once did.

Teachers' specialized sensitivities

As a teacher you will come to view children in a much more sensitive and differentiated manner than will persons without your professional training and experience. The sensitivity you develop will be similar to that of other professionals charged with specialized child development responsibilities. As a teacher, however, you will also develop a set of sensitivities that is specific to your speciality. Each child development professional (such as child welfare workers, child psychologists, pediatricians, speech pathologists, school nurses, school psychologists, and reading specialists) has a view of the child that is related to the particular services he or she performs. Within any of these occupations, moreover, there are marked differences between people in their degree of sensitivity. The more able the professional, however, the more comprehensive and differentiated will be the sensitivities developed in relation to the professional role.

RESPONSE SECTION

The specialized sensitivities of persons with different professional training and experience has been illustrated and discussed in what you have just read. To give them personal meaning, we suggest that you prepare a sheet of paper with a column for each of the jobs you have ever held and/or the volunteer work you have done. In each column, list the special sensitivities you now have as a result of that experience. For example, if you have worked in a greenhouse, you may have become sensitive to evidence of plant disease, to healthy signs of growth, and to soil variations, which others, without this kind of experience, are unlikely to note.

If possible, compare your lists with those prepared by persons who have had different experiences. Consider the contrasting perspectives and concepts each of you has as a result of your differing work experiences.

Contrasting Views of the Child: Three Major Orientations

Making sense of encounters

All of us are constantly trying to make sense out of what we encounter. Having things make sense to us is so important that we often distort what we see or hear in an effort to make it more sensible. Consider the child, for example, who asked to hear the song "Oh, Suzanna" sung repeatedly until she could sing it for herself. Lacking knowledge of a banjo, however, she sang, "Oh Suzanna. Oh, don't you cry for me. I come from Alabama with a Band-Aid on my knee." She distorted what she heard so it would make sense to her. Band-Aids were something she knew could go on knees; banjos were unfamiliar to her. What is "out there" is constantly being filtered by each of us so that it will fit with what we have previously learned about the world.

Professional psychologists and educators who study children's development, like everyone else, are constantly trying to fit current observations into their respective orientations. They emphasize or deemphasize certain aspects of behavior in order to build a "sensible" (that is, a consistent and patterned) view of children. As a teacher you will benefit from being aware of the major concepts about children and the rationale or tradition behind each particular view.

Benefits from multiple perspectives

For each historical period, for each different society, for each individual family, the view of the child that is currently held usually feels "right and natural" to those who hold it. Contrasting views usually produce feelings that range from vague uneasiness to outright rejection or hostility. Yet once the contrasting views are added to one's original conception, they typically enrich one's appreciation and understanding and make possible more flexible and intelligent decision-making.

In the following discussion we urge you to become familiar enough with the three perspectives presented that you can understand how the adherents of each organize and interpret their observations of children. An adherent of each of these respective orientations, upon viewing the same set of childhood behaviors, would probably make rather different observations and express quite different concerns. It will significantly increase your sensitivity if you can observe and interpret the behavior of children through each of these perspectives.

ENVIRONMENTALIST ORIENTATION

The first orientation, often referred to as environmentalist or behaviorist, can be historically traced from John Locke to Edward Thorndike and subsequently to B. F. Skinner, the formulator of the principles of operant psychology. John Locke viewed the human infant's mind as a *tabula rasa*, a blank slate upon which a variety of experiences could be imposed to create quite different sorts of development. The view that external influence can and should be used to **shape** the developing child is central to the tradition of environmentalism.

THE BEHAVIORIST VIEW OF HUMANS

B. F. Skinner's behaviorist view of humans is exemplified in statements such as the following (Skinner, 1971):

> In the scientific picture a person is a member of a species shaped by evolutionary contingencies of survival, displaying behavioral processes which bring him under the control of the environment in which he lives, and largely under the control of a social environment which he and millions of others like him have constructed and maintained during the evolution of a culture. The direction of the controlling relation is reversed: a person does not act upon the world, the world acts on him. (p. 202)

Shaping of behavior

Operant psychologists who work with an environmentalist orientation are primarily concerned with determining how environmental influences shape particular kinds of behavior in an individual. They have traditionally examined how events that either precede or follow particular behaviors appear to increase or decrease the occurrence of those behaviors. Their goal is the better arrangement and management of those events so that desirable behaviors can be encouraged and undesirable behaviors eliminated or decreased.

Operant psychologists' views of the child seldom include attention to such factors as the child's self-concept, physical maturation patterns, or internal thinking processes. They tend to feel it is irrelevant to try to infer how a child feels or how he is viewing the world. Only observable behavior is felt to be worthy of study. They feel quite justified in this emphasis since behavior-management principles have been demonstrated as effective (when appropriately applied) in bringing about and maintaining specific behavior changes. B. F. Skinner and his colleagues, in studies of both animal and human behavior, have repeatedly demonstrated that to influence behavior you need only have knowledge of (1) what is rewarding or reinforcing and (2) how to systematically schedule these reinforcements according to empirically derived principles. No knowledge of feelings or motivations is necessary to alter behavior, they point out, only knowledge of behavior.

A particular person's reinforcements are determined by observation, by noting those stimuli (events or objects) that seem to increase the desired behavior. For example, it is is noted that a child tends to persist with an activity after receiving a smile or verbal praise, it is thought likely that these social acts are reinforcing for that child. Or perhaps a food or trinket reward or a special privilege is more effective in maintaining or encouraging a given behavior.

Premack principle

David Premack, another behaviorist, has provided further elaborations of operant psychology which are of particular interest to educators. He points out that those behaviors that an individual engages in frequently on a voluntary basis can be assumed to be reinforcing for that individual. Once these behaviors are identified, they can be used as rewards for increasing the occurrence of other, less frequently exhibited behaviors. To illustrate, if a second-grader seldom engages in writing activities voluntarily but frequently uses Lego blocks, the teacher could increase the child's involvement in writing by making opportunities to play with Lego blocks contingent upon writing involvement. A child's preferred activities can thus be used as reinforcers just like food, trinkets, social approval, or other privileges. The proof of whether something is reinforcing for a given child is determined by whether or not it increases the specific behaviors made contingent upon it.

The principles of behaviorism, also referred to as principles of **operant conditioning,** behavior management, **contingency management,** or **behavior modification** by various writers, will be further elaborated in Chapter 14, where alternative kinds of programs are discussed. In brief, adherents of this orientation proceed in the following manner. First, they observe a child's behavior to see if any part of that behavior is undesirable. Second, they attempt to determine what might be reinforcing for the child and, therefore, potentially useful in altering the **target behavior.**

A technology to alter behavior

The basis for making judgments regarding what are desirable or undesirable behaviors may differ markedly. Behaviorists typically say that what they have to offer is a technology, a set of principles that, if appropriately applied, can alter behavior. Nothing in that technology offers judgments as to how any child *should* behave at any given age or stage. Behaviorists do, however, often point out specific instances in which a child's behavior is so obviously harmful that some effort toward change appears generally desirable for all concerned.

To date, the behaviorists as a group have been more successful in demonstrating the effectiveness of their methodologies in modifying discrete behaviors, such as kicking, crying, or work effort, than they have been in determining the cumulative effects of these modifications over an extended time period. For example, Brown and Elliott (1965) reported that teachers in the Hanover Nursery School at Dartmouth College successfully reduced the amount of aggressiveness among the boys in their group by ignoring these acts and attending to and praising only cooperative and peaceful behavior. They noted a remarkable change in two boys who "became friendly and cooperative to a degree not thought possible."

The study was conducted over a period of several weeks during which there was an observation period, a period of special treatment, further observations, and a second treatment period. There was ample evidence in the data collected to linking the degree of aggressive behavior with the degree of response and attention from teachers. Whether this kind of systematic reinforcement was continued with these boys was not reported. Nor was evidence presented as to whether this reduction of aggressive behavior had significant long-term consequences, either positive or negative.

It makes more sense to the behaviorist to concentrate on the altering of very specific behaviors which have immediate positive consequences for a child (making him or her more acceptable to others, who react favorably in return), rather than trying to deal with more obscure, long-term developmental patterns where equally reliable modification procedures have not yet been developed. The behaviorist position, as developed by the Skinnerian group, is clear-cut, limited in scope, and built upon principles that are easily learned. It results in a very detailed and specific view of children's immediate behavior and provides a definitive approach to altering that behavior in directions considered as desirable.

MATURATIONIST ORIENTATION

Regularities from within

The **maturationist** orientation contrasts sharply with that of the behaviorist. The focus of the maturationist is on those aspects of development that are least influenced by environmental forces. They are particularly prone to focus on the regularities with which all humans develop, and they argue that what comes from within the child is the most important aspect of development. Although environmental forces are seen as possible supporters or inhibitors of internal growth potential, the primary direction of that growth is seen as coming from within. Parental, educational, and societal influences are consequently viewed as aiding or facilitating growth rather than as directing it.

An unfolding process

The maturationist sees a child's behavior at any particular time as primarily reflecting one stage in a continuing and largely unalterable unfolding process that is universally experienced. Faulty development, as evidenced by a child's unhappiness or maladjustment, can be attributed to interference with the child's capacity to develop according to his or her own timetable and according to his or her own needs. The French philosopher Jean Jacques Rousseau, a believer in the basic goodness of human instincts, was an early maturationist. His expectation was that children, if given the opportunity to grow in natural ways, would develop to their full potential, and that teachers or parents should therefore primarily avoid impeding the child's natural inclinations.

ROUSSEAU'S VIEW OF CHILDREN

The following is quoted from Rousseau's (1712–1778) writings. Rousseau advocates that the inherent good in children be allowed to emerge and develop prior to attempting to educate them.

> Nature requires children to be children before they are men. By endeavoring to pervert this order, we produce forward fruits, that have neither maturity nor taste, and will not fail soon to wither or corrupt. . . . Childhood has its manner of seeing, perceiving, and thinking, peculiar to itself; nor is there anything more absurd than our being anxious to substitute our own in its stead. (Rousseau, 1963, p. 47)

Plant analogy   This orientation has often been expressed by using the analogy of the growing plant. Unless it lacks basic nutrients, the plant will sprout and thrive and grow to its maximum potential. The gardener must simply respond to evidence of its needs for water and sunshine, and the plant will become what it can become. There is no need for the gardener to try to alter or hasten its growth; the consequences will either be unsuccessful or undesirable. Educators of the maturationist persuasion liken themselves to the gardener caring for the plant's basic needs but leaving the growing process to the plant and the universal growth forces within it.

Sigmund Freud and many of his followers in **psychoanalysis** can be considered proponents of a maturationist orientation. They viewed the primary influences on development as coming from within the child and as being universally experienced. Erik Erikson, for example, examines the way the

Stage conflicts   child is able to face a series of **psychosexual conflicts** which are thought to be central to the maturational process. Particular discrete behaviors would not be seen by Freud, Erikson, or others of the psychoanalytic persuasion as important, except as these reflect a person's conflicts at a particular growth stage.

Erikson poses eight **developmental crises** encountered by each human across the life span: trust versus mistrust, autonomy versus shame or doubt, initiative versus guilt, industry versus inferiority, identity versus identity diffusion, intimacy versus isolation, generativity versus stagnation, integrity versus despair. The first few of these stages, which are thought to encompass the first years of life, are discussed in some detail in Chapter 5, which deals with emotional and social development.

Although very general guidelines can be derived from the maturationist's view of the child, there is little direct and immediate action proposed for altering or influencing children's development. The educator is advised to care for the child's expressed or observed needs rather than attempting to directly and systematically alter those behaviors that might be viewed as evidence of faulty developmental progress.

Others within the maturationist tradition, such as Arnold Gesell and his co-workers at Yale University, have focused on the regularities of children's

Normative studies   growth and development across time. Over many decades they sought to determine, through observation, testing, and parental interviewing, what children can do at various ages. From these studies have come carefully derived **norms** which describe children's characteristics and abilities at various age levels. Many of the normative statements made in this book are derived from their work.

A major focus of the maturationists has been the development of realistic expectations for children that will prevent their being "pushed" toward performance beyond their maturational level. By establishing a general picture of children's developmental patterns, educators and parents can better judge the appropriateness of their instructional efforts. Children with a chronological age of six, for example, might be determined on the basis of their overall physical development and performance to have a developmental age of only five. According to this view, they should not be expected to perform in academic areas like a six-year-old simply because of their chronological age. Given time to develop according to their own internal timetable, they could be expected to learn to read, count, and perform other tasks with greater ease at a later point. The important factor is their own internal maturational level, as evidenced by various performance indicators. Intervention to hasten maturation is considered undesirable by most maturationists. Behavior and abilities are thought to develop relatively independently of what occurs in the environment.

The "real" self The expectation that there is a "real" self from which one can become alienated is derived from a maturationist view. The educator or parent who has this orientation is very concerned about allowing children to "become" rather than influencing what they should become. When they look at children, it is primarily to see how they may be assisted in whatever they are attempting to do and be. The ideal direction and rate of development will occur naturally unless thwarted by external influences. The maturationist puts great faith in the positive growth forces believed to be central to the human organism.

HORNEY'S VIEW OF THE "REAL" SELF

Karen Horney's (1950) views regarding the phenomenon of the "real" self are expressed in the following statement:

> You need not, and in fact, cannot, teach an acorn to grow into an oak tree, but when given a chance, its intrinsic potentialities will develop. Similarly, the human individual, given a chance, tends to develop his particular human potentialities. He will develop then the unique alive forces of his real self: the clarity and depth of his own feelings, thoughts, wishes, interests; the ability to tap his own resources, the strength of his will power; the special capacities or gifts he may have; the faculty to express himself, and to relate himself to others with his spontaneous feelings. All this will in time enable him to find his set of values and his aims in life. In short, he will grow, substantially undiverted, toward self realization. And that is why I speak . . . of the real self as that central inner force, common to all human beings and yet unique in each, which is the deep source of growth. (p. 17)

INTERACTIONIST ORIENTATION

A third group can be referred to as **interactionists** to differentiate their ways of viewing children from the other two major orientations. The interactionists are concerned with how children attempt to make sense of the world, what means they use in their explorations and thinking, and, especially, how their interactions with the environment help them move toward a higher state of development. Interactionists assume that children's own active functioning guides their development, so in viewing children they note primarily the nature of the child's transactions with the environment.

Whereas the maturationist generally assumes that growth alone leads to a new developmental stage regardless of experience at previous stages, the interactionist considers appropriate experiences to be essential to progression. The richness and appropriateness of the stimulation encountered at each point of development are felt to have a direct bearing on how well a child moves through a series of developmental stages to the next level of functioning.

The interactionist is thus less concerned than the maturationist with attributes of a particular stage of development and seeks instead to understand the dynamic process by which the child is transformed from one stage to another. Both orientations accept the notion of a progression through a series of stages, but the interactionist does not see this progression as an "unfolding" process generated from within the organism due simply to innate and/or genetic patterning, but as the result of its interaction with the environment.

A child's characteristics, at any particular time, are the result of the constant interplay between environmental stimuli (encountered through exploratory behavior) and the intellectual structures through which those stimuli are filtered.

Interactionists contrast with environmentalists in that they do not see children only as passive recipients of reinforcing stimuli that lead them to perform particular behaviors. Nor do they see children as simply emerging "good and whole" as maturationists tend to do. They see children as active

agents constantly engaged in figuring out who they are and what the world is all about and going through some rather predictable developmental patterns and stages in the process. Interactionists are very aware of how children's experiences with the environment influence their values and judgments, and, consequently, they try to provide children with encounters that will lead to higher levels of functioning.

Each of the three perspectives also differs regarding its ultimate expectations for human development. Maturationists simply assume that the upper limits of human capacity are genetically determined. Environmentalists, on the other hand, can only "shape" humankind to levels of development that parallel their own current functioning—but not higher. Interactionists, in

turn, assume that by improving children's early interactions with the environment the children can ultimately be brought to a higher level of functioning than their parents and teachers. They assume that, while the upper limit of potential in any given individual is not likely to be attained, an enriched experience throughout the life span will foster higher levels of development than would otherwise have been achieved.

John Dewey was an interactionist. His views of knowledge and learning were concerned with the processes that would lead children to more effective inquiry and problem-solving strategies. Central to his philosophy was the human quest for knowledge. Children who learned to think and investigate were expected to ultimately make discoveries that would benefit society.

The work of Jean Piaget, the Swiss psychologist, is cited here and throughout other sections of this book. Piaget's extensive studies of children's thought processes have led to a clearer perception of how the child's own activity can be central to his or her understanding. Piaget describes how a child's motor explorations are gradually transformed into more sophisticated means of exploration and eventually into representational thinking via abstract manipulation of symbols and language.

Piaget's contributions

Piagetians have given us a set of fresh insights about children. It has been said that once one looks at a child as Piaget does, one can never view children in quite the same old ways again. Whereas a very few years ago many American teachers had not heard of Piaget or his ideas, at the present time it is unusual to find one who does not have at least some knowledge about Piaget's stages of development. The term **conservation** used to mean to almost all American educators the protection of natural resources. Now it is generally recognized as the Piagetian term for the marked "turn-around" in children's abilities to recognize permanent qualities in the objects they view despite transformations in physical appearance. We have learned much from Piaget, not the least of which is a more precise understanding of the interactionist position. Some psychologists and educators who generally fall within an **interactionist** orientation, as we have developed it here, prefer the term "transactionist." "Interaction," they say, does not imply the mutual modification of perspectives that characterizes human encounters. "Transaction," however, implies that children influence or modify the behaviors of teachers, parents, or peers at the same time that they are themselves being influenced by these other persons. In this text, the term "interaction" is used to denote the more complex process of mutual influence.

Some Basic Principles of Child Development

The preceding section has discussed some of the contrasting views of children's behavior and development. Each of these views of behavior will be developed further in subsequent parts of this volume. In addition to these differing views, the following principles of child development are generally accepted and may be useful for you to keep in mind.

Development is continuous, gradual, and orderly. While professionals may not agree on specific ways to explain or promote development, all agree that development occurs in a regular fashion. A child does not abruptly become something other than what he or she was previously. The striking thing about development tends to be the predictable nature of the changes within a given individual across time. Few specific acts or series of acts in teaching are likely to cause massive, irreversible changes in children. The effects that a particular program has upon its participants can thus be gradually assessed and modified without fear of dire consequences for any given child.

Photo by Barbara Dopyera.

Development proceeds from the general to the specific. All observers of behavior would agree that specific, differentiated responses gradually develop from more global and general behaviors. The examples are myriad. The infant flails about with his limbs and only later develops the ability to control movements and perform specific manual actions. The preschooler first discriminates only grossly between visual forms such as circles and squares before becoming able to note intricate differences between letters and words. Your own general awareness of preschool children's behavior will develop into a more differentiated awareness of specific facets of children's behavior as you study this section. Throughout the life span, human responses tend to become more detailed and specific.

Growth and development vary among individuals. While general patterns are predictable across individuals, each person has an idiosyncratic pattern of development which only becomes known through a study of his or her specific behaviors across time. While a child of a given age or stage may be expected to behave in predictable ways, which are common to others of the same level, there are many unique aspects to each child's pattern of development, growth, and behavior that require special consideration.

You have just read about three general orientations toward children and have considered some basic principles of child development. It may be helpful to you at this point to do the following.

1. Ask any assortment of people available to you what they believe to be true about how children should be reared and educated and why. Decide whether their views generally reflect the orientations of behaviorists, maturationists, interactionists, or some combination of these, or whether they have other views that are quite different from any of these categories.

2. Start collecting comments on child rearing and education from a variety of sources. Look at editorials, letters to the editor, and newspaper and magazine features. Listen to talk shows and opinion programs. Try to categorize the opinions you hear according to the orientations they express.

Becoming a Skilled Observer of Children

In training yourself to become a skilled observer of children, the following precautions should be considered. You should first become very familiar with the factors that tend to limit your personal sensitivity on any given occasion. Second, you should become aware of how your perceptions and sensitivity are consistently affected by your own needs, beliefs, and preferences. Third, you should become aware of how the behaviors of the child you are observing may be influenced by the particular context within which you are working. And fourth, once these three limitations are accounted for, there is still the matter of systematically recording observations. Each part of the remainder of this chapter addresses these respective issues.

IDENTIFYING FACTORS THAT LIMIT SENSITIVITY

Right now, you possess a specific set of understandings or discriminations that you are capable of making about any child you encounter. Of course, you do not always make all the discriminations of which you are capable. The child you see on the sidewalk as you hurry by on your way to an appointment may hardly take your attention at all; you may note only a few very superficial features. The important discriminations are those you make when you do attend to a child and are not otherwise distracted.

The major thrust of this section is to help you extend your sensitivity to children's behavior and development. It will also be valuable for you to identify when, and under what conditions, you fail to make even those discriminations of which you know yourself to be capable. You will do well to consider those factors now, prior to your efforts to further extend your knowledge of children. To assist you, it should be helpful to consider what factors interfere with your taking in and retaining information in any situation.

Let us assume for a moment that you are shopping for clothes at a local shopping center. As a potential consumer, it is to your advantage to take in as much information as possible as you move from store to store so that you can make sound purchases. You probably differ from your friends in how sensitive you are to such variations as size, style, texture, cut, construction, durability, and price. The question we would like you to ponder is, under what conditions do you take in the most and the least information?

Fatigue probably plays a major role. You are probably taking in and retaining much more information at the beginning of a shopping excursion than at the end. After a snack break, however, your abilities to note and remember may be revived. Your general physical condition also plays a part. A simple headache or toothache can leave you functioning less well, noting less, remembering less.

Mental overload can result in less attention to details. If, while shopping, you are simultaneously trying to resolve a personal hassle with a companion, trying to decide what would be an appropriate gift for a friend, or are engaged in some other distracting activity, you will probably be less sensitive to the merchandise before you.

Finally, there are general environmental factors that can also affect your perceptions. Factors such as crowds, noise, particular lighting effects, temperature, display arrangements, uncomfortable clothing, all affect people differently and, for any given person, may diminish his or her perceptual ability.

It is likely that your reaction patterns are similar across many situations, and that whatever factors limit your perceptions in shopping situations

RESPONSE SECTION

You have just read about some of the factors that can reduce your perceptual capabilities. To more fully assess the factors that limit your own sensitivity, we suggest that you try some self-monitoring over a period of two or three weeks. Once each day, at a regular time, stop and consider when, during the previous twenty-four hours, you were most in tune with the things about you, and when you were most distracted, rattled, or on edge. List any factors, either internal or external, that you feel may have contributed to that state.

As you continue this activity across time, try to determine whether any principles could be derived that would help you increase the number of "with-it" times and decrease the "out-of-it" times. If you identify these factors now you will be better prepared to combat them when teaching.

Identifying the distractors would also have the same effect when you are trying to observe and record information about children. Note the extent to which fatigue, hunger, noise, and clutter interfere with your attention and memory. For each of us there is an optimal range within which we function well. Some of us like quiet, others prefer some background noise; some of us do well with several cups of coffee, others become overstimulated with one cup. You must learn for yourself what conditions are optimal for you.

SORTING OUT "YOU" FROM WHAT YOU VIEW

When you are observing children you will, of course, interpret what you see. Your own idealized view of child behavior, based on your own childhood experiences or your current needs, can greatly influence what you read into situations. It is important that you recognize this tendency. You may, for example, find yourself thinking that a little boy is wishing he had friends, wishing someone would notice him and take care of him, when it is really the *The "child" in you* "child" in you who has these feelings far more than the child being observed.

Personal taboos As you observe children you may find you become so attentive to a particular aspect of behavior that is personally disturbing to you that you will fail to note other behaviors. For example, if you are confronted by a child who is picking his nose and then putting his finger in his mouth, are you likely to note that he is also tracing intricate patterns with the other hand, humming a sophisticated tune, and balancing first on one foot and then on the other? In other words, to what extent are your powers of observation likely to be obstructed by your own internal "taboos"?

You may also find that your assumptions regarding what is proper and improper behavior influence your perceptions. For example, you may find

Photo by Robert Burdick.

that you are quite turned off by a child whom you see as acting like a "smart-aleck," while another person seeing the same behavior may not find it particularly noteworthy, or may even report the child as spirited, confident, and appealing. It is quite common for two people who view the same set of behaviors to come to quite different conclusions about them. Furthermore, they may both assume that their own judgment is quite universally accepted. It is important that teachers become aware of their personal idiosyncracies in perceiving and interpreting behavior.

Reporting, inferring, evaluating

There are two ways in which you can begin to distinguish your personal biases. First, we recommend that you begin to clearly differentiate your observations in terms of whether you are **reporting, inferring,** or **evaluating.**

Reporting is simply focusing on what is before you in as much detail as possible. *Inferring* is going beyond what you actually see and trying to guess at the underlying feelings, goals, or causes that might explain the behavior. *Evaluating* is making a judgment about the behavior you see, whether it is desirable or undesirable, positive or negative, mature or immature. A teacher, of course, engages in all three types of observation, often simultaneously, and benefits from proficiency in each. It is useful, however, to clearly differentiate between these processes and, especially, to develop the habit of relating each inference and evaluative statement to the actual behavior that was observed. Only if a report of actual behavior is available for

---

EXAMPLES OF REPORTING, INFERRING, AND EVALUATING

1. *Report.* Sara is drawing on the chalkboard. She makes a circular figure about which she says, "Look at the cookie I made." Tom replies, "I'll eat that cookie," and with his hand reaches over and wipes across the drawing. Sara lunges toward him and pushes him away. In doing so the piece of chalk breaks, falls to the floor, and shatters into several pieces. Sara goes to the teacher and says, "Tommy broke my chalk."

2. *Inference.* Sara is pleased to be able to produce figures and wants Tom's recognition for her ability. Tom, however, is more interested in the social interchange than Sara's product and demolishes it, bringing forth her anger and physical aggressiveness. However, when the chalk breaks, she is unwilling to accept the responsibility for her own action and so attributes it to Tommy.

3. *Evaluation.* Both Sara and Tom are behaving less maturely than might be expected for children of their age. Sara needs help in learning to verbally express her displeasure rather than physically striking out. She also needs to be encouraged to "own" her own actions—even when they have unfortunate consequences. Tom may need help in understanding that the destruction of another's product is not likely to produce the positive social interaction he evidently desires. He should be shown other ways of relating in a situation where someone asks him to look at their work.

Each of us projects our own feelings and needs into our observations of others. To become more aware of how others see and interpret behavior, try some of the following activities.

1. Examine some of the things you have written in the past, such as personal letters and reports. Underline those portions that are straight reporting. Put two lines under portions that are inferences or evaluations. Consider how other persons who knew about the same events might have given a different report and might have made different inferences and/or evaluations.

2. The next time you view a behavior your consider as "outlandish," try this strategy while relating it to your friends. Instead of biasing your report at the outset by saying, "Did I ever see an outrageous thing," or "Let me tell you something really weird," simply relate what you saw in detail (without revealing your impression) and then ask, "What do you think about that?" Get several different reactions and compare them with your own.

3. Locate some photographs of children that provoke strong feelings in you. Write down your impressions of each photograph, including (a) a report of what you see, (b) inferences about the cause of the actions or conditions depicted, and (c) an evaluation of what you feel is worthwhile or appropriate in the actions or conditions depicted. Ask others to tell you their impressions in the same order. Compare their observation with yours.

consideration can alternative inferences and evaluations be considered. Without a descriptive report there is no possibility for considering whether other kinds of statements have validity.

Comparing your views with others   The second way to determine your observational biases is to systematically compare your impressions—your reports, your inferences, your evaluations—with those of others. Find out if what you see is consistently different from the observations of others, and then closely analyze the nature of these differences. Through such comparisons you may find that you can increase your awareness in some areas, while in others the accuracy of your perceptions may already be well developed.

RECOGNIZING THE INFLUENCE OF CONTEXT ON BEHAVIOR

In the previous discussion it was pointed out that you should support your own inferences and evaluations with as much evidence as you can acquire.
Obtain impressions in different contexts   This "supporting evidence" rule is also useful in recognizing the influence of context on behavior. Obtaining reports of behavior in several different contexts (such as in a free activity time, on a playground, and in group discus-

sions) is advisable before attempting to make inferences about a child's behavioral repertoire or developmental level.

Suppose, for example, you observe a five-year-old girl in a single setting—a school assembly. You may observe that she sits for ten minutes without talking, and for most of that time without even moving, while watching and listening to a play about school citizenship presented by some older children. She laughs and claps at two appropriate points. She only looks at (but does not join in) some tickling and giggling activity of other kindergartners sitting near her. By observing this behavior you have learned some valuable things that you can eventually combine with other similar reports to draw some inferences and conclusions about the child.

On the basis of these reports alone, however, it would be unwise to infer that she is bright or slow, social or unsocial, interested in citizenship, serious, good, inhibited, or possessing any one of a number of other attributes. Nor could you validly make any determination of the kind of instructional program that would be most appropriate. In this example much of the child's behavior is influenced by the particular context within which you are viewing her. You should combine these observations with reports from other situations before drawing inferences or making evaluations about the child.

While it is sometimes possible to learn a great deal on the basis of a single observation, especially if that observation includes a variety of social, physi-

Although you probably acknowledge that context influences behavior, you may fail to recognize the extent of this influence. To increase your own awareness, make a list of behaviors that are comfortable for you in each of the following situations. List no more than fifteen behaviors for any one, just enough to get an impression of the range.

Beach
Own room
Church, synagogue, or place of worship
Bus or taxi
Restaurant
Public park
University classroom

Note the difference in constraints imposed by different settings. In which setting would it be most difficult for an observer to gain an impression of the breadth of your behavioral repertoire? Where would it be easiest?

cal, verbal, intellectual, and emotional expressions, there is always a danger of inferring too much from too little evidence. Consequently, repeated observations in varied settings are always desirable in order to offset the limiting effects of context.

After reading and reflecting on the preceding material you should have an increased awareness of (1) the factors, both internal and external, that tend to diminish your sensitivity, (2) the possible ways in which your own needs, preferences, and behavioral taboos may limit or distort your perceptions, and (3) the ways in which context may limit or constrain the behavior of individuals on any given occasion. These factors should be periodically reconsidered as you continue to extend your sensitivity and as you begin to engage in systematic observations of children.

Alternative Formats for Recording Observations

Behavioral scientists have devised various ways of recording their observations. Books are available that index and describe these various strategies and formats. We will discuss only two very general methods that are particularly appropriate to teaching—the descriptive narrative system and the category system. We suggest that you use a combination of the two in making observations of individual children.

DESCRIPTIVE NARRATIVE

This first approach sounds quite simple, but can prove to be more difficult than you anticipate. In producing a descriptive narrative of a given child's behavior, the observer begins by recording the time and the setting and then proceeds to write down in as much detail as possible what the child does, including responses to the actions of others. The following is an example of a five-minute descriptive narrative.

Setting: Lucy's (age five) backyard
Time: 3:30 P.M.

Lucy is filling a plastic "swimming pool" with water from a hose. She directs the stream of water to make swirls and waves in the pool. She moves the stream of water as close to the pool's edge as possible and goes twice around in this fashion. George (neighbor, age five) asks Lucy to fill the watering can he is holding: "Gimme some gasoline." She guides stream of water into the one-and-a-half-inch opening and fills, saying, "That's all you get." Betsy (neighbor, age four) comes over with another can saying, "I want some gasoline." Lucy says, "You can't have any more 'cause you aren't my friend." Sprays hose on edge of pool and onto Betsy's feet. Betsy says, "My mother said not to get wet." Lucy does not reply but looks at her and then swings stream of water across her shorts. Betty shrieks. Lucy grins, then turns and walks about ten feet from pool pulling hose along at her side. Wets down concrete patio flooring. Turns hose toward each dry area until all is wet.

In recording behavior in descriptive narrative format, the goal is to describe only actual behaviors and to exclude statements of inference or evaluation. There are no set limits for the time span covered by such a narrative, but, since the writing load is intense, many observers restrict themselves to a brief episode. During this time observers are involved with rapid notetaking, after which they fill in the details. The initial episode can be followed by another stretch of observation, notetaking, and note expansion. To psychologists this practice of making a record for preset time periods at regularly recurring intervals is called **time sampling.** The observer assumes that by regularly sampling behavior across a period of time, sufficiently representative behaviors will be obtained to make reasonable inferences about that person's typical pattern of behavior.

Time sampling; event sampling

Another approach to sampling is called **event sampling.** Again, the observer does not try to record behavior continuously, but instead waits for some particularly relevant event or situation to occur and then records all behaviors that occur during that event. The observer may decide in advance, for example, to record only instances of conflicts, interactions with adults, or the use of toys. This kind of sampling is used when the observer (1) wants to have a controlled set of contexts for making better inferences about behavior, or (2) wants to assess the child's behavioral repertoire in a particular type of situation. As with time sampling, the observer records, as rapidly as possible, all relevant actions and reactions, and, upon termination of the event, makes sure the record is readable and complete.

Advantages and limitations

Especially in the initial observations of a child, detailed, descriptive narratives of segments of behavior are useful. The disadvantages of narrative descriptions stem from the fact that they are relatively time consuming and require at least a brief period of total concentration on the particular child to the exclusion of all others. Although such a period of concentration on each child is easily justified by the insights obtained, it is often difficult for a teacher who has responsibility for a group to find the opportunity to make such observations. It is an excellent way for a student to observe, however, since the novice observer of children typically follows the action of a group and misses the nuances of the individual child's ongoing behavior.

CATEGORY SYSTEMS

Another very different way of recording observations of children is to note only the occurrence of certain selected behaviors in which the observer may be especially interested. In this approach the observer typically watches an individual child for a set period of time (sometimes for regularly recurring periods) or during a particular event, such as a story time. The observer can record the occurrence of each kind of behavior in one of two formats: (1) whether it occurs at all, or (2) the frequency with which it occurs.

Any sort of discrete behavior can be included in such a system, and many kinds of behavior can be looked for simultaneously. The following are examples of the kinds of behaviors that are included in one observational schedule (Medley *et al.*, 1968).

1. Physical movement
   • high activity with locomotion
   • moderate activity with locomotion
   • high activity, no locomotion
   • moderate activity, no locomotion
   • low activity

2. Child-child contacts
   • aggressive toward peer
   • initiating peer contact
   • cooperating with peer
   • withdrawing from peer contact
   • resisting peer contact

The entire schedule contains nearly a score of such headings, covering many areas of child behavior. For each of a series of brief time segments, the observer indicates which of the alternative descriptions best characterize the child's behavior.

Advantages and limitations   The advantage of this kind of observational approach is that it forces a very particular focus. It is possible for several observers looking at the same situation to report essentially the same things because they are focusing on predetermined behaviors. Agreement between separate observers (interobserver reliability), after initial periods of training, is usually quite high. In contrast, two people preparing a descriptive narrative may focus on different aspects of behavior and may give quite different kinds of reports.

Both of the general methods of recording observations—descriptive narrative and category systems—are useful for a teacher's purposes. It is helpful to have full detail of happenings as provided by the descriptive narrative. On the other hand, the use of a category system ensures attention to specified behaviors. A method that combines the descriptive narrative and the category systems will be recommended for your use in the following part of this chapter. Further descriptions and illustrations of this combination method will appear in subsequent chapters in this section.

Making Observations of Individual Children

Full behavioral assessments

As an extension of your study in this section, we suggest that you arrange to systematically observe individual children. Our recommendation is that you prepare full **behavioral assessments,** according to specifications we will provide, for as many different children as possible. Ideally, you will arrange to make these assessments for at least nine children—three different children at three different age levels. This would enable you to gain a sense of age progression as well as of individual differences at a given age. Each of these behavioral assessments will involve the expenditure of substantial amounts of time and energy, so plan accordingly. We would emphasize, however, that preparing a behavioral summary based on a series of observations for even one child is far more valuable than simply studying the materials included in this section without any systematic application.

It is essential that you arrange for repeated observations of any child you wish to fully assess. You will need a situation where you can both observe the child and make notes about what you see. It is also important, that you be able to observe the child in various kinds of activities and that, during some of the observations, the child have some option of doing what he or she "wants" to do. It is difficult to get a sense of what children can do if you *only* see them in situations with limited options.

Perhaps you have observation opportunities available to you as part of your training program. If so, you are lucky. If not, we urge that you seek these opportunities for yourself. You might approach teachers, parents, program administrators, club leaders (such as Brownies and Cubs), playground directors, or other persons responsible for children, and request permission to observe a child or children in their care. If you offer to share your notes with them, they will perhaps be more willing to allow you to make a series of observations. You should emphasize that your major purpose is to develop your skills as an observer and that the reports you prepare are of course not professional. You will need practice and credentials before offering youself as a professional. Nevertheless, the observations you make will undoubtedly prove very interesting and helpful to the person responsible for the children.

Guidelines for observing

The following general guidelines for making observations apply to almost any setting. Most are just common sense and can be easily kept in mind.

- Children will be less distracted by your presence if you sit or kneel than if you are a tower within their visual "landscape."
- Be as unobtrusive as possible and do not become involved in the children's activity, or you will have little opportunity to be an observer.
- If a child tries to talk with you, asks for your help (of a nonemergency variety), or asks what you are doing, reply that you are doing your work, that you are learning about what children are like (or something of the kind), but do not encourage further conversation. Remove yourself briefly, if necessary, to lose a persistent child.
- Try not to laugh, frown, or in any way react to either the child you are observing or the other children in the setting, or you may find that you are not only recording but are influencing behavior.
- Never talk about a given child to other adults if either that child or the other children are within hearing. The old saying that "little pitchers have big ears" is sometimes truer than you may realize.
- Avoid casually discussing the behavior or characteristics of any particular children you have observed (especially by name) with anyone other than the responsible person who gave you permission to observe. Consider information you obtain through observation as privileged professional matter, which has no place in casual conversation.

We suggest the following very general procedures in observing and recording children's behavior. At the beginning, obtain only very basic information such as the child's name, age, sex, and the name and relationship to the child of the person giving your permission to observe. Learn as much as you can through observation before asking for additional information.

During your first observation try to gain a general impression of the setting and of the child's general appearance and demeanor and then prepare several narrative descriptions of approximately five-minute segments of behavior. Try to get down as much detail as possible. Be sure to save these for later reference.

Cross between descriptive narrative and category approach

In each of the next three chapters directions will be provided for recording observations in a way that is a cross between the descriptive narrative and the category approach. We are suggesting this format because of its usefulness for (1) immediately increasing your sensitivity to children's behavior, and (2) providing you with an ongoing record-keeping system that you can use as a teacher of young children.

A series of questions about the individual child's behavior will be posed, relative to the concerns of each of these chapters. Your task will be to study these questions (categories) and, in your observation of the child, to record in a descriptive narrative form (very briefly) any evidence that bears upon the questions. For example, one such question posed in the next chapter is, *What is the child's ability to use his/her body in rhythmic fashion?* During your observation you might see no evidence at all of rhythmic performance, or you might note something such as the following:

- Janey tries to skip across the room as her friend Suzy is doing; manages skipping pattern about half-way across and then runs the rest of the way
- Listens to "Funky Chicken" music from record player while writing on chalkboard; continues in activity of writing but moves in dance pattern while doing so.

In each of the three chapters a large number of such questions are posed to guide you in looking for specific behavior that might otherwise go un-noticed. By combining the category and narrative description methods of observation, you are able to obtain a record that is both wide ranging (category system) and sufficiently rich in details related to these categories (descriptive narrative).

Just prior to the questions, there will be some very specific suggestions for organizing your notes, using either a notebook or a card file system. More detailed guides for observing and recording are also included there.

We suggest that you arrange for at least one observation experience before studying the next chapter, recording what you see, as previously recom-mended, via straight descriptive narratives. Then, as you proceed through Chapters 4, 5, and 6, your observations will gradually broaden their focus to assimilate the content of each successive area of development. By the end of Chapter 6 you should be observing and recording behaviors related to three realms of development: **physical characteristics** and **motor behavior; affec-tive behavior** and **social behavior; cognitive behavior** and **intellectual behav-ior**.

You will be primarily engaged in reporting behavior in these chapters. In Chapter 7, however, we suggest procedures for analyzing and organizing your notes in order to compile a full behavioral assessment, which includes inferences and evaluative statements about the child's needs, interests, and progress. We will also recommend ways of supplementing your own obser-vations of children with information from other sources.

Summary

In becoming a teacher you must develop very specialized sensitivities to children and their development. You must learn to take in more comprehen-sive and more detailed information about certain aspects of children's behav-ior than persons in other professions, even those in closely related fields. The observations made of behavior are interpreted according to the beliefs of the observer as to the basic nature of development and learning. You will need to become familiar with the major contrasting orientations: environmentalist, maturationist, interactionist. Knowledge of some of the principles that underlie all development will also prove helpful in developing your own sensitivity.

To become a skilled observer of children, you must become aware of and control the influence of factors that tend to limit your sensitivity. You must also become aware of any biases and idiosyncratic reactions that cause you to distort or miss some behaviors. Context factors often influence behavior, and as an observer you must learn to observe in multiple settings before drawing conclusions about what you have seen.

In subsequent chapters you will be guided in making observations of children using a method that combines the narrative description and the category system. Although there are various other methods available, this approach will be most useful for your immediate goal—becoming more sensitive to the behavior and development of young children.

REASSESSMENT

Reread what you wrote for the preassessment as you began this chapter, comparing this with your current understandings. Now write on these topics again and incorporate your new insights and knowledge. Continue to update as you prepare for teaching. Save your materials for your portfolio.

Additional Reading

Try these first:

Environmental Engelmann, S., and Engelmann, T. *Give your child a superior mind.* New York: Simon and Schuster, 1966.

Sparkman, B., and Carmichael, A. *Blueprint for a brighter child.* New York: McGraw-Hill, 1973.

Then progress to these:

Skinner, B. F. *Beyond freedom and dignity.* New York: Alfred A. Knopf, 1971.

———. *Science and human behavior.* New York: Macmillan, 1953.

——— *Walden two.* New York: Macmillan, 1948.

Maturation Ames, L. B., and Chase, J. A. *Don't Push your preschooler.* New York: Harper & Row, 1974.

Beck, H. L. *Don't push me, I'm no computer: How pressures to "achieve" harm preschool children.* New York: McGraw-Hill, 1973.

Gesell, A., and Thompson, H. *The psychology of early growth.* New York: Macmillan, 1938.

Hymes, J. L. *A child development point of view.* Englewood Cliffs, N.J.: Prentice-Hall, 1955.

Interactionism Dewey, J. *Experience and education.* Reprint. New York: Collier, 1963. Original edition, 1938.

Hunt, J. McV. *Intelligence and experience.* New York: Ronald Press, 1961.

Kohlberg, L. Early education: A cognitive-developmental view. *Child Development,* 1968, 39, 1013–62.

Try these first:

Observing Children Brandt, R. M. *Studying behavior in natural settings.* New York: Holt, Rinehart and Winston, 1972.

Cartwright, C., and Cartwright, G. *Developing observation skills.* New York: McGraw-Hill, 1974.

Gordon, I. J. *Studying the child in school.* New York: Wiley, 1966.

Rasking, L. M., and Taylor, W. J. The teacher as observer for assessment: A guideline. *Young children*, 1975, 30, 339–44.

Then progress to these:

Barker, R. G. *Ecological psychology: concepts and methods for studying the environment of human behavior.* Stanford, Calif.: Stanford University Press, 1968.

Medley, D. M., and Mitzel, H. E. Measuring classroom behavior by systematic observation. In N. Gage, Ed. *Handbook of research on teaching.* Chicago: Rand McNally, 1973.

Wright, H. F. Observational child study. In P. H. Mussen, Ed. *Handbook of research methods in child development.* New York: Wiley, 1960.

———. *Recording and analyzing child behavior.* New York: Harper & Row, 1967.

CHAPTER 4
Increasing Sensitivity to Children's Physical Characteristics and Motor Behavior

Overview

Motor Behavior and Physical Characteristics of Infants and Toddlers

Motor Behavior and Physical Characteristics of Children Ages Three Through Seven
  SIZE AND WEIGHT
  BODY TYPES
  BODILY POSTURE
  PHYSICAL ATTRACTIVENESS
  GROSS MOVEMENTS
  SMALL MUSCLE DEVELOPMENT
  DOMINANCE
  PHYSICAL DEFECTS
  NERVOUS TRAITS
  HEALTH AND DISEASE INDICATORS

Observing Motor Behavior and Physical Characteristics of Individual Children

Transition into Resourcefulness Section

Summary

PREASSESSMENT

When you have completed this chapter you should be able to describe and compare the following:

1. *physical characteristics and motor behavior of infants and toddlers, three- to five-year-olds, and six- and seven-year-olds.*
2. *specific aspects of physical characteristics and motor behavior in young children that may be relevant for you to observe.*
3. *implications for programing of young children's physical development and motor behavior.*

Before beginning to read this chapter:

1. *take enough time to write what you already know about each of the above topics.*
2. *observe the physical characteristics and motor behavior of individual children and record your impressions.*

Save what you write for rereading, comparison, and elaboration after you have studied and discussed these materials.

Overview

The following account illustrates the primacy of physical activity in young children's behavior:

Curtis runs into the play room at full speed and slides to a stop with verbal screeching just short of a block tower Joey is building. "What 'cha doin'?" he says, but before Joey can answer he runs in the other direction, kicks shoulder high with his left foot at some imaginary target, and says, "Got 'cha!" He wheels about and returns to the exact spot again kicking shoulder high, this time with his right foot. Again he says, "Got 'cha!" He then turns about, runs up the four-foot sliding board attached to the jungle gym, pivots half-way up, and sits down to slide to the bottom. At the bottom he stretches out, completely relaxed, watching the block tower teeter as Joey adds a cube. "Watch it!" he shouts and leaps up in time to catch one of the falling blocks.

Curtis is four years old. He is full of energy and enthusiasm. His gross motor abilities appear to provide him with great satisfaction. His body gives him pleasure in both its appearance and its performance. If Curtis' teachers are unaware of the central role that physical abilities play in his development at this age, they are missing a critical aspect of his being. And Curtis is not particularly unusual in this respect. Most young children, although perhaps not as able as Curtis, judge themselves more on the basis of their **motoric competence** than on any other criterion. Teachers of young children need to become as sensitive to these aspects of development as they are to cognitive or social behaviors.

In this chapter we will first very briefly discuss the progress and significance of motor development and physical growth during the infant and toddler years. We will then describe in greater detail the motor and physical characteristics of children ages three through seven, including size and bodily proportions, bodily posture, physical attractiveness, **gross movement, small muscle coordination, dominance,** physical defects, nervous traits, and health and disease indicators. Third, you will be given some very specific guidelines for observing individual children's behavior. Finally, there will be some suggestions for taking those observations into account as you plan a program for children that is appropriate to their physical and motor development.

Motor Behavior and Physical Characteristics of Infants and Toddlers

The competent infant

When did you last hold and wonder at a newborn baby? The human infant, while quite helpless, has amazing competencies from the day of birth. The **differentiation** process begins immediately and continues throughout the life span. Much of the early learning consists of establishing the source of an experience—Is it coming from within or from outside oneself? Both are unknowns that must be learned.

The way the child develops these awarenesses has been well described by the Swiss psychologist Jean Piaget. Piaget has helped us to understand that, for infants, there is no **intellect** apart from **motor intelligence.** Infants' only mode for thinking about encounters with the world is through their own actions or through the sensory qualities of whatever is encountered. It is through their own motor activity that the **mental structures** are developed from which further thinking is derived.

The first year of life, according to Piaget, involves the development of successively more advanced schemas, or means for acting on the world and deriving information. At first, children use the schema of sucking (initially a **reflexive behavior**); later they use grasping (also initially a reflex). They taste and feel all that comes within range of their mouths and hands and visually examine the sights that surround them. Eventually they begin to coordinate the use of these separate ways of acting on the world and from this coordination come new schemas, or modes of learning. These include the awareness that something grasped is something to taste, things heard are something to look at, things seen are something to reach for and grasp. These new schemas are an improved means (beyond separate actions such as sucking and grasping) for obtaining information. Knowing that the feel of something is dependably associated with its appearance is a tremendous advance in knowing about that object; knowing that one can navigate a felt object into one's mouth to taste and explore orally is another significant realization about oneself as well.

The development of schemas

A bit later, children begin to show some anticipation about which actions will bring about particular outcomes. For example, Piaget describes how his five-month-old daughter Lucienne, upon looking at a doll hung from the hood of her bassinet, would consistently kick her feet to create movement and a swaying of the doll. In becoming aware that its own activity can effect what it sees or hears, the baby has acquired a very effective means for learning about the world. If you have ever watched a baby at this age, you might have observed how enthralled and delighted they appear to be with their newfound ability to make things happen.

Making things happen

Infants increasingly learn how their own actions bring about effects upon objects around them. By the end of the first year an infant with a rattle or a bell will experiment with vigorous shaking, slow movements, and pauses followed by more movements. There is a very active manipulation of any object within reach to determine what it is like and its possible uses. By age eighteen months children have begun thinking of themselves as a separate object in a world of permanent objects (that is, objects that still exist when out of sight). These new conceptions allow young children to more effectively manipulate objects to create effects and solve (simple) problems.

While these kinds of behaviors had been noted by parents and other close observers of infants long before Piaget's ideas had become known, they were typically considered to be the result of **biological maturation** and were not considered significant in terms of further development. Piaget's contribution has been to point out that it is the child's own functioning that transforms these initial schemas into more complex ones and that the higher forms of thinking and problem-solving have their genesis in the infant's motor explorations.

Functioning transforms schemas

A greater elaboration of the continuity from the **sensorimotor period** in infancy to the development of schemas for more complex thinking is presented in Chapter 6. In the present chapter we will limit ourselves to briefly tracing how the child's increased motor efficiency leads to the ability to move from place to place and to manipulate objects and tools with increasing skill. The child who at age three or four can run, climb, and use pencils and scissors has "come a long way" from infancy.

A child's increasing competence in moving about generally includes the following progression: lifting chin, lifting chest, sitting with support, walking when led, creeping, standing when holding on to furniture, standing with help, sitting alone, walking, walking and pulling a toy on a string, jumping, running—and then the world! This difficult and involved progression ranges from the helpless prone position to moving about very independently during the second year.

Handling and learning from objects

The ability to manipulate objects has its genesis in the baby's grasping. When the baby is able to sit alone, at around seven months, the handling of objects is greatly aided. By seven months, infants can grasp and explore objects with both thumb and palm (instead of just the palm alone). Infants shake and bang objects to create sounds, transfer them from one hand to the other, and generally become quite engrossed in examining anything that comes within reach, such as stones, blocks, toys, silverware, cookies, or cotton balls. They learn about such sensations as *prickly, soft, sticky, sour, pliable, hard,* and *rough*. They gradually learn how to use their hands in coordination with their eyes to control the object being explored.

The "letting go" of objects

A crucial ability and a difficult one to acquire is that of consciously letting go of an object in hand. This often is not accomplished until late in the first year. To effectively pick up and put down objects, the baby must have considerable control of the fingers, and especially of the opposing thumb. (Try to pick up and release an object without your thumb if you would like to gain a new appreciation of these carefully acquired skills.) After months of practicing hand manipulation of various objects, the two-year-old has typically learned such "advanced" feats as building a tower of six or seven blocks, making a train of three or more cubes, drawing misshapen circles and V's, turning individual pages of a book, or fitting square blocks into square forms in puzzles. Think of the learning this represents, the number of unsuccessful or partially successful efforts required before these tasks are mastered. Only the baby's parents or constant caretakers can appreciate how much effort this represents.

It is hoped that the preceding discussion will lead you to appreciate what has already been accomplished, both by the typical three-year-old and by those children who enter a preschool program without some of these motor skills. Some children will struggle much longer with these rudimentary skills of walking, balancing, and handling objects and will need far more tolerance than their more successful peers. Yet all too often they receive reprimands for their clumsiness simply because they do not equal the average attainment for their age.

The vast changes in physical characteristics and motor abilities during the early years have been emphasized in the preceding discussion, and the remarkable accomplishments of this period have been repeatedly cited. We suggest that you now focus on two additional areas of exploration.

1. Make a list of the things that you believe must be supplied to an infant and/or toddler to ensure his or her survival and healthy development. Then try to spend some time with someone who is caring for a baby. Observe the child and the caregiver for an extended period (while the child is awake), noting what is provided for the child. Then modify your initial list on the basis of what you learn.

2. Make a list of your own motor skills that you think are beyond the capabilities of a two- or three-year-old. Spend an hour or two observing a child of this age to check on the accuracy of your list.

Motor Behavior and Physical Characteristics of Children Ages Three Through Seven

When you see young children at the library, the laundromat, or at a concert, can you guess about how old they are? If you cannot, or if you feel unsure of your estimates, you might begin sensitizing yourself to the physical characteristics and motor abilities of children of various ages. You can do this by making it a practice to observe, predict, and verify (by asking the child or parent) the ages of children you encounter. You will find that your guesses will become more and more accurate. Besides, it is very interesting to compare the different responses of individual children and children of different ages to your question, "How old are you?"

SIZE AND WEIGHT

Growth is an individual matter

While tables of average heights and weights for varying ages may be interesting to study, any conclusions drawn from them about the appropriate size for an individual child at any given time can be thoroughly misleading. Any given child follows his or her own growth pattern, both in rate of growth and eventual size. Comparisons with agemates are virtually meaningless. For example, two six-year-olds who weigh exactly the same may be faring very differently. As judged by previous growth rates and by expectations based on size of parents, one could be undersized, and the other, by the same criteria, could be overweight.

Adequacy of size cannot be judged at any one point in time. The pattern of growth across time and the parents' statures are essential in making such a judgment, but even with this information it is difficult to say whether a given height or weight is "normal" for an individual child. Teachers need to be very wary in making such appraisals. Although it is a well-known fact that inadequate nutrition, especially in protein, restricts size, there are many nondietary causes of different growth patterns. It would be erroneous simply to assume that a small or thin child is not getting the proper diet.

Height and weight increases occur quite regularly during the early childhood years, but changes in bodily configuration are even more conspicuous. Six-year-olds are shaped much more like adults than when they were age two or three. It is during this period that the trunk and arms increase in length. Three-year-olds find the task of reaching over their heads and touching the opposite ear an impossible one, but most six- and seven-year-olds can do this easily because they have longer arms. You might enjoy testing this out with the children whose ages you are trying to guess. Tell them that you can do a trick, then touch your opposite ear and find out if they can do it also.

The advantage of size You may note that many children who are large for their age are more "advanced" in other respects as well, such as motor coordination, **reading readiness,** and social ability. Many explanations of this have been proposed. One is that such individuals have a genetic superiority that is evidenced in many ways. Another is that optimal diet, physical care, and a stimulating learning environment result in "advanced" growth and social and intellectual development. A third is that being initially larger than one's agemates produces a natural superiority in social relationships, and consequently a positive self-concept that facilitates development in all areas.

CORRELATES OF BODY SIZE

Stanley Garm (1966) comments, as follows, regarding the relationships between body size and characteristics and/or behavior:

> Body size from infancy through adolescence carries with it a variety of physiological, developmental, and behavioral correlates. For constant age, taller individuals have a larger basal oxygen consumption and in consequence they eat more because they need more. Taller children, like taller adults, have larger bones and in consequence their needs for calcium and phosphorus during growth must be proportionally larger . . . . Skeletal age tends to be advanced in taller children. Taller children are also slightly but consistently advanced in the number of teeth present at a given age. (pp. 540–41)
>
> Taller children tend to walk earlier. . . . Boys and girls with a larger lean mass tend to be advanced in gross motor development. A variety of studies report that "reading readiness" is positively correlated with stature. And most measures of "intelligence" appear to be loosely associated with body size during the growing period. (p. 542)

From the teacher's perspective, there is good reason to concentrate on helping all children view their current stage of growth as a launching point for further development. The teacher must also be very aware of those instances in which larger size is not accompanied by advanced abilities and must develop his or her expectations accordingly.

BODY TYPES

Consider for a moment those persons with whom you associate in your daily activities. Are some of them not tall and slim, and others stout and stocky? Do some not have heavy limbs whereas others have rather spindly arms and legs? Are you aware of whether the behavior of your friends is in any way related to their differing body types?

Three distinct body types were identified by Sheldon (1942) as **mesomorph, endomorph,** and **ectomorph.** The mesomorph is characterized as stocky, muscular, and very active. People generally expect a person with this build to be assertive and dominant. The ectomorph is tall and gangly, a "bean pole" often stereotyped as intelligent, withdrawn, dreamy, and a bit wishy-washy. The endomorph is round and pudgy and is expected to be unassertive and good natured. Although unaware of these categories, most of us operate toward others according to the characteristics we associate with the body type, such as "fat and jolly," or "skinny and sensitive." Certain behaviors have been shown to have a somewhat more than coincidental *Inherited* relationship with body type (Bayley, 1951; Davidson *et al.*, 1957; Hale, 1956; *characteristics or* Sheldon *et al.*, 1954); this has been shown even in young children (Walker, *social expectations* 1962; Douglas *et al.*, 1965). It is of course impossible to determine whether these personality characteristics stem from hereditary influences or social expectations.

It is important for you as a teacher to explore your own expectations and feelings. Are you turned off or on by certain physiques and, if so, how will this affect your teaching? Will you have different expectations for muscular as opposed to gangly children, expectations based on body type rather than behavior? How will your own reactions and attention patterns vary? Which type of child will you be most apt to smile at, an active mesomorph type or a dreamy ectomorph?

You may also find that the children you teach react to body types in ways that can have detrimental effects. To many children, being fat is very degrading, more so than, for example, using crutches, missing a limb, or having a facial disfigurement (Richardson, 1961). For such children, your example of acceptance as a teacher could be particularly valuable.

BODILY POSTURE

Posture is the result of various adjustments used to balance the whole body. Despite the frequent admonitions of parents and teachers to "Sit up" and "Stand straight," there is actually little a child can consciously do to improve posture. If opposing muscles are unequal, faulty balance between them results in poor posture. A better alignment of the body is not necessarily brought about by holding the head up or putting the shoulders back. It is achieved, instead, by good muscle tone, good skeletal development, and general physical and emotional good health.

Each child balances his or her body in the most functional way, given his or her individual mass and muscle tone. A stocky child balances the body in one way, a skinny child in another. While a beautifully balanced body is an indication of health, one child's stance should not be modeled on another's, since significant bodily differences usually exist. Bodily posture is something a teacher might note and possibly use to evaluate a child's physical and emotional health, but it is not something that warrants direct action to bring about change.

A low center of gravity in a living organism, as in an automobile, leads to a desirable stability. The young child has a high center of gravity that gradually shifts downward throughout the early years from just above the navel to just below it. This high center of gravity, along with incomplete muscle development, accounts for the frequent falls and comparative clumsiness of young children, in contrast to older ones. You may find it interesting to observe the number of times preschool children fall during active play, as contrasted with older children.

PHYSICAL ATTRACTIVENESS

Do you consider yourself physically attractive, and does it matter to you? Why? Despite all the admonitions to the contrary, such as "Beauty is as beauty does" and "Beauty is only skin deep," attractive features are a great asset. Although personal appearance is partly a matter of fashion, some people are never considered to be pretty or handsome. Worse yet, there are always some people whose features are so differently or unevenly arranged that they are universally seen as unattractive or ugly. Television and children's books have had a tremendous impact in broadening our image of attractiveness. Nevertheless, many children remain outside the current standards of attractiveness, and consequently may identify more with villains and clowns than with attractive heroes and heroines.

*Attractiveness is in
the eye of the
beholder*
As a teacher, you will be responsible for children who both match and deviate from your own and society's image of attractiveness. Can you care as much about a hollow-cheeked, sallow-skinned child with decaying teeth and large protruding ears as you can about a cute, freckle-faced redhead with an engaging smile and a stylish haircut? What effect will this have on the children you teach? You may wish to systematically examine your feelings about the appearance of others, especially children.

GROSS MOVEMENTS

Do you know how you look when you move? Do you have a vocabulary for describing these movements as well as the differences between your own movements and those of your best friend? Chances are, you do not. Most of us tend to perceive and articulate differences in physical appearance far more than differences in movement. We are usually quite unaware of how we look as we move, and we often find filmed or videotaped sequences of our movement quite surprising. Most of us are unable to describe the movements of others even though these may intuitively influence our reactions to them.

For children, movement is almost everything

In working with children it will be helpful to become consciously attuned to movement. For a child, movement is almost everything. Keturah Whitehurst (1971, p. 9), a physical educator, expresses this view as follows: "Movement means to young children, life, self-discovery, environmental discovery, freedom, safety, communication, enjoyment and sensuous pleasure." To be fully attuned to children you must learn to see movement and to differentiate its many aspects. Such as:

agility—the ability to move flexibly, to stretch, bend, twist, spin, arch, leap, turn, throw, run, jump.

strength—the effective alignment of body parts to push or release power.

endurance—the extent to which movement(s) can be continued without need for rest.

balance—the effective alignment of body parts to maintain the vertical center of gravity, which prevents falling.

rhythm—the ability to pattern movements in a predictable, repetitive sequence.

speed—the effective alignment of body parts to allow rapid and/or efficient movement through space.

The above movements do not necessarily develop simultaneously. A child may be quite skilled at climbing and tumbling, yet awkward at running, jumping, and throwing. Strength and power are often associated with body size and build, whereas balance and agility show little relationship to physique or strength. There is relatively little relationship between strength and speed. Therefore, when observing children you should look for and note specific movements rather than making broad judgments such as "well coordinated" or "poor motor development."

It will be useful for you to learn the "typical" patterns of motor development by age levels, despite the many exceptions to these developmental progressions within any group of children. As you read through the following section, we would like you to keep in mind that movements typical of four-year-olds are sometimes accomplished by three-year-olds and, conversely, are sometimes still unattained by children of ages five and six. Knowledge of the general progression is more useful than the specific ages at which these accomplishments are attained.

Three-year-olds

Three-year-olds can run smoothly and easily, increasing and decreasing speed, turning corners sharply and coming to screechingly quick stops. Many three-year-olds alternate feet as they climb steps, rather than placing both feet on each step. They can also, just for fun, jump from a bottom step to the floor with both feet together. They can jump up and down with both feet without falling and can even (but ever so briefly) balance on one foot. They can walk along a sidewalk crack or a line for distances of ten feet or so without falling off, and they can walk backward.

Most joyful of all, they can ride a threewheeler! On wheels they can go faster and with less effort, can turn, stop, and back up, and can extend the control they have gained over their own bodies to the vehicles. And they find it easy to do. Anyone who can do this, they seem to feel, could never be mistaken for a baby! In fact, one of the minor traumas for many three-year-olds in nursery school is the need to share their threewheelers. On such occasions, they often pucker up and howl like the wee ones they really are still—or were not long ago.

Four-year-olds Age four is the time for pushing out, for testing the limits of one's growing abilities and testing also the tolerances of caregivers. Four-year-olds, for example, are likely to climb as high as they can on equipment or in trees, often bringing fear to the hearts of observing adults. Many are expert jumpers, being able to make running and standing jumps, whereas most three-year-olds can only jump up and down in place. The threewheeler has been well mastered by age four and is used for stunting and all kinds of special variations, such as backing rapidly, turning hairpin corners, rounding curves at top speed, or riding standing up. Many of the skills practiced at age three with total concentration are, at age four, nonchalantly incorporated into elaborate fantasy play. The bike speeding around the circle is likened to a racing car or a space ship, and its rider may well be receiving and responding to vital messages from fellow pretenders as he or she navigates. At age four, though, few children can throw with any proficiency and most cannot do more than attempt to catch a ball thrown to them.

Five- and six-year-olds Five- and six-year-olds have efficient, coordinated skills for running, jumping, and climbing that, as at age four, are constantly employed in pretend play. They are also likely to become involved in jumping rope,

jumping over objects, hopping and standing briefly on one foot, balancing on narrow planks or chalk lines, roller skating, riding a twowheeler, and keeping time to music by walking or skipping. Skipping, in particular, requires considerable coordination of muscles as well as a good sense of rhythm and is often not mastered by five-year-olds and even some six-year-olds. Six-year-olds begin to catch balls with their hands rather than with outstretched arms or against their chests.

Seven-year-olds

Seven-year-olds skip easily and can gallop to rhythmic music. They can skip and jump with accuracy into small spaces, as in hopscotch. In throwing a ball, the proper footwork and shifting of weight is often mastered, while accuracy (such as hitting a four-foot target from a distance of fifteen feet) greatly increases. At age seven children run vigorously and can jump upward and forward with ease, using effective arm movements as they do so. Bike-riding skills are carefully rehearsed and perfected. Various motor skills are coordinated through games, races, gymnastics, and dramatic presentations.

New skills require concentration

When tackling a new motor skill, such as walking or jumping, children display remarkable concentration. Nothing else dilutes their attention. Only after much repetition can the new skill be combined with other behaviors in a more complex activity. For example, as children are learning to walk they concentrate fully on maintaining balance and shifting weight effectively; only after much practice can they look around while walking or simultaneously walk and talk. Two- and three-year-olds, with full concentration, can barely manage to throw a ball in the general direction they wish it to go; as likely as not, they will drop it behind them or misdirect it entirely. Even at age four only a small proportion of children have mastered throwing.

Between the ages of five and five-and-a-half approximately three out of four children learn to throw effectively. First attempts usually involve both hands and much body movement, but the movements gradually become more specialized. A patient adult who is willing to retrieve the ball is needed during the initial practice sessions. This practice often goes on and on, to the limits of adult tolerance for chasing off in all directions. Eventually, through patient and concentrated practice, the child acquires the balance and coordination needed to properly direct the ball. The practice continues with gradual improvement in strength, speed, and accuracy. The skill can then be employed in fantasy activities (such as, "Let's pretend that old box is a bear attacking us and that we throw rocks at it") or in organized games where throwing must be coordinated with running, jumping, and dodging in very complex and varied patterns.

Differentiation, then integration

These patterns of differentiation and **integration,** which are easily observed in regard to motor skills, are also descriptive of development in the social and cognitive areas and will be referred to repeatedly throughout this section. They should be considered as examples of the basic principle of child development presented in the previous chapter: Development proceeds from the general to the specific. *Differentiation* refers to the processes by which broad patterns of behavior are refined into more functional and precise abilities; for example, scribbling is practiced and refined to the skills of drawing and writing. *Integration*, on the other hand, is the process of bringing various behavior patterns into coordinated interaction with one another (such as the coordination of hopping, leaning, and balancing in a game of hopscotch). These processes can be observed at all levels of development, and for a teacher making observations of children it is very important to determine not only whether a child can perform a particular skill (differentiation) but also whether that skill has been sufficiently mastered to allow integration with other actions.

SMALL MUSCLE DEVELOPMENT

Continuity from gross to small muscle development

There is a direct continuity in the development of small muscle coordination, from gross movement through the processes of differentiation described above. Our presentation under the two separate headings of *Gross Movements* and *Small Muscle Development* are for convenience of presentation and should not be inferred to signify two distinct streams of development.

Two- and three-year-olds

Beginning with the ability to use the thumb in opposition to the fingers during the first year, hand and finger manipulation becomes increasingly skillful. While the toddler (before age two) typically carries little toys or blocks about individually and drops them in unstructured piles, two- and

Photo by Ursula Moeller.

Significant relationships are frequently found between children's functioning in perceptual motor tasks (such as copying forms) and academic achievement. In recent years many special programs have been instituted to improve motor and perceptual functioning in the hope of improving performance in other areas. Among the originators and advocates of such programs are Newell Kephart (1971), Gerald Getman (Getman *et al.*, 1968), Marianne Frostig (Frostig and Horn, 1964), and R. E. Valett (Valett, 1974).

Although perceptual-motor functioning is sometimes significantly improved by these special programs, which involve children in various motor and visual patterning activities, the anticipated concomitant improvement in reading or other academic areas does not necessarily follow (Jacobs *et al.*, 1968; Falik, 1969; Elkind and Deblinger, 1968; Larsen and Hammill, 1975; Robinson, 1972). Research findings have indicated the interrelatedness of these abilities, but the formal structured programs devised to date appear to be either unnecessary or ineffective for most children. L. E. Halverson (1971) points out that increased opportunities for children to explore, experiment, and practice all types of movement under a variety of situations could be more appropriate than formal training programs.

three-year-olds place objects carefully into rows, towers, and other formations. Most three- and four-year-olds can perform a large variety of hand movements, such as stringing large beads, copying a circle or cross, folding paper, or making large letters (especially those with vertical or horizontal lines only, such as *E, H, L,* and *T*).

Three- and four-year-olds At ages three and four many of the abilities needed for dressing have been developed. Most children at this age are able to pull on or wriggle into their clothing and do the simpler fastening tasks. Help is still needed with tying shoes, with smaller buttons and fasteners, with boots that are snug, and with complex outerwear.

Five-year-olds By age five most children can fold a triangle from a paper (if shown how), can copy a square or a triangle, and can cut along a line with scissors. However, the letters and numbers they make are still large and uneven and very frequently are reversed from left to right or from top to bottom. Although still laboring to write his or her name, the five-year-old has often achieved independence in dressing, except for tying shoes. In dressing, the children still need to see the fasteners they are trying to manipulate. It is not unusual to see young children straining their necks and bending themselves into odd postures to get a view of the zippers on the bottoms of their coats. By age six nearly all children have mastered ties and fasteners and need visual guidance only with unfamiliar articles of clothing. Try watching children of various ages as they get dressed and note the things that create problems for them.

Six- and seven-year-olds, although they have sufficient small muscle ability to form all letters, especially with good models and patient instruction, still reverse many letters and numbers and make them large and irregular in size. Some children can easily print letters about one-quarter-inch high that are level with each other. By this age most have sufficient control of their small muscles to become engaged in writing activities without great difficulty. The child's ability to draw a diamond is often used as an indicator of the development of perceptual-motor coordination. To increase your awareness of the development of children's abilities, try exploring what forms (such as the circle, square, triangle, and diamond) or letters children of various ages can copy from a model you make for them, and compare their performances. If children are able to make a particular form, they will usually copy you without any urging on your part.

Six- and seven-year-olds typically perfect skills such as carpentry, clay modeling, painting, and sewing to the point where they can use them to real advantage in creating objects. Their increasing ability and willingness to work on intricate tasks is in significant contrast to their preference for gross motor manipulations as preschoolers and kindergartners.

DOMINANCE

Infants initially use whichever hand comes in contact with an object. By age two, however, children have ceased to alternate between the use of both hands and have begun to establish dominance, the distinct preference for use of one hand over the other. A majority of children prefer the right hand, a few the left hand, and a few still show little preference at this age. Those who are undecided will in most instances have settled on the use of either the right or left hand for most manual activities by the age of five or six. By age five, most children not only prefer using one hand over the other but also

Photo by Laura Lehmann.

Downing and Thackray (1971) comment as follows on patterns of dominance:

> In any large unselected group of people, approximately 5 percent are left-handed, 35 percent are left-eyed, and 33 percent have mixed dominance. The most plausible explanation as to why left-eyedness should occur so much more frequently than left-handedness is . . . social conditioning. Right-handed people are more favoured than the left-handed, and as the hereditary disposition to handedness is slight, early social pressure which is brought to bear on the child to use his right hand succeeds in changing the disposition to left-handedness. In contrast, there is no social pressure for right-eyedness. (p. 26)

perform more efficiently with their preferred hand in tasks such as cutting along a line or filling a space with crayon markings.

Establishing handedness Despite massive speculation and research into the causes and effects of dominance in **handedness,** there remain more questions than answers. There is agreement, however, that much of our right-handedness is the result of a culture in which right-handedness is expected, modeled, and rewarded (often unconsciously) by adults and older children; that is, more children would become left-handed if they were not reared in a right-handed world. Handedness is, at least to some degree, a learned preference.

Handedness is thought to be a part of general **lateral** (or sided) **dominance**, which is also evidenced in use of one foot over the other and one eye over the other. Although for most people the preferred foot and eye is the same as the *Mixed dominance* preferred hand, it is not at all unusual to find a **mixed dominance**; for example, left-eyed, right-handed, and right-footed. Nor is it particularly unusual to find a child who writes with the right hand, throws a ball with the left, cuts with the right, and sews with the left. However, the tendency to perform more and more acts with the preferred side continues throughout the school years.

While being left-handed is not associated, as was once thought, with lower intelligence, achievement, or clumsiness (Young and Knapp, 1972), it can present certain problems for left-handed children. If you are right-handed you may never have realized that nearly everything is geared to your preference. Handshaking is just one example; the use of the right hand is the only "acceptable" way. Most scissors and other tools are constructed for right-handed use, while table settings and illumination are usually arranged to benefit the right-handed. Most instruction and modeling of such skills as pasting, cutting, folding, handwriting, and game playing are done with the right-hand perspective. It certainly is to the child's benefit, given these conditions, to be among the majority, that is, right-handed.

Opinions vary on the extent to which children in the toddler and preschool years should be encouraged or urged to use the right hand. According to one point of view, young children can learn to use either hand, and if there is no clear preference by age three or so, they should be encouraged strongly to use the right. Others, aware of a possible association between forced use of the "unnatural" hand and certain speech problems, especially stuttering, avoid directing the use of either hand. Only under certain conditions do most authorities recommend that a child systematically attempt to use the right hand. Hildreth (1950), for example, suggests that such an effort be made only if the child is under six years of age, uses both hands interchangeably, shows no difficulty in a trial period, is agreeable to eliminating left-hand use and concentrating action on the right, and is above average in intelligence. Because it can be traumatic for a child to be forced to use the right hand after he or she has already established some patterns and competence with the left, most preschool teachers permit continued use of both hands rather than try to influence the child to consistently use the right.

Cautions about "changing" handedness

PHYSICAL DEFECTS

Our image of the human race, and especially of its children, may be of glowing health and wholeness, but the image does not match up to reality. In your classroom there will most likely be a number of children with slight disabilities and some who have multiple and/or severe problems. In preparation for teaching you need to carefully assess your own feelings and reactions to disability and to increase your knowledge of particular disabilities and their effects.

It was once thought to be beneficial to segregate children with disabilities into "special" programs designed to accommodate their particular "problem." However, the benefits in terms of management ease for teachers was not necessarily accompanied with developmental benefits for the children. More normal participation in everyday school and neighborhood environments is increasingly believed to make greater contributions to functioning levels than special placements. Given this new perspective, it is your challenge to provide programs that will accommodate a variety of performance levels and disabilities. However, without some knowledge of what a particular disabled child is likely to be coping with, your efforts could be more inappropriate than helpful.

Mainstreaming and normalization

It will benefit you to think about each of the disabilities on the following list, one at a time. Consider what you know about the disability, its cause, and its effect on the afflicted person. But most of all, consider your own feelings about persons you have known with these problems. If your feelings about particular disabilities prevent you from helping these people feel "normal," then you need to investigate that area more fully. You may well find that your acceptance of each disability grows in direct proportion to your familiarity with it.

Your own reaction to handicaps

- dental problems (decayed teeth, braces, abnormal malocclusion)
- visual impairments (ocular misalignments, faulty vision improved by glasses, artificial eye, blindness)

- hearing impairments (hard of hearing, faulty hearing improved by hearing aide, deafness)
- orthopedic disabilities (club foot, conditions requiring braces, crutches, orthopedic shoes)
- central nervous system disorders (abnormalities of movement, speech, etc., due to cerebral palsy, birth defects; epilepsy)
- heart disturbances (heart murmur, heart valve damage, rheumatic fever)
- speech defects (sound omissions and substitutions, lisping, stuttering, inaudible speech, absence of speech)
- cleft palate/hare lip
- severe allergies
- skin problems (eczema, rashes, cold sores, moles, warts)
- abnormality of physique (webbed fingers, hunchback) etc.
- amputated limbs
- growth defects (dwarfism)
- scars from accidents and burns

Some of these are damaging to the child primarily in psychological terms because of negative social reactions, while others are damaging primarily in terms of physical functioning and development. As a teacher, you must be able to assess the developmental status of disabled children and plan for their

Photo by Mary Green.

continued development, just as you do for "normal" children. Your job is to assist the child in further extending whatever is currently within his or her repertoire, even though the rate of achievement and eventual goals may be affected by a particular disability. The assisting of children with disabilities does not ordinarily demand esoteric teaching and can usually be accomplished within the scope of the regular classroom. In this volume the discussion is limited to a brief overview of the kinds of disabilities you may encounter in the classroom, but we strongly recommend additional reading to prepare you for working with children with physical defects.

NERVOUS TRAITS

In observing children, you may note and wonder about certain motor behaviors that seem to have no particular function. These include such actions as body rocking (a rhythmic rocking back and forth in place, usually in a sitting position), grimaces (tics), rapid blinking, nail biting, teeth grinding, thumb sucking, eye rubbing. Among the many potential causes of such behavior are physiological immaturity, emotional insecurity, insufficient opportunity to engage in active purposeful activity, and substitution for other comforts.

Masturbation is another activity that teachers and parents wonder about. By age four children have usually discovered that touching their genitals is pleasurable and may often do so when not otherwise occupied or when tired or upset. Only when the preschool child masturbates to the exclusion of other activities should it be considered indicative of emotional upset or nervousness.

Speculation about the causes of nervous mannerisms and programs of preventive action are generally unrewarding for teachers. On the other hand, the teacher may find it profitable to note the conditions under which such behavior increases and decreases and to arrange circumstances accordingly.

HEALTH AND DISEASE INDICATORS

Hurlock (1964) describes a healthy and an unhealthy child as follows:

> In a healthy child, the mucous membranes (especially of the lips) are definitely pink; the facial expression is happy, often radiant; smiling is frequent; the eyes are bright and responsive; the skin is smooth and elastic; the limbs are rounded because of a sufficient layer of subcutaneous fat; the muscles are well formed, and their tonus is good; the stance is well balanced, erect and graceful; the limb muscles are almost straight; the spine is straight; the shoulder girdles do not droop; the arches of the feet are well formed; and the movements of the limbs and body in walking and running are characterized by elasticity, vigor and poise.
>
> By contrast, the child whose health is poor is either underweight or soft and flabby; his posture is poor, his shoulders are rounded, his legs tend to be bowed and his teeth are carious. The healthy child is full of

energy and anxious to be on the go; he shows an alertness that is rarely seen in the child whose health is poor. When given a choice of play activities, the healthy child will choose those which require bodily activity. The child in poor health will select sedentary activities, such as watching television or going to the movies. (p. 143)

The signs of poor health   This description should be useful in classifying those children whose general health may need attention. An especially difficult problem for teachers is recognizing the onset of a disease condition in a healthy child. In the first weeks and months of contact with children, it is especially difficult to tell whether they are engaging in natural, healthy "orneriness" when they clown, test, and rebel, or whether they are really reacting to some unusual internal state. Since each child's reaction to illness may be highly idiosyncratic, it is probably wise for a teacher to discuss this in initial contacts with the people who know the child best.

Crankiness, unreasonableness, or crying at the slightest provocation may

COMMON DISEASE CONDITIONS

Disease	Symptoms	How spread
Chicken pox (varicella)	Mild fever, upset stomach, headache; blisterlike rash appearing suddenly	Through air from sneezing and coughing and from rash
German measles (rubella)	Coldlike symptoms, headache, stiff neck; rash spreading from face and head to neck and trunk; slight fever; glands enlarged at back of head and neck and behind ears	Through sneezing, coughing, or contact with nose/throat secretions
Measles (rubeola)	Coldlike symptoms, nasal discharge, fever, cough, watery eyes; white spots in mouth; pinpoint rash from behind ears on forehead and face on third or fourth day.	Same as German measles
Mumps	Sudden onset of chills and fever; headache, swelling and pain in salivary gland(s)	Contact with throat secretions
Whooping cough	Nose and throat secretions; spells of coughing; fever (slight); cough worse at night	Direct contact with nose/throat discharge
Impetigo	Small blisterlike sores on skin surface; sores contain clear fluid at first, which changes to pus, followed by thick, yellowish crust	Highly contagious; contact with sores or objects that have become contaminated
Ringworm	Inflammation, typically on scalp but also elsewhere; circular scaling; itching	Primarily direct contact

be signs either of approaching illness or simply of weariness. Fatigue in young children is often very difficult to diagnose because of their tendency to deny it and, in fact, to increase their activity and excitement level. If allowed to continue without rest, they may become listless and inactive, or show puffiness and dark circles around their eyes. Once a teacher becomes aware of a particular child's early fatigue signs, the later stages may be avoided

RESPONSE SECTION

The preceding pages have provided you with basic information regarding the young child's size, body type, posture, appearance, movements (gross and small muscle), dominance, physical defects, nervous traits, and health and disease indicators.

We suggest that you gain additional understanding by doing the following:

1. Stand in front of a mirror and perform as many different discrete actions as you can think of (for example, bend forward and make complex circular movements with your hands at knee level). For each action, try to describe in words what you have done. Then, if possible, invite children at two different age levels to do the same. Compare their repertoire of actions and descriptive vocabulary with yours, and note the variance with age.

2. For a period of time, preferably several hours, try to use your non-preferred hand for all manual activities. Compare your performance on such tasks as drawing circles and squares and writing your name with your preferred versus your nonpreferred hand.

3. Reread Hurlock's descriptions of health and, point by point, assess your own health status. If you do not appear to be in glowing health, plan strategies to correct these conditions as part of your practical preparation for teaching.

4. Review your feelings regarding certain body physiques, types of appearances, defects, nervous traits, and disease conditions. If there are particular types, conditions, or states that concern or repulse you, plan some strategies for desensitizing yourself to these. The following exercises might be helpful: (a) take on the particular condition for a period of time (either through role-playing or in imagination) and try to feel what it would be like in the other's shoes; (b) investigate through reading and other study the cause, effect, and nature of the condition; (c) make a special effort to approach and talk with persons who have this condition about general topics of interest to you (not about their condition).

through diversion into more relaxing and sedentary activity. Some children are attuned to their own bodily conditions and will independently regulate their activity level. As a teacher, you need to become aware of young children's different reactions to their bodily states and to intervene where necessary.

Observing Motor Behavior and Physical Characteristics of Individual Children

On the following pages we pose some specific questions about the children you observe. Some of the answers will be obvious given a very brief observation; others will require repeated contacts. We recommend that you keep these questions handy and use them as the basis of your observing and notetaking when assessing the physical characteristics and motor behaviors of children.

Specificity in observational record　　What you record should be actual descriptions of the child, obtained as you are watching him or her. For example, in studying the child's hand dominance, record exactly what you see. You might note, "combs hair with left hand," "uses both hands in doing puzzle," or "marks with crayon using left, sometimes right." Avoid general statements such as "no hand preference." Only after repeated notations of specific behaviors would the inference that the child has not established hand dominance be justified. Beware of jumping to immediate conclusions on the basis of limited evidence. Even if your early impressions do turn out to be correct, you will be on safer ground if you can support your statement with repeated examples of the child's actual behavior.

The format for note-taking　　There are a number of ways to organize your notes. You may wish to put together a notebook for each child for whom you will make a full behavioral assessment, recording category heads and questions for motor and physical development across twelve or so pages, leaving sufficient blank space for writing in descriptions of the behaviors you see.

Or you may prefer to use a three-by-five-inch card file. If so, the questions might be written on dividers, with tabs indicating the numerical codes. Your notes could then be jotted on three-by-five-inch note pad sheets (one sheet for each note you make) and filed under the appropriate heading after each observation.

Whatever your organization of materials, we encourage you to be a liberal note taker. It is easier to discard later than to recall half-remembered details. It will probably help you to read through the list of questions just before your observation period. Make notes while you are actually observing if it is feasible to do so. Immediately after the observation period, reread the list of questions and record any additional behaviors that seem to be relevant to your records. Be sure to put a date on each entry so that you will have a means for following the child's behavior pattern across time.

Ample, detailed notes　　You will probably find that when you first begin to observe a child you will have countless notations and you will feel frustrated that you are seeing more than you can possibly record. However, you will soon find that what you miss will typically occur again and again and can be recorded later. As time goes by, new behaviors will become increasingly rare. The process of learning about a new child is always "heavy" initially, but stick with it! You will find that persistence pays off and that the task becomes increasingly manageable.

Each individual, whether adult or child, has at any given time a limited repertoire of behaviors that are used in daily interactions. While some individuals have a far greater repertoire than others, particularly in some areas, there is far greater repetitiveness than at first appears. Your task as observer is to assess this repertoire, making extensive notes at first contacts and determining new or previously unused facets of the repertoire through continued observations.

Questions as guides to observations A warning: in providing you with a series of questions and categories to guide your observations of children's development, we do not imply that this is the only way, or even the best way, to organize your investigations. Other equally valid category systems could be devised for investigating these and other aspects of children's behavior. We are simply suggesting that you follow this line of questioning initially and that as you become more aware of children's growth and development you should not hesitate to reorganize our questions and categories, especially by adding to or elaborating on them.

Here are the questions. You will note that examples are included to help you interpret the meaning of the question, but by no means should you limit your own entries to our list of examples.

1. Physical Characteristics
   You may wish to sketch or photograph the child to supplement your verbal responses in this section.

   1.1 *Is there anything particularly distinctive about the child's body build?*

   Examples: • tiny, small boned, slim
   • heavy proportions, small shoulders
   • overheard from peer, "You can't be Superman, you're scrawny."

   1.2 *Is there anything particularly distinctive about the child's posture?*

   Examples: • reclines or leans on most occasions
   • stands squarely; shoulders straight
   • sway back; protruding tummy

   1.3 *What are the child's attractive/unattractive features—to you, to other adults, to peers?*

   Examples: • sallow, pale skin coloring
   • long lashes framing brown eyes; very appealing
   • comment from peer, "You look like a witch. You play witch."

   1.4 *What is the nature of the child's grooming?*

   Examples: • hair unkempt; face and neck dirty
   • carefully braided hair; bright ribbons

2. Gross Movements

  2.1 *What is the child's action repertoire? What different actions does he or she perform?*

   Consider the following actions, but also include others as you observe them: crawls, rolls, walks, walks sideways, walks backward, climbs stairs, runs, hops, jumps, slides/shuffles, climbs (trees, ladders, equipment with rungs), swings suspended by arms, swings by legs, falls over (intentionally), swims, flips body over on bars, somersaults, does hand flip on floor.

   For each action, note whether it is being differentiated from a more gross activity and is practiced as a new skill requiring the child's whole attention, or whether it has been sufficiently mastered to be performed with little conscious attention and is integrated with other kinds of activities. You may wish to indicate with (D) those actions that are at the differentiation level and with (I) those that are integrated.

   Examples: • while playing Batman, walks, runs across room, falls over, slides to stop, climbs tree while shouting orders to "Robin" (I)
   • carefully and repeatedly swings self up by arms to flip feet over bars on climbing equipment and then hangs by feet. Goes through whole process several times, then goes to friend Joey and says, "Did you see what I can do?" (D)

  2.2 *How strong is the child? What actions give evidence of body alignment to physically alter the environment?*

   Consider the following actions, but also include others as you observe them: pushes, shoves, lifts, pounds/hammers, throws, pulls, bends object. Record the object or objects toward which the child is directing his or her strength. Indicate differentiation (D) and integration (I).

   Examples: • loads cart with twenty blocks and alternately pushes it from one side and pulls by rope from other side; adds more blocks and does both again (D)
   • playing Daniel Boone, shouts, "Okay, men, I'll save you. Here's the ammunition," while dragging the wagon filled with blocks across the room (I)

  2.3 *What is the child's ability to balance?*

   Consider the following actions, but also include others as you observe them: walks on a raised beam (indicate width and distance), walks along a crack or line (indicate width and distance), balances on an inclined plane (indicate width, whether still or walking, distance walked), skates, balances on platform over fulcrum, hops over rocks. Indicate differentiation (D) or integration (I).

   Examples: • walks fifteen feet along border of bricks (three inches wide) without falling off (D)
   • walks up and down inclined plane (board six inches wide) at about thirty-degree angle; stops at midpoint; turns around easily, while singing, "Tie a yellow ribbon. . ."

  2.4 *What is the child's ability to use his or her body rhythmically?*

   Consider the following actions, but also include others as you observe them: skips, gallops, dances, jumps rope, moves to music (in place), uses hula hoop. Indicate differentiation (D) or integration (I).

Examples: • tries to skip across room, imitating friend Suzy; manages skipping patterns about half-way, simply runs rest of way (D)
• listens to "Funky Chicken" music from record player; continues in activity of writing on chalkboard, but performs dance movements in the process (I)

2.5 *What is the child's ability to move quickly?*
Consider the following actions, but also include others as you observe them: runs, climbs, swims, gallops.

Examples: • runs across playground faster than all except two of friends
• when climbing often holds up those behind who are waiting to use same equipment

2.6 *What is the child's physical endurance? What is the duration of sustained physical activity?*
Consider the following actions, but also include others as you observe them: runs, pushes, jumps in place, climbs, skips rope, rides bike.

Examples: • climbs up three steps; walks down to the bottom step and jumps off fifteen times
• bounces ball continuously for fifteen minutes

2.7 *To what extent can the child coordinate several types of gross motor behavior into a more complex skill?*
Consider the following actions, but also include others as you observe them: runs and catches object that is moving through the air; throws to intended target; throws at moving target; runs and slides to base; rides twowheeler bicycle; roller skates; runs and dribbles ball.

Examples: • kicks large rubber ball to direct it around other toys and then kicks to friend who is several yards away
• rides twowheeler without difficulty once under way, but sways and sometimes must catch self with feet and give extra push from ground before getting off

3. Small Muscle Development

3.1 *What is the child's repertoire for self-help in areas of eating, dressing, and grooming?*
Consider the following actions, but also include others as you observe them: in eating: uses spoon, uses fork, cuts with fork, uses knife to spread, pours from pitcher to glass, serves self from serving dish with large spoon; in dressing: buttons, zips, puts on socks, puts on shoes, puts on tie; in grooming: washes face, combs hair, dries hands, puts toothpaste on brush.

Examples: • zips up jacket once lower ends are engaged
• puts on shoes; ties first part of bow and then asks for help
• drinks from glass without assistance but allows glass to topple when replacing on table
• goes through motions of drying hands but usually leaves hands wet

3.2 *What is the child's repertoire for manipulating materials and toys? For using tools?*

Consider the following actions, but also include others as you observe them: cuts with scissors, marks with crayon, draws or writes with pencil or crayon, uses hammer, uses saw, uses screwdriver, uses needle, pastes, uses pencil sharpener, turns book pages, puts puzzle together, uses games or construction toys with tiny parts. Indicate differentiation (D) or integration (I). You may wish to include examples of children's writing or drawing along with your written notations.

Examples: • removes one-half-inch wheels from small plastic car and replaces with ease (D)
• takes thumb tack out of bulletin board and replaces in exact spot by inserting into hole made previously (D)
• rips paper while trying to cut (D)
• reverses letters (*s*, *p*); writing otherwise even; approximately one-half inch in size (I)

4. Other Characteristics

4.1 *Has the child established left- or right-hand preference/dominance? Which hand does the child use? Which foot?*

Examples: • uses left hand to scribble
• uses right hand while eating; transfers fork from one hand to other
• uses right hand for combing hair
• uses left foot to kick ball
• uses left foot to kick blocks out of way

RESPONSE SECTION

You have been provided with questions to use as guides for observing the physical characteristics and motor development of children. We suggest that, along with these questions, you try the following:

1. Summarize the similarities and differences between the children you have observed.

2. Answer the list of questions in respect to your own physical characteristics and motor development. Summarize the similarities and differences between your own self-appraisal and those you make of the children you observe.

3. Reread the descriptive narratives you prepared in connection with Chapter 3. What differences exist between these observations and those made in response to the questions in this chapter?

4.2 *Does the child show any evidence of physical disability? Any prosthetic devices?*

Examples: • mouth hangs open; head tilts
• wears one shoe with heavy sole
• has hearing aid
• squints, rubs eyes when looking at book

4.3 *Does the child exhibit any behaviors that appear nonfunctional and that may be indicators of pervasive tension?*

Consider the following behaviors, but also include others as you observe them: body rocking, rapid blinking, tics, nail biting, teeth grinding, thumb sucking, eye rubbing.

Examples: • just before session is over puts thumb in mouth and stands by entrance
• bites nails while listening to story
• when not involved in muscle activity, rocks body in rhythmic fashion even while looking at books

4.4 *Does the child's behavior or physical appearance suggest symptoms of poor health or disease?*

Consider the following symptoms, but also include others as you observe them: runny nose, pallor, coughing, sores, hoarseness, inactivity.

Examples: • complains that head aches
• sneezes occasionally; coughs continually
• skin irritation on neck

Transition into Resourcefulness Section

As soon as you have collected a variety of descriptions of a particular child's physical characteristics and motor behaviors, you will have some basis for judging what kinds of physical activities will be easy, difficult, or impossible for the child to perform. For example, what do you know about a child whom you have determined can do the following actions:

walk
run
hop (two feet)
jump in place
climb stairs using one foot per step
move in time to musical rhythm
zip (once fastener is engaged)
use fork and spoon
scribble both vertically and horizontally
make very imprecise circles and *V*'s

but whom you never observed to do the following actions?

broad jump
climb rungs or ladders
gallop or skip
use scissors

Could you, on the basis of this information, make some kind of reasonable prediction about which of the following activities or materials would be appropriate or inappropriate for the child?

hopscotch
basketball
slide with four-foot platform
slide with eight-foot platform
follow-the-dot book
chalkboard drawing
tracing paper
folk dancing
tunnels or barrels to crawl through
Pick-Up-Stix game
bead stringing (leather and two-inch beads)
paper chain construction

Guidelines   The following guidelines are recommended for matching activities to children, based upon your observations of their physical characteristics and motor behavior.

1. Avoid urging the child to engage in an activity that requires behaviors very different than those you have already observed in his or her repertoire. If the child does become involved in those kinds of activities, be prepared for helping and, if necessary, for withdrawing him or her from the activity and finding something more in line with current abilities.

2. Avoid urging and encouraging the child to engage in any activity that is already well integrated into the repertoire. Consider, for example, cutting. You may observe that a given child can easily cut on a line while carrying on a conversation or while singing along with a record. It would therefore probably be inappropriate to expect the child to be interested in or benefit from a simple cutting task unless it is an integral part of a more complex endeavor; for example, he or she might be interested in cutting heart shapes to produce valentines. On the other hand, for children who are still just perfecting and practicing the cutting skill, cutting by itself is enough and they can be happily and profitably engaged in merely cutting pieces of newspaper into strips. For them, if the cutting task is part of a more complex construction activity it might be too demanding, and they might well "tune out" or become frustrated by the less appropriate aspects.

3. Encourage the child to participate in new activities or use new materials that require behaviors quite similar to those you have observed him or her using. If the child can run, hop, jump in place, climb up steps, and jump off the bottom one, and is just beginning to practice the running broad jump, look for practice possibilities that will provide some variety. Examples might be: (a) Provide some varying arrangements of steps with blocks and boards that he or she might maneuver around and over: (b) Create some spaces on

the floor to jump into and over, should the child care to do so, by attaching strings to the floor with masking tape or attaching masking tape to the floor. Say rhymes such as, "Jennifer, Jennifer goes jumpity hop, jumpity hop. There she goes, see her hop, here she comes, see her stop." (c) Construct an obstacle course with running spaces interspersed with blocks or old tires that can be climbed over or jumped from. You might take the child to a novel outdoor space that has varied terrain to run through and explore.

There are many possibilities for variations of activity that are perfectly matched to a given child's level of motor development. Your job, as a teacher, is to encourage a full use of the existing repertoire. Subsequent development is more keyed to a thorough development of existing skills (using many variants) than to a speedy introduction of new skills.

4. Provide the opportunity for the child to see others engaged in motor activities slightly more advanced than those he or she has mastered to date. This kind of "modeling" is typically available because of the developmental differences in almost any group of children. For the more "advanced," however, the adult must either provide the model or arrange for older and more skilled persons outside the group to occasionally join them. In all instances, however, avoid making overt comparisons between children's abilities.

If a child voluntarily engages in an activity or voluntarily continues an activity in the absence of adult or peer encouragement, you can feel assured that the activity is appropriate to the child's developmental level. There is something very satisfying to a child (and to an adult as well) in those activities that provide a slight challenge, just enough difficulty to require

The problem of the attention and effort but not so difficult as to be impossible. J. McVicker Hunt
"match" (1961) refers to this optimal degree of discrepancy as the "match," and to the teacher's task one of solving the problem of the "match." In other words, the teacher's job is to determine for each child what activities or situations will not be too easy or too difficult, but "just right." According to Hunt, if "just right" is found, the child will get intrinsic satisfaction from the activity and will not need to be praised, cajoled, threatened, bribed, or otherwise influenced to become and remain involved with the activity.

As a teacher whose task it will be to arrange these child-activity matches, you will first of all need sensitivity to what the child can and cannot do with ease. You are in the process of developing this sensitivity when you observe a child's physical repertoire. You must also be ready to provide the child with a variety of activities suitable to his or her developmental level. This is the business of Section Three.

Summary

The newborn's only mode of interacting with the world is through reflexive actions. The initial reflexes are gradually modified to become schemas, which are more effective for deriving information. It is from these sensorimotor schemas that more abstract thinking processes are derived, according to Piaget's views. Motor and physical development are thus seen to be closely interrelated with other aspects of development from the beginning of the life span.

From the rudimentary skills such as reaching and letting go, developed during infancy, come the more complex motor skills of the three- through seven-year-old. By age three, large muscle abilities are sufficiently developed to be considered as separate aspects, such as agility, strength, endurance, balance, rhythm, and speed. These abilities were described as developing through processes of differentiation and integration. A sensitive teacher can facilitate repertoire expansion in motor areas by carefully observing and assessing existent abilities in children and by making thoughtful matches with activities and experiences.

Physical characteristics of children influence their overall development in two major ways. Their size, posture, attractiveness, hand preference, physical defects, nervous traits, and health all influence the way they interact with the world (both physical and social) and/or the way they are perceived by the world. As a teacher you need to be particularly sensitive to both influences and, most importantly, to your own reactions to the physical characteristics of the children you teach.

REASSESSMENT

Reread what you wrote for the preassessment as you began this chapter, comparing this with your current understandings. Now write on these topics again and incorporate your new insights and knowledge. Continue to update as you prepare for teaching. Save your materials for your portfolio.

Additional Reading

Perceptual and Motor Development in Infants

Cratty, B. J. *Perceptual and motor development in infants and children.* New York: Macmillan, 1970.

Frichtl, C., and Peterson, L. W. *Early infant stimulation and motor development.* Champaign, Ill.: Illinois State Department of Mental Health, 1969. ERIC Document Reproduction Service No. ED 038 179.

Gordon, I., Dunagh, B., and Jester, E. *Child learning through child play.* New York: St. Martin's Press, 1972.

Levy, J. *The baby exercise book: The first fifteen months.* New York: Pantheon, 1974.

McDiarmid, N. J., Peterson, M. A., and Sutherland, J. R. *Loving and learning: Interacting with your child from birth to three.* New York: Harcourt Brace Jovanovich, 1975.

Physical Attractiveness

Berscheid, E., and Walster, E. Beauty and the beast. *Psychology Today,* 1972, 5, 42–46, 74.

Perceptual and Motor Development in Young Children

Cratty, B. J. *Perceptual and motor development in infants and children.* New York: Macmillan, 1970.

Feature on perceptual-motor development. *Journal of Health, Physical Education and Recreation*, 1970, 41, 30–47.

The significance of the young child's motor development: Proceedings of a conference. Washington, D.C.: National Association for the Education of Young Children, 1971.

Disabilities

Bangs, T. E. *Language and learning disorders of the pre-academic child.* New York: Appleton-Century-Crofts, 1968.

Crain, J. *Early childhood education for diversely handicapped children.* Illinois: Department of Exceptional Children, Office of the Superintendent of Public Instruction, 1974. Available through Bureau of Education for the Handicapped, U.S. Office of Education.

Denhoff, E. *Cerebral palsy—The preschool years: Diagnosis, treatment and planning.* Springfield, Ill.: Charles C. Thomas, 1968.

Gesell, A., and Amatruda, C. S. *Developmental diagnosis: Normal and abnormal child development.* New York: Hoeber Medical Division, Harper & Row, 1947.

Gotts, E. A., Compiler. *A bibliography related to early childhood education, child development and preschool handicapped children.* Austin, Tex.: University of Texas. ERIC Document Reproduction Service No. ED 061 687.

Granato, S. *Day Care: Serving children with special needs.* Washington, D.C.: U.S. Government Printing Office, 1972. Document No. 1791-0176.

Klein, J. W. Mainstreaming the preschooler. *Young Children.* 1975, 30, 317–27.

Learning to talk: Speech and hearing and language problems in the preschool child. Bethesda, Md.: National Institutes of Health, 1969. ERIC Document Reproduction Service No. ED 038 813.

Monahan, R. *Free and inexpensive materials for preschool and early childhood.* Belmont, Calif.: Lear Siegler/Fearon Publishers, 1973. Includes many listings on handicapped conditions.

Neisworth, J. T., and Madles, R. A. Normalized day care: A philosophy and approach to integrating exceptional and normal children. *Child Care Quarterly*, 1975, 4, 163–71.

Northcott, W. N. The integration of young deaf children into ordinary educational programs. *Exceptional Children*, 1971, 29–32.

Semple, J. E. *Hearing impaired preschool child.* Springfield, Ill.: Charles C. Thomas, 1970.

Pamphlets, directories of statewide services, and books (at reasonable cost) can often be obtained from:

Bureau of Handicapped
U.S. Office of Education
Washington, D.C. 20202

CHAPTER 5
Increasing Sensitivity to Children's Affective and Social Behavior

Overview

Affective Development
AFFECTIVE DEVELOPMENT IN INFANTS AND TODDLERS
AFFECTIVE DEVELOPMENT AT AGES THREE THROUGH FIVE
AFFECTIVE DEVELOPMENT AT AGES SIX AND SEVEN

Social Development
SOCIAL DEVELOPMENT IN INFANTS AND TODDLERS
SOCIAL DEVELOPMENT AT AGES THREE THROUGH FIVE
SOCIAL DEVELOPMENT AT AGES SIX AND SEVEN

Observing Affective and Social Behavior in Individual Children

Transition into Resourcefulness Section

Summary

PREASSESSMENT

When you have completed this chapter you should be able to describe and compare the following:

1. *affective and social behavior of infants and toddlers, three- through five-year-olds, and six- and seven-year-olds.*
2. *specific aspects of affective and social behavior in young children that may be relevant for you to observe.*
3. *implications for programing of young children's affective and social behavior and development.*

Before beginning to read this chapter:

1. *take enough time to write what you already know about each of the above topics.*
2. *observe individual children and record your impressions of their feeling states and their interactions with others.*

Save what you write for rereading, comparison, and elaboration after you have studied and discussed these materials.

Overview

Consider the following description, written by a teacher, of Thaddeus, age four, and his conflict with his classmate Carl.

Thaddeus comes toward me looking upset, puckering his face up but not quite crying. He stops and starts back toward Carl, a few feet from him, with his hand held into a fist and raised as if to hit. Carl raises his fist also and takes a threatening step in Thaddeus' direction. Thaddeus turns and runs to me, putting his arms around me as if for protection, looks back over his shoulder at Carl and says, "He hit me. I goin' beat his butt. Carl shouts, "He bump me first."

What in the above description would fit the label "affective" (emotional) behavior? Social behavior? Cognitive behavior? Physical behavior? Clearly there is anger, fear, and frustration, all affective states. They are evoked in a social situation. If there is to be a solution, however, it will require cognitive input. Thaddeus, Carl, and the teacher must use all of their combined repertoires for talking, thinking, and problem-solving if the current state, which appears to be uncomfortable for Thaddeus, and probably for Carl, is to be resolved.

The separation of real-life situations into physical/motor, affective, social, and cognitive/intellectual components is clearly artificial, made for the convenience of studying children's development. While each of the four components of development is related to the others, affective and social development are often closely aligned. It is far easier to sort out motor development and cognitive development as separate strands than it is to separate affective and social development. We are therefore presenting both affective and social development in this single chapter.

The chapter begins with a discussion of affective development at three age levels: infants and toddlers, ages three through five, and ages six through seven. This is followed by a similar discussion of social development. Both kinds of behaviors are then combined in the list of questions suggested as an observation guide. The final part of the chapter discusses the teaching implications of what has been presented.

Affective Development

AFFECTIVE DEVELOPMENT IN INFANTS AND TODDLERS

A baby's crying is a signal that something is amiss. According to Erik Erikson, who has provided helpful insights into these early periods, if parents attend to and consistently and appropriately respond to the baby's signals of distress, a major contribution can be made to initial affective development. If children's discomfort can be alleviated by caregivers, it is more likely that the children will develop a sense of goodness about the world, a sense that they can depend on their own organisms, their **signaling**

An orientation of trust **systems**, and the responsiveness of their caregivers to their needs. Erikson believes this infancy period is critical in developing a healthy balance between feelings of trust and mistrust.

If the baby's signals are ignored or attended to inconsistently, the infant will likely have a mistrustful orientation, will lack confidence in self and others. Most infants do receive sufficient "tender loving care" in this crucial period and do develop the expectation that their world is an "okay" place where their needs will continue to be satisfied.

Of course, this is not an either-or phenomenon. All infants, even with the most attentive and caring parents, suffer from distresses such as feeding upsets, hunger pangs, skin irritations, uncomfortable temperatures, and teething. Also, the best of parenting is sometimes inadequate to provide

Although many different perspectives on children's affective and social behavior are presented in this chapter, there are recurrent references to the stages of development as described by Erik Erikson. Erikson (1950) writes of eight stages of life, each dominated by a particular "theme." They can be briefly described as follows:

1. *Trust versus mistrust.*   Dependent infants develop expectancies about the extent to which their needs will be cared for by others.
2. *Autonomy versus doubt and shame.*   Early in childhood, children develop expectancies about whether they have the freedom and capability to take certain actions independently of others.
3. *Initiative versus guilt.*   As children "play," they develop expectancies about whether they can initiate their own projects.
4. *Industry versus inferiority.*   During the "school-age" years, children develop expectancies regarding whether they can perform "real" tasks competently and whether they can persist with activities they do not particularly enjoy.
5. *Identity versus identity diffusion.*   In adolescence, young people develop their own personal identity, imitating, experimenting, and attempting to integrate their views of self.
6. *Intimacy versus isolation.*   Young adults develop expectancies regarding the extent to which and the manner in which they can integrate their lives with others.
7. *Generativity versus stagnation (or self-absorption).*   The developmental challenge to adults is to become productive and creative and to nourish and nurture the young.
8. *Integrity versus despair.*   In later maturity, there is the challenge of accepting one's life with its disappointments as well as its joys and appraising its relationship to overall human endeavors, past, present, and future.

In each of these stages of development Erikson sees that there is a central problem to be solved, at least temporarily, if the individual is to proceed with confidence and vigor to the next stage.

sufficient comfort for infants. For infants with lower thresholds for these distresses the infancy period leads to less positive orientations and expectations and often to a reduced level of parental involvement.

It is very easy for the inexperienced teacher of young children (or a parent who has had a "happy" baby) to look at an edgy, mistrustful three-year-old and think, "If only he had had better parenting." Parents of such children may deserve some assurance that they have had a rough experience through no fault of their own and that their child's initial disadvantage can be overcome at a later age. While a sense of trust is thought to be most easily and effectively established in the first year, it can be gained at later ages, when the child has full assurance that significant others will care for his or her needs. If basic trust has not been achieved by the preschool age, the teacher's first concern may well be to collaborate with the parents or other caregivers to assure the child that they will care for his or her well-being.

Attachment bonds

At about age five months infants are becoming aware of themselves as objects that have a continuing existence just as other objects do. Mother is differentiated as a separate object from self. The child, aware of the distinction between self and mother, forms a very strong emotional **attachment** that becomes the mainstay of feelings of security. Younger infants will accept feeding and care from anyone, but at about age eight or nine months they begin to differentiate and shrink away from all except the major caregiver. They may even suffer a social-emotional setback if this central person "deserts" them. If this attachment is not abruptly terminated, however, the child can be expected to gradually learn to extend trust and acceptance to other adults as well.

A sense of separate autonomy

In the second and third year of life the basic affective issue becomes concern about whether or not one can act autonomously without forfeiting the care and concern of caregivers. As children grow they become more autonomous, asserting their own wishes and needs as separate from those of their mother or other caregivers. In thus asserting themselves, which is a very healthy and positive development, they need assurance that they can do so without alienating those persons to whom they have primary attachments. This can constitute a serious conflict, since toddlers know they are still very small and helpless and in need of the goodwill of caregivers. If saying no appears to be turning adults against them, children may become very distressed. By age two, the children may persistently refuse to do things they really want to do, despite an obvious anxiety if a confrontation should occur.

The "trying" two-year-olds

For parents and teachers, this is a difficult time. The two-year-old obviously cannot be given full rein to make decisions about such things as whether to wear new shoes to walk in puddles or whether to run across a busy street. Wise adults learn not to provide choices at this age where there really is no choice. They learn that a two-year-old (as well as many three-year-olds) will respond better to statements such as "We're going home now" than to "Are you ready to go home?" They learn to give assistance very directly rather than to pose questions such as, "Do you need help?" They learn that forced choice questions such as, "Do you want peanut butter or tuna sandwiches for lunch?" is a more effective way to get a two- or three-year-old to the lunch table than asking, "Do you want to have lunch?"

Erikson has helped us to understand that at this age it will be unfortunate if children are led to believe that they are silly or bad to be so assertive about what they do not want to do or have help with. The teasing or shaming of children, while often quite effective in stopping "silly" behaviors or arguments, can also have the unintended effect of making them doubt themselves just when they most seek and need confirmation that they are separate, viable persons. The provision of decision-making situations in which the two-year-old can legitimately decide, can acceptably say no or refuse help, are helpful to social-emotional development.

Erikson further points out that adult-child conflicts over toilet training are especially symbolic of this period. The child's ability to control elimination can either provide further evidence of developing autonomy or can become a battle ground in which the adult shames the child for his or her "accidents" and dependency. In this period, which Erikson describes as centering around a favorable balance between autonomy and doubt or shame, toilet training may be but one of the adult-child hassles, but it is a very representative one.

AFFECTIVE DEVELOPMENT AT AGES THREE THROUGH FIVE

Integration to disintegration
An interesting phenomenon is the apparent progression of the normally developing child from calm, cooperative, "together" periods to periods of disintegration in which the child's behavior and disposition are very trying to parents and teachers. Adults typically find the two-year-old period a very trying time, thoroughly enjoy their three-year-old, and then again find their patience, understanding, and tolerance put to test as their child turns to four.

If development has generally gone well in the previous years, three-year-olds typically have a certain delightful sense of assurance about who they are and what they can do. In fact, three-year-olds seem, especially after their "terrible twos" year, to emerge as quite delightful people. They are old enough to have well-developed, individual personalities, to have their own ideas and histories, but are still young enough to be quite guileless. Their thoughts and passions are quite easy to read. While teachers of children at this age may become exhausted, they are seldom bored or disillusioned by the behavior of the children in their charge.

An emergent sense of self
By age three, children have developed a relatively complete and stable sense of self that serves as an influence on further development. While many of their self-conceptions are still relatively fluid and will be modified by later experiences, many stable views have already been formed that will influence children's involvements, their reactions to various stimuli, and their expectations of others. The child at age three may well have formed a sense of him- or herself as being good or bad, attractive or ugly, weak or strong. All of these self-views have developed out of the interactions of the prior three years and, while they persist, they will strongly influence future interactions. Whereas the child's basic sense of identity is formed prior to age three, it is still quite pliable and susceptible to adult and peer influences during the preschool and early school years. Preschoolers' current self-concepts can be reinforced and strengthened, or they can be extended to include additional perspectives.

Four-year-old children typically want to know about the world, what people are like, what they do, and what they themselves can learn to do. They push vigorously into all kinds of activities. This is the stage Erikson *A sense of initiative* describes as centered around the development of initiative, where children tirelessly question, experiment, and act out various roles in an effort to understand the world around them. If thrusting is not thwarted, children learn that they can do many things. They can paint a picture, do "hard" puzzles, build forts, write, and plan and carry out involved play sequences in which they become daddy, mommy, doctor, teacher, Dracula, or the Cookie Monster. "Let's pretend" is planned and managed with increasing competence, the whole self being thrown into the role. It is not "just play," it is work; and if the child is frustrated in it there will be genuine tears and anger.

The "experimenting" four-year-olds

Without intending to be difficult, four-year-olds experiment with all sorts of "kooky" actions, such as wearing clothing backward, putting boots on their hands and mittens on their feet, eating with the handle of the fork, and cutting food up into miniscule bits or trying to eat huge pieces. They may cover their whole face, arms, and the mirror with soap suds when washing their hands, or even try out fancy patterns and positions when urinating. They may be full of "What if ———?" questions, such as "What if it snowed for ten years?", "What if we only had spaghetti to eat?", "What if it were always night time?", or "What if a big bear came in here?"

Four-year-olds love to try out behaviors that are shocking. Language or actions that are "bad" are gingerly tested at first but then practiced with increasing competence in a variety of settings. The particular objectionable language that is practiced varies according to the neighborhood. Giggles and laughter may surround such mild words as *pooh-pooh* in some settings, whereas getting the proper vehemence into stronger four-letter words may characterize other settings.

Four-year-olds can be frustrating to teachers and parents because their great interest in starting things is not followed by an interest in finishing them or in doing them "well." There is also little inclination among most four-year-olds to clean things up after play. While a three-year-old may cheerfully help adults restack blocks, for example, the four-year-old is much more likely to resist or secretly begin a big new building project while appearing to be sorting the blocks for storage.

The "focused" five-year-olds

Five-year-olds are typically more settled than four-year-olds. Perhaps by this age most of the antics have already been tried. They have established themselves as "doers" if they have been given a chance, and many, especially girls, are ready to give up trying everything to focus on doing some things, especially school-type activities, better and better. Activities last longer and products become more important. Five-year-olds have less need to prove themselves as persons but greater need to improve their skills. They are beginning to look ahead to the progression of their growing up. At this point the modeling of more advanced behaviors by older children becomes very important. Five-year-olds when in the company of older children can take on such grown-up behaviors as sitting quietly, taking turns, or expressing themselves as the older children do, whereas at age four they remained pretty much themselves regardless of the company.

This is an impressionable age. A teacher can easily gain "control" of a five-year-old's behavior, a fact that makes kindergarten teaching both easier and scarier than teaching either older or younger children. Kindergartners often, by mistake, call their teachers mommy or grandma, even if their teacher is male. They generally accept whatever their teacher says. Only occasionally will a strong-willed five-year-old rebel at a teacher's demands, saying, as one did, "You can't tell me what to do. You can't ruin my whole life. Only my mother is allowed to do that." If there is a strong influence within the peer group for silliness or misbehavior contrary to the teacher's expectations, many kindergarten children appear to suffer real conflicts in trying to serve two masters. A teacher—like the one described in Chapter 2—who tries to rigidly control children's behavior, but without success, would be especially poorly placed as a kindergarten teacher.

Sex-role learning   Of particular interest in the period from ages three through five is the way in which the child develops **sex-appropriate** behavior. Throughout this period **sex identification** becomes increasingly apparent. Some of these differences, such as the earlier maturation rate of females, are inborn rather than learned. Other differences, such as the greater activity level of boys, might be both inherited and learned. Boys are typically encouraged or at least permitted to be quite active, while girls are usually expected to be quieter and calmer. Certainly boys are more often provided with cars, trucks, and building blocks, toys that encourage activity, while girls receive dolls, books, and other quiet toys.

Photo by John James.

Whether sex-appropriate behavior is a result of the modeling done by adults, older peers, the media, or direct admonition ("Boys don't————" or "Girls don't like to————"), there is no doubt that children ages three through five learn these lessons well. The sex-related limitations imposed at this age are fewer for girls than boys. If they so choose, girls can play rough, ride tricycles, punch punching bags, and wear dress-up policeman hats and cowboy boots without comment from most adults. Boys, however, are apt to be scolded for crying or playing with dolls and be told that ladies' hats and purses are strictly girls' things; if they do not engage in active play, they may be prodded to do so. On the other hand, girls at this age may also be learning that since they receive fewer admonitions, they matter less than boys.

Parents and teachers, book publishers, television producers, and toy manufacturers have become increasingly aware of the limiting effects of many sex-role prohibitions, so that behavioral differences in the early years may become less pronounced. However, as long as there remains any suggestion within the culture that certain behaviors are "okay" or "not okay," most children of this age will readily comply with the norm.

AFFECTIVE DEVELOPMENT AT AGES SIX AND SEVEN

The "school" expectations

At age six or seven years the child makes a very sudden and sometimes traumatic entry into the middle childhood years. A great deal is typically expected of the child entering elementary school, not the least of which may be the boarding and riding of a bus to a destination that is relatively strange and far from home. Once in first grade, the six-year-old is often expected to work on assigned tasks for long periods of time, to follow complex directions, to form letters and numbers, and to remember all sorts of things. At almost no point in the life span are the expectations of the world so markedly altered as when the child makes this transition from the neighborhood or the typical early childhood program into the elementary school.

Developmentally, nothing has prepared the child age six or seven for a sudden increase of sedentary activity. Six-year-olds especially, retain babyish characteristics such as the desire to be hugged and cuddled. They still cry easily and many of them, particularly the boys, would be constantly on the go if left to their own devices. Rather than sit in a straight chair at a table or desk they prefer to lounge, stretch, sit on the floor, or sprawl out flat.

Most children at this point are eager to learn to read, write, and count, just as they want to learn all the jump rope rhymes, singing games, and other childhood customs. Although they are eager, serious learners, many of them, especially the boys, want their lessons served in light doses, preferably intermingled with play activities. The prolonged inactivity that accompanies "book" learning in many classrooms can create real tensions. Amazingly, a majority of children make whatever personal adjustments are necessary in their school situations. They learn to suppress their feelings of discomfort, to understand that their own wishes are not as important as they once thought, and to accept others' goals instead of their own. Despite such demands, six-

and seven-year-olds typically like their teachers and, if the teacher is kind and fair, are eager to win his or her recognition, praise, and special privileges. So going to school becomes their way of life, although recesses, if they are lucky enough to have them, may be the "best thing about school."

School-age children typically enjoy helping to make things go smoothly and are willing to modulate their activities to do so. They begin to think about things, to have ideas and plans that they do not show to the world. Although more difficult to "read," they become less bother to parents, teachers, and other caregiving adults. The demand for adult help and attention, which many preschoolers consider as their due, fades rapidly as they more clearly comprehend their actual position in the scheme of things and develop a capacity to hide their thinking and feelings.

A sense of industry   School-age children are not satisfied with mere activity, but want to produce something. Just pounding nails in a board is no longer enough; building a table is better. Pretend play, still a very important activity, is often transformed into "doing a play" for an audience. The staging and costumes become increasingly important and consume much enthusiastic effort.

Much more energy is devoted to projects, both short and long term. Girls, for example, may create all the props for a paper doll or a "Barbie" doll world, or they may set up a pretend school or hospital in which they play teacher, doctor, or nurse to younger siblings or dolls. Staging and the manufacturing of props for such activities become increasingly important, and the actual playing less important. Often the fantasizing about the play appears sufficiently satisfying in itself, and the acting may never materialize.

Boys spend equal time and energy building and arranging forts, space stations, barracks, and helicopter stations. Most of the time boys prefer playing with boys, while girls, either by choice or necessity, play with girls. However, when playing out a currently popular movie, play, or television show, boys and girls often join together to take sex-appropriate roles.

When not engaged in dramatic activity, children of ages six and seven devote much time and attention to practicing skills such as writing, reading, spelling, drawing, jumping rope, bouncing balls, and playing jacks. At first they do these things just to prove their ability, but they soon learn to enjoy using their skills to create something, such as a letter or sign, or to compete with each other.

The peer culture   Six- and seven-year-olds quickly tune into the peer culture in their community and school. They are significantly influenced by the older peer models available to them and eagerly learn and practice the songs, sallies, and superstitions of their age, sometimes to the dismay of adults. This is the age of riddles, "knock-knock" jokes, elephant jokes, or whatever is in vogue at the time. If children this age hear a joke from the older children, they become interested in it, even if they do not quite understand it.

The "symbolic" loss   The six- or seven-year-old, while grown-up in many ways, continues to be
of baby teeth   quite aware of his or her vulnerability. The loss of baby teeth is perhaps symbolic of the age. Having one's teeth loosen and finally hang by a thread is a very momentous happening. Analogous to this sudden loss of baby teeth,

the six- and seven-year-old is expected to cast aside all babyish traits. But the skills and experience of grown-ups cannot be accumulated suddenly, so the young school-age child must struggle to maintain the new image, often at the cost of spontaneity, openness, and ease. If parents and teachers can be aware of the nature of these struggles and have patience with the occasional regressions to tears, wet pants, wanting Mommy, wanting help with dressing, and silly fears, then the transition from early childhood to the middle school years can be greatly eased.

A potential time of tension Teachers often expect too much of first- and second-graders and thereby unknowingly create tensions that could have been avoided. Children's parents should be asked to inform the teacher if tensions are showing up at home. As one uneducated but concerned mother of a first-grader put it, "Listen here, my boy ain't no genius, and I ain't no genius. But you ain't no genius either. So lay off some." This appraisal of her son's school experience, while roughly stated, was probably far more accurate than the professional teacher's. Six- and seven-year-olds, unlike three-, four-, and five-year-olds, do not openly express their feelings, so the teacher may need help from families in assessing their affective states.

The "real" world of family life Children experience pressures at home as well as at school, and teachers need to be alert to such situations. Unfortunately, the stereotyped image of the American family, in which loving, mature parents always put their children's concerns first, is often more fiction than fact. There are many happy families, of course, but they too must endure hard times and internal strains that cannot be hidden from their young children. Six-year-old Kim, for example, from a secure and happy family, heard her teacher tell another child, who was trying desperately not to cry, "It's okay to cry. Even grown-ups cry sometimes." Kim came from across the room to confide, "That's right. My mommy was crying a lot last night because daddy goes to meetings all the time and all she ever gets to do is stay home with us kids."

Children's plights Some children carry very direct imprints of problems at home in their physical condition and behavior. Three-year-old Joey has a cigarette lighter burn, a memento of his father's drunken cruelty. Robert tells how his father hung him by his jacket from a coat hook on the wall because he "sasses him back." Janey, age four, teaches her friends at the child-care center how to play "pussy" the way her teenage mother does with her boy friends. Betsy, playing mommy in the doll corner, says calmly in a play phone conversation, "You know what that fuckin' husband of mine did? I gon' get rid of him. He just no good. He never did do no work."

Children usually cannot tell you about their upsets at home. Only occasionally do they have sufficient awareness of their own feelings and enough trust in you to be able to say, as did the following six-year-old, "Teacher, I didn't cry this morning because I was mad at you. My mother works and is gone by the time I get home from school every day. I hardly ever get to see her. She was going to stay home today, and I just wanted to stay home with her so badly. I just didn't want to come to school today."

It would be very easy for an inexperienced teacher to become immobilized by the tragedies and dramas of children's lives. Likewise, it is sometimes tempting to take the child-advocate role and allow yourself to develop hostile feelings toward careless and uncaring parents. Again, you might sometimes see your role as parental adviser or, in the case of children from undesirable backgrounds, you might simply write the child off as hopeless.

If the child is to be helped, however, it is important that you become as sympathetic to the plight and dilemmas of the parents as you are to those of their children. Given their view of the world and their resources, most parents are doing their level best to fulfill their conception of "good" people. While you may disagree with them as a teacher you cannot take responsibility for their behavior; your only responsibility is in the way you relate to them and their child. If you communicate understanding and optimism about the child along with your concerns, and if you can effectively describe what you are trying to do, most parents will cooperate far more than if you succeed in making them feel guilty about what they are failing to provide.

It is impossible for you as a teacher, even in a full-time day-care center, to take on the task of providing parental love to a child. You can provide consistency, respect, praise, physical protection, warm smiles and hugs, and new experiences. You can help the children improve their skills, but you cannot be a parent to the children you teach, and it is important that you not try to be. You must demonstrate to the parents (or caregivers) that you find them worthwhile and acceptable (although perhaps not all their behavior)

RESPONSE SECTION

The changing concerns, emotions, and interests from infancy through age seven have been discussed in the preceding part of this chapter. We now suggest that you further extend your sensitivity to affective behaviors by doing the following:

1. Observe an infant and/or toddler for a period of time and try to summarize the range of behavior and emotion displayed and the caregiver's reactions. Especially note your own reactions to the child. What do you consider cute and appealing? What is unpleasant or of concern to you? Why?

2. Try to recall and list at least three specific incidents that happened to you prior to age seven. Keeping in mind that recall of one's early experiences can be distorted by one's current perspectives and interpretations, try to recapture the following in regard to those experiences: (a) perceptions of your size relative to other objects and persons, (b) perceptions of competence or helplessness, (c) major concerns in the situation, and (d) the options available to you in the situation. Consider to what extent these experiences are comparable to those described in this chapter.

and that you join with them, rather than compete with them, in seeking the best for their child.

Social Development

SOCIAL DEVELOPMENT IN INFANTS AND TODDLERS

Social interest in peers begins at a very early age. Infants, when in the presence of other babies, are likely to make limited social advances, although these are usually ignored by the potential receiver. These initiations are in the form of looking, smiling, and grasping, behavior that is commonly directed toward almost any object.

SOCIALIZATION IN INFANTS

Lee Lee (1973) observed infants (less than one year old) in a group care setting at Cornell University and found that they varied in their interactions with other infants in the program. One of the infants, who was relatively inactive in making initiations herself but who was responsive to the contacts of others, received a greater number of advances. In contrast, the infant who received fewest overtures was one who initiated many himself but consistently terminated (looked away or turned away) the overtures of others. It would appear from this study of early peer socialization that, although infants may appear to be quite undifferentiated in their responses to each other, they are developing personal preferences and styles of socializing that at least temporarily affect their popularity.

Early social contacts

As infants grow into toddlerhood they develop increased interest in the activities of their agemates and often express this interest in conflicts over the use of toys. By age two, toddlers make contact with each other whenever they have the opportunity and appear to prefer being in the company of other children. At this age, however, most of the children's time together is spent in solitary play. They observe each other intermittently, and occasional contacts consist primarily of grabbing the other's toy, with only limited interaction of other kinds.

SOCIAL DEVELOPMENT AT AGES THREE THROUGH FIVE

Parallel play, then associative play

At ages three through five children increasingly interact with each other. At first, children may engage in **parallel play,** that is they play beside each other with the same kinds of materials but with little interaction. This pattern gradually gives way to **associative play**, where they exchange materials and take turns by mutual consent.

Preschool children assume that their thoughts and observations are obvious to everyone, and consequently their early attempts to communicate and

Egocentric thought and speech play with their agemates are fraught with difficulties. Piaget describes this kind of thinking as **egocentric**, that is, assuming that one's perception of the world is shared by all and that there is therefore no need to explain one's actions or wishes. There is no effort to understand another's point of view because there is no realization that other views exist. The child's cognitive abilities (or, more accurately, inabilities) directly influence the nature of social exchanges.

Adults find children's egocentrism frustrating but are usually tolerant and try to find out what the child sees and thinks and then react accordingly. When two children, age three, try to talk and play together, neither can understand the other's egocentric view, and consequently their play involves each child doing his or her own thing and making comments that are quite incomprehensible to the other child. Play and conversations at this stage are often hilarious to listen to, as in the following exchange:

Jane: The baby's hungry. You be baby in a buggy, okay?
Susan: Want a ride in my car?
Jane: Here, baby. Here's your bottle.
Susan: What's that, gasoline?
Jane: Drink it all up. Then I'll burp you. (begins thumping Susan on the back)
Susan: Stop hitting me. I'll have a wreck.

Photo by Barbara Dopyera.

Their contact with peers who do not understand thoughts or intentions provides children the necessary jolt for moving out of an egocentric view of the world. Children gradually learn that although their signaling behaviors, such as pouting, may communicate a specific message to their mothers, the same behavior has no effect on anyone else, especially preschool friends. Children find that they must learn to grab, ask, barter, or find other ways to communicate what they want.

Cooperative play

Children gradually learn to explain ideas and actions and to take into account the views and actions of others so that they can engage in **cooperative play** ventures. This appears to begin with the agreement to play out particular roles or functions in dramatic play. At the most rudimentary level, one child agrees to be the mother and the other to be the baby. Each may behave quite independently, but each maintains the role, and the net result gives more mutual satisfaction than earlier parallel or associative play. Increasingly, role actions are coordinated, families go out for a walk together, adults discuss the disciplining of baby, there are sibling fights, etc. From these beginnings emerge highly complex play scenes: moving vans and packers moving a family to California or Texas, or a hospital scene replete with doctors, nurses, a worried mother, scared and injured children, and ambulance drivers. Only with extensive opportunities for interaction can children develop the communication and planning skills needed for such elaborate play scenes. Children who do not attend preschools and who lack play companions in their neighborhoods are often "slower" in developing the necessary social abilities. Such play has affective, social, and cognitive benefits and is extremely important to children's overall personal development.

The frequency of social interaction

Given the opportunity, preschool children will increasingly interact with each other. In a study of children's activity in the Syracuse University Early Childhood Center, Lay (1972) found that three-, four-, and five-year-olds were talking with each other 45 percent of the time they were observed. Children in this age range will voluntarily engage in all kinds of play activity without adult urging. Simply by having materials, equipment, space, and the opportunity available they will become involved in chasing, climbing, dramatic play, building, drawing, writing, constructing, painting, and myriad other activities.

Not all interactions between children of this age are friendly. There may be increases in conflicts across the three-to-four-year-old age period in proportion to the increases in interaction. The height of aggressiveness is typically reached at age four, when it appears to be practiced more out of curiosity than animosity. If another activity is offered, four-year-olds can often be easily diverted from aggressive play. For example, one particularly skillful nursery school teacher repeatedly curtails the disruptive activities of groups of marauding four-year-olds by offering such alternatives as participation in a mock wrestling match, complete with cheering, bowing, and bells signaling the end of each round.

Sometimes fights in preschool are the result not of "feeling one's oats," but of real frustration and anger. Just as children of this age are insensitive to roles other than their own during dramatic play, so they fail to perceive the motivation behind the behavior of their peers. Events such as having one's tower bumped over, having to wait for a turn with a cherished piece of equipment, or having one's painting torn, are all taken very personally and may precipitate a battle, even though such actions may be quite unrelated to themselves. This also applies to name-calling. The preschool child does not yet understand that words are simply words and that saying something does not make it so. The child has not sorted out the symbolic function of language and assumes a real connection between the word and its referent. They seem to think that they can inflict real, as opposed to psychological, damage with words whenever they are angry. Conversely, they are themselves quite enraged by the words others use to attack them. Many a physical battle among preschoolers has been precipitated by an accidental event (such as a slight bump) followed by an awful name like *baby* or *dummy*. This appears to be a very threatening thing in the child's mind, and therefore is a suitable basis for conflict.

The potency of words for young children

SOCIAL DEVELOPMENT AT AGES SIX AND SEVEN

Given the opportunity, children of ages six and seven will continue the kind of cooperative, dramatic play ventures described as typical of four- and five-year-olds. If six- and seven-year-olds have not had ample group play experiences previously, it may be important that they be given this opportunity, not just for brief periods under a teacher's active direction but with as much time and autonomy as possible. The value of working cooperatively with peers and independently of adults in decision-making, planning, role-playing, and creating props and settings cannot be matched by teacher-directed activities.

The value of sociodramatic play interactions

Organized group games are increasingly popular for this age group, and children try hard to figure out how to play Spud, Duck Duck Goose, and various other games that they have had an opportunity to learn about. They begin also to participate in skill games such as Four Square, Dodgeball, and beginning versions of games such as basketball and softball. They assume that the rules they learn from older children are givens and tenaciously resist any attempt by adults to simplify or otherwise change them. They may refuse to play at all if things are not done "right." Again, this shows how cognitive abilities (or limitations) directly affect social interaction. They have not, as yet, figured out that rules have not always existed as untouchable entities. They may have no awareness that a rule is a social agreement and that it can be subsequently modified.

Organized games with rules

Many six- and seven-year-olds also enjoy participating in more formal group discussions, especially those dealing with problems they see as important, such as how to get older kids to stop teasing them, or how to become friends with someone you like who does not seem to like you. The more

Group discussions

> The child's interest in and ability to interact with others from infancy to age seven have been discussed in the preceding part of this chapter.
>
> We suggest that you further extend your awareness of these topics by thinking again of the early life incidents you listed in the previous response section. Consider whether any peers or siblings were also involved. If not, consider other incidents in which you *were* involved with peers at a relatively early age. Try to recall your feelings about these other children, especially if they were older than you.
>
> Can you, in retrospect, make any comparisons between your own repertoire for social behavior and those of the other children? If so, consider the personal significance of those differences on those occasions.

mature children have sufficient social and self-awareness at this age to enjoy comparing their own ideas and feelings with those of their classmates. Although some children of this age are still more interested in talking than in listening to the other children, there is sufficient other-awareness to make group talking a satisfying experience for most.

Social repertoire and adjustment   We have referred several times to the relationship between the child's cognitive limitations and his or her social ineptness. Research by Spivack and Shure (1974) into the relationship between cognitive and social functioning disclosed a significant correlation between children's repertoires of ideas for dealing with interpersonal situations and social adjustment. They conclude that children who are frequently involved in interpersonal conflicts, such as how to get a toy from another child, are frequently at a loss as to how this might be accomplished other than through aggression. By teaching children additional ways of dealing with social situations (including a more effective vocabulary for thinking about and expressing their desires), they found that they were able to reduce the child's aggressive behavior and improve his or her emotional condition. This kind of contribution to children's social competence is clearly within the teacher's sphere of influence.

Observing Affective and Social Behavior in Individual Children

The following pages contain specific questions about the affective and social behaviors of the children you are observing. You will need to follow the same procedures that you used in making observations and notes of motor behavior and physical characteristics.

We would like to point out again that the examples provided are only included to help you interpret the meaning of the question and to suggest the range of possible answers that might be given. Your actual responses will undoubtedly be quite different.

Photo by John James.

1. Expression of Affective States

    1.1 *What kinds of things give the child pleasure? What things, topics, or activities have particular appeal?*

        Examples: • grins happily when Melissa says she would save her place while she goes to the bathroom
                • laughs when going over bump on slide and falls off
                • smiles when Renee holds her hand and says, "I'm sorry"
                • cuts out all the pictures of lions she can find in magazines and toy catalogs

    1.2 *What kinds of things cause the child displeasure or discomfort? What things, topics, or activities are particularly aversive?*

        Examples: • goes and sits alone when Juney calls her "baby"
                • says, "I'm too hot. Turn down the heat," to teacher after vigorous running
                • rips up paper when gets letters in wrong order
                • says, "I don't like you to do that," when Simon kicks his chair

    1.3 *What kinds of things seem to frighten the child? How is fear expressed? What does the child do about fears?*

        Examples: • says afraid of bees (in dining room) but enters
                • moves closer to friend when dog comes near

- cries and hides face when psychologist wants him to go to another room "to play some games"
- goes to adult and says, "That noise scared me"

1.4   *What kinds of things seem to make the child angry? How is anger expressed?*

Examples:
- spits at Donna, who said she was stupid
- after shoving Connie for taking her place, notices that Connie went in the bathroom and gagged; follows her and says, "I'm sorry. I didn't know you was about to throw up"
- says two hours after hitting Shawn, "I hit Shawn. I was really mad"
- goes up to Sam and gives a shove, saying "Gimme that"

2. Orientation of Self in World

2.1   *In what actions or activities is the child dependent* (requires or wishes others to be present, supervise, or assist)? *In what actions or activities is the child independent* (engages self without help or attention from others)?

Examples:
- needs help in putting on boots
- asks teacher to watch after each attempt at performing flip on climbing equipment
- listens to story on tape with earphones by self
- plays in sand by self for half-hour

2.2   *What actions or activities does the child initiate* (participate with no direction or without concurrently seeing others thus involved)?

Examples:
- goes to book corner and takes out book when no one else is there
- tries to touch each finger, respectively, to a different space on chart paper
- makes obstacles with blocks to jump over
- makes painting about "me and my mommy chasing our dog"

2.3   *What actions or activities does the child appear to sustain or continue to a point of completion* (in contrast to engaging in and then stopping without any obvious point of completion)?

Examples:
- looks all the way through book
- does all of puzzle
- writes note to friend (done in two separate sittings)
- builds block tower as high as can reach

3. Concepts of Self

3.1   *What evidence is there in the child's behavior (including self-appraisal) of how he or she views his or her physical appearance? His or her body? His or her size?*

Examples:
- has inaccurate perception of size; tries to crawl into box that is much too small
- says, "I got ugly hair"
- admires self in mirror with new shirt on (pleased smile)
- says, "I'm bigger than you," to Tony

3.2 *What evidence is there in the child's behavior (including self-appraisal) of how he or she views his or her worthiness? Goodness or badness?*

Examples: • while waiting to have help from teacher points out, "I'm waiting and not fussing"
• says, "Ain't I nice?" when shares colander at sand table
• smiles as says, "Susy thinks I'm mean"
• in reading book about the bad duck Ping, says, "I be bad too"

3.3 *What evidence is there in the child's behavior (including self-appraisal) of how he or she views his or her sex role?*

Examples: • sorts out boy clothes from dress-ups as own to use, gives others to Jane
• says to Bryan, "You be daddy and build a house. I'll be mummy and wash dishes. Daddies don't wash dishes"
• when gets pants wet in snow and is looking for dry ones in box of extras, examines each to see if for boys (fly) or girls
• says, "I can too play with dolls," to other child who says that only girls like dolls

3.4 *What evidence is there in the child's behavior (including self-appraisal) of how he or she views his or her skills—motor skills, social skills, thinking skills, etc.?*

Examples: • says to new child, "Want to shovel? I'll show you how"
• says, upon doing a goof, "I'm so stupid"
• when teacher cannot push open the door, says, "I can do it, let me do it," and tries very hard
• says to self, "I can climb all the way up there"

4. Social Awareness

4.1 *What evidence is there in the child's behavior (including what he or she says about others) of sensitivity to other's feelings and views?*

Examples: • says, "Oh, oh, Neal won't like that" (broken top)
• asks teacher to help another child who is beginning to cry
• says to child on other side of chair, "Can you see my feet?"
• asks, "What are you going to do with that stick, Pam? Are you going to use it to poke Jane?" (fight earlier between two)

5. Social Interaction Levels

5.1 *In what types of play activities does the child primarily observe others?*

Examples: • in the outdoor yard
• rocking and holding doll

5.2 *In what types of play activities does the child primarily play parallel to others?*

Examples: • at sand table
• play with toy trucks and cars

5.3 *In what types of play activities does the child primarily play associatively with others?*

Examples: • using Tinker Toys
• doing puzzles

5.4 *In what types of play activities does the child play cooperatively with others?*

Examples: • dramatic play (doctor, hospital play)
• building large block house

6. Social Leader/Follower

6.1 *In what different ways does the child initiate contact with others?*

Examples: • says to Erica, "Come on, let's play house"
• says, "Want to be my friend?"
• just walks over and enters into activity
• says, "Do you want some candy?"

6.2 *What kind of ideas or suggestions does the child offer to others?*

Examples: • says, "Pete, you be the dog"
• says to Kim at lunch table, "Let's not pass her the milk" (mad at Debbie)
• says, "Try this one. It's harder" (puzzle)

6.3 *What suggestions of others does the child follow?*

Examples: • follows Sandy when she says, "Want to swing?"
• carries toy teakettle when friend says, "Pretend this is your purse"

7. Repertoire for Solving Social Problems

7.1 *When conflicts or disagreements with peers or adults occur, what does the child do to reach a resolution?*

Examples: • when Ronnie grabs his airplane, says, "You give that back, it's mine," and then, "I'll tell my mommy"
• threatens, "If you don't let me in, I'll rip up your paper" (wants to get in playhouse)
• when tips Tim's glass over and Tim is mad says, "I'm sorry. I won't do it any more"
• in disagreement over who will feed gerbil, says, "If I get to do it today, you can do it tomorrow"

7.2 *If the child is excluded from an activity or group he or she wishes to join, what does he or she do to resolve the situation?*

Examples: • says, "I won't invite you to my party if you won't be my friend"
• tells teacher, "They won't play with me"
• says, "I didn't want to play anyway," and goes elsewhere

You have been provided with questions to use as observation guides for affective and social behaviors. In addition to these questions, it might be helpful for you to try the following:

1. Summarize the similarities and differences between the children you have observed.

2. Answer the list of questions as they apply to your own affective and social behaviors. Try to summarize the similarities and differences between your own self-appraisal and those you made of the children.

3. Reread the descriptive narratives you prepared in connection with Chapter 3. What differences exist between those observations and those made in response to the questions in this chapter?

8. Formal (Teacher-led) Group Participation

   8.1 *What evidence is there in the child's behavior (including what he or she says) that he or she is either comfortable or uncomfortable in group discussions?*

      Examples: • comes immediately to discussion location and sits waiting
      • tries to hide in lavatory when group assembles
      • spends most of discussion time looking at child next to him and occasionally engages in tickling match
      • listens for about ten minutes and then plays with little puzzle that was in pocket

   8.2 *What does the child contribute to group discussion that indicates he or she has heard and understood what another child said?*

      Examples: • says, "I went to Florida once too" (Jimmy told about his trip to Florida)
      • says to Tom, "What did you do when no one was home?" (in response to Tom's tale of a lost cat)
      • says, "My baby sister has the chicken pox" (previous speaker said his father had a sore throat)

Transition into Resourcefulness Section

After observing and recording the affective and social behavior of several children, you have some basis for predicting what activities and social situations each will likely find satisfying, difficult, or uninteresting. For example, consider the child who knows the names of only a few other children; shows little awareness of others' feelings or perspectives; seeks adult proximity when other children are engaged in rough play; laughs when being hugged and when playing peek-a-boo; screams for Mommy when distressed; only observes others or engages in parallel play; does not initiate play contacts; avoids confrontation with other children.

THE IMPORTANCE OF PLAYFULNESS

The following excerpt is from a document prepared by Lichtenberg and Norton (1972) that summarizes extensive research findings on early development:

> It is common agreement in the field that growth, development, health, and high levels of cognitive and affective functioning in children are all associated with continuous, ongoing participation in actions and interactions that are full of pleasure and playfulness. There are no proponents of the stiff upper lip school of thought in respect to positive developmental processes. Stoicism, the inculcation of moral codes, the emphasis on humorless acquisition of mores and technology of the society, all are absent from the scene when positive development is under consideration. If parents and children have fun together, if caretakers and infants laugh, play at words, satisfy each other, act in an animated and joyful way, glory in their mutual liveliness, the infants and children will grow into intelligent, happy, searching, curious, creative human beings. If the parents are depressed, ritualistic, proper but not happily engaged, sincere but not vivid, there will be noticeable deficits. (p. 17)

Compare the above child with a second one who often shows awareness of other's perspectives and feelings; behaves independently in many activities; has a variety of ways of expressing emotions; frequently engages in cooperative play ventures (such as planning and presenting puppet shows); initiates play in a variety of ways; has numerous suggestions for others and accepts others' suggestions; terminates interaction simply by stopping and walking away or saying that he is stopping and giving a reason; has a variety of techniques for resolving social conflict; shows awareness of others' views in his contributions to group discussions.

The provision of matches   Both of these two children are age five, but their development in affective and social areas has progressed at quite different rates. Could you, on the basis of this amount of information, make some kind of reasonable prediction about which of the following activities will be appealing to each of these two children?

- Being sent to an adjoining building to find the school nurse
- Working with a couple of other children in repairing a rabbit hutch for a new bunny
- Holding the new baby bunny while the rabbit hutch is being repaired
- Playing hide-and-go-seek
- Picking apples in a nearby orchard
- Washing doll clothes from the doll corner
- Working with a group in building a fort ready for an attack by spacemen

- Playing baby role in dramatic play activity upon invitation from other children
- Playing leader of wild dog pack in dramatic play activity

Some activities in this list would likely interest both children, such as apple picking. Others, such as playing baby or holding the bunny, would probably have a great deal more appeal for the first child and somewhat less for the second. Many of the activities that the second would thoroughly enjoy would simply overwhelm the first.

Guidelines
In considering how to facilitate the affective and social development of the children you are observing or will observe, we suggest the following guidelines:

1. Try to provide opportunities for all children to engage in activities appropriate to their stage of development, and avoid involving them in activities that will likely prove uninteresting or stressful. There is some evidence that pleasure is related not only to emotional well-being in the young but also to other kinds of positive developmental outcomes, such as intellectual achievement. There is general agreement among those who study human development that children who are accustomed to playfully exploring the world of ideas and relationships become more competent than those whose lives are devoid of joy and playfulness. Even if this were not true, most of us would still wish to make children's lives enjoyable. Evidence that there may be long-term benefits from fun and playfulness simply make it easier for us to justify making programs pleasurable rather than boring and ritualistic.

In the next section of the book you will expand your repertoire of ideas for providing satisfying experiences for children at different levels.

2. Remember that young children's affective and social behavior is, in large measure, not the product of inborn characteristics and is consistently modified by experience. While basic orientations and self-conceptions are becoming established by age three, they are still amenable to your influence as a teacher, whether consciously or by default.

Imagine Butch, a child in your class who appears to consider himself a bad guy, a real toughie. He teases, attacks, breaks things, and appears to delight in being destructive and feared by the other children. He influences others to do what he wants by threat of physical harm. The children in your group are likely to view Butch just as he presents himself and will further reinforce the limited perspectives he has of himself. As a teacher, will you accept his conception of himself as a mean kid and act toward him as though this were true? Will you only admonish him for being bad, further solidifying his current self-view, or will you also act toward him with the expectation that he is kind, helpful, tender, and sympathetic as well? At age three, four, and beyond, being presented with a new set of expectations about what one is like can be an important influence in modifying one's self-conception. Your behavior toward children can help them extend their view of themselves. For example, if children have only identified themselves as being good, big, or similar "positive" attributes, you can help them see that they need not rigidly adhere to those, but rather can still be worthwhile persons if they occasionally act bad, little, dependent, or in other "negative" ways.

Undue emphasis on the "positive" virtues in a developing self-conception is nearly as harmful as conceiving of oneself in only "negative" ways. Teachers should strive to give young children a self-conception that is flexible enough to permit a variety of behaviors and states of mind. Children should celebrate themselves as unique, worthwhile persons who do both good and bad things, who sometimes act and feel grown-up but are sometimes babyish, who in some ways are attractive and in other ways not so attractive. The attempt to make young children believe only "positive" things about themselves is not likely to succeed because so much of their real behavior and thinking will not measure up to it.

As an example, imagine Mike, another child in your classroom. Mike appears to basically see himself as good, helpful, polite, careful, and nice. If Mike were in the same class with Butch he would probably be very aware of Butch's behavior, would probably insist that Butch be punished, and would expect the teacher and other children to like his own behaviors much better than Butch's. If Mike, at age four or so, also engages in aggressive acts, how might you as a teacher respond? Might you quickly draw him back into line by saying, "Why, Mike, that's not the way *you* behave. You're acting like Butch today. That's not the good Mike I know. I'm sure you won't do it again." Or might you say, "I see that you got in a fight today. That's something new for you, isn't it? How did it make you feel?" Of course, there are many other ways to respond. The point is that you, in your teaching role, can act to solidify the child's current self-conception or you can value and encourage explorations into new ways of behaving and feeling.

3. In your role as teacher it will be your responsibility to encourage children to develop, practice, and extend their repertoires for social interaction. To a great extent, simply providing opportunities for children to practice different ways of behaving is sufficient. However, the findings of Spivack and Shure (1974), referred to earlier in the chapter, suggest that some children simply repeat again and again the same stereotyped action in critical social situations without being aware that other options could have been tried. You can provide models for alternative ways of behaving and also quite directly point out other behaviors appropriate to the situation. If you can determine via your observations what individual children do in initiating social contacts, in trying to influence others, and in trying to resolve social conflicts, you will be able to determine the kind of additional awarenesses, instruction, and practice they need to improve their social relationships. In Section Three there will be many suggestions of how specific activities and materials can be used to extend children's social repertoires.

Summary

Erik Erikson has described the early years as the time for seeking successful resolution of several developmental conflicts—trust versus mistrust, autonomy versus doubt or shame, initiative versus guilt, industry versus inferiority. These have been elaborated throughout this discussion of affective development. Further, there has been discussion of the individuality of children (even as infants and toddlers), the emergent self-view, the adoption of sex-appropriate behaviors, the pressures of home problems and school expectations, and the influences of the peer group. The activity interests and the typical behaviors for each age level have also been described in considerable detail. Affective development was often directly or indirectly related to social development.

Children's social development was further described as progressing from parallel and associative to cooperative peer interactions. The interrelatedness of all development was evidenced in discussion of the limitations placed upon social effectiveness by preschoolers' egocentric thinking and of the relationship between children's repertoires of ideas for solving social problems and their social adjustment. Clearly, cognitive development directly affects social development. It is only for the convenience of discussion that the aspects of development are separated. As you make observations of individual children and seek matches based on those observations, you will recognize how directly one aspect of development can influence the others.

REASSESSMENT

Reread what you wrote for the preassessment as you began this chapter, comparing this with your current understandings. Now write on these topics again and incorporate your new insights and knowledge. Continue to update as you prepare for teaching. Save your materials for your portfolio.

Additional Reading

Individuality in Infants

Chess, S., Thomas, A., and Birch, H. G. *Your child is a person: A psychological approach to parenthood without guilt.* New York: Viking Press, 1965.

Bell, R. Q. A reinterpretation of effects in socialization. *Psychological Bulletin*, 1968, 75, 81–95.

Thomas, A., Chess, S., Birch, H., Hertzig, M., and Korn, S. *Behavioral individuality in early childhood.* London: University Press, 1964.

Affective Development of Infants and Toddlers

Ribble, M. *The rights of infants: Early psychological needs and their satisfaction.* 2nd ed. New York: Columbia University Press, 1965.

Salk, L., and Kramer, R. *How to raise a human being: A parent's guide to emotional health from infancy through adolescence.* New York: Random House, 1969.

Sex-Role Development Cuffaro, H. K. Reevaluating basic premises: Curricula free of sexism. *Young Children*, 1975, 30, 469–79.

Maccoby, E. E., and Jacklin, C. N. *The development of sex differences.* Stanford, Calif.: Stanford University Press, 1974.

Sprung, B. *Guide to non-sexist early childhood education.* New York: Women's Action Alliance, 1974.

Parent-Teacher Relations Caplan, G. *Emotional problems of early childhood.* New York: Basic Books, 1961.

Helfer, R. E., and Kempe, C. H. *Helping the battered child and his family.* Philadelphia: J. B. Lippincott, 1972.

Polansky, N. A., DeSaix, C., and Sharlin, S. A. *Child neglect: Understanding and reaching the parent.* New York: Child Welfare League of America.

Protecting children: Freeing them from mental and physical abuse. Five articles on the theme of child abuse. *Childhood Education*, 1975, 52, 58–75.

Sanders, L., Kibby, R. W., Creagan, S., and Tyrrel, E. Child abuse: Detection and prevention. *Young Children*, 1975, 30, 332–8.

CHAPTER 6
Increasing Sensitivity
to Children's
Cognitive and
Intellectual Behavior

Overview

Cognitive and Intellectual Development Prior to Age Three

Cognitive and Intellectual Development from Ages Three through Seven

CLASSIFICATION ABILITIES
NUMBER CONCEPTS
SERIATION
MASS AND LIQUID QUANTITY
CAUSALITY
SPACE CONCEPTS
TIME CONCEPTS
SPOKEN LANGUAGE
WRITTEN LANGUAGE
DECODING
ENCODING

Observing Cognitive and Intellectual Behavior in Individual Children

Transition into Resourcefulness Section

Summary

PREASSESSMENT

When you have completed this chapter you should be able to describe and compare the following:

1. *cognitive and intellectual behaviors of infants, toddlers, and young children ages three through seven.*
2. *stages in cognitive and intellectual development in young children (including language development).*
3. *specific aspects of cognitive and intellectual behavior in young children that may be relevant for you to observe.*
4. *implications for programing of young children's cognitive and intellectual development.*

   Before *beginning to read this chapter:*

1. *take enough time to write what you already know about each of the above topics.*
2. *observe individual children and record your impressions of their thinking and language abilities.*

Save what you write for rereading, comparison, and elaboration after you have studied and discussed these materials.

Overview

Much can be learned about children's cognitive and intellectual attainments by observing how they respond in situations where they have some freedom to act and talk as they wish. Consider, for example, the following situation:

Tina, age four, and Donna, age five, are playing with clay. Tina rolls out a long coil, chops it up into pieces with a tongue depressor, and says, "There—one, two, three, four, five. One, two, three, four, five snakes." She points to each as she counts the second time. "Oh, oh, too fat," she says. "I'll get you long." She rolls them into a longer and narrower form, aligns them at the edge of the table, and puts a tiny pat of pressed clay by each snake, saying, "Here's some cookie for you. And here's some cookie for you."

Donna, also rolling coils from clay, joins the ends of one piece to form a ring of clay and puts it on her finger, where it hangs loosely. She says, "This thing is too big around. I need to make it littler." She puts the clay back into the ball, rolls it all out again, and puts it into circular shape. Says to Tina, "Here's a ring for you." Tina puts it on with a smile. Donna makes another ring and puts it on herself saying, "Boys wear married rings. Claudia's brother has a married ring."

As Fred, age seven, walks into the room, Tina takes her ring off and holds it up to show him. "See what Donna made me," she says. Fred says, "What did she make you an O for? You can't read!" Tina replies, "It's no O. It's a ring." Donna says, "Don't show him. He might marry you." Tina looks startled and quickly hides the ring. Fred says, "Show me. I'm not going to marry you, for heaven's sake. You're too little."

Tina's use of clay includes manipulation of shapes, production and alignment of objects, counting, and consideration of proportions. Donna considers size and proportions in producing her objects, and is also involved in considering what concrete symbols (wedding rings) actually represent and how this representation occurs. Fred reacts to the younger girls' activities with a different perspective. If the observation of the three children were to continue there would be further evidence about variations in their internal representation of reality, their current concerns, and the upper limits of their thinking abilities. We might also be able to observe how each of them gradually takes in new information and uses it to modify his or her perspective and transform his or her internal representation of the world.

Events and viewpoints, such as an adult conversation, that are quite out of alignment with a child's current perceptions often appear not to even enter a child's awareness. The views or actions of another child, however, if only slightly different from their own, may be noted with enthusiastic interest and almost immediately cited or included in their activity. It is likely, for *Potency of peer* example, that Tina will begin making rings of clay and begin to call them O's. *influence* Donna may begin to consider how big a person needs to be before marriage rings become something to either seek or watch out for. Thus accommodations are gradually made in internal representations of reality.

Adaptation The means by which cognitive and intellectual structures develop are *processes:* described by Piaget as **"adaptation."** Adaptation is said to consist of two *assimilation and* complementary and simultaneous processes, **assimilation** and **accommoda-** *accommodation* **tion**. *Assimilation* refers to the process whereby new, external experiences (such as objects and events) are incorporated into existing mental organization. *Accommodation* is the process whereby the internal mental organization must be altered before it can incorporate certain of the new experiences that it was unable to assimilate. These terms represent difficult concepts, but they are crucial to understanding the Piagetian view of intellectual development.

It may help to apply the terms *assimilation* and *accommodation* to yourself to give them greater meaning. As you read this chapter, we hope you will engage in the processes of assimilation and accommodation. If you are already familiar with the intellectual development of the infant and young child, you may simply be assimilating the ideas presented here. That is, you will already have an organized network of intellectual concepts that includes the ideas we are presenting. In short, there will be no need for accommodation to occur; you can simply assimilate the material.

On the other hand, if the ideas we present are not similar to what you

---

PIAGET'S STAGES IN THE DEVELOPMENT OF INTELLIGENCE

Jean Piaget's views of the child are presented throughout this chapter, as well as in other portions of the book. The picture of the development of intelligence that emerges from Piaget's studies is one of continuous transformations in the organizations, or structures, of intelligence. The sequence of stages described by Piaget is as follows:

1. *Sensorimotor period* (birth to eighteen or twenty-four months). The inborn sensorimotor reflexes (such as crying, sucking, and grasping) are generalized, coordinated, and differentiated through direct action on "reality" to form the elementary operations, which begin to be internalized.
2. *Preoperational period* (eighteen or twenty-four months to seven or eight years). The first phase within the preoperational period, sometimes referred to as the preconceptual phase, is when symbols are constructed in which children imitate and represent what they see through actions and language. This phase lasts to about age four. During the second phase, sometimes called the intuitive phase, children are extending, differentiating, and combining their action-images and correcting their intuitive impressions of reality.
3. *Concrete operations period* (seven or eight years to eleven or twelve years). During this period the child's thinking becomes "decentered," that is, less dependent on either actions or immediate perceptual cues. Internalized thinking operations facilitate classifying, ordering in series, numbering, grouping, and subgrouping of action-images.
4. *Formal operations* (eleven or twelve years to fifteen or sixteen years, and beyond). At this stage children begin to systematize classification, ordering, and numbering, and to consider the logical extension of these systems beyond action-images. The central thinking processes become sufficiently autonomous to permit consideration of all possible instances, that is, beyond those present in any actual situation.

---

already know or believe about intellectual development, you will not be able to conveniently assimilate this information into your existing mental structures. You may then need to accommodate these differences, that is, in some way realign your existing network of concepts and beliefs to take into account the additional perspective or different view.

It may also be that what we offer will be either so discrepant or unmeaningful to you that you will dismiss it as irrelevant, and thus will neither assimilate nor accommodate it. What do you think? Will you be able to assimilate these ideas? Or will you find them irrelevant? For learning, or adaptation, to occur, the mutual processes of assimilation and accommodation must be operating. A change in your mental structure will not occur unless the ideas encountered can be assimilated into your existing mental structure with only a slight need for accommodation.

Intrinsic need to engage in adaptation

The human organism is considered by Piaget and other interactionists to have an intrinsic need to function, interact, learn, and grow, that is, to be engaged in processes of adaptation. Satisfaction is derived from situations in which there is a good balance between assimilation and accommodation. The provision of situations with that optimal balance, as was indicated in Chapter 4, is what J. McVicker Hunt (1961) refers to as "the problem of the match." Finding that match for children is the teacher's primary job. You will know that you have succeeded when children are fully engaged without external inducements. Watch any multiage group and note the differences between what engages an infant, a toddler, a preschooler, a school-age child, an adolescent, a young adult, and a mature adult. Note what each one appears to screen out of awareness and what each attends to and responds to.

Response to external events depends on internal constructions

It is Piaget's view that the human organism responds to external stimulation and instruction according to the internal constructions that have already been developed. There is a "growing edge" at which each person can be engaged fully. Even the brief description of Tina, Donna, and Fred gave a glimmering as to what their "growing edges" might be. To some extent there is a common human progression in these matters, although idiosyncratic differences between individuals do result from personal experiences.

In the first part of this chapter we present you with background on the common human progression in acquiring cognitive and intellectual abilities. The first part of this discussion will concern infants and toddlers, followed by a more extensive presentation on children ages three through seven. Then, as in the previous two chapters, we will pose questions to guide your observations of individual children that should further increase your sensitivity to cognitive and intellectual behavior.

Cognitive and Intellectual Development Prior to Age Three

Sensory organs well developed; experience lacking

As you observe infants you will note that most of what is going on about them is not within their sphere of awareness. This is not due to an undeveloped sensory apparatus. The organs for seeing, hearing, touching, smelling, and tasting are all functioning well. It is simply that infants have not had sufficient interaction with the environment to enable the mental structures to be developed that transform meaningless sensations into meaningful perceptions. As Piaget puts it, according to Flavell (1963, p. 105), "It is a remarkable thing that the younger the child, the less novelties seem new to him."

The sensorimotor period

During what Piaget calls the sensorimotor period, from birth to age one and one-half or two years, children develop schemas (organized patterns of behavior) that gradually enable them to meaningfully perceive more and more of what surrounds them. To study a person's cognitive and intellectual status is to inquire into their level of perception or awareness, which in turn stems from the schemas that have been developed in the ongoing adaptation process. Schemas are developed in the following sequence during the sensorimotor period:

1. use of reflexes only (such as sucking, swallowing, and grasping)
2. modification and coordination of reflexes (for example, something grasped becomes something to suck)
3. "intentional" repetition of actions that at first were chance occurrences
4. use of actions to make things happen (such as swinging, striking, rubbing, and shaking)
5. trying new actions to see what will happen; experimentation
6. use of symbolic representation (signs) to invent solutions instead of just engaging in trial and error (for example, how to keep a rolling object where it is placed, how to open a box, and how to get in a more convenient position for performing actions)

COGNITIVE STRUCTURES IN THE SENSORIMOTOR PERIOD

The following excerpt from Churchill (1958) describes how the child develops cognitive structures during the sensorimotor period:

> He has come to know two worlds, his own inner world and the outer world, and this response is possible because every response he makes is registered in the mental structure which is being built into the system from the beginning. Every new experience, every sensori-motor reaction makes links with comparable experience already registered. Every sensation mediated by the eye is caught and registered on inner structure, so also every movement sensation, every sound attended to, every touch. In this way cell assemblies of knowledge are being built into the mental life of the child. (p. 36)

The beginnings of symbolic representation

Once children are able to symbolize objects or events (by representing them in some way in order to mentally manipulate them) they begin passing from the sensorimotor period. Piaget (1952, p. 338) has given us an example of how symbolic action is initially attained. His child, Lucienne, at age one year and four months, is given a nearly closed match box containing a watch chain. She unsuccessfully tries to open the box using two schemas she has previously discovered through active manipulation of other objects. She first tries to turn the box over in order to empty it of its contents, and she then reaches inside the box with a finger. Neither is successful, because the opening is too small. Looking intently at the box, Lucienne opens and shuts her mouth several times, "at first slightly, then wider and wider" and then "unhesitatingly puts her hand in the slit, and instead of trying as before to reach the chain, she pulls so as to enlarge the opening." Piaget interprets this mouthing action as Lucienne's use of a motor symbol, or sign, which gives the same kind of assistance to her thinking about a problem situation that words and other imagery will later provide.

These early motor imitations (mimicking actions with the body) become the **signs** or **images** that allow some limited internal construction of reality. As the child becomes able to construct, via motor imitation, some rudimentary signs that can be mentally manipulated in problem situations, there is less dependence on purely motor learning. Piaget describes how the various types of representations invented by children help them move toward more and more reliance on symbols and less on actions. For Piaget's child, a piece of paper was made to represent food and a piece of cloth was made to represent a pillow. These objects were then reacted to with all of the actions and emotions usually reserved for eating or going to bed.

According to Piaget, the acquisition of language is made possible by children's experience with these early motor representations and the rudimentary internal manipulation of these symbols. The first use of these objects (such as the piece of cloth used to represent the whole going-to-bed

Early symbolic representations are the invention of the child

process) is a very private invention on the part of individual children and has little meaning to others who have not had intimate contacts with them. Similarly, the child's first words, even though they are imitated from language that is heard, will have very private and unique connotations that may not coincide with the "public" meaning. A word like *mama*, for example, may be used by the child to refer to many other things, such as wanting to be held, an opening door, or food, as well as the presence of mother.

Learning the "public" meanings

Many children by age one use several words whose meanings may or may not match the public usage. The task of gradually modifying the private meanings of words to coincide with their public meanings continues throughout the life span. Many of our jokes are made possible because of the errors that occur when a person misuses a word. We remember with a chuckle, for example, the child with a much older sister who said, "I used to have a sister but she's a grown-up woman now."

The discovery that everything has a name

From the time when the child first begins to use words as signs that represent something repeatedly experienced (whether or not that usage matches the public meaning), there are rapid increases in efforts to represent more and more experiences with words. At ages eighteen months to two years, children appear to become keenly aware that everything has a name, and they set about busily trying to learn the names for everything. At about this time children also begin to use words in combination. The phrase, "What's 'at?" is one of the combinations acquired relatively early and used constantly thereafter in the energetic quest for word symbols; the child begins to assume that these symbols exist as an integral part of every object.

Many multiword utterances, such as "all gone" or "go bye-bye," are often learned by children as though they were single words. They are later differentiated and separated into word components. In a family where formal terms were used for toilet functions, the youngest of three siblings had among her first "words" an understandable version of, "I wanna urinate." The referent matched that of the older siblings and the grammatical intent was appropriate, but the child had no awareness of the words as separate entities.

Children's amazing success in language learning

It is amazing how easily children learn to organize words into sentences that serve various grammatical functions, such as speaking of the present versus the future or the past, asking questions, making statements, or giving commands. Linguists vary in their explanations of how these abilities are achieved. Lenneberg (1967), among others, believed that there are inherent human propensities toward the acquisition of language structures and that these are simply triggered when children hear language being used. This maturationist view is supported by the remarkable success with which nearly all children learn whatever language they hear at certain developmental levels, even when it is only occasionally heard. Lenneberg proposed that language acquisition is due to a specific maturational schedule that is similar to, but separate from, motor development. Exposure to language, even minimal exposure, provides the stimulus for acquisition of all the basic grammatical constructions.

Constructing rules to make sense of language

Linguists Chomsky (1965) and McNeill (1970), however, describe the interactive process of language acquisition as follows: (1) as children mature they become increasingly able to hear language forms; (2) they make sense of what they hear according to their level of intellectual maturity; (3) they actively try to construct rules to make sense out of the language they hear; (4) they produce speech that is based on the rules they have formulated. This position contrasts with the view that speech is basically an imitative process. The interactionists point to the mistakes that children make as evidence that they are actively forming rules regarding what they hear. It is clear that children are not just repeating what they have heard when they say things like, "Me no go bed," or "See the mouses." This is a critical point. If the child were simply a passive receiver of language, teaching would require nothing more than a providing of correct models and appropriate social reinforcement (which is the environmentalist/behaviorist view). If, on the other hand, the child must act on and experiment with what is heard and figure out rules governing appropriate and inappropriate expressions, then the teaching process must be quite different: it must be attuned to the constructions the child is already using and, above all, it must allow the child ample opportunity to practice and receive feedback concerning the invented rules.

Whatever the processes of learning, there is amazing progress in language development in almost all children prior to age three. By that age the child can already have a vocabulary of some 1000 words, and most of what is said is intelligible even to strangers. The grammatical complexity of utterances is

Prior to age three, children have become quite word proficient and use language as well as actions for thinking and problem-solving. It would be fun to "read" children's thoughts and see the progression from nonverbal to verbal mental processes. While this kind of observation is not available, it is easy to tell what in the environment takes a child's attention and what does not, and by what modes his or her investigations are conducted, such as looking, feeling, pinching, or asking about. You can use your spare moments in places such as restaurants, laundromats, parks, and buses to note what infants and toddlers notice and how they investigate what they notice. When no infants or toddlers are available in those settings, try to note the processes you personally use to investigate things, such as watching, listening, or asking. Contrast your awareness and investigatory powers with those of the young children you observe.

roughly that of everyday, "spoken" adult language, although many mistakes still occur.

Although motor activity is critical to learning, the three-year-old has long since ceased to rely *only* on sensorimotor schemas for thinking and learning about the world. Language is now used to represent and manipulate reality, including the reconstruction of previous experiences.

Cognitive and Intellectual Development from Ages Three through Seven

Although we were tempted to split this section into two parts, one describing the preschool child and the other the school-age child, we decided there was no justification for doing so. The child's cognitive and intellectual development is gradual across this age span, although there are marked changes in thinking at the end of these years. The abrupt plunge into "academia" at the first-grade level, often forced on the child by educational programs, is not consistent with known child growth patterns, and consequently is not used as the organizational scheme in this part of the chapter.

The preoperational child

According to Piagetian formulations, the preoperational period begins with the early use of signs and symbols in the thought process at around age one-and-a-half or two, and continues to age seven or eight. During this period the child is "transformed from an organism whose most intelligent functions are sensory-motor overt acts to one whose upper limit cognitions are inner symbolic manipulations of reality" (Flavell, 1963, p. 151). However, during the age period from three to seven years, the preoperational child still largely relies on what is often described as **preconceptual** or **intuitive thinking**. The child is described as being dominated by the perceptions of how things appear at the moment, and has an apparent inability to consider how they appeared previously or how they can be anticipated to appear. The child seems to have no capacity for keeping one thing in mind while considering another and consequently has no way to make comparisons that might lead to greater understanding. At this age, children have no schemas for **operating** on their experiences to derive basic principles. They are thus described by Piaget as being in the **preoperational** stage. In the following discussion we give many examples of the characteristics of children's thinking at this stage.

CLASSIFICATION ABILITIES

Progression in how to "sort" objects

The ways in which children group and label objects are highly indicative of their conceptual abilities. Limitations in thinking are revealed when children are presented with an array of objects (or pictures) and asked to put together all the things that go together or, alternatively, are presented with one object within an array and asked, "Which of these other things goes with this?" Very young children usually group objects according to their momentary fancy, with little or no attention to common characteristics. By age five, however, they can sort the objects according to similarities such as size, color, shape, or, less frequently, function. However, they may change their grouping criterion from one choice to the next; that is, they might first match

Photo by permission of Department of Early Childhood Education, Syracuse School District.

a white toy rabbit with a white mitten (color), then put a hat with the mitten because both keep you warm (function). In general, three- and four-year-olds tend to sort more by color and size and less by form than do older children. Only a few children, even at age five, use function as a criterion for sorting.

Prior to age seven or eight, children are unlikely to be able to align or sort objects according to several dimensions simultaneously. Thus, children given large and small triangles and circles of red and blue cannot sort them into separate piles, such as large red triangles or small red circles, without intermediary sorting operations. With the assistance of an adult, young children can successfully sort according to any one dimension at a time; for example, they can classify color, putting red and blue in different piles, and can then sort each of those piles into large and small, and each of those into triangles and circles. If they concentrate on one dimension (shape, size, color, or function) they appear to become oblivious to all other dimensions. They can switch and attend wholly to another dimension, but will then forget the first.

Classification according to a single dimension

NUMBER CONCEPTS

One-to-one correspondence

An early step toward numerical competence is the ability to align objects in one-to-one correspondence. This simple task is far more difficult than it appears from the adult perspective. If you ask a very young child to put two different kinds of objects in lines so that there are just the same number in each line, you may be surprised to find that he or she cannot do so, or, at least, cannot continue to do so. Attending to the extension of the lines detracts from attending to their proper alignment. Conversely, the child can arrange two lines of objects but may have quite a different number in each line. Many five-year-olds and some six- and seven-year-olds still have difficulty with this kind of task.

Conservation of number

Even when children have developed the ability to align objects in one-to-one correspondence, they may not have a sense of invariance regarding the number of objects in each line. They may agree that each has the same number of objects after placing them out in matching, one-to-one rows, but if you either spread or bunch the objects in one row, thereby making it longer or shorter than the other, the child may say that one row now has more or fewer objects than the other.

Watch preschoolers aligning toy cars on top of blocks that they call garages. They line them up carefully, one car on each block, never two on a block, never an empty block. They are aligning them in one-to-one correspondence. If you were to ask them if there are the same number of cars and blocks, they would count both cars and blocks to prove it.

If you then help them clean up at the end of the period, putting cars in one box and blocks in another, and ask as you finish, "There are just the same number of blocks as cars, aren't there?", they may look at the two boxes and say, "No, there are more blocks." They do not keep in mind or even consider that they just finished setting them out one to one. They now confuse volume and number because the blocks, being larger, take up more room.

You may wonder whether children even understand you, since the terms *same* and *more* are difficult but essential to mathematical thinking. However, they will choose a dish with a spread-out array of Cheerios rather than one that actually has more cereal but in a more closely grouped arrangement. "I got the most," each declares as they devour them. Again, they were guided and fooled by "looks" without regard to number.

Fooled by how it looks

Piaget calls this the inability to conserve on number. Later, when the children are seven and eight, they will evidently have accumulated enough concrete experience with operations such as counting, rearranging, and recounting to no longer be fooled by appearances. At that point, once they have aligned and/or counted a group of objects they will "know" how many there are regardless of how they are subsequently arranged. At this stage, children can be described as having accomplished conservation of number, an early indication of movement from preconceptual to operational thinking.

Conservation of number is essential to the development of mathematical abilities. Effective number computation demands an awareness that the number of objects in any grouping remains the same regardless of how radically they are rearranged. A child must comprehend that a given grouping of, for example, nine objects, remains stable in number whether they are arranged as six and three, as two and seven, or as three, three, and three. For instruction in addition, subtraction, or other computational processes to be beneficial, the child must comprehend this concept of invariance of number.

SERIATION

Seriation is the ordering of objects or events according to a given dimension (such as size, weight, or distance from a given point). Just as children spontaneously engage in classification and one-to-one alignment activities, so they also spontaneously align objects according to such criteria as height and width. The difficulty of simultaneously perceiving two or more aspects of things is just as evident in the seriation efforts of preoperational children as in their classification efforts. Five-year-olds, for example, find it relatively easy to place a series of blocks of differing lengths in sequence from the tallest to the shortest, or vice versa, if allowed to build from one extreme to the other. They will likely have great difficulty, however, in finding the proper slot in an existing sequence for a single, midpoint block. By age seven or so children will be able to make the two-directional comparison necessary for such a placement, but before that time this kind of problem just leads to frustration. The task simply demands a cognitive feat of which they are not yet capable.

One dimension or direction at a time

MASS AND LIQUID QUANTITY

In using a material such as clay, children prior to age seven or eight typically confuse quantity with other physical attributes such as height, length, or width. They may form two balls that they declare to be "just the same," but upon rolling one to be longer or squashing it to be flatter, they will often insist that one or the other contains more or less clay. They lack conservation of mass, according to Piagetian terminology.

Again, fooled by how it "looks"

Similarly, when children pour liquids from one container to another, they may insist that the volume changes as the surface level falls higher or lower in relation to the proportions of the container. "Here, let's make it more," the children may say, as they pour from a soup-size can into a taller, thinner vial. As they pour it back, they may say, "Now there's not so much." They lack conservation of liquid quantity.

In each of these instances of nonconservation, children fail to see any need to account for what they had previously observed. The invariance of given amounts of things is not their concern. Only after repeated experience with **reversibility** (changing from one form to another and back again) will they doubt appearances and begin to conserve, that is, to hold in mind the previous states while viewing the current one.

CAUSALITY

Disinterest in investigating causal relationships is characteristic of children ages three through seven. They want to know all about things in a descriptive sense, but they give little thought to discovering why certain events occur. They assume that causations are linked to themselves—either caused by or for them—and consequently find further investigation irrelevant; the car is there to give them a ride, the rain comes to water their plants. Or the

No awareness of impersonal causation

child may assume that events happen because they are needed, they are "supposed to happen"; the tree just knows it is supposed to grow apples, the cloud wanted to send down rain. The possibility of impersonal causes is seldom considered.

Preoperational children, when quizzed about familiar phenomena, describe what they see and assume that this is a sufficient explanation, even though there may be contradictions in their statements. For example, in regard to the buoyancy of objects, the child may declare that a leaf floats because it is light; a ship floats because it is wood; a chair sinks because it is wood. Any consideration of the inconsistencies of these explanations are not long lived. The concept of general principles that can be derived through experimentation is quite beyond their comprehension.

SPACE CONCEPTS

Children learn to "see" spatial relationships

Children's conception of space is developed during the early years by their own actions. Their perceptions of space are thought to stem more from their tireless clustering and separation of objects than from merely viewing objects in space. The child must learn to "see" space and spatial qualities such as distance and position; this ability is not the product of simple visual maturation. A child who has not had opportunity to actively manipulate objects may have delayed or distorted space perception and faulty orientations.

By age three, this spatial awareness is often reflected in the use of terms such as *up, down, off, come, go, here, there, on, at, in, way up, up in, in here, in there, far away, back corner, over from, by, up on top,* and *on top of.* At age four, the following terms are likely to have been added: *next to, under, between, way down, way off, far away, in back of, under, out in, down to, way up there, way far out, way off,* and *behind* (Ames and Learned, 1948). Terms such as *left, right, opposite from,* and *across from* may not be acquired until age six or seven.

The space concepts mastered by children bear a clear relationship to their own bodies. Only later are objects perceived in relation to other objects. Four-year-olds, for example, may know that both you and a particular object are far away, but will not be aware of whether the object is behind, beside, or in front of you. They will especially not be able to perceive how an object might look from some vantage point other than their own, and will totally ignore any expectation that they should even try. One of the authors once tried to read what she considered to be a fascinating book to a group of bright kindergartners, which depicted how a mouse might view a cow differently from various positions within the barn—from above, behind, front, and side. They were totally disinterested. What young children see from their own perspective is of interest to them, and they consequently learn to recognize objects from whatever perspectives they might have used; but the hypothetical appearance of an object from a different position is of little interest to children ages three, four, five, and often at older ages as well.

TIME CONCEPTS

Time concepts from experiencing regularity in events

Children's conception of time develops from the experience of regular, sequenced events that are accompanied by time-oriented descriptions. The youngster learns through repeated experiences that breakfast is followed by "Captain Kangaroo," or play time by the mail delivery. As adults and older siblings talk about the events as "Know what you can do next?", "Not until after Captain Kangaroo," and "Did the mail come yet today?", the child gradually begins to anticipate the regularities of happenings through time and is assisted in this process by learning and using the vocabulary that others model. By age three, children may correctly use terms such as *now, going to, in a minute, today, after, morning, afternoon, some day, one day, tomorrow, last night, all the time, all day,* and *at lunch time.* They may also refer to what they will do tomorrow or at Christmas or that they are three years old (Ames, 1946). It is difficult to determine, in many instances, the actual meaning of time references for them. By age four, they may use many past and future tenses accurately and will use terms such as *for a long time, for years, a whole week, two things at once, it's almost time, in a month,* and *next summer.* They will often make errors in trying to describe time, such as "the next tomorrow" or "I'm not going to take a nap yesterday." However they do seem to have a clear understanding of the sequence of daily events at this age. Only a very few children, though, even at age six or seven, actually use clock hours to regulate or describe their activities, although they are very interested in clocks and watches and in learning to tell time. They are more apt to regulate their time by the passage of regularly occurring events, such as the time between television commercials, than by clock hours.

SPOKEN LANGUAGE

Children understand and use an amazing number of words. At age three, the child's vocabulary may consist of nearly 900 words; at age four, 1500; at age five, 2000; and age at six, 2500 (Smith, 1926). However, even after children begin to use certain words regularly, they may still be deciphering their exact meaning in relation to other similar words. Experimentation with words continues in various settings over long periods of time and results in gradual refinement of their meanings. Children hear words and phrases and try out what they think is the appropriate use until either their communication fails or new listening experiences lead them to revise their initial usage.

Learning concepts to match words

The process of language acquisition requires the learning of **concepts** along with words. The toddler may call "doggie" anything that has four legs. He or she not only must learn specific words such as *skunk, fox, kitten, cat, puppy,* and *lion,* but must also learn the characteristics that distinguish one animal from the other. The process of learning what is *not* "doggie" is incomparably more complex than the initial acquisition of the word. The sorting out of appropriate meanings is of course necessary for each word acquisition. Many three-year-olds still consider that all women are mommies and all men daddies. We know of a toddler who once wanted cold water when hot was coming from the faucet, and said, "Turn it to the other channel, Mommy." Why not? Learning the common usages of words is, indeed, a complicated task!

Names believed to be intrinsic parts of objects

Preschool children, however, are very concerned about learning the right names for things and do not like to be wrong. For them, there is nothing arbitrary about words; they believe the name to be an intrinsic part of the object. When Piaget asked a child how people knew that the sun was called the sun, he was told, "They say it was called the sun because they could see it was round and hot." This is a typical response.

To acquire new vocabulary and learn appropriate meanings, it is helpful for children to interact with verbally mature persons. Those children, for example, who benefited most from watching the educational television program, "Sesame Street," were found to be those whose parents watched with them and talked about what they had seen (Ball and Bogatz, 1970). The amount and richness of face-to-face language interactions appears to be critical in promoting language development.

Adults as intuitive language tutors

Adults' understanding of children's efforts to expand their language abilities is typically rather limited. They have little theoretical awareness of the complexity of language acquisition, but despite this lack of formal knowledge may be providing highly useful corrective feedback. For example, if the child says, "It isn't any more snow," the adult will almost automatically correct, "There isn't any more snow," and may add, to be conversational, "It all melted, didn't it?" If the child says, "What does this does?" the adult will probably repeat, "What does this do?", changing inflection for emphasis and then giving the answer.

By such verbal interaction adults provide the child with just the kind of help that many linguists feel benefits children most—simple talk, slightly more complex or correct or different than what the child said. This help is typically intuitive; the adults involved are usually unable to describe the nature of their corrections, the kinds of sentences they have modeled, or the kinds of sentences the child produced.

As a teacher, you will do well to emulate what the parent naturally does. However, you can also benefit from systematically studying children's language and selecting the kind of help that seems most appropriate. It is important to acquire the ability to listen and appraise children's language—what they are trying to say, their syntactical usage, and their vocabulary. We will try to help you do this by identifying in this part of the chapter some of the more typical language changes that occur. The questions we offer as a guide to your observations of individual children also pose some very specific things for you to look for.

The typical language changes

Between the ages of two-and-a-half and four, children begin using longer sentences (more words per sentence) and also begin including particular word structures that make their communication more specific. It is interesting to note that language development illustrates well the general child development principle introduced in Chapter 3: Development proceeds from the general to the specific.

Some of the changes most typical of this period can be summarized as follows (Pflaum, 1974):

1. Increasing use of *ing* with verbs as in "I mak*ing* coffee," "He go*ing* up ladder," and "I work*ing*."
2. Increasing use of auxiliary verbs to express tense, to indicate questions and negatives, and to show the passive voice, as in "Me *have* this one," "Daddy *did* it," "I *am* too cowboy," "*Want* take this?" and "I *been* good."
3. Acquiring the forms of the verb *to be*, as in "Doggie *is* here," "That*'s* a clock," "He*'s* going up the ladder," "There*'s* a fire and here*'s* a ladder," and "He *isn't* coming."
4. Developing greater facility with negative sentences, as from "He no bit you," or "I no want it," to "I don't want cover on it," "They not hot," "He didn't caught me," "I didn't did it," and "I am not a doctor."
5. Developing greater facility in asking questions, as from "Who that?" or "Ball go?" to "Where my mitten?", "Why you cry?", "Why not me go with you?", "Where my mommy go?", "What you doed?", and "Did I saw that in my book?"
6. Acquiring word parts that make nouns plural and produce noun-verb agreement. As they become aware of rules for this they may overgeneralize and make mistakes with some things they had previously said correctly.

By age four many children will use the following constructions:

Main clause conjunction, as in "Mary sang and Mary danced"
Conjunction with deletion, "Mary sang and danced"
Relative clause, as in "The man who sang is old"
Because sentence embedding, as in "You come here 'cause Mommy said so"
Particle separation, as in "Put down the box"
Reflexive, as in "I did it myself"

Although many four-year-olds use the following constructions, they are much more common among five-year-olds:

Imperative, as in "Shut the door"
Passive, as in "The boy was hit by the girl"
If sentence embedding, as in "You can go if you want to"
So sentence embedding, as in "I gave it to him so he won't cry"
Compound of nominal, as in "baby chair"

In assessing children's language development, teachers need to be aware that what may appear to be immature or incorrect forms of expression can be *Dialectical* quite correct within the dialect used by the child's subgroup. The language *differences* patterns of Black English, for example, should not be regarded as incorrect, even though they differ from the standard English spoken in schools and in the business and professional world. Children learn the structures of the language they hear. The irregularities that a standard English speaker hears in the Black dialect are actually quite regular and follow consistent, if somewhat different, language rules.

There is no doubt that the speakers of dialects, whether Black English or others, will benefit from learning the standard English forms. However, according to many linguists, these standard forms should be learned as a *Standard forms as a* language alternative, that is, not to replace the original speech, but simply to *"language* expand it through a new and different language pattern. Within the Black *alternative"* community the language used by the speakers of Black English will be far more functional and "correct" than standard English. Children must learn when to say, "Susy is sick," "It's his book," or "He's over at the school," and when to say, "Susy, she be sick," "He book," or "He over to the school." A child that feels comfortable with both speech patterns will be able to move easily and competently in either social environment.

Language not only represents past and present experience but also stimulates us to have new experiences. Once children recognize that words represent classes of actions, objects, or events, the existence of a new word *Words as cues to* signifies to them the possibility of something to be learned. After encounter-*new concept* ing an unknown word, the child is able to seek the referents for it and thus *possibilities* acquires abstract ideas that might otherwise have been overlooked.

Our language abilities influence us far more than most of us realize. There is considerable evidence that language influences thinking modes and behavior. For example, the work of Spivack and Shure (1974), referred to in Chapter 5, suggests that specific language concepts are prerequisite to the child's awareness of alternatives in problem situations. The terms *and, or,* and *not* are prime examples. A child that wants the toy another has, but does not have the language facility to tell himself, "I can grab it or I can ask for it or I can wait until he finishes," also does not have the means for considering alternative behaviors. Without the words *or* and *not,* the child cannot consider, "Should I do this *or* that?" or "Should I do this *and not* that?" Without these rudimentary language concepts, the child has no cognitive means for considering actions as choices, rather than as necessities.

Spivack and Shure suggest that children's awareness of those words that are closely related to their behavioral decision-making (such as *same, different, happy, sad, mad, if, then,* and *but*) can be developed by initially teaching their meanings in regard to the physical world. They recommend language modeling such as "Who is holding the hat? Who is *not* holding the hat?", "Is Carol standing *or* is she sitting?", "Is a hat the *same* as a flower?", and "Is stamping my foot the *same* as patting my head or is it *different?*" Once such concepts are clearly understood in reference to the physical world, their meanings can be transferred to social behavior, where children can be taught to think in terms of the alternative behaviors available to them. Without such words in their vocabulary, children appear unable to deal with *if-then* relationships such as "If I do this, then what might happen next?"

Teachers of young children sometimes overestimate children's capacities for understanding language, often by assuming that if children use a word "correctly" their meaning must coincide with the adult usage of the same word. In one classroom, for example, a kindergarten teacher discussed with the children an upcoming parent's meeting that was to be held in their classroom. There was eager discussion of what various children thought parents would like to see when they came for the meeting. Someone even volunteered to make a sign for the rat cage warning the parents that the rat had once bitten someone. However, when asked to take a note to their parents announcing the meeting, several children looked puzzled and asked, "What's a parent?" Investigation showed that the children's meaning for the word *parent* ranged from "some kind of teacher" to "bigger kids like teenagers." Only a few children were sure that a parent is a father or mother. Given the language exposure of this current television generation, who talk glibly of ranges, porpoises, Hawaii, the year 2000, etc., it is easy to be misled into believing that they know and understand far more than they actually do.

WRITTEN LANGUAGE

In the minds of many the three *R*'s—readin', 'ritin', and 'rithmetic—are the primary work of school, and often specifically of first grade. They mistakenly

Photo by John Young.

To study the gradual progression of children from listening and talking to reading and writing, consider the following notations made by teachers in a child-care center about one child's language development from age three to five. They illustrate how many small, personalized steps children typically take in developing their reading and writing skills.

> Tommy made some scribbled lines on paper and said, "What's that spell?" He then said, "That's a little monster. He's friendly though."
>
> I wrote Tommy's name. He grabbed some other chalk and made a dozen or so *T*'s. Tried to make the letter *m* but couldn't seem to get the parts together to satisfy himself that they looked right. Kept saying, "Oh, oh, made a goof."
>
> Tommy wrote name on paper. When I asked if he knew the name of letter *T* he said, "Me."
>
> Played with Alphabet Bingo cards after watching older children playing it. Easily matched most of the letters—except confused by *b*'s and *d*'s.
>
> Found all letters in his name from box of wooden letters. Also found *B* for Bobby's name and *J* for Joey's. Asked what the name of their letters were.
>
> Wrote on chalkboard—*T,R,B,C,H,I* (made *C* backward).
>
> Tommy looked at my pad and said, "My name's on there." Points to Tommy. Says, "Me and Tim have a *T*."
>
> Tommy talked about the names of other children, which all began with *T*—Tim, Terry, Tammy, Tina. Interested in how much Tammy's name looks like his. I also showed him how Tim's name looks when it is written out as *Timmy*. He paid close attention and went to get Tim to come and look too.
>
> Matched *T, H, K, s, f, m, u, y, o, b, q*, and *j* on the letter form board. Asked the name of *q* and whose letter it was. Very interested that we don't have anyone in our group that has a *Q* initial. Evidently had thought there would be a name for every letter.
>
> Wanted me to write on his picture, "This is a house." Indicated the left side when I asked him which side of paper the writing should start on.
>
> Tommy asked me to write *Happy Birthday* on the picture he painted for his mother. I said the names of the letters as I wrote them. He commented, "It has two of those, huh?" pointing to the *p*'s, and then added, "I got two the same too, right?"
>
> Used the typewriter. Said his mother has one at home. Found and typed *T* for *Tommy, B* for *Brenda* (sister), *m* for *mother*. Made rows and rows of periods.
>
> He drew a picture of his mother. Eyelashes first, and then *lots* of hair. He then told me to write, "This is Tommy's mother." He spoke slowly waiting for me to write the word before saying the next.
>
> As soon as Tommy saw the alphabet he went over and started putting

letters in. Said names of some of the letters as he did so but seemed to pay no attention when I said names of others.

Told me that I make the letter *m* wrong (means different from his mother, she makes it as capital letter—writes his name in all caps). I explained that both ways are right ways and that he can make it either way.

Asked, "Will you read me a story?" He went and got *Rabbit and skunk and the scary rock,* and said, "Hi, all you rabbits! What do you do?"

Found own name and Joey's name on list of children who would ride together in car on the way to the fire station visit.

When saw *ABC* book said, "Oh, *ABC* book." Read "*A,B,C. . .*" and then said, "book."

Tommy dictated story about fight he had had with his brother the night before. Wanted it read to him several times.

Tommy asked me to write a note to his mother and tell her that "I doed hard puzzles."

Found letters for last name from alphabet box (while looking at written model on card). Scrambled all the letters and rearranged in order. Took frequent looks at model as put back in correct sequence (started left, went right).

Wrote whole name looking at model of last name. Resaid each letter after all written.

Played Alphabet Bingo with two cards at once! Says that's how his mom plays Bingo.

Asked if he could have a notebook (loose leaf) for his papers (like Roger's). We found one for him and he made four sheets of "writing" to put in it, full of his name and other letters and pictures.

Tommy found the word *strawberry* on his ice cream cup lid after I showed him how the word *strawberry* looked where it was written on my cup lid. Checked other cup lids to see if they said some other flavor.

Tommy was telling an incident about how he got lost and then "founded." I started to write it down as story. He slowed down to my writing speed. Seemed pleased with the story. Wanted to read it to Joey.

After I read *Billy goats gruff* to Tommy and several others, he "told" it all the way through with great dramatic flourish. Kept his audience interested all the way.

Sat with books for forty-five minutes. Asked questions and very involved. Noticed in one picture that the man's feet were facing the wrong way.

Discovered all the places in *Green eggs and ham* where it says *Sam.* He differentiated between *Sam, see,* and *so,* saying, "Starts like *same* but it ain't *Sam,*" or "That there is *Sam.*"

Actually read several pages of *Little bear* using some context to help him figure out words; asked me for help with others. Reread these pages at least three times today.

The preceding notes about Tommy's progress toward becoming a reader and writer are of course but a sampling of the many instances in which he had involvement with words and books across three years. These notes are sufficient, however, to represent some principles common to the experiences of many children.

---

assume that most of the learning in these areas is accomplished through formal lessons. This is not and, in our opinion, should not be the case. A great deal of progress in these areas is made by children at much younger ages. Most children who become successful readers in early elementary school have typically had preparatory experiences that support their success.

In the absence of adult intervention that emphasizes another sequence, children generally seem to develop reading and writing abilities as follows:

Progression into reading

1. The child develops an awareness of the functions and value of the reading and writing processes prior to becoming interested in acquiring specific knowledge and skills.
2. The child is likely to give greater attention to words and letters that have some personal significance, such as his or her own name or the names of family, pets, etc.
3. The child develops both reading and writing skills simultaneously as complementary aspects of the same communication processes, rather than as separate sets of learning.
4. The child develops an awareness of words as separate entities (as evidenced when he or she dictates words slowly so that a teacher can keep pace in writing them down) before showing awareness or interest in how specific letters represent sounds.
5. The child becomes familiar with the appearance of many of the letters through visually examining them, playing games with them, etc., before trying to master their names, the sounds they represent, or their formation.
6. The child becomes aware of the sound similarities between high-interest words (such as significant names) and makes many comparisons between their component parts before showing any persistence in deciphering unfamiliar words by blending together the sounds of individual letters.

Any teacher of young children over age three can anticipate working with some children who already have interest in and abilities for reading and writing. As a teacher you should be aware of the various processes involved in learning to read and be able to assess and assist in their development. This is no less true for the teachers of three-, four-, and five-year-olds than for teachers of six- and seven-year-olds.

DECODING

Decoding, the process of obtaining meaning from written symbols, depends heavily on the ability to make **visual discriminations.** The infant learns to discriminate between such things as kinds of foods, between his mother and others, or between his own stuffed toy and other objects. The toddler makes further discriminations, such as between big cars and little cars, between dogs and cats and elephants, between bowls and plates, between tulips and dandelions, between happy faces and mad faces. The number of discriminations mastered by this age are phenomenal. The preschooler continues to develop finer and finer discriminations. They may include such fine points as the differences between dump trucks and cement mixers, between Porsches and Volkswagens, between zebras and horses, between kinds of sea shells, between kinds of leaves, or between individual letter forms.

Discriminations between word forms are gradually learned

From these increasingly fine discriminations come the abilities that are prerequisite to reading. Looking at two similar words such as *car* and *run*, the child must see how they are alike and how they are different. To a child still struggling with the difficult tasks of discriminating between words, these two may appear very alike—they both have three letters and they both have the same letter *r* in them. Neither has any "tall" letters or letters that extend downward. Even though young children, on the basis of these similarities, might erroneously conclude that they are the same word, they may not be unperceptive. At this point children are struggling with the same kinds of cognitive problems they encountered as two-year-olds when they worked out, with patient adult feedback, the fine points that separate four-legged animals called dogs into particular categories such as collie, Lassie, puppy, and St. Bernard. The question now, from the child's perspective, is what makes two words the same. What if only one letter is different? What if the letters are in capitals instead of lowercase?

The complexity of the decoding task

Sensitive adults will recognize the tremendous complexity of this learning process and will assist the child by providing feedback on what he or she is doing, whether it is right or wrong. In the case of the words *car* and *run*, the adult may recognize the reasonableness of the child's erroneous conclusion (because of the actual similarities between the two words) and then proceed to point out their differences, such as "In *run*, the *r* is at the beginning; in *car* it is at the end," or, "Notice that *car* starts like Carey's name; *run* starts like Rob's name."

The representational letter-sound relationship

The ability to decode is greatly accelerated when the child eventually learns, through repeated exposures, that the function of letters is to represent discrete sounds and that each spoken word can be represented by letters, just as each written word can be decoded. Once children become aware that the function of letters, either singly or in combination, is to represent portions of words, they are ready to become decoders.

To become efficient readers, children must eventually be able to recognize words as entities, as unique configurations of letters to which they can instantly attach meaning. The mature reader gives very little attention to individual letters. For example, when reading these sentences you respond immediately to the ideas represented by the words and do not decipher, letter by letter, the sounds that comprise the words. Also, as you write, you give very little attention to the sounds in the words you use. This attention to words, not letters, is what children must strive for as well. They will

Letter-sound analysis as a process aid, not the final goal

progress toward that goal with greater ease if they first understand how letters represent sounds and how these letters can be combined in different ways to form a variety of words. However, since the ultimate goal is to get meaning from words, it is important that the intermediate process of learning letter-sound relationships not be allowed to obscure that goal.

A few words—those seen frequently or those of particular interest to an individual child—are typically learned and recognized as whole words just by the way they look. Most children recognize several different words before they develop an awareness of how the letters comprising those words are representative of particular sounds. Awareness of letter-sound relationships

The analytic approach

comes from noting that some of the known words that contain the same letter also have similar spoken sounds. For example, Sally notes that *Santa, see,* and *cats* have her very own letter *s* and that they also have the same sound she hears at the beginning of her name. She then begins to generalize about the letter *s* and the sound it represents in words. This approach toward learning is often called the **analytical approach.**

The synthetic approach

An opposite approach to word learning is one in which children first learn that given letters represent certain sounds and then learn how to put together these sounds to create and discover words—*s* says "s-s-s," *a* says "a-ah," *d* says "duh," so *s-a-d* says "sad." Rather than starting from whole words as meaningful units and discovering their component parts, the child in this

---

LETTER AND WORD REVERSALS

Parents (and beginning teachers) sometimes note that children confuse those letters (*b* and *d*) and words (*on* and *no*) that are the reverse of each other, and conclude erroneously that these errors are caused by some basic learning disability. The following statement by Downing and Thackray (1971) contradicts this assumption:

> Actually the tendency to confuse *d* and *b, n* and *u,* etc. is more likely to be due to *good* perceptual development rather than the opposite because the child's experiences prior to coming to school will have taught him to ignore such mirror images. He has learned the lesson well that a walking stick is still a "stick" no matter in which direction the handle is pointing. When he learns to read he must learn that in reading and writing the direction *does matter.* The letters *b* and *d* are not both sticks with a handle. The one pointing to the left represents one sound while the one pointing to the right means something different.
>
> The retarded reader who continues to make reversals has failed to unlearn the generalization he had learned before coming to school. Thus it is much more likely that reversals are the symptom of reading failure than its cause. Hence, we conclude that the tendency to reverse letters and words at the beginning stage is quite normal and cannot be regarded as any indication of lack of readiness to learn to read or write. (p. 30)

alternate approach begins with the letter sounds and constructs the meaningful words through processes of combination. This is called the **synthetic approach**.

Whether a child's first steps toward independent decoding are based on the first or second approach depends both on his or her own preferred learning style and on the kind of instruction received. While some teachers prefer establishing a supply of known, whole words before introducing phonic comparisons, others prefer to begin with the introduction of discrete letter sounds, which are then blended together to form a word. Whichever approach is used, the typical child benefits from an early awareness of letter-sound correspondences as useful keys in the decoding process.

Prerequisite skills to reading and writing

The ability to decode is itself dependent on certain prerequisite skills and understandings. For example, to figure out the word *car*, even when one knows the sound each letter represents, one must know that the letters and their associated sounds are read from left to right. Typically children will have developed this left-to-right orientation if they have been in situations where they have had frequent opportunities to observe others' writing.

Also, before children can correctly match sound to letter in trying to decipher a word, they must be able to hear similarities and differences in spoken words. Awareness of rhyming words is typically the first such awareness for children, and even three-year-olds delight in creating chains of rhyming words, such as *zoon, soon, toon, boon, groon;* later (at age five, six, or seven) they become able to identify the rhyming portions (*quick* and *stick*) of jingles such as

> Jack be nimble
> Jack be quick
> Jack, jump over the
> Candlestick.

Even though a child can discriminate between letters, knowledge of individual letter names is not particularly necessary in learning to read, even though it is true that children who have become familiar with the alphabet through voluntarily using books, playing with letter games, and asking about letters are likely to be more successful. They gain a perceptual familiarity with the letter forms that is very helpful in the learning-to-read process. In other words, pleasant exposure to letter forms is useful; this may or may not include learning letter names. Drill on the names of the letters, even if successful, does not ensure that children will learn to read with more ease then if they lacked that knowledge. On the other hand, children who are still struggling to "see" the letters in order to perform simple sorting or matching activities probably still do not have sufficient knowledge to allow them to concentrate on the more complex analyses required in learning to read.

ENCODING

Encoding, the ability to record in writing ideas for others to read (and for oneself to read later), requires the same prerequisite skills and under-

Throughout this chapter the intellectual development of the normally developing child has been presented. There are, of course, sizable proportions of the population that do not develop as described. When adaptation processes proceed much more slowly than for the average child, the person may be referred to as mentally retarded. Retardation can be caused by birth defects, diseases of the nervous system, toxins and poisons, or brain injury. The American Association on Mental Deficiency has classified the mentally retarded into four groups according to intelligence quotients (IQ), as follows:

Profound retardation: 0–24 IQ
Severe retardation: 25–39 IQ
Moderate retardation: 40–54 IQ
Mild retardation: 55–69 IQ

It is now generally recognized, however, that there is no such thing as a fixed IQ score and that at least some young children who are found to be retarded can be helped to reach much higher levels of functioning through programs of early identification and stimulation. According to Karnes and Zehrback (1972), 70 to 80 percent of children in special classes for the educable mentally retarded are from low-income families. Preschool education can potentially help many of these children to function at a higher level than is possible without intervention.

Children who have severe physical handicaps may also have retarded mental development. As Caldwell (1973) points out,

> The environment of the young handicapped child is, by definition, depriving. If there is sensory deprivation, he cannot take in the best of the environments that are around him. If he has any kind of motor dysfunction, he cannot get up and move himself to find something better, or at least cannot move himself to a situation where the environment might be a better match with his own developmental state. (p. 7)

In working with children who are retarded, the approach may not be markedly different than for any other child. There is the need, first, for sensitivity to what the child can already do, even though that may be quite different in quality and quantity than his or her agemates. Second, there must be the same kind of provision for the ample use of the existent abilities as well as provision for a very gradual expansion into additional areas of functioning. Retarded children primarily need full acceptance as human beings and encouragement to behave as normally as possible. You may find that the book by Robert Perske (1973) (see Additional Reading section), prepared for parents of retarded children, can also help you to understand retarded children and your own reactions to their retardation.

standings as decoding—visual and **auditory discriminations** between letters, an understanding of the representative functions of letters, left-to-right orientation, and a familiarity with the alphabet. Encoding is the reverse side of the decoding process, but mastery of one does not ensure mastery of the other. Children can often decode words that they cannot independently encode or, conversely, they can sometimes independently encode words that they cannot later decode.

Encoding, a reverse but separate process from decoding

Reading and writing, although closely related processes, require distinct learning experiences. As with Mark Twain's Mississippi River, learning the landmarks in one direction helps with but does not ensure knowledge of the river as one travels in the other direction. Most children become skillful, independent readers well before undertaking much independent writing, and a few become highly involved and skilled at encoding their own ideas before voluntarily and independently reading. The extent to which children engage in writing activities prior to reading is in large measure a function of the expectations, provisions, and encouragement of adults. Some approaches to reading (particularly **language experience** approaches) are closely tied to early writing, while others make no such provision. Given the slightest encouragement and assistance, most children become engaged very early in writing activities (composition, not copying).

Writing can precede reading

One encoding success story involved a very resourceful kindergartner who found himself in a situation that stretched his meager writing ability to the limit. When Nicky arrived home from kindergarten, he found that his mother was not there. He had been given prior permission to go to a friend's

RESPONSE SECTION

Children aged three through seven have been described as eager explorers who are often misled and hampered by an inability to concentrate on more than one thing at a time. Since the thinking of young children is so markedly different from that of adults, we often misjudge what they should be able to do or understand, and consequently give them mismatched explanations and tasks.

To increase your sensitivity, observe adults in interaction with children and note, in writing, all of the instances where it becomes obvious that they are not in tune with the child's thinking level. Note, for example, when the adult says something that confuses the child or asks that the child do something of which the child is not capable. To observe instances of these mismatches, visit classrooms or watch adults and children in informal interaction. In almost any situation where there are adult-child interchanges, you will find some mismatches to analyze. From these, derive guidelines that will help you become more sensitive in similar situations.

house to play but had been told to come home and have lunch with his mother first. He waited a while, but when his mother still did not arrive, he fixed and ate a peanut butter sandwich for lunch. When his mother arrived home two hours later, expecting to find Nicky upset and troubled, she found instead the remnants of his lunch and a message in his wobbly handwriting that used three of the ten or so words he knew. They managed to communicate what he wanted her to know. The note said, "I go. Nicky."

Observing Cognitive and Intellectual Behavior in Individual Children

On the following pages are very specific questions about the cognitive and intellectual behaviors of children you are observing. Follow the same procedures that you used in making your observations and notes on the other aspects of development. You may find that many of the questions posed in this chapter cannot be answered as readily as those listed in the other chapters—the children you are observing simply may not behaviorally demonstrate their cognitive abilities within the limited time span you have for observing. You must be especially attuned to the cognitive processes that our questions probe and to the physical and verbal behavior of the children relative to these processes.

If both simple and complex behaviors are present, record only the complex ones. For example, if a child can match word forms, it would be irrelevant to also record that he or she can match identical toys or other objects since the more advanced ability would not be possible if the simpler ones had not first been mastered.

Record all behaviors that might be indicative of the child's thought processes, even if you question whether the child actually understands the actions or words. You may also wish to record in your notes your doubts about your interpretation of the behavior. For this area of development, it will also prove useful to record observations that demonstrate the child's *inability* in a particular area of thinking. For example, in response to the question regarding the child's performance with one-to-one correspondence, you might wish to note something akin to the following: "Starts to line up pairs of red and black checkers, placing a red one beside each black, but soon loses track of that and simply makes two uneven lines, one red and one black, without one-to-one correspondence."

1. Classification

    On what basis does the child note objects or situations to be alike or different?

    Examples: • sorts poker chips into red, blue, yellow piles
    • puts animals in barn and people in house while playing with blocks
    • puts all of what he calls "girl stuff" (purses, aprons, dolls) outside of housekeeping corner before he begins to play there
    • finds all of the words on a page that begin with *t*

2. Number

   2.1 *What is the child's ability to align objects in one-to-one correspondence?*

   Examples: • aligns cups and spoons for juice and puts one to each place
   • places small cars one-by-one on a tongue-depressor road
   • fastens single dot (from the paper punch) on each of her toenails and fingernails

   2.2 *What is the child's ability to count objects?*

   Examples: • counts the pieces of a carrot at snack time: "One, two, three, four, five, eight, ten
   • asks for cotton balls and when I ask "How many?" says, "Five," and counts them correctly as I place them in her hand
   • counts how many baby chicks have hatched; counts six instead of actual five when one moves to a different place

   2.3 *On what basis does the child make comparisons in total number between groups of objects?*

   Examples: • rolls two dice and decides which one she wants (it has more dots) without counting; only visual inspection
   • says, "We got five chairs and only three kids. Wanta sit down?" (to me)
   • in comparing his baseball cards with Rob's, puts them out in one-to-one correspondence to see who has more

   2.4 *Does the child show recognition that different subgrouping arrangements may be made without changing the total number?*

   Examples: • when playing Candyland game with two dice, says, "You got the same as me," when Sue throws the numbers three and three right after he throws four and two
   • shows me that eight glasses can be arranged as four groups of two or two groups of four, but seems unaware of other possible arrangements
   • puts out five Tinker Toy pieces and sings, as she alternately takes some away and replaces them, "Now there are three. Now there are five. Now there are two. Now there are five," etc.

3. Seriation

   On what basis does the child appropriately order objects or events? How many?

   Examples: • lines up six bottles according to height
   • says correctly that she is older than Tod and he is older than Benjie; looks puzzled when I ask if she is older than Benjie
   • when given an array of six sandpaper sheets of varying roughness, discriminates between the two with greatest contrast, but says others are "just the same"

4. Mass and Liquid Quantity

   How does the child appear to think about mass and liquid quantity?

   Examples: • says everyone will "get the same" while pouring juice, and then fills all the glasses to comparable heights even though there are glasses of quite different diameters

- when playing with salt clay makes "pancakes" for everyone at the table; squashes one down very flat and gives to Tina, saying, "Here, you can have the biggest one"
- carefully measures out two cans of water for each of the animals into their watering dishes so they will "all have the same"

5. Causality

What, if any, explanations does the child either seek or give for physical phenomena? For his own or other's behavior?

Examples:
- "I've got to wear my raincoat because it's raining"
- "It's raining today 'cause the sun got so tired of shining all the days"
- "It broke 'cause she was too rough and it's fragile" (*fragile* was a term the student teacher had used earlier)

6. Space Concepts

What evidence does the child give of awareness of space, position, location, or spatial perspectives?

Examples:
- says to self upon standing back and looking at opening she has made in block construction, "That wagon ain't goin' to git in there"
- asks, "Why you put my pictures up so high? I want them down here"
- says, at sharing time, "We going to visit Grandma out in Wyoming. It's so far we'll stay in a motel two nights"

Photo by Robert Burdick.

7. Time Concepts

What evidence does the child give of awareness of time perspectives (past or future) or of the duration of happenings or activities?

Examples: • says, "I liked that swimming yesterday. Can we go today?"
• says to Robin, "I will call you up when Captain's done" (meaning after the "Captain Kangaroo" TV program)
• says, "Who was borned first, me or my mother?"

8. Spoken Language

8.1 Vocabulary

8.1.1 What is the child's use of relational and opposing terms?

Consider terms such as and, or, not, same, different, more, less, instead, if, then, because. Cite sentences in which terms are used.

Examples: • when asked whether he wanted a fork or a spoon, says, "I want a fork and a spoon"
• when hat is misplaced, cries because the one offered to replace it is said to be "not the same: it's too big"
• says indignantly, "I'm not little"

8.1.2 What words in the child's vocabulary appear to represent the greatest degree of differentiation regarding the following categories? Cite the words that the child uses.

animals	dog, cat, rat, chipmunk, alley cat, Siamese cat, cougar
people	grown-up, kid, baby, mommy, daddy
family relationships	sister, brother, grandma, auntie, uncle
colors	red, black, yellow
space	big, little, over here, right there, someplace
time	now, today, yesterday, when I'm big, at three-thirty
shape	round, circle, square, triangle
containers	box, cup, dish, suitcase
machinery	lawnmower, vacuum, mixer, fire engine pump
vehicles	truck, car, jeep, boat, jet, helicopter, Datsun
clothes	coat, shirt, pants, socks, shoes, jacket, hat, raincoat, leotards
weather	raining, hot, cold, sleet
foods	apple, milk, ice cream, hot dog, catsup, chili
tools	hammer, pencil, scissors
furniture	chair, table, bed, rocker, bean bag chair
body part	arm, leg, head, eyes, nose, mouth, knee, hand, fist
body movements	run, walk, jump, go away
feelings	happy, don't like, like, mad, fun
toys	ball, doll, blocks, gun, Steiff bear
liquids	water, milk, orange soda, juice, drink
plants	tree, flower, leaf, poinsettia

8.2 Sentence Structure

8.2.1 *Does the child use the following types of sentences?*
Subject/predicate/object?

Examples: • "I'm going to be a nurse"
• "We are big"
• "He's a baby"

Questions?

Examples: • "What's that?"
"Is it almost time to get up?"
• "You going too?"

Imperatives?

Examples: • "Shut the door!"
• "Bring me that book!"
• "Get your nasty mouth outa here!"

8.2.2. *Does the child use the following structures?*
Compound sentences?

Examples: • "Tommy hit me and Sammy hit Tommy"
• "I saw him but I didn't tell"
• "I like my kitty but my kitty bites me"

Complex sentences (main clause/subordinate clause)?

Examples: • "I came in 'cause it's raining"
• "I'll play with you 'lessen you hit me"
• "He got too heavy so I left him there"

Relative clauses?

Examples: • "The girl who came here is my sister"
• "You know that hat what I always wear is lost"
• "The rabbit that has the big ears is the nicest"

8.3 Syntactical Forms

8.3.1 *Does the child use the following syntactical forms?*
Forms of to be?

Examples: • "I *am* big"
• "Doggie *is* here"
• "June *was* in the house"

ing *endings?*

Examples: • "Susy is cry*ing*"
• "Jimmy is sleep*ing*"
• "Dog bark*ing*"

Infinitives?

Examples: • "I want *to go*"
• "He like *to play*"
• "It feels good *to eat* a good lunch"

Future tense?

Examples: • "I'll be next"
• "He'll help you"

8.3.2 *Does the child use the following questioning forms?*
Wh-*word in question?*

Examples: • "What did you do?"
• "Why did it stop?"
• "Where is it?"

Subject and auxiliary verb inverted?

Examples: • "Can Sally play with me?"
• "Will you give me that?"
• "Does he want to be your friend?"

8.3.3 *Does the child differentiate between singular and plural noun forms?*

Examples: • "I got two dogs"
• "Put your shoes on your feets" (overgeneralization of rule)
• "Stand on both feets"

8.3.4 *Does the child use possessive forms?*

Examples: • "That Jane's coat"
• "I wash my baby's face"
• "You like Donna's boy?"

8.3.5 *Does the child differentiate between singular and plural verb forms?*

Examples: • "The baby likes it. Big kids don't like it though"
• "My daddy makes pancakes. Mommies can't make good stuff like that"
• "The dog barks. Cats meow; dogs bark"

8.3.6 *What is the child's use of pronouns?*

Examples: • "*It* is *theirs*"
• "*Nobody* would call *you* ugly"
• "*She* gotta get *her* ears pierced"

8.3.7 *What is the child's use of adjectives?*

Examples: • "I got *new* pants"
• "This is no *hard* puzzle"
• "That's a *heavy* box"

8.3.8 *What is the child's use of prepositional phrases?*

Examples: • "What you got *under you coat*?"
• "I want to go *in front of you*"
• "What's that *beside Stevie*?"

8.3.9 *What is the child's use of adverbs?*

Examples: • "He can *sure* go *fast*"
• "I wish he would get here *quick*"
• "I been playing very *nicely*"

9. Written Language

9.1 *What evidence is there of the child's knowledge of left-to-right orientation in written language?*

Examples: • when copies words (his own or other's names) starts at left and goes right
• points to left when I ask him where to start writing
• asks, "Where you start?" when starting to write

9.2 *What evidence is there of the child's abilities in auditory discrimination? (Does the child note or produce rhyming words or sounds? Does the child note whether words begin, end with, or contain similar sounds?)*

Examples: • says "pop, hop, slop," laughs and says it several more times
• supplies rhyming endings when I pause at the end of the line in reading poetry;
• says, "You can hear that 's-s-s' when you say *Miss*"

9.3 *What evidence is there of the child's ability to make visual discriminations? (Between objects? Two-dimensional forms? Pictures? Letters? Numerals? Word forms?)*

Examples: • sorts shells according to similar appearance
• finds all the *w*'s on the page he is looking at correctly
• confuses *q* and *g* in Alphabet Bingo game

9.4 *What evidence is there of the child's awareness of how written words represent spoken words?*

Examples: • asks, "What does that say?" about sign on the door
• asks me to write on his painting, "This is Jimmy with his baby sister," and points to each word as he "reads" it back to me after I have written it
• says to child who is looking at pictures and telling story, "Are you reading the words or making it up?"

9.5 *What evidence is there of the child's awareness of how letters represent sounds?*

Examples: • writes letter *v* and says, "Does that say 'm-m-m'?" and when told that it does not, says, "What letter is for 'm-m-m'?" as I am writing *mom*
• tries to figure out the word *pop* by saying to self " 'p-p-p'."
• when asked how to write *car*, I tell him *c* and *a* and then suggest that he could figure out the last letter by the way the word *car* sounds, and he writes *r*, very pleased with himself

9.6 *What evidence is there that the child recognizes (or can quickly figure out) some word forms? What words (or types of words)?*

Examples: • goes through several pages of *Cat and dog* book finding all the places it says either *cat* or *dog*; also identifies *I, see, can, go, and, to,* and *the*
• reads several pages of *Are you my mother?*, and only asks for help with *will* and *with*
• knows most words from high-frequency list; only confuses *what, who; was, saw; there, where; with, will; did, put*

9.7 *What evidence is there that the child is able to obtain messages (meanings) from written language?*

Examples: • laughs as reads funny parts of story to herself
• asks for clarification when things do not make sense to him: asks, "What does that mean?" about the line, "Look into my eyes"
• reads the sign on the classroom door that says "Don't forget to put Jell-o in the refrigerator," and reminds the student teacher, who had placed it there

Transition into Resourcefulness Section

On the basis of your observations of children's cognitive and intellectual behaviors, you will be able to make some initial judgments about the tasks and problems that will interest and satisfy them and about the kind of instruction you might provide in your interactions with them. It will increasingly become second nature to take in information about children's behavioral repertoire that you can then use to draw inferences about the kind of experiences to provide for them. In making transitions from the assessment of children's current abilities to deciding about the experiences and instruction you as a teacher might provide, there are four guidelines we think you should consider (or reconsider):

Guidelines

1. Instead of trying to push the preoperational child on to more advanced functioning, provide new contexts, new "twists" for the application of his or her existing repertoire. The opportunity to adapt what has already been mastered to a variety of situations leads to consolidation and confidence. Ample opportunities to use current abilities should usually precede expectations for further achievement.

2. Most children in the preoperational stage (prior to age seven or eight) benefit far less from following adult directions than from structuring their own actions. Adults can use children's initiations and activities as the basis for developing vocabulary, concepts, and insights. Children are more likely to attend to and profit from such interactions than from more formal instruction.

✓ 3. Children will benefit from opportunities to observe and interact with peers who are operating at a slightly more advanced level than theirs. The modeling of a child with a more advanced thinking and language pattern and with skills that are almost, but not quite, within the ability level of the less-advanced child, provides a potent stimulus to cognitive and intellectual development.

4. The preoperational child's intellectual and cognitive development will proceed better if there is an abundance of zest, joy, pleasure, surprise, and fun in learning situations. This is in contrast to monotony, boredom, and

grimness. Play and gratification are the basis for all growth, including growth in cognitive functioning. For a child who is really learning there is no separation of work and play. There is no need and, in fact, great disadvantage in equating learning with the absence of pleasure. The more playful the child can be while learning, the better the learning will go. Perhaps this is also true of adults. What do you think?

Summary

According to Piaget, adaptation through mutual processes of assimilation and accommodation occurs across the life span. The rate of adaptation, however, is particularly rapid in the early years. Cognitive and intellectual development is accelerated when the child from age one-and-a-half to two years and upward discovers ways to symbolize aspects of reality so that it can be internally represented.

The child progresses from the initial use of motor signs to the use of language and visual imagery to construct mental representations of external reality. Only to the extent that there is a matching internal construction can aspects of the surroundings be meaningfully perceived. Across the preoperational years children gradually become capable of more effectively representing to themselves the things they experience. They gradually become able to go beyond their immediate perceptions to consider a phenomenon from other perspectives. Also, they begin to take into account what has been previously perceived. This "decentering" process occurs within several areas of cognitive and intellectual activity—classification, use of number concepts, seriation, understanding of mass and liquid quantity, causality, space concepts, time concepts, and language usage. Only to the extent that you as a teacher can accurately assess children's current thinking abilities in these areas, will you be able to determine the kinds of learning experiences that might further enhance this functioning.

REASSESSMENT

Reread what you wrote for the preassessment as you began this chapter, comparing this with your current understandings. Now write on these topics again and incorporate your new insights and knowledge. Continue to update as you prepare for teaching. Save your materials for your portfolio.

Additional Reading

Learning in Young Children

Brackbill, Y., and Thompson, G. G. *Behavior in infancy and early childhood.* New York: The Free Press/Macmillan, 1967.

Brackbill, Y., Ed. *Behavior in infancy and early childhood.* New York: The Free Press/ Macmillan, 1967.

Bruner, J. Up from helplessness. In P. Cramer, Ed. *Readings in developmental psychology today.* Del Mar, Calif.: CRM Books, 1970.

Gesell, A. *Infant development.* New York: Harper, 1952.

Gordon, I. J. *Baby learning through baby play*. New York: St. Martin's Press, 1970.

Landreth, C. *Early childhood: Behavior and learning*. New York: Alfred A. Knopf, 1967.

Sklar, M. *How children learn to speak*. Beverly Hills, Calif.: Western Psychological Services, 1969. ERIC Document Reproduction Service No. ED 033 508.

Slobin, D. I. Children and language: They learn the same way all around the world. *Psychology Today*, 1972, 71–74, 82.

Stone, L. J., and Church, J. *Childhood and adolescence: A psychology of the growing person*. 2nd ed. New York: Random House, 1968.

About Piaget

Beard, R. M. *An outline of Piaget's developmental psychology for students and teachers*. New York: Basic Books, 1969.

Elkind, D. Misunderstandings about how children learn. *Today's Education*, 1972.

————. What does Piaget say to the teacher? *Today's Education, NEA Journal*, 1972, 47–48.

Furth, H. G. *Piaget for teachers*. Englewood Cliffs, N.J.: Prentice-Hall, 1970.

Ginsberg, H., and Opper, S. *Piaget's theory of intellectual development: An introduction*. Englewood Cliffs, N.J.: Prentice-Hall, 1969.

Hawkins, F. P. *The logic of action: Young children at work*. New York: Pantheon/Random House, 1969.

Pulaski, M. A. *Understanding Piaget*. New York: Harper & Row, 1971.

Sharp, E. *Thinking is child's play*. New York: E. P. Dutton, 1970.

By Piaget

You may find Piaget's own writings difficult to read and comprehend. It will be useful, however, to sample at least enough to gain a sense of how he studied children, of the kind of records he kept, and of his way of thinking about his observations. The volumes *about* Piaget will be more meaningful after an exposure to writings he has authored.

Inhelder, B., and Piaget, J. *The early growth of logic in the child: Classification and seriation*. New York: Norton, 1964.

Piaget, J. *The child's conception of number*. New York: Humanities, 1952.

————. *The child's conception of the world*. London: Routledge & Kegan Paul, 1951.

————. *The origins of intelligence in children*. New York: Norton, 1952.

————. How children form mathematical concepts. *Scientific American*, 1973.

Piaget, J., and Inhelder, B. *The child's conception of space*. London: Routledge & Kegan Paul, 1956.

————. *The psychology of the child*. New York: Basic Books, 1969.

Language Development in Young Children

Cazden, C. B. *Child language and education*. New York: Holt, Rinehart and Winston, 1972.

Cazden, C. B., Ed. *Language in early childhood education*. Washington, D.C.: National Association for the Education of Young Children, 1972.

Chukovsky, K. *From two to five*. Berkeley: University of California Press, 1965.

Engel, R. C. *Language motivating experiences for young children*. Van Nuys, Calif.: DFA Publishers, 1968.

Hess, R. D., and Shipman, V. C. Early experience and the socialization of cognitive modes in children. *Child Development*, 1965, 36, 869–86.

Lavatelli, C. S. *Language training in early childhood education*. Urbana: University of Illinois Press, 1971.

Menyuk, P. *Sentences children use*. Cambridge, Mass.: MIT Press, 1969.

Pflaum, S. W. *The development of language and reading in the young child*. Columbus, Ohio: Charles E. Merrill, 1974.

Reid, W. R., Engel, R. C., and Rucker, D. P. Language development for the young. *Audio-visual Instruction*, 1966, 11, 534–37.

Reading and Writing Development in Young Children

Allen, R. V., and Allen, C. *Language experiences in reading: Teacher's resource book*. Chicago: Encyclopaedia Britannica Press, 1966.

Aukerman, R. C. *Approaches to beginning reading*. New York: John Wiley, 1971.

Aukerman, R. C., Ed. *Some persistent questions on beginning reading*. Newark, Del.: International Reading Association, 1972.

Barbe, W. B. *Educator's guide to personalized reading*. Englewood Cliffs, N.J.: Prentice-Hall, 1961.

Carrillo, L. W. *Informal reading readiness experiences*. New York: Nobile and Nobile, 1971.

Chall, J. *Learning to read: The great debate*. New York: McGraw-Hill, 1967.

Chan, J. M. T. *Getting your child off to a good start in reading*. Iowa Falls, Iowa: General Publishing and Binding, 1974. Available from Dr. J. Chan, 425 West Race Street, Visalia, California 93277.

Chomsky, C. Write now, read later. *Childhood Education*, 1971, 47, 296–99.

Downing, J., and Thackray, D. V. *Reading readiness*. London: University of London Press, 1971.

Durkin, D. *Teaching young children to read*. Boston: Allyn and Bacon, 1972.

Gans, R. *Fact and fiction about teaching phonics*. New York: Bobbs-Merrill, 1964.

Hall, M. A. *Teaching reading as a language experience*. Columbus, Ohio: Charles E. Merrill, 1970.

Lee, D. M., and Allen, R. V. *Learning to read through experience*. New York: Appleton-Century-Crofts, 1963.

O'Brien, C. A. *Teaching the language-different child to read*. Columbus, Ohio: Charles E. Merrill, 1973.

Smith, N. B., and Strickland, R. *Some approaches to reading*. Washington, D.C.: Association for Childhood Education International, 1969.

Spache, G. D., and Spache, E. B. *Reading in the elementary school*. Boston: Allyn and Bacon, 1973.

Stauffer, R. G. *The language experience approach to the teaching of reading*. New York: Harper & Row, 1970.

Veatch, J. *How to teach reading with children's books*. New York: Scholastic Book Services, 1968.

Retardation in Children

Dybwad, G. *The mentally handicapped child under five*. Arlington, Texas: National Association for Retarded Children, 1969.

Caldwell, B. M. The importance of beginning early. In *Not all little wagons are red: The exceptional child's early years*. Arlington, Virginia: The Council for Exceptional Children, 1973.

Gotts, E. A., Compiler. *A bibliography related to early childhood education, child development and preschool handicapped children*. Austin, Texas: University of Texas, 1971. ERIC Document Reproduction Service No. ED 061 687.

Granato, S. *Serving children with special needs*. Washington, D.C.: Department of Health, Education, and Welfare, Office of Child Development, 1972. U.S. Government Printing Office. Document No. 1791-0176.

Karnes, M. B., and Zehrback, R. R. Flexibility in getting parents involved in the school. *Teaching Exceptional Children*, 1972, 5, 6–19.

Perske, R. *New directions for parents of persons who are retarded.* New York: Abingdon Press, 1973.

Neisworth, J. T., and Madle, R. A. Normalized day care: A philosophy and approach to integrating exceptional and normal children. *Child Care Quarterly*, 1975, 4, 163–71.

CHAPTER 7
Assessments of Individual Children

Overview

Integrating and Summarizing Observations

Obtaining Information from Other Sources
    THE FAMILY
    SCHOOL RECORDS
    STANDARDIZED TESTS
    PROGRAM PERSONNEL

Planning for the Whole Child

Summary

PREASSESSMENT

When you have completed this chapter you should be able to describe and compare the following:

1. *components of useful behavioral summaries for individual children.*
2. *sources of information on individual children other than your own observations.*
3. *guidelines for planning educational programs for individual children.*

Before beginning to read this chapter:

1. *take enough time to write what you already know about each of the above topics.*
2. *attempt a behavioral summary for an individual child using observational data you have already obtained.*

Save what you write for rereading, comparison, and elaboration after you have studied and discussed these materials.

Overview

The first part of this chapter deals with how to summarize the behavioral records you have compiled into a form that is useful for program planning and for communicating with others. The second part suggests some additional sources of information about children beyond your observations of their behavior. Third, recommendations are given for using this information about children to facilitate their continued development.

Integrating and Summarizing Observations

The process of preparing a summarizing statement that profiles a child you have been observing requires that you review your notes, which are already organized by topics, and write a brief summary of your overall assessment and/or evaluation of the child on the particular topic in question. For example, under the topic of *strength*, you may have several notations of how the

The following topical outline, based on the questions in Chapters 4, 5, and 6, is included here for review and for ease of reference.

Physical Characteristics and Motor Behavior

1. Physical characteristics
    1.1. General physical appearance
    1.2. Body build
    1.3. Posture
    1.4. Attractive/unattractive features
    1.5. Grooming
2. Gross movements
    2.1. Action repertoire
    2.2. Strength
    2.3. Balance
    2.4. Rhythm
    2.5. Speed
    2.6. Endurance
    2.7. Coordination into complex skills
3. Small muscle
    3.1. Self-help in eating, dressing, grooming
    3.2. Manipulation of materials, toys, tools
4. Other
    4.1. Dominance
    4.2. Physical disability
    4.3. Tension indicators
    4.4. Health/disease

Affective and Social Behaviors

1. Expression of affective states
    1.1. Pleasure
    1.2. Displeasure/discomfort
    1.3. Fears
    1.4. Anger
2. Orientation of self in world
    2.1. Dependence/independence
    2.2. Initiation
    2.3. Persistence
3. Concepts of self
    3.1. View of physical appearance
    3.2. View of worthiness of one's behavior
    3.3. View of sex role
    3.4. View of skills
4. Social awareness

5. Social interaction
    5.1. Observer
    5.2. Parallel
    5.3. Associative
    5.4. Cooperative
6. Social leader/follower
    6.1. Repertoire for initiation
    6.2. Ideas or suggestions to others
    6.3. Ideas or suggestions of others followed
7. Repertoire for solving social problems
    7.1. Conflicts
    7.2. Exclusion
8. Formal group participation
    8.1. Comfort/discomfort
    8.2. Contributions

Cognitive and Intellectual Behaviors

1. Classification
2. Number
    2.1. One-to-one correspondence
    2.2. Counting
    2.3. Comparing groups
    2.4. Conservation of number
3. Seriation
4. Mass and liquid quantity
5. Causality
6. Space concepts
7. Time concepts
8. Spoken language
    8.1. Vocabulary
    8.2. Sentence structure (syntax)
9. Written language
    9.1. Left-to-right orientation
    9.2. Auditory discrimination
    9.3. Visual discrimination
    9.4. Word concepts
    9.5. Letter-sound relationships
    9.6. Word recognition
    9.7. Reading skills

---

child used his or her body to move, lift, or push objects. If you have noted, "Pushes wagon filled with blocks," "Tries unsuccessfully to push open locked door," "Lifts other child almost his size," and "Holds door shut against two others trying to enter the building," you might summarize all of these by writing: "Appears to use body strength effectively." It is very important that you include with your statements, whenever possible, reports of the specific behaviors responsible for your assessment. Note the format of the following report.

Behavioral Assessment

Name: Lucy
Age: four, just prior to fifth birthday
Sex: female

Parental education: college/professional training
Based on two two-hour observations at Lucy's home on two successive days. Others present at some point during observations:

> male friend, age four—George
> female friend, age four—Donna
> female friend, age four—Betsy
> toddler brother, age two—Matt
> caregiver/maid—Thelma
> caregiver's teenage daughter—Lena

Physical Characteristics. Lucy is of average proportions. Although not particularly large boned, neither would she be described as petite. She is slim and stands straight and firmly with easy balance. She has long, light brown, curly hair, light skin, and blue eyes. Although neat and clean at the beginning of each observation, Lucy was not at all concerned about remaining that way and gradually became increasingly wet, muddy, and "disheveled." For example:

- Lucy takes the hose and runs water onto dry dirt, muddying it. She swishes it with her free hand and then slaps the water, splashing herself and others. She wipes her hand on her bathing suit and stomach.
- Lucy slides into the plastic wading pool on her stomach, head first, totally submerging and arising with dripping hair.

Gross Motor Behavior. Lucy has a broad repertoire of large muscle actions, which include running, skipping, hopping on both feet, hopping on one foot, jumping from heights of up to two and one-half feet, crawling on hands and knees, sliding on stomach, sliding on rear, taking a running jump over two-foot barriers, swaying from left to right, catching body weight with hands, swinging arms and objects in all directions, running up sliding board, striking with open hand, stamping feet, kicking and splashing vigorously in water.

Her strength was displayed in pushing and pulling a bulky wooden cover (two-and-a-half by five feet) for a sand table to the wading pool, approximately twenty feet away. She also was observed to support her entire body weight by her elbows. She can also stop herself at midpoint on the sliding board and on an inclined pole.

Lucy's balance seemed particularly excellent, as evidenced by her hopping on one foot more than ten times in succession. She easily stood on the narrow (three-inch) edge of a sofa and balanced first on two feet and then on one foot for a period of time before jumping to the floor. She also stood and balanced on the edge of the teeter-swing arrangement and then lightly jumped and ran off.

Rhythmic actions were a regular part of Lucy's activity. She skipped, hopped, stamped her feet, swung her arms, and swayed in repetitive patterns, some quite complex. She often accompanied her movements with vocal chants or singing. For example:

• Lucy swings her arms in time to

   Chucken, goody, goody, doody
   Chucken, goody, goody, doody

• Says "Ding Dong" (the *Dong* at a lower pitch) twenty or so times as she stands at the top of the sliding board and sways her body from side to side in rhythm with her words.
• Energetically hops in rhythm with music on record player. Stops and moves arms in full arc to same rhythm.

Lucy moved relatively quickly in both total body movement and in arm actions. She ran from place to place as she played and crawled for short distances almost as fast as other four-year-olds run. When spraying water from the hose, she periodically created a whirlwind of water by twirling the hose rapidly in large arm movements.

The longest continuous effort observed was a twenty-minute stretch of spraying water from a hose. Her persistence in moving the sand table top across the play yard—several minutes of sustained pushing and pulling—was the greatest physical effort. Otherwise, her running, jumping, etc., were interspersed with somewhat less vigorous activity.

Nearly all of Lucy's involvements throughout the two observation periods included motor activity. Only when she was watching television was this not the case. Even then she was seldom completely inactive. For example, during this time she was rubbing her leg with her foot and rubbing the backs of her hands together.

Lucy's gross motor activities were frequently well integrated with more complex actions. For example:

• Lucy, as mother in pretend play, says to George, playing her son, "You've got to start sinking, Georgie, and then I'll crawl in the water with you." She runs and jumps feet first into play pool, grabs George, and pulls him to the side, supporting his body with her arms and holding him against her chest.
• Lucy runs about the yard, pulling hose with her and spraying other children who are trying to elude her.
• Lucy moves sand table top to different locations in relation to wading pool

to create slide (inclined plane from edge of pool), dock (extending over pool), and bridge (extending across pool).

Small Muscle Coordination. Lucy was very independent in dressing, eating, etc. She put on and took off her own clothing, zipped, unzipped, snapped button fasteners, dried herself, wrapped herself in a towel. She served milk for herself and friends from a carton in the refrigerator, opened a peanut butter jar and spooned out peanut butter, climbed on a chair and took candy from the freezer.

Lucy demonstrated capability in eye-hand coordination by manipulating a record player mechanism, TV knobs, a water faucet, and in directing a stream of water from the hose into specific target locations, such as the top of a watering can. She also quite proficiently altered the stream of water into spray of varying intensities and directions with her alternate hand. During the span of observation, she did not use pencil, chalk, scissors, or make any effort to manipulate any tool in small area, with the single following exception:

• Climbs onto chair to get candy from top section of refrigerator. Takes out piece about one inch by one-half inch. Places it on counter and takes table knife and tries to cut through it, pulling upright knife toward herself with right hand while holding candy with her left. She is partially successful.

Lucy predominantly used her right hand but often switched to her left and sometimes used both simultaneously for certain tasks. For example:

• Uses mostly left hand for holding hose and right for directing spray. Interchanges sometimes.

Photo by Mary Green.

- Digs up one spoon of peanut butter with her right hand, and while sitting and eating it, uses her left hand to fill another spoon to hand to George.

Other. Lucy appears to have no physical disability or health problem. She did, however, consistently breathe through her mouth. Her emotions appeared to be directly expressed in behavior and there were almost no other indicators of tension. For one brief period, she sucked her finger while watching television.

Expression of Affective States. Lucy's pleasure and displeasure and other emotions were very directly expressed. She appeared to especially enjoy having others note her actions. She smiled and laughed and bounced with pleasure when playmates or adults commented on what she had done. For example:

- Says to George, "Let me show you a trick." Looks delighted with his close attention as he watches her slide into the water and tries to do the same thing himself.
- Asks, "What are you doing now?" (to observer). When told, "About all the things you do," she smiles and giggles.

She also expressed pleasure when she successfully manipulated physical materials, such as moving the sand table top successfully, supporting the side of the wading pool with the wagon so the water did not spill out, and making mud "muffins." Her greatest pleasure, however, appeared to come from successfully distressing others without any reprisal other than vocal protests or crying. For example:

- Lucy turns hose on toddler brother with greater and greater gusto and at closer and closer range until he bellows and runs away. She giggles in delight. Repeats same pattern with varying degrees of finesse and/or aggressiveness with all playmates, adult neighbor, and observer. Says to adult neighbor, in own yard and on other side of fence, "Here comes the rain cloud, Mrs. C. Don't get wet." Sprays her and laughs. Says, "Get away from the rain storm," sprays her again, and as she protests, laughs and runs away.
- Swings four-foot pole very close to George without actually hitting him until he draws back in fear. Laughs.
- Other pleasures appear to be movement, especially rhythmic movement, saying rhymes and singing, creating effects with water, and role-playing (kitty, mother, sister). Pleasure is primarily expressed in smiling, laughing, and "bouncy" movements.

Lucy's expression of displeasure was immediate whenever she was not allowed to do something she felt entitled to do. For example:

- Caregiver's daughter, Lena, tells Lucy that she cannot turn water on until her (Lena's) mother arrives at the house. For a period of ten minutes Lucy pouts, flounces, cries, wails, sniffs, argues ("My daddy said I could"), threatens to do it anyway, tries reasoning ("My legs need that water"), and questions ("Why can't I do that? Why can't I?"). When Lena still refuses to let her, Lucy says, "I'm going outside [means without turning hose on] but I'm going to git some potato chips and git Matt some and git Donna some." Lena does not respond. Lucy gets potato chip can. Lena grabs it from her and says, "You didn't ask." Lucy again cries and stomps floor with her foot and shouts, "I was *telling* you. Why can't I? Why can't I?" When Lena says, "Because you've been so nasty." Lucy walks into another room and stands behind a chair. Lena says, "If I give you some potato chips, will you go outside then?" Lucy hesitates, "I want them [brother and friends] to have some too." Lena agrees and begins to give each some. Lucy demands that they all be given more. "I want more than that. Give them more than that." She gets as many as she demands and walks outside, saying calmly to her friends, "We're going to go swimming when Lena's mother gets here."

She expressed displeasure at her brother and friends whenever they obstructed her activity or plans. For example:

• Lucy wants to slide, but George is ahead of her. She says, "Georgie, let me slide." George points out in distress that Matt is ahead of him. Lucy says, "He can go if he wants to. Beat it, Matt! You want a spankin'? Git!" Pushes around George and bumps Matt on down the slide. Matt cries and Lucy says loudly, "Matt, why did you do that when I didn't do anything?"

Lucy also expressed displeasure when she lost in a game, as in the following instance:

• Lucy is playing a record that suggests a musical chair game. She gets a chair and tells George that they should play. They walk around it and the first time the music stops, Lucy gets the chair and laughs, saying, "Georgie, you're out." As they begin to play again, the music stops very soon and George sits down ahead of Lucy. She says, "Georgie, he didn't say to stop!" Then as she notes that the music did stop, she says, "Who cares, Georgie?", and starts to walk away. She turns back and strikes George on his arm and says, "I'm not going to play." Continues, "You aren't gonna git anything, either. I'm goin' to git something you ain't goin' to git."

Lucy became very angry when her friend Donna sprayed her with the hose *once*, after repeated instances of Lucy's doing it to others despite their protests and tears. The following describes that incident:

• Donna picks up hose Lucy has put down. (She previously repeatedly begged for a turn, without success.) After hosing Matt and George the way Lucy had with similar results (crying from Matt and verbal protest from George), turns hose directly on Lucy. Lucy pauses, appears surprised, takes deep breaths, sobs a couple of times. She then shouts, "I'm tellin' [pause] cause you shouldn't have wet my hair." Runs to door and screams at full volume, "Thelma, Thelma, Thelma, Thelma!" When Thelma does not come to the door, she rushes over to Donna and raises her arm as if to hit her, saying, "You ———." Donna puts the hose down and runs. Lucy then picks it up and squirts everyone while they loudly protest.

During the observation periods, Lucy showed no particular fears. Although lightning appeared to frighten playmate George at one point, Lucy simply said in a matter-of-fact way, "You'd better go in so you don't get electric shock," and went in herself. In dramatic play sequences, the following were posed as "scary" things: sharks, rough persons, and poisons.

Orientation of Self in World. Lucy is a very independent child. She constantly initiated activities and almost always carried them out without assistance. These activities included play on equipment, sand play, dramatic play, water play, watching TV, obtaining snacks. The only things she appeared unable to do were to tie a bow to assist her friend in dressing and to secure a piece of play equipment in the location she wanted it. Although she called for the caregiver on several occasions, it appeared to be done as a threat to playmates and not in a real bid for assistance. In each instance, she was ignored by the caregiver and continued on with her activities without delay. On the couple of occasions when Lucy initiated an activity that required a sustained effort for completion, she continued through until it was done. This included filling the wading pool, wetting down the porch, replacing snack materials (carton to refrigerator), and some dramatic play episodes.

Lucy evidently views her appearance positively, as evidenced by her pointing out with some interest that she and Donna looked the same (had the same hair style) and by the way she pushed at and flounced her clean, combed curls. She seems to view herself as a worthwhile person and seems confident that she can and should initiate interactions with peers and adults and that her wishes and directions are worthy of being followed. She also appears to easily incorporate both "good" and "bad" behaviors into this positive view of herself, as evidenced by the following incidents:

• Bumps Matt over, making him cry, and then pats and comforts him singing,

Hush, little baby, don't say a word
Mommy's going to buy you a mockingbird

• Says to observer very matter-of-factly, "I wet you yesterday. You turned the water off. I know cause I was squirting you." Later says, "I'm going to hose off the patio [where observer is sitting]. Shall I get you a chair first?"
• What was probably (although not observed) a long hassle with caregiver over Lucy's refusal to nap, Lucy describes to observer thus, "If I take my nap I can play, but I don't want to right now. After awhile I'll take my nap, and then I'll be able to play all right."

Lucy frequently called others' attention to her skills and appears to feel that she should be good at things. She appeared to be surprised (showed signs of embarrassment) when she did not excel and reacted with aggressive behavior. For example:

- When Donna insists that her pinafore should be tied in bows at the side, Lucy stops immediately and says, "I can't tie in a bow," and begins to tickle her.
- After successfully sliding underwater holding her breath, she once gets a nose full of water and coughs and sputters. She appears to be quite embarrassed, looks around quickly to see if George has noticed (he hasn't), and then walks over and pushes Matt off his feet.

During the period of observation, Lucy showed the following interest in whether or not behaviors or objects were sex-appropriate:

- While the girls are changing into their swimsuits, the caregiver asks George to leave the room "while the ladies dress." Lucy immediately visually checks each person present to determine if they should stay or leave. She indicates that Donna and the female observer can stay, hesitates over Betsy, her black female friend, but then says, "You're a girl. You can stay." She then firmly insists that Matt should leave. Matt is not at all attentive to her efforts to exclude him and she immediately gives in and changes into her swimsuit.
- Lucy becomes angry at George and insists that he not use the toy truck he is playing with because it is "a *little* boy's truck." She appeals to the caregiver, saying that it is Matt's truck and George should not play with it. The caregiver takes it from him to his great displeasure. George then appears to be trying to get even (observer's inference) by saying he has an airplane that Lucy cannot play with because "girls can't play with boys' things and it has a picture of boys on its wing." "Who cares?" replies Lucy, apparently for lack of a better answer, but she is very attentive to George.

"I'm going to get a camper, too," says George.

"I'll get a camper, too," says Lucy.

"I'll get a racer. That's not for girls," says George.

"I'm going to buy me a woman that won't move like Barbie," says Lucy. "Like Randy—a Barbie that won't move."

George appears not to understand.

Lucy continues, "I'm going to buy all girls' stuff."

George says, "I'm going to buy a rifle. That's for boys. I'm going to buy two guns. And a Planet of the Apes."

Lucy replies, "Well, I'm going to be a cowboy and when I catch that Planet of the Apes, I'll swing it around and around."

George appears to be confused but says, "That's what I'm going to do, too. I'm going to buy a police hat and a pistol. I'm gonna get a new pistol."

Lucy stands considering this without reply.

George, having "stopped" her (an inference), broaches another topic, one he had tried unsuccessfully to talk with Lucy about twice the previous day. He says, "I'm growing onions."

"Yeah, but you ain't growing radishes like me," replies Lucy.

Before George can reply to this, she says, "And goodbye. I'm going outside." Whereupon she runs outside and begins vigorous swinging and singing.

Lucy was obviously intrigued with learning about sex-roles. She assigned herself female roles in dramatic play (sister, mother) while giving George male roles (father, brother, boy named Stevie, bad man), but she also played hunter, cop, and tough guy. Soon after observing George urinating on the lawn (after his unsuccessful attempt to get in the house to go to the bathroom), she pulled her bathing suit down, held the hose between her legs with the end of it extending outward, and, giggling, said, "Look, George." However, she appeared to feel generally pleased with herself as a girl and incorporated into the female image a wide range of behaviors.

Social Awareness. Lucy showed only glimmerings of looking at the world from another's point of view. She often behaved in very gracious ways, taking care of others' needs. She was very selective in doing this, however, and usually did not take others' preferences and concerns into account. For example:

- Lucy offers George peanut butter. He refuses. She says, "Well, you can't have nothin' else."
- Lucy asks Betsy to come over and play hunter. When Betsy says she does not want to be squirted with the hose or her mother will be mad at her, Lucy points the hose at her, wetting her thoroughly, and says, "Then stop getting next to us."

Social Interaction. Lucy's solitary play included singing and dancing by herself, watching TV, sand play, and some dramatic play. Associative and parallel activities included the use of the play set (swings and slide) and many of the water play activities. Cooperative play was primarily in "pretend" activities involving kitties, drowning child, drowning mother, bad man (then father) in jail, hunters shooting, cops, etc.

Social Leader/Follower. Lucy's initiations to others were typically verbal and direct. She often addressed people by name in initiating contact with them. For example:

- "Georgie, want to get on the dock?"
- "Here comes the rain cloud, Mrs. C."
- "Betsy, did your mother say you could go swimming?"

She constantly gives suggestions or orders to companions but only very selectively accepts suggestions from them. During cooperative play ventures, virtually all of Lucy's suggestions were enacted; and few or none from the other children were included. When the suggestions of others were taken into account and followed (or modified) by Lucy, it was definitely because of the idea's appeal rather than an attempt at cooperation. More frequently, Lucy gave directions. For example:

- "Betsy, you're supposed to kill him."
- "Georgie, you've got to save your mother when I say it. The first time I say it you got to help, Georgie."
- "We're in jail, but I get out. I breaked the bars but not on you 'cause you're the bad man."

Repertoire for Solving Social Problems. Lucy's repertoire for solving social conflict appeared to be limited to those actions that induced others to accept her point of view and give up their own. These included hitting, shoving, shouting, threatening, calling for adult support, ordering, promising later turns ("I'll let you later"), and ignoring. Her actions are typified by the following comments:

- "You ain't goin' to git any more 'cause you ain't my best friend."
- "Well, you can't [play with toy]."
- "I'm tellin' cause you shouldn't."

In no instance did any of the three friends or the little brother persist with wishes that were contrary to Lucy's. She has a very broad and effective repertoire for resolving problems to her own satisfaction, but little capacity for accommodating others' interests. There was no effort by others to seriously confront or exclude her.

Formal Group Participation. No opportunity to observe.

Classification. Lucy did not engage in any actual classification activity during the period of observation, although there was some evidence of awareness of concepts and dimensions for classifying. For example:

- Points out, "See, we got the same hair. Our hair's the same, see!" Both she and her friend have their hair in pigtails. (Aware of the concept, *same*.)
- Locates "Sesame Street" on TV, and then as she and Donna begin to watch, "What's My Part," a parody of "What's My Line," comes on. Donna says, "That's not 'Sesame Street'." Lucy looks puzzled and then says, "Oh, that's Smiley [character]. See, it's *on* 'Sesame Street'."

Number. Lucy showed no evidence of being aware of one-to-one correspondence during the periods of observation, except in her provision of food to each friend on several occasions. There was, however, the following evidence of a developing understanding of number concepts and terminology:

- In obtaining potato chips and in water play activity, uses term and concept of *more*. She says, "I want more than that. Give them more than that," and "Do you want more gasoline?"
- In discussing whether Betsy should play in the pool, says, "I don't need

three, only two. If I have three, it will bust the whole thing."
- Frequently counts, "One, two, three, go!" before starting to run, jump, etc. Also chants counting rhymes such as "One, two, buckle my shoe."
- She obtains one piece of candy and tells Donna, "Only one piece so I'm going to *halve* it."
- Tells George, "I'll be five before you, and I'll be five and a half [before he is five]."

Mass and Liquid Quantity. Lucy showed no evidence of awareness of mass and liquid quantity except for the concept *more* (already mentioned). Filled glasses of different dimensions with milk for herself and Donna but did not seem to attend to any comparison of size or quantity.

Causality. Lucy commented on certain causal phenomena but seemed uninterested in investigating or asking about causality.

Space Concepts. Lucy's manipulation of her own body and of materials and equipment reflected excellent spatial awareness. In four hours of play, mostly active movement, Lucy only misjudged her position (bumped knee while jumping on sofa) on one occasion and then only slightly. Her judgment of distance and velocity in directing the stream of water with the hose was quite accurate. In a few instances she showed considerable awareness of herself in relation to the location of other persons, objects, or places. For example:

- Says to observer about to drive away in car, "You can go that way [motions a corner] to the same place. Go up the hill. It's the same." (Indicates correctly a different route to main street from her house.)

Lucy's references to broader space and place designators showed a beginning awareness of places, along with the confusions to be expected at her age level:

- Pulls Florida map from drawer. Unfolds it and says, "Want to see the map? Want to see how big it is? It's the whole world."
- Brings doll to observer and says, "I was born in Germany and my people gave me this." Immediately thereafter takes five-foot pole and holds it upright at her side and says, "Here's United States, Georgie. It is." (Inference: may mean that it is a flag of the United States.)

In dramatic play, she displayed some representational knowledge of land forms.

- Calls squirting upright hose a volcano and then says, "This ain't a volcano. It's water."
- At different points during play, calls the wading pool a pond, a river, an ocean, for different activities. For shark play, says, "That's not a pond; it's a big ocean."

Time Concepts. Lucy used many time indicators and showed awareness of events as they occurred in time sequence. For example:

- "I'm going to take a nap *before* my dad comes home."
- *"After awhile* I'll take my nap."
- "I'm making a little kite *today.*"
- "Next day's Bible School [means *tomorrow*]."
- "My mother comes home *at five.*"
- "I wet you *yesterday.*"

Spoken Language. Lucy had a great many relational and opposing terms in her vocabulary. Among those noted were *same, not, off, on, another, else, more, bigger, little, in, out, if, cause.*

As evidenced by her vocabulary during the period of observation, Lucy's discriminations in the following categories were:

animals	*shark, birdies, kitty, kitty cat, fly*
people	*little boy, cowboy, bad man, cop, hunter, lady, girls, waiter*
family relationships	*daddy, mother, sister, brother, baby brother*
colors	*blue*
shapes	(no words designating shapes were used)
vehicles	*truck, car*
clothes	*shoes, swimming suit, pants, barefoot, clothes*
weather	*air, cooler, sky, rain, rainstorm, blue sky, rain cloud*
foods	*potato chips, muffins, candy, salad, flavoring, radishes*
liquids	*water, milk, wet, Kool-Aid*
furniture	*chair, TV, dryer*
body parts	*leg, head, nose, eyes, barefoot, hair, bird* (penis)
feelings	*mad*
toys and play equipment	*kite, doll, truck, wagon, swimming pool*
buildings/ structures	*garage, dock, bridge, jail, patio, building*
plants	*grass, tree top*

Action words used by Lucy were *dried, throw, chase, hop, change, wish, forget, tie, wait, crashed, breaked, sleeping, washing, starts, stops, open, pretend, watch, listen, walk, buy, catch, disappeared, pulled, help, kill, know, say, watch, drown, fall, hold, take, swim, sunk, spray, swing, shoot, squirt.*

Lucy used a variety of sentence structures. For example:

- "I'm making muffins with mud" (subject / predicate / object)
- "You're supposed to be the father" (subject / form of *to be* / predicate nominative)
- "You're getting wet" (subject / predicate / predicate adjective)

- "Why can't I do it?" (question—*wh*-type)
- "Would you help him, please?" (question—inverted subject, auxiliary verb)
- "You get the wagon" (imperative)
- "I'm the sister and this sister is going to get you" (compound)
- "If you want to, you can have some salad" (complex)
- "Are you the lady my mommy said would come?" (relative clause)

She also uses various grammatical forms:

- "I'm a bigger cop than you" (forms of *to be*)
- "We're going to go swimming" (*ing* ending)
- "I'm going to find something" (infinitive)
- "I'll let you later" (future tense)
- "That's the lady's car" (possessive form)

She was not heard to make errors with use of single and plural noun or verb forms.

The pronouns Lucy used included *you, me, my, I, he, his, it, we, your, them, she, someone, us.* Her only "error" in use of pronouns was in the sentence, "I want they to have some, too." Few adjectives and adverbs were noted in Lucy's speech. Among the adjectives were *deep, big, rough, whole* (world), *little, biggest, best.*

Lucy has excellent command of prepositional usage. Those she used included *off, on, into, out of, around, under, from, over, with, in, than, before, outside, inside, about, in front of.*

Written Language. Lucy obviously has the concept that written symbols record spoken language. On several occasions, she asked about the writing being done in her presence by the observer, saying, "What does that say right here?", pointing to a specific place on the written page. She pointed first to the top of the page and then asked about each line as she moved her finger downward. She also moved her fingers from left to right as she insisted that she be told, "Right here—what does it say right here?"

There was no opportunity to observe Lucy's ability to discriminate visually with two-dimensional materials. However, she did appear to be aware of similar sounds at the endings of spoken words, as shown by her improvisations in chanting. For example:

- Says, "Boom, zoom, doom. Boom, zoom, doom," as she taps her knees with her hands.
- Sings to herself, "Chucken, goody, goody, doody," as she rotates her arms in large arcs.

The preceding comprehensive statement about Lucy is based on a relatively brief period of observation. It was done in only one setting, Lucy's own home. Additional observations in other settings (such as nursery school) would be useful to determine whether her patterns of behavior are significantly influenced by context. The strength of the report is that it is derived from direct behavioral evidence rather than conjecture. In most instances, the evidence can be clearly differentiated from statements of inference. This differentiation is particularly important in that it facilitates the consideration of alternative interpretations. The detail also allows a more precise comparison with observations that could be made of the same child at later points and in other settings.

You probably noted in the summary of Lucy's behavior that, for some categories, no statements were attempted. It is far more preferable to refrain from going beyond what is observed than to attempt to draw a conclusion from sketchy information. What is important for you, in preparing statements of this type, is to note where you lack information. Information gaps may be due to the absence of particular actions on the part of the child you are observing or may be due to your own insensitivity to particular types of behaviors. You will need to give special attention in subsequent observations to those aspects of behavior for which you lack information to make sure you are not simply overlooking them.

In addition to summarizing your observations, as illustrated in the previous pages, you should be able to prepare answers to the following questions based on your knowledge of the child's behavior. Append these evaluative statements to your report.

1. In what areas is the child currently striving (attempting to perform or understand with full attention and concern)?
2. What characteristics, skills, or attitudes appear to represent the child's strengths?

For Lucy, the following comments were made in response to the above questions.

Evaluative Statements Regarding Lucy

Lucy appears to be currently striving for more precise material manipulations and more precise motor skills. Much of her attention and energy during the observations were devoted to these concerns.

The other major area of concern, which recurred throughout the observation periods, was the manipulation of others' wishes or behaviors to be more closely aligned with her own. As her repertoire for maintaining a dominant position is quite extensive, she was typically successful in getting others, even adults, to accommodate her desires. However, this effort required considerable energy and attention and typically reduced others' involvement with her. Relating to Lucy often appeared to produce tensions in both adults and children, despite their obvious respect for her and their interest in continuing to interact with her.

Lucy also appears to be absorbed by word and sound manipulations, representing objects and events in dramatic play, age (being four versus five/impending birthday), and others' interest in her activity. Any of these represent excellent avenues for relating to her.

Lucy's strengths include her orientation of independence and competence. She approaches situations with great confidence and this proves an important personal asset. Her motor and language abilities are particularly well developed and she constantly uses them to accomplish her objectives. She impresses one as being very capable in most spheres. Upon developing a greater repertoire for accommodating herself to others in cooperative endeavors, she should derive greater satisfaction and benefit from social encounters. More relaxed interchanges would also enable Lucy to devote more energy and attention to acquiring new knowledge and developing additional skills.

Your involvement in observing, note-taking, and summarization throughout this section is meant to increase your own sensitivity to children's development. Few practicing teachers attempt this kind of extensive written summary for all of the children they teach. Much note-taking by sensitive and experienced teachers is done mentally. However, this is a constant, ongoing part of the teaching responsibility, and all teachers, even the most *Written* sensitive and able, benefit from whatever note-taking they can manage. Even *observations* if they can remain attuned to their children's current status, changes in a *important aid in* child across time are not so easily recalled. Without written notes, it is *assessing changes* difficult to document the extent and nature of a child's progress, and conse-*across time* quently many teachers attempt to write down as many of their observations as possible.

At this point in your development, you should continue note-taking and

RESPONSE SECTION

In the preceding material you have learned a great deal about a child called Lucy. You have also read the observer's evaluation of Lucy's current strivings and strengths.

There are, of course, many alternative interpretations of the behaviors reported. You may find it useful to reread the behavioral descriptions and then to try your hand at formulating an alternative evaluative statement. Discuss the possible interpretations with others who have studied the same material. Also consider the following questions:

1. How do you personally feel about Lucy's behaviors as reported in the summary?
2. Would you enjoy having Lucy in your classroom?
3. What aspects of Lucy's behavior would you find appealing?
4. What aspects of Lucy's behavior would you find difficult?
5. How would you react to Lucy if she behaved as described in your classroom?
6. What experiences do you feel would be most beneficial for her?

periodically try to summarize your notes. This will solidify your observational skills and your sensitivity to the developmental progress of young children.

Obtaining Information from Other Sources

It was suggested in Chapter 3 that you not seek extensive background on the children you are observing until you have obtained as much information as possible through observation. Upon making repeated observations of the children and summarizing these into a Behavioral Assessment Statement, you may wish to consider other sources of information that will give you additional perspectives on the child and how he or she is viewed by others.

We suspect that some of these sources will not actually be available to you at this point. Do not attempt to obtain further information from the sources we are about to suggest without the express permission of the person who first gave you permission to observe. Once you assume full teaching responsibility, however, you will want to routinely use the following sources of information about the children you teach.

THE FAMILY

The most useful source of further information and insights about children is their own families. It is a rare parent who, upon hearing of your sincere and knowledgeable interest as expressed in your report of school behavior and areas of competence, will not try to help you better understand and interpret behavior. If, on the other hand, you begin with negative evaluations or inferences, parents will typically become defensive or hostile and will avoid further exchanges with you. If you communicate acceptance of them and optimism about their child, parents can become a prime ally in your efforts. Continuous dialogue with the parents about your joint efforts will eventually have positive outcomes for all. The following are among the things that parents may be uniquely able to tell you about in regard to their child: signs of tension; signs of impending illness; signs of approaching fatigue; physical problems such as allergies; fears; favorite toys, TV shows, films, stories; sibling relationships; special interests, strengths, and abilities.

SCHOOL RECORDS

In most educational or caregiving institutions some form of ongoing record is kept of the child. Some such records are extensive, some sketchy. Such records will routinely include children's home addresses. Teachers often find *Knowing the living* it instructive to drive through the neighborhood where the child lives and *circumstances may* have a look at the living environment. Familiarity with the family living *be helpful* circumstances is sometimes very helpful in understanding what the child is talking about as he or she tries to relate home experiences.

The record sometimes includes information on the parents' educations, occupations, and the ages and names of other siblings. Health reports are also routinely available. These include any special health problems as well as the results of routine checks on functions such as hearing and vision. Attendance is often included, which gives some indication of the extent to which the child is present or absent from the program.

STANDARDIZED TESTS

You may also see scores derived from the administration of standardized tests in the records. While extensive discussion of the meanings of test scores is not appropriate in this volume, some brief comments may be helpful.

A **standardized test** is one that has been previously administered to a large number of subjects under specified conditions, which may vary according to the specific test. The performance of these groups has been carefully analyzed and norms, which are published in a **test manual**, have been determined for comparison with the score of an individual child.

Standardized tests have been developed for a vast range of purposes, but most are used to assess either intelligence or achievement (including readiness for younger children). The most reliable intelligence tests are administered on an individual basis by a trained person and may require an extensive time period (fifty to seventy-five minutes) for complete testing. The most commonly used individual intelligence tests for children are the revised

Intelligence tests Stanford-Binet (S-B) and the Wechsler tests—the Wechsler Preschool and Primary Scale of Intelligence (WPPSI) and the Wechsler Intelligence Scale for Children (WISC). Each of these has **verbal items** and **performance items**. The verbal items require an understanding of and/or command of language, whereas the performance items require the manipulation of materials.

Scores may be noted in the school records in terms of **mental age** (MA) or **intelligence quotient** (IQ). The mental age is derived by determining where on the normed scale a particular child's total "raw" score falls. If a tester were examining Lucy on the Stanford-Binet, for example, he or she would first derive a raw score by summing the number of correct responses in each of the subsections. From the tables of norms the tester would find that her score is higher than is typical for her age group. In fact, her score is comparable to what children at age six years and two months achieve on the average. The tester may therefore indicate on Lucy's record form something like the following:

(current date) Stanford-Binet MA 6–2

IQ calculation Or the tester may calculate and record the intelligence quotient using the following formula, which takes into account her actual chronological age (CA) as well as her mental age:

$$IQ = \frac{MA}{CA} \times 100 = \frac{74 \text{ months}}{60 \text{ months}} \times 100 = 123$$

Lucy's IQ would thus be approximately 123, as of this testing. Thus Lucy's record card might show an entry such as the following:

(Current date) S-B 123

Sometimes tests intended to measure intelligence are administered to groups rather than individually. The tester gives oral directions and each individual marks his or her response in a test booklet. These group tests are occasionally administered in kindergarten, but they are more valid for older children. Some intelligence tests typically administered in a group situation are the Pintner General Intelligence Tests, Lorge-Thorndike Intelligence Tests, and Cole-Vincent Group Intelligence Tests.

Readiness tests and achievement tests　You may also find that scores from various readiness or achievement tests are in the record. These tests, which are typically group administered, attempt to measure what a child's performance is in particular areas. The child's score, which is derived from comparisons with the norms for previously tested groups, may be expressed in the following different ways: (1) **age score equivalents,** which, like Mental Age, indicate the average age at which previously tested groups achieved the particular score; (2) **grade score equivalents,** which indicate at which year and month in school the previously tested groups achieved the particular score. In grade scores, a figure like 1–6 typically refers to first grade, sixth month, or six-tenths of the way through the first-grade year, assuming a ten-month calendar; (3) **percentile scores,** which indicate the percentage of children of the same age or grade level in the original norm population that scored below that point. For example, if a raw score total of thirty-five were determined to be at the sixtieth percentile, this would mean that 60 percent of all of those of comparable age (or grade) in the norm group scored thirty-five or below, while 40 percent scored thirty-six or above.

Some commonly used readiness tests, which include items in areas such as vocabulary, visual discrimination, matching, auditory discrimination, and following directions, are the Metropolitan Readiness Tests, Lee-Clark Reading Readiness Test, Gates-MacGinitie Readiness Tests, and Stanford Early School Achievement Test. These and the many other available readiness tests are intended to help predict whether children will be successful in academic learning tasks. Achievement tests such as the Metropolitan Achievement Tests, Stanford Achievement Tests, and California Achievement Tests are frequently administered in group settings to determine primary children's progress in basic skills areas.

Cautions on test results　While scores on standardized tests can provide some general indication of how a child performs in the areas assessed as compared with other children of the same age or grade, you should carefully note some qualifying factors before simply accepting scores as a guide for your educational decision-making. The first qualifier is the nature of the test itself. Unless you have access to a copy of the test and the tested child's actual responses, you will be unable to interpret and meaningfully use the test results. Knowledge of how a child ranks with others, which is all that a test score typically reveals, does not give much information in itself. In fact, overall test scores are really composites of various subsections, each of which measures a different mental operation.

One of the criticisms of standardized tests, especially intelligence tests, is that they reflect the orientation of the middle-class professionals who devised them. If the language or the experiences and objects referred to in test items are not within the experience of the child being tested, the failure of that child to give a correct response may well reflect the inappropriateness of the item rather than the cognitive or intellectual inability of the child. Children from city slums, poor rural communities, or minority ethnic groups may have quite different life experiences than the norm groups, and consequently the test may be an inaccurate indicator of the actual competence of these children. Such a test score is, at best, a good predictor of how these children will perform in a school program built upon the same kinds of cultural expectations. The very real competence that a child may have developed relative to his or her particular life experience may not be tapped via the particular testing situations and/or items; your own observations are far more likely to give a valid assessment of the unique capabilities of a child, especially if the child is poor or ethnically different.

A middle-class bias

The second qualifier is the condition under which a test is administered. An individually administered test is likely to be more valid than a group administered test as an indicator of what the child can do, especially a young child. In both individual and group testing, interpretations of test scores are impossible unless the specific recommendations of the manual are followed regarding factors such as group size, amount of assistance and explanation given, and length of testing sessions. Many well-meaning educators who are not aware of the significance of these matters administer tests in "willy-nilly" fashion and therefore invalidate overall interpretations of the results.

A third set of qualifiers are the individual proclivities of the tested child. Among these factors are the extent of previous test or testlike experience, willingness to follow the directions of the tester, motivation to perform well, and personal associations with the content of the items. Typically, middle-class children "test" better than do the children of lower socioeconomic groups, that is, they are motivated to please the adult tester and so, with a little encouragement, are willing to persist with difficult and (to them) meaningless tasks. For a child who lacks this adult orientation, a low test score may reflect disinterest rather than inability. As a general rule, a score should be interpreted to mean that the child can do at least as well as the score indicates, but no assumption should be made that he or she cannot do better.

Test motivation

To summarize, for purposes of program planning you should consider your own observations more valid than standardized test scores. At best, a test score provides some estimation of how the child compares with a peer group in responding to the given set of items in a given testing situation. Individual scores on even the most "reliable" tests have repeatedly proved highly unreliable, especially with young children. A child that is tested and then retested within a few days or weeks on a comparable version of the same test may obtain a markedly different score. A high score is generally a more trustworthy indicator of a child's ability than a low score, since a child can easily fail to show all that he or she knows or can do in a test situation, but can seldom, by sheer effort or by guessing, score far beyond the actual achievement level. However, because overall test scores are really composites of various subsections, each of which measures a different mental operation, the overall score is very difficult to interpret.

PROGRAM PERSONNEL

In most program settings the adults who have had previous contacts with the child provide a far richer source of information than formal records. The prime sources, of course, are the child's former teachers. You may also wish to talk with the program director or school administrator, the school secretary, the cafeteria workers, the aides who supervise hallways and playgrounds, the bus drivers, the corner-crossing guards, and the custodians. All of these persons may interact with the children you teach and could contribute meaningful observations to a detailed and well-rounded profile.

Specialists as sources of information   Some program personnel, by the nature of their specialized training and position, are uniquely qualified to comment on certain aspects of children's development. These specialists include the social worker, the school nurse, the school psychologist, the reading specialist, the speech and hearing specialist, and the parent-education worker. It is important that you as a

RESPONSE SECTION

On the preceding pages you have read about the various sources of information that can supplement the observations you make of children's behavior. Reflect on what a person might learn about you by going to such sources and how this might enrich or distort their observations of you.

What would be learned from your family? What would be learned from the records kept by the institutions with which you have been affiliated? What would be learned about your basic abilities, achievements, health, and previous experiences? What would be learned by contacting the various professionals you have consulted in the past? From nonprofessionals who see you frequently?

What would constitute the best and most useful source of information for someone who wanted to assist your learning and development? Would the best information come from observing your behavior, from consulting other sources of information, or from a combination of the two? Would such data-gathering efforts be equally valid in profiling children?

teacher learn early what specialists are available to you and the nature of the services they can provide. Some of these specialists may have already had contacts with some of your children, their parents, and their siblings. In communicating with these persons, you are likely to obtain more practical help if you can present them with your own observations relative to their area of concern.

Planning for the Whole Child

Reiteration of guidelines

When you have developed the kind of behavioral assessment described in this section, you are ready to consider the planning implications of such information. At the conclusion of each of the three previous chapters, some general guidelines were proposed for moving from observation to practice. Although these were initially recommended as ways of reinforcing and sharpening the developmental focus of those specific chapters, they are rephrased in the following summary to point out their broader applicability to all areas of development:

- Avoid urging children to engage in activities that require behaviors very different than those you have already observed in their repertoires.
- Avoid urging children to engage in activities that only require behaviors that are already well integrated into their repertoires.
- Provide new activities and materials that require behaviors similar to those you have already noted in their repertoires.
- Provide opportunities for children to see others engaged in activities that are somewhat more advanced than those they have already mastered.
- Keep in mind that children's behavior is only partially determined by genetic inheritance; much of it is learned and is therefore modifiable by experience.
- Keep in mind that it is your responsibility as a teacher to facilitate the development of a broad behavioral repertoire in your children.
- Provide opportunities for children to structure their own actions and make their own initiations; then use their activity as the basis for your instruction by providing concepts, insights, vocabulary, problem-solving models, and questions.
- Let there be an abundance of zest, joy, pleasure, surprise, and fun in learning situations, instead of monotony, boredom, and grimness.

Interactionist approach

You may recognize that the preceding reflects some bias toward the interactionist view of the child. In this view, you may recall, children are active agents in promoting their own development. The needs to know, to understand, and to make sense of the world are considered innate human proclivities. Children are seen as constantly acting according to their perceptions of the world and of themselves, which are in accord with their experiences to date; life is always "logical" to them within their frame of reference.

For interactionists, the child's own perspective forms the basis for educational planning. They view the child's cognitive functioning as the key to understanding his or her behavior, and close attention is paid to this coordinating area of development.

A teacher of interactionist persuasion, in planning for Lucy, would likely try to perceive the world as Lucy does and would then think of ways to further extend this perception. For example, having noted Lucy's absorption in the physical manipulation of materials, the teacher might provide many additional materials such as tools, containers, planks, barrels, boxes, and blocks. The teacher might also provide obstacles for climbing around and through, which Lucy could herself arrange in various locations. While Lucy used these, words describing their characteristics (such as *thin, smooth,* or *heavy*) and the variations in her actions (such as *slowly, carefully,* or *quickly*) might be interjected into conversations with her.

Since in Lucy's view of the world there seems to be little awareness of the advantages of cooperation, a range of new social experiences might prove useful. Her egocentric view is understandable since she is an eldest child with a much younger brother, and since her friends appear to have no repertoire for modifying her sense of dominance. An interactionist teacher might hypothesize that children slightly older than Lucy be used both to model compromise behavior in cooperative play ventures and to force some modifications in her play patterns.

A range of special materials and activities might be planned for Lucy's upcoming birthday to create involvement in the pretend play she enjoys and to lead her into related involvements. These might include:

- real cake making, with activities such as measuring, baking, decorating, etc.
- making pretend birthday cakes with clay dough and sticks as candles
- making party invitations
- receiving and examining birthday cards
- examining, discussing, and sharing photographs of herself at earlier ages.

Each of these activities offers many possibilities for Lucy's learning and development.

This discussion presents only a brief version of the kinds of activities that might be included in a program plan for Lucy based on observations of her behavior. Nevertheless, it illustrates how interactionists use a child's own interests, concerns, and strivings as the basis for planning. Let us now contrast this hypothetical interactionist plan with others that might be representative of the maturationist and environmentalist views.

Maturationist   Maturationists, as you may recall, assume that a child will progress as
approach   rapidly as the internal, maturational clock allows and that, beyond providing an emotionally supportive setting within which the child's special age and stage conflicts can be resolved, not much else is necessary. While recognizing that the child's experience helps to determine what the child knows, maturationists are unlikely to think that the educational program will significantly influence the child's rate or level of development.

A maturationist teacher would probably feel that no special provisions should be made for Lucy beyond a continuation of her free and accepting environment, within which she would gradually "unfold" and become the person she is capable of becoming. Although the maturationists might note with some satisfaction any incidents in which Lucy's brother or friends convince her to take their wishes more into account, they would probably not arrange for contrasting social experiences.

Behaviorist/ environmentalist approach

Behaviorists (environmentalists), on the other hand, would have far less faith in the positive outcome of a "hands-off" policy. While recognizing the effect of physical maturation on the child's current behavior, behaviorists see this influence more as a limitation. Behaviorists try to determine how a child can most rapidly and effectively be moved toward desired levels of functioning through environmental manipulations. They consider the child's current status as largely a reflection of past exposures and past reinforcement patterns—children behave as they do because they have been rewarded for similar behaviors in the past. A change in reward contingencies brings about a different set of behaviors, and the task of program planning is to: (1) learn what is specifically reinforcing to the child, (2) learn the specifics of current behaviors, and (3) set particular objectives for future behaviors.

Using this information, the child is "shaped" in a direction that, from the behaviorist's view, will be more satisfying to the child as well as more useful to society. The task of the behaviorist teacher is to systematically regulate reinforcements that move the child via small steps from the current behavior to the desired behavior. In the case of Lucy, the behaviorist teacher might wish to make some of her favored activities, such as water play, listening to records, and being "noticed," contingent (dependent) first, on nonaggressive behavior, and later, on accepting playmates' suggestions. Depending on the particular objectives, rewards might also be tied to other activities such as small muscle efforts or use of school-related tools.

Each of these views, although unique in its emphasis, overlaps with the others in some significant ways. Basic care, for example, would be of major concern to all. At other points they show marked contrasts, both in what is planned and how it is accomplished.

You may find that it is useful to be able to step back and view the child from each of these three perspectives. Consider one of the children you observed. Try to think about the child as the maturationist would—as being controlled by internal maturation mechanisms. You will see the child "unfolding" to his or her highest potential unless thwarted in some way, restricted only by universal forces and conflicts over which neither the child, the family, nor you have much control. What is needed most from adults is love, respect, nurturance, care, and acceptance for what the child is and will become. From this perspective one gains a sense of appreciation and patience. It is reassuring to accept children as they are, to be relieved of responsibility for guiding their development, to think that all one must do is live with them and learn to love them as they are. How do you respond to this view?

Now try to view the same child from the behaviorist's perspective. Do you

To get further insights on how different people view children, discuss with others (preferably those who have not studied this section) what they think about the children you have described in your behavioral summaries and what they think a teacher should do for those children. Try to place their views within one or more of the three orientations that have been considered.

Try discussing with your own parents the children you have observed and ask for their reactions. Their handling of you as a child will probably parallel what they recommend for these children; this could provide you with greater insight into your own orientation.

wish the child to become something other than what he or she currently is? What reinforcements can you control that will "shape" the child in the directions you desire? What does the child respond to? What influences his or her behavior? How is the child being influenced already? Can the child gain a more positive view of self by being gradually reinforced to behave in more acceptable or mature ways? From this perspective, one gains a sense of potency and power. You do not have to accept the child as he or she is; change behaviors instead! What feelings does this view evoke in you?

Finally, look at the child from the interactionist view. The child's life is an adventure in learning to use the developing mind and body to explore and understand the world. This is your adventure, as well, because part of your reality now includes the child (or would if you were in the role of teacher). Can you make enough sense of the child's thoughts and aspirations to be helpful? Are you resourceful enough to know how to do that? The interactionist position affords a sense of challenge, searching, exploring, creating, and optimism about children, since their eventual development can potentially outstrip our current capabilities.

You must decide for yourself what your predominant orientation will be. Keep trying all three, as well as any others you may encounter, until you can decide what makes the most sense to you.

Summary

This chapter provided a model for summarizing observations in a report on an individual child. The strength of such a report is in the inclusion of direct behavioral evidence to support statements of inference and evaluation, with an emphasis on areas in which the child is currently striving and has strength.

To obtain information about children beyond that obtained through your own observations, you may be able to consult the child's family, school records, program personnel, and standardized test scores. However, the results of standardized tests are not always reliable and should be viewed in light of several possible qualifiers.

In planning for the whole child, several guidelines were cited that tended to reflect an interactionist view. Interactionists, maturationists, and environmentalists would be likely to plan quite different programs for a child, based on the same set of observations. You are advised to try different perspectives until you can decide what makes most sense to you.

REASSESSMENT

Reread what you wrote for the preassessment as you began this chapter, comparing this with your current understandings. Now write on these topics again and incorporate your new insights and knowledge. Continue to update as you prepare for teaching. Save your materials for your portfolio.

Additional Reading

Intelligence Testing Feather, B., and Olson, W. S. *Children, psychology and the schools.* Glenview, Ill.: Scott, Foresman, 1969. See Section IV.

Ginsberg, H. *The myth of the deprived child: Poor children's intellect and education.* Englewood Cliffs, N.J.: Prentice-Hall, 1972.

Hoepfner, R., Stern, C., and Nummedal, S. G. *CSE-ECRC preschool/kindergarten test evaluations.* Los Angeles, Calif.: UCLA Graduate School of Education, 1971.

Horrocks, J. E., and Schoonover, T. I. *Measurement for teachers.* Columbus, Ohio: Charles E. Merrill, 1968.

Justman, J. Assessing the intelligence of disadvantaged children. *Education,* 1967, 87, 354–62.

Tarczan, C. *An educator's guide to psychological tests: Descriptions and classroom implications.* Springfield, Ill.: Charles C. Thomas, 1972.

SECTION
THREE
RESOURCEFULNESS

Teaching resourcefulness is the ability to provide children with experiences and instruction that match their needs, interests, and capabilities. The ability to assess these factors was the focus of the previous section. This section is designed to extend your repertoire for (1) providing activities for children, and (2) posing questions and making comments that advance their learning. It is our belief that the more extensive your repertoire for providing varied activities and instruction, the greater the likelihood of your being an effective teacher.

The activities included in this section are grouped as follows: (1) the manipulating of materials such as sand, water, clay, and blocks, (2) encounters with living creatures, (3) encounters with children's literature, (4) pretend play, and (5) sharing activities. Each of these topics is the focus of one chapter. Their choice is somewhat arbitrary on our part; other topics (such as music, art, and playground equipment) would be equally useful. The activities we have selected are typical of what is encountered with children regardless of the program structure or curriculum being used. The organization of the material within chapters is according to the developmental categories used in the prior section—motor and physical development, affective and social development, and cognitive and intellectual development. This should assist you in matching activities and instruction with your assessment of a child's developmental status and needs.

We do not believe that teachers' efforts to increase their resourcefulness need necessarily be tied to any particular organizational scheme. Although it is traditional to organize such training under subject matter "methods" categories, such as reading or mathematics, we believe that these tend to foster a "mental set" that is somehow apart from daily living situations. This detracts from the development of awareness of the many possibilities for learning that are always at hand. Although you will at some point in your preparation probably benefit from traditional methods training, we feel a better initial approach is one that fosters the broadest possible repertoire for teaching in varied everyday settings. We would propose, for example, that you could increase your resourcefulness by analyzing the contents of the various rooms in which you are currently living. The basic elements central to children's learning (such as variations in color, size, form, number, volume, and pattern) are all around you. The intent of this section is to make you sensitive to their presence as a result of habitually analyzing the teaching-learning possibilities around you. In Chapter 13 we discuss the application of your teaching resourcefulness to prepared curricula and within programs for various age levels.

CHAPTER 8
Resourcefulness
with
Manipulative Materials

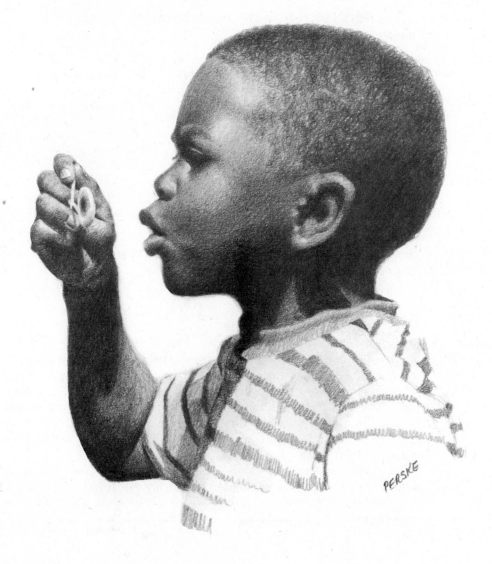

Overview

Your Resourcefulness and Children's Development

MANIPULATIVE MATERIALS: RELEVANCE FOR MOTOR DEVELOPMENT

MANIPULATIVE MATERIALS: RELEVANCE FOR AFFECTIVE AND SOCIAL DEVELOPMENT

MANIPULATIVE MATERIALS: RELEVANCE FOR COGNITIVE AND INTELLECTUAL DEVELOPMENT

Further Extensions and Applications

Summary

PREASSESSMENT

When you have completed this chapter you should be able to describe and compare the following:

1. *kinds of manipulative materials.*
2. *techniques for facilitating children's use of manipulative materials.*
3. *relevance of children's involvement with manipulative materials for motor, affective, social, and cognitive/intellectual development.*

Before beginning to read this chapter:

1. *take time enough to write what you currently know about each of the above topics.*
2. *reflect on the child or children you observed as you studied Section II; consider what your current repertoire is for involving this child (these children) with manipulative materials in ways that will enhance development.*

Save what you write for rereading, comparison, and elaboration after you have studied and discussed these materials.

Overview

Adaptability to developmental level

Materials such as sand, water, clay, and blocks offer rich learning possibilities for children. These unstructured materials take on whatever meaning and form a child imposes upon them, in contrast to most games and toys, which replicate something very specific in the real world. The child adapts unstructured materials to his or her own purposes, and consequently they are used in different ways at different points in development. A three-year-old, a five-year-old, and a seven-year-old will each use the same materials in quite different ways.

Although miniature toys, with their intricate replication of reality, immediately attract children, they tend to be quickly discarded or ignored. On the other hand, unstructured materials, which allow children the opportunity to explore and replicate reality according to their own perceptions, serve month after month and year after year. Dorothy Cohen (1972) points out the need to provide these kinds of materials for children who lack natural access to them:

> In the past parents bought their children the structured play materials, and the children found the unstructured ones in the natural world around them. Dirt, mud, sticks, stones, sand, clay, plant debris, and whatever else nature offers are all fair game for children's use. In industrialized, urban society such natural riches are harder for children to come by. Blocks, paint, manufactured clays, crayons, and various manipulative construction materials are the replacements both at home and at school for nature's gifts. (p. 91)

Symbolic representations of reality

The appeal of unstructured materials to children is undeniable, whether they are used at early ages or for very complex constructions as their abilities grow. Activity becomes increasingly elaborate and detailed as the children mature and become more experienced with the possibilities inherent in the material. When children construct a highway with a sand tunnel, or create a rain storm at the beach or water table, they symbolize these objects and events in their thinking. Sometimes their activity leads them to new discoveries. For example, as the sand caves in on the cars in the highway tunnel, they may begin to wonder what keeps the ground from falling on cars in real tunnels. As the incompleteness of their knowledge becomes apparent, their curiosity will lead them into more precise observations and further experimentation.

SETUPS FOR SAND, WATER, CLAY, AND BLOCKS

Sand

Basic Equipment
- Container—commercially sold sand table; wooden box lined with heavy plastic; child's small plastic swimming pool; plastic baby's bath; plastic dish pan; flat cardboard box (12″ × 8″ × 3″)
- Sand—beach quality, clean
- Boxes for storing accessories

Preferred Location

Locate where floor covering will be least likely to be damaged by sand, such as a cement area or outside; or use large plastic, canvas, or cloth sheeting with weighted corners under sand play area.

Accessories

Shovels (miniature), scoops, funnels, containers (varying sizes/some duplications), pans, measuring spoons, cups, plastic see-through containers, spoons, tin cans, gelatin molds, muffin tins, chunks of wood, beach rocks, large marbles, shells, string, miniature boats, trucks, cars, animals, rigid plastic tubing, magnifying glass, bottle caps, tongue depressors, rollers, balance scale, plastic letter forms, netting, cardboard tubing

General Guidelines
- Sometimes use sand dry; sometimes wet for contrasting experiences. Dry sand pours easily through tubing, sieves, sifters, funnels. Wet sand molds more easily and facilitates use of various-size containers to create different-size molds; use miniature toys, plastic letter forms, tongue depressors, etc. in making impressions.
- Keep accessories in boxes rather than in sand container. Take out only some accessories each day. Vary them to create fresh experiences.
- Set firm limits early for keeping sand in box, sand table, or whatever container is in use.
- Have floor brush and dustpan on hand and teach children how to use them to clean up spills.

Alternatives
- Rice or cracked corn or wheat, beans of various sizes, wood shavings, pebbles, sawdust, salt (large-grain variety) if you can keep it dry and covered between uses. For salt, a plastic cake pan (with cover) serves well for one child's use.
- Where climate permits, sand play may be predominantly an outside activity. Providing a variety of accessories is equally important, and there might be an additional need for larger containers such as pails and pans, and for tools such as hoes, shovels, and trowels.

Water

Basic Equipment
- Container—commercially sold water table; child's small plastic swimming pool; plastic baby's bath; dish pans; water pails; galvanized small tub
- Boxes for storing accessories
- Plastic or rubberized coverups for children to wear to keep their clothing dry

Preferred Location

Locate where dampness or spills will not damage surroundings, and close to sink or other water supply for ease of filling and emptying.

Accessories

Floating soap or soap flakes; measuring cups; funnels; plastic baster or other syringes; rotary eggbeater; pieces of hose; plastic squeeze bottles; blocks of wood; toy boats, animals, people, etc.; small watering can (spray attachment); plastic straws; floating/sinking objects—corks, sponges, wooden ball, hollow rubber ball, eraser, buttons, shells, etc.; food coloring; medicine droppers; clear rigid plastic tubing (6" to 24" long with varying diameters); marbles (giant size); tin cans (varying sizes); materials for boat making—aluminum foil, waxed paper, sticks, tongue depressors, manila paper, masking tape.

- Establish expectations with children that coverups will be worn for water play; be prepared to provide dry changes of clothing even with use of coverups.
- Drain water often, typically each day if water play is routinely available.
- Keep a small plastic pail and sponges on hand and teach children how to sponge up spilled water.

Alternatives
- If a large water table is routinely available, occasionally place small plastic dishpans in it so that children have individual spaces.
- On warm days outdoors provide a bucket of water and brushes. Children will create designs and intriguing effects as they "paint" with water on walls, sidewalks, play equipment, and bikes.
- Fill water table with ice, frost, or snow for variation in experiences.

Clay

Basic Equipment
- Clay-type material—ceramic potter's clay, salt clay or play dough, plasticene, sawdust mixed with wheat paste. *Note:* Potter's clay can be purchased ready for use in a sturdy plastic bag or it can be obtained in powdered form and mixed with water.
- Storage container with tightly fitting cover, such as crock, plastic garbage pail, or large covered bowl
- Masonite boards (about fifteen inches square)
- Coverups (aprons or smocks)

Preferred Location

Locate relatively close to water supply or sink for ease of cleanup, and away from games and other nonwashable materials.

Accessories

Tongue depressors; rollers (round wooden cylinders); cookie cutters; yarn; buttons; leather thongs (pieces); sturdy plastic knives and forks; scissors; table knives; wooden mallets; spools; blocks; bits of aluminum foil, waxed paper, or small pieces of plastic; cracked eggshells; toothpicks

General Guidelines
- When providing clay to children, test to see whether it is in malleable condition before giving it to them. Clay is used and reused by most young children without interest in creating a product to preserve. If potter's clay becomes dry, it can be reconditioned for further use. If it is at all malleable, mold it into small balls (tennis ball size), make an indentation in each ball with thumb, and place in storage container under wet toweling. Seal overnight or longer. Upon removal work it

well before providing for children. If the clay becomes too wet, leave cover off for a period of time and then rework. If it dries into hard, unmalleable lumps, place in a cloth bag and pound with hammer or other instrument until it is reduced to powder form, and then remoisten.

- When children reach the stage of wishing to preserve their products, potter's clay can be left to harden and can be fired, either with or without glaze, if a kiln is available. Pieces that are not fired tend to be very fragile, although they can be kept if children wish to care for them.
- Plasticene must be relatively warm to be usable by children. Store in a warm place, if possible, or warm through your own hand manipulations.
- Salt clay or play dough may be mixed from one cup salt, one cup flour, one tablespoon alum, and water sufficient to bring it to the consistency of putty. Food colorings can also be added. The products will eventually dry, but if the mass is very large the drying time is usually prohibitive.
- Place newspapers under the work areas to ease cleanup tasks, even when the clay is used on masonite boards.
- Distribute or set out clay in balls intended for individual use, but be prepared to "serve" more if a child has a project under way for which the allotment is insufficient.
- You may wish to encourage children to use clay by sitting with them and manipulating clay while they are working. Beware, however, of making representational objects that they might then try to imitate rather than attempting to develop their own ideas. In clay and other art media, children benefit most by representing their own perceptions and experiences.

Blocks

Basic Equipment
- Large wooden hollow blocks and auxiliary pieces; large cardboard hollow blocks; small unit blocks
- Open shelving for unit block storage

Preferred Location
- Locate in an out-of-the-way area so that those passing by will create minimal interference with construction activities.
- Carpeting can be used for noise reduction.

Accessories
- For use with larger constructions in which the children are themselves the users: large steering wheel affixed to sturdy base; large foam rubber balls; short pieces of rope; rug remnants; linoleum squares; pieces of sturdy cardboard; pieces of plexiglass; cardboard boxes (various sizes); boards; barrels

- For use in smaller constructions in which the children create miniature worlds and imaginatively manipulate the actions: colored cubes; pail of smooth beach stones; empty thread spools, empty tin cans; string; Easter grass; objects replicating those familiar to children, such as humans, animals, transportation, furniture, etc. *Note:* Children will be more likely to attempt representations of their own experience in block play if the accessories include toy replicas that are familiar to them. Buses, taxis, cranes, traffic officers, etc. may be most appropriate for urban children. Cows, sheep, horses, and pickup trucks might facilitate richer play in rural areas. Try to include regional and subcultural representational toys to the extent possible.

General Guidelines

- Arrange blocks in storage by size and shape. Place unit blocks in open shelving. Indicate the correct placement of the respective blocks by taped-on configurations.
- Expect that block structures will be regularly knocked down, both by accident and intentionally.
- Always give advance notice of the termination of an activity period in which there is block play under way. This will avert the disappointment of children who spend long periods of time preparing a construc-

RESPONSE SECTION

You have just been given guidelines for children's activities with sand, water, clay, and blocks. Before you read how a teacher can enhance the benefits of these materials for children, consider the following:

1. Try to think back to your own childhood experiences and recall the situations in which you played with sand, water, clay, blocks, or other construction or manipulative materials. Think about your feelings, problems, frustrations, and successes. Consider how adults interfered with or assisted your efforts, how environmental factors encouraged or discouraged you, etc.

2. If you have difficulty in recalling experiences of this kind from your childhood, consider why that might be the case. Do you think you actually did not engage in these kinds of activities? Or are there other reasons for your lack of recall?

3. What recent experiences have you had with media such as sand, water, clay, or construction materials? What were your feelings about these experiences?

4. If you lack enjoyable and rewarding experiences with such materials either in your early years or in recent years, how might you now develop an appreciation of their benefits so that you can more enthusiastically provide them for children?

tion in anticipation of a particular kind of play, only to have the actual play abruptly canceled.

- Block cleanup can be made fun and interesting through the use of one of the following techniques: say to the children, "You bring them to me and I'll put them away," or vice versa; assign particular children to bring all blocks of a given size; sing or play a lively record to accompany cleanup.

Alternatives
- Use cardboard cartons, taped tightly closed, as a substitute for large blocks.
- Use cardboard milk cartons, washed and trimmed to angular shape, as substitutes for cardboard hollow blocks. Cover with adhesive shelf covering.

Your Resourcefulness and Children's Development

As you read this chapter, try to attune yourself to the many possibilities that unstructured materials afford. To make the study particularly meaningful, we suggest that you actively search through the ideas and suggestions to locate those that would be good matches for the interest levels of the children for whom you prepared behavioral assessments in Section Two.

MANIPULATIVE MATERIALS: RELEVANCE FOR MOTOR DEVELOPMENT

Gross motor activities Large muscle activities are predominant in block play and in outdoor sand play. For example, if there is any opportunity to do so, children will constantly transport sand and large blocks and, in the process, will develop strength, balance, endurance, and broadened action repertoires. They gradually increase their ability to perform these actions with ease and agility. The tasks of lifting, pulling, and pushing are practiced initially as separate endeavors and are then gradually interwoven into more complex play actions.

To further encourage gross motor involvement, you may wish to use the following types of arrangements and activities with manipulative materials:

- Arrange storage of blocks so that some are as high as children can reach and others are low, to mandate reaching and bending.
- Use blocks to build bins for target shooting with bean bags or foam rubber balls. Mark a starting line on the floor (with masking tape) and let the children "shoot." Lengthen the distance between bin and starting line to increase the difficulty of the task.
- When you are filling or emptying the water table or washing the clay or painting tables, a few helping children can be encouraged to engage in water carrying activities. If suitable containers are provided in outside water areas, children will spontaneously become involved in carrying and balancing tasks. Expect spills, of course!

Photo by John James.

- Erect a pulley system that children can use for transporting blocks placed in a sling or blanket, or pails of sand (outside).
- Blocks can periodically be used along with other materials (such as large cardboard boxes, hoops, chairs, and tables) to create "obstacle" courses. Masking tape or string can be used to mark the trail to be followed through the series of obstacles. To follow the trail children might need to crawl over objects or through, under, around, and between them. Large wooden hollow blocks can be used with the longest unit blocks to create tunnels, arches, and steps.
- Children can be encouraged to construct and use a series of blocks in the form of walking rails. The blocks can be placed end to end to provide narrow or wide ridges, or a combination if you are uncertain about the difficulty level. Children can be encouraged to try to walk forward, backward, sideways, halfway, and all the way. This provides excellent practice in balance and motor control.
- Arrange two outdoor sand areas, close together but with one higher than the other. Provide boards for the construction of inclined planes, and wagons or wheelbarrows, and place steps between the levels.

Small muscle activities   As children use sand, water, clay, and blocks, they also quite spontaneously engage in activities that foster small muscle development. Especially when an abundance of varied accessories is available, children gradually extend their repertoire and skill. The following arrangements can prove particularly useful in encouraging children to engage in actions that improve eye-hand coordination and small muscle control.

- For sand play, be sure to provide sifters, sieves, scoops, various-size containers, funnels, and miniature toys, cars, trucks, people, etc.
- For water play, provide cups, spoons, various-size containers, basters, funnels, tongs, rigid plastic tubing, and rotary beaters. As children use these tools they become more precise and skilled in their movements. Encourage precision and experimentation with suggestions such as, "Can you pour like that into the bowl from way up high?" and "Can you fill this bottle with the watering can without spilling any water?"
- With clay activities, provide tongue depressors, wooden meat skewers (with points blunted), or other marking tools. Comment on the "marks" children make with these tools, such as "I see you are making curvy lines," or "Those crisscross lines look interesting." Or if a tool is used for cutting, you might say, "I see that you have two pieces now that you cut that in half," or "Oh, look, you made a square when you cut off those curved edges."
- When children are playing with dry sand, encourage experimentation with different actions by asking, "How many different ways could you get sand in that bowl [or whatever container is in use]?" Suggest ways the child has not thought of, such as scooping with hands, scooping with spoon, scooping with another container, through a funnel, through a tube, etc.

These ideas are not intended to include all of the things that might be done to promote motor development in the context of children's use of manipulative materials; they simply illustrate some of the possibilities. Once you become aware of how children quite spontaneously become involved in motor activities with sand, water, clay, and blocks, you will undoubtedly think of many additional ways to extend these activities.

MANIPULATIVE MATERIALS: RELEVANCE FOR AFFECTIVE AND SOCIAL DEVELOPMENT

Tension-reducing activities

Manipulative materials are useful in helping anxious children to relax or angry children to settle down. Concentration on the responsive material and their own manipulation of it can help children regain their composure. To calm an angry child or relax a tense one, suggest water play, or ask for help in washing tables with warm, sudsy water. Show the child how to use a sponge in *both* soaking up and letting out water. Demonstrate procedures such as wetting the sponge, large muscle scrubbing, bringing in water, and rewetting the sponge, and notice whether the child's tensions dissipate as he or she becomes involved in these actions.

Sometimes the amorphous manipulative materials serve as targets of feelings generated in other situations. For example, you may note that children quite spontaneously use clay as the object of their aggressive feelings. You may also be able to encourage a child who appears to be having a series of pugnacious encounters to use clay for this purpose, perhaps by saying, "This clay would do better if it was worked around a bit." You might punch it vigorously yourself a few times and then ask, "Would you like to pound this up until it is mixed very well?" Praise vigorous slapping and pounding, saying, "Good, that should be better mixed now."

At other times children may use the materials to enact a situation that has created conflict. A child who is feeling angry about his or her treatment from others may retaliate in vigorous representational play—with blocks, clay, or sand—in which something or someone really "gets it."

The unstructured quality of these manipulative materials makes them especially useful for the indirect expression of affective states. Teachers may wish at some point to help a child broaden his or her repertoire for dealing with problem situations that have generated tensions and anger, but the immediate value of manipulative materials for indirect emotional release should not be overlooked.

Since there is no right or wrong way to use manipulative materials, especially water and sand, these materials—more than structured toys such as tricycles, dominoes, puzzles, or dolls—allow a child who lacks confidence to experience satisfaction. The following techniques may therefore be appropriate to use with children whose abilities to initiate activities and to be independently involved are not well developed:

• Go with the child to the water or sand area and begin to play there yourself. Smile and praise the child if he or she begins to use the materials. Continue frequent visual contact, smiling and offering periodic comment as long as the child remains occupied. Make your attention contingent on continued activity. With an initial positive experience built upon adult support and attention, the child is likely to find that this type of involvement is within his or her repertoire, and he or she will therefore be likely to independently initiate involvement on subsequent occasions.
• For a child who has only used water or sand play, suggest other manipulative materials (such as blocks, clay, or painting) rather than an activity that would require more specific skills, especially those involving social interactions.
• After children, especially those who lack confidence, have created a block structure or some other similar product, ask if they would like to see themselves with the work. Hold a mirror (preferably the large, stand-up, metal variety) so they can see themselves standing beside it. Or take a Polaroid picture.

Contact with manipulative materials can facilitate more comprehensive participation for the hesitant child. The teacher must get the child to handle the materials initially and then to follow up with warm attention and quiet praise. Since all levels of performance are well integrated in manipulative

Photo by John James.

play, children are very likely to see their efforts as quite adequate when viewed positively by others.

Multiple levels of social interaction   Social interactions between children when they are using manipulative materials range from early parallel and associative play to the most advanced cooperative play activity. The myriad possibilities for working together, especially with sand, clay, and blocks, can incorporate very advanced social functioning. Children who have not been involved with peers often have first contacts at the water table or sand area. As they work side by side, one child's action frequently leads to imitation or comment by others and subsequently to increased interaction and joint activity.

Play activities with manipulative materials can also lead to interpersonal conflicts and other social problems, thereby providing opportunities for helping children develop their social sensitivity and problem-solving abilities. The following types of teaching strategies are among those that may prove useful in this regard:

• Demonstrate to children alternative behaviors for obtaining a particular material that someone else is using, instead of grabbing, crying, or other relatively ineffective behaviors. These possibilities might include asking the other child if they can use it; trading something else for it; looking for something like it; waiting; getting the other child more interested in another activity; or finding a good substitute. If they fail to understand the basic idea of having different options for their actions, concentrate first on developing such concepts as *and, or, same,* and *different* with the concrete manipulative materials. Suggest, "There is a shovel *and* a hoe," "We have blocks this size *and* blocks this size. Which do you want?", "Do you want to shovel in the sand *or* do you want to swing?", "You have a big pail. Do you want the *same* kind or do you want a *different* kind next?", or "You usually play in sand first when you come to school. Today you are doing something different." When you have evidence that children understand the meanings of these terms in regard to their materials and their actions with materials, you may also be successful in helping them apply those terms in their thinking about alternative social behaviors. To make them more aware of their actions, ask, "Do you want to ask Jimmy for it *or* do you want to wait?", or "That didn't work, did it? Is there a *different* way you could do it?"

- If children become bothersome by knocking down others' block structures, suggest alternative activities, such as building their own structures for the express purpose of knocking them down; trying to build structures that are very easy to knock down and some that are so strong that it is almost impossible to knock them down (show them how the base is essential to a building's stability); standing blocks up on end like bowling pins and trying to knock them down with balls or bean bags.
- After children engage in an alternative behavior, explain why that is better than their previous actions, and praise this current activity.
- Watch for the positive alternatives employed by children in solving social conflicts. Make sure that the other children understand the nature of the conflict and are aware of the original, inappropriate behavior as well as the substitute behavior you are praising.

MANIPULATIVE MATERIALS: RELEVANCE FOR COGNITIVE AND INTELLECTUAL DEVELOPMENT

The opportunities for helping children develop cognitively and intellectually are particularly abundant when they are using manipulative materials. Children will benefit if their teachers have a broad and varied repertoire for furthering development in each of the following areas.

Classification, seriation, number

Manipulative materials and the accessories used with them offer many diverse opportunities for classifying, ordering, counting, grouping, regrouping, and various numerical operations. The following are among the possibilities:

- Help children classify blocks by size as they put them away—all large cylinders on this block shelf, smaller cylinders here, the longest blocks on another shelf.

- Commercial unit blocks are carefully graduated in size, which facilitates learning. They can be sorted according to size or ordered in sequence to form "stairsteps." Smaller units can be combined to replace larger ones, while the teacher says, "This is half as big as that. I'll need two of the smallest ones to match it."
- If you provide a variety of containers for use with wet sand, children will be able to make forms of various sizes and shapes, such as round, square, flat, tall, big and round, little and round, etc. These provide the opportunity for labeling and classification.
- With tweezers or kitchen tongs and objects in sand or water, the child can become involved in classification activities such as those involved in picking up "everything that is red" or "everything that floats." Through conversational interchange, descriptors and classifications can be modeled very effectively, such as by saying, "There, you got that large blue boat. Now can you pick up the little red one?"
- In using water, children will soon learn that items such as a cloth, sponge, or paper towel will soak up water, whereas others will not. The classification of a group of things according to which are absorbent and which are not might be insightful to older children.
- As more mature children construct block buildings, ask about the kinds they are making. Talk with them about other kinds of buildings, such as those for living in, for storage, for selling, for making things, for conducting schools, and for caring for sick people.
- If children are pretending that materials such as water and clay are other things, help them extend their thinking even further; for example, if they are serving "Coca Cola" in pretend play with water, ask for something else to drink besides Coca Cola. See what they can think of and then mention others as well, such as orange juice, milk, or root beer. Or if you are served a pretend apple made of clay, ask whether they have additional fruits to go with the apple. Start with their "pretend" item and try to extend their awareness of other items within the same category.
- Provide smooth, weathered sticks or beach stones of differing sizes, and encourage children to place them in order according to length, size, and weight.
- As a child is manipulating clay, note what he or she is making and draw comparisons. Say, for example, "You have such a big round shape. That's the shape of a cookie. It's the shape of a plate too. And let's see, what else?" If the child does not contribute, continue, "The clock face is sort of like that, isn't it? So is the dial on the telephone. So is the top of that can."
- Children will quite spontaneously make piles and rows of blocks, mounds of sand, series of clay balls, etc., all of which can be noted, counted, and described: "You have two blocks here and three blocks there," and as the child places another with the two: "Now you have the same number in each group." As he or she places another: "Now they have different numbers. There are more in that pile." By reacting to children's manipulations you can reinforce those concepts they have not yet mastered, such as *more, same, less,* and *different.*

- Sifting objects out of sand is particularly intriguing to the child who has only a meager sense of cause and effect. Counting how many objects are thus retrieved on each sifting is also fun: "That time you got two feathers, three shells, and a piece of string. Let's see how many things that is altogether."
- Supplying real candles or small sticks along with wet sand or clay on a child's birthday will almost inevitably lead to cake making. This allows all kinds of discussion about topics such as how many candles various cakes have, how many years older six is than four, and how many more candles you need for a "four-year-old" cake if you already have two. If a teacher then makes a numeral to match the number of candles on each cake, children can begin to make associations between numerals and counting.
- When children are using blocks, look for opportunities to initiate counting as the blocks are distributed, stacked, and replaced. And use chances to divide blocks, saying, "One for Jim. One for Jack. . . ." Point out the equality of the groups formed in this way.
- With blocks, also look for opportunities to ask children questions such as, "*How many more* do you want?", or "Do you want me to hand you big blocks *first* or do you want *little* ones first and big ones last?"
- Children involved in playing with clay will often place their objects in one-to-one correspondence—a cookie for everyone at the table, a hat for every snowman, a banana on every plate. Note and encourage this, especially if it is not typical for the given child. Point out to younger or less mature children what others have placed in one-to-one correspondence.
- If children become engaged in activities such as shooting bean bags or foam rubber balls into bins constructed with blocks (as suggested earlier), they might enjoy keeping score as follows:

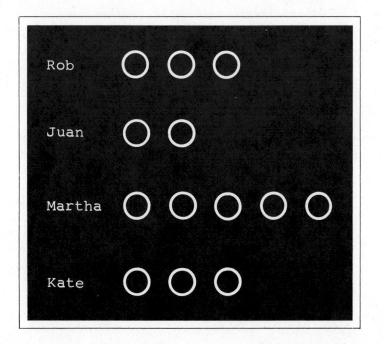

- Children create wares, which they pretend to sell; blocks are sometimes used as hot dogs, clay as cookies, water as lemonade. This simple dramatic play provides a good opportunity to increase number awareness by asking about cost and then very elaborately counting out money (made from other blocks, bits of paper, etc.). Comments can accompany the interchanges, such as, "I owe you three cents for the other one, right?", "Let's see, that's one, two, three, four, five, six. Is that right?", or "I have only two cents left. What can I buy for that?"

TEACHING STYLES

Hess and Shipman (1965, 1967) investigated the differing styles of middle- and lower-class mothers in teaching their children to perform toy and block sorting tasks. The more successful mothers tended to rely on praise and on engaging the interest of the child in the activity, rather than on coercion. While mothers in general made greater use of coercive control than of attempts to interest children, only the middle-class mothers used techniques other than coercion.

Differences were also noted in mothers' abilities to abstract the essentials of the task, to communicate them in words their children understood, and to interpret and respond to the behaviors of their children. The successful mothers appeared able to make an analysis of the task, abstracting the essentials into an organized sequence of subparts leading to the ability to sort. They transmitted necessary information early in the task, engaged in an interaction in which the child participated actively, asked questions, and generally showed evidence of involvement. The less successful mothers failed to provide labels for sorting criteria, either in initial instructions or in feedback.

For insights into teaching-learning interactions between adults and preschool children, you may wish to study the examples of successful and unsuccessful teaching strategies provided in the Hess and Shipman research reports.

Mass and liquid quantity

Conservation insights Children need many experiences in observing through their own manipulations the reversibility of liquids and other substances. Until they have accrued sufficient experience and maturity to hold in mind how the thing was before being transferred to another container (in the case of liquid and sand) or manipulated into another shape (in the case of clay), they will deny or doubt the sameness of its quantity. They will declare it to be either "more" or "less," depending on how it appears. Although most children will not fully develop these conservation insights until age six or seven or later, prerequisite understandings are being accrued in the child's play with unstructured materials throughout the early years. Conservation cannot be imparted by teaching; it is gradually acquired through the child's own activities and observations. Through the following arrangements, however, the likelihood of involvements leading to conservation are enhanced.

• For sand and water play, make sure that some containers have a definite relationship to others; for example, one might hold exactly twice as much as another. Also try to have two or more different shapes that hold the same amount. Observe and question children to help them discover these relationships and use the terms for describing what they discover, such as "twice as much" and "half as much."
• Encourage children to count the number of times they use a small container to fill a large one. They could be helped to make a chart that shows what they have discovered.

It takes 6 little cans

to fill one big bowl.

• Encourage children to figure out which container in a set holds the most water or sand. Help them label each according to the number of cups it holds.
• A child who has shown considerable interest in learning how many small containers are required to fill a larger one might be led to first guess

(estimate) how many, before figuring out the actual number.

- If you supply a large and sturdy homemade balance scale for use with blocks, clay, sand, and water, those children who already have some awareness of conservation of mass and liquid quantity can experiment with balancing different sizes and shapes of containers to find further confirmations of weight variance despite variations in appearance.

Causality

What children typically learn about cause and effect are specific associations: "If you do this, that will happen." Most young children appear cognitively incapable of either **inductive thinking** or **deductive thinking**. By acquiring many sets of specific associations during their early years, children build up an experience base that will eventually help them master the notion of predictability. To provide this kind of experience base, the following sorts of activities may prove useful.

An experience base

- Let children help make play dough. Make sure they note the appearance, feel, and smell of the ingredients prior to and throughout the process of mixing. Before adding the water to the salt and flour, ask, "What do you think will happen when we add the water?" Note with them the change from dry to lumpy to sticky. Later ask, "Can you remember what we did to make the clay?"

Play Dough

flour

salt

food coloring

water

Mix it all together.

- Let children help you smash up the pieces of hardened potter's clay (in a cloth bag) with wooden mallet or sturdy wooden block, to prepare it for reuse. Let them also assist you in adding water, stirring, kneading, and inspecting to see if the clay has reached a desired consistency.
- Encourage children to make various-size holes in paper cups for use with sand and water. Note with them the sizes of the streams of water or sand that escape through the holes. Lead them to predict and then experiment to find out which varieties of small objects will wash through different-size holes and which will be caught and retained in the cup through repeated washings.
- For water play, prepare a set of tin cans of identical size and that have "leaks" of various sizes in various positions. Make one with a large hole, one with a small hole, one with several fine holes, and one with two holes of different sizes. Other cans might have different numbers of small holes punched into the side. *Note:* Stuff can with paper or cloth to prevent collapse while hammering holes.
- Both sand and water play lead children into experiences with gravity and centrifugal force, and teachers can sometimes help extend this interest. For example, if some of the tin cans with holes positioned in different locations (as described above) are suspended from strings, the differences in their rotation as water is poured into them may encourage experimentation. If a small windmill, pinwheel, or waterwheel is provided, children will delight in using falling water and sand to make it go around. Observing water

running downhill often leads to experimentation with dams, waterfalls, and channels.

- In water play, as children are tipping containers underwater, point out the bubbles of escaping air. Ask, "I wonder if you could hold your bottle in a way so you could make big bubbles?", or "Can you make little bubbles?"
- If children are supplied with a magnifying glass while playing with sand, they might enjoy examining sand crystals. The source of the sand may be of interest to some children, especially if different types of sand from different sources are available for close examination.
- Provide the children with sandstone for examination. If mallets are also available, they can pound the sandstone into a sand, which could be added to the sand table after thorough washing.
- Blocks or block structures (and objects such as sticks or dowels), when stuck into sand or clay, cast shadows in different directions and of different lengths according to their distance from the light source. Experimentation in creating shadows of different lengths and shapes can follow. Outside shadows can then become the subject of careful observation across different points of the day as well, as in Beatrice Schenk de Regnier's *The Shadow Book* (New York: Harcourt Brace Jovanovich, 1960).
- For more mature six- and seven-year-olds, combine water and clay play with the challenge, "Can you make a clay boat that will float?" If children can successfully do this, let each test his or her boat to see how many paper clips (or similar light objects) the boat can take aboard, and in what position, without sinking.
- Children will experiment with sounds of water splashing or being poured, blocks bumping together and against other objects, and clay as it is pounded against various surfaces and with varying intensity. Encourage this experimentation by suggesting significant variations, such as filling containers to different levels and then striking with other objects (such as a digging spoon, wooden stick, or block), or arranging blocks according to length to produce a xylophone effect.

In each of these instances children are gaining a greater awareness of specific causal relationships. As they acquire a rich base of these kinds of associations, they will be better prepared to appreciate the general rules at some later point in development. Without specific associations from personal experience to use as a basis for drawing conclusions, magical and intuitive thinking patterns will tend to persist.

Space concepts

Some of the most useful experiences children can have in developing spatial orientations come through manipulations of concrete materials. As children build low block barricades around themselves and then add even more *Object* blocks to make enclosures with walls as high as they can reach, they gain *manipulation* valuable perspectives. They learn how large a space must be in order for them to go through it or take other objects through it. They learn that when the largest blocks have been used, several smaller ones can be combined and substituted. And as children build roads, lakes, and towns for their toy cars and people, using sand, water, and clay, they quite literally become cartographers. As a teacher, you can extend these experiences in the following ways.

- Space concepts such as *inside, outside, around,* or *between* are natural learnings in sand and block play. For example, as children engage in activities such as constructing barriers to contain the turtle they have found, you can help them learn the vocabulary that describes their actions through your commentary, such as "Do you think he will be able to go *between* those two blocks?", "Who ever would have thought he could climb *over* that block? Why, it's as high as he is!", or "I see you are making a tunnel for the turtle to crawl *through.*"
- If a child is stretched out on the floor in the block area, place one block on all four sides to mark "how big he [she] is" and invite him or her to look. Or involve children in placing blocks at distances they think will allow them to lie down between them. Ask, "How far do you think it is from your head to your feet?" When the blocks are placed you might wish to more permanently mark the child's size by replacing each block with masking tape on which you write the child's name. You might also give the children string, which you and they can measure out to be just their height.

Photo by John Young.

- As a child manipulates a miniature horse or other type of toy along a sand trail, you can describe the actions using space vocabulary. For example, "I wonder how *far* that rider is going? There she goes *around* the bend and *over* the hill. Here she comes to the crossroads. She's making a turn to the *right*. And another turn to the *right*. And another, and here she is back where she started. You know, she went in a *square*."
- If children have constructed what amounts to a three-dimensional map using sand or blocks, examine it admiringly and ask where various things are in relation to each other; you might wish to photograph or sketch it as the children watch. You might also involve them in trying to determine distances and perspectives, saying, for example, "Suppose the driver of that jeep ran out of gas right where he is, what would he do? Would he go back into town or go this way to the airport?", and "Why do you think it would be better for him to do that?"
- The opportunities for sign making in sand play or in unit block play are vast. Directional signs are usually made by or at the request of the children and are helpful in language learning, in spatial orientation, and in considering perspectives other than one's own.

Time concepts

Sequence of activity

Children's involvement with manipulative materials provides a meaningful context for helping them become more aware of time sequences and ways to describe the passage of time. For example, simply reiterating to them what they did first, next, and last while creating a clay form or a block scene is helpful. The following suggestions exemplify other possibilities.

- Look for opportunities to relate children's current activities with what they have done previously. Use terms such as *yesterday, last week, this morning, last year,* or *in the fall.* For example, say, "Remember when you made strawberry shortcakes from clay *last week.* You made a big one, a little one, and a middle-size one. And *yesterday* you made big-, little-, and middle-size bowls like the three bears. *Today* I see you are making something in three sizes again!"
- Help children keep track of time as they wait for potter's clay or salt clay products to harden. For example, say, "Let's see, you made this on *Monday.* Then *yesterday* was *Tuesday* and *today* is *Wednesday.* Let's check it *today.* You might have to wait until *tomorrow* but it should be dry before *Friday.* I'm sure of that. It usually takes three or four *days.*"

Spoken language

Vocabulary and concept learning

The ability to "teach" while talking naturally about children's activities is the real essence of resourcefulness. A resourceful teacher can make an exciting learning experience out of the most insignificant events—a lost mitten, too much milk money, a dripping faucet. Almost any situation contains stimuli capable of provoking learning in children. You can improve your ability to enhance children's language development by noting the rich possibilities contained in the dialogue accompanying manipulative activities.

- With block play, look for opportunities to use words such as *more, fewer, same, tall, taller, short, shorter, high, higher, wide, many, several, long, even, uneven, same, different, and, or, first, next, last,* etc.
- With water play, look for opportunities to use words such as *dry, wet, soaked, damp, how much, full, empty, thin, wide, deep, shallow, fast, slow, float, sink, evaporate,* etc.
- With sand play, look for opportunities to use words such as *damp, dry, sprinkle, pack, rough, smooth, wide, narrow, thin, thick, short, tall, round, curved, straight, flat, full, empty, half full, half empty, heavy, light, how much, fine, coarse, deep, shallow,* etc.
- In using balance scales with water, blocks, clay, or sand use words such as *heavy, heavier, light, lighter, balanced, more, less, same, fewer, how many, how much,* etc.
- Ask questions such as, "Is your clay too hard, too soft, or just right?", "How much water should we add to this salt clay—just a little, a cupful, or a half cupful?", and "What size trucks do you want for your highway?"
- Children like to hide things in sand for others to find. Encourage them to verbally describe something about the object they have hidden to allow guesses as to its identity before you or another child begin to look for it.
- Particular kinds of vocabulary can be encouraged by the kinds of "props" provided for sand and water play. Funnels, tubing, and containers encourage terms such as *into, out of, through,* and *half full.* Containers of three different sizes enable discussion of *smallest, middle size, largest, more,* and *less.*

Many children who have retarded speech development or who lack confidence in their talking abilities can be more effectively helped while they are happily involved with play materials than in a special "instructional" session. For example, it might be useful to place at the water and sand areas accessories and toy objects whose names or descriptions require sounds that are difficult for a particular child. It is often easier to model the correct pronunciation and to engage the child in producing these sounds in informal, nonpressured situations. While children are involved in play with sand, water, or clay it is often possible to provide elaborations of sentences and phrases and to ask them questions that encourage a more precise language expression than they typically attempt. Ask open-ended questions such as, "What are you going to do now?"

Written language

Visual discrimination learnings The visual discrimination abilities prerequisite to success in reading develop as children sort blocks and compare and match identical accessories (buttons, cups, etc.). The following types of activities are among those that are especially helpful in leading children to look for visual similarities and differences.

- Roll out a clay slab of any size and shape and provide an assortment of small objects, such as blocks, spools, buttons, straws, pieces of wire screening, coins, paper clips, and old keys. Encourage children, especially pre-readers, to make imprints on the flat surface. Help them note which ones look alike, and which are different. Later, have them match the objects with the imprints.

- For children becoming familiar with letter forms, provide a set of small plastic lower-case and upper-case letters for making imprints on clay slabs, as described above.
- Help children become aware of the features of repetitive patterns, such as a series of lines or markings that either you or they make in sand or in clay. Help them note whether there is continuous repetition of one figure or whether there is an alternation of two or more figures or movements. Encourage children to try to continue with simple repetitive patterns that you have started.
- Children who are becoming interested in letter forms might enjoy fitting narrow coils of clay to cover the outlines of letter forms you provide on cardboard. While they are in the process of making a coil replica of the letters, you can talk with them about the letter name and features or words that use the letter (such as names of persons they know or words they are especially intrigued by). Their visual attention to the letters will lead to a more precise awareness of letter forms.

Many opportunities for recording ideas in writing are related to play with sand, water, clay, or blocks. Whether children remember the words or not, the more words they see, the more they will understand that the written

Aa	Bb	Cc	Dd	Ee
Ff	Gg	Hh	Ii	Jj
Kk	Ll	Mm	Nn	Oo
Pp	Qq	Rr	Ss	Tt
Uu	Vv	Ww	Xx	Yy
		Zz		

word represents the spoken word, that words are definite units, and that words are written and read in a left-to-right direction. Consider the following possibilities for involving children in written language.

- Invite children to dictate stories to you about their block structures or other products of their manipulative materials. Print clearly in lower-case and upper-case letters. If children are not yet aware of the need to match their talking speed with your writing speed as they dictate, take down rough notes, and then carefully print out what is said and read it back, "to be sure you have it right." A Polaroid photograph to go with the dictated story would add to its continued appeal.
- Look for opportunities to make signs to embellish block structures. The builder of a hot dog stand, for example, would likely appreciate having the name of the business and a listing of wares and prices printed out on signs, or perhaps having messages to customers placed on signs.
- While with children during sand play, you might write their names or other personal messages, such as "I like Becky," in the sand. If they are interested, read, discuss, point out words and similar letters, and cross out and change parts ("I like Sally") for as long as their interest is maintained.

Whenever you are doing the kind of writing for children described above, try to print their exact words. Be sure to read it back to the child when you finish writing. Depending on the child's awareness of word forms, point out similarities between words and identical words. Help the child to locate his name and any other high-interest word that appears in the writing. Try to make sure that others note and appreciate the messages that the words represent.

You should also encourage children's efforts to engage in writing activities themselves. The following are some possible ways for doing so:

- Involve children in putting their names on papers and beneath their clay products (or other expressive products) to the extent that they are able. This may involve writing a child's entire name, making all but a few difficult letters, or making one part of one letter. If necessary, make a model (showing only one letter at a time) for them to copy, or write (again one letter or stroke at a time) very faintly on the paper so that the child can mark over it. The important thing is to give the child a feeling of being a writer, a successful writer. As you write the letters for beginners, sometimes discuss their features; for example, say, "The *l*'s in your name are just tall straight lines, aren't they, Bill?", or "That is an interesting letter, isn't it, Meg? Look how it goes straight down and then curves up under itself."
- Comment appreciatively on forms, letters, numerals, and symbols that children form on sand or clay. Note especially the aspects that are correctly formed. You might comment, "That's almost a perfect *s*, Sally," or "I can tell that's an *H*, Hank." Only if the child is proficient and secure in his or her writing abilities will you find it helpful to note letter reversals or other errors.

You have been presented with scores of suggestions, both general and specific, for the use of manipulative materials to enhance children's learning and development. Out of these many alternatives, identify the ten that you feel would be most appropriate for each of the children you observed in your study of Section Two. Browse back through the suggestions under motor, emotional, social, and cognitive/intellectual development and draw out, modify, and/or enlarge on specific suggestions until you are well satisfied that your sets of ten manipulative activities would be appropriate "matches" for the developmental levels of the respective children.

For each of the items you have identified, try to determine whether the activity would provide a new opportunity for the application of acquired skills and concepts, the development of new skills and concepts, or both.

Further Extensions and Applications

This chapter has provided numerous suggestions of how children's development can be facilitated through the active manipulation of sand, water, clay, and blocks. We hope that these presentations have attuned you to the educational possibilities of these and of other similar materials.

Table toys
The same kinds of activities suggested here can also be very appropriate for the host of manipulative and construction materials that are sometimes referred to as "table toys." Included among this group are items such as Tinker Toys, Lincoln logs, counting blocks, parquetry blocks, dominoes, design cubes, marbles, checkers, Cuisenaire rods, attribute blocks, Lego blocks, mosaic shapes, peg boards, and nuts and bolts (assorted sizes). Each of these can serve many of the same functions and be used in the same ways as blocks.

Natural materials and industrial castoffs
Many other materials can serve some of the same functions. Some of these are natural materials readily available in many outdoor situations, such as mud, leaves, rocks, plant debris, and snow. Other manipulative objects can be obtained in industrial and commercial settings, such as barrels, packing cases, ladders, bricks, cement blocks, tires, planks, cardboard cartons, styrofoam packing materials, cardboard tubes, pipes and pipe fittings, pails, hoses, and baskets.

Whether manipulative materials are natural or manufactured, free or costly, they offer wide opportunities for children's learning; any teacher should continue to extend his or her repertoire for using these materials to stimulate particular learnings and skill development in children.

Summary

The use of unstructured manipulative materials changes with children's development. The nature of these materials allows the imposition of increasingly elaborate use as children move to higher levels of conceptual and physical development. Without adult assistance and intervention, there are benefits to children from access to sand, water, blocks, clay, and similar materials; with skillful arrangements of materials and appropriate commentary from adults, the benefits increase.

Large block play and outdoor sand play can especially contribute to gross motor development. Challenges for small muscle manipulation can be heightened by the skillful introduction of tools and other props and through verbal recognition and encouragement of their varied uses.

Tensions are lessened through concentration on the manipulation of materials such as water and sand. Concerns can be actively explored through projective activity, and children's repertoires for resolving conflicts can be extended in the context of activities with these materials.

The use of manipulative materials provides especially abundant possibilities for experiencing classification, seriation, and number groupings; for assessing quantity, causality, and space and time concepts; and for oral and written communication. Whatever children's functioning level in these categories of cognitive and intellectual development, there are varied opportunities for enhancing and extending their understanding.

The involvements and learnings provided by the four materials discussed in this chapter can also be provided through the small manipulative materials referred to as "table toys," through many natural materials available in the outdoor environment, and through industrial and commercial castoffs.

REASSESSMENT

Reread what you wrote for the preassessment as you began this chapter, comparing this with your current understandings. Now write on these topics again and incorporate your new insights and knowledge. Continue to update as you prepare for teaching. Save your materials for your portfolio.

Additional Reading

Manipulative Play   Anker, D., Foster, J. McLane, J., Sobel, J., and Weissbourd, B. Teaching children as they play. *Young Children,* 1974, 29, 203–13.

Blum, S. Puddles: Other than wet feet and the sniffles, what are they good for? *Learning,* 1975, 3, 22–25.

de Regnier, B. S. *The Shadow Book.* New York: Harcourt Brace Jovanovich, 1960.

Elementary Science Study. *Teacher's guide to geo blocks.* New York: Webster/McGraw-Hill, 1969.

Elementary Science Study. *Teacher's guide for pattern blocks.* New York: Webster/McGraw-Hill, 1970.

Hammerman, A., and Morse, S. Open teaching: Piaget in the classroom. *Young Children*, 1972, 28, 41–54.

Hawkins, F. P. *The logic of action: Young children at work*. New York: Pantheon, 1969.

Lorton, M. B. *Work jobs*. Reading, Mass.: Addison-Wesley, 1972.

Seefeldt, C. Boxes are to build . . . a curriculum. *Young Children*, 1972, 28, 5–12.

Sharp, E. *Thinking is child's play*. New York: E. P. Dutton, 1970.

Whiren, A. Table toys: The underdeveloped resource. *Young Children*, 1975, 30, 413–19.

Sand Activities   Elder, C. Z. Miniature sand environments: A new way to see and feel and explore. *Young Children*, 1973, 28, 283–6.

Elementary science study. *Teacher's guide for sand*. New York: Webster/McGraw-Hill, 1970.

NAEYC publication. *Water, sand and mud as play materials*. Washington, D.C.: National Association for Education of Young Children, 1959.

Water Activities   Boys, C. V. *Soap bubbles: Their colors and forces which mold them*. New York: Dover, 1959.

Eggleston, P. J., and Weir, M. K. Water play for preschoolers. *Young Children*, 1975, 31, 5–11.

Elementary science study. *Teacher's guide for sink or float*. New York: Webster/McGraw-Hill, 1971.

Simon, S. *Soap bubbles*. New York: Hawthorne Books, 1969.

Clay Activities   Elementary science study. *Teacher's guide for clay boats*. New York: Webster/McGraw-Hill, 1971.

Block Activities   Cartwright, S. Blocks and learning. *Young Children*, 1974, 29, 141–6.

Hirsh, E. S. *The block book*. Washington, D.C.: National Association for the Education of Young Children, 1974.

Johnson, H. *The art of blockbuilding*. New York: Bank Street College of Education, 1945.

Robinson, H. F., and Spodek, B. *New directions in the kindergarten*. New York: Teacher's College Press, 1965.

Starks, E. B. *Blockbuilding*. Washington, D.C.: American Association of Elementary/Kindergarten/Nursery Education, 1960.

CHAPTER 9
Resourcefulness with Animals

Overview

Your Resourcefulness and Children's Development
    ANIMALS: RELEVANCE FOR MOTOR DEVELOPMENT
    ANIMALS: RELEVANCE FOR AFFECTIVE DEVELOPMENT
    ANIMALS: RELEVANCE FOR SOCIAL DEVELOPMENT
    ANIMALS: RELEVANCE FOR COGNITIVE AND INTELLECTUAL DEVELOPMENT

Further Extensions and Applications

Summary

PREASSESSMENT

When you have completed this chapter you should be able to describe and compare the following:

1. various animals relevant to the classroom.
2. techniques for facilitating children's involvement with animals.
3. relevance of children's involvement with animals for motor, affective, social, and cognitive and intellectual development.

   Before *beginning to read this chapter:*

1. take time to write what you currently know about each of the above topics.
2. reflect on the child (children) you observed as you studied Section Two; consider what your current repertoire is for involving this child (these children) with animals in ways that will enhance development.

   Save what you write for rereading, comparison, and elaboration after you have studied and discussed these materials.

Overview

The appeal of living creatures

Children are typically fascinated with other living creatures. They like to see them, examine them, play with them, experiment with them, and care for them. Animals are the ultimate in responsive "toys"; they act and react. As a teacher you will want to be prepared to help children grow and learn through the activities that arise from their interests in animals.

   Animals are readily available to children for observation in almost every situation. Spiders, houseflies, chipmunks, dogs, ants, lizards, earthworms, robins, pigeons, palmetto bugs, and grasshoppers are among those frequently present, depending on the geographic location. These common creatures are often as interesting to children as pet store purchases such as gerbils, hamsters, or parakeets. Children will search out anything alive in any setting, whether a play yard, a park, ponds, the seashore, woods, swamps, city streets, or simply indoors in corners, on walls, and by windows. In this chapter, we suggest ways to use children's interest in animal life to support their development and learning.

The following will give you only very general ideas about how to house and care for some types of animals in the classroom. Additional information can be obtained from the suggested references listed at the end of the chapter.

Woodland Terrarium

Animals
- Frogs
- Toads
- Salamanders (newts)
- Land snails
- Box turtles

Preparation
- Use any sizable glass container with a cover, such as gallon food jars, aquariums, or bowls. Cover the bottom of the container with a combination of gravel and charcoal. Cover this with rich soil. Plant tiny plants and bits of moss collected from a woodsy area. Add a rock or two. Sprinkle with a bit of water and cover. Keep out of direct sunlight.

Feedings
- Place live insects (houseflies, fruit flies) in the terrarium for frogs, toads, and salamanders whenever possible. Otherwise provide meal worms, or put raw hamburger bits on the end of a string and wave slowly back and forth in front of animals. They will respond only to moving objects! Some food is necessary each day, even on weekends.
- Snails will eat bits of lettuce; feeding every two days is sufficient.
- Turtles eat raw meat bits, apple slices, berries, and live insects.

Basic Information
- If box turtles burrow themselves into the bottom of the terrarium, they are hibernating and should be put in a cool place. It is probably preferable to return them to their natural habitat as winter approaches.
- Children's tendency to squeeze frogs, toads, and salamanders to keep them from escaping can be injurious. Show them how to cup their hands around the creatures without squeezing. Frequent handling is to be avoided.

Freshwater Aquarium

Animals
- Fish: goldfish, neons, angelfish, catfish, guppies, etc.
- Snails
- Freshwater mussels or clams
- Tadpoles
- Mud turtles

Preparation
- Acquire aquarium or glass container large enough to accommodate the number of fish or other creatures you will care for. Each small fish will need approximately one gallon of water, and larger fish, more. Clean container thoroughly, using salt for scrubbing, not detergent.
- Cover bottom of container with aquarium gravel or clean coarse sand. Anchor small plants, either purchased or collected from lake or pond, into the gravel or sand.
- For tadpoles, mud turtles, and fish captured in lake or pond, use water from the same source; otherwise condition water before using by letting it stand in an open container for twenty-four hours. When adding water to container, you may wish to cover gravel and plants with a layer of newspaper before pouring in the water. Once the container is filled, remove newspaper. This prevents the dislodging of anchored plants.
- Provide tadpoles and turtles with rock surfaces out of the water.

Feeding
- Give fish *small* amounts of commercial fish food. A little goes a long way.
- Turtles eat water plants and bits of lettuce. Float lettuce in the water, turtles do not eat on land surfaces.
- Tadpoles eat tiny bits of cooked lettuce, raw liver, and drops of raw egg yolk.
- Snails and catfish require no special feeding; they consume wastes from fish.

Basic Information
- Goldfish are very hardy, and are therefore excellent choices as classroom residents.
- Guppies multiply rapidly, with about fifty babies born (live) to each female every month or so. Babies need to be quickly removed to other quarters upon birth or given many weeds for hiding, otherwise they will be eaten by the adults. Disposing of or caring for the many baby guppies is often a problem for the teacher.
- To raise tadpoles from eggs, collect just a few eggs from a pond. Most will soon hatch, or none will (the incubation period for some species is longer), so taking a large supply of eggs is unnecessary and ecologically unsound. When tadpoles become frogs or toads, move to a terrarium, providing separate homes for each you intend to keep. If eggs do not hatch within a few weeks, return to pond.

Mammal Cage

Animals
- Rabbits
- Guinea pigs
- Gerbils

- Hamsters
- Rats
- Mice

Preparation
- Provide a wire or metal cage large enough for the given animal. A cage that measures four by six feet is appropriate for a rabbit. Cages should provide light and air and be kept dry and clean. A smaller hideaway section within a larger cage is desirable. Place out of direct sunlight and away from drafts.
- Supply separate quarters for different mammals.

Feeding and Watering
- Provide animal food pellets routinely (from pet shops or feed supply stores); also offer seeds or grains, fresh greens (in small amounts). bread crusts, apple bits, carrot pieces.
- Keep a constant water supply by obtaining glass or plastic bottles with rubber stops into which plastic tubing can be inserted. Hang these, inverted, onto the side of the cage.
- Supply rabbits with salt.

Basic Information
- Layers of papers should be placed beneath the cage or in the waste drawer (where this is part of cage construction). Replace daily.
- Wash the cage at intervals with disinfectant.
- Give rabbits the opportunity to hop about the classroom for exercise *at quiet times.* They will often become nervous and agitated if children are noisy and active, but will hop freely about when there is quiet.
- A male and female pair of gerbils, rats, mice, or hamsters will reproduce regularly, giving many opportunities for children to learn about birth. Finding homes for the many offspring can become a problem.

Insect Cage

Animals
- Caterpillars/cocoons, chrysalis/moths, or butterflies
- Praying mantises
- Crickets
- Grasshoppers
- Other insects

Preparation
Obtain two identical (in circumference) shallow cake pans and a piece of window screening twelve by thirty-six inches. Make a roll of the window screening that will fit into the cake pan. Sew or otherwise secure in that position, fitting tightly where screening overlaps. Stand screening roll in one pan and invert the other pan and place on top. You may also wish to add forked branches, sprinklings of soil and dry grass or leaves.

- Feed caterpillars the kind of foliage on or near which they were found, or consult a resource book on the subject. Different kinds of caterpillars eat different vegetable matter; for example, monarchs eat milkweed leaves.
- Crickets will consume small bits of lettuce, corn, and bread. Remove uneaten food daily and replace. Provide a small dish of water.
- Praying mantises will catch and consume flies placed in the cage and will also eat pieces of fruit.

Basic Information
- As caterpillars approach mature size, be sure to provide a branch upon which they can attach themselves while forming their cocoon or chrysalis. Incubation periods in the dormant stage vary, so consult resource books for particular species. When moths or butterflies emerge and are fully developed, the cage will not provide them with sufficient space, and they should then be taken to a natural setting.
- In parts of the country where praying mantises are common, children will find and bring to school their egg nests (tan and very light-weight).When these hatch there will be countless miniscule babies, so store egg cases in a glass container or, better yet, return them to the outdoors after examining them—before they hatch!

Snake Cage

Preparation
- Provide a large aquarium or a similar large glass container with a cover and a weight to keep cover securely on. Rocks and forked branches can also be placed in the container. Ample room is important for the snake's comfort.

Feeding and Watering:
- Place live insects, earthworms, mealworms in cage.
- Provide a small container of water and spray-mist the cage occasionally.

Basic Information
- When handling snakes, hold one hand behind the snake's head and the other hand under the snake's body. Show the children how to hold securely to prevent the snake from wriggling and trying to prevent itself from falling. Also point out how a snake can be lowered to the ground or floor to get a better hold, rather than just squeezing it tighter, which can injure it.

Ant Farms

Preparation
- Locate a clear glass jar (gallon or half-gallon). Scoop ants and sand from any ant hill into the jar. Cover the jar immediately with cheese cloth or a double thickness of nylon netting and hold in place with a rubber

band. Cover the sides of the jar with dark, opaque paper or the ants will only build their tunnels on the interior sections of the jar. Leave the paper in place for several days initially, but then remove it whenever you or the children are observing the ants. Provide a flashlight and a magnifying glass for easier viewing.

Feeding and Watering
- Place a small piece of wood, foil, or other similar material on top of the soil and put two small bits of sponge on it, one that has been dipped in honey water and the other in plain water. Remoisten often.
- Ants, especially some kinds, will also eat small bits of fat or cooked egg white. Provide bits of overripe fruit periodically. Remove those they do not consume.

Basic Information
- The ant farm will thrive longer if the queen (larger with wings) is captured along with the worker ants. In most cases this is not easy to do, and for the purpose of immediate observation is not important.
- If ants from another colony are placed in the ant jar they will likely be attacked by the other ants and killed.

Earthworm Jar

Preparation
- Fill a large glass jar with garden soil, peat moss, leaf mulch, and a few earthworms. Sprinkle lightly with water. Cover the sides of the jar with dark, opaque paper. Leave the sides covered except when observing worms and their tunnels. Provide a flashlight and a magnifying glass for easier viewing.

Feeding and Watering
- Place bits of lettuce, damp oatmeal, and bread crumbs soaked in milk on top of the soil.
- Add a layer of peat moss every month or so.
- Sprinkle the soil very lightly with water every few days, but not to the point of muddiness.

Basic Information
- If you sprinkle a handful of cornmeal on top of the soil, the earthworms will carry it into their tunnels, making them easier to see.
- If the temperature is approximately seventy degrees, breeding is encouraged.
- Earthworms are bisexual; any two can reproduce. Earthworms attaching themselves to each other at the light-colored band around their bodies are mating. Each will produce an egg case soon thereafter.

Mealworm Jar

Preparation
- Fill a glass jar three-fourths full with bran, put in the mealworms, cover the top with wet burlap and secure firmly.
- Keep in warm location; eighty-five degrees is ideal.

Feeding and Watering
- Place a slice of raw potato or apple in the jar; this provides both food and moisture.

Basic Information
- Mealworms are the larvae of black beetles and can be purchased at pet stores. The worms develop into beetles, which lay eggs and then die. The eggs hatch and the cycle continues.

RESPONSE SECTION

The previous pages give guidelines for housing and caring for animals in the classroom. Before you read about how a teacher can enhance the benefits for children of their interest in these and other animals, consider the following:

1. Try to think back to your own childhood experiences and recall your own pets and the other animals, insects, etc. that you observed or captured. Think about what these experiences meant to you and whether they made positive or negative contributions to your development.
2. If you have difficulty in recalling experiences of this kind from your childhood, consider why that might be the case. Do you think you actually did not have many contacts with animals? Or are there other reasons for your lack of recall?
3. What recent experiences have you had with animals that you found interesting, rewarding, or insightful?
4. If you lack enjoyable and interesting experiences with animals, either from your early years or in recent years, how could you now develop a greater appreciation of their attributes so that you can more enthusiastically respond to children's interests in them?

Your Resourcefulness and Children's Development

As in the previous chapter, we present here ideas about how children's spontaneous interests, in this case in animals, can be used to facilitate their motor, affective, social, and cognitive and intellectual development. Again, we urge you to try to match these activities to the needs and interests of the children you observed in your study of Section Two.

ANIMALS: RELEVANCE FOR MOTOR DEVELOPMENT

Imitations of animal movements   Children enjoy pretending that they are animals by imitating animal movements. Crawling, hopping, and galloping children are a common sight in preschools and on elementary school playgrounds. You can encourage children to engage in a greater variety of movements, and consequently to improve muscular development and control, by making the following types of suggestions:

- Can you wriggle like a snake? Can you twist and bend your body to make yourself move across the floor?
- Look how slowly the turtle walks. Did you notice how its feet are turned in and its knees are pointed out? Can you move slowly?
- How would you move if you wanted to pretend you were a moving worm? (Perhaps by bending over, touching the floor with hands and feet, walking forward with the hands, then with legs, then with hands, etc.)
- Can you walk like a dog, with hands and feet touching the floor?
- Remember how the baby goats climbed and ran so quickly? Can you move that quickly?
- Look how high and far that grasshopper jumped. I can jump that far, can you?

There are often other large muscle benefits from children's contacts with animals. Trying to keep abreast of a running dog, sheep, bunny, or even a playful pussycat is excellent practice in the alignment of the body in moving quickly and making abrupt turns and stops. Children who are not active can often become involved in large muscle activity for extended periods with a playful animal. As a colleague once remarked, "An open field and two baby goats lead children to have more good exercise than a score of gym instructors."

Photo by Laura Lehmann.

Animal care requires eye-hand coordination

Small muscle development is not necessarily furthered by children's interaction with animals, although, if you are resourceful, you can often invent ways to convert an interest in animals into activities requiring eye-hand coordination. The following are only a few examples of the activities that could be suggested to children:

- Cut carrots or other vegetables up into small bits for a bunny or other animal to eat (with a knife that is not particularly sharp, of course).
- Pick "stick-tights" or other burrs out of a dog's coat.
- Make tiny hamburger bits and wave them on a toothpick in front of toad or frog, or suspend them on a string.
- Cut papers to fit the bottoms of cages for insects, small mammals, birds, etc.

ANIMALS: RELEVANCE FOR AFFECTIVE DEVELOPMENT

When animals are born in the classroom, grow up, mate, give birth, become sick, get hurt, grow old, and eventually die, children express concern as well as curiosity about these phenomena. They often ask blunt, simple questions and expect blunt, simple answers in return. An involved or delayed reply will tend to discourage further questioning, so answers should be as brief and direct as possible. If an immediate and honest response is given, there

Fundamental concerns

Photo by Robert Burdick.

will be many more opportunities to give more detailed information in response to the same questions or similar ones that will follow.

As a prospective teacher, it will be useful for you to think through what you will answer to children who ask the varieties of fundamental questions that are always asked by each new generation. You must become prepared to answer in your own way, in your own language—briefly, accurately, and clearly, without avoiding the question that has been posed. Generally, it is a good idea not to give more-detailed information than has been requested, even if you are sure the child lacks complete understanding. Answer what is asked and then be ready for more questions. The following are typical of the questions young children ask:

> What does being *born* mean?
> Why does a baby chick come out of an egg?
> Did I come out of an egg?
> Where is the seed?

Reproduction   There are many useful references for adults and books for children that you will find helpful in considering what to tell children about reproduction. Among those that describe animal reproduction are Millicent Selsam's *All about eggs and how they change into animals* (New York: William R. Scott, 1952); Robert Foran's *Animal mothers and babies* (New York: Warne, 1960); Carla Stevens' *Birth of Sunset's kittens* (New York: William R. Scott, 1969). The real facts on human reproduction are beautifully presented in *Did the sun shine before you were born?* by Sol and Judith Gordon (New York: Third Press, 1975). Your own version, however, must be your own. Be sure that you are well prepared with actual facts, including accurate names for body parts and functions, so that you are ready to respond to whatever questions are posed. It is probably important that you use actual names like *vagina*, *penis*, and *uterus*. Children may not necessarily remember them, but they will learn that these body parts have names and that it is appropriate to use them.

Death   When classroom animals die or wild animals are found dead, children's concerns and questions about death often surface, and your responses could have significant impact. It is helpful to children if you reflect a reverence for life in the way you care for living animals, and an acceptance of the inevitability of death in the gentle, matter-of-fact disposal of animal remains. Many teachers have found Margaret Wise Brown's sensitive book, *The dead bird* (New York: William R. Scott, 1958), to be very useful to share with children on such occasions as a model for their own behavior.

A few parents may prefer that you not attempt to answer their children's questions about issues such as birth and death. It may be useful to establish early in your experience with the parents whether this is the case. Most parents feel that questions should be answered when and where they are asked but will be interested in knowing about their children's inquiries and your answers. You may also wish to note and discuss with parents the misinformation or apprehensions that you note in children's conversations, so you can decide together whether and how these might be corrected.

In teaching, you will occasionally encounter differing family orientations being expressed during children's confrontations with each other, and you may have to serve as arbitrator. In one classroom, a goldfish's death led to a discussion between two six-year olds about whether or not there is a God. One was insisting that the other would go to hell if he did not believe in God. The other was insisting with equal zeal that he certainly would not go to hell because God does not really exist. He insisted that God was just made up like Santa Claus, because his father said so. Their question to their teacher was, "Do you believe there's a God?", and they waited expectantly, as though hers would be the final word on the matter! How will you respond to questions like this?

ANIMALS: RELEVANCE FOR SOCIAL DEVELOPMENT

Social substitutes

Animals housed in the classroom often provide a social substitute for children who are socially immature or who appear to mistrust others. This may be one of the most important reasons for having animals like gerbils, bunnies, and guinea pigs in the classroom as permanent residents. Socially isolated children often gravitate toward cuddly and gentle animals and spend long periods of time looking at them, stroking them, and holding them. A common interest in a classroom pet can also prove a first step toward friendship between very young or socially immature children. Little social skill is required to sit together and look and pat a cooperative animal. Many reticent children find their first friends at the animal cages.

Conflicts over animals

You will find, however, that social conflicts often arise over who will hold or care for classroom animals, especially those recently acquired. A child holding a soft little gerbil is usually reluctant to give it up, and the resultant struggle could require quick adult intervention to save the animal from injury. These incidents provide the opportunity to help children see that there are several different ways to equitably resolve their conflicts. Among these are: (1) let all those who want to hold the animal sit in a circle and gently pass it on to the next person at the end of a set period of time (as indicated by timer—sand type or mechanical—or clock settings); (2) let each "holder" have as long a turn as he or she wishes, but establish who will have the next unlimited turns; (3) let all interested children sit so they form an enclosed circle, which allows the animal to move freely and enables each of them to pat the animal as it comes near them.

The safety and comfort of animals brought into classrooms is of primary importance. Children often do not realize that they can easily hurt a small animal, and may unintentionally maul it in their efforts to be affectionate. Sometimes they deliberately hit, squeeze, or otherwise endanger animals in the course of experimenting with them. Just as they have difficulty taking another person's point of view, so they fail to realize that an animal can suffer from rough treatment and that some kinds of animals become distraught with fear in strange situations. Adults play an important role in modeling concern for animals, taking whatever actions are necessary to ensure the animals' (as well as the children's) safety and well-being.

Experiences with animals give excellent opportunities for children to engage in processes of observing, measuring and assessing of space and time, classifying, inferring, and predicting. Although these thought processes accompany all childhood investigations, the special appeal of animals makes them a particularly valuable stimulus. Animals promote all sorts of communication activities as well. The extent of these benefits for children will be dependent in large measure on how resourcefully you can guide them into investigative and communicative activities on their natural interests and curiosity.

Classification, seriation, and number

The world of animals is especially rich in possibilities for classification, number, and seriation. While classification of animals for very young children may be restricted to broad terms, such as *doggie, horsie, birdie, fish,* and *bug,* learning is quite rapid. Some seven-year-olds make relatively complex differentiations, such as between animals that have live births versus those that lay eggs, or between carnivores and vegetarians.

Animal classifications

The following factors are all useful in classifying animals. Keep them in mind as you seek to help children gradually learn to make more detailed discriminations.

- Habitat (farm, forest, jungle, grasslands, desert, ground, shrubs, trees, ponds, rivers, lakes, oceans)
- Movements (swim, fly, jump, walk, creep, swing, slide, float)
- Speed of movements
- Size (as babies and adults)
- Maturation rate
- Dependence or independence of babies
- Similarity or change of appearance across life span
- Diet
- Reproduction (eggs versus live births)
- Skin covering (fur, feathers, scales, none)
- Body parts (number of legs, kinds of feet, ears, teeth, tail, eyes, tongue)
- Life span
- Eating modes
- Excretory habits (shape of droppings)

The following are examples of specific actions you can take to encourage children in making more adequate classifications and discriminations:

- Draw comparisons for children between the different animals they encounter. For example, you might say, "Notice the bunny's teeth. They are quite different from dog's teeth, aren't they? Remember how the dog we looked at the other day had long, sharp teeth on either side and tiny little teeth in between? Are your cat's teeth more like a dog's or a bunny's?" And later, on a farm visit, "Did you notice the cow's teeth? Aren't they big? Are they more like a bunny's or a dog's? Let's see if we can find out what the horse's teeth look like."

- When children have shown interest in some physical aspect of an animal (such as a bushy tail), be ready to provide picture books or animal pictures so they can see if any other animals have similar features.
- Develop a mix-and-match set of adult and baby animal pictures, some of which show similarities between parent and offspring and some of which show differences (for example, tadpole and frog; caterpillar and butterfly; yellow duckling and white duck).
- Provide children with a selection of picture books that make comparisons between different kinds of animals on some dimension. You may wish to include the following:

Branley, Franklyn, M. *Big tracks, little tracks*. New York: Thomas Y. Crowell, 1960.
Fisher, Aillen. *Where does everyone go?* New York: Thomas Y. Crowell, 1961.
Garelik, May. *What's inside the eggs?* New York: William R. Scott, 1955.
Green, M. *Everyone has a house and everyone eats*. New York: William R. Scott, 1961.
Ipcar, Dahlov. *Wild and tame animals*. New York:Doubleday, 1963.
Selsam, Millicent. *All kinds of babies and how they grow*. New York: William R. Scott, 1953.
Ylla (Pseud.) Koffler, Camille, *Whose eye am I?* New York: Harper & Row, 1968.

Seriation with living creatures   Careful observations of animals afford many varied opportunities for children of ages four, five, six, and seven to experiment with seriation. The following are examples of activities that might encourage children to order their impressions in more precise ways:

- Make a life-size silhouette that approximates the shape of any animal brought into the classroom. Keep these on a bulletin board or in available storage so that they can be used for comparisons with each successive animal visitor. Comparisons can be made for height or length, with a different ordering emerging for each emphasis. Compare a mouse, poodle, Great Dane, goldfish, bee, etc.
- Chart the quantity of food or water consumed by various animals in a day.
- Chart animal growth across time.
- Make a "draw-around" outline of each kind of egg your children have contact with across a year. Keep these outlines so they can compare and order the sizes of chicken eggs, duck eggs, frog eggs, turtle eggs, ant eggs, snake eggs, and robin eggs (or other eggs you or the children can locate without disrupting nests).
- Get animals to make muddy tracks on paper so that children can examine the tracks and then cut them out to save. Across time, as more are collected, compare and order according to size.

You will find it very easy to use children's interests in animals to provide experiences with number. Counting will occur quite naturally. The following

How much did the animals eat?

Rabbit

Guinea Pig

Hamster

sample questions illustrate the many instances in which you can stimulate consideration of number when children are attending to animals:

- How many baby chicks are hatched now? How many eggs are left?
- How many goldfish are there in the aquarium? How many neons? How many snails?
- How many of our cocoons have already hatched? How many are left to hatch?
- How many kittens did your cat have?
- How many milkweed leaves did our monarch caterpillar eat up today?
- How many times will your dog fetch a ball for us, do you suppose, before he gets tired of doing it?
- We had six mouse babies, but two of them died. How many are there now?
- How many cardinals are at the feeder? How many starlings? How many birds altogether? Is that the most we've ever seen at one time?
- We just put two worms in that jar last fall, remember? There are a lot now. Let's find out how many.
- Give the rabbit one cup of water, but give the guinea pigs *more*. They will drink at least two cups, maybe three.

By focusing on these kinds of opportunities for developing counting abilities and number concepts such as *more, same, less, add to,* and *take away from* children can be helped to develop in mathematical thinking. An effective way to help children toward conservation of number is to help them become aware that the total number of animals (for example, in a litter of kittens or a flock of chicks) is not different, regardless of how they may group themselves. By noting, for example, that the same number of chicks seems like fewer when they all huddle around the heat than when they are running about, children become more aware of number constancy. Repeated experiences of counting and recounting guppies, mice, gerbils, or crickets in different physical arrangements can lead toward the ability to conserve number, and are far more interesting for children than the counting of circles or symbols on a workbook page or the manipulation of counting blocks in formal instructional situations.

Mass and liquid quantity

There are many possibilities for increased sensitivity to the invariance of mass and liquid quantity in the feeding of animals, since, in this situation, children can understand that it is the actual measure of food, rather than its quantitative appearance, that is important. When children help in feeding and watering animals, indicate to them in precise terms how much should be given, whether measured by scoop, cup, or weight.

Use various-shaped food and drink containers for the animals, so children can see that a measured amount looks different, depending on the container shape, but that it remains the "right" amount despite the appearance. Talk with children about this, and sometimes pour the liquid back into the measuring container as proof. While children are caring for the animals you can check their perceptions; for example, "Did you give the praying mantis two spoonfuls or is it more?" Or, in the case of solid foods that the child has weighed, "Is that just one ounce of hamburger? Now that you have it in those little bits it looks like much more. Why don't you weigh it again to see if it is just one ounce?"

If scales are available, five-, six-, and seven-year-olds can document the increasing weight of growing animals and compare the weights of different animals within and across species. Myriad questions can be addressed by young scientists with a set of scales. In relation to animals, they include the following:

- How long does it take a guinea pig to eat food equal to its own weight?
- How long does it take a newborn puppy or a newly hatched chick to double its weight? A hamster? A rabbit?
- What is the total weight of a litter of mice? Is this more or less than the weight of the mother before giving birth? After giving birth?

Causality

Animals provoke children's curiosity. A child will exercise his or her questioning skills as he or she looks at an unfamiliar animal or has an unfamiliar experience with animals. For example, during a brief period of watching eggs in the process of hatching, a group of children asked the following questions:

- Why does that bulb keep going off? [incubator heat source]
- Will that one chick that got out of his egg get the others out too?
- [to teacher] Are you turning that light on and off?
- Why does he [chick] got just one leg standing up?
- Why do they lie down after they get out of the egg?
- Do they get tired of being born?
- Can they fly?
- [to teacher] If they can fly, will you let them?
- Will they eat? What do they eat?
- When will all these others [unhatched eggs] come out? [points to nearby picture of egg] If those were real, could they open too?
- They'll get this big? [indicates size with hands]

When children ask such questions, teachers do well to answer quickly and briefly if they know the answer, or to respond, "I wonder about that too," if they do not. Knowledge about the everyday phenomena that fascinate children is a great asset, and we encourage you to systematically and continually increase your stock of such knowledge. Learn as much as you can about whatever animals the children in your care are likely to encounter. For example, learn as much as you can about spider habits by reading or doing some observations for yourself, before drawing attention to the one spinning its web across your classroom window. If you note that the grasshopper population is increasing in your play yard, bone up on grasshoppers; you will probably be asked questions about them. With younger children, even

Photo by John Young.

six- and seven-year-olds, being taken off to look something up in a library book is seldom as satisfying as being given an immediate answer. Of course, children can also benefit from going to the library to find books with additional information. You will need to continually increase your own store of knowledge about living things, both plants and animals, and other physical phenomena, if you are to be a resourceful teacher. But keep in mind, if you do not have an answer, say so—do not give children answers that are probably untrue.

Wondering is "catching"

The other part of your teaching responsibility, in regard to questioning, is the modeling of good questions. Let children see you as an inquirer like themselves. Wondering is likely to be "catching." The following kinds of questions about animals might well lead to experiments that would be of interest to many children, especially older ones:

- I wonder if the rabbit would eat more if we gave him food both in the morning and the afternoon, instead of just feeding him in the afternoon?
- I wonder if your dog could find you if you hid behind the door where he couldn't see you?
- I wonder whether the guinea pig will choose to hide in this little bag or in a big one?
- I wonder, if we put some bits of thread and yarn on the bush outside the window, if the birds will come and take it away for their nest building?
- I wonder, if we put a pan of water out, if anything would drink from it or come and take a bath?
- I wonder whether any animals ever walk here?
- I wonder if there is anything alive under this rock?
- I wonder whether the salamander will eat a piece of fruit?

Space concepts

Children will delight in constructing habitats such as homes, runways, pastures, tunnels, caves, and ponds for the animals they acquire. Through trial and error they make discoveries about the size of the animals and the appropriate size of the space they are arranging for them. Even quite young children can become proficient in determining which of a collection of jars, cans, and boxes of various sizes will most appropriately contain a praying mantis, a lady bug, a mouse, a snake, a daddy longlegs, or a full-grown bunny. Teachers can increase space awareness in older children by pointing out how animals behave in different spatial arrangements—the discomfort (foot thumping) of a bunny in a small box, the preference of the guinea pig for his small cage over the open classroom, the contrast between the behavior of a snake in a small jar and in a roomy aquarium.

Animal housing and spatial awareness

An animal's point of view

Six- and seven-year-olds can also be encouraged to speculate about what an animal can see from its vantage point, if a teacher asks questions such as, "Do you think the bunny can see that dog outside? Can she see the mice up on the shelf? Do you think she can see this carrot if I hold it here? What if I hold it here?" Questions like these make children aware that the bunny's perspective is different than their own and encourages them to think about what that different perspective might be.

For younger children still developing their spatial orientations, and far from being able to take another's perspective, it will be more useful to simply use the animal's activity and position in space as another opportunity to reinforce spatial concepts and the understanding of spatial words such as *around, under, over, behind, between, in back of, half-way, all the way, backward, across,* and *into.* Comments such as "Where is he now?", "Now why do you suppose he wants to get *behind* that food dish?", "Look at him run *between* the bushes," "Now he is *turning around,*" "Where did he go now?" are useful.

Time concepts

Keeping an account of how the passage of time is marked by changes in animal maturity contributes to children's developing time sense. For young

Records of sequence of animal growth and development

children, this is probably best done through a photographic record. Polaroid or other photographs of the sequence of development from tiny caterpillar, to large caterpillar, to chrysalis, and finally to emerging butterfly will help children recall the events in the life span. If pictures of eggs, baby ducks, half-grown ducks, and full-grown ducks are placed along a calendar time line, the passage of time becomes meaningful for children, even the youngest. Schematic drawings, although less authentic than photographs, can be substituted, and may even help children comprehend how symbols are used to represent aspects of reality.

The provision of stopwatches will encourage older children to time animal activity and thereby gain a better sense of time measurement. You or they may suggest the following sorts of investigation:

- How far can a caterpillar go in a minute? A turtle?
- How long will the lizard hold perfectly still?
- How long will it take a dog to run to its owner from across the playground?
- How long will it take the praying mantis to catch and eat the fly placed in its cage?
- How long will a fly sit on one window before flying away to another spot?
- How long will the gerbil run on his exercise wheel? What is the record run?

Spoken language

When an animal is brought to the classroom it will cause much talking among children. Children of all ages are usually eager to tell about their pets or the animals they have seen. Because conversations flow so easily when the topic is animals, there are many opportunities to engage children in using unfamiliar expressions and vocabulary. Encourage children's expression by unqualified acceptance of anything they say, while simultaneously modeling for them target vocabulary and sentence constructions.

A child learns to talk partly by listening, but also by engaging in talk. Picture collections, flannel board figures, and puppets are among the "props" many teachers use to keep children's talk about animals flowing. Pictures of animals from magazines and old picture books can be mounted on cardboard or heavier paper and periodically made available for children's examination, discussion, and sorting. Or the animal figures can be cut out and backed with sandpaper to make them adhere to the flannel board. Children will likely tell stories and describe actions as they manipulate these figures or play with animal puppets.

Children's libraries are packed with books about real animals and about "pretend" animals with human characteristics; both kinds appeal to the growing child. The following are among the books about real animals with which you may wish to become familiar:

Adelam, Leone. *Please pass the grass.* New York: David McKay, 1960.
Brandenburg, Aliki. *Green grass and white milk.* New York: Crowell, 1974.
Brinkloe, Julie. *The spider web.* Garden City, N.Y.: Doubleday, 1974.
Collier, Ethel. *Who goes there in my garden?* New York: William R. Scott, 1963.
Fife, Dale. *The little park.* Chicago: Albert Whitman, 1973.
Garelik, May. *About owls.* New York: Four Winds, 1975.
Graham, Margaret. *Be nice to spiders.* New York: Harper & Row, 1967.
Ironmonger, Ira. *Alligator smiling in the sawgrass.* New York: William R. Scott, 1965.
Mizumura, Kazue. *Opossum.* New York: Thomas R. Crowell, 1974.
Schoenherr, John. *The barn.* Boston: Little, Brown, 1968.
Zim, Herbert S. *What's inside of animals?* New York: William Morrow, 1953.

Written language

The presence of animals gives very meaningful opportunities for children to see their ideas and observations being recorded in writing. If you print carefully, either on chart paper or on smaller sheets, what children dictate or what you hear them saying to each other about animals, you can create very useful teaching tools. Children can be helped to understand that written words correspond to spoken words, that writing and reading proceed from left to right, that a word is a unique arrangement of the letters that represent the sounds in the spoken word, that some words are written repeatedly since they are spoken repeatedly, that words can be "remembered," and that the spelling and pronouncing of words can be figured out by knowing about letter sounds.

If you are resourceful you can use children's interest to create writing that either specifically represents their own language or is very closely related to their own experiences. Sometimes these dictating and reading experiences are done with only one child, and at other times with a small group, where each child suggests additions to a common story theme. Sometimes six- and seven-year-olds can work together as an entire group to create a piece of writing about something they have all experienced or are planning. The following are some specific ways that interest in animals might be used to stimulate writing experiences:

• Each animal habitat can be well labeled with its occupant's name, how it

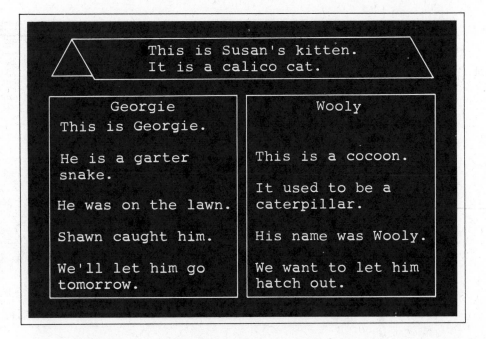

This is Susan's kitten.
It is a calico cat.

Georgie

This is Georgie.

He is a garter snake.

He was on the lawn.

Shawn caught him.

We'll let him go tomorrow.

Wooly

This is a cocoon.

It used to be a caterpillar.

His name was Wooly.

We want to let him hatch out.

came to be in the classroom, and whatever additional information children may wish to include.

- Records about animals can be made across a period of time and may involve a continuous listing of observations.

Animals we saw out our window

sparrow

pigeon

dog

chipmunk

earthworms

What a mouse can do

run

eat

drink

stand on two legs

sleep

climb on a wire

turn wheel

```
              The Big Bite

Joggle, the gerbil, was lost yesterday.

Sara found him in the cafeteria.

She tried to catch him.

He was scared so he bit her.

He wouldn't let go.

Finally, he did.

Rob said, "Joggle was probably in the
cafeteria to get a bite to eat but Sara
was just too big a bite for him!"
```

- Funny or exciting events make especially good stories.
- Children's questions about animals, both answered and unanswered, can be placed on a chart to encourage further questioning.
- Reminders about animal needs can be written on the chalkboard or on

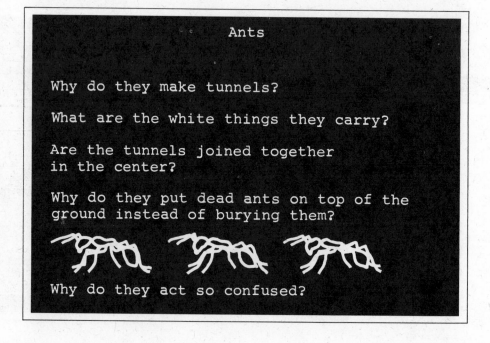

```
                 Ants


Why do they make tunnels?

What are the white things they carry?

Are the tunnels joined together
in the center?

Why do they put dead ants on top of the
ground instead of burying them?




Why do they act so confused?
```

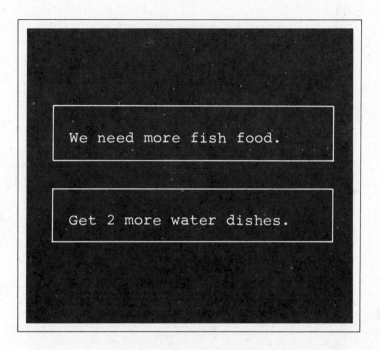

signs for the bulletin board. Children should be made aware of the specific needs and of the exact words you write.

- Directions for animal care can be written out so that it is easier to keep track of what needs to be done (with adult help).

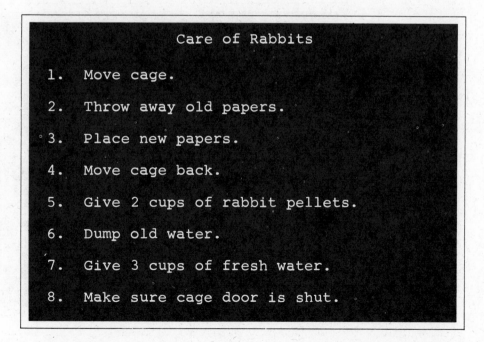

Children also like to write their own stories about animals once they have developed some abilities in letter formation and word awareness. At first they may dictate a sentence to you, which they will then want to copy—perhaps only a word or two. Most children gradually become more ambitious and skilled and wish to write stories of several sentences. At this point their writing is facilitated if they have an easily viewed set of the most frequently used words. Such a set might be written on nine-by-twelve-inch poster board sheets that they can take to the table where they are writing. Another way is to put the collection of words on a large sheet on the wall. Or, if there is an alphabet display at children's eye level along one wall, the words might be written below the particular letter that is the word's initial sound. Although children will not initially know where to look for a word on any of these lists, when they ask how to write a listed word you can simply point it out. They typically learn the positions of words very quickly and, in the case of the alphabet display, become able to transfer their grasp of beginning letter sounds to new, unlisted words.

Assist children in writing about animals

Picture dictionaries are also useful aides for children's writing, such as Alla McIntier's *Follett beginning to read dictionary* (Chicago: Follett, 1969), and special dictionaries can be made that are very specific to classroom animals. Children involved in writing stories will of course want to know how to spell many words not on the high-frequency lists that are specific to their own ideas at the moment. A teacher must be prepared to help children spell these

Aa	Bb	Cc	Dd
and	be	come	do
all	but	could	did
at	by	call	down
as	been	cat	don't
are	before	can	day
an	big	can't	dog
about	back		

words as they are writing. A resourceful teacher might wear a smock with lots of pockets, or have a "teacher basket" close at hand containing paper and pencil in order to quickly write any word a child needs.

Phonics teaching can often be done in the context of helping children figure out how to spell the words they ask about. As a child comes to you and asks, "How do you write *cow*?", you should be able to quickly recall whether or not this particular child can figure out any of the letters that are needed, that is does he or she know any words that have similar endings, like *now* or *wow*? If not, the word is simply written for the child; if so, you may be able to help the child see the connection between what he or she already knows and what he or she is asking.

As children begin to accumulate some known words (that is, can correctly identify them whenever they see them—on charts, in their own writing, in others' writing, in books), they will thoroughly enjoy using some of the delightful "easy to read" books about animals. You will want to be ready to offer such favorites as the following:

Easy-to-read animal books

Averill, Esther. *Fire cat*. New York: Harper, 1960.
Eastman, P. D. *Are you my mother*? New York: Random House, 1969.
Berenstain, Stan and Jan. *Bears in the night*. New York: Random House, 1971.
Geisel, Theodore (Dr. Seuss). *The cat in the hat*. New York: Random House, 1957.
———. *The cat in the hat comes back*. New York: Random House, 1958.
———. (Theo LeSeig). *I wish I had duck feet*. New York: Random House, 1965.
———. *The foot book*. New York: Random House, 1968.

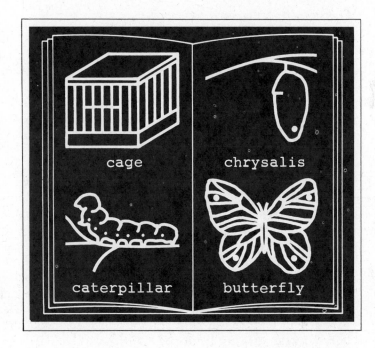

Lobel, Arnold. *Frog and Toad are friends*. New York: Harper & Row, 1970.

Minarik, Else. *Little Bear*. New York: Harper & Row, 1957.

———. *Little Bear's visit*. New York: Harper & Row, 1961.

———. *Little Bear's friend*. New York: Harper & Row, 1960.

———. *A kiss for Little Bear*. New York: Harper & Row, 1968.

———. *Father Bear comes home*. New York: Harper & Row, 1959.

Myrick, Mildred. *Ants are fun*. New York: Harper & Row, 1962.

Selsam, Millicent. *Benny's animals and how he put them in order*. New York: Harper & Row, 1966.

Zion, Gene. *Harry the dirty dog*. New York: Harper & Row, 1956.

———. *No roses for Harry*. New York: Harper & Row, 1958.

———. *Harry by the sea*. New York: Harper & Row, 1965.

RESPONSE SECTION

> The previous pages contain many suggestions, both specific and general, for using children's interests in animals to enhance their learning and development. Choose the ten activities that you feel would be most appropriate for each of the children you observed in your study of Section Two. As you formulate your list of activities, browse back through the chapter and modify the activities to match the developmental levels of the respective children. For each of the activities you have chosen, determine whether it will provide new skills or concepts, a new application of existing skills and concepts, or both.

Further Extensions and Applications

This chapter has presented extensive discussions of the possibilities for using children's natural interests in other living creatures to further their development and learning. Nevertheless, the varied suggestions contained here represent only a beginning repertoire for a truly resourceful teacher. You should now be able to find further learning possibilities in the vast array of animals that surrounds you—bees, ponies, gophers, cockroaches, armadillos, fireflies, ducks, hermit crabs, horned toads, or whatever animals are found in your area.

Parallels to other natural and physical science phenomena
You should also feel better equipped to generate ideas on how other natural and physical science phenomena can promote development and learning. What you have learned about children's exploration of animals in this chapter closely parallels the investigations they might make of other objects and events. Children are as intrigued, for example, with observing, measuring, classifying, inferring, and predicting about growing plants as about animals. And they have similar interests in rocks and minerals; heat, light, and sound phenomena; physical and chemical changes; and weather events and conditions. In each of these areas, the well-informed and resourceful teacher can help children develop increasingly adequate understanding and foster habits of inquiry, experimentation, and observation.

Summary

Animals are available in almost every situation and offer children countless opportunities for learning; with resourceful teaching, they can support many other aspects of development as well.

Children develop their action repertoires as they imitate animal movements or actively cavort with playful animals. In caring for animals they can also become involved in various small muscle activities requiring eye-hand coordination.

Since animals' life events parallel those of humans, children often become involved in thinking through fundamental concerns about birth, life, and death; the feelings generated about animals' life cycles have direct implications for their own lives.

Animals often serve as social substitutes for immature or mistrustful children, and a common interest in a pet can lead to a first friendship between such children. On the other hand, conflicts over animals are frequent and may require adult intervention and supervision.

Experiences with animals give excellent opportunities for children to engage in the processes of observing, measuring, assessing space and time, classifying, inferring, predicting, and communicating. By becoming familiar with the learning possibilities inherent in children's interest in animals, a teacher can become better equipped to see the parallel possibilities in other areas of intense interest.

REASSESSMENT

Reread what you wrote for the preassessment as you began this chapter, comparing this with your current understandings. Now write on these topics again and incorporate your new insights and knowledge. Continue to update as you prepare for teaching. Save your materials for your portfolio.

Additional Reading

Activities with Animals

Blackwell, F. F. *Starting points for science*. Vol. 1. Oxford: Alden Press, 1968.

Elementary science study. *Animals in the classroom: A book for teachers*. New York: McGraw-Hill, 1970.

Hammerman, D. R., and Hammerman, W. M. *Teaching in the outdoors*. Minneapolis, Minn.: Burgess, 1973.

Russell, H. R. *Ten-minute field trips: Using the playground for environmental studies*. Chicago: J. G. Ferguson/Doubleday, 1973.

Woodland Terrarium

Freshet, Bernice. *The old bullfrog*. New York: Scribner's, 1968.

Howes, Judy. *Spring peepers*. New York: Thomas Y. Crowell, 1975.

Kramer, Jack. *Pets and plants in miniature gardens*. Garden City, N.Y.: Doubleday, 1973.

Zappler, George and Lisbeth. *Amphibians as pets*. Garden City, N.Y.: Doubleday, 1973.

Zim, Herbert. *Frogs and toads*. New York: Morrow, 1950.

Freshwater Aquarium   Caras, Roger. *A zoo in your room.* New York: Harcourt Brace Jovanovich, 1975.

Mammals   Caras, Roger. *A zoo in your room.* New York: Harcourt Brace Jovanovich, 1975.
Walker, E. P. *First aid and care of small animals.* Animal Welfare Institute, P.O. Box 3492, Grand Central Station, New York, N.Y. 10017. Also has additional inexpensive materials.

Insects   Earle, Olive L. *Praying mantis.* New York: William Morrow, 1969.
Goudey, Alice E. *Butterfly time.* New York: Scribner's, 1964.
Hussey, Lois J., and Pessins, Catherine. *Collecting cocoons.* New York: Thomas Y. Crowell, 1953.
Sammis, Kathy. *The beginning knowledge book of butterflies.* New York: Macmillan, 1965.
Stevens, Carla. *Catch a cricket.* New York: William R. Scott, 1961.

Snakes   Gross, Ruth. *Snakes,* New York: Four Winds, 1975.

Ants   Epple, Anne O. *The beginning knowledge book of ants.* New York: Crowell-Collier, 1969.
Hutchins, R. E. *The ant realm.* New York: Dodd, 1967.

Earthworms   Darling, Lois, and Darling, Louis. *Worms.* New York: William Morrow, 1972.

CHAPTER 10
Resourcefulness with Children's Literature

PERSKE

Overview

Your Resourcefulness and Children's Development
CHILDREN'S LITERATURE: RELEVANCE FOR PHYSICAL AND MOTOR DEVELOPMENT
CHILDREN'S LITERATURE: RELEVANCE FOR AFFECTIVE DEVELOPMENT
CHILDREN'S LITERATURE: RELEVANCE FOR SOCIAL DEVELOPMENT
CHILDREN'S LITERATURE: RELEVANCE FOR COGNITIVE AND INTELLECTUAL DEVELOPMENT

Further Extensions and Applications
Summary

PREASSESSMENT

When you have completed this chapter you should be able to describe and compare the following:

1. *kinds of children's literature.*
2. *techniques for facilitating children's involvement with literature.*
3. *relevance of children's involvement with literature for motor, affective, social, and cognitive and intellectual development.*

Before *beginning to read this chapter*:

1. *take time to write what you currently know about each of the above topics.*
2. *reflect on the child (children) you observed as you studied Section Two; consider what your current repertoire is for involving this child (these children) with literature in ways that will enhance development.*

Save what you write for rereading, comparison, and elaboration after you have studied and discussed these materials.

Overview

Love of literature
Among the more delightful gifts you can bestow on children as a teacher is a love of literature. To do this you must yourself have a deep appreciation of literature. Do you get "turned on" by books? Have books, stories, poems, and articles made significant contributions to your life?

If children are to expend the time and energy necessary to successfully learn to read, they need to have a strong conviction that reading is its own reward, that it is not something done to please others or as a means to another end. To convince children that books are worthwhile, you had better believe it yourself! But do not despair if your current feelings about literature are less than enthusiastic. Many an adult has developed a new appreciation for books and reading through new exposure to children's literature. In the last twenty years children have been blessed with an abundance of stories that have an appeal to grown-ups as well. Begin familiarizing yourself with some of these.

You might start with Roger Duvoisin's tale, *Petunia* (New York: Alfred A. Knopf, 1950), about the silly goose who found a book and thought that she was therefore qualified to give opinions to all the other animals. She had heard that "he who owns BOOKS and loves them is wise." A series of mishaps resulting from her misadvice to her friends eventually leads to her realization that it is not enough to carry wisdom under her wing, that she must put it into her mind and heart. To do that she must learn to read!

"Turn on" to books

After you have mused over Petunia's ignorant arrogance, seek out some of the following books and see if you can resist their appeal. These or other books by the same authors will likely be available in the children's section of any public library.

Burton, Virginia Lee. *The little house*. Boston: Houghton Mifflin, 1942.
Fujikawa, Gyo. *Gyo Fujikawa's A to Z picture book*. New York: Grosset and Dunlap, 1974.
Keats, Ezra Jack. *The snowy day*. New York: The Viking Press, 1962.
Lionni, Leo. *Inch by inch*. New York: Obolensky, 1960.
Sendak, Maurice. *Where the wild things are*. New York: Harper, 1963.
Ungerer, Tomi. *Crictor*. New York: Harper, 1958.
Wildsmith, Brian. *Wild animals*. New York: Franklin Watts, 1964.
Yashima, Taro. *Crow boy*. New York: The Viking Press, 1955.
Zaffo, George. *The giant nursery book of things that go*. Garden City, N.Y.: Doubleday, 1959.

Benefits of literature to children

We expect that by the time you have become familiar with these particular volumes you will be eager to share them and others with children. Children who have had regular exposure to children's literature have been found to use more complex linguistic structures (Chomsky, 1972) and to develop reading abilities earlier and more successfully than children who lack such exposure (Cohen, 1968; Plessas, 1964; Durkin, 1966). You can help children learn the value of reading first by getting "hooked" on books yourself and then by developing your repertoire for sharing that enjoyment with children. In this chapter you will learn of the specific contributions books can make to children's physical and motor, affective, social, and cognitive and intellectual development.

SETUPS FOR CHILDREN'S LITERATURE

At least two types of physical arrangements need to be considered. The first is for a literature and language arts area that will be used independently by children and within which you will also informally read to and with individual children (as well as assisting them in recording their own ideas in writing). This area is often called the *book corner* or *reading area*. The second arrangement is for group presentations. Sometimes these two areas can be combined. To encourage thoughtful consideration of both individual and group needs, we have presented each separately here.

Book Corner

Basic Equipment
- Low open shelving; low tables and chairs; carpeting (not mandatory but very desirable); one hundred picture books (minimum), thirty to fifty easy-to-read general resource materials; well-illustrated encyclopedias; magazines

Suggested Location
- Locate apart from heavy traffic areas. Isolate from art and snack areas, which foster "messes," and from noise-producing activities such as blocks and dramatic play.

Accessories
- Small rugs, rug samples, a couch or overstuffed chairs, display rack, bean bag chair

General Guidelines
- Books crowded together on shelves are less likely to attract children's interest than books standing so that their covers show.
- A fresh supply of books selected to stimulate new interests and to supply known enthusiasms will increase usage. Try to borrow some new books each week to supplement those in the basic collection. Sources for borrowing can include the central school library collection, the public library, other classroom collections, and parents' collections.
- Include on the shelves the books and stories children have produced themselves.
- Sit with individual children as often as possible while they are looking at or reading books. Make it a point to talk informally with each child about books as often as possible. You might wish to keep a record of these contacts to make sure that you do not inadvertently miss certain children. Try to sit even more frequently with those children who resist the group story sessions.
- Children at ages five, six, and seven may enjoy having books classified according to reading level or subject. All the easiest-to-read and easy-to-read books might be kept in particular sections, with others classified topically (such as *animals*) or generically (such as *pretend, real, Mother Goose*, etc.). Pieces of colored tape on the binding can be used to indicate the shelf location.
- As you are talking with children about the books they have selected, note their interests and be alert to ways of using these books to facilitate the learning experiences you have designed for them.

Alternatives
- Arrange trips for children to the school or public library to examine and select books.

Story Time

Basic Equipment
- Chairs or floor space (preferably rug) for seating; low chair for teacher or other story reader

Preferred Location
- Locate in open area away from activity and toys, with light source behind children.
- Keep the group as close together as comfort permits.

Accessories
- Pictures or flannel board cutouts (with flannel board) representing story theme or sequence
- Objects relating to books to be read; for example, real blueberries to go with Robert McCloskey's *Blueberries for Sal* (New York: The Viking Press, 1948), or a flower to introduce Munro Leaf's *The story of Ferdinand* (New York: The Viking Press, 1969).

General Guidelines
- Whenever possible arrange to read or tell stories to a small group of children rather than to large groups. At ages three and four, five or six children at a time is preferable; at age five, ten or so; even at age six or seven, small groups are occasionally desirable because they allow more opportunity for interaction, questions, and discussion.
- It pays to use great care in selecting books to read. Avoid reading a book you have not previously read yourself. In making your selections consider the interests and attention span of the children and the general appeal of the books. Look at picture books from the distance at which children will be sitting to determine whether the illustrations are large enough to be effective. You may find that it will be more effective to read two or more short stories that have great appeal than to read a longer story that is less interesting.
- Always have alternatives on hand. If, once under way, you find that the book you selected has no holding power for the particular group, tell the rest of the story instead of reading it—as you quickly turn the pages, give only the most salient points and sketchy information. Then go on to one of your alternative choices.
- Plan to have stories read at a relaxed time of day—not during cleanup or just before outdoor play! Reading after outdoor play might be preferable, or as the last thing in the day. Reserve enough time, however, for leisurely enjoyment.
- In introducing a book, mention the title and point to the words that give the title. (For children from age five on you will also wish to give the name of the author and illustrator, making sure that children know the meanings of those terms.) Otherwise keep the introduction brief. A few sentences or less will probably suffice. "This book is about ————," or "Can you guess what this book is about? I thought you'd like to hear it because ————" and then start reading.

• In reading a book aloud, you may find these guidelines useful:

1. Maintain eye contact with the listeners as much as possible.
2. Hold the book open toward the children, turning it as necessary for all to see the illustrations before turning to the next page.
3. Show your regard for the book by turning the pages very carefully and handling the book gently.
4. Start the reading in a clear tone and at a lively pace. Once you sense that you have the children's full attention, lower or raise your voice and quicken or slow your pace as appropriate to the text. Lengthen your dramatic pauses to let your listeners savor the words and ideas.
5. From time to time, point out things in the illustrations to which the text refers.
6. Periodically, sweep your fingers under the sentences as you read them to reinforce for the children your left-to-right pattern of reading.
7. When reading rhymes, word repetitions, or predictable outcomes, pause to let the children finish phrases for you. It maintains children's involvement and gives them a feeling of confidence when they can use relevant cues to predict what is coming.
8. Have the children save their discussion until the story is finished. Some interruption will inevitably occur among young children, but if your request to "Tell us later" is consistent and if you immediately continue with the story, they will accept the delay and a more satisfying story reading experience will be maintained.
9. Should your story not hold everyone's attention, continue on without interruption if at all possible. Sometimes a hand on a child's shoulder will regain attention, or a rejoinder can be interwoven into the story, such as, "And, Toby, whatever do you suppose will happen now?" Keep the story going, more dramatically than ever. If stopping does become unavoidable, make it as brief as possible and then continue on without additional comment.
10. As you conclude a book, you may wish to avoid asking, "Did you like that story?" and the inevitable shouts of yes and no. Instead of asking for comment you may find it more effective to simply turn back to the beginning of the book and slowly, without comment, turn through the pages again. Typically, children will be reminded of the things they wished to say or ask and may spontaneously comment, "That's a good book."
11. After spontaneous discussion, you may wish to pose other questions or suggestions related to what has just been heard, such as, "What other things might [character] have done to solve the problem of [whatever]? Would you be interested in trying [whatever]?"

The previous pages give guidelines for how you might introduce young children to literature. Before you read about how books can enhance children's development and contribute to their learning, consider the following:

1. Try to think back to your own childhood experiences with literature. Make a list of the books, stories, and poems you remember and decide what significance these materials or selections had for you. Also try to recall the settings and situations within which you had contact with books in your early years and how they contributed to your feelings about what you heard or read.

2. If you have difficulty in recalling experiences of this kind from your childhood, consider why that might be the case. Do you think that you actually had little contact with books, stories, and poems? Or are there other reasons for your lack of recall?

3. What recent experiences have you had with children's literature that you found enjoyable?

4. If you lack enjoyable experiences with children's literature, either from your early years or in recent years, how could you now develop a greater appreciation so that you can more enthusiastically provide these experiences for children?

Alternatives
- Flannel board stories: prepare cutouts of major characters and props for a story and position them on the flannel board in coordination with the reading or telling of the story. To most easily prepare effective cutouts, place fabric lining material (Pellon) over the figures you wish to reproduce from illustrations and trace with a black felt pen. Fill in with felt color pens the areas you wish to brighten (such as clothing). These pieces will adhere firmly to the flannel or felt surface of the board.
- Young children can learn to use commercial or teacher-prepared tapes of children's books at listening stations with a minimum of help. In preparing tapes, read the text of a book you have selected into the tape as clearly as possible, pausing at the finish of each two-page spread. Play a signal of some kind at this point so that the listening children will know that it is time to turn the page. It is easy to flick a fork against a glass while you are reading, and this sound makes an effective and nondistracting "turn" signal.

- Records of many excellent children's books can be obtained. Among those available are:

    I know an old lady (Rose Bonne and Alan Mills). Scholastic Book Service.
    Horton hatches the egg. MGM, Leo 1013.
    The house at Pooh Corner and now we are six. Golden, GW 228.
    The tale of Benjamin Bunny. Golden, GW 227.

Your Resourcefulness and Children's Development

Despite the wealth of good children's literature available today, young children are totally dependent on their adult caregivers for contact with these materials. It is up to you as a teacher to familiarize yourself with these books so that you can help children read those that are appropriate for them.

CHILDREN'S LITERATURE: RELEVANCE FOR PHYSICAL AND MOTOR DEVELOPMENT

An array of "character types"

Children learn about themselves from books. If they cannot find characters with physical characteristics similar to their own, they may become insecure about their own social acceptability. Fortunately, books recently prepared for young children are displaying a mix of sexes, races, and physical features. It is hoped that this array of "character types" is communicating to children the belief that social acceptability is not dependent upon physical appearance. Children should have exposure through books and other media to the universal human needs, concerns, and abilities running through all people despite their physical differences.

Some books are available that deal directly with individual and racial differences in physical appearance. In a series of books produced by Thomas Y. Crowell Publishers, the reader is given a closer look at the functions of various parts of the body and at physical variation among human beings. Among these are Aliki Brandenburg's *My hands* (1962); Augusta Goldin's *Straight hair, curly hair,* (1966); and Paul Shower's, *Look at your eyes* (1962); and *Your skin and mine* (1965).

Stimulating movement activities

In addition to helping children understand and accept their own physical characteristics and those of others, books can also be instrumental in stimulating motor activities that develop agility and coordination. Quite spontaneously, children often imitate the movements and activities they hear in stories. Given teacher suggestions, their motor participation will become even more extensive and varied, as follows:

- The children are listening to Esphyr Slobodkina's *Caps for sale* (New York: William R. Scott, 1957). As they listen, they cannot resist duplicating the monkey's imitation of the peddler whose wares (caps) the monkeys have stolen. With delight, they shake their right hands, their left hands, both hands, stamp their left feet, both feet, and finally toss an imaginary cap as the story concludes with the peddler collecting the caps and continuing to shout, "Caps for sale!"

- Many four- and five-year-olds, inspired by George Zaffo's *The giant nursery book of things that go* (Garden City, N.Y.: Doubleday, 1959), have spent their activity period chasing fires, pulling on coats and boots, winding hoses, and climbing imaginary ladders.
- A few three- and four-year-olds have just heard the book by Wanda Gag, *Millions of cats* (New York: Coward-McCann, 1938). In this rhythmic tale, a little old man and a little old woman who wanted just one cat find themselves with "millions and billions and trillions" of cats. As their teacher puts some lively music on the record player, they act out their impressions of the playfully mewing, pawing, pouncing, and fighting kittens. Their activity is so appealing that many other children join in. Crawling "kittens" appear to be everywhere, just as in *Millions of cats*.
- The seven-year-olds have thoroughly enjoyed rehearing Theodore Geisel's [Dr. Seuss] Christmas classic, *How the Grinch stole Christmas* (New York: Random House, 1957). They ask their teacher to read it again, so that they can act out the parts of the Whoville citizens who almost lost their holiday. At the conclusion, with their teacher's help, they consider the many different ways particular parts of the story could be portrayed. All the children quite spontaneously try out each action suggested, which involves a wide range of posturings and gestures.

Rhythmic verses and movement

Verses can be even more effective in leading children into a variety of motor activities. If you have memorized a series of rhythmic verses that you can recite at any point, you will find it easy to involve children in the actions suggested by the cadence, whether they are in the classroom, on the playground, on a field trip, or simply waiting for the bus to arrive. The nursery verse "The Grand Old Duke of York" has good marching rhythm:

"The Grand Old Duke of York"

The grand old Duke of York,
He had ten thousand men.
He marched them up to the top of the hill,
And he marched them down again.

And when they were up, they were up,
And when they were down, they were down,
And when they were only halfway up
They were neither up nor down.

Or children can try stalking to:

"Grizzly Bear"

If you ever ever meet a grizzly bear
You must never never never ask him where
He is going or what he is doing,
For if you ever dare

To stop a grizzly bear
You may never meet another grizzly bear.
                                          Mary Austin[1]

Fun and relaxation   Such light verses often prove useful in reducing the tensions of hyperactive
or emotionally upset children. It is also very helpful to have an array of
humorous stories and poems in your repertoire to share with children who
are "up tight" for any reason. Laughter can be an effective relaxant. Try some
of Seuss's tales such as *Yertle the turtle* (New York: Random House, 1958);
And to think that I saw it on Mulberry street (Eau Claire, Wisconsin: E. M. Hale,
1937); and *Horton hatches the egg* (New York: Random House, 1954) for this
purpose. Some of the stories in *The Sneetches and other stories* (1961), also by
Theodore Geisel, are dependably funny. The one that children laugh most
uproariously about is the story of Mrs. McCabe who had twenty-three sons
and named them all Dave. It is worth memorizing. Mrs. McCabe, as the verse
relates, wishes that she had named them otherwise:

> And often she wishes that, when they were born,
> She had named one of them Bodkin Van Horn.
> And one of them Hoos Foos. And one of them Snimm,
> And one of them Hot-Shot. And one Sunny Jim.
> And one of them Shadrack. And one of them Blinkey.
> And one of them Stuffy. And one of them Stinky.
> Another one Putt-Putt. Another one Moon Face.
> Another one Marvin O'Gravel Balloon Face.
> Another one of them Ziggy. And one Soggy Muff.
> One Buffalo Bill. And one Biffalo Buff.
> And one of them Sneepy. And one Weepy Weed.
> And one Paris Garters. And one Harris Tweed.
> And one of them Sir Michael Carnichael Zutt.
> And one of them Oliver Boliver Butt
> And one of them Zanzibar Buck Buck McFate.
> But she didn't do it. And now it's too late.
>
>   Theodore Geisel (Dr. Seuss)[2]

The advantage of memorized rhymes is that they can be repeated and
repeated at the drop of a hat and gradually become more and more beloved,
and so are consistently associated with fun-filled and tension-free moments.
A resourceful teacher will have a range of light-hearted rhymes and rhythmic
tales memorized. You might try the following:

---

[1] From the book *The Children Sing in the Far West*. Copyright 1928 by Mary Austin. Copyright
renewed 1956 by Kenneth M. Chapman and Mary C. Wheelright. Reprinted by permission of
Houghton Mifflin Company.
[2] From *The Sneetches and Other Stories*, by Dr. Seuss. Copyright 1953, 1954, © 1961 by Dr. Seuss.
Reprinted by permission of Random House, Inc.

One misty moisty morning
    When cloudy was the weather
I chanced to meet an old man
    Clothed all in leather
He began to compliment
    And I began to grin
How do you do? And how do you do?
    And how do you do again?

Traditional Mother Goose

"I Know an Old Lady"

I know an old lady who swallowed a fly.
I don't know why she swallowed a fly!
I guess she'll die!

I know an old lady who swallowed a spider,
That wriggled and wriggled and tickled inside her.
She swallowed a spider to catch the fly,
But I don't know why she swallowed the fly!
I guess she'll die.

I know an old lady who swallowed a bird,
How absurd to swallow a bird!
She swallowed the bird to catch the spider, etc.

I know an old lady who swallowed a cat.
Now fancy that, to swallow a cat!
She swallowed the cat to catch the bird.
She swallowed the bird to catch the spider, etc.

I know an old lady who swallowed a dog.
My what a hog, to swallow a dog!
She swallowed the dog to catch the cat, etc.

I know an old lady who swallowed a goat.
Just opened her throat, and in walked the goat!
She swallowed the goat to catch the dog, etc.

I know an old lady who swallowed a cow.
I don't know how she swallowed a cow!
She swallowed the cow to catch the goat, etc.

I know an old lady who swallowed a horse!

She's dead of course!

   Also available is a wide array of verses that have been set to music for fun
and action. You probably already have a repertoire of these from you own
childhood. Many of these include actions that children enjoy performing,
some of which contribute to conscious coordination and motor development.

Among those you may wish to include in your teaching repertoire are "London Bridge," "Pop Goes the Weasel," "Here We Go Round the Mulberry Bush," "Here We Go Looby Loo," "Farmer in the Dell," "Skip to My Lou," "Did You Ever See a Lassie?," "If You're Happy," "Hokey Pokey," "A Tisket a Tasket," "This Old Man," "Bingo." What others do you know?

CHILDREN'S LITERATURE: RELEVANCE FOR AFFECTIVE DEVELOPMENT

There are at least two major ways in which literature can contribute to children's emotional development. The first is simply the provision of beauty through words, images, and ideas. The second is through the vicarious experience that results from identifying with the major characters.

Books as aesthetic experiences

Many children's books are pure aesthetic delights. Even though most children will not respond as vigorously and directly to the visual beauty in books as to humor and adventure, they do appreciate and benefit from this dimension also. For the youngest children there are volumes like Ruth Krauss's simple tale of the awakening animals' discovery of a flower in spring, *The happy day* (New York: Harper, 1949).

The Caldecott Medal is awarded annually by the American Library Association to a book selected as the outstanding picture book. The media used, the themes, and the level of appeal to young children vary greatly among the books selected for this award. Some exposure to the winning titles (given here with last names of illustrators and the publishers) is recommended.

1976 *Why mosquitoes buzz in people's ears* Dillon and Dillon (Dial)
1975 *Arrow to the sun* McDermott (Viking)
1974 *Duffy and the devil* Zemach (Farrar)
1973 *The funny little woman* Lent (Dutton)
1972 *One fine day* Hogrogian (Macmillan)
1971 *A story—a story* Haley (Atheneum)
1970 *Sylvester and the magic pebble* Steig (Windmill/Simon & Schuster)
1969 *The fool of the world and the flying ship* Shulevitz (Farrar)
1968 *Drummer Hoff* Emberley (Prentice-Hall)
1967 *Sam, Bangs and Moonshine* Ness (Holt)
1966 *Always room for one more* Hogrogian (Holt)
1965 *May I bring a friend?* Montresor (Atheneum)
1964 *Where the wild things are* Sendak (Harper)
1963 *The snowy day* Keats (Viking)
1962 *Once a mouse* Brown (Scribner's)
1961 *Baboushka and the Three Kings* Sidjakov (Parnassus)
1960 *Nine days to Christmas* Ets (Viking)
1959 *Chanticleer and the fox* Cooney (Crowell)
1958 *Time of wonder* McCloskey (Viking)
1957 *A tree is nice* Simont (Harper)
1956 *Frog went a-courtin'* Rojankovsky (Harcourt)
1955 *Cinderella* Brown (Scribner's)

1954 *Madeline's rescue* Bemelmans (Viking)
1953 *The biggest bear* Ward (Houghton Mifflin)
1952 *Finders keepers* Nicolas (Harcourt)
1951 *The egg tree* Milhous (Scribner's)
1950 *Sing of the swallows* Politi (Scribner's)
1949 *The big snow* Hader (Macmillan)
1948 *White snow, bright snow* Duvoisin (Lothrop)
1947 *The little island* Weisgard (Doubleday)
1946 *The rooster crows* Petersham (Macmillan)
1945 *Prayer for a child* Jones (Macmillan)
1944 *Many moons* Slobodkin (Harcourt)
1943 *The little house* Burton (Houghton Mifflin)
1942 *Make way for ducklings* McCloskey (Viking)
1941 *They were strong and good* Lawson (Viking)
1940 *Abraham Lincoln* d'Aulaire (Doubleday)
1939 *Mel Li* Handforth (Doubleday)
1938 *Animals of the Bible* Lathrop (Lippincott)

In addition to the visual delights of picture books, young children often relish the accompanying word sounds and images. As a teacher you have the opportunity for sharing delightful words, such as those of the gingerbread man as he says,

Run, run as fast as you can,
You can't catch me,
I'm the gingerbread man.
I've run away from the little old woman
And the little old man
And the bunny
And the bear cub
And I can run away from you, too,
I can, I can.

Perspectives on feelings and behavior

Books provide children with models of what is acceptable and admirable and of what is undesirable or deplorable. By exposing them to a variety of character roles with contrasting experiences and feelings, they can begin selecting and clarifying their own roles and feelings. Through books you can offer children a rich set of perspectives for thinking about their own feelings and behaviors.

Children's books have broadened appreciably during the 1960s and 1970s. Before the 1960s they tended to be much more stereotyped in their portrayal of the world. Females, for example, were portrayed as either nice mommies and lovely princesses, or as mean old stepmothers and wicked witches. You may wish to take advantage of the new wave of books depicting a variety of male and female roles and behaviors. Among those volumes you will find books such as Joe Lasker's *Mothers can do anything* (Chicago: Albert Whitman, 1972), in which mothers are portrayed as fixing pipes, making films, fixing teeth, flying, and climbing.

The current world of children's books is far from being a fairy tale world of good and evil, beauty and ugliness, wisdom and stupidity. The characters in many children's books are now quite believable, exhibiting real problems and human frailties that children can easily identify with. Things sometimes go quite badly for these new heroes of children's literature, just as they do for us. In Viorst's *Alexander and the terrible, horrible, no good, very bad day* (New York: Atheneum, 1972), Alexander woke up with the gum he had been chewing the previous evening stuck in his hair. From that point right through bedtime, when his cat deserts him to sleep with his brother, everything goes wrong. Knowing about Alexander should make any young child a bit more tolerant of his or her own bad days and the negative feelings that accompany them.

Through books children can learn that their own occasional "bad" feelings are felt by others as well. Storybook children often are not any happier with their siblings, for example, than are real children. In Charlotte Zolotow's *If it weren't for you* (New York: Harper & Row, 1966), the main character tells another child about all the things "I would do if I were the only child. . ." but concludes ". . . except I'd have to be alone with the grown-ups."

Storybook children have very realistic problems as when Mary Jo, in Janice May Udry's *Mary Jo's grandmother* (Chicago: Albert Whitman, 1970), has her first independent visit to her grandmother's home in the country during one Christmas vacation. Everything goes as expected until in the middle of a big snowstorm, Grandmother falls, hurts her ankle, and cannot move at all. Mary Jo faces a problem situation that could happen to any child, and children relish thinking about such dilemmas. In another book, Joe Lasker's *He's my brother* (Chicago: Albert Whitman, 1974), the problem is an ongoing one

Photo by permission of Bernice Wright
Cooperative Nursery School.

involving a slow-learning younger brother whose odd behaviors are sometimes difficult to understand and accept.

As children vicariously encounter and live through these experiences by identifying with the book characters, they gain emotionally. Especially important are those books that deal with situations similar to ones confronted by the young reader or by persons close to him or her. Through books we can all extend our experiences and emerge as stronger people because of it. As a teacher you can consciously choose books that will facilitate such emotional growth for children.

CHILDREN'S LITERATURE: RELEVANCE FOR SOCIAL DEVELOPMENT

Understanding social relationships

Books can contribute much to children's appreciation and understanding of their own feelings in social relationships. Even the best of friendships have their ups and downs and this range of feelings is reflected in children's literature. Charlotte Zolotow's *My friend John* (New York: Harper & Row, 1972) celebrates all that is good about having a friend. "I know everything about John," reads the text, " and he knows everything about me." What each knows about the other is lovingly recounted, "John's the only one besides my family who knows I sleep with my light on at night . . . and how to get into each other's house if the door is locked." Young listeners respond warmly to this message, one that they are just learning—that it is very good to have a close friend.

That friendships, however good, have their rough moments is delightfully conveyed in Udry's *Let's be enemies* (New York: Harper & Row, 1961). Two good friends have a falling out. "James used to be my friend," reads the text, "but not today." Three- and four-year-olds echo agreement as they hear the problem, "James always wants to be the boss." Evidently, they often see their friends in the same light and recognize the uncomfortable mixed feelings in being mad at your friend. The tension begins to break as the angry one declares, "I'm going over and poke James," and then, "I think I'll put his crayons in the soup." What comic relief from the preschoolers' perspective!

How social discontent gets passed along in a chain of events becomes a bit more understandable to children who hear Byron Barton's *bzz, bzz, bzz* (New York: Macmillan, 1973). A bee stings a bull so hard that he runs madly around until he makes the cow nervous, and she kicks the farmer's wife, who goes home and yells at the farmer, until a full circular effect is created. In a more complex but similar tale, Zolotow's *The quarreling book* (New York: Harper & Row, 1963), the same kind of chain of events is presented. Mr. James, on a gray rainy morning forgets to kiss Mrs. Jones good-bye, whereupon she . . . and the chain begins. In this latter tale, however, when the chain reaction finally reaches the dog, who has not been affected by the rainy weather, he does not react in kind and his positive response to ill treatment starts a new chain of positive reactions. The parallels between the two books are interesting for six- and seven-year-olds to ponder and discuss.

Story punch lines can often help teachers and older children cope with

As you become familiar with a variety of children's books you will note there are a number of different types, each of which may need to be presented and used in a different way. If children are helped to approach books with expectations appropriate to their purposes, they will respond to them in more positive ways and benefits will likely be greater. You may therefore find it useful to ask yourself the following kinds of questions about each book you examine:

- Does it tell a story?
- Does it teach a concept?
- Does it provide an aesthetic visual experience?
- Does it provide an aesthetic language or an internal imagery experience?
- Does it stimulate imagination?
- Does it reflect imagination?
- Does it reflect reality?
- Is the intent of the book fulfilled primarily by the illustrations? By the text? Or both?
- Does it provoke an emotional reaction?

Developing social repertoire

situations similar to the ones depicted in books. A reference such as, "I guess you feel like putting his crayons in the soup," or "bzz-bzz-bzz," can serve as ready reminders of the universality of negative feelings and the need for greater tolerance and altered behaviors.

Books can also play a crucial role in helping children consider alternative responses to social situations. Recall the discussion, in Chapter 5, of the work of Spivack and Shure (1974) in developing children's awareness of alternatives for social problem-solving; books can help you develop these abilities in children. By pausing at critical decision points within a story and asking the children what they would do in that particular situation, they will become more aware of the diverse decision-making possibilities in most situations. Such discussions should probably not interrupt the initial reading of a story, however, as it might detract from the story's impact; they can be reserved until the end of the initial reading or until subsequent readings.

Some stories provide built-in opportunities for children to respond. One such book is Norma Simon's *What did I do?* (Chicago: Albert Whitman, 1969). In this book, Consuela faces many small issues in her Puerto Rican neighborhood, such as "I want to play but I can't find my doll. What do I do?" and "Joe wants my wagon. What do I do?" Consuela only tells the reader of the one option she took, that is, she looked for her doll, she suggested to Joe that they take turns. It is only through a teacher-led discussion that listeners can learn that Consuela had many other possible choices.

Book characters often demonstrate their cleverness in solving social problems. In Crosby Bonsall's *I mean it, Stanley* (New York: Harper & Row, 1974), the main character tries to lure his balky dog Stanley to come and play with him. Failing, he proceeds to make something he declares to be simply marvelous and puts it off limits to Stanley. Of course, Stanley comes right over. In Ezra Jack Keats' *Goggles* (New York: Macmillan, 1969), some older bullies are foiled in their efforts to take some motorcycle goggles away from Archie, Peter, and their dog Willie. Cleverness prevails over size. However, in the Udry book, *What Mary Jo shared* (Chicago: Albert Whitman, 1966), the heroine cleverly solves the very common problem of what to show during sharing period at school. In each of these books a single solution is offered to some common childhood dilemma. In such cases, teachers can extend the book's usefulness by leading a group discussion of alternative solutions.

CHILDREN'S LITERATURE: RELEVANCE FOR COGNITIVE AND INTELLECTUAL DEVELOPMENT

On the following pages we offer examples of books that are appropriate to the various types of learning discussed in Section Two: classification, number, seriation, causality, space and time concepts, and spoken and written language. It should be noted, however, that books defy pigeonholing. Clever teachers can adapt most books to a variety of teaching responsibilities.

Classification

Many books demonstrate classifications to children. In books such as Richard Scarry's (New York: Random House) *Great big school house* (1969), and *Great big air book* (1971), or George Zaffo's (New York: Doubleday) *The giant nursery book of things that work* (1967), and *The giant nursery book of things that go* (1959), animals or objects are grouped according to form or function. Children can discover or can be shown why particular things are grouped in the same book or on the same pages.

Implicit and explicit classifications

In other books, such as Bernice Kohn's *Everything has a shape* (Englewood Cliffs, N.J.: Prentice-Hall, 1964), and Millicent Selsam's *All kinds of babies and how they grow* (New York: William R. Scott, 1953), the classification criteria are explicitly discussed in the text. In the latter volume baby animals that resemble their parents are contrasted with other animals that go through a series of radical developmental changes during their life spans (frogs, moths, eels, crabs, and swans).

Number

All sorts of number books are available that encourage children to count pictured objects and recognize written numerals. Among the wide array are such volumes as Ulf Lofgren's *One-two-three* (Reading, Mass.: Addison-Wesley, 1970), the tale of Farmer Featherstone trying to figure out how many animals he has on his farm. The reader sees *"One* fat friendly dog," *"Two* slim smiling cats," *"Nine* quacking ducks with flat floppy feet." Farmer

Counting books

Featherstone not only counts his animals, but has five of his giddy goats chase him across the field while two others just stand and stare. With adult help many young children become involved in counting, adding, and thinking about numbers as they read or listen to this kind of book.

Counting books are available that deal with all kinds of topical interests. For urban children there is Eve Merriams' *Project 1-2-3* (New York: McGraw-Hill, 1971). The housing project takes up *one* whole block, the number *two* is represented by two front doors, two elevators, and two walls covered with mail boxes. When the number *six* is presented, it is in a laundromat scene with six double-load washers and six giant dryers. *Eight* depicts garbage collection, with eight trash cans. This book demonstrates that anything can be counted. In Keats' *Apt. 3* (New York: Macmillan, 1971), which is more of a story than a counting book, Sam and little brother Ben go from apartment to apartment noting apartment numbers while searching for the music they have heard. Finally, in Apt. 3, they find a blind tenant who not only plays the harmonica but also knows all about what goes on in the building, including Sam's interest in the little girl who lives in Apt. 2.

Benjamin Elkin presents the tale of *The six foolish fishermen* (Chicago: Children's Press, 1959) who never get beyond *five* when counting themselves. That each has forgotten to count himself is obvious only to the most observant child. Other particularly appealing counting books are Helen Oxenbury's *Numbers of things* (New York: Franklin Watts, 1968), James Kruss's *Three by three* (New York: Macmillan, 1965), Arthur Gregor's *1 2 3 4 5*

Photo by Laura Lehmann.

(Philadelphia: Lippincott, 1964), Dahlov Ipcar's *Brown cow farm* (Garden City, N.Y.: Doubleday, 1959), and Maurice Sendak's *One was Johnny* (New York: Harper & Row, 1962).

Seriation

Alignment according to size or other dimensions is best learned by children's active manipulation rather than through books. However, a number of books can help a child formalize or crystallize his or her developing concepts of how objects can be compared with each other. Books that help children with size *Comparisons* comparisons are Bernice Kohn's *Everything has a size* (Englewood Cliffs, N.J.: Prentice-Hall, 1964), Miriam Schlein's *Heavy is a hippopotamus* (New York: Dodd, Mead, 1956), Alexi Tolstoi's *The great big enormous turnip* (New York: Franklin Watts, 1969), and Charles and Martha Shapp's *Let's find out what's big and what's small* (New York: Franklin Watts, 1959). Relative speed is the focus of Miriam Schlein's *Fast is not a ladybug* (New York: William R. Scott, 1953).

Causality

Many fine books covering virtually all subjects are available to help explain various real phenomena to young children. By spending time in the nonfic-*Simple* tion section of any children's library, you will not only learn what is available *explanations and* to children but will also inevitably sharpen your own perspective on many *activity ideas* topics. Study carefully the presentations that are made in these books, especially those in the natural and physical science areas, and you will gain many valuable ideas for demonstrating cause and effect.

Some books suggest a variety of possibilities for children's investigations of the common things that surround them. In Harvey Milgram's *Egg-Ventures* (New York: E. P. Dutton, 1974), for example, suggestions are given for measuring the length, width, and volume of eggs; for examining their buoyancy in fresh and salt water; for rolling them and comparing their rolling patterns with those of balls and other objects; for examining the effects of heating and beating them. Seymour Simon's *A tree on your street* (New York: Holiday House, 1973) gives more complex suggestions for various activities in measuring, examining, and analyzing changes in a tree.

Space concepts

While the preschool-age child most effectively builds space concepts through active manipulation of objects and self in relation to objects, five- to seven-*Measurement and* year-olds can benefit from simple book presentations on measurement and *directionality* directionality. Among the books that may be useful at this point are Ethel Berkeley's *Big and little, up and down* (New York: William R. Scott, 1960), and Rolf Myller's *How big is a foot?* (New York: Atheneum, 1962). There are also books that help the child consider him or herself relative to larger spatial contexts. Herman and Nina Schneider's *You among the stars* (New York: William R. Scott, 1951) is one such volume; another is James Hengesbough's *I live in so many places* (Chicago: Children's Press, 1956), which attempts to help the child understand that he lives simultaneously in a house, in a town, in a state, in a country, and in a world.

A beginning sense of geography can be facilitated by books depicting children's lives in other parts of the globe or travel through space. However, while children welcome hearing stories such as Len Yiang's *Tommy and Deedee* (New York: Henry Z. Walck, 1953), which describes some of the likenesses and differences between two children living on opposite sides of the world, any realistic conception of what is presented will be acquired at a later age. To a child, the moon or China may seem closer than his or her grandmother's house several hours' drive away, and book descriptions are unlikely to affect that view.

Time concepts

Passage of seasons and years

While young children's sense of time and history remains quite sketchy from ages three through seven, their awareness may be heightened by attention to the time concepts presented in many children's books. For example, Virginia Lee Burton's *The little house* (Boston: Houghton Mifflin, 1942), the story of a country house that is increasingly surrounded by city structures, contains beautiful illustrations of the passage of time. The little house is portrayed through days and nights, through passages of seasons, through the passing of years and generations. The same kind of direct or indirect reference to time is included in many other children's books and can contribute to the child's awareness of these dimensions. Among these are Miriam Schlein's *It's about time* (New York: William R. Scott, 1955), Franklyn Branley's *Snow is falling* (New York: Thomas Y. Crowell, 1963), and Maurice Sendak's *Chicken soup with rice: A book of months* (New York: Harper & Row, 1952).

Spoken language

Modeling syntax and vocabulary

The improvement in children's language abilities through exposure to literature is ample justification for reading to them frequently and regularly. New vocabulary and more complex sentence constructions become familiar through pleasant listening experiences. When literature provides children with models that basically fit but slightly stretch their existing language abilities, the benefits are great. For those children who lack language facility because English is their second language or because they typically use a nonstandard dialect, stories with simple and clear wordings and phrasings are best. The old nursery tales are good choices: "Goldilocks and the Three Bears," "The Three Billy Goats Gruff," "The Three Little Red Hens," "Chicken Little," "The Gingerbread Boy."

The language in many newer tales is almost as clear and simple, such as Beatrix Potter's *The tale of Peter Rabbit* (New York: William R. Scott, 1957), H. A. Rey's *Curious George* (New York: Coward-McCann, 1941), and C. W. Anderson's *Billy and Blaze book bag* (New York: Collier, 1973).

Assessing language difficulty level

It is important that you determine the level of language difficulty in books you plan to read. Some picture books that initially seem appropriate for young children actually have very complex vocabulary and language structure. These are "just right" for linguistically gifted children and should be reserved for them. Exemplary of this kind of book are the Mellops series by Tomi Ungerer, such as *The Mellops go spelunking* (New York: Harper & Row, 1963). In these books a family of pigs have quite fascinating adventures, but the vocabulary level is quite different than that found in the tale of the three little pigs. For example, the text reads, "A sharp stalagmite punctured the raft. The Mellops' sons cried out in despair."

By age six or seven many children can follow stories without help from pictures. They begin to enjoy stories in which the illustrations support the text, as well as the other way around. There are some excellent transition books that wean children from total reliance on picture books to enjoying simple stories conveyed primarily in language. During group story time, try the following as first experiences with such books: Alice Dalgleish's *The bears on hemlock mountain* (New York: Scribner's, 1952), and *The courage of Sarah Noble* (New York: Scribner's, 1954); Miriam Mason's *Caroline and her kettle named Maud* (New York: Macmillan, 1951); Richard and Florence Atwater's *Mr. Popper's penguins* (Boston: Little, Brown, 1938); and Alice Rothschild's *Bad trouble in Miss Alcorn's class* (New York: William R. Scott, 1959).

Advantages of memorizing stories to tell and poems to share

Language impact is further heightened when teachers can tell rather than read stories, due to better voice inflection and eye contact. Choose at least five stories that you thoroughly enjoy and learn to tell them well. Not only will your students benefit linguistically, but you will also be able to profitably fill those difficult waiting periods (for example, because of buses, special events, and slower group members) that plague every teacher.

Similarly, poetry should be recited to children, not read, if it is to have maximum impact. Unless you have the poems you want to share with children on the tip of your tongue, the chances are they will never be heard. Memorize and practice reciting several poems and then look for opportunities to share them.

Written language

Relationships of literature to children's own reading

If children's natural inclinations to imitate "grown-up" literary behavior are encouraged and assisted over a span of years, most children will find learning to read and write a relatively easy task. If they have continuous opportunities to dictate their ideas for a teacher to record and read, they will gradually learn to recognize their own "high-frequency" words and then spot them in books. Of course, this will occur more easily for some children than for others. However, competence in written language will be hastened for all children if they are given regular opportunities to hear stories, look at books, and record their own thoughts in books they produce (with a teacher's help).

Preprimers and "easy-to-reads"

By the time children recognize ten or so different words, they will be delighted to discover that, given a little help, they can actually read certain books. This initial reading experience typically involves books labeled "preprimer" or "easy to-read." Both labels signify books whose vocabulary is

FREQUENTLY USED WORDS

The following are words determined to be most used in speaking vocabularies and in reading materials (including basal readers) (Dolch, 1941). They are arranged here in groupings according the frequency of occurrence:

a, an, he, in, is, of, that, the, to, was

and, are, as, at, be, but, by, for, from, had, have, his, I, it, not, on, or, they, this, with

about, after, again, all, always, any, around, away, because, been, before, best, better, big, both, came, can, come, could, did, do, does, done, don't, down, every, find, first, for, found, four, get, give, go, going, good, got, has, her, here, him, how, if, into, its, kind, know, let, like, light, little, look, long, made, make, many, may, me, much, must, my, never, new, no, now, off, old, once, one, only, open, our, out, over, own, past, put, right, said, saw, say, see, she, small, so, some, take, their, them, then, there, these, think, those, three, too, under, up, upon, us, use, very, want, we, will, went, were, what, when, where, which, white, when, who, will, work, would, you, your

Reprinted by permission from E. W. Dolch, *Teaching primary reading* (Champaign, Ill.: Garrard Press, 1941), pp. 205–207.

Photo by permission of Bernice Wright Cooperative Nursery School.

BOOKS FOR EARLY READING

Children who are at the very beginning stages of word recognition receive a tremendous boost along the road to becoming literate if they discover that there are some interesting books that they can actually "read." For this reason many teachers of young children search for a supply of books with intriguing pictures and real plots that are related with a limited vocabulary and a "lilting" phraseology. Among these "satisfying" books for early reading are the following:

Averill, E. *Fire cat*. New York: Harper & Row, 1960.
Eastman, P. D. *Are you my mother?* New York: Random House, 1969.
Eastman, P. D. *Go, dog, go*. New York: Random House, 1961.
Geisel, Theodore (Dr. Seuss). *Green eggs and ham*. New York: Random House, 1960.
Guilefoile, E. *Nobody listens to Andrew*. Chicago: Follett, 1957.
Hoff, S. *Who will be my friend?* New York: Harper & Row, 1960.
Minarik, E. *Little bear*. New York: Harper & Row, 1960.

limited to a few familiar words that can be learned relatively easily by most young children.

In their initial reading experiences, some children may only read a couple of lines from a page, while others may read an entire book six times over. Unless this early reading experience is guided by some instructional system, this variation will continue. Some children will read only the easiest materials as rapidly as they can, while others will skip directly to hard materials that they must slowly and painstakingly plow through. Still others will alternate between easy and difficult reading. Most children can find an array of books that suit their reading levels and interests, given reasonable access to the multitude of early reading materials that have been produced over the past two decades.

Your role as a teacher is to remain constantly aware of what each child can do—which words the child knows, what similar words the child could learn easily, and what cues the child uses in attempting to decipher unfamiliar words. If you regularly spend time with each child in looking at books and talking about books in the prereading stages, you can easily help them make transitions into reading. As children gradually master the mechanics of word recognition, more and more of your book corner time will be spent in discussing the content of books, and in helping them write their own stories.

Underlying the whole venture, however, is your ability to motivate children to explore books, whether this involves looking at, listening to, reading, writing, or sharing them. To the extent that this ongoing process continues to be enjoyable, full of small successes and few failures, the children you teach will gradually become competent at reading and writing.

The previous pages contain many suggestions, both specific and general, for using literature with children. Choose the ten books, or activities that you feel would be most appropriate for each of the children you observed in your study of Section Two. As you formulate your list of books or activities, browse back through the chapter and modify your choices to match the developmental levels of the respective children.

For each of the books or activities you have identified, try to determine whether it will provide new skills and concepts, a new application of existing skills and concepts, or both.

Further Extensions and Applications

Need for continued effort in becoming familiar with children's literature

This chapter is only a brief introduction to what you will need to know about children's literature. You should continue to extend your knowledge in this area through independent study or through coursework. While other areas of preparation require field experience, familiarity with children's literature can be accomplished without having direct responsibility for children. It is important that you become familiar with a broad array of literature on a variety of topics. Select and rehearse those poems and stories that you would like to be able to share extemporaneously, and keep in mind those books that you would especially want to make available to children you will teach.

You may find it helpful to browse in the children's sections of bookstores and libraries whenever you have the opportunity. As you are doing so, observe the children. Note which books they are most drawn to. Whenever possible, observe the story hours in children's libraries. Note at what points children of various ages seem most involved and when they become most bored and restless. Watch the librarians to see which reading and story-telling techniques seem most successful and try to master them yourself.

Summary

As a teacher, it is your responsibility to lead children to an appreciation of literature. You are not likely to satisfactorily fulfill this obligation unless you have developed an appreciation of this literature yourself. Children depend on adults to introduce them to books, stories, and poems that can enhance their development.

Recent children's book characters include a mix of sexes, races, and physical features that can contribute to self-acceptance and self-understanding among a more diverse group of readers than in times past. Many books and verses also stimulate engagement in various motor activities. Humorous selections help children laugh and relax, so they are more able to participate in all of the opportunities available to them.

Books can contribute to children's affective development by providing aesthetic experiences that, for many, are not otherwise available. Through books they learn to understand and accept their own and others' feelings and, with adult help, to expand their social awareness and behavioral repertoires.

Excellent books are currently available for assisting children with virtually every area of cognitive and intellectual development. Some of the books explicitly emphasize classification, counting and numbers, seriation, causality, space and time concepts, and language development. Others, while focusing on other subject matter intriguing to young readers, also include ample material for the development of these basic abilities. With enough exposure to books and continuous adult help, children gradually and successfully learn to read and write.

Your task is to continue the process, begun in this chapter, of gaining familiarity with children's literature so that you can assist children in becoming, first, enthusiastic about reading, and then, readers.

REASSESSMENT

Reread what you wrote for the preassessment as you began this chapter, comparing this with your current understandings. Now write on these topics again and incorporate your new insights and knowledge. Continue to update as you prepare for teaching. Save your materials for your portfolio.

Additional Reading

Children's Literature   Anderson, W., and Groff, P. *A new look at children's literature.* Belmont, Calif.: Wadsworth, 1972.

Arbuthnot, M. H., and Root, S. L. *Time for poetry.* Glenview, Ill.: Scott, Foresman, 1968.

Arbuthnot, M. H., and Sutherland, Z. *Children and books,* 4th ed. Glenview, Ill.: Scott, Foresman, 1972.

Cathon, L. E., Haushalter, M. McC., and Russell, V. A. *Stories to tell to children: A selected list.* Pittsburgh: University of Pittsburgh Press, 1974.

deRegniers, B., Moore, E., and White, M. M. *Poems children will sit still for.* Englewood Cliffs, N.J.: Scholastic Books Service, 1969.

Fagerlie, A. M. Using wordless picture books with children. *Elementary English,* 1975, 52, 92–94.

Griffin, L. *Books in preschool.* Washington, D.C.: National Association for Early Childhood Education, 1970.

Hall, M. A., and Matanzo, J. Children's literature: A source for concept development. *Elementary English,* 1975, 52, 487–94.

Huck, C. S., and Kuhn, D. A. *Children's literature in the elementary school*. New York: Holt, Rinehart and Winston, 1968.

Jacobs, L., Ed. *Using literature with young children*. New York: Teachers College Press 1965.

Larrick, N. *A parent's guide to children's books*, 3rd ed. Columbus, Ohio: Charles E. Merrill, 1969.

Larrick, N. *A teacher's guide to children's books*. Columbus, Ohio: Charles E. Merrill, 1963.

McIntyre, M. Books which give mathematical concepts to young children: An annotated bibliography. *Young Children*, 1969, 24, 287–91.

Stawicki, C. *Children's books: Awards and prizes*. New York: The Children's Book Council, 1973.

Periodicals on Children's Literature

The Booklist. American Library Association, 50 E. Huron St., Chicago, Illinois 60611

The Calendar. Children's Book Council, 175 Fifth Ave., New York, New York 10011

Language Arts (formerly *Elementary English*). National Council of Teachers of English, 704 S. Sixth St., Champaign, Illinois 61820

The Horn Book Magazine. Horn Book, 585 Boylston St., Boston, Massachusetts 02116

School Library Journal. R. R. Bowker, 1180 Avenue of the Americas, New York, New York 10036

Children's Songs

Bailey, C., and Holsaert, B., Compilers. *Sing a song with Charity Bailey*. New York: Plymouth Music Company.

Chroman, E. *Songs that children sing*. New York: Oak Publications, 1970.

Jenkins, E., Krane, S., and Lipschutz, P. *The Ella Jenkins songbook for children*. New York: Oak Publications, 1966.

Landeck, B. *Songs to grow on: A collection of American folk songs for children*. New York: William Sloan/Morrow, 1954. See also *More songs to grow on*, 1954.

McConathy, O. *et al. Music for early childhood*. Morristown, N.J.: Silver Burdett, 1952.

Reynolds, M. *Little boxes and other handmade songs*. New York: Oak Publications, 1964.

Seeger, R. C. *American folk songs for children*. Garden City, N.Y.: Doubleday, 1948.

Smith, B. N., Harter, T. C., Walter, M. W., and Hyman, T. S. *Let's sing this-a-way*. LaSalle, Ill.: Open Court, 1970.

Winn, M. *et al. The fireside book of children's songs*. New York: Simon and Schuster, 1966.

Periodicals for Children

Children's Digest. Parents Institute of Parents Magazine. 52 Vanderbilt Ave., New York, New York 10017

Ebony Jr.! 820 S. Michigan Ave., Chicago, Illinois 60605

Highlights for Children. 37 East Long Street, Columbus, Ohio 43215

Humpty Dumpty's Magazine for Little Children. Parents Institute of Parents Magazine, 52 Vanderbilt Ave., New York, New York 10017

Jack and Jill. Saturday Evening Post Company, 1100 Waterways Blvd., Indianapolis, Indiana 46202

Ranger Rick's Nature Magazine. National Wildlife Federation, 1412 16th St. N.W., Washington, D.C. 20036

Sesame Street Magazine. North Road, Poughkeepsie, New York 12601

Guide to Children's Magazines, Newspapers Reference Books. Association for Childhood Education International, 3615 Wisconsin Avenue N.W., Washington, D.C. 20016

CHAPTER 11
Resourcefulness with Children's Pretend Play

Overview

Your Resourcefulness and Children's Development
PRETEND PLAY: RELEVANCE FOR MOTOR DEVELOPMENT
PRETEND PLAY: RELEVANCE FOR AFFECTIVE DEVELOPMENT
PRETEND PLAY: RELEVANCE FOR SOCIAL DEVELOPMENT
PRETEND PLAY: RELEVANCE FOR COGNITIVE AND INTELLECTUAL DEVELOPMENT

Further Extensions and Applications
Summary

PREASSESSMENT

When you have completed this chapter you should be able to describe and compare the following:

1. *varieties of pretend play.*
2. *techniques for facilitating children's involvement in pretend play.*
3. *relevance of children's involvement in pretend play for motor, affective, social, and cognitive and intellectual development.*

   Before beginning to read this chapter:

1. *take time to write what you currently know about each of the above topics.*
2. *reflect on the child (children) you observed as you studied Section Two; consider what your current repertoire is for involving this child (these children) in pretend play in ways that will enhance development.*

   Save what you write for rereading, comparison, and elaboration after you have studied and discussed these materials.

Overview

Given time, props, and opportunity, most children will act out in fantasy the relationships and events that are important to them. Pretending is serious business for children. They will create their fantasy worlds with whatever objects are at hand and will act out their roles in pretend. "Pretend you are————" and "Let's play that I'm————" are such common phrases to *A central role in* children that there seems little doubt that pretend play fulfills some central *development* role in development. Only in those few cultures where children are thrust into adult responsibilities from an early age is the kind of role-playing so familiar to us in Western culture not often observed (Ebbeck, 1971). While the amount of fantasy play differs from one culture to another, there appears to be a relationship between it and the richness of the adult culture (Whiting *et al.*, 1953). Within the more complex cultures, fantasy activities abound among the young and are assumed to be a necessary preparation for more mature and differentiated adult roles.

In pretend play, or **dramatic play**, as it is often called, children take on an identity not their own (Let's pretend I'm———), convert common objects into imaginary uses (Let's say this is a———), and set up imaginary conditions (Let's pretend we're downtown and ———). A child can engage in dramatic play alone, with a single friend, or in a group. In your observations of individual children, you have noted the extent to which they engage in **sociodramatic play**, that is, play involving others. When engaged in sociodramatic play, children act out complex social situations that involve the reconciling of players with differing needs and background experiences and contradictory views.

Powers of observation and abstract thought

According to Smilansky (1968), sociodramatic play contributes to children's development by providing practice in adapting their scattered experiences to the demands of a particular role; they must discern the central features of the role behavior and simultaneously take into account the physical context and the ideas and actions of others. Such complex involvement is believed to develop powers of observation and abstract thought.

"Just playing"

Despite the observations of Smilansky and others regarding the value of sociodramatic play, adults and children alike commonly refer to it as "just playing." Parents may wonder about the value of this kind of school activity. Since children play at home and in the neighborhood, why should they do the same thing in school? This is a legitimate question, and as a teacher of young children you must be prepared to answer it often. In fact, unless you can develop your resourcefulness for arranging productive play environments that will extend understandings and skills, there is little reason that special program time should be used for what healthy children will naturally do on their own. Each of the following sections presents a rationale for including pretend play in the program setting and ideas for making these activities more beneficial than when they occur spontaneously outside the school.

SETUPS FOR PRETEND PLAY

Part of your contribution in establishing beneficial pretend play will be in providing settings that encourage particular and varied kinds of dramatic activity. Only the most basic "staging" arrangements are included here.

Basic Equipment

- Child-size furnishings are commercially available to stock "house-keeping areas" for children's dramatic play. These include refrigerators, kitchen ranges, sinks, rockers, ironing boards, chests of drawers, beds, and doll carriages that all beautifully replicate real home furnishings. Children certainly enjoy these ready-made replicas, and young children especially can benefit from them, since their imaginations may be inadequate to the task of "making do" with common objects, as older children can. The following materials are very desirable for children ages three through seven: low tables, child-size chairs, shelving, full-length mirrors (metal), sturdy crates, boxes (perhaps reinforced beverage boxes or other sturdy containers), small barrels, smooth and sturdy boards, dress-up clothes (older boys' and girls' sizes are more appropriate than adult men's and women's, such as simple gathered skirts, vests, etc. of washable material), a rack for hanging dress-ups, floor cushions, small bean bag chairs, rug samples, toy telephones (at least two), durable dolls (both sexes, varied features and skin coloring), doll clothing and accessories, small metal or sturdy plastic dishes, silverware, pots, pans, bowls.

Preferred Location

- Within "walls," either in a miniature house or within screens, room dividers, etc.
- Within a space sufficiently large to allow easy movement of several children both inside and outside the "wall" boundaries.
- Near the block area, since blocks often are used as props for various pretend activities.

Accessories

- Old sheet, blanket, bed spread, tarp
- Cloth remnants of different textures (cotton, satin, velveteen, terry cloth, silk, nylon netting)
- Other remnants (fur, fish net, heavy plastic)
- Ties (pieces of lace, ribbons, sashes, scarves)
- Carrying cases (suitcase, briefcase, satchel, shoulder bag, lunch box, shopping bag, mailing boxes)
- Dress-up extras (eyeglass frames [without glass], purses, billfolds, jewelry, neck ties, bow ties, gloves)
- Odds and ends (note pads, calendar, clock, pillows, grocery bags, small boxes, cans of food, food boxes, cash register)
- Dramatic play kits: the following collections of materials might be stored in boxes and made available to support or stimulate particular types of dramatic play activities:

  1. *Office*—discarded portable typewriter, pads, paper, envelopes, pencils, pens, rubber stamp and ink pad, pictures of office settings
  2. *Restaurant*—tray, pads, tablecloths, napkins, paper dishes, real food, pictures of restaurant scenes
  3. *Store*—paper bags and boxes, play money, note pads, cash register, cartons, cans, pictures of store scenes
  4. *Fire station*—firefighters' hats (plastic), hose lengths, ladder lengths, tall boots (older children's sizes), pictures of fire fighters in station and in action

Kits might also be prepared for a hair salon, a library, camping, fishing, a train, a bakery, a picnic, a clinic or hospital, a post office, a gas station, etc.

General Guidelines

- An ample period is necessary for children to have satisfying experiences in dramatic play. A half-hour is probably minimal and a longer time is preferable. A warning that a time period is almost over should be given somewhat prior to terminating children's activity in dramatic play.

- At the start of each activity session make sure that the dramatic play area is clean and orderly, with dress-ups, dishes, and other props neatly arranged.
- Frequently launder all dress-ups and cloth remnants and remove, repair, or discard all articles that are broken or torn.
- Establish a clear policy on whether or not water, clay, and other "messy" materials may be used in the area established for pretend play. In some situations, it is easy to accommodate and clear away spills as they occur at the water table or in the clay area. In other situations, the carpeting, flooring, or the nature of the "props" preclude the use of these materials with dramatic play.
- Establish a clear policy on whether toy guns or other kinds of "props" children will inevitably bring from home may be used in pretend play. Keep in mind that the nature of the play will be significantly influenced by the kinds of props available.

RESPONSE SECTION

The previous pages give guidelines for children's pretend play. Before you read about how a teacher can resourcefully enhance the benefits of pretend play, consider the following:

1. Try to think back to your own childhood experiences and recall the situations in which you engaged in pretending. Were these solitary situations or were you involved with others? Try to recall your feelings, problems, frustrations, and successes. Consider how adults interfered with or assisted your efforts.

2. If you have difficulty in recalling experiences of this kind from your childhood, consider why that might be the case. Do you think you actually did not engage in pretend activity? Or are there other reasons for your lack of recall?

3. What recent experiences have you had in engaging in pretend, fantasy, or dramatic activity? What were your feelings about these experiences? What were the benefits?

4. If you lack enjoyable and rewarding experiences with pretend play, either from your early years or in recent years, how could you now enhance your appreciation of the benefits so that you can more enthusiastically provide these opportunities for children?

Alternatives

- Puppets of all varieties often serve to engage children in dramatic representation. An impromptu stage can be created by simply turning a table on edge and allowing the performers to be behind the table (between the table legs) while the audience sits on the other side. Durable and attractive hand puppets are commercially available from many sources, and others can be easily constructed for or by children. These can include hand puppets made of fabrics, socks, mittens, etc.; finger puppets; paper bag puppets; and papier-mâché puppets. Almost anything can be turned into a puppet, given a bit of imagination.

Your Resourcefulness and Children's Development

Beyond setting the stage for dramatic play, you will often have the opportunity in your teaching role to interact creatively with children, to suggest, lead, praise, question, and embellish. Knowing when and how to interject yourself in the play activity, and when to simply observe, calls for real artistry on your part. The following pages provide guidelines to help you decide how and when to manage this involvement.

PRETEND PLAY: RELEVANCE FOR MOTOR DEVELOPMENT

Constant motion

While children are "just playing" at being firefighters, pioneers, monsters, wild dogs, horses, Batman and Robin, or other such roles, they often appear to be in constant motion. They may pause for plans and consultation (for example, "Let's say I find a note one of the bandits left"), but when the action resumes, so does the incessant running, diving, rolling, dodging, sneaking, crawling, jumping, and climbing. The healthy child in pretend play quite naturally practices and perfects motor skills, and especially muscle coordination.

Action repertoire

Pretend play can also be used to encourage motor activities that are not performed spontaneously. Children's repertoires of movements can be expanded as they follow your suggestions, and they can pretend to be jack-in-the-boxes, rubber bands, firecrackers, balloons, popcorn, alligators, snails, fish, skaters, Raggedy Ann or Andy dolls, soldiers, giants, clowns, racing cars, puppets, tightrope walkers, propellors, jumping beans, rocking boats, jeeps, bouncing balls, jets, helicopters, tops, trees, or daisies. The possibilities for things to imitate and the related actions are nearly limitless. Almost any child will enthusiastically respond to suggestions that he or she pretend to be something else. The following role suggestions may encourage children to practice particular motor skills:

- Body alignment for strength: strong man at the circus pushing and lifting "heavy" objects; football lineman pushing against opponent; farmer lifting hay bales or bags of feed; horse pulling heavy load; sanitation workers moving heavy garbage cans; movers pushing pianos, sofas, refrigerators; bulldozers pushing heavy rocks

- Body alignment for balance: high wire performer at the circus; animals or people crossing stream on log or series of rocks; firefighter walking narrow ledge to save stranded kitten; ballet dancer on toes; construction worker on steel girder
- Rhythmic movements (can have musical or clapping accompaniment): bouncing balls; swimmers; dancers; marionettes; sea gulls; grass blowing in the wind; rowing or paddling; shoveling or chopping
- Body alignment for speed: Superman; power boat; jet plane; baseball player; racing cars; race horse

Endurance

Children's physical endurance is more likely to be encouraged through participation in dramatic activity than by any other means. In normal play they may take quick runs, gallop across the room, or turn a somersault, but they are not likely to sustain these activities for as long a period of time as they will when playing a role. As wild horses they may gallop about for long periods of time, neighing enthusiastically through it all. As a lame dog trying to get back to its master against all kinds of obstacles, a child will struggle long distances on two hands and one foot. While scooting along on their backs with knees up and feet on the floor, pretending to be submarines, children will traverse great distances, turning and changing directions but continuing to sustain these rather tiring actions.

While you seldom wish to interrupt children's spontaneous sociodramatic activity to suggest beneficial motor movements, you will find ample opportunity to make such suggestions when children are not involved, and some of these suggestions will later become incorporated into their impromptu dramatic actions, often in more complex and creative ways than you imagined.

Tensing alternated with relaxation

Hyperactive and impulsive children may especially benefit from your direct suggestions for engaging in dramatic actions. Activities that involve conscious tensing followed by relaxation can be particularly effective for these children. Suggest, for example, that children become racers. Begin with preparatory actions that are fun (such as shaking hands and giving autographs to the fans). Next, encourage them to become tight, set, muscles hard, waiting for the starting signal. Then get them to run a hard quick race followed by total relaxation—collapsed, stretched out, exhausted, "like the bones are all out of the muscles." Again, let them pretend that they are fierce lions, all tense and waiting for a chance to pounce. Then let them quickly capture the prey and devour it before taking a carefree lope over the grasslands. Finally, let them find a place in the sunshine for a nap, stretched out in total relaxation like a big, tame pussycat. Practice on yourself, when you are tense. What kinds of dramatic imagery help you alternatively tense and relax your muscles? Perhaps you can translate your own imagery into suitable relaxing activities for the hyperactive, tense child.

The impulsive child might especially benefit from dramatic activities that require conscious control of movements, alternately moving slowly and quickly. To this kind of child, you may suggest series of actions; for example,

A shockingly large number of American children are currently under medication to reduce their hyperactivity. A very real issue is whether their behavior should be considered deviant and in need of correction, or whether schools and homes should provide for a higher level of activity than at present. There is some reason to believe that many children labeled "hyperactive" are well within normal ranges of wanting to move and act, and yet they are placed under medication because their activity is annoying to the adults responsible for them.

When forty four- and five-year-old children were given options for locating themselves within three different areas—an active, expressive, and a task area—during a study (Lay, 1972) conducted to determine where they actually spent their time, it was found that nearly all of them spent more time in the active area than in the other locations. Yet, all too few program or home settings have arrangements to accommodate children's preferences for lively activity.

a cat stealthily approaching and pouncing on a mouse; a little dog trying to steal a big dog's bone; a mechanical man performing a variety of activities; or someone fishing, slowly reeling in a line to change the bait and then rapidly reeling when there is a catch. Any of these roles must of course be embellished with suggestions not related to the desired movements; for example, *Quick movements* the dog might stop to scratch a flea, or the person fishing might wave away *alternated* the mosquitoes and wipe his or her forehead. Within a "fun" context, it is *with slow* possible to insert many suggestions that require the conscious control of movement rates.

Small muscle While it is relatively easy to think of ways that dramatic activities can *actions* encourage large muscle movements, it may not be so easy to find ways of promoting eye-hand coordination and use of unfamiliar small muscle skills. It is possible to supply raw materials that encourage small muscle activity, such as apples and carrots that can be cut up and served in a play restaurant, or scissors and paper for children wishing they had "money." It requires real resourcefulness and sensitivity, however, to offer these at the appropriate moment, so that the main thread of play is not interrupted.

PRETEND PLAY: RELEVANCE FOR AFFECTIVE DEVELOPMENT

The "therapeutic" value of fantasy play is frequently cited in books about early education, to the exclusion of motor, social, and cognitive development. It is easy to understand this emphasis; pretend activities do offer *"Therapeutic"* children possibilities for (1) exerting control over a situation rather than *benefits* being controlled; (2) safely expressing negative feelings and unacceptable impulses; (3) working out feelings about disturbing situations and coming to better understand them; and (4) reliving or anticipating pleasurable experiences. In pretend play children are free to deal with their particular concerns and to pursue their interests at their own pace.

Teachers have only limited possibilities for assisting with the "therapeutic" aspects of dramatic play. Perhaps the most important ways of helping are simply by providing play time and recognizing when not to interfere. For example, when a child in the role of mother or teacher is scolding or beating a doll-child, this is probably not the time to interject alternative views on how a teacher or mother might treat a misbehaving child. When some child, playing a big sister role, is ruthlessly teasing a little sister, there is no need for moralization. Nor should you infer that such actions necessarily reflect the true reality of the child's experience. A teacher need not understand precisely why a child acts a role out in a certain way; it is often sufficient to recognize and respect the intensity of the child's involvement.

It is sometimes possible to provide specific experiences and "props" that stimulate children's role experimentation in critical areas. For example, having the props (such as a chair, stethoscope, syringe, Band Aids, carrying cases, white jackets) to act out the traumatic experience of blood tests for lead poisoning was helpful to children in one day-care center. In another situation, when several kindergartners expressed resentment about their treatment from "that school patrol boy," their teacher set out the school patrol

Photo by John James.

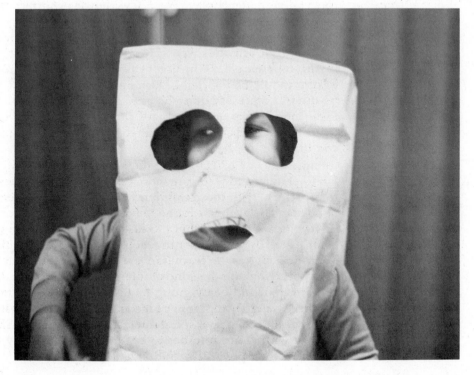

insignia along with other paraphernalia needed for a street scene. Their experimentation with the roles of patrol boys and girls, bus drivers, and children were intense and pointed.

After seeing an older group acting out a rather frightening "Snow White" drama, a group of first-graders, gingerly at first but with increasing confidence, tried on the witch costume and mask their teacher had borrowed. They gradually began to enjoy feigning the fierceness of the witch and the fright of Snow White. Of course, children should never be forced or even encouraged to play out frightening or puzzling experiences. Some children will refuse even if given the props and the opportunity. However, many will benefit from such play, as evidenced by their increased confidence in similar, real situations thereafter.

PRETEND PLAY: RELEVANCE FOR SOCIAL DEVELOPMENT

Sociodramatic benefits

In dramatic play children have more opportunities to work cooperatively with a greater variety of children than they do in the home and neighborhood. Sociodramatic play typically represents the first effective social education in a child's life. As mentioned earlier, the regulation of personal fantasies so that they mesh with those of others, in a way that is mutually satisfying to all, is a challenging task. This kind of sustained and mutually satisfying sociodramatic activity, when it occurs, reflects a milestone in social development.

Teacher intervention to instigate sociodramatic play

Most children need only the opportunity, time, and props to stimulate cooperative pretend play. For a few, however, direct teacher intervention may be necessary to get them under way with this very specialized type of social interaction. When children appear unable to successfully engage in sociodramatic activities, you may wish to invite them to play a specific role, saying, for example, "Why don't you pretend that you are the customer at the bakery and I'll be the clerk?" Demonstrate to them how specific objects can be used to represent other objects, saying, for example, "We can pretend these long blocks are bread and the round ones are cakes," and set the fantasy stage verbally, saying, "Pretend that you are coming into the bakery and that you are *very* hungry."

Smilansky, in investigating the lack of sociodramatic play activities in Israeli children from socioeconomically deprived families, induced teachers to participate with those children who had previously engaged in very little or no dramatic play. She found that these children's involvement in dramatic interactions with each other increased markedly both in total amount and in complexity. By demonstrating how to translate specific experiences into dramatic activity, the teachers were able to significantly increase the children's repertoire for this kind of interaction. Thereafter, the children's ability to learn from and enjoy group fantasy play increased markedly. When the children you teach appear to be incompetent or uninterested in dramatic play and appear to have poor social interactions, you may wish to take the lead by playing with them, in order to ensure their familiarity with the processes involved in cooperative sociodramatic play.

The line between helpful and nonhelpful intervention in children's dramatic play is often difficult to determine. However, when children already skilled in group pretend play are having conflicts over who will take which role, your intervention to solve their problems would probably be inappropriate. For example, in playing house, children like to have someone play the role of baby, but they may not be willing to take the role themselves. And many children will vie with each other for the lead role in whatever drama is under way at the moment. You will frequently be asked by children to intercede to make sure that they are fairly treated: "He [or she] always wants to be Peter Pan and won't let anyone else." A helpful rejoinder might be, "I can see why you wouldn't like that. How might you get him [or her] to take turns with you?" This may be ineffective in solving the immediate problem, but could set the stage for more effective problem-solving later. It is seldom helpful for a teacher to assign roles in a voluntary dramatic activity; the playing typically disintegrates, everyone is dissatisfied, and nothing is learned about problem-solving.

The noting and commending of children's social problem-solving is especially effective in regard to cooperative play. For example, "That was really a good idea you had about Jimmy playing your dog, wasn't it? He wanted to play dogs and Janie wanted to play house and by suggesting that he be the family dog, everyone was happy. That was certainly a smart idea!" As another example, "When you and Tanya both wanted a purse to carry to play secretaries, I really like the way you pretended the hat was your purse. It worked out well, didn't it?"

As a reinforcement for children who have done especially well in merging their separate fantasies in a coordinated play theme, you can invite them to act out their "play" before the class at sharing time. Six- and seven-year-olds,

and even some five-year-olds especially enjoy "doing a play," and this is the natural progression into more formalized cooperative endeavors. The tasks of jointly creating individual scenes and then sequencing these in a coherent presentation leads to the satisfactions inherent in all cooperative drama.

PRETEND PLAY: RELEVANCE FOR COGNITIVE AND INTELLECTUAL DEVELOPMENT

While children are engaged in pretend play, they often attempt to better integrate new and puzzling encounters and situations into their understanding. As they structure their activities they invent ways to make the actions they have seen in adults, peers, or the media fit within their own conceptions of the world. Things that have been accommodated in their actual experience

are re-created in fantasy, reworked, and gradually assimilated. The greatest values from pretend play are derived from these self-initiated processes. Adults can make additional interjections that stimulate further explorations and learning in play situations. It is these special arrangements and situations, secondary though they may be to the value of pretend play, that are primarily discussed in this section. You will need to keep in mind that while many of the following ideas for intervention can prove useful, they may have far less significance for children's cognitive and intellectual development than the processes in which children spontaneously engage.

Classification, number, seriation

Without detracting from children's ongoing play, there are many indirect strategies you can use for involving them in thought about classification, numbering, and ordering. The most effective way is to stock their dramatic play areas with materials that invite these processes. The following are examples of props that will serve this function:

- Silverware, dishes, pots and pans, napkins, and other kitchen items, selected so that they represent differing kinds, shapes, sizes, and colors
- Fabric samples (differing fabrics—satin, cotton, corduroy; differing sizes—four by four, eight by eight, and sixteen by sixteen inches; differing colors)
- Cans and cartons of differing sizes and colors
- Dowels that vary in diameter and length
- Play coins (varying in size and composition)
- Doll clothes (differing in size, fabric, and design).

Planned variations in props   If these materials have been carefully selected to provide several instances of each variation, children will quite spontaneously use and reuse them to classify, order, and count. Frequently, these processes will be interwoven with dramatic play sequences after a child or group of children has been given direct practice with them. For example, in an instructional situation a group could be presented with fabric samples to sort according to color, type

Photo by John Young.

of fabric, and size. In this situation, deliberately help the children learn the differentiating concepts (size, color, and texture). When the materials are then returned to the dramatic play area, you can observe whether the children have incorporated any of the words or concepts into their spontaneous play. This, of course, is the ultimate test of your teaching effectiveness.

There are many opportunities to unobtrusively work numbers into the exchanges that children initiate with you while playing. For example, playing store offers constant opportunities to ask eager sellers, "How much will that cost?" When the baker, for example, says, "Ten dollars," or "Three pennies," you can count out something (bits of paper, play money, twigs, or simply hand-pats) to match the number cited. Also, when children are assembling "props" for a particular set and ask you for something, a sensible reply would be, "How many do you need?" Or, after counting out two or three, "Is this enough or do you need more? How many more do you need?"

Responsive instruction

Mass and liquid quantity

In pretend activities in which products are produced and sold, children sometimes express concern about quantity. At a lemonade stand, for example, with only a limited supply on hand, it behooves both the buyer and seller to note how much various containers hold. By age six or seven some children are ready to begin making comparisons on a more accurate basis than appearance. By providing them with measuring utensils, weighing instruments, and a varied array of containers, you can increase the likelihood of their investigating and learning about conservation of quantity.

Causality

As children are acting out various pretend experiences, questions about phenomena that they only partially understand are likely to surface. Most children will stop only long enough to ask a quick question and get a quick answer. They usually do not want to become involved in doing an experiment, looking in a book, or listening to a long answer; they just want quick information in terms they can understand, based on what they already know. In fact, rather than asking questions, some children will simply create their own answers, announce them, and wait to see whether they are countered. What kind of response would you make to the following children's comments?

Partial understandings

- Jimmy is playing car wash outside on a sunny day, washing bikes for two cents (stones) each. He suddenly notes that the pavement, which had been wet, is now dry. "Where did that wet go," he asks, "into the ground?"
- Janey has spread her doll clothes out on the grass on a hot day and has gone to get the dolls. When she comes back she notices that the dark cloth feels much hotter than the white. "This one was in the oven," she says, looking at you for confirmation.
- The light suddenly goes out during an electrical storm. Several children

playing house say, "Who did that?" One says, "Probably Mrs. Dubrey [the principal] didn't pay the bill."

- Randy and Elmer are playing policemen. They are trying to tell some children who are engaged in another kind of playing that they must stop and be searched. The other children declare that they do not have to. Randy says, "You have to do what police say 'cause they got guns." Elmer adds, "And they can shoot anyone they don't like!" They look to you to support their contentions.

In each of these situations, you must make two decisions. First, how to explain the immediate question; and second, how to provide for future elaboration. By carefully listening to and observing children while they are involved in dramatic play, you can often identify potentially productive areas for later instruction.

Time and space concepts

The essence of pretending is the manipulation of space and time. Most pretend play involves superimposing a different time and setting on the real "here and now." A single dramatic play episode can even include several locations and several points in time. Consider the following excerpts, taken from the planning segments of children's play:

- "Now let's say that's over and now it is much later, and we've gone out to the park."
- "Hey, let's pretend I go to the movie. Okay, I'm at the movie show now. Pretend you are the person who sells tickets. Wait, let's make the chairs and stuff for the movie first, okay?"
- "Let's say we feed the baby and then she cries a lot so we have to spank her and then she goes to sleep. When she wakes up, it's the next day. And let's say she's sick, so I will be the doctor in my office and you can call me up. Okay?"

Precursors to an appreciation of literature and history

Perhaps such mental excursions are the precursors of an appreciation of literature and history: each situation requires keeping in mind a time and place and then considering a series of events within that context.

Between the ages of three and seven spatial understanding is derived from the creation of settings for children's role-playing or the manipulation of miniature toys in pretend activities. To successfully convert the same props and the same space into such diverse settings as a movie theatre, museum, motel, office, or hospital, as many five- through seven-year-olds will do, requires considerable spatial expertise. Of course, those children who have already become adept at playing house are more likely to tackle more imaginative staging enterprises. Less-experienced children will remain content with domestic scenes.

Staging enterprises

The beginnings of sense of geography can be spawned through children's efforts to create play worlds for their dolls, toy soldiers, and miniature animals. In one elementary school a bear fad—involving tiny three-inch

Steiff bears—developed and spread throughout the entire student body. Nearly every child kept a bear close at hand and many children even created and furnished tiny bear homes. Some of the older children created a factory in which their bears produced bear furniture, which was sold to other bears—at a good profit, of course.

At the height of the bear mania, the first- and second-graders, with the help of their teacher, created a miniature bear world on a six-by-eight-foot wooden platform. Using a mix of sawdust and wheat paste, they formed a continent with mountains, hills, valleys, and a couple of small islands. Surrounding these land forms was an ocean, and within the continent were an inland lake and two rivers. For weeks, little bears sailed the oceans, built houses on the land, fished in the rivers, climbed the mountain, and skated on the lake. The children "lived" geography through their little bears' adventures. The creating of miniature worlds for their small objects is an excellent way for children to develop their spatial understandings.

Spoken language

Children's participation in sociodramatic play puts intensive demands on their language abilities, and at the same time motivates them to become more precise in their use of language. They must verbally influence their fellow players if their own ideas are to be included in the play activity, so most children work at learning how to express themselves effectively.

Play settings to encourage reenactments Teachers can also enhance language development through the medium of pretend play. This can be done by arranging play settings that encourage the reenactment of new experiences and their associated new words. When

Photo by Robert Burdick.

children have been to a fire station, on a picnic, or to a library, it is likely that the trip will be reenacted via dramatic play if visited objects (or replicas) are available in the play setting during activity periods. Also, if photographs or illustrations of the places visited or similar settings are posted nearby, children will continue to talk and play through those experiences and, in the process, will add some of the new words to their vocabulary.

Language development can also be stimulated by introducing new objects into the dramatic play area. For example, you might bring in **realia** from your excursion to the seashore, if you think this would represent a new experience for some children. You might show them your shells, sunglasses, beach towels, beach chairs, and a collection of representative postcards or photographs. If you then leave these objects in a box near the dramatic play areas, some children will incorporate them into their play, and will ask, "What did you call this? What do you do with that?" In short, by thoughtfully introducing new objects into the play area, you can ensure children's exposure to new vocabulary and, depending on the degree to which they incorporate these objects into their play, you may succeed in expanding their permanent vocabulary.

Vocabulary expansion through provision of varied objects

You might consider the following kinds of objects for this purpose: scuba diving equipment, bathroom scales, real flowers, vacuum cleaner, flashlight, backpack, life vest, plastic thermos jug, crutches, rubber boots, coil of heavy rope, parachute, picnic basket, rowboat. Many other such objects can be used to enrich children's play and vocabulary.

Written language

The making of signs, labels, and other written materials can become an integral part of many dramatic play activities. Because written language abounds in the real world, the re-creation of this writing adds authenticity to children's play. If children are making a restaurant, for example, they may want any of the following: a large sign bearing their restaurant name, duplicated menus, a wall price list, order pads, advertising posters, table signs, and name tags. As children create play settings from what they perceive as the essence of the situation they are depicting, you can be alert to opportunities to ask, "Do you want a sign?" or "Do you want me to write that out for you?" Children will usually be delighted to add this extra dimension of reality. If they do want such assistance, you can use the opportunity to teach basic "speech-to-print" fundamentals such as left-to-right directionality, correspondence between the spoken and written word, word recognition, sound-and-letter correspondence, and punctuation.

Re-creation of writing in pretend settings

Reading and writing skills

Once children of age six or seven have begun producing plays for others to see, you can often involve them in preparing their "play bills," which tell the audience the name of the play, the scenes, the actors, and offer short character sketches. Whether these are duplicated to be passed out or are read by a child announcer, such writing enhances both the dramatic endeavors and the children's competency in reading and writing.

Even the very young, who are still uninterested and unaware of written

Readiness experiences language, can sharpen their visual discrimination skills within the context of dramatic play. By interjecting into their plays props such as rubber stamps (library, post office), stick-on forms (post office, stores), playing cards (homes, camping), picture collections (stores, homes), play money (stores, homes, restaurants), and price tags (stores), children will typically examine and sort them according to their likenesses and differences.

Further Extensions and Applications

Our consideration of pretend play has been within the context of the activity periods in the typical early education setting. It may also be useful to consider how a child's pretending experiences can be extended through other expressive modes or in other settings. For example, a vivid representation of the world as seen and imagined can be created in dance. Bruce (1965) suggests that movement accompanied by music may be a prime means of expression for children:

> The child expresses through dramatic movement ideas which are of his imagination and arise from his experience. Pictures, stories, the world around, television and cinemas provide the stimuli. He can be like an animal, a bird, a space man, or father digging the garden. He can also be like a train or a river, the wind or the snow, a rock or a star. In children, music will often excite movement which is spontaneous and unself-conscious. A child responds especially to the rhythm with gestures which is unplanned and on the whole unremembered. (pp. 7–8)

For this kind of movement activity, a large open space may be preferable to the regular classroom. A gymnasium, hallway, or other large space without furnishings provides opportunities to freely create in movement without psychological or physical impediments.

Sound effects Children are typically enthralled with pretending through the production of sound effects. They delight in making sounds with their voices and by the manipulation of objects—striking, scraping, tapping, etc. The sounds children produce are frequently disturbing to adults, and there are often sanctions against shrieks, whistles, motor imitations, etc. While such noise prohibitions may be necessary to preserve the well-being of most adults and some children, there perhaps should be some recognition of the fact that the producing of sounds is an important avenue of pretending for many children. Within each child's daily experience, there perhaps should be some time and place where the creation of sounds in all variations—loud, raucous, soft, rhythmic, staccato, shrill—is allowed and encouraged.

Because children prior to age seven or eight, as Piaget (1969) points out, do not have the capacity for internally representing movement and change, but instead think in terms of static imagery, it is small wonder that creating and re-creating scenes in pretend play is so important to development.

The previous pages contain many suggestions, both specific and general, for furthering children's development through the medium of pretend play. Choose the ten activities that you feel would be most appropriate for each of the children you observed in your study of Section Two. As you formulate your list of activities, browse back through the chapter and modify the activities to match the developmental levels of the respective children. For each of the activities you have chosen, determine whether it will provide new skills and concepts, a new application of existing skills and concepts, or both.

Through pretending, children can reexperience changes and sequences of events so as to better understand them. Sound and motion can contribute to this understanding.

Summary

The benefits of pretend play for young children are many and varied. They typically engage in "pretend" activities without instigation, but under adult guidance can derive even greater benefits.

Through pretending, children can be encouraged to engage in a wide variety of gross muscle actions and will often sustain them, without urging, for long periods. Positive outcomes can be derived for some children from movement imitations in tensing and relaxing, slowing and speeding, and other contrasting actions. The provision of appropriate props encourages involvement with small muscle actions.

Given the opportunity, children will typically engage in spontaneous dramatizations of episodes that concern them. A teacher may be able to further encourage this "therapeutic" use of pretending by furnishing props related to situations that appear to be stressful.

Participation in sociodramatic play is particularly valuable and demanding. Teachers may need to initially help some children translate specific experiences into dramatic activity. In general, however, direct involvement of teachers in sociodramatic play is counterproductive.

Particular kinds of props may encourage classification, consideration of number and seriation, awareness of quantity, spatial awareness, and language usage. The situations that arise during play may present further opportunities for considering causality, time sequences, and written communication.

Given the developmental status of children ages three to seven, it is not difficult to understand why pretending has positive consequences, nor is it difficult to understand that movement and the production of sound effects might contribute significantly to children's pretending.

REASSESSMENT

Reread what you wrote for the preassessment as you began this chapter, comparing this with your current understandings. Now write on these topics again and incorporate your new insights and knowledge. Continue to update as you prepare for teaching. Save your materials for your portfolio.

Additional Reading

Pretend Play   Almy, M. Spontaneous play: An avenue for intellectual development. *Young Children,* 1967, 22, 265–80.

Bender, J. Have you ever thought of a prop box? *Young Children,* 1971, 24, 164–9.

Blackie, P. *et al. Drama: Informal schools in Britain today.* New York: Citation Press, 1972.

Gillies, E. *Creative dramatics for all children.* Washington, D.C.: Association for Childhood Education International, 1973.

Herron, R. E., and Sutton-Smith, B. *Child's play.* New York: John Wiley, 1971.

McCaslin, N. *Creative dramatics in the classroom.* New York: David McKay Co., 1968.

Robison, H. F. The decline of play in urban kindergartens. *Young Children,* 1971, 26, 333–41.

Smilansky, S. *The effects of sociodramatic play on disadvantaged preschool children.* New York: John Wiley, 1968.

Stecher, M. B. Concept learning through movement improvisation: The teacher's role as catalyst. *Young Children,* 1970, 25, 143–54.

Sutton-Smith, B. The role of play in cognitive development. *Young Children,* 1967, 22, 361–70.

CHAPTER 12
Resourcefulness in Helping Children Share Ideas and Experiences

Overview

Your Resourcefulness and Children's Development
SHARING: RELEVANCE FOR PHYSICAL AND MOTOR DEVELOPMENT
SHARING: RELEVANCE FOR AFFECTIVE DEVELOPMENT
SHARING: RELEVANCE FOR SOCIAL DEVELOPMENT
SHARING: RELEVANCE FOR COGNITIVE AND INTELLECTUAL DEVELOPMENT

Further Extensions and Applications

Summary

PREASSESSMENT

When you have completed this chapter you should be able to describe and compare the following:

1. *informal and formal sharing.*
2. *techniques for facilitating children's sharing of experiences and ideas.*
3. *relevance of children's sharing for motor, affective, social, and cognitive and intellectual development.*

Before beginning to read this chapter:

1. *take time to write what you currently know about each of the above topics.*
2. *reflect on the child (children) you observed as you studied Section Two; consider what your current repertoire is for involving this child (these children) in ways of sharing that will enhance development.*

Save what you write for rereading, comparison, and elaboration after you have studied and discussed these materials.

Overview

Informal sharing
There are both informal and formal ways of promoting children's sharing. **Informal sharing** refers to the kind of talking that occurs in an unstructured situation. For younger children, informal sharing in which they initiate talk about themselves or show off their possessions and creations should predominate. To promote this kind of sharing there must be many opportunities for spontaneous exchanges among children and between children and adults.

While the greatest benefits for young children are typically derived from informal sharing, from the ages of four through seven they also become increasingly capable of engaging in **formal sharing,** which refers to those situations especially structured by the teacher for interchanges within a group.

Formal sharing
The most common type of formal sharing is sometimes referred to as *show and tell*. Children take turns talking about anything they wish, whether or not it is related to what others have said. These sessions are usually a potpourri of topics, objects, and experiences. They are also referred to in some situations as *sharing time*, *news time*, *talking time*, or *circle time*.

A second type of formal sharing revolves around the accomplishments of the school day. Between ages five and seven, many children begin to appreciate the end products of their creative efforts, rather than the mere physical manipulation of materials, and at this stage they are encouraged in further efforts if they have frequent opportunities to share what they have produced. At the end of a work session or a program day, they may be given the opportunity to hold up or talk about things such as paintings, constructions, inventions, written stories, books they have read, or fights they have resolved.

A third type of formal sharing involves group planning or group problem-solving. Individuals are invited to share the ideas they have about a particular topic. In group planning, children are told of an upcoming situation, such as a trip to an apple orchard to pick apples, and are then invited to contribute their ideas about what could be seen, investigated, and learned there and about what preparations should be made. This kind of discussion is typically initiated and led by the teacher but can be quite open-ended in allowing children's expressions of concerns, questions, and thoughts about the subject in focus.

Group consideration of a problem, in which individuals are invited to share their ideas for resolution, can be initiated and conducted by either the teacher or a concerned child. A child who is personally confronted by a problem situation may request that others join in and give their views of the situation. The child, rather than the teacher, can then recognize speakers and manage others' participation. Initiative of this sort, of course, usually requires prior experience in sharing situations in which adults or older children have demonstrated these procedures. Examples of the problems that young children may wish to discuss with their peers are disruptive incidents on the playground or during work periods, damage to possessions, unfairness, and invasions of privacy. Typically these sessions do not resolve the immediate concern of the child, but if such sessions occur consistently over a period of time, a greater sensitivity to the needs and feelings of others evolves and fewer such incidents arise. The discussion process itself usually seems to satisfy the offended or concerned child.

As a teacher you should know how to provide the settings within which children can develop an ability to both informally and formally share their ideas, experiences, and concerns. You will also need to learn how these sharing activities can be used to satisfy a variety of developmental needs.

SETUPS FOR SHARING

Informal Sharing

Basic Arrangements
- As children arrive from home, be available to them at or near the entrance to the classroom or center. You can simultaneously assist with

wraps and listen to them as they make the transition from home and neighborhood to school. This of course requires that all advance preparations for the school day be completed before the children's arrival.

- Intermingle with the children during indoor activities and outdoor play so that you can be the recipient of their sharing. Circulate in much the same manner as a host or hostess at a social function.
- Try to be available to children as they complete their activities and share with them their final enjoyment of the process or the product. Be ready to label objects they have made with their names and a caption or a full description.
- Arrange display spaces within the classroom—a bulletin board, open table space, or open shelf space. These will typically accommodate a random assortment of items rather than a coordinated or thematic display. For younger children, display items can simply be labeled with their names. As children mature in their awareness of written communication, the amount of labeling will increase. Displays will change frequently, even daily, as a reflection of children's shifting interests.
- To facilitate the transformation from oral to written sharing, have on hand felt pens, crayons, newsprint sheets, file cards, strips of paper, and stand-up display cards (fold 5" × 8" file card in half). You may wish to prepare a special container with these raw materials so that they can be kept close at hand. Some teachers keep these supplies and others

Photo by John Young.

(such as scissors, tape, safety pins, paper clips, stapler, and Band Aids) in a "teacher basket," which can be carried from place to place in the program setting (even outdoors).

General Guidelines
- You can encourage children to share by staying at their eye level at least part of the time, kneeling or sitting rather than standing above them. Establish eye contact and signal with a smile your willingness to listen.
- Learn to decipher children's nonverbal body language (their bearing, expressions, and gestures). For example, note the way a child bounces newly styled hair or carefully wipes off new shoes. Note looks of dejection or pride. Verbal expression is only one of many ways young children communicate about themselves.
- Note any objects children are carrying. Anything valuable enough to children to be transported from home to school or from one location to another within the classroom is likely to have some personal significance.
- Avoid being monopolized by children who want to share constantly. Make sure that you give roughly equal attention to all children over the course of a week, if not daily.

Alternatives
- When you cannot be personally available to children, arrange for another adult or for more mature children to assume your role. Their effectiveness will depend in large measure on your ability to communicate what is expected of them.

Formal Sharing

Basic Arrangement
- Some teachers prefer to have children sit on chairs during group discussions. They feel there is less confusion once the chairs are placed. It is more difficult to move about in a chair, they point out, and thereby to divert attention away from the speaker. Other teachers prefer having children sit on the floor, which eliminates the need for transporting and arranging chairs as well as the temptation to tilt them precariously on two legs. Still others prefer to use seating mats that identify each child's spot, which also eliminates the problem of transporting and arranging chairs.
- Most teachers find that a circular arrangement promotes attentive listening better than either rows or random groupings. Masking tape is often used to indicate the circle size and to help children arrange themselves for group discussions.

Preferred Location
- It is important that the discussion circle not crowd the children. Any large open space, such as the block or reading areas, can be converted into a discussion area. Ideally, the space should be separated from the

room entrance and from other activity areas that might be used simultaneously.

Accessories

- The display spaces mentioned in regard to informal sharing should be close at hand. The bulletin board, table, or shelves that children use to mount and store their materials should be easily accessible during the sharing activity.
- A chalkboard or an easel stocked with chart paper and felt pens can be used to record the sharing experiences. The extent of this recording will of course vary with the maturity of the children.

General Guidelines

- Transitions from informal to formal sharing are best made very gradually, beginning with very short periods and limited expectations for order and formality. These transitions are most easily accomplished when younger children can simply join or observe older peers who have already learned to share their ideas in an orderly manner. Taking turns, listening to others, and questioning or commenting on others' ideas are more easily learned through observation and imitation than through verbal instructions.
- If older children are not available to model formal group discussion, then it becomes your job to make the transitions as painless and productive as possible. Initially, you might ask for volunteers to join you in a "talking time" (or whatever label you want to use). You will need to repeatedly model the appropriate behaviors and procedures. Try to do this with your most dramatic flair! Demonstrate how to sit or stand while listening or talking, how to talk in bold tones to make sure everyone hears, how to listen to and later question the speakers, and how to signal readiness to talk or stop talking. Make your points clearly, dramatically, and definitively.
- Your guidelines for group discussion should emphasize what to do rather than what not to do. There must be fun, ceremony, pride, and recognition. If the sharing becomes a time of prohibition, of child misconduct and teacher scolding, it will take a great deal of effort to rebuild a positive atmosphere. Careful attention to keeping the sharing periods brief, lively, and pleasurable will do much toward making it a time for real communication.
- Emphasize all positive behaviors and good efforts while ignoring less desirable behaviors. In the long run you will find that the praising of specific desirable behaviors is more effective than general instructions or the correcting of inappropriate behavior. Praise the child who is attending to the speaker; ignore the child who is clowning while another speaks. Comment on the child who speaks in audible, well-modulated tones; pass over your concerns for the child who speaks too loudly. In other words, praise and reward all those who model the kind of communication you desire in the group sharing situation, and avoid

attention to those who do not. When you find that you must attend to a disruptive or inappropriate behavior, do it swiftly and briefly, and then continue on without further delay.

- Clarification of the following procedural concerns may be especially helpful to children just learning to participate in group discussions:

1. How to indicate that they wish to tell or ask something, such as whether to raise their hands, put their hands on their heads, just wait until no one else is talking, or some other signal

2. How to recognize when it is their turn to talk or ask a question, such as a teacher or child leader recognizing them by name or pointing to them; the last speaker handing them a signal object; or noting that no one else is talking

3. What topics are appropriate to talk about, such as family, toys, pets, sights and experiences, jokes, accomplishments, creative products, problems, and plans

4. Where they should stand or sit when it is their turn to talk, such as beside the teacher, at their regular place, beside the discussion leader, or in a special "talking" chair

5. Where to keep the things they want to show, such as in their lockers, in their desks, in their hands, behind them, or on the display table or shelf

6. How to terminate their comments, such as just stopping; saying, "That's all I wanted to say"; or saying, "Any questions or comments?"

Although the adoption of one procedure over another is strictly arbitrary, having an initial set of procedures provides security for the novice. Modifications can easily be made as children mature. Rigid adherence to

SMALL GROUP DISCUSSIONS

James Moffett in his book *A student-centered language arts curriculum, grades K-6: A handbook for teachers* (1968) points out that whole group discussion, because of the number of participants involved, precludes the kind of active interchanges (picking up ideas and developing them, corroborating, qualifying, and challenging) that are the essence of real discussion. He recommends instead the extensive use of small group discussion with no more than six participants per group. He suggests two types. One is teacher-led, for the purpose of developing discussion skills. The other is a problem-centered type, with a focused topic related to ongoing projects. For this second type several small groups might discuss at the same time in different locations in the classroom. While the actual examples of successful small group focused discussion, as cited by Dr. Moffett, are from second grade or above, he proposes that this approach be used for the entire span of kindergarten through sixth grade. His major thesis is that "to develop their language powers, children must talk a lot. They must use language and use it an enormous amount."

The previous pages give guidelines for encouraging both informal and formal sharing among children. Before you read about the various ways in which sharing can contribute to children's development, consider the following:

1. Try to think back to your own childhood experiences and recall the situations in which you shared your own feelings, ideas, and experiences (a) informally with peers or adults (outside your family), and (b) formally in a group situation. Recall your feelings in these settings and situations.

2. Think about the current situations in which you most easily and effectively relate your ideas, feelings, and experiences in informal discussion and in group settings. Consider also the situations in which you find this most difficult.

3. As you consider your own sharing, past and present, are there any generalizations you can make about what facilitates it? Think about whether these generalizations have any relevance as you plan for children's sharing.

a set of procedures is of course inadvisable and might discourage communication rather than enhance it. For young children, though, the "ceremony" of sharing is half the fun and will typically encourage participation rather than discourage it.

Your Resourcefulness and Children's Development

The following pages explore ways in which sharing experiences can be used to facilitate children's development. There are also suggestions for using the ideas that are shared as a stimulus for related learning activities. As in the prior chapters, you will find it useful to relate the following discussion to the needs of the children you observed and assessed in Section Two.

SHARING: RELEVANCE FOR PHYSICAL AND MOTOR DEVELOPMENT

Topics such as becoming half as tall as Mother, losing a tooth, learning to swim, learning to ride a twowheeler, jumping off a fence "as tall as me," and outgrowing last year's snowsuit are typical sharing fare. These topics reflect children's keen awareness of their physical and motor development.

Sharing with movement as well as words   The resourceful teacher can use children's reports of physical feats as a springboard for involvement with motor activities. Given a bit of encouragement and direction, the child who is showing or telling about something can also act out what he or she did, saw, or created. Young listeners are also able to relate better to what they have heard if it is accompanied by motoric expression. The following are examples of how teachers encourage motor participation in regard to sharing activities:

- When Julie reported that she had gone to a local amusement park, she was encouraged to enact as well as describe the things she saw there: the "dodgem" cars that twirled and careened as they narrowly missed or bumped into each other, the undulating animals on the merry-go-round, etc.
- Stevie told about his birthday party and about the games and presents there. He was invited to demonstrate as well as tell about how the biggest balloon expanded and expanded and then *popped!* All of the listeners enjoyed joining him in the Hokey Pokey when he mentioned it as one of the activities.
- As Jimmy arrived at school he described to the teacher the TV show he had watched the previous day. He was asked to demonstrate how the cowboys stopped the oncoming train to save it from derailment and then how they captured the "bad guys" without firing a shot. As others gathered around to see, he pretended to climb a pole holding a jacket in his teeth and then waved it vigorously. As he described the capturing of the bandits, everyone became involved in crawling, hiding, rolling, dodging, feigning, hitting, and being hit.

Photo by permission of Bernice Wright Cooperative Nursery School.

Many teachers feel that, by sharing important thoughts and experiences, children develop positive feelings about themselves that significantly influence other aspects of their physical, social, and cognitive development. When you observe children who seem to be lacking in independence, initiative, and persistence, note whether they also appear to lack awareness of themselves as individuals who have distinct characteristics. Considerable self-awareness is usually necessary to support a healthy sense of autonomy. For those children who do not seem to have developed such self-awareness, you might wish to use both informal and formal sharing situations to increase their acceptance of themselves. While most children in the preschool and early school years are already developing a healthy self-awareness, some may benefit from your assistance in these areas. If so, the following types of activities may prove useful:

Developing positive self-awareness

- Help children develop books, pictures, or object collections that contain items of personal significance. Label these with their names and help them share the collections with others. A book might include such items as photographs of themselves, and of their families and pets or pictures selected from magazines. It is important that they have something concrete to share (easier than verbal sharing) that they identify as very personally theirs.
- Note the new skills children develop, which they may not have considered sharing with others, and suggest that they do so. You might say, for example, "Susan, I was wondering if you might want to show everyone how you have learned to skip." Emphasize that what is important is the newness of the experience for that particular child, whether or not it has been mastered by others.
- Point out to others things about the child of which he or she may have only a dim awareness. For example, "Have you noticed what a good friend Tim is? He————", or "Have you noticed how carefully Susan holds the bunny?"
- Have smiling, sad, and mad faces prepared and attached magnetically to a metal chalkboard (or with Velcro to a felt board) and ask a child undergoing an obvious emotion whether any one of these faces show how he or she feels. Encourage children to tell how they feel, that is, to "own" their own feelings.
- When you note that a child has distinctive clothes, looks particularly well groomed, or has a special possession, creation, or a newly acquired skill, encourage self-observation in front of a full-length mirror. Such visual awareness can lead to heightened self-awareness.

Children with developmental retardation or physical disabilities may need the encouragement of teachers in order to share their feelings and experiences. Children who feel themselves to be different than others may equate their differences with inadequacy, and consequently may avoid attention. When this appears to be the case, it is wise to intercede very directly to make

THE MAGIC CIRCLE

Bessell and Palomares (1967) have developed a program for children from prekindergarten through fourth grade that is intended to promote a sound emotional orientation. It focuses on three problem areas: (1) understanding and accepting others, (2) insight into and acceptance of one's own feelings, and (3) achievement of responsible competency. The program uses the *magic circle*, which consists of an arrangement of eight or so children and the teacher in a small inner circle, with the remaining children in the group in a larger outer circle. The inner circle participates; the outer circle observes as the teacher initiates discussion about feelings and perceptions. Daily sessions last for twenty minutes, and a theme from one of the problem areas is pursued across a period of several weeks. Different children rotate into the circle on a daily basis. There is an emphasis on the clarification of feelings and on the development of a vocabulary for expressing feelings. The developers feel that this kind of sharing prevents mental health problems and that early affective education is far more viable than remediation of emotional ills in later life.

Intervention to initiate sharing

sure that each child does have a successful sharing experience. Sometimes this requires close cooperation between home and school. Parents might be asked about important events that the child could be led to talk about with you or the classroom group. Personal day-to-day observation of a child's behavior is another way of identifying special characteristics that might be shared with others.

Keep in mind that each of us has unique traits and abilities and that sharing these with others usually enhances our own appreciation of them. Children who lack the confidence to talk about themselves or who fail to recognize what about themselves is worthy of sharing, will benefit from your tactful acknowledgement and publicizing of their special characteristics. By first soliciting and accepting the feelings, concerns, and experiences of insecure children in one-to-one discussions, you can gradually lead them to further self-disclosure and eventually to group sharing.

SHARING: RELEVANCE FOR SOCIAL DEVELOPMENT

Until children have reached the stage of voluntarily entering into sustained cooperative play with other children, it is unlikely that they will participate with any competence in formal group discussions. Prior to this point, informal sharing strategies are generally preferable, although some children may feel comfortable in group discussions if their roles involve listening but no active participation. Conversely, some young children who find cooperative play very enjoyable may be quite uncomfortable with the restrictions imposed by formal group discussion. As suggested previously, unpleasant group experiences will contribute nothing of value to children's development and can even delay the willing acceptance of group discussion activities.

However, once children have successfully participated in group sharing situations of the *show and tell* variety, they are also usually ready to participate in group planning or problem-solving discussions. The following examples illustrate likely themes for these kinds of discussions:

- After recess, Lynn and Janey asked for a group discussion to talk about a problem. Lynn announced to all those who came to listen that she and Janey did not like the way some big kids were teasing little kids. The teacher interjected, "Do you want us to help you think what *you* could do when you see something like that happening?" The girls indicated that that was what they wanted and Lynn called on children who had suggestions. The ideas offered included,

> You could go over to the mean kids and say, "Pick on someone your own size!"
>
> You could tell the mean kids' mothers or the teacher.
>
> You could be especially nice to the little kids yourself.
>
> You could tell the mean kids' mothers or the teacher.
>
> You could tell the little kids that if they don't pay any attention, the mean kids will probably get bored and stop.

- Mr. Whitney calls the children to the circle and says, "Some of the sixth-graders have discovered a nest of baby garter snakes on the playground. They want to show them to you, but they want to be sure that you know how to catch and hold snakes without hurting them. What do you think we should do?" Answers included the following:

> I don't want to catch no snakes anyway.
>
> Maybe they could show us.
>
> I know how. You cup your hands like this and don't squeeze.
>
> Only people who know how should catch them.

- Miss Jones uses her special piano chord signal to call the children to the circle for discussion. Some continue to work quietly at their previous activities, an option that has been established in this classroom. She addresses those who gather around her, "I wanted to talk with you because we have a problem. Miss Peters just told me that some of her children had to stop their work when we went out to the playground today because we were so noisy. She said she didn't like that. I told her we would talk about it. What do you think we could do to help us all remember to go out more quietly?" The children's ideas flowed freely as she called on the many who indicated they wanted to talk. They had the following ideas:

> We could put up a sign outside our door that says, *Be Quiet.*
>
> You could always remind us just before we go out the door.
>
> We could have someone whose job it is to stand by the door and say "*shhh*" to everyone.

We could go out to recess at the same time as Miss Peters' class.

They could keep their door closed.

We could all try harder to remember.

These kinds of sharing sessions, focusing around topics of genuine concern, contribute substantially to children's social development. The rapidity with

---

ASHTON-WARNER'S "ORGANIC" APPROACH

Sylvia Ashton-Warner in *Teacher* (1963) describes her "organic" approach to teaching the Maori children of New Zealand. Her daily plan included an alternating rhythm of "breathing out" and "breathing in" periods. Breathing in periods were for convergent efforts; breathing out periods were for expressive activities. In the morning breathing out period, for example, there were the following types of activities: conversation, painting, creative writing, clay play, sand play, water play, singing, daydreaming, crying, quarreling, block play, creative dancing, and doll play. It was at the beginning of this period, "when the energy is at its highest," that she took the *key vocabulary*, which she describes as follows:

> I take it the minute they come in before they touch any other medium, because I don't like to interrupt them later when they are deep in blocks of clay. Also I want to catch the first freshness.
>
> The preparation is modest enough. A number of cards at hand, about a foot long and five inches wide, of cheap drawing-paper quality, and a big black crayon. And a cardboard cover a size or two larger than the cards. And their old cards tipped out on a mat.
>
> I call a child to me and ask her what she wants. She may ask for "socks" and I print it large on a card with her name written quickly in the corner for my own use. She watches me print the word and says it as I print, then I give it to her to take back to the mat and trace the characters with her finger and finally replace it in the cover nearby. I call them one by one until each child has a new word. (pp. 43–44)

The greater the emotional significance to the child of the word asked for and written, the greater the probability that it will be remembered as a "one-look" word. Only remembered words are retained and accumulated as key vocabulary in the child's folder.

> It may sound hard, but it's the easiest way I have ever begun reading. There's no driving to it. I don't teach at all. There is no work to put up on the blackboard, no charts to make and no force to marshal the children into a teachable and attentive group. The teaching is done among themselves, mixed up with all the natural concomitants of relationship. I just make sure of my cards nearby and my big black crayon and look forward to the game with myself of seeing how nearly I hit the mark. And the revelation of character is a thing that no one can ever find boring. (p. 45)

---

which children become sophisticated in these kinds of group discussions sometimes surprises their teachers. For example, by age seven or so, children can often carry on a coordinated discourse without adult intervention. Their commentary reflects their understanding of each others' comments; for example, they might say, "The problem with Tod's idea about . . . is that . . . might. . . ." or "I agree with you, Jay, but I think a better way might be to. . . ." or "I disagree with what Chris said because I'm afraid that what would happen is. . . ." or "Would you tell me your idea again, Rob? I didn't understand what you meant when you said. . . ." Children's abilities to interact usually depend on their having had ample opportunity to hear their teachers or older children engage in such discussions. In terms of developmental benefits, these discussions not only build discussion skills, but increase awareness of alternatives for social problem-solving.

Discussion skills from observing older peers or teachers

SHARING: RELEVANCE FOR COGNITIVE AND INTELLECTUAL DEVELOPMENT

There are many opportunities to use the content of children's show and tell sessions to develop skills, concepts, and knowledge. A resourceful teacher can see abundant learning possibilities in almost any object or event. The trick is to select from among the many possibilities those that are particularly appropriate for a given child or group. This is sometimes called *incidental teaching*, since the teacher does not know in advance precisely what will be emphasized. There is nothing incidental, however, about the teacher's constant watching for situations or incidents that can be used to introduce or reinforce appropriate learnings.

"Incidental" teaching as a function of constant watching

Classification, seriation, and number

Very often the collections of things that children bring to school for sharing lend themselves quite naturally to classification, seriation, and counting activities. Among these are such items as shells, buttons, leaves, nuts, cones, pebbles, flowers, picture collections, baseball cards, playing cards, marbles, bottle caps, feathers, seeds, and seed pods.

Diverse objects provide instructional cues

Children also can be led to classify the object they show with other similar objects already present. For young children such classifications might be limited to aspects such as color, size, and shape. For older children, more advanced classification criteria, such as the function or derivation of objects might be used. The following are examples of ways an alert teacher might use a shared object to trigger involvement in classification:

- Felt pen—What else in our room can we use to write with?
- Clay bowl—What else do you see that might be used to hold water like this bowl?
- Plastic raincoat—Do you see some other people who are wearing something made of plastic today?
- Transparent sheet of acetate—Do you see anything else in this room that is transparent, that we can see right through?

- Miniature horse—Did you know that the word *miniature* means something that is made smaller than it would naturally be? What else is there around here that is miniature?

The opportunities to focus on numbers are particularly plentiful during sharing sessions. The following are only some of the many possibilities:

- *Clothing*—How many buttons? How many of each kind of button? How many pockets? How many pockets in both shirt and pants? How many of each kind of decorative item [flowers, birds, loops, etc.]?
- *Birthdays*—How old were you last year? How old next year? How many candles are on the cake? How much older are you than your brothers and sisters? How much younger? How many years until you are eight?
- *Trips*—How many went? How many were in the seat where you sat? In other seats? How many stops did the bus make?

A teacher should be resourceful enough to see that there may be other more interesting and productive possibilities, or children may be too often asked, "How many?" in regard to the things they share.

Causality

Sometimes sharing sessions can be used to encourage children to make careful observations and to speculate about causality in a rudimentary way. If you wonder aloud about phenomena, as in the following examples, children may take the cue and become "wonderers" also:

Sharing instigates "wondering"

- *Icicle*—Where did it come from? What causes it? What happens to it [in the classroom]?
- *Pussy willows*—What will happen if we just put them in a vase without water? With water?
- *Toy cars*—Why will some cars roll such a long way while others stop so soon?
- *Rock*—That rock looks very heavy. I wonder which weighs more, the rock or one of our large blocks?

Space concepts

When children talk about places they have been, you may be able to improve their typically fuzzy grasp of distance and location. They may speak easily of going to California, visiting Grandmother in the adjacent city, going across the ocean, or getting a present from Africa, without any idea of the relative distances or the directions involved. They may know that Japan is "far away," but have no idea whether it is a country, an ocean, a state, or a city. All of these things, are of course learned very gradually, those that have the greatest personal significance serving as a reference point for later learning.

Personal linkage for building space concepts

For this reason children's sharing activities provide an excellent basis for developing such understandings. The state and city where the child's grandmother lives will likely be learned first and will serve as good examples for further comparisons. Similarly, a TV show that children report on is a better reference point for understanding geographical relationships than something they do not identify with. The following types of comments and questions may help children clarify terms and concepts:

- Do you know what street your new friend lives on? What is your street? There are lots of streets in our city. Does your friend live on your street or on a different one?
- Were you farther from home when you went to Cleveland to visit your aunt or when you went to Florida at vacation time? Let's look at our big globe and see if we can find Cleveland, Ohio and Orlando, Florida.
- How many days will it take you to drive to Texas? Texas is a big state. It's the biggest state in our whole country. Do you know what city or town in Texas you are going to? What city do we live in? What state is *our* city in?

Time concepts

Inquiry into time sequences

As children talk about their experiences, teachers can help them clarify the time frame within which the events took place. Children's talk is full of *and then*'s. A teacher can gently inquire whether events happened this morning, yesterday, the day before yesterday, last week, last year, or a long time ago; and whether anticipated events will be in a few minutes, today, tomorrow, the day after tomorrow, next week, next month, or next year. Even when children do not know the answer, they can become aware that there is terminology related to time that can be learned and used to good advantage.

The recording of shared events on a calendar can also be helpful in developing a time sense. Upcoming birthdays and holidays can be anticipated as the number of days to the event are marked off. The dates of plantings and the record of growth can be recorded for children who share their experiments with gardening. Children's reports of seasonal events can be recorded on a calendar until it is obvious that the season has fully arrived. For example, as spring approaches, the flowers, returning birds, people in summer-type clothing, kites, bees, and swimming can all be recorded as "firsts" of the new season.

Spoken language

Translating the child's imagery into language

Many children still in the egocentric stage are unable to share experiences in a way that their listeners can understand. Trying to tell a group of peers about incidents such as "flying a kite on the golf course with Daddy yesterday" so that they appreciate the event is a language task of the highest magnitude. Without teacher assistance, trying to share such experiences may be too frustrating for many children. Consequently, a resourceful teacher will try to capture the child's imagery and, through questions such as the following, will supply some of the words and concepts the child is struggling for. Was the wind blowing very much? How big was the kite? As tall as you? Could you reach across it? Did it have a tail? Was it shaped like this [drawing on chalkboard] or was it different? How did your daddy get it started? Was it difficult to hang on to the string? What would have happened if you let go?

Photo by Robert Burdick.

Did it go as high as the door? Did it go as high as this room? As high as this building? As high as birds fly? As high as airplanes go? Did it hold still or did it move about?

Teachers are in a far better position to assist children in sharing out-of-school happenings if they are familiar with the child's family, home, and neighborhood. The more a child's socioeconomic, cultural, or ethnic background differs from that of the teacher, the more important it is that the teacher make a special effort to become familiar with what the child is likely to talk about. Knowing such things as what the family members are called, the ages of siblings, who the prominent neighborhood adults are, and what holidays are celebrated, all aid in understanding the child who is struggling to relate some personal experience.

Listening- *questioning* *patterns* This kind of knowledge helps the teacher become engaged in productive listening-questioning patterns. In describing a study conducted in the British infant schools, Brandt (1975) points out the predominance of these patterns of behavior in the exemplary teaching he observed, and elaborates as follows:

> Often this took the form of a child's showing his teacher something he was working on; asking for assistance, information, or permission; or telling about an experience he had. Although the teacher occasionally provided information, reaction, or direction, more often her response consisted of raising questions designed to draw the child out further with respect to his feelings, plans, or experiences. Hughes (1959) maintains that such eliciting of additional thinking in response to students' bringing up potential instructional content represents the essence of

good teaching. In the classrooms she studied, however, she found it occurred infrequently and accounted for less than 20 percent of most teachers' behavior.

Because of the greater evidence for this type of behavior in the British infant school, it seemed important to study the specific types of questions teachers raised. I made a tape recording, therefore, of a "show-and-tell" class discussion that teacher A conducted one Monday morning. Although weekend experiences constituted a major portion of the discussion, children were permitted to bring up anything that seemed important to them. Opening questions such as "Who has something he wants to tell us?" encouraged them to talk. The teacher would ask the child responding a number of questions about the experience until a rather full elaboration of its details was forthcoming. Typically, this listening and questioning on the teacher's part took the form of an open dialogue between child and teacher; other children were permitted to ask questions, furnish additional details (if they had been involved also), and make related comments only after the responding child seemed to have completed his story. The teacher would often hush another child momentarily with such remarks as "We are listening to John now; your turn will come." At other times she would purposefully bring other children into the discussion by asking such questions as "Who else has been to see the Cutty Sark?" (i.e., the item being described). This particular morning the show-and-tell period was kept going for over an hour, until almost all forty children had shared one or more experiences and until obvious restlessness appeared.[1]

While a show and tell session of this length is very unusual with young children, even for this skilled British teacher, the interest of children in listening to others can often be extended by skillful adult interjections and enthusiastic responses.

When a child is attempting to share an experience with you or with peers, this is obviously not the time for training in pronunciation or grammar. As a teacher you may wish to echo back the child's message in clearer speech or better language, but you should not break the sharing mood by pointing out incorrect usage.

Written language

There are many ways to encourage children's interest in writing down what they have told about. As you greet children upon their arrival at school, you will find opportunities for recording what they say to you. For example, a chart can be used to record whatever news children informally share as they arrive at school.

[1] From R. M. Brandt, Observational portrait of a British infant school. In B. Spodek and H. J. Walberg, Eds., *Studies in open education* (New York: Agathon Press, 1975), pp. 111–112. Reprinted by permission.

News

Jim has a carpenter's apron.

Peter knows an elephant joke.

Nancy said, "It is 10 days to Christmas!"

Jane said, "Our car got stuck in the snow."

B.J. has new orange mittens.

Steve can count to 10 in French.

News charts, news sheets

Later, the chart can be read to the entire class, or it might be posted in a prominent spot where visitors could read and enjoy its messages throughout the day. At the end of the day such a chart can be cut into individual strips so that interested children can take their news home to show their families.

During group sharing sessions, you may occasionally wish to prepare such a news chart while the children are talking, and then conclude the session by reading the things you have heard them say or by letting them read their own messages, if they can. For variation, the news can be written on a master sheet and duplicated so that each child has a copy. Or, instead of making a compilation of news items on a chart or master sheet, you may wish to make

Stand-up signs

individual stand-up signs to be placed on the display table.

Teachers can also write down children's descriptions of paintings, drawings, and constructions. Children often enjoy talking about their creations,

Sharing work products via written descriptions

and these descriptions can either be written as they are dictated or, at a later stage, written by the children with whatever adult help is necessary. This writing can take the form of brief labels, longer captions, stories, or even a book text (to accompany a series of paintings, illustrations, or other products).

When children write down their descriptions of their creations, these can be available for later sharing periods at school or to take home. Such writings often culminate their productive effort and for some may even serve as the major vehicle for learning the mechanics of writing and reading.

This is what I got for
my birthday.   Kathy

Why did the chicken
cross the street?   Ask Betsy

This is a hard puzzle
but I can do it.   Carlos

This is a piece of a
robin's egg.   Lynn

In addition to recording what children say as they arrive at school, a resourceful teacher will look for interesting labels and directions on the objects that are brought to share. Depending on the maturity of a particular child or group of children, you may wish to discuss titles of books, prominent phrases (*made in USA; caution; open here*), or directional signs (*on; off; stay off the grass*). Children will become increasingly word-conscious as you draw their attention to the written language attached to their personal possessions.

RESPONSE SECTION

The previous pages contain many suggestions, both specific and general, for furthering children's development through their sharing activities. Choose the ten activities that you feel would be most appropriate for each of the children you observed in your study of Section Two. As you formulate your list of activities, browse back through this chapter and modify the activities to match the developmental levels of the respective children. For each of the activities you have chosen, determine whether it will provide new skills and concepts, a new application of existing skills and concepts, or both.

CHAPTER 13
Guidelines for Resourceful Teaching

Overview

Mental Sets to Enhance Your Resourcefulness

Applications of Resourcefulness to Prepared Curricula and Instructional Packages

Applications of Resourcefulness in Varied Settings
NURSERY SCHOOL
CHILD-CARE CENTERS
KINDERGARTEN TEACHING
PRIMARY TEACHING

Summary

PREASSESSMENT

When you have completed this chapter you should be able to describe and compare the following:

1. *teaching perspectives and practices derived from* **mental sets**.
2. *different ways of using* **packaged curricula.**
3. *varied applications of resourceful teaching to different early childhood education settings.*

   Before beginning to read this chapter:

1. *take time to write what you currently know about each of the above topics.*
2. *reflect on the child (children) you observed as you studied Section Two; consider how you would "instruct" this child (these children) in ways that would*
   a. *use a large proportion of your repertoire.*
   b. *facilitate maximum development.*

   Save what you write for rereading, comparison, and elaboration after you have studied and discussed these materials.

Overview

Each of the preceding chapters in this section has demonstrated how you can create and manage various contexts in an effort to support children's physical, social, emotional, and cognitive growth. In addition to the contexts already discussed, a full coverage of early childhood education would involve similar chapters on music, art, and outdoor contexts, to name but a few. Without being exhaustive, our goal has been to communicate an overall perspective, or *mental set*, that generates ideas on how children's development can be enhanced in any context.

On the following pages we will explore more precisely these mental sets and how they can be applied to various curriculum approaches and instructional packages. Finally, we will discuss the specialized areas of resourcefulness you will need for work with specific age levels and types of programs.

Mental Sets to Enhance Your Resourcefulness

What you do in any particular interaction with a child depends on two factors: (1) your repertoire of ideas, and (2) your mental set about what you *should* do in that situation. Chapters 8 through 12 have provided you with a broadened teaching repertoire. Whether or not you fully use that repertoire in your interactions with children, however, depends on the assumptions you hold about what you should do in teaching situations, or, stated differently, on your mental set.

If your mental set is that you should not engage in teaching unless you are conducting a formal lesson, the teaching repertoire you have developed thus far will be used far less than if your mental set is that you can informally teach in any interchange with a child. Many teachers assume that teaching consists of applying a **lesson plan** (a series of preplanned actions and tasks with carefully selected materials, an evaluation, and a followup). Such lessons, well planned and executed, do make significant contributions to children's learning. However, if children were dependent for their learning on what is presented in this manner, there would be little cognitive or intellectual progress. A lesson can crystallize a learning or arouse interest in a new topic, but children learn most in less formal circumstances.

Learning can happen anywhere and at any time

If you are to be truly effective in teaching, you must hold the mental set that learning can happen anywhere and at any time and that most settings can provide the stimulus for teaching and learning, whether the setting is a desert island, a living room, a bowling alley, a hardware store, or a street corner. As part of that mental set, you will have an awareness (at the very least) of the following characteristics of situations:

1. The physical characteristics of available objects
   size—What are the size relationships between objects? Which is larger? Smaller? Wider? Taller?
   shape—What is round? Square? Rectangular? Cylindrical?
   color—What is red? Yellow? Brown? Dark? Light?
   texture—What is smooth? Rough? Bumpy?
   transparency—What can be seen through?
   reflectivity—What reflects light, serving to mirror objects?
   weight—What are the weight relationships? Which is heavier? Lighter?
   mass—What is the area or volume of objects?
   composition—Which objects are metal, glass, wood, plastic, paper, fabric, manufactured, natural?
   symmetry—Which objects are symmetrical, nonsymmetrical, have symmetrical aspects?
   patterns—Which objects display patterns or, together with other objects, form a pattern?

2. The potential uses of available objects
   containability—What can hold or contain what?
   combining ability—What can be combined with what else?
   malleability—What can be molded, folded, or bent into different forms?

changeability—What can be changed into different states (evaporated, melted, frozen, dissolved, burned)?

reversibility—What changes can be reversed, returning objects to their original states?

sound production—What can be used to produce sounds or variations in sounds?

marking—What can make marks on other surfaces?

3. The language requirements of specific situations

vocabulary needs—What words are necessary for naming and describing various objects and actions?

grammar and syntax needs—What will involve the child in language expression of various kinds?

4. The written communications already available and the potential for introducing new writing activities

5. The possibilities for fantasy

movement—What movement activities are suggested by objects and situations?

emotion—What emotional tones or expressions are suggested by objects or situations?

Photo by John James.

human roles—What human roles are suggested by objects or situations?
literature—What stories or poems are suggested by objects or situations?

6. The social possibilities within situations
   interactions—What interactions might the situation foster? Which social repertoire is necessary?
   conflicts—What kinds of conflicts might the situation engender? What alternatives can be modeled for conflict resolution? For cooperative effort?

Practice in "low-demand" situations

You will find that, with practice, you will increase the speed and ease with which you can size up situations and draw conclusions about the learning potential available for given children. You will find it extremely beneficial if you can begin practicing now in "low-demand" situations. Take yourself into different locations and, using the preceding criteria, evaluate the learning potentials there. Almost any situation will do, but you may find the following ones especially valuable:

- Involve yourself in using various art media—finger paint, clay, printing, weaving, etc. Once immersed in the activity, consider the physical characteristics of the objects, the possibilities for oral and written language, for projective activities, for social actions.
- Go to a playground. Swing, slide, and do whatever else is available there for children. Watch any children present for ideas. Then stop and reflect, as suggested above.
- Collect a variety of musical and rhythmic instruments and other sound-producing apparatus and begin experimenting with them. Then stop and

---

TEACHER-CHILD INTERCHANGES

In commenting on her visits to schools in England and Wales, Courtney Cazden (1971) pointed out that the key word for British teachers is *extension*. For example, Margaret Roberts of the University of London Institute of Education was said to describe good teaching as "sensitive observation," a "mental companionship" between teacher and child, which in turn leads the teacher to *extend* the child's ideas and language.

Cazden also cited comments of Mr. Norfield, head of a primary school in London, as follows:

> If the teacher is not aware of particular aspects of experience, she can't pay attention to them; if she's not aware of the intellectual skills and concepts in the simplest activity, she cannot nourish those skills and concepts in the context of children's play. (p. 121)

These comments of British educators are quite in accord with the views being expressed in this chapter.

For further reading on teacher-child interchanges designed to teach, see Additional Reading section at the end of the chapter.

Photo by Ursula Moeller.

consider how a resourceful teacher might use them to foster children's development and learning.
• Make a tour, such as children would be taken on, of some interesting sites—a bakery, an apple orchard, a pond, a dairy farm, a turkey farm, a forest—and generate a list of possible learning activities.

RESPONSE SECTION

Pause for about ten minutes and evaluate your current environment in terms of its teaching potential. First, without rereading the first part of this chapter, list all those aspects of your environment that suggest teaching-learning possibilities. Draw a line at the end of your list and read back through the criteria described as characteristic of resourceful teachers. With these in mind, add to your list (below the line) any new teaching possibilities that you can now identify in your current setting.

Reflect on whether these conscious efforts to extend your awareness of teaching possibilities seem helpful.

- Go to everyday places, such as a gasoline station, a restaurant, a motel, a street corner, the inside of a car, or the inside of a bus, and analyze them as suggested above.

Evaluation of surroundings as "second nature"

Ideally, the evaluation of surrounding environments will gradually become "second nature," so that most of your attention can be focused on the children with whom you are working.

Applications of Resourcefulness to Prepared Curricula and Instructional Packages

Curriculum guides provide general statements

Teachers sometimes have available to them prepared **curriculum guides** that specify objectives and offer instructional strategies for achieving those objectives. Sometimes these guides are prepared locally by teachers, parents, and administrators, and sometimes they are developed by state departments of education or by federal agencies specifically for the programs under their administration and funding. In almost all instances these guides are restricted to very general statements, which require the individual teacher to exercise considerable independence and resourcefulness in order to implement them. The extent to which programs voluntarily or involuntarily follow an existing guide varies enormously. In many situations, such guides do not even exist; teacher resourcefulness is assumed to be sufficient to determine curricula in these instances.

Specificity of commercial materials

In almost all program settings **instructional packages** (sets of learning materials designed for use in developing particular concepts or skills) or collections of commercially prepared curriculum materials will be available. Unlike curriculum guides, these often include very detailed directions for the teacher concerning the use of materials. The developers of these materials even try to make them as specific or **teacher-proof** as possible, assuming that the adults using them will lack sensitivity and resourcefulness. In your initial years of teaching you may wish to follow some of the excellent suggestions contained in the **teacher's manuals** that accompany commercial materials. However, do not assume that following the procedures suggested in these manuals is sufficient to fulfill your responsibilities as a teacher.

Modify and supplement

As you gain teaching experience you will increasingly find that you will need to modify and supplement the procedures outlined in these teacher's manuals according to your own assessment of your children and your teaching situation. Eventually, the major portion of your instruction should revolve around your own ideas and resourcefulness. However knowledgeable the developers of instructional materials may be, there is no way they can individualize instruction to meet the needs of particular children and specific teaching situations. We have observed well-meaning teachers take children away from potentially rich learning involvements, in favor of prescribed lessons and activities that are quite inappropriate for the children's current development or interests. A prime example is the teacher who unthinkingly called her children in from outdoor play, where they had been capturing and examining ants, to engage in a "prepared" science lesson on

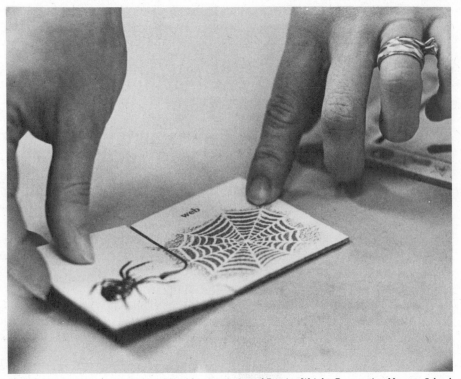

Photo by permission of Bernice Wright Cooperative Nursery School.

insects. A similar example is the teacher who daily required all children to stop their outdoor play on the jungle gym, monkey bars, tunnels, and walking rails in order to engage in simple movement exercises prescribed in a curriculum guide. The teacher ignored the fact that most of the children were already performing much more advanced actions.

If, as a teacher, you are provided with a particular set of **objectives**, whether commercially or locally prepared, you should periodically examine each objective in terms of the diverse ways in which it can be accomplished. As an example, your curriculum guide may direct you to develop in primary-grade children the ability to perform **multiple classifications** and may offer a specific lesson sequence for this purpose. Let us suppose the ultimate goal is to enable children to simultaneously sort things into two major categories (for example, animals versus dishes) and then into subcategories (dinosaurs versus farm animals; cups versus plates). You can teach the lessons exactly as suggested; some children will probably benefit, others will not. What they learn will depend, first, on the match between their readiness and the instructional level, and second, on their familiarity with and interest in the particular materials recommended.

The more resourceful you are, the more alternative strategies and materials you will be able to offer the children to develop their proficiency with classifications, both single and multiple. You may decide to substitute alternative strategies for what is prescribed, or possibly to supplement the lessons with more personalized and varied instruction. As a beginning teacher you will probably wish to study any curriculum guides available to you and often will wish to follow their suggestions. At the same time, however, you should gradually begin to develop your own ability to provide comparable instruction more closely aligned to the needs and interests of the particular children you are teaching.

The need for personalized alternatives

COMMERCIALLY PREPARED MATERIALS

The following commercially prepared materials (instructional packages and series) are cited as examples of the many that are available for use in programs for young children. Descriptive brochures can often be obtained from the publishers. Addresses can be found in the Appendixes.

Alpha One: Breaking the Code (New Dimensions in Education)
Bank Street Readers (Macmillan)
Basic Reading (J. P. Lippincott)
Building Blocks (Steck-Vaughn)
DETECT (Science Research Associates)
DISTAR (Science Research Associates)
Dubnoff School Program (Teaching Resources/Educational Service of the New York Times)
ESLI—Elementary Science: Learning by Investigating (Rand McNally)
Fairbanks-Robinson Program (Teaching Resources/Educational Service of the New York Times)
Frostig Program for the Development of Visual Perception (Follett)
Getting a Head Start (Houghton Mifflin)
Goldman-Lynch Sounds and Symbols Development Kit (American Guidance Service)
Language Experiences in Reading (Encyclopaedia Britannica Educational Corporation)
Magic Circle Film Curriculum (Human Development Training Institute)
Open Court Basic Readers (Open Court)
PEEK—Peabody Early Experiences Kit (American Guidance Service)
Peabody Rebus Reading Program (American Guidance Service)
Piaget program: Early Childhood Curriculum (American Science and Engineering)
Programmed Reading (McGraw-Hill)
Readiness for Reading (Lippincott)
SRA Reading Program (Science Research Associates)
Structural Reading Series (L. W. Singer/Random House)
Sullivan Decoding Kit (Behavioral Research Laboratories)
TRY: Experiences for Young Children (Noble and Noble)

To test your resourcefulness with prepared curricula and instructional packages, select an instructional segment from an educational television program (for example, "Sesame Street," "Electric Company," "Mr. Roger's Neighborhood," "Romper Room") for which there are identifiable educational objectives. Filmed instruction is the ultimate in instructional packaging. While written lessons and teachers' guides to some extent prescribe instructional content and methods, filmed instruction actually presents it. For the particular objectives in the sequence you select, generate as many alternative ideas as you can for presenting the same concepts. You may benefit from working with others in generating these ideas. Finally, select from your total list those you feel would be particularly appropriate for the children you observed in studying Section Two.

Applications of Resourcefulness in Varied Settings

In preparation for teaching young children, you will need to develop a repertoire broad enough to permit working with children ages three through seven, and in a range of settings—nursery schools, child-care centers, kindergartens, and primary grades. Preparation for a single age group in a single setting is insufficient for coping with the unexpected contingencies that normally arise in one's professional career. Even when you work with a single age level, you will encounter broad ability levels. Therefore, throughout this section, we have focused on a broad preparation and have not differentiated between the various preschool, kindergarten, and primary-grade settings. At this point, however, it may be useful for you to consider the application of your resourcefulness to particular situations.

NURSERY SCHOOL

Nursery-school programs are less than four hours in daily duration, two or three hours being usual. The children typically range in age from three to five years and attend programs that meet from two to five days a week. The availability of public school or special kindergarten programs often determines the upper age range of the nursery school.

Informal teaching

In nursery school, children's primary interests are likely to be social. While parents may be very interested in the academic side of nursery school, the children themselves are more likely to be preoccupied with playing with the other children. They are even likely to show a greater interest in academic activities, such as learning letters and numbers, in the home setting than in the nursery school. Children of this age will benefit most from the integration of learning and skill development into their total activity pattern. While they may react uncomfortably to a formal lesson in number sets, for example, they will respond very positively to the same content interjected into their play activity.

There will be a broad range of social repertoires among the nursery-school children, which complicates the task of arranging for successful and satisfying social experiences. Since many children in nursery school are encountering, perhaps for the first time, peers who neither understand nor care about their interests and desires, the potential for conflict is high and the teacher's *Conflict resolution* resourcefulness with conflict resolution becomes paramount. If you are planning to teach in a nursery school, you should not only be resourceful in helping children resolve their conflicts, but you must also be able to communicate effectively with parents about the progress of their children in this regard. Children who have little initial conflict often experience a rapid increase in conflict at some point and then a gradual decline as their reper- *Parent* toire for cooperation increases. This is a very important development and is *communication* an essential one to communicate to concerned parents. This is especially true when parents assume that an absence of conflict is a desirable state of affairs and worry as they see their child increasingly involved in "fights" as he or she settles into nursery school.

The nursery-school teacher also needs special resourcefulness in explain- *Providing* ing physical phenomena to children and in providing clear instructions and *explanations* directions. Contrary to common-sense expectations, the younger the child, the greater the need for the teacher to have strong conceptual abilities. At the drop of a hat, a nursery teacher must provide succinct, accurate, and interesting verbal explanations and directions. It is very difficult to capture and communicate the essence of something without careful planning; teachers of young children must be prepared to spontaneously discuss clearly and accurately all the complicated things that children may ask about.

Caregiving The nursery-school teacher must fulfill more caregiving needs than teachers of older children. The prekindergarten teacher must cheerfully and efficiently be unable to undo "hard" knots, force on and remove tight boots, clean up spills, attend to children's toilet "accidents," and match children with stray possessions and clothing. These are but a few of the bothersome but necessary tasks that constantly confront teachers of the very young.

CHILD-CARE CENTERS

For teachers who work in programs where children attend for more than four hours, there is need for additional kinds of resourcefulness. Since more time *Feeding, napping,* is spent in caregiving functions (such as feeding, napping, and grooming), it *grooming* becomes important that teachers have patience with these duties and that their teaching skills be adaptable to such functions. A child-care worker, for example, might prepare for the kinds of learnings that can be fostered at meals. What can a group of children learn about each other, about the foods they are eating, and about classification, number, and causality while they

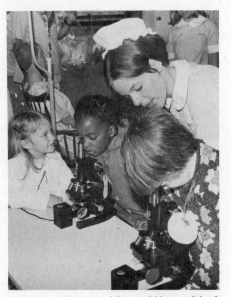

Courtesy of Carousel Nursery School.

are eating? There are many possibilities and the resourceful teacher is alert to them.

Integrating events from the outside world into the program

Teachers in child-care centers must be able to integrate events from the outside world into the program. Whereas a child at home is normally taken along to the grocery store, to the bank, and to the homes of friends and relatives, and is therefore exposed to a variety of persons, these experiences are far less available to the child in a full-day program unless the program is structured to provide such contacts. Resourceful child-care workers make sure that children have chances to interact with visitors whenever possible. Children are invited to watch (at a safe distance) when repairs are being made; they are sometimes taken to local shops to obtain supplies needed for their activities; and they are given ample opportunity to watch interesting events near their center, such as street repairs, building construction or demolition, landscaping efforts, and truck deliveries. These experiences foster valuable learnings when shared with adults who help supply needed vocabulary, draw discriminations, and make comparisons. In a child-care center it becomes the responsibility of the teaching staff to make sure that the children are not isolated from these everyday learning experiences because of the length of the program day.

Describing children's activity and development to parents

It is also especially important that child-care workers have a facility for describing the child's activity and development to parents. When a major portion of a child's life is spent in a program setting, it becomes especially critical that there be full and continuous school-family communication. Notetaking regarding the child's behavior is helpful in this effort, as illustrated in Section Two. It is also important, however, for the parents to know about the everyday experiences made available to the child and the rationale for their inclusion. Children of ages three and four cannot effectively communicate what is happening to them, and consequently the teacher and parents must communicate with each other so that an integrated set of home-school experiences can be maintained.

In addition to performing these specialized tasks, the child-care teacher needs all of the types of resourcefulness described as necessary for the nursery-school teacher.

KINDERGARTEN TEACHING

Providing a program organization to accommodate diversity

Teachers of five- and six-year-olds must be especially skilled at helping children make gradual transitions from very active to more sedentary involvements. Individual children's readiness for these transitions come at very different points in time. Some children enter their kindergarten year already interested in paper-and-pencil "school" activities, while others, even at the end of the kindergarten year, may find this kind of sustained inactivity very difficult, preferring instead to run, jump, climb, and engage in all kinds of large muscle activity. The kindergarten teacher has the difficult task of providing satisfactory experiences for all and, in the process, making sure that there is increasing exposure to reading, writing, counting, and problem-solving. For those children who are still in a very "active" stage, the teacher's resourcefulness in integrating academic learnings into other activities, as described in the previous chapters, is particularly important.

Program organization in the kindergarten is especially important since the sessions are often quite short and children typically have such a wide range of readiness skills. These issues will be fully considered in Section Four.

PRIMARY TEACHING

Reading, writing, and mathematics instruction

As a primary teacher you will need to be especially resourceful in helping children with the basic academic skills of reading, writing, and mathematics. The preceding chapters have discussed how to provide such instruction in a variety of contexts. Your repertoire for this kind of teaching will be especially crucial if you are working with six- and seven-year-olds. Even if you teach in a primary situation that prescribes a particular system of instruction for the basic academic areas, you will find that you can better adapt that system to the needs of your children if you have developed a wide repertoire of teaching activities. The more spontaneous and flexible your instruction, the more effective it will be.

Accommodating a range of abilities and interests

Arranging for children's independent work

Program organization that complements your teaching resourcefulness is especially important in the primary grades. The older the children you teach, the broader the range of abilities and interests you can anticipate. A program structure that accommodates this diversity is therefore even more critical in the primary grades than with younger children. Arranging for children's independent endeavors while you provide instruction for individuals or small groups is especially important. The materials in Section Four address these organizational issues.

The preceding section has attempted to differentiate your teaching repertoire in terms of different age levels and types of programs. If you have not already done so, arrange to observe, in a regular daily session, each of these kinds of situations. As you observe, try to imagine yourself working in the setting and try to determine what extensions of your repertoire would be necessary for you to perform competently.

Summary

Three topics have been considered within this chapter. First, a delineation of the kinds of mental sets resourceful teachers use to identify teaching possibilities within any given setting. Second, the relationship of teaching resourcefulness to the use of prepared instructional materials. And third, the kinds of resourcefulness that are particularly critical in certain settings—according to the type of program and the age of the children.

Throughout this chapter and section we have emphasized that your resourcefulness will increase in proportion to your efforts to expand your teaching repertoire. A certain minimal level of resourcefulness is necessary for mere survival in teaching; beyond that point, however, your own satisfaction as well as the extent of children's development and learning, will be significantly influenced by the efforts you make to continue extending your own personal resourcefulness.

REASSESSMENT

Reread what you wrote for the preassessment as you began this chapter, comparing this with your current understandings. Now write on these topics again and incorporate your new insights and knowledge. Continue to update as you prepare for teaching. Save your materials for your portfolio.

Additional Reading

Teaching Resourcefulness Association for Childhood Education International. *Creating with materials for work and play.* Washington, D.C.: ACEI, 1969.

Biggs, E. E., and Maclean, J. R. *Freedom to learn: An active learning approach to mathematics.* Ontario, Canada: Addison-Wesley (Canada), 1966.

Burie, A. A., and Heltshe, M. A. *Reading with a smile: 90 reading games that work.* Washington, D.C.: Acropolis Books, 1975.

Carmichael, V. S. *Science experiences for young children.* Pasadena, Calif.: Southern California AEYC, 1969.

Cherry, C. *Motivational curriculum chart for early childhood.* Belmont, Calif.: Fearon Publishers, 1969.

Clark, B., Lay, M., and Tryon, B. *And so there was me: A potpourri of creative art experiences for children 3 to 6.* Syracuse, N.Y.: Syracuse University Early Childhood Education Center, 1973.

———. *A space to discover me: Books, games, puzzles and other quiet things for children 3 to 6.* Syracuse, N.Y.: Syracuse University Early Childhood Education Center, 1973.

Cratty, B. J. *Creative learning: Games to enhance academic abilities.* Englewood Cliffs, N.J.: Prentice-Hall, 1971.

Croft, D. *Recipes for busy little hands.* Washington, D.C.: Day Care and Child Development Council of America.

Croft, D. J., and Hess, R. D. *An activities handbook for teachers of young children.* Boston: Houghton Mifflin, 1975.

Engel, R. C. *Language motivating experiences for young children.* Van Nuys, Calif.: DFA Publishers, 1970.

Garvey, M. *Teacher displays: Their purpose, construction and use.* Hamden, Conn.: Shoe String Press, 1972.

Golick, M. *Deal me in! The use of playing cards in teaching and learning.* New York: Jeffrey Norton, 1973.

Greenberg, P., and Epstein, B. *Bridge-to-reading.* Morristown, N.J.: General Learning Corporation, 1973. Eight-book set.

Hamilton, D. P., Flemming, B. J., and Hicks, J. D. *Resources for creative teaching in early childhood education.* New York: Harcourt Brace Jovanovich, 1976.

Hodgen, L., and Koetter, J., Laforse, B., McCord, S., Schramm, D. *School before six: A diagnostic approach.* Vols. I and II. St. Louis, Mo.: CEMREL, 1974.

Jorde, P. *Living and learning with children: A handbook of activities for children from three to six.* Paula Jorde, 217 B 10th Street SE, Washington, D.C. 20003.

Karnes, M. B. *Helping young children develop language skills: A book of activities.* Washington, D.C.: Council for Exceptional Children, 1968.

Lorton, M. B. *Workjobs: Activity-centered learning for early childhood education.* Menlo Park, Calif.: Addison-Wesley, 1972.

Marzollo, J., and Lloyd, J. *Learning through play.* New York: Harper & Row, 1972.

Montgomery, C. *Art for teachers of children.* Columbus, Ohio: Charles E. Merrill, 1967.

Nuffield Mathematics Project. *Mathematics Begins.* New York: John Wiley, 1967. Others in series: *Shape and Size; Beginning; Computation and Structure;* etc.

Pitcher, E. G. *et al. Helping young children learn.* Columbus, Ohio: Charles E. Merrill, 1966.

Rudolph, M. *From hand to head: A handbook for teachers of preschool programs.* New York: Webster/McGraw-Hill, 1973.

Russell, H. R. *Ten-minute field trips: Using the school grounds for environmental studies.* Chicago: J. G. Ferguson/Doubleday, 1973.

Sharp, E. *Thinking is child's play.* New York: E. P. Dutton, 1969.

Stant, M. A. *The young child: His activities and materials.* Englewood Cliffs, N.J.: Prentice-Hall, 1972.

Taylor, B. J. *Child goes forth: A curriculum guide for teachers of preschool children.* 2nd ed. Provo, Utah: Brigham Young University Press, 1970.

Tryon, B., Clark, B., and Lay, M. *I can do it: A collection of action-oriented experiences for children 3 to 6.* Syracuse, N.Y.: Syracuse University Early Childhood Education Center, 1973.

Voight, R. C. *Invitation to learning: The learning center handbook.* Washington, D.C.: Acropolis Books, 1971.

Teacher-Child Interchanges Blank, M. *Teaching learning in the preschool: A dialogue approach.* Columbus, Ohio: Charles E. Merrill, 1973.

Cazden, C. B. Language programs for young children: Notes from England and Wales. In C. S. Lavatelli, Ed. *Language learning in early childhood education.* Urbana, Ill.: ERIC Clearinghouse on Early Childhood Education, 1971.

Cook, A., and H. Mack. *The teacher's role: Informal schools in Britain today.* New York: Citation Press, 1971.

Karplus, R., and H. Thier. *A new look at elementary school science.* Chicago: Rand McNally, 1967.

Sparling, J. J., and M. C. Sparling. How to talk to a scribbler. *Young Children*, 1973, 28, 333–41

Nursery-School Teaching

Gardner, D. E. M., and Cass, J. E. *The role of the teacher in the infant and nursery school.* Oxford: Pergamon Press, 1965.

Goodlad, J. *et al. Early school in the United States.* New York: McGraw-Hill, 1973.

Landreth, C. *Preschool learning and teaching.* New York: Harper & Row, 1972.

Leeper, S. H., Dales, R. J., Skipper, D. S., and Witherspoon, R. L. *Good Schools for young children*, 3rd ed. New York: Macmillan, 1975.

Read, K. H. *The nursery school: A human relations laboratory*, 5th ed. Philadelphia: Saunders, 1971.

Tarnay, E. D. *What does the nursery school teacher teach?* Washington, D.C.: National Association for Education of Young Children, 1965.

Todd, V. E., and Heffernan, H. *The years before school: Guiding preschool children,* 2nd ed. New York: Macmillan, 1971.

Vance, B. *Teaching the pre-kindergarten child: Instructional design and curriculum.* Monterey, Calif.: Brooks/Cole–Wadsworth, 1973.

Day-Care Teaching

Child development/Day care resources project. Philadelphia: Research for Better Schools, 1971. ERIC Document Reproduction Service No. ED 058 966.

Day-care pamphlets (in Spanish and English). New York: Curriculum Development, 1971. Sample titles: Dawson, B. *A child's questions about death;* Curtis, C. *Preparing the child for the day care center.*

Fein, G. G., and Clarke-Stewart, A. *Day care in context.* New York: John Wiley, 1973.

Hildebrand, V. Trips for preschoolers. *Childhood Education*, 1967, 43, 524–7.

———. *Guiding young children.* New York: Macmillan, 1975.

Katz, L. G. *Teacher-child relationships in day care centers.* 1972. ERIC Document Reproduction Service No. ED 046 494.

LeLaurin, K., and Risley, T. R. The organization of day-care environments: "Zone" versus "man-to-man" staff assignments. *Journal of Applied Behavior Analysis,* 1972, 5, 225–32.

Pizzo, P. D. *Operational difficulties of group day care.* Washington, D.C.: Day Care and Child Development Council of America, 1972.

Prescott, E., and Jones, E. *Day care as a child rearing environment.* Washington, D.C.: National Association for the Education of Young Children, 1972.

Weir, M. K. Establishing, operating and using day care. *Child Care Quarterly*, 1975, 4, 141–9.

Kindergarten Teaching

Foster, J., and Headley, N. *Education in the kindergarten.* 4th ed. New York: American Book, 1966.

Heffernan, H., and Todd, V. *The kindergarten teacher.* Boston: D. C. Heath, 1960.

Hymes, J. L., Jr. *The child under six.* Englewood Cliffs, N.J.: Prentice-Hall, 1963.

Latting, L. H., and Stephens, B. L. *Kindergarten guidebook*. Denver, Colo.: State Board of Education, 1960. ERIC Document Reproduction Service No. ED 001 713.

Robison, H. F., and Spodek, B. *New directions in the kindergarten*. New York: Teachers College Press, 1965.

Rudolph, M., and Cohen, D. H. *Kindergarten: A year of learning*. New York: Appleton-Century-Crofts, 1964.

Weber, L. *The kindergarten*. New York: Teachers College Press, 1969.

Willis, C. D., and Lindberg, L. *Kindergarten for today's children*. Chicago, Ill.: Follett, 1967.

Primary Teaching ALERT: *A sourcebook of elementary curricula, programs and projects*. Pleasantville, N.Y.: Docent Corporation, 1974.

Anderson, M. et al. *Activity methods for children under eight*. London: Evans Brothers, 1962.

Dawson, M. A. *Language teaching in kindergarten and early primary grades*. New York: Harcourt, Brace and World, 1966.

Engelmann, S. *Preventing failure in the primary grades*. Chicago, Ill.: Science Research Associates, 1969.

Imhoff, M. *Early elementary education*. New York: Appleton-Century-Crofts, 1959.

Jarolimek, J., and Foster, C. D. *Teaching and learning in the elementary school*. New York: Macmillan, 1976.

Morrison, I. E., and Perry, I. F. *Kindergarten-primary education*. New York: Ronald Press, 1961.

Shuster, A. H., and Ploghoft, M. E. *The emerging elementary curriculum: Methods and procedures*. Columbus, Ohio: Charles E. Merrill, 1970.

Stahl, D. K., and Anzalone, P. M. *Individualized teaching in the elementary school*. West Nyack, N.Y.: Parker, 1970.

SECTION FOUR
ORGANIZATIONAL
ABILITIES

As a teacher you will probably have responsibility for such things as the specification of objectives, the organization of time segments, the arrangement and use of space, the selection and use of equipment and materials, and the establishment and maintenance of ground rules for children's behavior. The organization and management of all of these elements can be likened, in some respects, to that of an orchestra conductor, who must coordinate and bring harmony out of various musical elements; the organizational task of the teacher is even sometimes referred to as orchestration. Different educational effects are achieved through different arrangements of the basic program elements. Organizational skill depends on the ability, first, to create a plan, and second, to implement that plan to achieve particular educational objectives.

Many different configurations have been created from the basic program elements, which are often referred to as "models." Two extensive federally funded studies, Head Start and Follow Through, have compared the outcomes of various early education models. These, as well as other smaller studies, show that programs generally achieve most when they have well-articulated objectives and careful planning that directs program elements to the attainment of those objectives.

You will find it helpful to carefully study some of the early education models currently being used throughout the nation. As you become familiar with their orientations and objectives, their distinctive arrangements of time, space, and equipment, and their pattern of classroom management, you will be in a far better position to evelute employment opportunities and to set up and manage your own program once you are teaching.

This section begins with a presentation of the types of programs favored by those who emphasize the environmentalist, the maturationist, and the interactionist views of development. Program models compatible with each view are described in Chapter 14. In Chapter 15 some of the critical decisions regarding programs will be more fully analyzed in regard to the organization of time, space, and equipment, ground rules for children's behavior, and relationships with parents.

Chapter 16 attempts to help you (1) match program decisions to objectives, (2) prepare to implement your plans, and (3) assess your outcomes. The value of carefully thinking through these issues before you begin to teach cannot be overemphasized.

CHAPTER 14
Contrasting Program Models

Overview

The Environmentalist View of Programs
    CHARACTERISTICS OF ENVIRONMENTALIST PROGRAMS
    THE TRADITIONAL ELEMENTARY SCHOOL APPROACH
    REINFORCEMENT TECHNOLOGY
    PROGRAM APPLICATIONS OF REINFORCEMENT TECHNOLOGY: DISTAR,
        BEHAVIOR ANALYSIS, DARCEE
    FURTHER COMMENTARY ON ENVIRONMENTALIST PROGRAMS

The Maturationist View of Programs
    MATURATIONIST PROGRAMING PRINCIPLES
    A PROGRAM COMPATIBLE WITH THE MATURATIONIST VIEW: BANK STREET
    PROGRAM CRITIQUES FROM THE MATURATIONIST VIEW
    FURTHER COMMENTARY ON MATURATIONIST PROGRAMS

The Interactionist View of Programs
    PROGRAM CONDITIONS FAVORED BY INTERACTIONISTS
    PROGRAMS COMPATIBLE WITH THE INTERACTIONIST VIEW: MONTESSORI,
        BRITISH INTEGRATED DAY, COGNITIVE CURRICULUM, AND SYRACUSE
        RESPONSIVE CARE
    FURTHER COMMENTARY ON INTERACTIONIST PROGRAMS

The Prevalence of Eclectic Practice
Summary

PREASSESSMENT

When you have completed this chapter you should be able to describe and compare the following:

1. *patterns of program organization for young children.*
2. *ideological origins of programs for young children.*
3. *common elements of programs for young children.*

   Before beginning to read this chapter:

1. *take time to write what you currently know about each of the above topics.*
2. *reflect on the child (children) you observed as you studied Section Two and for whom you planned involvements in Section Three; consider what kind(s) of organized educational program(s) would be most suited for this child's (these children's) development.*

   Save what you write for rereading, comparison, and elaboration after you have studied and discussed these materials.

Overview

Young children in the United States are currently undergoing a variety of educational experiences on both the local and national levels. Some three-year-olds may already have had extensive experiences in child-care settings, and many of these will continue on a full-time basis until they are enrolled in elementary schools. As five-year-olds, these children sometimes attend a half-day kindergarten program and then return to the child-care center for the remainder of the day, and thus have two program experiences simultaneously.

At the same time, many other children in the same community will have had no program experience until they are enrolled in kindergarten or first grade. They spend their days at home, in the neighborhood, at a baby sitter's, or in a family day-care home. Some children have limited nursery-school experiences, and others attend nursery school from ages three through five.

Just as there is marked variation in preschool settings, so there are differences between the various types of organized programs. Nursery schools, child-care centers, kindergartens, and primary grades may all be organized in quite different ways, and a variety of curriculum approaches may even be employed within the same school.

To assist you in understanding the varieties of education experienced by American children from ages three to eight, it will be useful to examine different programs based on the three views of learning and development discussed in Section Two. Each of these views—environmentalist, maturationist, and interactionist—leads to different types of program arrangements, and within each view there are contrasting (although compatible) approaches. Distinct program configurations are referred to in this book, and in educational literature generally, as **models**. Over the past decade the developers of contrasting perspectives have made intensive efforts at model-building. In what follows, each of the three basic views is reintroduced, along with its implications for program organization. The specific model or models derived from or compatible with the view are individually presented and then compared with other approaches.

The Environmentalist View of Programs

Environmentalists, as was discussed in Section Two, emphasize that humans are constantly being shaped by impinging environmental forces. They urge that the shaping of behavior in teaching be done intentionally and be directed toward desirable goals. They see developmental progress in terms of small increments of change: knowledge and skills are acquired piece by piece, in cumulative fashion. Since the mastery of simpler learnings is considered a prerequisite to the accomplishment of more complex learnings, the primary task of teaching is the careful sequencing of what is to be learned. The program is thus structured to allow for step-by-step assessment of important objectives so that children can move as rapidly as possible toward more advanced levels of performance.

CHARACTERISTICS OF ENVIRONMENTALIST PROGRAMS

Those programs most compatible with the environmentalist view of development often have the following characteristics:

1. There is a focus on very specific objectives.

2. Disciplines or subject fields are viewed as sources of knowledge that must be simplified (broken into pieces) and carefully graded or sequenced for transmission to children. The sequence is "preprogramed" so that each step provides a gradual transition from simpler to more complex tasks.

3. The nature of a particular teaching sequence is primarily based on the subject matter being considered, not on the characteristics of the individual learner or the inclinations of the teacher.

4. Distinctions are made between intellectual, social, emotional, and perceptual-motor development. Objectives for each of these areas are usually formulated separately.

5. The teacher very actively directs children's activity. Intensive training, especially in areas where children seem "retarded" or weak in comparison with their age peers, is seen as especially necessary. It is the teacher's role to direct, correct, and reinforce behavior in desired directions.

6. The learner is seen as relatively passive, shaped by the teacher through reinforcement. It is the teacher's role to control reinforcements to the children, thereby directing them into desired learnings and behaviors.

7. Children are moved as quickly as possible from concrete (involvement with real materials and actions) to abstract manipulations of subject matter. Much of the instruction is verbal—oral or written. Language is seen as synonymous with thought, so training in correct language usage and logical statements are viewed as the main avenues for promoting intellectual development.

THE TRADITIONAL ELEMENTARY SCHOOL APPROACH

Much of traditional elementary school practice is based on an environmentalist view. Textbooks, workbooks, and lesson plans, as you may recall from your own early education, are based on the assumption that curriculum objectives can be formulated apart from any knowledge of the individual learner. The teacher's task is to find the most effective means to get all students to meet these objectives. In programs based on this view, individual rates of progress may vary as children move through materials and instructional sequences, but little individualization of content or approach is provided.

Textbooks,
workboooks, and
lesson plans

Teachers typically reward children (with praise, gold stars, grades, or privileges) for appropriate behavior and accomplishments, and sometimes punish them for nonaccomplishment or lack of compliance. The success of teachers in meeting academic objectives is dependent on their ability to keep children learning. In the past, however, teachers were often left to their own devices in managing the learning process, and often even the successful teachers were unable to explain the principles that guided their practice.

REINFORCEMENT TECHNOLOGY

In recent years the technology for managing reinforcements to accomplish desired objectives, as formulated by B. F. Skinner and his followers, has become increasingly available to teachers. These reinforcement principles have been used as guides for environmentalist classroom practice.

Operant behaviors

According to Skinnerians, there are two kinds of behaviors. The first are *reflexive behaviors* (such as the knee jerk or eye blink); these behaviors are not under volitional control. The second type are described as **operant behaviors**; these are engaged in voluntarily, presumably to bring about some effect on the environment that is considered desirable and rewarding.

Consider the following example: Jimmy, age three, is hungry. At first he cries and fusses but is ignored by his mother. He then tries unsuccessfully to reach into the cookie jar for a cookie. Finally, he says, "I want a cookie." His past experience has taught him that *all* of these behaviors will lead to his being given a cookie. In this instance, only the asking behavior proves effective in achieving his "cookie" goal. Since the asking was instrumental in producing food, he is more likely to use verbal requests when next hungry and is less likely to attempt the other strategies. If, on the other hand, the crying and fussing had proved successful in bringing forth attention and food, the frequency of these behaviors would then be maintained or increased.

Control effects to control behavior

Thus, according to Skinnerians, it is not preceding stimulus conditions (in this case hunger), but rather the effects brought about in prior situations under similar conditions, that lead to the particular choice of behaviors. The frequency with which one engages in any behavior, according to this line of thinking, depends upon the effects that have been produced by the same or similar actions in the past. This is a critical point: What must be controlled in influencing the behavior of others are the effects that follow the behavior.

Knowing this, a teacher can systematically lead a pupil to desired behaviors or learnings. Whatever the child finds reinforcing must be made contingent (dependent) upon the desired behavior. The child's behavior is thus *shaped* by denying something he or she wants (reward) until a desired behavior (teacher objective) is made or approximated.

Four steps

The implementation of these principles requires four steps. The first is clarification of the desired behavior. The second is the determination of the closest approximation to the desired behavior that the child is already exhibiting. The third is the determination of what is reinforcing to the child.

And the fourth is making those reinforcements contingent on the child's behaving in the desired way. If these four steps are successfully completed, the principles of behavior modification can be applied toward specified learning goals.

Positive reinforcement

A **reinforcement** is defined as anything that increases the frequency of a given behavior. **Positive reinforcement** often consists of rewards such as attention, praise, and recognition. These social reinforcers are most effective for young children whose family lives have connected these rewards with the gratification of primary needs (such as feeding, affection, and warmth). Where these associations have not been formed, as in chronically disorganized or deprived families, smiles or praise from a teacher may have little, if any, effect on child behavior. In such cases physical materials such as food, toys, or money are more likely to serve as effective positive reinforcers. One should not assume that what is reinforcing for oneself or for most other people, will necessarily be reinforcing for everyone. Only careful observation of the rewards that actually increase the frequency of a given behavior can produce dependable information regarding reinforcement possibilities.

The Premack principle In addition to food, objects, and social acts, positive reinforcements can come from the opportunity to engage in particular kinds of activities. This principle, as expressed by Premack (1959; 1965), states that voluntary, high-frequency behaviors can be used to reinforce low-frequency behaviors. Thus, a child can be influenced to spend more time practicing writing skills, an activity that he or she would not typically engage in, if rewarding activities, such as outside play or access to toys, are made contingent upon demonstrated accomplishment in writing. To apply the **Premack principle,** the teacher must carefully observe the child to determine his or her preferred activities so that they can be used to reinforce other, low-frequency behaviors the teacher considers desirable.

Negative reinforcement

Negative reinforcements have also been demonstrated to alter the frequency of behaviors. Negative reinforcements involve the cessation of some undesirable stimulus (such as pain or teacher scolding). For example, if you want children to walk in straight lines, you might scold them whenever they do

Avoiding aversive stimuli otherwise, until they do as you wish. If they find your scolding unpleasant, they may conform to your expectations of walking in lines because they find the lack of scolding reinforcing. You should be aware, however, that just as individual children vary in what is positively reinforcing, so they vary in what is negatively reinforcing. To some children scolding may not be particularly aversive; a few may even be positively reinforced by the attention scolding produces and may therefore be led to increase rather than decrease their objectionable behavior.

Nonreinforcement

Ignore undesired behaviors; reinforce desired behaviors

According to the operant psychology position, when a behavior brings no reinforcement, either positive or negative, it will gradually be dropped. To most effectively eliminate undesired behaviors, however, you should, in addition to ignoring the undesirable behaviors, positively reinforce any opposite and desirable behaviors. For example, if whining behavior in a child is to be reduced, it is best ignored (without scolding or otherwise giving any attention). At the same time, any cheerful positive acts by the child should immediately and consistently be followed with attention, privilege, or whatever is reinforcing to the child.

Punishment

The aversive consequence; uncertain effects

Punishment refers to the application of something aversive (such as scolding, spanking, or deprivation of a privilege) as the consequence of particular undesirable actions. You may find the difference between negative reinforcement and punishment difficult to understand. Think of punishment as an aversive consequence of the child's noncompliance with parents' or teacher's wishes, and of negative reinforcement as the child's ridding him or herself, through compliance, of something he or she finds aversive. The latter is more dependably effective than punishment.

For punishment to be effective it must be severe and applied immediately after the objectionable act. While the effects of punishment on subsequent behavior are still a matter of debate, there is agreement that the use of positive or negative reinforcement and nonreinforcement are far more effective. Unless punishment quickly modifies the undesirable behavior, there is little likelihood that its continuation will eventually produce the desired modification.

Schedules of reinforcement

Continuous reinforcement/ intermittent reinforcement

The other important aspect of reinforcement technology is the **scheduling of reinforcements.** If a reinforcement is applied to every instance of the target (desired) behavior, it is described as **continuous reinforcement.** To most effectively bring about behavior change, continuous reinforcement is initially more effective. This requires great vigilance on the part of the teacher when attempted in a classroom. If, for example, you wished to use reinforcements to get a child to pay attention to your presentations, you would try to note and reward each instance of the desired attending behavior. In practice this is difficult. Nevertheless, continuous reinforcement is generally more effective than **intermittent reinforcement** in initiating a modification in behavior. Skinner and his followers have also thoroughly investigated the effectiveness of different schedules of intermittent reinforcements.

Fixed interval/variable interval

The first aspect of intermittent reinforcement is the interval of time between reinforcements. One approach is to have reinforcements occur according to a **fixed interval schedule** (such as every two minutes, two days, or two months). An example of fixed intervals might be the teacher who each morning gives out "stars" or praise for the previous day's accomplishments.

The contrast would be the teacher who at varying unpredetermined intervals throughout the day praises or otherwise rewards children's work efforts. This latter is called a **variable interval schedule.**

The second aspect of reinforcement schedule involves the number of responses or behaviors necessary for each reinforcement to occur—this is referred to as a **ratio schedule.** Instead of reinforcing according to a particular time schedule, the teacher may, for example, give out gold stars or praise on the basis of some predetermined amount of accomplishment, such as a finished puzzle or a correctly done row of number problems. This is called a **fixed ratio schedule.** If the ratio of responses necessary for reinforcement keeps changing, this is called a **variable ratio schedule.** For example, the teacher would initially praise each correct response and then would gradually begin to reserve praise until successively larger groups of correct responses were made.

Fixed ratio/variable ratio

It is not particularly important that you remember the terminology at this point. However, the varying interval and ratio schedules do have predictable effects that are important for you to understand. To bring about behaviors that will persist across time, the most effective reinforcement schedules will be those with variable intervals rather than fixed intervals, and variable ratios rather than fixed ratios. Thus, while continuous reinforcement of specific behaviors will most rapidly bring about initial modifications, varying reinforcement schedules (interval and ratio) have proved more successful in maintaining those behaviors than fixed reinforcement schedules. The basic reinforcement principle is to make rewards contingent upon behaviors in a person's current repertoire that are closest to the desired behavior, and, simultaneously, to avoid reinforcing actions that are incompatible with the desired behavior.

Effects of reinforcement schedules

PROGRAM APPLICATIONS OF REINFORCEMENT TECHNOLOGY: DISTAR, BEHAVIOR ANALYSIS, DARCEE

The technology provided by the Skinner group makes it possible for teachers to more systematically attain traditional learning goals. Several model programs developed during the last decade stem directly from reinforcement theory and research. Most exemplary are the DISTAR, or Academic Preschool, model and the Behavior Analysis model. A third model, developed at the Demonstration and Research Center for Early Education (DARCEE), represents less of a departure from traditional school practice but also emphasizes systematic reinforcement practices.

The Academic Preschool, or DISTAR, model

Described as an academically oriented preschool program, DISTAR was initially developed at the University of Illinois by Carl Bereiter and Siegfried Engelmann. It is described in considerable detail in their book, *Teaching disadvantaged children in the preschool* (Bereiter and Engelmann, 1966). The program was based on the idea that waiting for academic readiness to develop in children is a highly inappropriate educational practice, especially for the disadvantaged population. To quote Engelmann, "When you say a kid's not ready, you've decided that he's not going to learn and you're blaming him for it. That's irresponsible" (Divoky, 1973). Bereiter and Engelmann emphatically made the point that the maturationist's practice of following children's inclinations and patterns in a play-oriented program was a disservice, since these children could be led to greater achievement in academic settings where reinforcements were reserved for work-related behaviors.

Revolutionary and controversial

When first developed, this program was highly controversial and received a great deal of publicity. It was further developed and elaborated for commercial distribution, by Siegfried Engelmann and Wesley Becker, as DISTAR. The approach was selected for use in two major projects commissioned to evaluate various approaches for teaching young disadvantaged children—Head Start Variation and Follow Through. At that point it was renamed the *Engelmann-Becker Model* and its implementation was coordinated from the University of Oregon.

The program emphasizes instruction in three areas—reading, language, and arithmetic—and its goal is to provide children with very specific skills. In reading, children are to look at written symbols (letters) and quickly say the sounds in a series of letters from left to right, the goal being the blending of letters into words.

In language, they are to answer the question, "What is this?" in regard to pictures of objects and symbols, in both the affirmative and the negative. They are taught to use oppositional terms and relational concepts—*if-then* statements and the terms *not* and *or*—in making deductive statements.

In arithmetic, they are taught to count forward and backward and to count in groups. They are taught the functions of symbols such as +, −, and =, and to answer questions about numbers that are expressed with these symbols.

Group instruction

Children are organized into groups for instruction. Group sizes vary from three to eight children, and are arranged according to ability. In a classroom group of twenty-five children in the primary grades, at least one teacher and two aides are required to conduct the program. Children attend three classes of twenty minutes each—one in each of the subject areas—within the daily session. During the teaching session they sit in a semicircle around the teacher. The teacher follows the very specific directions provided in a handbook as to what to say, what to do, etc. The distinctive characteristics of the program are (1) a fast pace, (2) strong emphasis on total group verbal responses from the children, often in unison, (3) carefully planned instructional units with continual feedback, and (4) heavy work demands during the sessions with little tolerance of nonwork behavior.

Reinforcement strategies

The key to the program appears to be getting children to make the right responses in the presence of the right stimulus, so that these can be positively reinforced. Rapid-fire questioning by the teacher regarding a page of pictures, letters, or figures held up in front of the group brings shouts in unison as a typical response. Questions are carefully sequenced to facilitate correct responses from the children, and there is much "ado," especially at first, over correct responses. The teacher gives cookies, praises, shakes hands, tells the children how smart they are, etc. Incorrect responses are not accepted, and the question is posed again until the correct response is forthcoming. It is then reinforced before the teacher proceeds further. "Good!" is probably the most frequent pronouncement of the able DISTAR teacher. Tight control is achieved through carefully specified objectives for children's conduct and learning. Children are rewarded for attending and responding. The following is typical of the directions provided in the teacher's manual (Science Research Associates, 1969) for a DISTAR lesson:[1]

Start the Program Here

Objective: Teaching *mmmm* as in "him"
Task 1: (Identify New Sound)

  a. "Everybody, look at the book." (Praise children who look.)
  b. (Point to letter *m* in book.) "Mmmm. This is *mmmm*. Good."
  c. (Point to picture of ice cream cone in book). "Is this *mmm*?"
  d. (Wait. Praise the response—"no.") "What is this?"
  e. (Trace *m*.) "Mmmm, say mmm." (Wait.) "Good."
  f. (Point to letter *M* in book.) "Look at the book. Mmmm. This sound is *mmmm*. Say it loud. Mmmm."
  g. (Wait.) "Good."
  h. "Look at the book." (Point to a picture of an ice cream cone in book.) "What is it?"
  i. (Wait.) "You fooled me! What is it?"

The Behavior Analysis model

The Behavior Analysis program was developed by Don Bushnell, Jr. at the University of Kansas. Like the DISTAR program, it uses principles of systematic reinforcement to provide children with the skills and behaviors that are deemed necessary for success in school. Like DISTAR, it has been a Head Start and Follow Through model used with children from poor homes, many of whom are from nonwhite ethnic and cultural groups. However, Behavioral Analysis has been used with students at varied ages and from varied backgrounds.

This approach first diagnoses each child's level of functioning, then prescribes his or her ability grouping, and finally uses systematic reinforcement to maximize the learning rate. The program focuses on the academic skills of reading, mathematics, spelling, handwriting, and on certain nonacademic and essential skills such as **attending** and **task persistence.** Various commercially available **programed materials** are used, which provide carefully graduated presentations, each step requiring responses from the pupil. Students have their own workbooks and work sheets and pace themselves through the

Programed materials; individual progress

[1] From *Distar*® *Reading I* An Instructional System by Siegfried Engelmann and Elaine C. Bruner. © 1969, Science Research Associates, Inc. Reprinted by permission of the publisher.

materials (in contrast to the DISTAR system, in which most of the children's involvement is in group instruction and requires oral responding). The materials (1) specify and sequence the behavior the child is to master, (2) provide clear criteria for the correct response (often through providing a forced-choice response between correct and incorrect instances), and (3) provide for periodic testing to allow the teacher to determine whether the child should move to a more advanced level or be recycled within the same level.

Token reinforcements

Token reinforcements are used in this system. Plastic chips are awarded for good work and desirable behavior and may be exchanged at a later point for a range of rewards according to the child's preference. Rewards may consist of free time, a special game, diet supplements, arts and crafts work, story time, music, and science projects. Recess might cost ten tokens; story time, five. Periodic changes are made in the types of rewards and their costs.

Instructional periods are interspersed with activity periods during which children exchange the tokens they have earned. It is up to the teacher to make sure that desirable (reinforcing) events are available, but each child makes his or her own decision about which of the available options will be purchased. For three-year-olds the instructional time may be only ten minutes in duration, followed by a longer activity period. At later ages, activity periods may be reduced to ten or fifteen minutes, with instructional time extended to forty-five or fifty minutes.

During instructional periods a small group of four to six children are seated around a table, each with his or her own workbook or work sheet. An adult supervises the work and systematically awards tokens for attending, following instructions, completing tasks, and accompanies the reward with a

Photo by John Young.

remark designed to communicate the nature of the behavior to be reinforced, for example, "That's good writing, Thomas." What a given child must do to receive tokens varies at different points in time since the contingencies are changed to match performance levels. By small increments, each child is expected to develop the skills or behaviors set as program objectives.

The DARCEE or Early Training Program model

The DARCEE program was developed by Susan Gray and associates at the Demonstration and Research Center for Early Education at George Peabody College for Teachers in Nashville, Tennessee. It was initiated in 1961 and is one of the earliest of the current set of intervention programs developed for the early education of young disadvantaged children. Its goal was to offset the progressive retardation (or cumulative deficit) that had been observed in poor rural black children during their early years of schooling. The development of attitudes and skills that would facilitate active participation in the learning process was the expressed concern of the DARCEE group. It is included in this chapter to illustrate another variation of the environmentalist approach to programing. In many ways the DARCEE program directly reflects the elementary school curriculum for which the children were being prepared.

Group activities related to unit theme

The DARCEE session starts with a large-group activity followed by two small-group sessions, often directed around a particular theme. The two small-group sessions are interspersed with an outdoor play period. The session ends with a second brief large-group gathering to review the day, sing songs, etc.

The major components of the program are the large-group activities and the small-group work. The large-group activity is usually built around a unit of study, or around themes such as "Pets and other animals," "The farm," "Autumn," etc. The units may last for a three-week period. The "Autumn" unit, for example, includes a focus on weather and plant changes during the first week, clothing and activity changes during the second week, and animal changes during the third week. Units are described in detail in DARCEE curriculum guides, and various activities are specified along with the basic skills which they are to develop.

For example, a small-group activity for one day is to have the children make collages of an autumn tree using the autumn colors. Children are given pieces of construction paper on which the teacher has colored or pasted a representation of a tree trunk and branches. Children are to paste small pieces of construction paper on the branches of the tree and on the ground underneath the tree. Through this activity, the children are thought to de-

Emphasis on readiness skills

velop visual skills, auditory skills, conceptual skills, association skills, verbal skills, and motor skills. These are considered by the DARCEE group to be important readiness abilities that prepare the child for later success in responding to instructional demands in elementary school.

The lessons are planned to fit the differing ability levels that characterize the small groups. The sequencing of activities is based on the premise that each task should be of "just manageable" difficulty. What will be "just manageable" is determined by the lead teacher and the assistants (paraprofessionals or parent assistants). For every class of twenty-five to thirty children, there is one lead teacher, one full-time assistant, and two aides. The recommended ratio of adults to children is one to seven or eight.

FURTHER COMMENTARY ON ENVIRONMENTALIST PROGRAMS

Program guides and manuals specify teacher behaviors

The DISTAR, Behavioral Analysis, and DARCEE models focus on early, direct instruction in academic areas and on certain nonacademic behaviors that are thought to be necessary for academic success. All require a higher-than-usual ratio of adults to children. Because of the degree of specificity built into teacher's guides and manuals, paraprofessionals can function as teachers, assuming that professional guidance is nearby.

In discussing the common traits of "structured" programs, Chow and Elmore (1973) concluded:

> While no one "structured" program necessarily includes all of the characteristics which follow, several of the traits will be recognizable in each. The classroom is teacher controlled, tightly scheduled, and highly charged. The teacher does not wait for the child to reveal what he is interested in because this is not necessarily what he needs to know for success. The teacher is confident that he or she knows what the child needs and when he needs it and that with this knowledge, skillful, intense instruction and the promise of rewards, the child's basic development schedule can be shoved ahead. The program organizers have minutely analyzed all of the skills that go together to make it possible for a child to master a task. The teacher always knows what skill ("behavioral objective") he is teaching, and where it comes in the "hierarchy." The curriculum emphasizes the fundamentals—language development, reading, mathematics. The teaching may be done by programmed instruction, carefully managed experiences, or group drill which capitalizes on the exuberant morale of a group working together out loud. . . . In order to keep up the learning pace the child may need to be rewarded "extrinsically" with praise from the teacher, tokens that can be exchanged for candy or trinkets, or special privileges such as recess, movies, or free-choice activity. The ultimate reward, of course, is success in school. (p. 12)

While the programs discussed above all have a traditional academic focus and are directed toward success in traditional schools, this is not necessarily the case with all program developers of the environmentalist persuasion. Others may emphasize the early or remedial acquisition of social skills, foreign languages, musical skills, or athletic skills. The common view, however, is that the child's interests and current abilities are not as important in

You have just read about environmentalist programs for children. These same features often characterize programs for adults as well. List any situations in which you have been a participant, as a child or as an adult, that were of this type. As your criterion for identifying environmentalist programs, decide whether there was a concerted effort to train you to do something or learn something that had been identified as an objective for all program participants. After you have identified several programs of this type in which you have been involved, try the following:

1. Identify the general advantages of these programs for you personally.

2. Identify the general disadvantages of these programs for you personally.

3. Consider which among the environmentalist programs were most effective in your view, and which were least effective. Try to identify the nature of the differences between them.

constructing a program as the adult conceptions of what the child can become, given appropriately structured and managed experiences. While environmentalists may not always agree on what the child should become, they would agree that it is the adult prerogative and responsibility to make that determination and then to find the most effective and efficient means for structuring programs to bring about the desired state.

The Maturationist View of Programs

Maturationists were described in Section Two as giving far less recognition to environmental influences on development and emphasizing instead the regularities within the organism. Following the view of Rousseau (and later G. S. Hall), the child is seen as inherently "good," and the child-rearing emphasis is therefore on facilitating the "unfolding" of these positive forces from within the child.

Little need for out-of-home programs
Strictly speaking, maturationists would not see the need for any "out-of-the-home" programs, especially for young children. This view is well articulated by Moore and Moore (1973):

> For highest and best cognitive, affective and physiological development, we should do all we can to develop a wholesome home and keep [the child] there—a place where the child can grow in an undisturbed environment, sharing the freedom with one or two adults (preferably his parents) in a warm, close, consistent and continuous relationship. (p. 14)

Only if the home environment is lacking in nurturing qualities would maturationists feel the need for outside programs. These conditions might include instances in which (1) there is a lack of parental awareness regarding the child's natural needs for play and activity; (2) there is an absence of opportunities for interaction with peers in the neighborhood setting; (3) the home is lacking in consistency, in opportunities for sensing orderliness, or in the valuing of children's developing language and curiosity; (4) the neighborhood or home is unsafe or "unsavory" in terms of vice or other "objectionable" influences. The enrollment of children in "school" programs may be delayed for as long as possible, that is, until ages seven or eight.

The maturationists' motivation for program development comes from a concern for providing all children with a "normal" setting. The conception of normality is derived from what is normal (typical) for the era and culture. Within the "normal" setting, all children are expected to develop at whatever rates their own innate capacities permit. James Hymes, Jr., an eloquent spokesman for this general perspective, proposed the following in his book, *A child development point of view* (1955):

> Children inherit their rate of growth. At the moment of their conception the speed at which they will mature is bred into them. As soon as the two cells join, a child's particular private horsepower is established. The way you treat the youngster can lower his capacities. You can make him function on only three of his four cylinders or on seven of his eight. But you cannot build an extra cylinder into him. A youngster has to be himself. Get the force of this. A child is the product of his mother and father. He inherits from them the genes which set the pace of his rate of development. But he inherits, too, from grandmothers and grandfathers; two on each side of the family. What each of them was like has a bearing on how fast this child will grow. . . . You see an endless chain stretching forever back. This chain has the power, not the child. A youngster simply must be himself. (pp. 54–55)

To maturationists, teaching and child-rearing involve the provision of an accepting and comfortable setting within which children can follow their own interests and needs within socially acceptable (normative) frames of reference. Instructional materials and educational experiences may be provided for children as they show interest and readiness, but instruction that is poorly timed and imposed on an unwilling child is considered not only likely *The inherent nature* to fail but also to have a negative effect. When programs are provided, *of development of* therefore, maturationists prefer to foster the development of the "whole" *the "whole" child* child in directions inherent within him or her—rather than toward specific isolated objectives, academic or otherwise.

MATURATIONIST PROGRAMING PRINCIPLES

Maturationists are in relative agreement about the following general principles:

1. Children will spontaneously select activities appropriate to their developmental level if given a range of options and a minimum of adult intervention.

2. A variety of materials should be available for children to use to nourish their development. Adults should provide materials that are appropriate to the child's interests and stage of development. If children do not use the materials provided, this is an indication that the materials are inappropriate to their particular developmental level.

3. Specific types of activities should be available at regular time periods each day, with a balance between active and inactive, group and individual, directed and nondirected activities. The particular balance is determined by age, the amounts of group and directed activities increasing with age.

4. Children should not be pressured or enticed to perform beyond their current level; if they are given an unpressured, nurturing atmosphere, they will gradually develop their capabilities in all important areas.

5. The optimum placement for children is with a group of peers at the same developmental level. When maturational readiness indicates successful participation at the next level, the child should be advanced. Children who are developmentally delayed or are suffering from handicaps that limit their functioning are best grouped with others like themselves.

6. There should be only a minimum of correction of children's efforts in work or play. Actions or responses are "right" given the child's developmental level and experiences. Additional real experiences can be provided to correct erroneous impressions or to develop more advanced skills. These, however, should be presented as possibilities rather than as requirements. What the teacher does not do is often viewed as more important than what the teacher does. Acceptance, gentle guidance, and facilitation of children's

Photo by John Young.

wants and interests are desirable, while directing, correcting, or actively modifying behavior are questionable or undesirable.

7. Children primarily respond to growth forces within themselves. It is the teacher's role to help them understand and accept themselves. Given a nurturing and accepting environment, outcomes for children will ultimately be positive even though particular phases may be experienced as difficult.

8. Experiences seen as desirable and feasible for children should be provided for them without explicit contingencies. Attempts to sway children from their natural inclinations by systematically providing reinforcements is shortsighted and counterproductive to overall development.

Maturationists believe that adults must accept children as they are. Teachers must help them in ways they want and need to be helped. In planning for *The major needs of* young children, for example, Dorothy Cohen (1971), of the Bank Street *young children* College of Education faculty, proposes that the following four major needs are relevant for all children and must be continuous over several years:

1. All young children need and want warmth, affection, and respect for their individuality.
2. All young children need help in coping with their feelings.
3. All young children need help in their social relations and group life.
4. All young children need encouragement and support in their symbolizing efforts with materials and in dramatic play.

A PROGRAM COMPATIBLE WITH THE MATURATIONIST VIEW: BANK STREET

Persons of maturationist persuasion may find programs such as DISTAR, Behavior Analysis, DARCEE quite abhorrent and inappropriate to their concerns for children. Maturationists are often sharply critical of the subject matter orientation of elementary schools, including the primary grades. However, most nursery-school and kindergarten programs have traditionally *"Child* offered a "child development" orientation that is quite compatible with the *development"* maturationist view. Examples of these were the university nursery schools of *orientation* the 1930s, 1940s, and 1950s. During this period there was a consensus among early educators concerning appropriate programing for the preschool child. This consensus was gradually destroyed in the 1960s as contrasting points of view came to the fore during the "war on poverty." At the present time, it is difficult to find a pure example of the "child development" point of view that pervaded nursery school education in prior years. The Bank Street College of Education staff, leaders for decades in determining programs for young children, still provide the closest approximation among well-known program models to the maturationist position.

The Bank Street model for Head Start and Follow Through implementation, developed by Elizabeth Gilkeson and her associates at Bank Street College of Education in New York City, has great appeal to many teachers of maturationist persuasion and reflects a philosophy developed over several decades. The approach is intended to develop children's self-images and a sense of self-direction in learning based on spontaneous play activities.

Specific goals are not prescribed in the Bank Street guidelines, but instead evolve according to each individual teacher's continuous analysis of children's progress. The Bank Street approach does, however, require a learning environment that allows children to choose from a large variety of activities, including a wide range of sensory and motor experiences. Materials such as play blocks, dress-up clothes, dolls, sand toys, pets, books, games, and counting objects are provided. Both teacher- and child-made materials supplement those commercially obtained. While there is no single prescribed way of organizing the classroom, there are always numerous interest areas provided for children's use. Teachers are encouraged to use a variety of materials and methods for the teaching of concepts, but children's spontaneous play is seen as the prime medium for self-development and learning.

Choices from varieties of activities

Interest areas and children's spontaneous play

Motivation is supplied by the pleasure inherent in the activities themselves—extrinsic rewards are not systematically used to influence children's learning, choice of activities, or behavior. It is also anticipated that the teacher will gain the children's cooperation through consistently showing concern, care, and support.

There is no typical lesson in the Bank Street approach, although group activities are regularly provided within the daily program. An overall theme or unit is often adopted by the Bank Street teacher, and many theme-related activities are then encouraged and supported. One activity is expected to lead naturally into another, and often several kinds of learning involvements result from a single activity. A teacher-initiated group project, such as making applesauce, might lead to counting, measuring, weighing, observing, reading, and writing in the various subgroups that become involved in some aspect of the activity.

Curriculum flexible and emergent

Reading and writing are considered just some of the many enjoyable activities available in the classroom. They are closely linked to children's individual expressions and choices. Children write their own books and read from books that other children have written. Teachers read to children daily, and a wide selection of picture books and simple readers are used for individualized reading instruction. Children accumulate a reading vocabulary through charts, labels, stories, games, and writing prior to being provided with a preprimer, which they usually find they can read through, with a little assistance, from beginning to end.

In the Bank Street program children are helped by teachers to attain skills and to become involved in a wide variety of activities that encourage the use and mastery of academic and social skills. There is little teacher "push," either directly or indirectly, to make sure that all participants acquire any particular set of skills. The child who does not learn something is not "ready" for that learning, but will be at some later point, assuming that current pressures do not produce a learning resistance in that area.

Few program "prescriptions" for teachers or children

PROGRAM CRITIQUES FROM THE MATURATIONIST VIEW

By definition, maturationists reject programs that set out to direct and channel children's development, and endorse those that confine themselves to supporting and extending children's natural inclinations. The maturationist tradition is clearly reflected in some of the rhetoric of the recent "free school" movement. Dennison (1969), for example, points out: "To give freedom means to stand out of the way of the formative powers possessed by others." The doctrines of John Holt, Herbert Kohl, A. S. Neill, James Herndon, Paul Goodman, George Dennison, Edgar Friedenberg, and other proponents of alternative education are eagerly read by those who are dissatisfied with the environmentalist orientation of "traditional" schooling. They would rather place greater reliance on children's internal directions and less on molding and hastening their learning and development.

To some extent the "open education" movement gained support in this country because of the greater freedom it afforded children to structure their own time and efforts. It allowed them to engage in concrete or expressive "child-like" activities, rather than being directed into "unnatural," abstract endeavors. Within the maturationist tradition, however, there has been a persistent strain that is incompatible with the open education and alternative school, or "free school," movement. As cited earlier, many maturationists assume that quality education depends on classes organized around similar developmental levels—the key to effective schooling is to place each child in a class with others who are ready for similar learnings. According to Arnold Gesell and his successors at the Yale Child Study Institute, the greatest teaching-learning problems stem from inappropriate class placement. Ilg and Ames (1964), for example, have said:

> Possibly the greatest single contribution which can be made in guaranteeing that each individual child will get the most out of his school experience is to make certain that he starts that school experience at what for him is the "right" time. This should be the time when he is truly ready and not merely some time arbitrarily decided by custom or the law. (p. 14)

In addition, they indicate that

> a child needs not only to go at his own pace, but also benefits from the stimulation of others who are progressing as he is. He thrives on an environment geared for him. When he is in a group that is operating more as a unit, his own adjustment is more easily discerned. (p. 13)

While placement by age appears to this group to be preferable to an "ungraded" or mixed age group, they prefer the use of developmental tests to ensure that a child is placed with those learners most like him or her in overall development. The use of age alone, they feel, is likely to lead to some misplacement due to individual differences in development rates.

This entire thrust toward homogeneous placement is contrary to the philosophy of those who have been foremost in the alternative school and open education movement. They value highly heterogeneous groups—mixed ages, mixed cultural and ethnic backgrounds, mixed levels of performance. It is within these open or alternative classrooms that the most rapid movement is currently being made toward the integration of developmentally delayed and handicapped children with normal children. In contrast, most maturationists continue to support special classes for developmentally deviant children. Such special programs, they reason, can best provide for the unique needs of these children, including a comfortable atmosphere where they can associate with others like themselves.

FURTHER COMMENTARY ON MATURATIONIST PROGRAMS

Unlike the programs developed from the environmentalist perspective, maturationist programs lack specificity. The role of the teacher is thought to be critical, but programing is left to the artistry of the individual teacher. The Bank Street teacher, for example, works under very general guidelines. Faith in the inherent goodness of humankind sustains the efforts of the maturationist teacher. There is a pervasive expectation that children's growth

Essentials: predictability, trust, warmth

will be positive in a setting that supplies predictability, trust, and warmth. What is actually done in the classroom, however, depends upon ongoing judgments about what will best meet children's needs. There is less predictability from classroom to classroom with this approach than with any other, and far less than in environmentalist programs.

RESPONSE SECTION

> You have just read about maturationist programs for children. The same features sometimes characterize programs for adults as well. List any situations in which you have been a participant, as a child or as an adult, that were of this type. As your criteria for identifying maturationist programs, decide whether the situation was established to generally accommodate persons of your age and ability and whether within that general structure you were generally left to your own devices (with no attempt to either assist or assess your efforts). After you have identified several programs of this type in which you have been involved, try the following:
>
> 1. Identify the general advantages of these programs for you personally.
>
> 2. Identify the general disadvantages of these programs for you personally.
>
> 3. Consider which among these programs were most effective in your view, and which were least effective. Try to identify the nature of the differences between them.

The Interactionist View of Programs

Interactionists assume that development, behavior, and learning are substantially influenced by both environmental influences and maturational processes. They strongly emphasize the activities of individuals in trying to construct a view of the world, which then serves to regulate further learning and development.

The interactionist view, as currently expressed by Kohlberg (1968), Langer (1969), and others, is derived from insights provided by Piaget. According to Piaget (1952), cognitive processes emerge from a process of development which is neither maturation nor learning in the usual sense but is, instead, a reorganization of psychological structures resulting from organism-environment interactions.

Life encounters are of crucial importance to interactionists, in contrast to maturationists. And unlike environmentalists, interactionists assume that learning experiences must be built upon the activity of the learner and cannot be effectively prestructured or appreciably accelerated.

All aspects of experience synthesized in cognitive transformations

For interactionists, the cognitive aspects of development are crucial to the total behavioral pattern. Development is thought to consist of successive transformations of internal cognitive structures, which are the basis for the individual's behavior. Each individual is constantly engaged in cognitive restructuring based upon the evidence gained from operations performed on the social and physical environment. Intellectual, social, affective, and perceptual-motor experiences are inseparable. According to this view, significant changes in behavior occur because of cognitive extensions and elaborations (the development of new and more adequate schemas) gained through operations on the environment. From ages three to seven, schemas are modified into increasingly complex and internalized operations. The child's behavior gradually becomes less dependent on new incoming perceptions and more influenced by logical internal manipulations of objects and events.

Interactionists do not expect that any specific learning (such as letter recognition) or any small modification of behavior (such as frequency of "attending" behavior) will significantly influence long-term development. The acquisition of particular bits of knowledge or specific academic behaviors is generally assigned a lower priority in programing than involving the child in finding order and relationships through operations such as classification, seriation, and generalizations.

Massive general experience, not specific instruction

The cognitive structures that form the basis of all specific knowledge are thought by interactionists to be acquired through "massive general experience" with phenomena of the physical and social world. The fullest and richest development stems from a broad range of child-initiated experiences, coupled with encouragement, guidance, and constant interchanges with teachers and peers. Through alternation between student-initiated activities and inputs from teachers, children develop increasingly varied and functional schemas.

PROGRAM CONDITIONS FAVORED BY INTERACTIONISTS

The program conditions that interactionists favor for young children can be summarized as follows:

1. All kinds of experiences should be available—not merely those labeled *academic*. Learners are provided with many possibilities for active "hands-on" involvement with physical materials, which is the basis for later abstract thought processes.

2. Long unstructured activity periods should be provided so that children can engage in the independent planning and execution of projects.

3. A variety of peers should be available for social interaction so that personal views can be validated or modified.

4. Adult input is largely provided on a one-to-one basis or through small groups formed for a specific purpose (for example, to compose a group story or learn to set up a terrarium) and disbanded immediately thereafter (in contrast to being maintained over a period of time).

5. Adults frequently request input from children that requires recall, synthesis, conjecture, estimation, demonstration, and experimentation.

6. There is a constant focus on better conceptualization of the physical and social world. A document prepared by the Educational Products Information Exchange Institute (1972) describes interactionist goals as follows:

> Students should understand differences in amounts and sizes of things in the physical world, establish a basic framework for orientation in space and time, develop a concept of numbers through handling of sets of objects and the study of relationships, extend their understanding of numbers through carrying out measurement operations, learn to communicate through graphs, charts, and numerals.
>
> Students should develop facility with abstract symbols (numbers, letters) through familiarity with the physical and human environment, achieved by exposure to participatory experiences and active symbolic communication (verbal and nonverbal); increase their use of thinking processes by stimulation of grouping and the noticing of differences and similarities in objects, functions, personal roles, and personal feelings.
>
> Students should develop a repertoire of actions to perform on objects; an ability to predict regularity of cause and effect, and to figure out means towards ends; language to communicate precisely, knowledge of language conventions, and ability to see others' points of view; an ability to classify on similarities and differences; increased mobility of thought; ability to sort by comparing differences among objects, in the structuring of space and time, in representation ability; symbols and signs. (pp. 31–32)

PROGRAMS COMPATIBLE WITH THE INTERACTIONIST VIEW: MONTESSORI, BRITISH INTEGRATED DAY, COGNITIVE CURRICULUM, AND SYRACUSE RESPONSIVE CARE

The following pages describe programs that promote children's development through active involvement with rich and varied materials and social settings. All assume that children's innate potentialities are best cultivated through appropriate encounters within a carefully arranged setting. Despite this common emphasis, however, the programs differ significantly in other respects. Four program models—Cognitive Curriculum, British integrated day, Montessori, and Syracuse Responsive Care—are briefly described in turn and then are comparatively analyzed.

The Montessori method

At the turn of the century Maria Montessori, the first woman physician in Italy, developed ways of working with children that contrasted markedly with previous practices. Although her original work was with children who were considered mentally deficient, she derived and proposed general principles of education that had wide appeal and were adapted for use with normal children. Montessori programs became very popular in many parts of the world, including the United States, during the early 1900s, and were then gradually dropped in the United States as a total approach. Some aspects of the Montessori methods were broadly incorporated into other early childhood programs, however, and there was a rebirth of interest in Montessori programs during the 1960s. At the present time Montessori programs, or adaptations, have again become prominent as a viable alternative in early education.

In many ways Montessori's ideas were early expressions of the interactionist view. She believed that the child's development consists of an unfolding of inborn characteristics, but she also insisted that certain environmental conditions must exist if these inborn traits and abilities are to develop normally. Unlike Arnold Gesell, a contemporary maturationist, Maria Montessori did not believe that normative behaviors at given ages should be accepted as necessary behaviors for that age level. She especially disagreed with the maturationist view that periods of disruptive behavior are simply a "stage" that, if tolerated, will naturally disappear as the child matures. She pointed out that whenever children are provided with appropriate activities, their "disturbed" behavior changes to concentration, self-confidence, and self-acceptance. Her entire effort therefore revolved around constructing environments within which children would have opportunities for appropriate "occupations." Montessori proposed that children should choose their own activities in the classroom, and saw it as the educator's job to provide choices appropriate to the concentration of the individual child. She wrote, "The child left at liberty to exercise his activities, ought to find in his surrounding something organized in direct relation to his internal organization which is developing itself by natural laws" (Montessori, 1964, p. 70).

Montessori became skilled at designing special apparatus whose educational appropriateness for children were measured by the children's degree of concentration as they interacted with them. It is the Montessori equipment that is best known by educators, and which is sometimes mistakenly considered as the whole Montessori method. The materials are of four types: (1) those associated with activities of daily living (such as personal grooming, cooking, and cleaning); (2) sensory materials (visual, tactile, auditory, and olfactory); (3) academic materials (language, reading, writing, and mathematics); (4) cultural and artistic materials. Some of the sensory and academic materials are designed to be "self-correcting," so the child can tell whether his or her use of the materials is appropriate. Variations are carefully introduced to provide a gradual transition from simple to complex manipulations.

Once a child has learned the precise use of the material—typically in a brief, individualized session called a *fundamental lesson*—the child is then invited to use the material whenever and however he or she wishes. Children are taught how to take the materials from a shelf, how to arrange them on a mat provided for that purpose, and how to return them for use by the next person. After the initial instruction, the child does not typically require the teacher's assistance. According to Montessori (1964):

> The child not only needs something interesting to do, but also likes to be shown exactly how to do it. Precision is found to attract him deeply, and this it is that keeps him at work. From this we must infer that his attraction toward these manipulative tasks has an unconscious aim. The child has an instinct to coordinate his movements and bring them under control. (p. 179)

If the activities correspond to the inner development of the child, he or she will delight in the repetition of these activities and will continue to use them as a self-directed learning tool. At a later point, after the child has fully absorbed the possibilities inherent in the particular equipment, the teacher introduces the vocabulary that represents the concepts the child has been exploring. First, the names are provided; then, it is determined if the child associates the names with the appropriate concepts; and finally, it is determined whether the child correctly uses the new vocabulary.

Less well known than the equipment are some of the other program emphases. For example, Montessori stressed the importance of the child's having contact with the natural environment. She also emphasized the growing sense of community that evolves from including children of differing ages in each classroom. Each child in the Montessori classroom has full dominion over his or her own activity, unless it interferes with the activities of the others. Without urging, however, children gradually begin to seek each other out and work together. There are few teacher-planned group activities in the Montessori system, and children need not share their individually chosen equipment until they desire to do so.

The role of the teacher in the Montessori program contrasts markedly with that in other program approaches. There is no effort, for example, to establish a close relationship in which the child will wish to please the adult, as advocated in the Bank Street approach. Nor is there any effort to systematically reinforce children, thereby accelerating and directing their learning and development. The design and maintenance of appropriate environments, based on careful observation of the children, is the Montessori teacher's concern. The teacher serves as a model for the children in extracting learning experiences from the environment, but ideally this is done without intruding too much of the teacher's personality into the situation. The child's autonomous functioning is the goal, and it is considered unfortunate if the child's attention is drawn away from his or her own interests and occupations by a desire to relate to or receive approval from the teacher. The focus of the program is intended to be on the child and his or her occupations—not on the relationship between the child and the teacher.

The goal: autonomy and intrinsic satisfaction

British integrated day

The integrated day approach evolved over several decades in the British infant schools and has now been adopted in many American schools as well. "Open education," as this approach is sometimes called in the United States, is said to be used in approximately one-third of the British infant schools (Featherstone, 1967). The ideas of Jean Piaget, John Dewey, Froebel, and Maria Montessori were influential in this movement. Much of the practice, however, has been derived from the practical experiences of classroom teachers and school "heads" who sought effective ways to help children acquire academic skills while simultaneously developing social independence and responsibility.

In the United States a prime source for this movement has been the Education Development Center (EDC), in Newton, Massachusetts, whose personnel have served as advisers to schools in designing classroom environments that are responsive to the needs of children and the talents of teachers. The EDC Open Education model was one of the approaches selected for the Head Start and Follow Through implementations and evaluation.

The interactionist view is clearly expressed by Roland Barth (1970), a proponent of the integrated day approaches, in the following commentary:

> Open education views the child not as a passive vessel waiting to be filled nor as an amorphous lump of clay awaiting some form-giving artist but as a self-activated maker of meaning, an active agent in his own learning process. He is not one to whom things merely happen; he is one who by his own volition causes things to happen. Learning is seen as the result of his own self-initiated interaction with the world. The child's understanding grows during a constant interplay between something outside himself—the general environment, a pendulum, a person—and something inside himself—his concept forming mechanism, his mind. (p. 99)

While integrated day classrooms vary greatly in their ability to meet the needs and interests of particular children and in the styles of their teachers, they have characteristic features. Children plan many of their own activities with teacher guidance and, ideally, are free to explore an interest as deeply as they wish for as long as they wish. Typically, a variety of activities are going on simultaneously and interchanges between children and cooperative efforts are encouraged. An abundance of varied physical materials stimulates exploration and discovery.

Individual choice from varieties of activities

The approach is clearly educative, in that teachers are constantly involved with children in the development of expressive (speaking and writing) skills, encoding and decoding skills, generalizing from experiences, defining and solving problems, and improving motor skills. As Joseph Featherstone (1967, p. 14), wrote, "It is this deep pedagogical seriousness, the attention paid to learning in the classroom, that makes the British primary school so different from progressive education which was all too often unconcerned with pedagogy." Instruction, however, is viewed as more effective when drawn from or directly related to an activity in which the child is immersed, so that its relevance is as apparent to the child as to the adult.

An educative approach

Children's responses to environmental stimuli provide many of the starting points for learning. There is little recognition of traditional subject divisions, and most of the children's work efforts simultaneously encompass several academic areas—mathematics, art, language arts (writing, reading, discussion), and science.

Continuous record-keeping on individual progress

Teachers keep continuous records of the children's progress in various areas, often on specific matters such as knowledge of the number line, new vocabulary or concepts, and ability to decode. By allowing the children time, space, and materials within which they can structure their own activities, and by interjecting highly focused instruction into that setting, open education teachers attempt to combine the development of cognitive skills with the development of positive attitudes and orientations. Their intent is well expressed in the introduction to *Fundamentals of the first school* (Brearly et al., 1969):

> It is clear that a complex of development such as has been described cannot be distilled into a set of "lessons," nor can it be left to "happen" even in a well-furnished school. The genesis of it all is the self-chosen activity which arises as the result of a child's own response to a set of circumstances. The wise teacher joins this forward thrust and helps a child to define, fix and organize his responses, genuinely preparing for more structured approaches in later work. This can be clearly seen in every area of work we have studied: a child's natural movements of elation or anger can be isolated and repeated with intention to bring about planned effects; a child's own vocalization can be matched to an instrument or recorded on paper and therefore can be "fixed" and repeated for a purpose. So it can be with painting, reading, number, science and the rest. Even many early experiences of moral behavior may be developed in this way. A child's spontaneous generosity or control of

himself can form the basis for his learning. The initiative comes from the children, their referral to the developed systems is done by the adult parent or teacher. This should be done, of course, without laboring too many points. The objective is not tied to these specific points but is a more global one; to set up the mental habits of structured thinking. (p. 9)

The Cognitive Curriculum

The Cognitive Curriculum, developed by David Weikart and associates at the High Scope Institute in Ypsilanti, Michigan, is an attempt to translate Piaget's theory of development into an education program. It is primarily concerned with children's cognitive development, or, stated more specifically, with the way children organize and interpret relationships between objects and events in the environment. Three areas are emphasized within the curriculum—cognitive skills, levels of representation, and levels of operation.

Program emphasis: cognitive skills, levels of representation; levels of operation

In the first area of concern, cognitive skills, there is a great deal of attention to classification, seriation, spatial relationships (concepts of position, direction, and distance), and temporal relations (time sequences). Within the cognitive program, children are actively involved in learning—through manipulating concrete materials and having real experiences—prior to the introduction of abstractions or symbols.

After being encouraged to act on the environment, they are asked to represent it. This is the second major area of program emphasis. Progression through three levels of representation—**index, symbol,** and **sign**—are considered important. At the index level, the child learns about what he or she sees and to recognize objects from minimal cues (for example, only part, visible, only heard but not seen, or with parts hidden). At the symbol level, the child has a clearer mental image of objects and can represent them through means such as drawing, modeling, and make-believe actions. At the sign level, symbols such as letters, words, and numbers are used to abstractly represent objects and events. The program tries to provide for the maximum amount of information and exploration on each level for each child.

The third area of emphasis in the Cognitive Curriculum is on levels of operation—motoric and verbal. The goal is to provide many opportunities for motoric experiences with equipment and materials, and, at the same time, to help children verbalize their experiences.

Teacher planning for instructional emphasis

The teachers in the Cognitive Curriculum develop their daily and weekly plans based on their assessment of the developmental levels of their children within these three areas of emphasis. In the skill area of seriation, for example, children might be provided with blocks or dolls of two sizes (large and small), and the teacher constantly emphasizes the size relationship until the children begin to use terms that differentiate size. Or, within the skill category of temporal relations at the symbol level, teachers might emphasize the symbolic terms *beginning* and *end* as children use books and listen to stories. Children are encouraged to verbally note the *start* and the *finish* of these and similar activities.

Teachers regularly provide special materials and events (such as trips) to further their objectives. They also use opportunities throughout the daily program to develop cognitive skills; for example, in cleanup, classification and seriation are emphasized as children are asked to tell why they are putting materials in a particular place.

Children's planning of central concern

Children's planning efforts are of central concern in the Cognitive Curriculum. During a period referred to as *work time*, children make and post their own plans and must identify them by placing their symbols (a two-dimensional shape with the child's picture and name) on a board used for that purpose beside each work area. As children move from area to area during the work period they take their symbols with them and place them on the planning board in the new area.

The Cognitive Curriculum, as developed and implemented by Weikart and associates, is only one of the many programs based on Piagetian theory. Although there are many differences between these Piagetian programs, they are similar in emphasizing an active involvement by children with materials and events arranged in an appropriate setting.

Syracuse Responsive Care

The Responsive Care educational program was developed by the authors at Syracuse University in Syracuse, New York. It is derived from principles of cognitive development and incorporates "open environment" educational principles. It has primarily been used in full-day child-care settings.

An essential feature of the Responsive Care approach is the division of the program space into large, clearly marked areas for large-motor, expressive, and task-oriented activities. Except during mandatory lunch and nap time, all children have free access to each of these areas throughout the day. Behavior requirements and maintenance expectations remain constant throughout the day and the year. By basing the program structure around spatial organization rather than a time schedule, the Responsive Care program accommodates the varying interests and activity levels of the children. For example, a child who is immersed in constructing an airplane at the work bench is able to complete the project without being interrupted for a scheduled change of activity. Similarly, a child who needs physical movement can go to the large-motor area, where such behavior is appropriate, instead of having to wait for a scheduled play time.

Structure in spatial organization not a time schedule

Responsive instruction

Another essential feature in the program is a mode of instruction termed *responsive*. Following this method, when a child is immersed in a self-initiated activity, teachers try to extend the child's experience within the context of that activity through comments, suggestions, questions, explanations, or material manipulations. While the initial interest is provided by the child, the teacher's intervention helps to enrich the experience by suggesting new, undetected findings, approaches, or meanings.

The program is designed for a class group of thirty-five to forty-five children of mixed ages, with a ratio of one "teacher" for every seven to ten children (depending on age). At least one adult is always present in each of the three areas of the center, leaving other teachers free to "float" or attend to individual children. Children choose their own activities while at the center and are invited but not required to attend additional regularly scheduled teacher-directed group activities such as story time or films. In addition to supervision of areas and preparation for invitational group activities, each teacher has further responsibilities for a small group of children. These re-

One-to-one *sessions* sponsibilities include providing weekly individual sessions with each child, making home visits, keeping progress records on the child, and informing other adults of the child's needs and appropriate instructional strategies.

The Responsive Care program structure is designed to facilitate the development of children's social and cognitive processes. Based on the premise that the primary impetus for development is the child's active interchanges with his or her environment, the program provides a rich physical and social setting that maximizes the opportunities to expand children's repertoires through responsive instructional techniques.

FURTHER COMMENTARY ON INTERACTIONIST PROGRAMS

Although there are marked differences between the four program models described as interactionist—Montessori, British integrated day, Cognitive Curriculum, and Syracuse Responsive Care—they are similar in their emphasis on children's activities. They all pay particular attention to those portions of a child's behavior that indicate the extent of his or her involvements and the nature of his or her conceptualizations. It is not assumed in

Programs based on *the active child* these programs that placing the child in a nurturing and age-appropriate environment will be sufficient for optimal development, nor is it assumed that a systematic presentation of skills and knowledge will suffice.

To interactionists, the things that a child encounters must mesh with the child's mental constructions. The ultimate source of the curriculum for the interactionist teacher is therefore the active child engaged with aspects of the environment that appear to intrigue him or her. The behavior and language expression of the child then provides the teacher with cues regarding what further explanations or materials are needed to extend the child's understanding. As Dewey (1897) expressed it in his pedagogic creed:

> There is, therefore, no succession of studies in the ideal school curriculum. If education is life, all life has, from the outset, a scientific aspect, an aspect of art and culture, and an aspect of communication. It cannot, therefore, be true that the proper studies for one grade are mere reading and writing, and that at a later grade, reading, or literature, or science, may be introduced. The progress is not in the succession of studies, but in the development of new attitudes towards, and new interests in, experience. Education must be conceived as a continuing reconstruction of experience; the process and the goal of education are one and the same thing. (pp. 11–12)

The many evaluative studies conducted in the past decade have provided few definitive answers to the questions. What program is best? and What model should be adopted? Studies sophisticated enough in design and execution to adequately address these questions have arrived at no clear-cut conclusions. However, these studies do indicate two factors that should be considered in designing an early education program.

First, *program outcome depends on program goals.* Several studies have found that different emphases in programs result in different outcomes. For example, when twelve different models were compared in the *Head Start Planned Variation* studies, it was found that the programs that specifically emphasized the names of letters, numerals, and shapes (for example, the Behavior Analysis and Engelmann-Becker models) produced children better at these skills than did the other models. The Cognitive Curriculum, on the other hand, clearly produced greater increases in scores on the Stanford-Binet intelligence test (Smith, 1975).

Stallings (1975) has reported somewhat similar findings from her study of first- and third-graders in programs representing seven Follow Through models. According to her findings, time spent in reading and math activities and a high rate of drill, practice, and praise contributed to higher reading and math scores. It was also learned that children taught by these methods tended to accept personal responsibility for their failures but not for their successes, which they tended to attribute to their teachers and instructional materials. Children in the more open and flexible instructional approaches had higher scores on a nonverbal problem-solving test of reasoning. They took responsibility for their own successes but not for their failures. Further differences were found in absence rates. Children were absent less from classrooms in which there was a high degree of child independence, child questioning, adult response, individualized instruction, open-ended questions, and positive affect. Child absences appeared to be more frequent in classrooms where children often worked in large groups, where adults used direct questions in academic work, and where corrective feedback was used frequently (Needels and Stallings, 1975).

The finding of these and other studies confirm that the program encounters of children do make significant differences in what they learn and become. There is no evidence, however, that any particular model has such widespread effects, as contrasted with other models, that there is reason to say it is a "better" model. The findings to date suggest only that a model should be selected that particularly emphasizes the goals deemed desirable by the decision-maker.

Second, *program outcome depends on the children.* Different children benefit from different kinds of programs. Prescott (1972), for example, observed children identified as *thrivers* or *nonthrivers* in both "open" and "closed" day-care center programs, and concluded that different kinds of children appear to thrive in each situation. She indicated that a closed structure appeared to offer a more useful experience for children who (1) trusted adults and were ready to meet task expectations, (2) did not trust adults and felt more secure with the clear expectations of the teacher-directed situation, and (3) tended to manipulate adults and children and needed exposure to limits that were firm and relatively impersonal. Open structures were seen as particularly useful for children who (1) needed experience in dealing with other children and adults in settings where they could learn coping skills other than compliance with adult expectations, (2) were shy and needed individual support for the development of initiative, and (3) could handle task demands but needed leeway for creativity and experimentation. Thus, different kinds of children, or the same children at different points in their development, might benefit from different kinds of program structures.

The Head Start Planned Variation studies also noted that for "passive" and "less competent" children greater gains on the Stanford-Binet intelligence measure occurred in the more directive models. The "more competent" and "less passive" children gained more, however, in the less directive models (Smith, 1975).

Soar (1973) summarized his findings from a series of studies conducted over a period of many years, first, with middle-class children, and then with

RESPONSE SECTION

You have just read about interactionist programs for children. These same features sometimes characterize adult learning situations as well. List any situations in which you have been a participant, as a child or as an adult, that were of this type. As your criteria for identifying these situations, decide whether (1) you were encouraged to choose your own activities from among diverse possibilities and in interaction with a range of different people, (2) whether you were then observed by someone interested in assisting you, and (3) whether you were then offered instruction, clarification, and possibilities for further involvement based on those observations. After you have identified several programs of this type in which you have been involved, try the following:

1. Identify the general advantages of these programs for you personally.

2. Identify the general disadvantages of these programs for you personally.

3. Consider which among the interactionist situations were most effective in your view, and which were least effective. Try to identify the nature of the differences between them.

low-income children in Follow Through programs, by pointing out the contrasts in findings for the different groups. He found that middle-class school-age children appeared to benefit (in achievement) from moderate degrees of freedom and benefited least from either very high or very low amounts of teacher-imposed structuring; the pattern was different for the Follow Through pupils: their achievement gains were greater under greater control and structure convergence.

These studies imply that a given program needs to be matched not only to the goals deemed desirable, but also to the characteristics of the children. And even within the same program there may be a need for differing degrees of teacher structuring to provide the best situation for the range of children enrolled.

The Prevalence of Eclectic Practice

Few "pure" models in real-life settings

We hope this examination of contrasting models for early education has helped you clarify your own views on programing. You should be forewarned, however, that it may be difficult to find any "pure" models or approaches in real-life settings. A program model, as conceived by its original designer(s), is typically modified each time it is implemented. Such modifications are due, in part, to the difference between the rational "ivory tower" atmosphere within which the planning often occurs and the hectic realities of the classroom. They also reflect the preferences of staff members who unconsciously modify a given program to fit their own personal teaching philosophy.

Each subsequent implementation of a program model brings further modifications that may or may not be in keeping with the original. Eventually, it becomes difficult to see much similarity between the original model and some of the programs that bear its name.

Incompatible practices sometimes adopted

Often the more innovative features of the well-publicized models are adapted in programs that have little similarity to the original model. Practices that are quite incompatible in both purpose and practical execution may even be included within the same program by teachers who are eager to "try new things," but who have little understanding of the rationale behind the various programs. Eclectic early childhood programs are more common than any other kind.

Summary

This chapter described teaching models and programs in terms of their compatibility with the three major developmental orientations described in Section Two—environmentalist, maturationist, and interactionist. The goals of this chapter were to acquaint you with the wide range of programs available for young children, as well as the developmental perspectives associated with each. It was also suggested that you examine and clarify your own views regarding children's programs in preparation for choosing and developing your own teaching program.

An effort was made to more thoroughly elaborate the practices and techniques associated with each of the three orientations. Thus, major concepts and practices of reinforcement technology from the research of Skinner, Premack, and others were discussed relative to the environmentalist orientation; principles and practices of child study and development and the views of researchers Gesell, Ilg, and Ames were described relative to the maturationist orientation; and Piagetian theories, concepts, and diagnostic practices were presented relative to the interactionist orientation.

Early childhood programs compatible with each of the developmental orientations were presented. The environmentalist orientation was seen as providing the major rationale for the traditional elementary education programs—DISTAR, or Academic Preschool; Behavior Analysis; and DARCEE, or Early Training model.

The maturationist orientation was characterized as leading to the absence of formal programs (except in special conditions where home care is inadequate) or to the provision of "child development" programs such as the Bank Street model, and some "open" and "free" schools. Most maturationists were said to favor grouping practices that place children with peers at similar developmental and performance levels.

The programs cited as most compatible with the interactionist orientation were the British integrated day approach, the Montessori method, Weikart's Cognitive Curriculum, and the Syracuse Responsive Care model. While differences between these four models were pronounced, they were described as being similar in that they all use the child's activity as the focus for curriculum implementation.

In addition to the models described in this chapter, there are several others that are less representative of a particular view, but nevertheless have distinctive configurations. You may wish to become familiar with some of these, so that you can make further comparisons with the models that have been presented. In some instances, you will encounter mixed orientations within a single model; others will more closely be compatible with one of the three orientations.

PROGRAM CONTACT PERSONS AND AGENCIES

Contact persons and/or agencies for the programs cited within this chapter are listed below. The names and developers of a number of other model programs, which are not described in this text, are also included.

Academic Preschool
    See *Engelmann-Becker Model* and *Conceptual Skills Program*

The Ameliorative Program
    Merele B. Karnes
    University of Illinois
    Champaign, Illinois

Anisa Model
    Daniel C. Jordan
    University of Massachusetts
    Amherst, Massachusetts

Appalachia Preschool Program
    Roy Alford
    Appalachia Educational Laboratory, Inc.
    Charleston, West Virginia

The Bank Street Model
    Elizabeth Gilkeson
    Bank Street College of Education
    New York, New York

BEEP—Brookline Early Education Program
    Burton White
    Harvard University
    Cambridge, Massachusetts

Behavior Analysis Model
    Donald Bushnell, Jr.
    University of Kansas
    Lawrence, Kansas

CHILD Curriculum
    Helen F. Robinson
    Bernard M. Baruch College/City University of New York
    New York, New York

The Cognitive Curriculum
    David P. Weikart
    High/Scope Educational Research Foundation
    Ypsilanti, Michigan

Conceptual Skills Program
    Carl Bereiter
    Ontario Institute for Studies in Education
    Toronto, Ontario, Canada

DARCEE—Demonstration and Research Center in Early Education
    Susan W. Gray
    George Peabody College for Teachers
    Nashville, Tennessee

DISTAR
    See *Engelmann-Becker Model*

Early Education Project
    Martin Deutsch
    Institute for Developmental Studies
    School of Education, New York University
    New York, New York

The Engelmann-Becker Model
    Siegfried Engelmann, Wesley Becker
    University of Oregon
    Eugene, Oregon

Montessori Method
    American Montessori Society
    Upper Lake Avenue
    Greenwich, Connecticut

New Nursery School
    See *Responsive Environment*

Open Education Model
    Educational Development Center
    Newton, Massachusetts

Parent Education Model
    Ira Gordon
    University of Florida
    Gainesville, Florida

Preschool Based on Piaget's Theory
    Constance Kamii
    Ypsilanti Public Schools
    Ypsilanti, Michigan

The Primary Education Project
    Lauren B. Resnick
    Learning Research and Development Center
    University of Pittsburgh
    Pittsburgh, Pennsylvania

Responsive Care Model
    Margaret Lay
    Syracuse University
    Syracuse, New York

The Responsive Environment Model
    Glen Nimnicht
    Far West Laboratory for Education Research and Development
    1855 Folsom Street
    San Francisco, California

TEEM—Tucson Early Education Model
    Ronald Henderson
    Arizona Center for Early Childhood Education
    University of Arizona
    Tucson, Arizona

Tutorial Program
Marion Blank
Albert Einstein College of Medicine
Bronx, New York

REASSESSMENT

Reread what you wrote for the preassessment as you began this chapter, comparing this with your current understandings. Now write on these topics again and incorporate your new insights and knowledge. Continue to update as you prepare for teaching. Save your materials for your portfolio.

Additional Reading

Behavior Modification

Becker, W. C. *Reducing behavior problems: An operant guide for teachers.* Urbana, Illinois: National Laboratory on Early Childhood Education, 1969. ERIC Document Reproduction Service No. ED 034 570.

Givner, A., and Graubard, P. S. *A handbook of behavior modification for the classroom.* New York: Holt, Rinehart and Winston, 1974.

Neisworth, J. T. *et al. Student motivation and classroom management: A behavioristic approach.* Lemont, Pa.: Behavior Technics, 1969.

Sheppard, W. C., Shank, S. B., and Wilson, D. *How to be a good teacher: Training social behavior in young children.* Champaign, Ill.: Research Press, 1972.

Stainback, W. C. *et al. Establishing a token economy in the classroom.* Columbus, Ohio: Charles E. Merrill, 1973.

Sulzer, B., and Mayer, G. R. *Behavior modification procedures for school personnel.* Hinsdale, Ill.: Dryden Press, 1971.

DISTAR

Becker, W. *Teaching children: A child management program for teachers.* Champaign, Ill.: Engelmann-Becker Corp., 1969.

Bereiter, C., and Engelmann, S. *Language learning activities for the disadvantaged child.* New York: Anti-Defamation League of B'nai B'rith, 1968.

————. *Teaching the culturally disadvantaged child in the preschool.* Englewood Cliffs, N.J.: Prentice-Hall, 1966.

Science Research Associates, Inc. *DISTAR.* Chicago: Science Research Associates, 1972.

Behavior Analysis

Buchanan and Sullivan Associates. *Programmed reading,* 3rd ed. New York: McGraw-Hill, 1973.

Bushnell, D., Jr. *The Behavior Analysis classroom.* Lawrence, Kans.: Department of Human Development, University of Kansas, 1970. Also ERIC Document Reproduction Service No. ED 047 775.

————. *A token manual for Behavior Analysis classrooms.* Lawrence, Kans.: Department of Human Development, University of Kansas, 1970. Also ERIC Document Reproduction Service No. ED 047 776.

————. The Behavior Analysis classroom. In B. Spodek, Ed. *Early Childhood Education.* Englewood Cliffs, N.J.: Prentice-Hall, 1973.

Bushnell, D., Jr., Wrobel, P., and Michaelis, M. Applying "group" contingencies to the classroom study behavior of preschool children. *Journal of Applied Behavior Analysis,* 1968, 1, 55–62.

DARCEE Camp, J., and others. Curriculum guides. Nashville, Tenn.: DARCEE, George Peabody College for Teachers, 1971. For example: *Unit 2: Plants; Unit 6: Forest Animals.*

Gray, S. W., and Klaus, R. A. An experimental pre-school program for culturally deprived children. *Child Development,* 1965, 36, 887–8.

Gray, S. W., Klaus, R. A., Miller, J. O., and Forrester, B. J. *Before first grade.* New York: Teachers College Press, 1966.

Klaus, R. A., and Gray, S. W. The early training project for disadvantaged children: A report after five years. *Monograph of the Society for Research in Child Development,* 1968, 33(4).

Maturationist Programs Biber, B. Goals and methods in a preschool program for disadvantaged children. *Children,* 17, 1970, 15–20.

Biber, B., and Franklin, M. The relevance of developmental and psychodynamic concepts to the education of the preschool child. *Journal of the Academy of Child Psychiatry,* 1967, 6, 5–24.

Biber, B., Shapiro, E., and Wicken, D. *Promoting cognitive growth: A developmental-interaction point of view.* Washington, D.C.: National Association for the Education of Young Children, 1971.

Gilkeson, E. *Bank Street approach to Follow Through.* New York: Bank Street College of Education, 1969.

The Montessori Method Carinato, M. E. *et al. Montessori matters.* Cincinnati, Ohio: Sisters of Notre Dame de Namur, 1967.

Lillard, P. P. *Montessori: A modern approach.* New York: Schocken, 1972.

Montessori, M. *The absorbent mind.* Wheaton, Ill.: Theosophical Press, 1964.

———. *The Montessori method.* New York: Schocken, 1964.

———. *Dr. Montessori's own handbook.* New York: Schocken, 1965.

———. *Spontaneous activity in education.* New York: Schocken, 1965.

National Association for the Education of Young Children. *Montessori in perspective.* Washington, D.C.: NAEYC, 1966.

Rambusch, N. McC. *Learning how to learn: An American approach to Montessori.* Baltimore, Md.: Helicon Press, 1962.

The British Integrated Day Barth, R. S. *Open education and the American school.* New York: Agathon Press, 1972.

Blackie, J. *Inside the primary school.* New York: Schocken, 1971.

Brown, M., and Precious, N. *The integrated day in the primary school.* New York: Agathon Press, 1969.

Featherstone, J. *The primary school revolution in Britain.* A Pitman/New Republic reprint. New York: Pitman, 1967.

———. *Schools where children learn.* New York: Liveright, 1971.

Nyquist, E. B., and Hawes, G. R., Eds. *Open education: A sourcebook for parents and teachers.* New York: Bantam, 1972.

Rogers, V. R. *The English primary school.* New York: Macmillan, 1970.

Sargent, B. *The integrated day in an American school.* Boston: National Association of Independent Schools, 1970.

Silberman, C. *Crisis in the classroom.* New York: Random House, 1970.

Silberman, C., Ed. *The open classroom reader.* New York: Vintage/Random House, 1973.

Spodek, B., and Walberg, H. J. *Studies in open education*. New York: Agathon, 1975.

Weber, L. *The English infant school and informal education*. Englewood Cliffs, N.J.: Prentice-Hall, 1971.

The Cognitive Curriculum

Kamii, C., and DeVries, R. *Piaget-based curricula for early childhood education: Three different approaches*. ERIC Document Reproduction Service No. ED 087 518.

Weikart, D., Deloria, D., Lawser, S., and Wiegerink, R. *Longitudinal results of the Ypsilanti Perry Preschool Project*. Ypsilanti, Mich.: High/Scope, 1970.

Weikart, D. P., Rogers, L., and Adcock, C. *The cognitively oriented curriculum: A framework for preschool teachers*. Washington, D.C.: National Association for the Education of Young Children, 1971.

The Syracuse Responsive Care

Clark, B., Lay, M., and Tryon, B. *And so there was me: A potpourri of creative art experiences for children 3 to 6*. Syracuse, N.Y.: Syracuse University Early Childhood Education Center, 1973.

———. *A space to discover me: Books, games, puzzles and other quiet things for children 3 to 6*. Syracuse, N.Y.: Syracuse University Early Childhood Education Center, 1973.

Lay, M. *The responsive care manual: A handbook for administrators*. St. Ann, Miss.: CEMREL, Inc., 1973.

———. *The responsive care model: A program manual and report of implementation*. Syracuse, N.Y.: Syracuse University Early Childhood Education Center, 1972.

CHAPTER 15
Analysis of Program Decisions

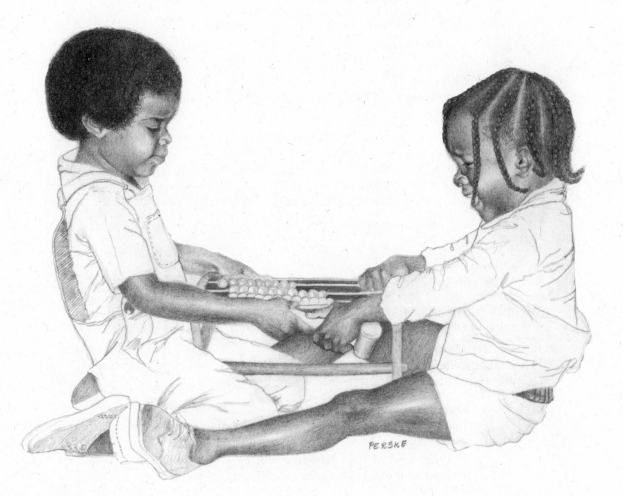

PERSKE

Overview

Decisions about the Organization of Time
THE ENVIRONMENTALIST ALTERNATIVE: INSTRUCTIONALLY FOCUSED TIME
    PERIODS
THE MATURATIONIST ALTERNATIVE: BROAD AND BALANCED TIME PERIODS
THE INTERACTIONIST ALTERNATIVE: OPEN SCHEDULING

Decisions about Facilities: Space, Equipment, and Materials
THE ENVIRONMENTALIST ALTERNATIVE: INSTRUCTIONAL FOCUS
THE MATURATIONIST ALTERNATIVE: DEVELOPMENTAL CONCERNS
THE INTERACTIONIST ALTERNATIVE: "HANDS-ON" DIVERSITY

Decisions about Ground Rules
THE ENVIRONMENTALIST ALTERNATIVE: IMPOSING RESTRICTIONS
THE MATURATIONIST ALTERNATIVE: ESTABLISHING "ROUTINES"
THE INTERACTIONIST ALTERNATIVE: PROVIDING FREEDOM WITHIN STRUCTURE

Decisions about Relationships with Families
PARENTS AS BYSTANDERS, OBSERVERS, LEARNERS
PARENTS AS TEACHERS AT HOME
PARENTS AS AIDES AND VOLUNTEERS
PARENTS AS PARTNERS AND POLICY MAKERS

Summary

PREASSESSMENT

When you have completed this chapter you should be able to describe and compare the following:

1. *environmentalist, maturationist, and interactionist perspectives regarding major program decisions.*
2. *contrasting program decisions regarding time, facilities, ground rules, and relationships with parents.*
3. *consequences for children's experiences of alternative decisions.*

Before *beginning to read this chapter:*

1. *take time to write what you currently know about each of the above topics.*
2. *reflect on the child (children) you observed as you studied Section Two and for whom you planned involvements in Section Three; consider which arrangements of time, facilities, ground rules, and relationships with parents would most facilitate development for this child (these children).*

   Save what you write for rereading, comparison, and elaboration after you have studied and discussed these materials.

Overview

In organizing a program for young children many kinds of decisions must be made, such as:

1. What kind of time schedule will be arranged?
2. How will available space be utilized?

3. What equipment and materials will be selected and how will they be arranged within the classroom space?
4. What ground rules will be established to direct pupil's participation?
5. What kind of relationship with parents will be established?

In each of the above areas, there are many alternative arrangements from which a teacher can choose. Decisions regarding each of these program elements are mandatory; the absence of a decision is in itself a kind of decision—decisions made by default typically result in chaotic and unsuccessful programs. Ideally, these decisions should grow out of the goals that characterize a specific program. The objective of this chapter is to inform you of the diverse answers currently being made to these questions within various programs and to help you understand how these answers are related to the respective programers' goals.

Decisions about the Organization of Time

Importance of predictability

Most early educators emphasize the importance of predictability in the time schedule. While some teachers may enjoy varying the time schedule for the sake of variation, young children are thought to function best within a dependable and predictable time structure.

People in general, and children in particular, gain a sense of security from predictable time schedules. Many emotional upsets can be directly attributed to unfulfilled expectations. Some adults and children are obviously much more affected by irregularities than others. If children are to develop a degree of independence in their daily activities, however, some known boundaries are mandatory, and among these are reliable time arrangements. Children can adjust to a variety of patterns, but they function best if the chosen pattern is generally adhered to. The younger the children, the more likely it is that regular time patterns will prove beneficial.

Early educators take three general approaches to time scheduling: (1) instructionally focused time periods, (2) broad and balanced time periods, and (3) "open" scheduling. Each of these generally corresponds to a respective orientation to child development and learning.

THE ENVIRONMENTALIST ALTERNATIVE: INSTRUCTIONALLY FOCUSED TIME PERIODS

Subject matter focus

The environmentalist approach to time schedules is to impose subject matter labels on the major time periods. These subject-oriented time periods are arranged to extend for as long as the attention span of the pupils permits. Reading or mathematics instruction is often scheduled early, when children are assumed to be fresh and attentive. Conversely, story time and music are relegated to those periods in which children are thought to be fatigued and less likely to benefit from instruction. However, if the development of musical knowledge and abilities were a major program concern, environmentalists would undoubtedly advise the teacher to schedule music during prime

Table 15.1 Academic Preschool Time Schedule for a Two-Hour Day

	Group 1 5 children	Group 2 5 children	Group 3 5 children
Period 1 (10 minutes)	Unstructured activity		
Period 2 (20 minutes)	Language	Arithmetic	Reading
Period 3 (30 minutes)	Toilet, juice, and music		
Period 4 (20 minutes)	Arithmetic	Reading	Language
Period 5 (20 minutes)	Semistructured activity		
Period 6 (20 minutes)	Reading	Language	Arithmetic

Source: Carl Bereiter and Siegfried Engelmann, *Teaching disadvantaged children in the preschool,* © 1966, p. 67. Reprinted by permission of Prentice-Hall, Inc., Englewood Cliffs, N.J.

morning time. Recesses or free periods are planned as breaks, so that children can then return to important activities with renewed vigor, but breaks are likely to be kept as brief as possible to allow generous time for academic focus.

Extrinsic reinforcement necessary for implementation

By arranging time periods with a subject matter focus, environmentalist programers ensure that adequate attention will be paid to high-priority academic areas. This approach has the advantage of emphasizing selected areas of highest concern and deemphasizing others. Since children are not naturally inclined toward brief, focused exposure to one subject area after

Table 15.2 Academic Preschool Time Schedule for an Eight-Hour Day

	Group 1 5 children	Group 2 5 children	Group 3 5 children
Period 1 (10 minutes)	Unstructured activity		
Period 2 (20 minutes)	Language	Semistructured activity	
Period 3 (20 minutes)	Semistructured activity	Language	Semistructured activity
Period 4 (20 minutes)	Semistructured activity		Language
Period 5 (40 minutes)	Toilet, juice, and singing		
Period 6 (60 minutes)	Unstructured activity and lunch preparation		
Period 7 (60 minutes)	Lunch, cleanup, and toilet		
Period 8 (20 minutes)	Arithmetic	Semistructured activity	
Period 9 (20 minutes)	Semistructured activity	Arithmetic	Semistructured activity
Period 10 (20 minutes)	Semistructured activity		Arithmetic
Period 11 (20 minutes)	Toilet and rest		
Period 12 (20 minutes)	Music		
Period 13 (20 minutes)	Reading	Semistructured activity	
Period 14 (20 minutes)	Semistructured activity	Reading	Semistructured activity
Period 15 (20 minutes)	Semistructured activity		Reading
Period 16 (50 minutes)	Unstructured activity		

Source: Carl Bereiter and Siegfried Engelmann, *Teaching disadvantaged children in the preschool,* © 1966, p. 69. Reprinted by permission of Prentice-Hall, Inc., Englewood Cliffs, N.J.

Table 15.3 Time Schedule for a Traditional Primary School

8:45–9:00	Opening—announcements, calendar (day, weather, temperature recording), collections (milk money, lunch count), pledge flag
9:00–10:40	Reading (milk break at 10:00)
10:40–11:15	Mathematics
11:15–11:40	Language arts (such as instruction in manuscript printing, spelling)
11:40–Noon	Story
Noon–12:30	Lunch
12:30–1:00	Free time; individual help
1:00–1:15	Silent reading period
1:15–2:00	Social studies (such as *Weekly Reader*) or science
2:00–2:45	Special activity (such as art, music, gym)
2:45–2:50	Dismissal

another, or toward one formal teacher-directed activity after another, it often becomes necessary to use reinforcement systems.

It may be helpful to examine some actual time schedules proposed by various environmentalist programers. For example, the schedules recom- *Academic Preschool* mended for four-year-olds by Bereiter and Engelmann for the Academic Preschool (with a one-to-five adult-child ratio) are shown in Tables 15.1 and 15.2.

Note that, with few exceptions, the time periods are labeled with the specific subject matter to be taught during that time. While the program schedules proposed for longer days (six hours or more) include more unstructured and semistructured activity periods, these are arranged so they provide maximum support for the instruction periods.

The schedule for the Academic Preschool is similar to that found in many primary classrooms (see Table 15.3), in that time segments are designated by the subject matter concerns of the program planner. Reading is scheduled for a longer period than any other subject. This period is usually one where the teacher spends a portion of time working with each of three ability-based subgroups. Each child spends approximately thirty minutes in teacher-directed activity with others who are thought to be at the same reading level. The instruction may include introduction of new vocabulary, word study activities, silent reading, oral reading, discussion, or practice exercises. During the remainder of the reading period, the children work independently on a reading-related assignment or some other quiet task. This is the most common pattern for reading instruction in the primary grades, and is designed to differentiate reading instruction according to readiness or ability levels. Given this arrangement, it is imperative that teachers carefully develop both ground rules and quiet "seat work" assignments so that disrup-

Table 15.4 Time Schedule for the DARCEE Program

9:00	Arrive
9:00–9:45	Group activity
9:30–9:45	Juice and crackers
9:45–11:45	Small group activities
11:45–12:30	Washup, lunch
12:30–12:50	Small group activities
12:50–1:00	Group activity; review; prepare for dismissal
1:00	Dismissal

Source: S. W. Gray, R. A. Klaus, J. O. Miller, and B. J. Forrester, *Before first grade* (New York: Teachers College Press, 1966), p. 79. Reprinted by permission.

tions are minimized and learning is maximized. This is one of the traditional teacher's most difficult tasks.

DARCEE   The DARCEE program seeks to provide systematic instruction in the skills and attitudes necessary for school success. Table 15.4 gives a time schedule recommended for this program.

In all of the schedules just described there is little variation in daily schedules across time (for example, during a school year) and children have *Behavior Analysis* very little choice of activity within the time periods. However, the Behavior Analysis program, also an environmentalist program, has three general pe-

Photo by John Young.

riods of time: planning, formal instruction, and exchange periods. Exchange periods provide children with the opportunity to exchange the tokens they have acquired during the instructional periods. A wide range of appealing activities are made available during this period. Early in the year, formal instruction and exchange periods alternate very frequently, with perhaps ten to fifteen minutes of work effort being followed by twenty to twenty-five minutes of activity. Gradually the pattern is reversed, and longer earning periods are interspersed with briefer exchange periods. Contingencies are changed to require more work effort to earn a given number of tokens or to require more tokens in exchange for given privileges. The exact balance between the various types of activities is regulated by progress toward specific objectives.

THE MATURATIONIST ALTERNATIVE: BROAD AND BALANCED TIME PERIODS

Child-development preschool

Many early childhood educators, especially those with maturationist and "child development" orientations, recommend a balance of contrasting types of activities—rest and play, indoor and outdoor, quiet and active, individual and group, teacher directed and child directed. Broad time periods of individual activity interspersed with shorter times for group activities are often suggested. Tables 15.5 and 15.6 gives a suggested framework for half-day and full-day preschool programs.

The time schedules recommended for several of the "model" programs for children ages three through seven provide broad and flexible time periods similar to those cited by Hildebrand (1971). Among those are the Bank Street

Table 15.5   Time Schedule for a Half-Day Preschool Program (A.M. or P.M.)

9:00–10:00	1:00–2:00	Self-selected activity indoors.
10:00	2:00	Cleanup time (can vary a few minutes either way). As child finishes helping with cleanup, he or she goes to the toilet, if necessary, and washes hands.
10:15–10:25	2:15–2:25	Snack. With older children, sharing time[a] goes on at the same time as snack time.
10:25–10:45	2:25–2:45	Children move to a story group or groups. They select a book for "reading" as they pass the shelf, and look at the book or just talk quietly. The teacher finishes the period with some songs, a special story, planning, or discussion.
10:45–11:30	2:45–3:30	Outdoor, self-selected activity.
11:30–11:40	3:30–3:40	Cleanup time. Preparation to go home.
11:45	3:45	Dismissal.

Source: Verna Hildebrand, *Introduction to early childhood education* (New York: Macmillan, 1971), p. 56. Reprinted with permission of Macmillan Publishing Co., Inc. Copyright © 1971 by Verna L. Hildebrand.

[a] A period when children are called on to share an object or news they have brought from home.

Table 15.6 Time Schedule for a Full-Day Program (presented in time blocks[1])

Time Block I	Self-selected activity (indoors)

Art	Music
Science	Dramatic play
Table games	Small wheeled objects
Blocks	Language arts
Books	

Time Block II — Teacher-instigated activity

Cleanup
Toileting, washing hands
Snack
Quiet Time: looking at books, music, story time and dis-
   cussions

Time Block III — Self-selected activity (outdoors)

Climbing	Riding tricycles
Swinging	Sand play
Running	Science

Time Block IV — Lunch period

Washing hands, toileting
Resting prior to lunch
Eating
Washing hands
Going home or preparing for nap

Time Block V — Nap time

Dressing for bed	Toileting
Sleeping	Dressing

Time Block VI — Self-selected activity

New activities
Snack
Outdoor play

Source: Verna Hildebrand, *Introduction to early childhood education* (New York: Macmillan, 1971), p. 57. Reprinted with permission of Macmillan Publishing Co., Inc. Copyright © 1971 by Verna L. Hildebrand.

[1] Blocks I, II, and III are typical of half-day programs in nursery schools and kindergartens where lunch is not served. The six blocks are more typical of day-care centers. Blocks I and III may be interchanged for variation and for meeting the needs of the children, as discussed elsewhere.

model, the Responsive Environment model, and the Cognitive Curriculum.

In arranging a sequence of time periods with a balance of activities, the program planner typically tries to ensure that children have exposure to activities deemed appropriate for their developmental level and to guard against the overemphasis of particular activities. The disadvantages are that some children must be interrupted in the middle of very productive involvement to move, along with the rest of the group, to whatever activity is prescribed for the next time period. It is rare to find a stopping point that is mutually satisfactory for all learners, and consequently some children's needs and interests must always be sacrificed during transitions.

Skilled and experienced teachers who use such schedules find it beneficial to announce to children that a particular time period is drawing to a close. Children who are deeply involved in a block construction project, for example, need time to either terminate their project or adjust themselves to the notion of completing it later. A reminder, such as, "In just a few minutes we will put everything away so that we can have a snack," helps alleviate the disappointment and frustration of leaving a project unfinished.

Planning for transitions

Teachers often need to plan for transitions between one kind of activity and another. For example, if children must walk somewhere as a group after an individual work period, it is useful to have some transitional activity during this time. Resourceful teachers often use these periods for showing children interesting pictures, singing favorite songs, saying chanting rhymes, doing finger play activities, or telling short lively stories. Without careful planning, transition periods lead to frustrations for both children and teachers.

THE INTERACTIONIST ALTERNATIVE: OPEN SCHEDULING

In several of the programs discussed in the previous chapter, there is neither a tightly scheduled program aimed at very focused objectives nor a structuring of broad time periods to achieve a balanced program. Instead, these programs feature an "open" time arrangement, or *integrated day*, in which individual children pace themselves through activities of varying duration throughout the program day. The integrated day and the open education programs derive their names from their use of open time scheduling and the integration of many academic areas into children's self-selected activities. Brown and Precious (1968) describe the integrated day as follows:

The integrated day/open time arrangement

> The integrated day could be described as a school day which is combined into a whole and has the minimum of timetabling. Within this day there is time and opportunity in a planned educative environment for the social, intellectual, emotional, physical and aesthetic growth of the child at his own rate of development. Our definition extends this day to encompass the whole life of the child during the six years of primary education.
>
> The natural flow of activity, imagination, language, thought and learning which is in itself a continuous process is not interrupted by artificial breaks such as the conventional playtime or subject barriers. The child is encouraged to commit himself completely to the work in hand which he has chosen. The child also has the time to pursue something in depth even though it may take several days. As he works, problems common to various subjects will arise but within the integrated framework he can make easy transition between any areas of learning. (p. 13)

In most British integrated day schedules and in the American "open education" equivalent, a part of the day is scheduled for whole group meetings, but, for most of the time, the children are free to move from activity to activity. In some situations the children are even permitted to go outside to work or play as they wish, without a scheduled recess period.

Montessori

The open time arrangement of the British system is also characteristic of the Montessori approaches. In the Montessori *prepared environment,* children are free to move about at will and, ideally, to go outside for "open air space" as well. It is thought desirable that children be permitted "to go and come as they like, throughout the entire day" (Montessori, 1964, pp. 4–5). The day is left open to the child so that there will be no unnecessary interruption of work. According to Nancy McCormick Rambusch (1962, p. 18), who in 1960 helped organize and subsequently became the first president of the American Montessori Society, "Three hours of activity will not fatigue these children, who shift from task to task with pleasure, now resting, now redoubling their efforts over a thorny problem."

Syracuse Responsive Care open time arrangement

The Syracuse Responsive Care model (Lay, 1972) also advocates an open time arrangement in which the children have "many diverse options throughout the day to select activities that interest them and to set their own pace in those activities." The program day, however, while continually providing the child with options, maintains a regularity in regard to invitational events (story, snack, musical and dramatic events, or cooking activities). These events are offered to the children in a predictable schedule, but they are not required to participate. Only lunch and rest are mandatory in the full-day program.

The development of independent activity in children is seen as one of the prime advantages of open time structures. Individual differences among children are easily observed as they move from activity to activity under this arrangement. Given this freedom, some children will persist in a task for hours or even days, deriving great satisfaction from the uninterrupted pursuit of their interests. Others, or even the same child at other times, will move frequently between activities.

Further comparisons of organization of time

To many interactionists, it is extremely important that children be permitted sustained exploration of whatever phenomena currently interest them and that they be allowed to terminate contacts that do not interest them. From other perspectives, the child's own interests are not seen as sufficiently dependable to serve as the basis for program structure. Environmentalists, especially, see far less value in time devoted to "messing about with materials" or, especially, to extended fantasy play and social interactions. These, of course, are precisely the kinds of activities that many interactionists see as highly valuable. Maturationists would also see great value in these activities, but would point out that there would be a smoother flow of the day if there were time markers to help the children make transitions into other kinds of age-appropriate involvements.

The kind of time arrangement adopted for a given setting is directly linked to the programer's theoretical view of child learning and development,

You have just read about three different types of time scheduling in early childhood programs: (1) instructionally focused scheduling, (2) broad and balanced time periods, and (3) open scheduling. Consider the early childhood centers or classrooms with which you are most familiar, and try to answer the following questions:

1. Do the time arrangements identify the center or classroom as being one of the above types? If not, how would the time schedule be characterized?

2. Do the time arrangements appear to be conducive to accomplishing the goals of the teacher(s)?

3. What aspects of the children's behavior do you attribute to the time arrangements?

4. What conclusions, if any, can you draw from your answers to the above questions that might prove helpful in planning for your own work with children?

which, in turn, determines the nature of instructional activities. Broad and balanced time arrangements tend to suit maturationists, because the child is not pushed into particular occupations and yet experiences the time regularity deemed appropriate for his or her age. Brief and focused periods, on the other hand, assure environmentalists that sufficient attention is being given to the areas deemed most crucial to the child's development. And open time arrangements suit interactionists because individual children have the opportunity to pursue their own interests without external interruptions. Each type of arrangement represents valid practice from one of these points of view; each is to some extent discordant with alternative perspectives.

Decisions about Facilities: Space, Equipment, and Materials

Decisions about program facilities such as space arrangements, equipment, and materials are also keyed to the programer's perspective on development and learning and, more specifically, to the particular objectives or goals embodied in that perspective. The terms *equipment* and *materials* are sometimes used interchangeably. *Equipment*, however, typically refers to furniture and other long-lasting and costly materials, whereas the term *materials* denotes the smaller and less expensive items, some of which are expendable and routinely replaced.

THE ENVIRONMENTALIST ALTERNATIVE: INSTRUCTIONAL FOCUS

If the major concern of a program is with formal, centrally directed instruction, as with the environmentalist perspective, it is important that space be arranged so that distractions are minimized. Manipulative materials (such as toys, sand, water, and clay) may be viewed as distracting clutter, and consequently may be eliminated from the instructional setting.

Academic Preschool instructional spaces

As an example, in the highly structured Academic Preschool it is considered desirable to arrange three separate instructional spaces, usually small rooms. One of these also houses the unstructured and large group activities at certain time periods. The rooms are kept as small and plain as possible. Small separate rooms are believed to minimize environmental distractions that could tempt the child to run about and explore. Acoustical arrangements to reduce distraction between groups are considered very important, but there are few other requirements for the facilities. The tendency to overstock the classroom is warned against by Bereiter and Engelmann (1966). Toys are limited to form boards; jigsaw puzzles; books; drawing and tracing materials; Cuisenaire rods; a miniature house, barn, and set of farm animals; paper, crayons, and chalk.

Traditional primary school spatial arrangement

Although the traditional primary classroom differs from the Academic Preschool in having a large rectangular space instead of several small rooms, there is a similar emphasis on nondistracting arrangements. For example, children are typically seated in rows, with spaces separating them to discourage social interchange. Seating is often arranged so that it faces the source of instruction. Small group instruction is usually conducted at the side of the room in a grouping of small chairs facing the teacher and away from distracting stimuli. Only books, workbooks, charts, and other instructional materials are permitted in the area. The classroom may include some decorative objects such as plants, posters, pictures, and displays of children's art or written work; a table may display collections of objects related to science lessons; maps and globes may be seen; counting materials may be placed on shelves and accessible to children. There are, however, few games or other objects that foster "messing about" or play; play materials are typically stored out of sight, except during recess or "free" periods.

Behavior Analysis spatial arrangement

The Behavior Analysis program is organized somewhat differently than either of the above. In the classrooms children sit around tables that also accommodate token-dispensing adults during the work periods. The work materials for the Behavior Analysis classrooms include several different types of programed instruction booklets and work sheets. The "reward" materials (such as games and puzzles) for which students exchange their tokens are present in a special area within the classroom or in an adjoining room.

THE MATURATIONIST ALTERNATIVE: DEVELOPMENTAL CONCERNS

The facilities described above are in considerable contrast to those of maturationist programers, who provide materials designed to stimulate large muscle activity, to promote cooperative play, to encourage dramatic play, and to stimulate expression of ideas and feelings through a variety of activities with blocks, music, clay, and paint, as well as to encourage quiet activities.

Most nursery schools, kindergartens, and many primary classrooms with a "child development" or maturationist orientation contain a recognizable set of materials that includes, in addition to child-size tables, chairs, shelving, and lockers, a range of other types of equipment and materials (see Appendix 5).

Activity centers   The materials are carefully arranged in activity centers, so that materials often used together (such as blocks and dress-up materials) are in close proximity, and materials not appropriate for simultaneous use (such as paints and books) are separated from each other. There may be dramatic play areas, large muscle areas, water play areas, book corners, and science tables. The following are some of the guidelines followed in placing the equipment and materials:

1. Equipment and materials requiring close eye work should be placed in adequate light.
2. Creative construction work, such as block building and clay modeling, should be placed away from the major traffic areas.
3. Space for quiet activities should be placed apart from those materials and equipment that stimulate noisy play.
4. Water and wet activities should be placed together, near a source of water and drainage and away from objects such as books that should not get wet.

THE INTERACTIONIST ALTERNATIVE: "HANDS-ON" DIVERSITY

Many new kinds of materials are now available to children in many United States classrooms. This influx is partly due to an increased awareness of the concept of Piagetian stages, with its emphasis on the manipulating of materials in order to help children develop conservation learning. Another major impetus has been the example of British education. Information regarding the material richness of British classrooms has helped many teachers break away from the stereotyped view of a fixed environment and a fixed daily schedule of separate subjects and activities.

The British influence   The British classrooms, described in books such as *The integrated day in the primary school* (Brown and Precious, 1968), appear to have great flexibility both in the basic setting and in regard to the materials that are introduced. Working surfaces, for example, include a wide variety of tables—stack tables, pull-down wall tables, small occasional tables, benches, boxes, and raised platforms. Seating accommodations include wooden chairs, cane chairs, benches, cushions, rugs, carpets, and easy chairs. Ingenious arrangements for setting off work areas, for storing diverse materials, for arranging work space, and for displaying work are described in books such as *Room to learn: Working space* (Dean, 1973).

In a guide for teachers, Anderson *et al.* (1950) advise:

They [children] will sometimes play without any apparent purpose; they will paint pictures and perhaps spend long periods just looking at

The following kinds of materials are introduced into classrooms by teachers interested in extending children's experiences and activity options:

Cameras
Stethoscope
Clocks (old)
Strong light source (for shadow-making)
Duplicating machines (for children's use)
Loom
Printing sets/press
Typewriter (for children's use)
Calculators
Balancing bars
Balsa wood
Ball bearings
Balls of all sizes/weights
Hoops
Ladders
Mats, large and small
Planks
Ropes
Rope ladders
Bamboo pieces
Cardboard potato chip or pretzel cannisters
Binoculars
Styrofoam or cardboard meat and vegetable trays
Bubble pipes and rings
Used wrapping and ribbons from gifts
Carbon paper
Tracing paper
Cardboard cones (from spinning mills)
Cardboard tubes
Crayon pieces and old candles
Chains
Clinical thermometer
Eye droppers/basters
Compass
Pine cones
Concave/convex mirrors

Empty sewing spools
Dyes
Metals, all kinds and weights
Egg cartons
Pendulum frame/pendulum
Cardboard pieces
Hinges
Wheels (all types)
Tires
Abacus
Adding machine tape
Adhesives of all varieties
Aerators
Aluminum foil
Balance scales
Balloons
Calendars
Calipers
Blotting paper
Bathroom scales
Old magazines
Batteries
Small boxes (cardboard, metal, plastic)
Bellows
Small plastic jars and bottles with lids
Bicycle pump
Net
Electric bell and gear
Pipe cleaners
Plaster of paris
Maps
Locks/keys
Kitchen scales
Leather pieces
Kites
Graph paper
Gauze
Food coloring
Foam rubber
Tiles/linoleum squares

Magnets, all shapes and sizes	Stopwatch
Playing cards	Shells
Printing ink	Slinky toy
Wallpaper sample books	Sawdust
Trundle wheels	Wheat paste
Turntable	

See Appendix 5 for a listing of more basic equipment and materials for equipping a classroom.

---

things. So, in addition to the usual school-cupboard equipment, they will need plenty of waste material; boxes, rags, sacking, cardboard of all sorts, bits of wood, old catalogues, as well as natural objects like stones, shells, cones, chestnuts, etc. They will want picture books, a pocket lens, and little interesting things which can be magnified, a magnet and objects it will pick up and some that it will not, a kaleidoscope, a few small mirrors, sometimes an old nest and any curious things which stimulate investigation. If changes are to be made throughout the school, materials can perhaps be pooled and redistributed; the time-table may be rearranged so that such equipment as bricks, the large sand-tray, the screen house and a few large black boards can be shared. If it is possible to buy anything new and there is no large building material in the school, I should certainly set bricks of assorted sizes (particularly big ones) and a good supply of damp sand in a large deep tray. (p. 76)

Montessori prepared environment
A quite different view of classroom facilities can be seen in Montessori classrooms. Essential to the Montessori approach is the prepared environment. Maria Montessori believed that the environment must be a nourishing place for children. As cited earlier, she believed that the environment should be matched to the child's potential, thereby leading to a fruitful interaction. Montessori (1963) identified her interactionist philosophy in the following statement:

Plainly the environment must be a living one, directed by a higher intelligence, arranged by an adult who is prepared for his mission. It is in this that our conception differs both from that of the world in which the adult does everything for the child and from that of a passive environment in which the adult abandons the child to himself . . . . This means that it is not enough to set the child among objects in proportion to his size and strength; the adult who is to help him must have learned how to do so. (p. 224)

There is no time structuring for most of the Montessori session, but there is a definitive space structuring. Materials must be located in a known place (although this place may be changed across time) and must be continuously accessible to the child in that place (unless they are being used by another child). Materials are grouped according to similarity of function and are arranged in sequence according to degree of difficulty.

The Montessori environment is also designed to bring the child into closer contact with reality and away from his or her fantasies and illusions. Therefore, toys such as replicas of furniture or dress-ups are not included. Children use real things instead of playthings, real tasks are performed, and in modern Montessori classrooms a real refrigerator, stove, sink, and telephone are available. Silverware is polished when it is tarnished; shoes are shined; nourishing food is prepared, with sharp knives available for cutting; a heated iron may be used for ironing. A child is not encouraged to play at being an adult in the Montessori setting; instead, he or she is provided with the tools for doing adult tasks.

Real objects, not "pretend"

There is in Montessori classrooms only one of each type of equipment. Children must wait until another child is finished if the equipment they want is in use. This helps them learn to respect the work of others and to cope with the realities they meet in daily life.

Some of the Montessori equipment is thought to develop the skills necessary for future academic work. An example of this are the materials for handwriting preparation. Children are shown how to lift and manipulate knobs on metal stencils, developing finger and thumb coordination as they do so. They are then provided paper and pencil and shown how they can use the stencils to guide their pencils in drawing basic forms. They are then provided sandpaper letters to develop a "muscle memory" of letter patterns. Thus, it is believed by the time they are motivated to write they will have abilities that allow them to do so without failure or frustration. In this respect, Montessori shows her environmentalist inclinations.

Self-correcting materials

Many of the Montessori materials are **self-correcting,** which affords children far greater autonomy and freedom to pace their own learning efforts.

RESPONSE SECTION

The facilities provided for early childhood programs should ideally be arranged to facilitate the accomplishment of program goals. Consider the early childhood centers or classrooms with which you are most familiar, and try to answer the following questions:

1. Do the physical arrangements identify the center or classroom as being (a) instructionally focused, (b) developmentally appropriate, or (c) rich in diversity?

2. Are the physical arrangements conducive to accomplishing the goals of the teacher(s)?

3. What aspects of the children's behavior do you attribute to the physical arrangements?

4. What conclusions, if any, can you draw from your answers to the above questions that might prove helpful in planning for your own work with children?

Materials are expected to be treated with respect, however, and never used improperly. When a child decides to use a particular "exercise," he or she brings all the materials and arranges them on a mat or rug. The child is not interrupted while using the materials, either by other children or by the teacher. When the child is finished, the materials are returned to the shelf, in good order for the next child.

The Montessori environment is typically an evolving one. Rather than having all the equipment available from the start of the program, new pieces are gradually introduced in response to the children's developing abilities. The appropriateness of materials is measured by the degree of concentration, involvement, and satisfaction the child experiences. When the child begins to experiment with possible new uses or begins to use an apparatus in fantasy play (such as using the rods as airplanes), it is time for the introduction of a similar apparatus that presents greater difficulty.

Syracuse Responsive Care: structured via space arrangement

Another contrasting model for space facilities is the Syracuse Responsive Care model (a full-day child-care program). In this program there are three basic spaces—an active area for large muscle play, an expressive area, and a task area. Children are able to move from area to area as they wish almost all day. Each area includes permanent equipment and temporary equipment, the latter being constantly changed by the supervising adult. An abundance of diverse materials are thus made available to children at all times. Because the program is organized around a space rather than around a time arrangement (similar to the Montessori program), the child becomes more familiar with the environment and is more likely to express independence and autonomy than in the typical time-structured program.

Further comparisons of organization of facilities

Just as there are different ways to arrange the use of time in early childhood programs, so there are different ways to arrange the environment. The objectives of a program determine what does or does not "make sense" in any given situation. It would be foolish for the programer who is primarily concerned with direct academic instruction to stock an environment with enticing distractors, as it would be foolish for the programer concerned with the "whole" child to stock the environment only with programed instructional materials. Unfortunately, this simple objectives-facilities relationship is sometimes overlooked, and purchases or arrangements are made on the basis of "tradition" or "expediency" rather than logic.

Decisions about Ground Rules

In any group situation a common set of expectations concerning personal behavior and the proper use of the physical environment needs to be established. Each of us must communicate our expectations and values to those around us, or effective interaction becomes very difficult. This is especially the case in teaching. As a prospective teacher, you should be able to communicate your own expectations for children's behavior consistently and in a positive manner. Otherwise you will find yourself reacting to children negatively and after the fact.

Ground rules, the
teacher's
responsibility

Despite a general consensus among program planners that it is the teacher's responsibility to establish and maintain ground rules either for or with children, programs vary in their formulations of ground rules, in the means by which rules are established, and in their methods of enforcement.

THE ENVIRONMENTALIST ALTERNATIVE: IMPOSING RESTRICTIONS

Behaviors are carefully regulated in environmentalist programs. Systematic reinforcement strategies or restrictive disciplinary measures are often used to keep the children's activities in accord with the programers' intentions.

Ground rules of the
Academic Preschool

In the Academic Preschool, children are expected to be quiet and restrained, even during the unstructured periods. It is felt that "letting off steam" during free periods does not pacify children, but rather makes it more difficult for them to get back to work during the next study period. At the end of the unstructured periods the children are expected to terminate their activities promptly and are rarely granted permission to finish nonacademic work such as drawings. Cleanup periods are brief. If cleanup will take more than two minutes of the children's time, teachers are expected to do it later. The teaching schedule clearly has a higher priority than cleanup or other nonacademic involvements.

Children are required to walk single file, without pushing or crowding, as they move from one classroom to another. They sit in assigned seats during the instructional periods, leaving their places only with the teacher's consent. They are required to participate, answering the teacher's questions in a loud, clear voice and to work hard at the tasks presented them. They are not allowed to interrupt and are discouraged from relating personal experiences or otherwise interjecting ideas irrelevant to the teacher's presentation. Only when the teacher invites children to express their own ideas may they do so.

Principles from
Bereiter and
Engelmann

The recommended means for establishing these ground rules are based on reinforcement theory. Several principles are recommended by Bereiter and Engelmann (1966):

1. *Reward the child who tries.*
2. *Try to avoid rewarding undesirable behavior* (for example, by holding the misbehaving child or taking him aside and talking with him).
3. *Avoid shaming and coaxing.* The teacher matter-of-factly tells children what to do and expects that they will perform and work hard, that they will be "smart," and that he or she will be proud of them.
4. *Preserve the spirit of the group.* Teachers avoid children's rejection of each other through tattling. Teachers only act to correct behavioral offenses that they personally see, not those reported by other children. In response to tattling they may say, "If he did that, he broke a rule," but they avoid encouraging children to turn against each other. The group should never be punished for the offense of any one child.
5. *Emphasize the rules of behavior that must be maintained, not the child's adequacy.*
6. *Exploit work motives rather than play motives.*

7. *Provide the child with a realistic definition of success and failure.* Teachers are not to approve incorrect or inadequate responses. If the child works hard he or she is rewarded for doing a good job but is not led to believe that his or her incorrect responses were correct.

The children are rewarded or punished according to whether they follow the established rule for the situation, and the teacher is careful to communicate that both he or she and the children are governed by the rule and that rewards are not related to the teacher's feelings about a child. During the first month of the program, punishment is sometimes used to clarify the rules. Physical punishment is used only for behavior that is unthinking and automatic; isolation is used for behavior that is more calculated. Two warnings are given before a child is placed in isolation. Rewards include verbal approval, and, to strengthen their rewarding power, verbal praise is initially paired with concrete rewards such as cookies, toys, games, and special privileges.

Traditional primary school ground rules

The ground rules of the Academic Preschool do not appear to be significantly different than the requirements of many traditional primary classrooms, except for their increased emphasis on rewarding desirable behaviors. For example, a second-grade teacher in a traditional primary school reports that on the first day of school she talks with the children about rules and why they are necessary. She then tells them that they should (1) sit down in their seats and remain silent as soon as the bell rings in the morning, (2) raise their hands to speak, (3) ask her permission to leave their seats to go to the bathroom, (4) return to their room after lunch and again sit quietly in their seats, and (5) never interrupt her during reading groups for any reason other than a real emergency.

Rather than systematically rewarding "good" behavior, however, this teacher simply expects it, and reprimands individual children as inconspicuously as possible if infractions occur. If a child persistently ignores one of the rules, however, she talks with the class about it and discusses what should be done to the person who breaks the rule or whether the rule should be revised. She reports that she has no real problems with rule-breaking, and that her practices are similar to those of the rest of the faculty. She teaches in a low-income suburban school where there is a high proportion of blue-collar workers who have similar expectations for their children's school behavior. Obviously, this emphasis on passivity is quite opposite to the behavioral expectations of maturationists and interactionists.

THE MATURATIONIST ALTERNATIVE: ESTABLISHING "ROUTINES"

Few restrictions

Maturationists try to carefully match their programs with the developmental level of the children so that only a few ground rules are necessary. They are likely to refer to ground rules as "establishing routines" for washing, toileting, going outside and coming indoors, resting and eating, or participating in group activities. It is anticipated that many children will not readily accept these routines and that patience will be needed. Leeper (1974), for example, states:

> The rigid conformance once required in nursery school or kindergarten routines has given way to a more relaxed and informal pattern that permits children to establish these requirements at their own pace, consistent with the demands of maturation attained at the time. Like most learned activities, changes occur gradually in keeping with the stage of development. It is, therefore, undesirable to expect the same level of conformity and perfection from all children. (p. 75)

The "don'ts" of child care

The teacher is often advised to indirectly divert the child and redirect his or her unfavorable behavior into more constructive channels. Reminders are frequently given; for example, "Remember that we use the blocks for building," is told to the child who is about to throw a block across the room. Even in those nursery schools or day-care centers that permit the child extensive freedom and self-direction, certain behaviors require adult intervention and redirection. In the publication *Away from bedlam*, Lois Murphy and Ethel Leeper (1970) point out that all good child-care centers forbid the children to (1) throw or destroy toys, (2) break or deface walls or furniture, (3) interfere with another child's play, (4) play with other's towels, washcloths, or combs, (5) throw sand, stones, or any hard object, or (6) bite, spit, hit, push, or otherwise try to hurt another child. Although teachers certainly show varying degrees of tolerance for these behaviors (for example, interfering with others' play), most would agree on this list of "don'ts." Actual observations in preschool classrooms, however, often reveal the following additional behaviors that elicit teacher praise or reprimand (Dopyera, 1969; Lay, 1972):

Implicit and unrecognized ground rules

1. Being involved and busy versus being at "loose ends"
2. Being in a desired place versus "out of place"
3. Doing things at the right time versus doing things at the wrong time
4. Sitting or standing correctly versus having inappropriate body postures
5. Not talking or talking quietly versus talking noisily
6. Being quiet and still versus being noisy and moving rapidly
7. Being personally careful versus being careless and harming self and others
8. Using equipment and materials in appropriate locations versus taking them to inappropriate locations
9. Being careful with equipment and materials versus harming and wasting materials
10. Being orderly, neat, and clean versus being "messy" and dirty

Many teachers who describe themselves as having only a few ground rules for children's behavior actually spend much time and energy aligning children's behavior with their inarticulated views of how they "should" behave. They appear to be quite unaware of the constant efforts they are making to control or direct children's behavior in the above ways.

The following are among the guidelines that have been advocated by various writers for verbally guiding the activities of young children:

1. Give positive suggestions rather than negative ones. Say, "Sit down when you slide," rather than, "Don't stand up when you slide"; say, "Wipe your brush on the jar," rather than, "Don't drip paint on the floor."
2. Speak directly to the child. Rather than shouting directions from distance, approach or sit by the child so that you can speak in a calm, friendly voice and maintain eye contact.
3. Speak in short meaningful sentences that the child will understand. Give a reason for your request but avoid lengthy explanations.
4. Give the child a choice, if possible, but only present realistic choices that you are prepared to accept.
5. Be consistent about behavioral limitations.
6. Use ingenuity rather than confrontation to make situations go smoothly. Help the child establish patterns of happy performance instead of negativism.
7. Allow children time to make transitions to the desired behavior. Avoid forcing children to conform quickly or to turn abruptly from one activity to another.
8. Make the desired behavior seem interesting and attractive.
9. To stop a particular type of activity that is objectionable, provide an alternative. Children are more responsive to new suggestions than to reprimands.
10. Use a variety of methods. If a first request is not successful, word the second request in a different way.
11. Give directions one at a time, if possible, and no more than two at a time. The younger the child, the fewer the number of directions he or she can remember and follow.
12. Give children directions for specific activities at the time and place you want the behavior to occur, not in advance of the situation and setting. For example, give playground directions on the playground, not inside.

Maturationists emphasize that if the program arranged for the child is appropriate for his or her development level, there will be little need for imposing restrictions beyond giving verbal directions. However, if a child is extremely upset and is disturbing to a group, teachers are often advised that *Isolation as the* a child may need to be isolated from the group to calm the entire situation. If *final resort* this action is taken, there should be concern for (1) making the isolation as brief and safe as possible, (2) ensuring that the child understands why he or she was removed, (3) assessing the child's reaction (frightened, calmed, or pleased), (4) establishing some means of terminating the isolation (child's decision or teacher's decision), and (5) explaining the action to the other children. It is important the child not be isolated from the peer group until all other means have proved ineffective. The group situation should be structured so that children are kept from reaching the point of upset that requires such treatment. A disruptive child's behavior should be carefully studied to determine what would provide him or her with more satisfying and instructive involvements.

Teachers are typically advised that neither verbal threats nor physical punishment are desirable alternatives. It is expected that the teacher will have a repertoire of methods for positively guiding children and will not need to rely on physical punishment. However, teachers are expected to take whatever action is needed to preserve the health and safety of the children in their charge, even if this occasionally necessitates physical restraint.

The Bank Street emphasis on the teacher-child relationship

The Bank Street staff emphasizes the teacher-pupil relationship and the establishment of mutual trust. In establishing trust it is believed that teachers must have realistic expectations concerning children, and that children in turn must accept teacher guidance until they become capable of self-direction; children who are destructive and hostile can become responsible and sensitive only by recognizing and accepting the authority of adults who care for and respect them. According to this view there must also be understandable rules and well-defined structures so that children can then learn to regulate and direct themselves.

THE INTERACTIONIST ALTERNATIVE: PROVIDING FREEDOM WITHIN STRUCTURE

Maturationists and interactionists are both concerned with the whole child. Their concern with children's interests, values, and emotions, as well as with their achievements, is reflected in their program ground rules. Interactionists differ from the maturationists, however, in the way their programs are structured, and consequently their ground rules are somewhat different. The major emphasis among interactionists is on rules that facilitate independent activity, especially the planning, initiation, and self-monitoring of "learning" involvements. Related to this are supporting ground rules concerning the treatment of materials, the environment, and peers.

Emphasis on positive attitudes toward school

In the British integrated day programs, for example, the emphasis is on establishing programs in which children are positively inclined toward their work, each other, and their teacher. If successfully implemented, such programs make ground rules secondary to activity and learning. According to Barth (1972), children's enjoyment of school is related to (1) the number of significant options available to them in a day, (2) being given the opportunity to determine the activity in which they will be engaged, (3) being allowed to pose their own problems and to determine how these problems will be solved with respect to the materials and activities available to them, (4) the extent to which there is a climate of consistency and order, and (5) the extent to which competition is minimized.

In regard to a climate of consistent order, Barth (1972) elaborates as follows:

> Open schools are not laissez-faire places where anything goes. The teacher knows and the child knows that an authority is present and that the teacher, no matter how personal and supportive he may be, is that authority. Teachers believe that although a child may appear to work for disorder, no child enjoys disorder. All recognize that unless *someone* is

in charge they will not be able to move freely, explore freely, and choose freely. In many open classes there are only two rules: (1) no destroying equipment, (2) no destroying or interfering with the work of other children. These rules seem sufficient for establishing and maintaining a climate in which learning can flourish. (p. 100)

Expectations of British teachers

After intensively studying the directions and reinforcements given by British infant school teachers, Brandt (1975) concluded:

1. Children were generally expected to have something to do.
2. Children were generally expected to finish something already started before starting something else.
3. Children were expected to have something tangible to show or tell to account for time spent.
4. Children were expected to maintain materials being used and to return items to their proper place after using them.
5. Children were expected to participate in group discussion and to permit others to talk.

Experienced and successful interactionist teachers, who are concerned about developing independence and responsibility in children, often involve them in planning their own activities. Yardley (1973) reports the following comments from one such teacher:

> Each time I take over a new class, I spend the first three or four weeks of the term working out with the children how we shall organize and run our workshop. For example, "Where shall we put the paint easels?", "How can we make sure that when Peter has finished using his rubber apron, it will be ready for Susan to use?", "Can you find a quiet corner where we can read our new books?" All this takes time and each group of children works things out in a different way. After all, the classroom is a workshop which belongs to all the people who work in it, and I'm only one amongst forty. (p. 39)

Children who have experienced this kind of procedural involvement generally work in the same acceptable ways whether the teacher is on hand or not. Once children have accepted responsibility for their own behavior, it becomes possible to use less supervisable spaces—the outdoors, hallways, adjoining rooms.

General guidelines for ground rules

Despite the wide variation in practice regarding ground rules between programers of differing orientations, the following principles appear to underlie all of the approaches:

1. A consistent set of expectations promotes feelings of security and encourages cooperation. Fluctuating expectations, on the other hand, make children's adjustment difficult and prevent a sense of order and mutual trust from emerging. Children's energies, in such unstable situations, are diverted from productive learning involvements into a continuous testing of the situation to find out what is and is not acceptable behavior.

You have just read about variations among program ground rules and how they are established and maintained. Consider the early childhood centers or classrooms with which you are most familiar, and try to answer the following questions:

1. What ground rules are made very explicit for children?

2. Beyond the explicitly stated ground rules, what other behaviors are typically commented upon, either positively through praise or reward, or negatively through scolding or punishment?

3. To what extent are the expectations (both explicit and implicit) likely to contribute to accomplishing the goals of the program?

4. What conclusions, if any, can you draw from your answers to the above question that might prove useful in planning for your own work with children?

2. The clear specification of desired behavior is crucial to developing group norms and thereby guiding individual behavior.

3. Praise or other rewards for positive behavior accomplish far more than negative reactions. Negativism reduces rather than promotes cooperative behavior. General misbehavior from a group of children requires more effective planning strategies on the part of the teacher and more careful specification of desired behaviors. A scolding or punishment is likely to be less effective than a more positive approach.

4. It is important that peer norms develop in the desired direction (from the teacher's standpoint). Once a group begins to accept and identify with teacher expectations, group discussion concerning ground rule modifications becomes feasible and desirable, and has very positive outcomes.

Decisions about Relationships with Families

The importance of involving parents in the education of their children is now commonly recognized by early childhood personnel. Experiences in recent intervention programs such as Head Start and Title I (Elementary and Secondary Education Act) have heightened this awareness. After an extensive study of a variety of school- and home-based programs for disadvantaged children, Bronfenbrenner (1974) concluded that "intervention programs which place major emphasis on involving the parent directly in activities fostering the child's development are likely to have constructive impact at any age, but the earlier such activities are begun, and the longer they are continued, the greater the benefit to the child" (p. 297).

Parent involvement benefits the child

Whether in planning an overall program or in merely teaching within an established program, parent relations are a reality that cannot be avoided. Sometimes that relationship is accidental and undirected. There is increased recognition, however, that the nature of the relationship between the important persons in children's lives—parents and teachers—should not be left to chance. As Grotberg (1972) points out:

The defense of this position rests on moral grounds as well as on research evidence. It does not seem possible for a society to morally justify the encouragement of parent abdication. Parents must be involved in decisions affecting their children, and their role in influencing early development must be recognized. Research in minority, ethnic, and socioeconomic groups makes exceedingly clear the importance of the parents in the early learning of children. There is also research evidence to indicate the parents, when trained, may be as successful in teaching their young children as are the professionals. While this evidence is heartening, the justification for parent participation in decisions and programs affecting their children could be made solely on moral grounds. (pp. 318–19)

Several types of parental involvement now exist, as Gordon (1969) points out. Parents may be viewed as (1) bystanders, observers, and learners, (2) direct and active teachers of their own children at home, (3) aides and volunteers in the school program, or (4) partners and policy-makers.

Photo by permission of Bernice Wright
Cooperative Nursery School.

PARENTS AS BYSTANDERS, OBSERVERS, AND LEARNERS

The traditional view of parental involvement in programs for young children sees parents as bystanders, observers, and learners. Within this view a series of class-teacher (PTA) meetings and a periodic one-to-one conference between teacher and parent are considered ample provision for parent involvement. The meetings typically interpret program practices or inform parents in areas that relate to the care and education of their children. Only in the event of a particular problem is further home-school contact considered important.

PARENTS AS TEACHERS AT HOME

In recent years many other models have been developed for involving parents very directly in the education of their children. The model programs discussed in this section have developed a variety of parental programs. For example, in the Weikart Cognitive Curriculum, the classroom teacher makes regular (weekly) home visits and, in the parent's presence, conducts a typical learning activity that models what is going on at school and also shows the parents how they might assist in the learning process. It is hoped that the parents can be enlisted as active teachers of their children.

In other programs, home visits are made by special liaison personnel other than classroom teacher, called *home visitors, parent educators,* or *child development trainers.* The parent may be taught very specific activities that can be done with the child. These activities may be related to either current development or future school success. Home visitors also show strong approval of parental efforts at working with their children. Such parent education efforts usually benefit all the children in a family even when only one particular child is the objective of the home visitor. Arrangments of this type are made in the DARCEE programs and the Florida Parent Education Follow Through model, among others.

PARENTS AS AIDES AND VOLUNTEERS

The third type of parent involvement involves parents as aides and volunteers in the school program. Parents are required to participate in or contribute to the program in some way as a precondition of their children's enrollment. This arrangement is often referred to as a **cooperative** and is found in both nursery schools and full day-care centers. The rationale for this kind of involvement is twofold. First, it educates the parents regarding what children of that age can do and learn under skilled guidance. Second, it has the practical advantage of appreciably reducing school personnel costs. Whatever the reason for the cooperative plan, the periodic participation of parents in the program, whether on a rotating or a sporadic basis, leads to a closer coordination of home-school efforts.

Cooperatives

Employment as paraprofessionals

In some of the Follow Through models parents are employed, whenever possible, in paraprofessional roles. This is especially the case in programs that have very explicit objectives and procedures, such as the Behavior Analysis and DARCEE programs. The children who benefit the most from these programs are thought to be those whose parents learn and practice the recommended approaches in their daily lives. The most thorough learning takes place with those parents who are employed as aides in the classroom programs.

PARENTS AS PARTNERS AND POLICY-MAKERS

Increasingly, parent groups are accepting a partnership and policy-making role. In this role they assume the initiative by advising professionals of the objectives they have for their children and the practices they prefer. Parent groups are sometimes active in establishing and maintaining new programs that are more in keeping with their own views of child development and learning than programs formerly available to them. They are also becoming increasingly influential within existing programs. This appears to be a very healthy trend—parents who view themselves as active agents regarding their children's care and education generally provide better conditions for their children than parents who feel "impotent" and "inept."

Policy decisions regarding organizational structures for early education are providing for increased parent participation. As one example, the Federal Interagency Day Care Guidelines mandate (1) that parents have the opportunity to become involved in decision-making regarding the nature and operation of the day-care facility in which their children are enrolled; (2) that they

RESPONSE SECTION

You have just read about four types of parent participation: (1) as bystanders, observers, and learners; (2) as teachers at home; (3) as aides and volunteers; (4) as partners and policy-makers. Consider the early childhood centers or classrooms with which you are most familiar and try to answer the following questions:

1. Which of the above roles do the parents take?

2. What actions or arrangements (or lack thereof) do you see as contributing to parents taking one role versus another?

3. What actions or arrangements might the center or school personnel modify if they wished to change the parents' role?

4. What role for parents would contribute most to accomplishing the program goals?

5. What conclusions, if any, can you draw from your answers to the above questions that might prove useful in planning for your own work with parents and children?

have the opportunity to observe or participate in the program; (3) that in centers of forty or more children there be a Policy Advisory Committee that includes not less than 50 percent parents or parent representatives. In federally supported programs such as Head Start, Follow Through, and Parent-Child Centers, parent participation in policy-making is also mandatory. As Hess *et al.* (no date) point out:

> The rationale for parent participation in decision-making is based on the belief that people will not be committed to decisions in which they have no involvement. Furthermore, it is believed that the processes of considering information, decision-making, and implementation are, in themselves, educational and aid in developing leadership skills. It is also argued that parents know their own situations best, and hence must be involved in planning for their children's education. (p. 277)

Summary

Program decisions regarding time, space utilization, ground rules, and relationships with parents are usually directly related to the orientation of the programers. In relation to time organization, environmentalists tend to favor instructionally focused time periods, while maturationists favor broad and balanced time arrangements. Interactionists prefer open time scheduling, in order to facilitate the child's pursuit of involvement for whatever period of time is satisfying.

In arranging the classroom facilities, environmentalists focus on instructional objectives and eliminate items that distract children from instruction and tasks. Maturationists tend to arrange activity centers with equipment and materials that stimulate spontaneous play or activity. Interactionists, following the example of the British, add an array of diverse materials to those maturationists select. In Montessori classrooms very specific pieces of equipment are included to provide satisfying activities for children, some of which are designed to lead directly to academic goals as well.

In regard to ground rules, there are wide variations in terms of both the programers' expectations and the ways in which rules are implemented. Such common themes as consistency, clarity, and positiveness underlie all orientations.

Parents can be involved with programs at four levels: (1) as bystanders, observers, and learners; (2) as teachers at home; (3) as aides or volunteers; (4) as partners and policy-makers. A variety of approaches, matched to the styles and needs of the particular parents, is more likely to prove successful than a single approach.

There are other program decisions, such as relationships with administrators, colleagues, and ancillary staff; assignment of children to "class" groups; and access to facilities with other groups, which we have not addressed directly in this chapter. Some of these decisions will be made by others, such as your administrator or the legislators who enacted the program; some will involve you. Obviously, the particular developmental orientation that is held will play a part in these decisions, as it did in those areas already discussed. Other factors do, however, often enter in, especially community and program administrative factors, and these are discussed in Chapter 16.

REASSESSMENT

Reread what you wrote for the preassessment as you began this chapter, comparing this with your current understandings. Now write on these topics again and incorporate your new insights and knowledge. Continue to update as you prepare for teaching. Save your materials for your portfolio.

Additional Reading

Facilities Planning   *Children's things: A construction guide.* Conway, Mass.: Stone Mountain Educational Projects.

Cohen, M. *Learning centers: Children on their own.* Washington, D.C.: Association for Childhood Education International, 1970.

Educational Facilities Laboratories. *The early learning center.* New York: Educational Facilities Laboratories, 1970.

————. *Found spaces and equipment for children's centers.* New York: Educational Facilities Laboratories, 1972.

————. *Schools for early childhood.* New York: Educational Facilities Laboratories, 1970.

Gross, D. W. Equipping a classroom for young children. *Young Children,* 1968, 24, 100–3.

Jacoby, S. What makes Sue Monell's classroom work? *Learning,* 1973, 1, 58–62.

Kritchevsky, S., and Prescott, E. *Planning environments for young children: Physical space.* Washington, D.C.: National Association for the Education of Young Children, 1969.

Monahan, R. *Free and inexpensive materials for preschool and early childhood.* Belmont, Calif.: Lear Siegler/Fearon, 1973.

Osmon, F. L. *Patterns for designing children's centers.* New York: Educational Facilities Laboratories, 1971.

Palmer, R. *Space, time and grouping: Informal schools in Britain today.* New York: Citation, 1971.

Preschool equipment. Conway, Mass.: Stone Mountain Educational Projects.

West, R. H. *Organization in the classroom.* Oxford: Basil Blackwell, 1967.

Ground Rules   Becker, W. C. *Reducing behavior problems: An operant conditioning guide for teachers.* Urbana, Ill.: ERIC Clearinghouse on Early Childhood Education, 1969. ERIC Document Reproduction Service No. ED 034 570.

Dreikurs, R. *Psychology in the classroom: A manual for teachers.* New York: Harper & Row, 1968.

Hymes, J. L., Jr. *Behavior and misbehavior.* Englewood Cliffs, N.J.: Prentice-Hall, 1955.

Kounin, J. S. *Discipline and group management in classrooms.* New York: Holt, Rinehart and Winston, 1970.

Madsen, C. H., Jr., and Madsen, C. K. *Teaching/discipline: Toward a positive approach*. Boston: Allyn and Bacon, 1970.

Purkey, W. W., and Avila, D. Classroom discipline: A new approach. *Elementary School Journal*, 1971, 71, 325–8.

Read, K. *The nursery school: A human relations laboratory*. Philadelphia: W. B. Saunders, 1971.

Stone, J. G. *A guide to discipline*. Washington, D.C.: National Association for the Education of Young Children, 1969.

Tood, V. E., and Heffernan, H. *The years before school*. New York: Macmillan, 1970.

Relationships with Families

Auerbach, A. B. Parents' role in day care. *Child Care Quarterly*, 1975, 4, 180–7.

Bender, S. A technique for involving parent helpers in a day care setting. *Child Care Quarterly*, 1975, 4, 53–57.

Bromberg, S. L. A beginning teacher works with parents. *Young Children*, 1968, 75–80.

Cory, C. T. Two generations of volunteers: Parents. *Learning*, 1974, 3, 76–79.

Gordon, I. J. *Parent involvement in compensatory education*. Urbana, Ill.: University of Illinois Press, 1968.

Gordon, I. J., and Breivogel, W. F., Eds. *Building effective home/school relationships*. Longwood, N.J.: Allyn and Bacon, Longwood Division, 1976.

Gotkin, L. G. The telephone call: The direct line from teacher to family. *Young Children*, 1968, 24, 70–74.

Honig, A. S. *Parent involvement in early childhood education*. Washington, D.C.: National Association for the Education of Young Children, 1975.

Howard, N. K. *Education for parents of preschoolers: An abstract*. Urbana, Ill.: ERIC/ECE Publication, 1974.

————. *Working with parents in the primary school: An abstract*. Urbana, Ill.: ERIC/ECE Publication, 1974.

Lane, M. B. *Education for parenting*. Washington, D.C.: National Association for the Education of Young Children, 1975.

Marion, M. C. Create a parent space: A place to stop, look and read. *Young Children*, 1973, 28, 221–4.

Seney, H. Two generations of volunteers: Grandparents. *Learning*, 1974, 3, 80–83.

Symposium on parent-centered education. *Childhood Education*, 1971, 48, 126–39.

CHAPTER 16
Your Own Program Decisions

Overview

Describing a Setting and Context for Teaching

Making Your Program Decisions
    YOUR DECISIONS ON GOALS AND OBJECTIVES
    YOUR DECISIONS ABOUT THE ORGANIZATION OF TIME
    YOUR DECISIONS ABOUT FACILITIES: SPACE, EQUIPMENT, AND MATERIALS
    YOUR DECISIONS ABOUT GROUND RULES
    YOUR DECISIONS ABOUT RELATIONSHIPS WITH PARENTS
    RECORD-KEEPING AND EVALUATION IN YOUR PROGRAM
    FURTHER COMMENTARY

Summary

PREASSESSMENT

When you have completed this chapter you should be able to describe and compare the following:

1. *your own goals for programs, and those derived from the three major early childhood perspectives.*
2. *your own program decisions, and those derived from the three major early childhood perspectives.*
3. *methods of record-keeping for children and for your own program performance.*

   Before *beginning to read this chapter:*

1. *take time to write about your current thinking on each of the above topics.*
2. *reflect on the child (children) you observed as you studied Section Two, and for whom you planned involvements in Section Three; plan a comprehensive program for this child (these children) that would facilitate development, explaining why you would choose this program arrangement rather than some other arrangement.*

   Save what you write for rereading, comparison, and elaboration after you have studied and discussed these materials.

Overview

The previous chapters in this section have presented various program models and have shown how each handles time, space, facilities, ground rules, and relationships with parents. You should now consider the type of program that you personally would like to provide for children. Good planning, however, requires an awareness of the social, geographical, economic, and administrative contexts within which your program will operate. In this chapter, therefore, you are asked to (1) consider broad contextual influences that might affect your program, (2) specify, in writing, your preferred context, and (3) make some organizational decisions, given this context.

Describing a Setting and Context for Teaching

Contextual constraints

Decisions about programs must always take into account the particulars of a given setting and context. Decisions that are sound in one situation may be inappropriate in another. For example, scheduling long outdoor activity periods may be appropriate in suburban settings with ample, grassy play space, whereas structured walking trips may be one of the few outdoor options available in urban centers that lack safe outdoor surroundings; climatic factors may also have the same kind of influence on scheduling outdoor periods. Whereas most activities might take place outside in a program located in southern California, children will be mostly indoors in programs in northern New York.

To help you become aware of these contextual factors, we recommend the following two-phase process. First, it will be useful for you to describe the type of setting in which you would most like to work. You will then be asked to make specific program decisions concerning space and time utilization, materials, ground rules, and so forth that are in keeping with your idealized program setting.

Consider the following setting and context factors:

1. *Within what geographical setting would you like to work?* What region of the country? Of the world? What climatic conditions? What seasonal influences? What topographical setting? What proximity to mountains, desert, bodies of water? What demographic considerations: rural, urban, suburban?

2. *What are the characteristics of the children and their families with whom you would like to work?* What ages? What racial, ethnic, linguistic backgrounds? What socioeconomic backgrounds? What performance levels? What value orientations? Which combinations of the above characteristics do you prefer?

3. *What type of sponsorship do you prefer?* Private enterprise? Franchise? Church or charitable organization? Nonprofit agency? Public school system? Industry or institution (providing services for employees or clientele)? Local cooperative? Federal or state supported?

4. *What kind of physical facility do you prefer?* New? Old? One built specifically for educational purposes, or one adapted from other purposes (such as a house, church, or store)? What provisions for toileting, resting, food preparation and serving, outdoor play, active indoor play, storage, etc. do you want?

5. *In what type of school or learning center do you prefer to teach?* How many classes or groups? What size classes or groups? Do you prefer working within a small autonomous center or would you rather be in a subunit of a large organization that consists of many such centers?

6. *What administrative and/or staffing arrangements do you prefer?* Full-time administrator or teaching head? What proportion of professionals to paraprofessional or volunteer staff members? What child-to-adult ratios? Self-contained, departmentalized, or team-teaching arrangements? What ancil-

lary support staff—custodial, food preparation, medical, dental, social work, secretarial, special teachers, librarians, home visitors, psychologists? What type of working relationships with these specialists—assigned, formal, on call?

7. *What general time structure would you like to work within?* What length of sessions? Full day? Half day? Continuous (ten- to twenty-four-hour child care)? Number of days per week? Length of year (term or semester, academic year, full year)?

8. *What type of school location do you prefer in relation to your own residence and those of your students?* Within walking distance? Bus ride? Car transport necessary? To what extent will you wish to participate in the community life of the children and their families? To what extent will you expect to use the community resources for program purposes?

9. *What budgetary provisions would you wish to work within?* What total amount per child? What amount for basic furnishings and equipment? For expendable supplies?

The answers you give to each of the above questions not only reflect your values, but may also affect the kind of program decisions you make. Using the above questions as your guide, write down your preferred specifications for a teaching setting—even though your preferences may not be particularly strong in some areas. Keep these specifications in mind as you attempt to make specific program decisions while studying the rest of this chapter. Even though your actual teaching may not correspond to what you now identify as preferred, due to factors such as practical constraints of the job market, it will be helpful for you to consider how setting and context influence program decisions.

RESPONSE SECTION

You have just been asked to respond to a set of questions regarding the circumstances in which you would most like to work. We suggest that you also reflect on the extent to which you have actually had exposure to some of the variations in program settings suggested by these questions. Are there areas in which you have no direct or second-hand knowledge? Look back over the set of questions and identify those areas in which you lack experience. For the most glaring of your "gaps," consider how you might gain some of these experiences. Might you, for example, make an effort to visit a greater variety of centers within your immediate area? Might you visit programs when you go elsewhere (on vacation, etc.)? Might you talk with persons who have had experiences different from your own?

Making Your Program Decisions

The following discussion will guide you in formulating your own program plans in relation to (1) your overall goals and objectives, (2) time arrangements, (3) arrangement of facilities—space, equipment, and materials, (4) ground rules for children's behavior and involvement, (5) relationships with parents, and (6) record-keeping and program evaluation.

YOUR DECISIONS ON GOALS AND OBJECTIVES

You have been urged repeatedly throughout this text to consider alternative views of child development and learning. At this point, it will again be useful for you to review these perspectives as you choose a set of goals and objectives to fit your idealized program setting. In Chapters 14 and 15 you saw how a programer's developmental orientations provide a guiding framework for selecting a set of program goals and objectives. Maturationists, you may recall, prefer global goals aimed at facilitating the natural growth forces within the whole child. Environmentalists, in contrast, set very precise measurable goals related to specific skills and knowledge. Interactionists, on the other hand, focus on extending children's cognitive repertoires for understanding the social and physical world.

Maturationist goals? What is your own inclination at this point? Do you tend to take the maturationist view that providing emotional support, a secure environment,

---

HEAD START OBJECTIVES

The aims for Head Start, as stated in *Project Head Start: Daily Program I* (1967), are to help children:

- learn to work and play independently, at ease about being away from home, and able to accept help and direction from adults;
- learn to live effectively with other children, and to value one's own rights and the rights of others;
- develop self-identity and a view of themselves as having competence and worth;
- realize many opportunities to strive and to succeed—physically, intellectually and socially;
- sharpen and widen language skills, both listening and speaking;
- be curious—that is, to wonder, to seek answers to questions;
- strengthen physical skills, using large and small muscles;
- grow in ability to express inner, creative impulses—dancing, making up songs, painting, handicrafts, etc.
- grow in ability to channel inner destructive impulses—to turn aggression into hard work, talk instead of hit, understand the difference between feeling angry and acting angry, feel sympathy for the troubles of others. (p. 8)

The following objectives were proposed by Carl Bereiter and Siegfried Engelmann (1966) for the Academic Preschool:

1. Ability to use both affirmative and *not* statements in reply to question "What is this?" "This is a ball. This is not a book."
2. Ability to use both affirmative and *not* statements in response to the command "Tell me about this _____ (ball, pencil, etc.)."
3. Ability to handle polar opposites ("If this is not _____, it must be _____") for at least four concept pairs, e.g., big–little, up–down, long–short, fat–skinny.
4. Ability to use the following prepositions correctly in statements describing arrangements of objects: *on, in, under, over, between*. "Where is the pencil?" "The pencil is under the book."
5. Ability to name positive and negative instances for at least four classes, such as tools, weapons, pieces of furniture, wild animals, farm animals and vehicles. "Tell me something that is a weapon." "A gun is a weapon." "Tell me something that is not a weapon." "A cow is not a weapon." A child should be able to apply these class concepts correctly to nouns with which he is familiar, e.g., "Is a crayon a piece of furniture?" "No, a crayon is not a piece of furniture. A crayon is something to write with."
6. Ability to perform simple *if-then* deductions. The child is presented a diagram containing big squares and little squares. All the big squares are red, but the little squares are of various colors. "If the square is big, what do we know about it?" "It's red."
7. Ability to use *not* in deductions. "If the square is little, what else do we know about it?" "It is not red."
8. Ability to use *or* in simple deductions. "If the square is little, then it is not red. What else do we know about it?" "It's blue or yellow."
9. Ability to name the basic colors, plus white, black and brown.
10. Ability to count aloud to 20 without help and to 100 with help at decade points (30, 40, etc.).
11. Ability to count objects correctly up to ten.
12. Ability to recognize and name the vowels and at least 15 consonants.
13. Ability to distinguish printed words from pictures.
14. Ability to rhyme in some fashion to produce a word that rhymes with a given word, to tell whether two words do or do not rhyme, or to complete unfamiliar rhyming jingles like "I had a dog and his name was Abel: I found him hiding under the _____."
15. A sight reading vocabulary of at least four words in addition to proper names, with evidence that the printed word has the same meaning for them as the corresponding spoken word. "What word is this?" "*Cat*." "Is this a thing that goes 'Woof-woof'?" "No, it goes 'Meow.'" (pp. 48–49)

Source: From Carl Bereiter and Siegfried Engelmann, *Teaching disadvantaged children in the preschool,* © 1966, pp. 48–49. Reprinted by permission of Prentice-Hall, Inc., Englewood Cliffs, N.J.

The following statements of program goals are from Weikart's Cognitive Curriculum (Weikart *et al.*, 1971):

1. To help the child develop logical modes of thought through concept formation
   a. to gain knowledge about himself and objects
   b. to see relationships between himself and things in his environment
   c. to group and order objects and events
2. To help the child develop the capacity to manipulate symbols and thus to act on and represent the environment. (pp. 6–7)

and a balance of different types of activities should be the prime consideration in your programing? Are you inclined to accept children's current performance as "right" for them at their particular stage, rather than trying to modify their behavior or hasten their learning?

Environmentalist goals? Or do you see teaching and programing as the environmentalist does, as best directed toward very specific measurable objectives within carefully selected domains? Do you feel that your role as a teacher should be to quickly move children toward such precise but limited objectives? Would you, for example, agree with Bereiter and Engelmann (1966) that certain minimum standards of academic attainment should be precisely stated and should be the primary focus of instruction so that both the students and the program can be more readily evaluated?

Or do you see both of these approaches as inadequate—the first too global, the second too narrow? Do you feel that they are both too uniform and unrelated to the development of individual children? Do you see the child's self-initiated activity as central to the whole educational process? Do you *Interactionist goals?* view the teacher's role as a process of interacting with children in learning experiences that have been carefully tailored to fit their current level of cognitive functioning? Do you feel that learning should be organized around environmental resources—whether they be butterflies, numbers, words, or mud pies—rather than around academic disciplines (such as math and social studies)?

At this point, try to write down your own teaching goals, taking into account the characteristics of the program setting that you specified. Do not try to do this all in one sitting, however. For best results, work on it, put it away, take it out again, and revise it until it gradually begins to feel "right" to you.

In doing this you may find it helpful to examine program guides, textbooks, and curriculum statements. Talk with others about their program goals and objectives. Modify your own statements until you feel satisfied *A cumulative folder* with them. Keep this list along with subsequent planning documents called for in this chapter in a cumulative folder. You may also wish to collect divergent plans that contrast with your own to sharpen your own views. In short, try to develop your ability to articulate your own point of view, why you prefer one kind of objective and reject others.

YOUR DECISIONS ABOUT THE ORGANIZATION OF TIME

The previous chapter outlined different programing practices in relation to time schedules. Three major patterns of time were described: (1) broad and balanced time periods, (2) periods with an instructional focus, and (3) "open" time arrangements. Broad and balanced time periods with structured transitions between periods were favored by maturationists, as most in keeping with the developmental levels of young children; environmentalists preferred periods with a subject matter focus; interactionists generally favored "open" time arrangements that allow individual children to complete their involvements. Each of these general approaches to scheduling is viable, of course, given the respective orientation and objectives of the programer. At this point, you must determine the approach to time scheduling that will best support the goals and objectives you have described.

Appropriateness of time arrangement for program setting described

In making your decisions about the organization of time, keep in mind the program setting you described previously. For example, does your schedule fit within the program day that you specified? Work out a time schedule that (1) gives the name of each activity or instructional segment, and (2) suggests the average duration and sequencing of these periods. If you are inclined toward the more open time structures, include optional activities for each period. Consider, also, whether time constraints such as the use of shared facilities or the need for special teachers must be accommodated in your program setting. If the setting you described includes these features, they should be taken into account in arranging your time schedule.

Congruence with goals

Try to make your time plan congruent with your previously defined goals and objectives. Think about the sequence of activities from a child's point of view. Try to visualize how the child (children) you observed while studying Section Two would fare within the time structure you are proposing. Also try to view it from your own perspective as a teacher. Think through factors such as the preparations that would be necessary at particular points, or what management problems might result. If possible, ask experienced teachers to examine your proposed schedule for unanticipated effects.

Another way to view the organization of time is through a larger base. Rather than using the day as your basic unit, you might organize around the month or the year. This approach, combined with daily schedules, has the advantage of forcing you to consider gradual modifications in scheduling across a broader time span.

Finally, file your time schedule with your goals and objectives in your cumulative folder, along with any supporting or contrasting views that might prove helpful in explaining your plan to others (such as parents or supervisors).

YOUR DECISIONS ABOUT FACILITIES: SPACE, EQUIPMENT, AND MATERIALS

In the discussion of facilities in Chapter 15, we saw how both maturationists and interactionists (and especially the latter) favor a materials-rich environment where children can have "hands-on" experiences. Conversely, we saw how environmentalists were more interested in textbooks and verbal instruction than in manipulative materials. Environmentalists would even emphasize that a setting devoid of distracting toys and materials makes instructional sessions easier to manage. In planning your own facility arrangements, you must again examine your goals and objectives and then try to determine what would best facilitate these goals.

Selection of equipment and materials

Keeping in mind your two previous planning documents—your statement of goals and objectives and your time schedule—begin your planning of facilities by preparing a list of the equipment and materials you would ideally wish to include in your program. Plan within the budgetary figures you listed for basic furnishings and expendables—you will need to acquire current school supply catalogs in order to plan realistically. In making your selections, keep in mind the activities you want to provide, as well as factors such as safety, durability, quality, functionality, and flexibility. If your budget does not accommodate the equipment and supplies you need, you will have to consider free or inexpensive sources.

Arrangement of equipment and materials

Once you have prepared your basic list of equipment and materials, your next task is to make decisions about the placement of these materials in a room or rooms you consider ideal for your program. Make a general outline of the space within which you visualize yourself working. It may be useful to draw this space to scale on graph paper, and to draw the major pieces of equipment to scale so that they can be cut out and moved around on the scaled drawing to determine the most advantageous arrangement. Do this planning in as much detail as possible, thinking of the consequences of one kind of placement or storage versus another. Keep in mind considerations such as quiet versus noisy, group versus individual, wet versus dry, etc. Do your planning in terms of "starting" your program, but also consider whether and how you might wish to change that arrangement across time.

You should also consider how to make your program space attractive and appealing. The judicious use of color, shape, and texture can assist you in creating a good learning environment. Although it may not be practical at this time to actually acquire the fabrics, objects, and other raw materials that you plan to use in your classroom, you might do well to begin making plans for their acquisition. Many a beginning teacher has been alarmed at encountering a barren classroom and has belatedly scurried around trying to collect things to make it warmer and to appear more attractive. Some forethought could ease this process. Note, for example, things seen in program spaces (such as bulletin boards, walls, and floor coverings) that appeal to you, and gradually accumulate a list of these materials and their possible sources.

As with your other plans, try to obtain as much feedback as possible about the facilities you are planning. Imagine the mix of children you are planning for and try to anticipate their responses to the space you are creating. Think again about the child (children) you observed in Section II and consider how they might react to your arrangements. What would individual children do in the various locations within the classroom(s)? Visualize your own position at various points throughout your time schedule and decide whether your spatial arrangement will facilitate or inhibit the attainment of your goals.

Finally, you should continue to update and modify your plan for facilities in terms of new materials, equipment, or arrangements that you encounter, and to accommodate any basic shifts in your program orientation.

YOUR DECISIONS ABOUT GROUND RULES

The relationship between program goals and expectations for children's behavior was discussed in Chapter 15. Attentive, task-oriented behaviors are carefully reinforced by environmentalists, whereas social and exploratory involvements are discouraged. In contrast, interactionist ground rules help establish a setting within which children can autonomously initiate, explore, and experiment. Maturationists emphasize a gradual acceptance of "routines" by the children, with few explicit ground rules.

In making decisions about ground rules, you might find it useful to formulate three lists: (1) the ground rules *you* will set for children's behavior and involvement, (2) the ground rules you will develop *with* the children, and (3) the procedures you will use to enforce your ground rules. The following two exercises will help you think about the ground rules that will be necessary in your classroom.

Ground rules for various locations
First, use an object to represent a child and place it in various locations in your classroom drawing. As you move the "child" from place to place, consider what he or she should and should not be doing in each of these locations. For example, is it permissible to climb on the window sills, to crawl under the tables, to run, or to experiment with mixing paints at the easel?

Ground rules for various time periods
Second, for each of the time periods in your scheduling document, consider whether children in your classroom might engage in the following activities (Dopyera and Lay, 1975) should they care to do so:

- go to the bathroom
- get a drink of water
- rest, be left alone, have privacy
- move freely around the room
- engage in large muscle movement (except running)
- practice fine-muscle coordination (other than with pencil or crayon)
- run, play, tease, chase other children
- talk informally with other children
- receive responsive undivided individual attention from you on something important enough to the student that he or she initiates contact with you
- have informal involvement in dramatic play

- have informal involvement with music (singing, dancing, rhythm, etc.)
- have informal involvement with art (painting, clay modeling, woodworking, etc.)
- have informal involvement with math, science, nature study
- have informal involvement in reading and writing (p. 141)

As you consider your ground rules, try to keep in mind your program goals and objectives. Avoid assuming that any behavior is right or wrong simply because it follows your own childhood school experiences. Examine your reasoning for each of your judgments. Try to align your program goals as closely as possible with what you allow or prohibit in the program setting.

When you have formulated the three lists, file them with your other planning documents. Make comparisons, whenever possible, between your plans and (1) what you find yourself actually doing with children, and (2) what you observe other teachers doing in their early childhood programs. As you gain further experience you may want to modify your statements on ground rules to accommodate new insights regarding child behavior or the role of teachers.

YOUR DECISIONS ABOUT RELATIONSHIPS WITH PARENTS

Crucial questions on relationships with parents

Given the diversity of views regarding child development and schooling, a "perfect" meshing of your own views with those of the parents you serve is highly improbable. In most instances, you will find that at least some of the parents will have expectations that are quite different from your own regarding the care and education of their children. The crucial questions then become:

1. How can you find significant points of agreement that will establish a strong enough communication base to permit rational discussion of other, more controversial issues?
2. How can you learn which of the parents' concerns are most significant to them, so that you can find ways to accommodate these despite your contrary convictions?
3. How can you most effectively demonstrate and communicate your own views so that they will be accepted and adopted by the parents?

The care with which you have planned each of the previous decision areas presented in this chapter will have a bearing on how convincingly you can present your program to parents. The answers to all three of the above questions must come, however, through continuous exchanges with parents in which you ask, listen, and talk—in that order. Parent meetings, parent conferences, home visits, newsletters, and parent participation will prove beneficial to the extent that they lead to a continuous exchange of views.

Accommodating individual differences among parents

It is your responsibility as a professional to find ways of relating to the parents you serve. Notes or phone calls requesting help or expressing concern, or gifts that relate to the child (such as photographs or simple toys), may be helpful in making parent contacts. Some will respond well to conversations about educational topics or about the specific accomplishments of their child. Other parents will interact with you more comfortably while engaged in some manual task, such as construction, cooking, or materials preparation. Some prefer home visits, others prefer to talk at school. Rather than relying on a single approach to parents, develop alternatives that can be matched to individual preferences. It goes without saying that the degree and quality of your relationship with parents depends on your attitude toward them. If you expect involvement on their part, you will likely get it. Conversely, if you expect apathy or if you actively wish to avoid their involvement, you will probably see these expectations fulfilled.

You will find it beneficial to write out a general plan for parent involvement that is logical in terms of your program setting. You may wish to make at least two lists: (1) the principles and goals you would use to guide your interactions with parents and (2) the particular strategies you might possibly employ.

RECORD-KEEPING AND EVALUATION IN YOUR PROGRAM

Thus far, you have been considering how to best organize your program and you have prepared documents describing (1) your goals and objectives, (2) your time schedule, (3) your space and facility arrangements, (4) your ground rules, and (5) your relationship with parents. There is yet another plan you need to make—a plan for keeping records.

Record-keeping maintains focus

Record-keeping is important for several reasons, but the foremost one is to keep you focused on your major goals and objectives and to avoid being distracted by lesser concerns. One of our colleagues has a sign that reads, "When one is surrounded by hungry alligators, it is difficult to keep in mind that one's goal was to drain the swamp." The distractions in teaching are not as threatening as hungry alligators, but it is important that you maintain a focus on your primary goals. This can be difficult in the middle of demands such as collecting milk money, cleaning up spilled paint, helping with stuck zippers, and keeping children supplied with sharpened pencils.

What you keep track of, you are most likely to accomplish. As an illustration of this point, consider the dieting phenomenon. You may decide that you need to lose weight and must therefore cut back on high-calorie foods. Many people make such decisions; only a few actually lose weight. Obstacles keep getting in the way—they are invited out to dinner; leftovers need to be eaten; there is only time for a candy bar. For many of us, it is only when we actually calculate on an ongoing basis the number of calories we consume that we manage to achieve our weight reduction goal. Record-keeping makes an important contribution to achieving the goal. It has a similar function in teaching.

Two types of records

There are two major types of records that you may wish to keep for purposes of evaluation and future planning. The first deals with the effectiveness of the program itself, including your own performance. The second deals with the children's participation and achievements.

Several approaches are available for either type of record-keeping. One involves *descriptive narrative,* which records significant happenings in writing, sometimes in the form of a daily log. This approach is highly flexible in that the writer records in as much detail as necessary whatever seems interesting. Its disadvantage is that the writer's interests may be too limited to produce a broad, well-balanced record.

A second approach uses *category systems,* which focus the observer's attention on particular kinds of behavior. Any behavior within the category description is noted by the observer. The feedback obtained is of a quantitative nature (for example, frequency counts) and therefore can be compared across time. This approach does not provide the richness of description of the narrative approach.

In Section Two, you used a combination of the category system and descriptive narrative. Categories or questions were provided to guide your observations, but you were also asked to write in narrative form the incidents that fell within each of these categories. For purposes of comprehensiveness and subsequent communication, this mixed type of record has a considerable advantage.

A third approach involves rating certain behaviors, achievements, or involvements against some normative rating scale—letter grades are the most common example. The advantages of rating scales are (1) the ease and speed

Photo by John Young.

with which they can be used, (2) their ability to produce a comparative record across time, and (3) the ability to be used simultaneously by a variety of persons. The disadvantages of rating scales are (1) the difficulty of knowing what observations led to the rating, (2) their limited usefulness in communicating with others due to their lack of information, and (3) the inability to offer clues concerning what might be done to improve the rating. Ratings are therefore best used in conjunction with other, more descriptive records.

Record-keeping and your own performance

Records on actual time use

Let us now examine more specifically the kind of records that you might wish to keep on your own program and teaching performance. In regard to the program, you may wish to keep a weekly record of your time allotments and compare these data with your idealized time schedules. For example, if you feel that a range of experiences with art media is desirable, you may wish to calculate the portion of your weekly program that children have access to these materials.

Records on contact with individual children

Again, you may wish to periodically go through your class list and reflect on the extent and nature of your interactions with each child relative to your program goals. For example, you might have decided in your planning to work individually with each child, helping him or her to write about some high-interest topic. Such an activity would fit well with the maturationist or interactionist approaches to language arts and reading instruction. However, plans often fall short of reality. Checking through your class list at regular intervals is one way to review your interaction and to align it more closely with your program goals.

Narrative accounts of teaching performance in daily log

Adaptations of record-keeping procedures can sometimes be beneficial in monitoring your own teaching behavior. A narrative account, for example, might be kept in the form of a daily log. The log would probably center around incidents that are easily compared with your ideal view of teaching, incidents that either support or refute your model. Your "highs" and your "lows" are most likely to be recorded. The following are log entries of two beginning teachers. The first teacher, Cynthia, briefly recorded the incidents about which she felt most positive or negative. The second, Anne, wrote a more involved account. The following excerpt is from Cynthia's log:

- Didn't react to Alex's clowning. What an accomplishment!
- Found a "just right" book to go with Lisa's sharing of her shell collection.
- Wasn't unduly rattled by Ginger's insolence and was able to show her the necessity for replacing things after use. Better than my behavior with Peter yesterday.
- Gave in finally to one of Renne's whining bids for attention. Probably will generate another whole stream of whining behavior. Well, try again tomorrow!
- Wasn't well enough prepared for planting activities and spent more time in trying to get it organized than in listening and teaching.

The following excerpt is from Anne's log:

What a day! Everything happened today. I guess I should have been better prepared for what would happen on Halloween. Next year I will be!

A lot of kids dictated fantastic stories today about the paintings they made of witches, pumpkins, ghosts. Real emotion attached to those topics which made them super interested in telling stories and asking about which words said which things. Really strong involvement—just like Sylvia Ashton-Warner says in *Teacher*. Ricky wanted me to write, "Witches and ghosts are real scary. Boo to you!" on his picture of ghosts. (Having that white paint at the easel got it started.) After I wrote what he wanted, he said, "What's a ghost really? I don't mean like dressed up in a sheet. *I mean really!*" Egads, I'd never thought about how to explain ghosts to five-year-olds. I mumbled something inadequate about some people thinking that people who died had invisible spirits which continued living after their bodies died. Wish I had asked him more about what he already knew about ghosts and why he was wondering and wish I had been better prepared to answer that kind of question. But, gosh, what can you say to a question like that?

The biggest problem today was the confusion about whether or not kids were to wear costumes. Some did from the beginning of the session and behaved in keeping with their get-ups most of the time. Peter, as a tiger, kept pretending to eat people and when he had his mask on really terrified Bridget and Aaron. And Rusty, with his pillow stuffed inside a shirt as a fat man, was a real "invite" for punching for the other kids. For a while he appeared to enjoy it but then it was evidently more than he could handle. I tried to explain to him that if he took his costume off the hitting would stop. I also tried to explain to the other children that he didn't want to be hit . . . but it continued.

But worst of all, was the upset of the kids who didn't have costumes. Mary [colleague across the hall] was well prepared with a sack full of new dress-ups but I hadn't thought of that. Was pleased with my ingenuity though. In a hurry with brown bags, a bit of paint and some masking tape, I made Rudy, Martin and Michelle into chipmunks.

But then, *horrors,* what with the "seven" sets of treats the kids brought to share, plus all the excitement, Willie vomited on Pansy's "dancer" outfit. Oh, wow. At least most kids got lots of involvement in counting, arranging, recounting, eating, rearranging, recounting, eating, recounting, out of those goodies before they did Willie in.

Next Halloween, I'll be a smarter teacher. I'll have clearer communication with parents on dress-ups and on treats. And I'll give some thought to explaining "adult" conceptions of ghosts, witches, and the like.

At least, T.G.I.F. today. Nothing boring about my job though. Keeps me on my toes . . . and sometimes on my knees . . . cleaning up!

Another approach is to have others observe your teaching behavior and provide you with (1) descriptive narratives of your performance during specified periods or activities, or (2) a numerical count of some specific behavior you are interested in. One former first-grade teacher, Jane Stallings, now a prominent researcher, often describes how she gained feedback on her performance as a reading teacher. She hired someone to watch her work with reading groups and to tally the frequency with which she engaged in certain behaviors she thought were important. She even paid for this service from her own earnings. In your own case, friends, aides, or colleagues might be asked to periodically sit in on your classroom and provide such feedback. The following list suggests the kinds of behaviors you might wish to have described or counted during particular segments of your teaching day:

- The amount of approval versus disapproval that you dispense.
- The amount of time that you spend controlling behavior versus instructing.
- The complexity of the language you use in giving directions.
- How frequently you interact with students on a personal versus an impersonal basis.
- The frequency with which you attend or talk to certain children.
- The frequency with which your talk is directed to an individual versus a group.

Table 16.1 Sample Teacher Appraisal Scale
1–inferior; 2–weak; 3–adequate; 4–good; 5–outstanding;

1. Personal qualities (posture, voice, dress, grooming, poise, temperament, manners)	1 2 3 4 5
2. Professional characteristics (attitude toward pupils, relationships with colleagues, acceptance of criticism, general use of language, classroom control and management)	1 2 3 4 5
3. Knowledge of subject (general background, specific preparation, use of resources, familiarity with materials, organization of material)	1 2 3 4 5
4. Teaching skill (motivation, pupil participation, skill in providing for individual differences, skill in using chalkboard and other aides, skill in questioning, in drills, in making assignments, in directing class activities, and in evaluating pupil progress)	1 2 3 4 5

Once you have identified the behaviors that you wish to have assessed, your performance will probably improve simply as a result of increased awareness. Keeping ongoing records of your own behavior is a time-consuming but highly effective way of improving your teaching performance.

In many situations you will routinely receive ratings by supervisors and administrators. Table 16.1 shows a sample teacher rating system. Ratings alone, however, give you little information other than how you compare with whatever norm the rater is using. To benefit from ratings you must find out what the observer had in mind when making the rating. This might be especially important for items on which you receive a "low" rating.

Tape recording or videotaping

In some situations, you may also find that you can periodically tape record or videotape yourself in the act of teaching. If videotape or tape recordings are objectively assessed against a set of idealized criteria, their usefulness will be greatly enhanced. Some examples of what you might look for in a videotape recording are: (1) Do I look directly at children as I talk to them? (2) Do I speak clearly and audibly? (3) Does my "body language" (facial expressions, postures, and movements) facilitate my teaching objectives? (4) To what behaviors in children do I respond positively? Negatively?

Record-keeping of children's behavior and development

In the rush of daily activity, keeping records of children's involvements and achievements is easily slighted unless it is built into the overall teaching plan. Keeping records of children is important for three reasons. The main reason, as with program and teacher record-keeping, is to provide an ongoing focus for your efforts. Since you are more likely to accomplish the things that you track, you should see to it that your record-keeping is directed toward significant matters. A second reason for keeping records is to evaluate your program's impact on the children you teach. Changes in children's performance levels and behaviors occur very gradually and are quite hard to recall and assess without written records or other visible evidence. Finally, it is only with precise records that one can adequately communicate about the progress of a given child or group of children to parents and other concerned professionals who may be able to assist your work.

Record-keeping provides focus

Accumulation of children's work

The most important records that you can keep are those that will help you determine the extent to which you are accomplishing the particular goals and objectives you have set for your program. There are many ways of keeping these records. One of the most effective is to simply accumulate the products of the children's creative and written efforts. Weekly or monthly samples of a first-grader's attempts at handwriting, for example, can show dramatic change and may become a revelation to the child, the parents, and even to you as the teacher.

If the tape recording or videotape equipment is available, you may find it very worthwhile to record real-life behavior sequences in areas related to your objectives. These might focus on academic objectives, such as the use of books, or on social matters, such as interaction with peers. You must determine for yourself what kind of behavior needs to be recorded given your program objectives.

If you have rather broad objectives, you may wish to write anecdotal descriptions that record the important events in your program related to those objectives. Some teachers keep notebooks with a separate section for each child. The following is a sample entry from a record on Danny, age three:

- Played with play dough for 45 minutes to an hour. Engaged in much conversation with others around the table about the objects they were making—wheels for cars, pumpkins, bananas, hot dogs, balls, etc. Also talked about big mean kids who might hit them and how they were going to do that to them when they got bigger than them.
- After hearing the story "The Meanest Man," he asked, "Why was he so mean?" I asked what he thought about why he was so mean and he said, "Because nobody likes him."
- Did one puzzle five times without stopping. As he finished it each time, said to himself, "All by myself."
- Danny invited Susan to ride in his block "car." He said that it wouldn't start and suggested that they take a bus or plane instead.
- Danny has quite good control of his pencil and crayon considering that he holds them so awkwardly.
- Brought his toy car to school but the wheel kept falling off. He and I tried to guess how far it would go before the wheel would fall off. He really enjoyed it and then tried to find all kinds of ways to hold the wheel in place. White glue finally did the trick.

The following are excerpts from a record on Nancy, age seven:

- Dictated and illustrated a very imaginative book on the *Adventures of the mouse who married a rabbit.* The major point of it all appeared to be the problem of the male mouse finding something to stand on so he would be higher than his rabbit bride for the ceremony. (Those sex roles stereotypes again.) Later in the day she wrote her own story about "The adventures of the dog who won a prize." She spelled, figuring words out for herself, *prize* as *prys, won* as *one,* and *eyes* as *Is.* The prize the dog won was a pair of glasses because he had bad "*Is.*"
- Figured out for herself all the combinations which can make seven. Really pleased. Said, "Tomorrow, I will do eight and the next day, nine, and the next day, ten. Then I'll rest for awhile."

Anecdotal records within preset categories

You will also need to gain periodic feedback concerning general, non-goal-oriented behavior patterns. Observations of a broad range of behaviors, such as those posed in Section II, are appropriate for this purpose. For example, you might keep a notebook section on each child in your classroom that contains standardized questions and space for writing observations. The particular format is less important than the fact that, from time to time, you stop and consider how children are developing in a broad range of areas. Whether your program is oriented toward cognitive or social and emotional goals, you will still need to make a periodic assessment of your children's development in other areas. You may be surprised at developments, both positive and negative, that have taken place in nontargeted areas.

Your own informal classroom assessments can be supplemented by standardized testing, which provides feedback on how your children compare with the broader population on certain kinds of tasks. Such normative information, while valuable for broad comparative analysis, cannot help you assess the attainment of your program goals unless the test items agree with those goals. Although this seems obvious, many teachers assume that the items on "formal" tests automatically correspond with program objectives. In reality, there is no necessary correspondence between what is easily measured and normal and what is most worthy of program emphasis.

Standardized tests may be highly appropriate to environmentalist objectives and quite unrelated to those of maturationists. In the same manner, Piagetian conservation or classification tasks may be irrelevant to environmentalists, but highly appropriate to interactionists. While a broad base of information is generally useful in program evaluation, it is important to recognize whether a testing device is providing only supplementary information, or information directly related to the program objectives. Evidence relating to program objectives is obviously your top priority in evaluating program efforts.

We recommend that you make some preliminary decisions at this point about the kinds of records you wish to keep. Briefly write out your record-keeping plans for inclusion with your other planning documents, or, if you are so motivated, try designing actual record-keeping instruments (notebook size) that reflect your program goals. Should you find an opportunity to use these, even on a brief trial basis, you will undoubtedly see ways they can be improved for later use.

FURTHER COMMENTARY

There are, of course, other program decisions made prior to or in the process of teaching that are not discussed in this chapter. For example, many studies on teaching behavior report that, on an average day, teachers make thousands of spontaneous, on-the-spot decisions. Beyond these momentary decisions, many other program-related decisions must be made, such as how

to relate your program to broader school and community contexts. In some communities local organizations such as the Chamber of Commerce, Red Cross, Parks and Recreation Department, and local industry provide tours, demonstrations, or films that can enrich the school program. You need to learn about such options, so that you can decide whether or not to use them in your program.

Most programs make provisions for children to have access to resource persons beyond those found in their immediate classrooms. Examples are counselors, nurses, specialized therapists (such as for speech and hearing difficulties), and reading specialists. Most public schools have supporting professional and paraprofessional staffs that provide such services to children both inside and outside the classroom. Although teachers rarely have

In this chapter you have been asked to make decisions about the kind of program you would like to conduct. As you have grappled with these decision areas, you have probably also considered your state of readiness for conducting such a program. At this point, it should prove useful to do the following:

1. Make a list of the areas in which you feel a need for further development in preparation for the kind of teaching you hope to do.

2. For each item on the above list, think of as many different ways as you can for how you might develop your abilities in this area. Consult others for further ideas.

3. From the ideas you generate, establish a plan for your further development that includes a way of determining to what extent you are meeting your program goals.

any control over the availability of such specialists, they are responsible for deciding how to work with them. Although you cannot make specific plans in this area until faced with a specific problem setting, you should become aware of such services and what to expect from the individuals who provide them.

Synthesis into a comprehensive and coherent program

Running throughout this chapter is the view that there is a broad array of options to choose from in planning your program. For ease of presentation we have discussed these as separate topics. The major issue of program organization, however, is how to combine these separate features into a comprehensive and coherent program that facilitates growth and learning in individual children, that is satisfying for you personally, and that meets the demands of both your school and the broader community.

Summary

In this chapter you have been urged to consider several aspects of program planning in order to prepare documents that implement your general view of teaching in a concrete program. The documents you were asked to prepare included:

a statement of your goals and objectives
your decisions about the scheduling of time
your decisions about facilities (space, equipment, supplies)
your decisions about ground rules
your strategies for relating to parents
your strategies for keeping program records and evaluating your own program

At this point, whether your planning documents meet your criteria for comprehensiveness or logical coherence is not the issue. Their immediate value lies in their ability to make you face the various realities associated with teaching. You will of course have to modify these paper plans in order to adapt to the realities of a particular teaching situation. However, you now should at least be able to approach your professional career with somewhat more awareness and confidence than if you had not engaged in these endeavors.

REASSESSMENT

Reread what you wrote for the preassessment as you began this chapter, comparing this with your current understandings. Now write on these topics again and incorporate your new insights and knowledge. Continue to update as you prepare for teaching. Save your materials for your portfolio.

EPILOGUE

Throughout this book four qualities have been emphasized as essential to becoming a successful teacher of young children. In Section One you examined your *commitment* to teaching. This quality was stressed initially since only when you have realistically identified yourself as a teacher can you devote the time and energy necessary for the other tasks of preparation.

Without a keen awareness of children's behavior and development you will not be able to determine whether a particular activity or material is appropriate for individual children. Section Two was designed to develop this *sensitivity* to children's behavior and development.

Although sensitivity to children's behavior is essential in determining what general types of activities and instruction may be appropriate, it is not sufficient in itself. Beyond this, you need to have a broad repertoire for identifying learning possibilities within a variety of situations and with diverse materials. Section Three contributed to the development of your teaching *resourcefulness*.

In Section Four you learned of alternatives for the *organization* of programs and made some preliminary decisions about arrangements for the setting you specified as the one in which you would most like to teach. In Sections Two and Four you also considered how you may tend toward one or more of the three basic orientations regarding child development—environmentalist, maturationist, and interactionist. With these perspectives, you are prepared to make program decisions and develop strategies that will produce a coherent and effective program.

If you have thoughtfully studied these sections and engaged in the suggested activities, you have made an excellent start toward preparation for teaching. And, what may be even more important, you now have an idea of the kinds of activities in which you can continue to engage to prepare yourself more fully prior to actual employment. Regardless of your current level of accomplishment in preparing yourself, you cannot expect to perform as a "veteran" until you have accrued considerable experience. The program you provide in your first years of teaching will not be as comprehensive or as individualized as those you will ultimately be able to provide. While the eventual goal—at least from our bias—is to provide programs that contribute to the broadest possible development in the most individualized way, it is only as you mature in experience, competence, and confidence that this goal can be approached. We therefore emphasize continued development within the broad framework we have proposed. You will continue to expand your sensitivity, resourcefulness, and organizational abilities throughout your teaching career.

Your continued activity will prove especially beneficial in two areas: (1) modification of your program plans in light of the actual circumstances of your eventual employment, and (2) consideration of how you will sustain your own basic intentions in the face of forces and situational factors in the "real world." Your survival, effectiveness, and satisfaction in teaching will depend on how you adapt to the situation in which you will actually teach, and on whether you find ways to both fulfill your own personal needs and meet your teaching goals.

However, any attempt to project the circumstances you may face during your professional career is clearly impossible. In Chapter 16 you considered some of the possible variations in situational factors that can markedly influence what you encounter as a teacher. These included variations in geographical settings; characteristics of children and families; sponsorship of programs; size of organizations; administrative and staffing arrangements; calendar and hours; and budgetary provisions. You will benefit from further analyses of these factors in advance of seeking employment. Take advantage of any opportunity to visit and learn about characteristics of different programs. First, determine the settings within which you personally could or could not find satisfaction in teaching, and, second, learn how teachers operate differently, according to their own convictions, within similar settings. Through the latter kind of observation, you may learn to what extent particular contextual factors can support a range of different styles and orientations—including those similar to your own. Clearly, there is significant variation between organizational structures, and it will also make a tremendous difference to you whether you are within a child-care context, a half-day nursery, or a primary classroom. You can best learn of these and other similar situational effects, however, through direct experiences. Make sure, for example, that you know the characteristics of the various program settings within your local community. Use the set of questions posed at the start of Chapter 16 as a guide in this effort. You can also use your vacations and trips to other locations and regions as opportunities to visit various types of early childhood programs. You will gradually acquire a very realistic view of variations among programs for young children that are influential in supporting or constraining teachers' efforts.

Beyond the immediate context, there are also, of course, broader cultural influences that will affect your practice as a teacher and about which you will wish to be informed. The cultural expectations for schooling and the role of teachers have changed markedly from the beginning of this century to the present, and can be expected to change at an ever-increasing rate as we move toward the twenty-first century.

In 1900, for example, schooling for the very young was not typically available or deemed desirable. While most cities provided some nursery schools and kindergartens, attendance in these programs was more the exception than the rule. Children were typically enrolled in the school program for the express purpose of being taught to read, write, and "reckon," and entered at an age when this instruction could begin. Because the population of the United States was still predominantly rural, farm activities often took precedence over school activities. The teacher, in many instances, had no particular training for teaching. A high school education was considered a sufficient education for a teacher, and less than that was often acceptable. The applicant for a teaching position usually had only to demonstrate literacy and some knowledge of the state and nation through a written examination and an oral defense.

Throughout the early part of the century, the rural teacher, in addition to full responsibility for teaching grades one through eight, also served as the school's administrator, custodian, nurse, social worker, and school psychologist. In a word, the teacher did whatever had to be done in the school. This included starting and maintaining the wood or coal fire in a heating stove during cold weather and the maintenance of the one-room school building and outside toilets.

The teacher in these situations was directly responsible to a local board of education, which did the hiring. A district superintendent visited very infrequently. Teaching success was typically judged by the "discipline" of the schoolroom. In fact, the critical problem for teachers was often how to keep the older boys in line. Physical punishment was not uncommon.

The one other assessment of the teacher's competence was the success of the pupils in passing eighth-grade examinations. When children had worked their way through the grades, using the same books they had seen and heard older students using in "recitations" during previous years, they were eligible for the examination. This was often written out in longhand by the school superintendent, and it was not unusual for many pupils to fail the exam. If those who failed cared to finish their grade school education, they studied another year, hoping to have better success the next time.

At the turn of the century 85 percent of all students enrolled in school were in the elementary grades. Further education was for only a few. Occasionally students who passed the eighth-grade examination became teachers the following year in schools that included students older than themselves.

By 1950, kindergartens were still primarily provided only in towns and cities. One-room schools were rapidly being replaced by "consolidated" schools, and young rural children who had formerly walked to school were bused long distances to attend school in larger, "modern" buildings. In the centralized school, teachers typically taught a single age or grade level or no more than two or three levels in combination. Specialized personnel relieved the teacher of most duties other than instruction. Teachers had far more extensive learning aids than had been available in the one-room schools, including audiovisual aids such as films and records.

At midcentury, kindergartens were provided primarily for learning "routines," for social development, and for attitude development. It was rare to find a kindergarten teacher who provided reading or other "academic" instruction, even for the most able and motivated children. In first grade, however, children were immediately provided with readiness workbooks and predictably progressed through the preprimer, primer, first reader, second reader, etc. of whatever basal series the school district had adopted. There was a general consensus about how and what to teach and at what age things should be taught.

Today we have far less consensus about these matters. Based on the theoretical and research evidence provided by Bloom (1964), Hunt (1961), and many others, a tremendous effort was launched during the 1960s to counteract the "cumulative deficit" of children from homes that were thought not to provide appropriate early stimulation. The varieties of program models with which you are now familiar were in large measure the result of this "war on poverty" waged via the provision of Head Start programs. This effort continues, although there is now a far more realistic appraisal of what massive and continuous efforts are necessary to make significant differences in children's development.

The tremendous activity and experimentation in early education during the 1970s and the general cultural turmoil in this period have left us with great program diversity. You will therefore enter the teaching field with a far greater number of options than your predecessors. However, there are several current trends that might greatly influence your teaching career, should they continue. Currently, there is a renewed demand for greater direct emphasis on the "basics," and for accountability to the educational "establishment" in traditional academic areas. There is a mounting concern, in the face of inflation and a depressed economy, about any expenditures considered not absolutely necessary. There is continued interest in using media technology to more efficiently as well as inexpensively educate children. These and many similar current trends may aid and abet or complicate what you consider to be your mission in teaching—depending on your goals, objectives, and overall orientation.

By the year 2000 these current trends may have dissipated and have been subsequently replaced by scores of others. The one trend that does seem quite stable is an ever-accelerating rate of change. A solid perspective on oneself and one's basic values will be essential for maintaining both stability and flexibility in light of new demands, expectations, and opportunities. At this point, you can profitably begin to adapt strategies both for your survival and growth as a beginning teacher and for your continued development in the years ahead. In concluding, therefore, we suggest the following strategies for this effort:

1. *Be as realistic as you can be in your endeavors.* Strive to make accurate discriminations about the requirements of situations, your own needs, and the extent to which your own commitment, sensitivity, resourcefulness, and organizational abilities are adequate for the responsibilities you are accepting. Keep your goals and priorities within reason, seeking a balance between personal and professional efforts. No one can do everything; sort out your priorities, plan, and work hard, but also reserve time for relaxation.

2. *Take active responsibility for continuing your own professional development.* Do this systematically. You are now familiar with the areas in which you need further work. Build and strengthen these.

Develop a classification scheme for storing plans, points of view, illustrative materials, activities for self-development, and ideas for things to do with children. Test out the usability of the scheme by periodically trying to locate something on short notice.

Start or join a professional work group and find a "buddy" with whom you can test out and share ideas, plans, materials, problems, solutions, and who will help you keep on target regarding your goals. Develop other support systems; find people who can help you out on short notice, sources of inexpensive and free scrap materials. Continue to get as much diverse experience as possible with the kinds of settings and children with whom you will ultimately specialize. Practice explaining ideas to children and to both sympathetic and hostile adults.

Your ultimate goals are survival, effectiveness with children, and personal satisfaction in teaching. We have suggested that this means the provision of the most comprehensive and individualized program possible, given the constraints of the setting, the resources you are able to muster, and your own teaching repertoire. With these goals in mind, you can perhaps see why the realistic assessment of your professional commitment and the continual enhancement of your repertoire for sensitivity, resourcefulness, and organization are so essential in becoming a teacher of young children.

APPENDIXES

1. Outline for Portfolio
2. Resource Organizations
3. Periodicals
4. Publishers' Addresses
5. Equipment and Materials
6. Sources for Equipment and Materials
7. Guidelines for Job-Hunting

1. Outline for portfolio

We recommended in the Introduction that you develop a portfolio of materials related to your professional growth. Whether or not you actually ever show others the materials in your portfolio, you will value their accessibility in projects related to teacher preparation and actual teaching.

You will probably acquire materials in diverse forms—loose papers, clippings, Xeroxed sheets, pictures, photographs, booklets, books, notebooks, etc. You may decide to keep them in file folders, in card files, in loose leaf notebooks, in envelopes, in boxes, or in filing cabinets. Keeping track of such a variety of materials so that you can find what you need when you need it requires a fairly detailed system for classifying and labeling. The following is a suggested outline for classification. It is intended to be only illustrative, because any such system is highly arbitrary and dependent on the particular bent of its designer. Most importantly, the outline or scheme you use must make sense to you. Second, it should be comprehensive enough to encompass quite diverse sets of materials on a range of topics related to early education. Third, the outline should be constructed to allow for expansion, through branching of the original categories.

One advantage of the following classification system may be that it follows the general format of this text and should therefore be easier for a text-user to learn and remember. The numerical divisions and the logical extensions of this outline are especially functional because they facilitate expansion, and they are easily applied to collections of materials in various forms through consistent numerical labeling and sequencing. To look for materials on a particular subject you need only know the category number to turn to that part of each type of collection—cards, files, etc.

A further suggestion is that you arrange for two kinds of entries under each category. The first, labeled *A*, would be reference materials prepared by others that you feel are of value and that you would like to keep in your possession. The second, labeled *B*, would be materials you produce. Thus for a category such as *Personal qualifications for teaching*, you would have two sections:

1.4–A Personal qualifications (reference materials prepared by others)
1.4–B Personal qualifications (materials produced by you)

Under the first, 1.4–A, you might have a Xeroxed article about a successful teacher, tape recordings of talks you have heard, a review of a book on the attributes necessary for teaching, a summary of research from a text, etc. Under the second, 1.4–B, you might include a profile of your own qualifications, your responses to Response Sections in this text that are related to this topic, your own critique of your interactions with children, etc.

Whatever classification outline you use initially, you should continue to modify it to make it more nearly fit your own ideas about important topics related to teaching. The following sample outline is intended to get you started thinking about your own outline:

1 Commitment
   1.1 General information about the profession
   1.2 Training programs
   1.3 Job requirements
      1.3.1 General
      1.3.2 Specific to a given state, program, etc.

1.4 Personal qualifications for teaching
2 Sensitivity
  2.1 Perspectives on children's growth and development
  2.2 Physical growth and development
  2.3 Affective and social development
  2.4 Cognitive and intellectual development
  2.5 Assessment and record-keeping
3 Resourcefulness
  3.1 Resourcefulness in activity-specific situations
    3.1.1 Manipulative materials
    3.1.2 Animals
    3.1.3 Children's literature
    3.1.4 Pretend activities
    3.1.5 Sharing
    3.1.6 Art media
    3.1.7 Music
    3.1.8 Cooking
  3.2 Resourcefulness in subject-matter areas
    3.2.1 Language development
    3.2.2 Reading
    3.2.3 Language arts (listening, writing, etc.)
    3.2.4 Natural and physical sciences
    3.2.5 Mathematics
    3.2.6 Social sciences
4 Organizational abilities
  4.1 Models (general types)
  4.2 Program descriptions (for specific programs)
  4.3 Time scheduling
  4.4 Space arrangement
  4.5 Facilities (equipment and materials)
  4.6 Ground rules/management
  4.7 Program planning
  4.8 Evaluation
  4.9 Home-school relationships
5 Foundations
  5.1 History
  5.2 Cultural and socioeconomic influences
  5.3 Current trends
  5.4 Future perspectives

2. Resource organizations

American Association of Hearing and Speech Agencies, 919 18th Street N.W., Washington, D.C. 20014

American Association of Psychiatric Services for Children, 1701 18th Street N.W., Washington, D.C. 20009

American Foundation for the Blind, 15 West 16th Street, New York, New York 10011 (visual problems)

American Physical Therapy Association, 1156 15th Street N.W., Washington, D.C. 20005

American Psychiatric Association, 1700 18th Street N.W., Washington, D.C. 20009

American Speech and Hearing Association, 9030 Old Georgetown Road, Washington, D.C. 20014

Association for the Aid of Crippled Children, 345 East 46th Street, New York, New York 10017

Association for Childhood Education International, 3615 Wisconsin Avenue N.W., Washington, D.C. 20016

Association for Children with Learning Disabilities, 2200 Brownsville Road, Pittsburgh, Pennsylvania 15210

Child Study Association of America, 9 East 89th Street, New York, New York 10028

The Child Welfare League of America, 44 East 23rd Street, New York, New York 10010

Children's Bureau, U.S. Department of Labor, Washington, D.C. 20210

Closer Look, Box 1492, Washington, D.C. 20012 (information on services for children with special needs)

The Council for Exceptional Children, 1411 S. Jefferson Davis Highway, Arlington, Virginia 22202

Council of Organizations Serving the Deaf, 4201 Connecticut Avenue N.W., Washington, D.C. 20014

Day Care and Child Development Council of America, 1426 H Street N.W., Washington, D.C. 20005

Education Development Center, 55 Chapel Street, Newton, Massachusetts 02160

Educational Facilities Laboratory, 477 Madison Avenue, New York, New York 10022

ERIC Clearinghouse in Early Childhood Education, University of Illnois, 805 West Pennsylvania Avenue, Urbana, Illinois 61801

International Reading Association, 6 Tyre Avenue, Newark, Delaware 19711

Library of Congress, 1291 Taylor Street N.W., Washington, D.C. 20542 (national reference and referral service)

National Association for Autistic Children, 621 Central Avenue, Albany, New York 12206

National Association for Retarded Citizens, 2709 Avenue E, East Arlington, Texas 76011

The National Easter Seal Society for Crippled Children and Adults, 2023 West Ogden Avenue, Chicago, Illinois 60612

National Reading Center, 1776 Massachusetts Avenue N.W., Washington, D.C. 20036

Office of Education, Bureau of Education for the Handicapped, Seventh and D Streets S.W., Washington, D.C. 20202

Office of Education, U.S. Department of Health, Education, and Welfare, Washington, D.C. 20202

President's Committee on Mental Retardation, Washington, D.C. 20201

United Cerebral Palsy Association, Inc., 66 East 34th Street, New York, New York 10016

United Epilepsy Association, 111 West 57th Street, New York, New York 10019

Women's Action Alliance, 370 Lexington Avenue, New York, New York 10017

3. Periodicals

American Education U.S. Department of Health, Education, and Welfare, Office of Education; Superintendent of Documents, U.S. Government Printing Office, Washington, D.C. 20402

Child Care Quarterly Human Services Press, 72 Fifth Avenue, New York, New York 10011

Child Development The University of Chicago Press, 5801 Ellis Avenue, Chicago, Illinois 60637

Childhood Education Association for Childhood Education International, 3615 Wisconsin Avenue N.W., Washington, D.C. 20016

Children's House P.O. Box 111, Caldwell, New Jersey 07006

Children Today U.S. Department of Health, Education, and Welfare, Office of Child Development; Office of Human Development, U.S. Government Printing Office, Washington, D.C. 20402

Early Years Circulation Service Center, P.O. Box 7414, Chicago, Illinois 60680

Education University of Wisconsin, P.O. Box 5504, Milwaukee, Wisconsin 53211

Education Digest Prakken Publications, Inc., Ann Arbor, Michigan 48107

Educational Leadership Association for Supervision and Curriculum Development, NEA, 1201 Sixteenth Street, Washington, D.C. 20036

Elementary School Journal The University of Chicago Press, University of Chicago, 5835 Kimbark Avenue, Chicago, Illinois 60637

Exceptional Children Council on Exceptional Children, 1499 Jefferson Davis Highway, Jefferson Plaza, Arlington, Virginia 22202

The Instructor The Instructor Publications, Inc., Dansville, New York 14437

Keeping Up with Elementary Education American Association for Elementary/ Kindergarten/Nursery Education, 1201 Sixteenth Street N.W., Washington, D.C. 20036

Language Arts (formerly *Elementary English*) National Council of Teachers of English, 508 South Sixth Street, Champaign, Illinois 61822

Learning Education Today Company, Inc., 530 University Avenue, Palo Alto, California 94301

Parent's Magazine Parent's Magazine Enterprises, Inc., 52 Vanderbilt Avenue, New York, New York 10017

The Reading Teacher International Reading Association, 6 Tyre Avenue, Newark, Delaware 19711

Science and Children National Science Teachers' Association, 1201 Sixteenth Street N.W., Washington, D.C. 20036

Teacher Macmillan Professional Magazines, Inc., Greenwich, Connecticut 06830

Today's Education National Education Association, 1201 Sixteenth Street N.W., Washington, D.C. 20036

Voice for Children Day Care and Child Development Council of America, 1426 H Street N.W., Washington, D.C. 20005

Young Children National Association for the Education of Young Children, 1834 Connecticut Avenue N.W., Washington, D.C. 20009

4. Publishers' addresses

Abingdon Press, 201 Eighth Ave. S., Nashville, Tennessee 37202

Acropolis Books, 2400 17th Street N.W., Washington, D.C. 20009

Addison-Wesley Publishing Co., Inc., Jacob Way, Reading, Massachusetts 01867

Agathon Press, Inc., 150 Fifth Avenue, New York, New York 10011

Allyn and Bacon, Inc., 470 Atlantic Avenue, Boston, Massachusetts 02210

American Book Co., 450 West 33rd Street, New York, New York 10001

American Guidance Service, Inc., Publishers' Building, Circle Pines, Maine 55014

Appleton-Century-Crofts, Croft Educational Services, 100 Garfield Avenue, New London, Connecticut 06320

Atheneum Publishers, 122 E. 42nd Street, New York, New York 10017

Basic Books, Inc., 10 E. 53rd Street, New York, New York 10022

Behavior Research Labs, c/o Sullivan Language Schools, P.O. Box 577, Palo Alto, California 94302

Behavior Technics, Lemont, Pennsylvania 16851

Basil Blackwell, Publisher, 108 Cowley Road, Oxford, England OX4 1JF

R. R. Bowker, Co., 1180 Avenue of the Americas, New York, New York 10036

Brigham Young University Press, 205 University Press Building, Provo, Utah 84602

Children's Press, Inc., 1224 W. Van Buren Street, Chicago, Illinois 60607

Citation Press, Scholastic Book Services, 906 Sylvan Avenue, Englewood Cliffs, New Jersey 07632

P. F. Collier, Inc. (subsidiary of Macmillan, Inc.), 866 Third Avenue, New York, New York 10022

Coward, McCann and Geoghegan, Inc., 200 Madison Avenue, New York, New York 10016

Thomas Y. Crowell, Co., 666 Fifth Avenue, New York, New York 10003

Curriculum Development, Inc., 144 W. 125th Street, New York, New York 10027

Dell Publishing Co., Inc., 1 Dag Hammarskjold Plaza, New York, New York 10017

DFA Publishers, Van Nuys, California 91409

Dial Press, 1 Dag Hammarskjold Plaza, New York, New York 10017

Docent Corporation, 430 Manville Road, Pleasantville, New York 10570

Dodd, Mead and Company, 79 Madison Avenue, New York, New York 10016

Doubleday and Company, 245 Park Avenue, New York, New York 10017

Dover Publications, Inc., 180 Varick Street, New York, New York 10014

Dryden Press (division of Holt, Rinehart and Winston, Inc.), 901 N. Elm, Hinsdale, Illinois 60521

E. P. Dutton, and Company, Inc., 201 Park Ave. S., New York, New York 10003

Encyclopaedia Britannica Educational Corporation, 425 N. Michigan Ave., Chicago, Illinois 60611

Evans Brothers, Ltd., Montague Ho., Russell Square, London, England WCIB 5BX

Farrar Books, P.O. Box 2029, Roosevelt Field Station, Garden City, New York 11530

Follett Education Corporation, 1010 W. Washington Blvd., Chicago, Illinois 60607

Garrard Publishing Co., 2 Overhill Road, Scarsdale, New York 10583

General Learning Press, 250 James Street, Morristown, New Jersey 07960

Grosset and Dunlap, Inc., 51 Madison Avenue, New York, New York 10010

Harcourt Brace Jovanovich, Inc., 757 Third Avenue, New York, New York 10017

Harper & Row, Publishers, Inc., 10 E. 53rd Street, New York, New York 10022

Hawthorne Books, Inc., 260 Madison Avenue, New York, New York 10016

Helicon Press, Inc., 1120 N. Calvert Street, Baltimore, Maryland 21202

Holiday House, Inc., 18 E. 53rd Street, New York, New York 10022

Holt, Rinehart and Winston, Inc., 383 Madison Avenue, New York, New York 10017

Houghton Mifflin Co., One Beacon Street, Boston, Massachusetts 02107

Human Development Training Institute, 7574 University Avenue, LaMesa, California 92041

Humanities Press, Inc., Atlantic Highlands, New Jersey 07716

Alfred A. Knopf, Inc., 201 East 50th Street, New York, New York 10022

John Knox Press, 341 Ponce De Leon Ave. N.E., Atlanta, Georgia 30308

J. P. Lippincott, 521 Fifth Avenue, New York, New York 10017

Little, Brown and Company, 34 Beacon Street, Boston, Massachusetts 02106

Liverwright Publishing Corporation (subsidiary of W. W. Norton Co., Inc.), 500 Fifth Avenue, New York, New York 10036

Lothrop, Lee and Shepard Company (division of William Morrow and Co., Inc.), 105 Madison Avenue, New York, New York 10016

McGraw-Hill Book Co., 1221 Avenue of the Americas, New York, New York 10036

David McKay Co., Inc., 750 Third Avenue, New York, New York 10017

Macmillan Publishing Company, Inc., 866 Third Avenue, New York, New York 10022

Charles E. Merrill Publishing Co. (division of Bell and Howell Co.), 1300 Alum Creek Drive, Columbus, Ohio 43216

M.I.T. Press, 28 Carleton Street, Cambridge, Massachusetts 02142

William Morrow and Co., Inc., 6 Henderson Drive, West Caldwell, New Jersey 07006

New Dimensions in Education, Inc., 160 Dupont Street, Plainview, New York 11803

Noble and Noble Publishers, 1 Dag Hammarskjold Plaza, 245 E. 47th Street, New York, New York 10017

Jeffrey Norton Publishers, Inc., 145 E. 49th Street, New York, New York 10017

W. W. Norton, and Co., 500 Fifth Avenue, New York, New York 10036

Open Court Publishing Co., P.O. Box 599, LaSalle, Illinois 61301

Pantheon Books (division of Random House, Inc.), 457 Hahn Road, Westminster, Maryland 21157

Parker Publishing Co., West Nyack, New York 10994

Parnassus Press, 4080 Halleck Street, Emeryville, California 94608

Pegasus (affiliated with Bobbs-Merrill Co., Inc.), 4300 W. 62nd Street, Indianapolis, Indiana 46268

Pitman Publishing Co., 6 E. 43rd Street, New York, New York 10017

Rand McNally and Co., Box 7600, Chicago, Illinois 60680

Random House, Inc., 457 Hahn Road, Westminster, Maryland 21157

Research Press Company, 2612 North Mattis Avenue, Champaign, Illinois 61820

The Ronald Press Co., 79 Madison Avenue, New York, New York 10016

Routledge & Kegan Paul, Ltd., 9 Park Street, Boston, Massachusetts 02108

Russell Sage Foundation (distributed by Basic Books, Inc.), P.O. Box 4000, Scranton, Pennsylvania 18501

St. Martin's Press, Inc., 175 Fifth Avenue, New York, New York 10010

W. B. Saunders Co. (subsidiary of Columbia Broadcasting System), 218 West Washington Square, Philadelphia, Pennsylvania 19105

Schocken Books, Inc., 200 Madison Avenue, New York, New York 10016

Scholastic Book Services (division of Scholastic Magazines), 906 Sylvan Avenue, Englewood Cliffs, New Jersey 07632

Scott, Foresman and Co., 1900 E. Lake Avenue, Glenview, Illinois 60025

William R. Scott, see *Addison-Wesley*.

Charles Scribner's Sons, Shipping and Service Center, Vreeland Avenue, Totowa, New Jersey 07512

Shoe String Press, Inc., 995 Sherman Avenue, Hamden, Connecticut 06514

Silver Burdett Co. (division of General Learning Co.), 250 James Street, Morristown, New Jersey 07960

Simon & Schuster, 630 Fifth Avenue, New York, New York 10020

Stanford University Press, Stanford, California 94305

Teachers College Press, Columbia University, 1234 Amsterdam Avenue, New York, New York 10027

Teaching Resources (Educational Service of the New York Times), 330 Madison Avenue, New York, New York 10017

Third Press, 444 Central Park West, New York, New York 10025

Charles C. Thomas, Publishers, 301–327 E. Lawrence Avenue, Springfield, Illinois 62703

University of California Press, 2223 Fulton Street, Berkeley, California 94720

University of Chicago Press, 11030 Langley Avenue, Chicago, Illinois 06028

University of Illinois Press, Urbana, Illinois 61801

University of London Press, Ltd., St. Paul's Ho., Warwick Lane, London, England EC4P 4AH

University of Pittsburgh Press, 127 N. Bellefield Avenue, Pittsburgh, Pennsylvania 15260

The Viking Press, Inc., 625 Madison Avenue, New York, New York 10022

Wadsworth Publishing Co., Inc., 10 Davis Drive, Belmont, California 94002

Walck, Henry Z., Inc. (division of David McKay Co., Inc.), 750 Third Avenue, New York, New York 10017

Frederick Warne and Co., Inc., 101 Fifth Avenue, New York, New York 10003

Franklin Watts, Inc. (subsidiary of Grolier, Inc.), 845 Third Avenue, New York, New York 10022

John Wiley and Sons, 605 Third Avenue, New York, New York 10016

H. W. Wilson, 950 University Avenue, Bronx, New York 10452

5. Equipment and materials

The following list of equipment and materials is abstracted from a comprehensive set of recommendations for equipping and arranging kindergartens distributed by the State Education Department/Bureau of Child Development and Parent Education for the State of New York (1966). The listings are similar to those prepared by other agencies and organizations.

Furniture

Tables
2   20–22" high, 24" wide, 24" long
3 or 4   20–22" high, 24" wide, 48" long
1   20–22" high, 36" diameter (for library corner)

Chairs (wooden posture chairs with saddle seats)
4–6 :   11" high, 13½" wide, 11½" depth of seat
10–12   12" high, 13½" wide, 11½" depth of seat
4–6   13" high, 14" wide, 12" depth of seat
1 or 2   adult size for parents or other visitors

Wooden lockers for wraps and personal possessions
(1 per child and a few extra)
60" high, 12" long, 12" deep with compartments for: plastic mats or rugs, personal possessions, wraps, and footwear

Shelf units and storage space
3   38" high, 50" long, 12" deep, 12" between shelves for unit blocks and accessories, housekeeping corner equipment, etc.
1   38" high, 50" long, 26" deep, 11" between shelves for hollow blocks

1 or 2 38" high, 3–4' long, 12" deep, 11" between shelves for doll accessories and miscellaneous equipment
1 library display rack, 48" high, 48" long for books and other reading materials
1 storage cabinet with doors, 6' high, 36" long, 12" deep for teacher's supplies
1 filing cabinet, 12" long, 28" deep, 2 drawers for teacher's records

Corkboards and screens

36–40 lineal feet per room corkboard, 4' high, at children's eye level
1 or 2 screens, 32" high, 48" long, with 14" firm base

Other Equipment and Materials

Block-building

Solid unit blocks

110–200 units
70–80 half-units
156–200 double units
120–180 quadruple units
24–40 small pillars
12–16 large pillars
16–24 small columns
16–24 large columns
24–30 small triangles
24–30 large triangles
12–16 quarter-circle curves
12–16 elliptical curves
4–8 half circles
8–14 small buttresses
4–8 large buttresses
12–16 ramps
4–6 large switches
4–8 small switches
4–8 arches
4–8 half arches
32–40 roof boards
20–30 floorboards

Hardwood hollow blocks
1 doz.+ 5½" by 5½" by 11"
1 doz.+ 5½" by 11" by 11"
1 doz.+ 5½" by 11" by 22"

Hardwood playboards
1 doz.+ ¾" by 5½" by 22"
1 doz.+ 1" by 5½" by 44"

Accessories
1 doz.+ miniature family figures
1 doz.+ miniature farm and zoo animals
2 doz.+ small colored cubes
1 or 2 sets interlocking wooden trains

several boats, tugboats, barges
1 wooden platform truck
2–3 rope-and-pulleys
1 cash register

Science supplies
1 animal cage
1 or 2 magnifying glasses
2+ horseshoe magnets
1 large thermometer
1 aquarium
1 terrarium
3 ft. rubber tubing, ½" diameter
1 or 2 trowels
1 or 2 cultivators, hand type
1 watering can
2–3 plant beds (low wooden boxes or nursery flats)
seeds and bulbs
plastic refrigerator dishes
3–4 sponges
1 hotplate
2+ wooden cooking spoons
1 or 2 measuring cups
1 set aluminum measuring spoons
1 eggbeater
1 or 2 saucepans (2-qt. or 4-qt. capacity)

Housekeeping
1 or 2 doll beds, approx. 32" by 17"
1 or 2 doll carriages, at least 24" by 14"
doll bedding
3+ dolls (light and dark skinned, boy and girl, at least two washable)
doll clothing
1 stove, 12" deep, 20" wide, 24" high
1 chest of drawers or substitute, 12" deep, 20" wide, 26" high
1 cupboard, approx. 12" deep, 22" wide, 40" high
1 sink, 12" deep, 36" wide, 24" high, removable dish pan
1 or 2 washboards
clothesline, clothespins, clothesrack
dishes and cooking utensils, adult size
1 ironing board, 7½" wide, 30" long, 23" high
1 iron, child size
2+ telephones
2+ brooms
1 or 2 mirrors, full-length
dress-up clothes

Art supplies
2 easels or substitutes (double and adjustable)
10–12 easel clips for holding paper

18+ brushes, long-handled, sturdy bristles (¾"
    or ⅝")
18+ paint containers, unbreakable with covers
1 cabinet large enough for storing easel paper,
    approx. 20" deep, 25" wide, 24" high, at least
    two shelves
1 rack for drying children's paintings
1 or 2 clay jars and covers
8–12 clay boards, approx. 14" by 18"
12 scissors, good quality, about 6" long, blunt
1 pan for wetting finger paint paper, 18" or 19"
    wide
1 galvanized pail for cleaning up

Expendable art supplies (approx. 1 year's supply;
18–22 children)
8 reams newsprint, 18" by 24"
6 reams manila construction paper, 12" by 18"
1 roll brown wrapping paper, 36" wide
2 pkg. each colored construction paper: red,
        blue, green, yellow, black, white
5 pkg. finger paint paper
4 rolls heavily glazed shelf paper, 16" or 22"
    wide
8 lb. each easel powder paint: red, yellow,
        blue, green
2 lb. each easel powder paint: black, brown,
        white
3 qt. each finger paint: red, yellow, blue, green
200 lb. potter's clay (moist), or 100 lb. dry
3 qt. library paste
3 doz. each crayons, large ⅜" diameter: red,
        green, blue, brown
2 doz. each crayons, large ⅜" diameter: orange,
        yellow, violet, black
odds and ends of cellophane, tinfoil, feathers,
    etc.

Music and rhythms
1 or 2 tone blocks or xylophones
2 tympani sticks padded with lamb's wool
5 drums, assorted (large Chinese tom-tom with
    pigskin head, large barrel drum with
    buckskin drumhead, bongo drums, small
    Indian drums)
2 musical triangles
1 or 2 bells on sticks
1 or 2 maracas
1 set Korean temple bells
1 or 2 tamborines

1 cymbal
1 piano
    collection of song and rhythm books
1 or 2 record players
1 record table
1 record holder
25–30+ collection of good records

Book corner (minimum of 50–80 books for 18–22
children)

Quiet pursuits
4 picture Lotto games
10–20 puzzles, wooden inlays, varying degrees
    of difficulty
1 puzzle rack
1 set hand puppets, family
5 play people, bendable, rubber
15–20 nuts and bolts, assorted sizes
1 set pipe fittings, assortment
1 flannel board
    pieces of different-colored flannel
1 or 2 hole punchers, ¼" round he
1 or 2 milk or cola carriers (wooden carrier with
    6 wooden bottles)
2 interlocking passenger trains, hardwood
2 interlocking tugboat sets, hardwood
    box of old colored postcards
    scraps of cloth of different colors and textures
1 sand box (if there is plenty of room)
    sand toys (wooden spoons, scoops, etc.)
1 wide sink or deep pan, approx. 6" deep or
    washtub
4–6 plastic aprons
2 eggbeaters
3–4 sponges
1 or 2 strainers or sieves
1 or 2 pails, 1 or 2 qt.
2–3 scoops
2–3 large funnels
2–3 measuring cups, tin or aluminum
3–4 boats, small
10–12 corks, assorted sizes

Carpentry
1 workbench, 54" long, 22" wide, 24" to 27"
    high
1 tool board, approx. 54" by 20", or tool cabinet
4 hammers, flathead, 10 oz. or 13 oz.

2 saws, crosscut No. 8, 12″	dowels, 36″ cylinders, ½″ and 1″ in diameter
2–3 iron clamps, mouth opening 4″	
2 screwdrivers, long handled, blades ¼″ and ⅜″	nail containers, coffee cans, plastic containers, or silverware tray
1 bit brace	
6 auger bits, ¼″, ½″, ¾″	wood container: baskets, wooden box with casters, or wood storage shelves
1 pliers	
9 lb. nails, assorted sizes	miscellaneous accessories: sandpaper (medium weight), button molds, washers, roofing caps, varied lengths of rope and string, etc.
screws, large heads	
tacks, both large headed and upholstery	
wood, soft pine in various small sizes	

6. Sources for equipment and materials

ABC School Supply, Inc., 437 Armour Circle N.E., Atlanta, Georgia 30324

Advance Crayon and Color Corporation, 136–138 Middleton Street, Brooklyn, New York 11206

American Guidance Service, Inc., Publishers' Building, Circle Pines, Minnesota 55014

American Seating Company, 901 Broadway, Grand Rapids, Michigan 49502

Beckly-Cardy Company, 1900 North Narragansett, Chicago, Illinois 60639

Cambosco Scientific Company, 432 Western Avenue, Boston, Massachusetts 02135

Carol School Supply, Union Turnpike, Flushing, New York 11366

Child Life Play Specialties, Inc., Holliston, Massachusetts 01746

Childcraft Equipment Company, Inc., 144 East 23rd Street, New York, New York 10010

Children's Music Center, Inc., 5573 West Pico Boulevard, Los Angeles, California 90019

Community Playthings, Department 81, Rifton, New York 12471

Constructive Playthings, 1040 East 85th Street, Kansas City, Missouri 64131

Creative Playthings, P.O. Box 1100, Princeton, New Jersey 08540

Cuisenaire Company of America, Inc., 12 Church Street, New Rochelle, New York 10805

Dick Blick, P.O. Box 1267, Galesburg, Illinois 61401

Edmund Scientific Company, 100 Edscorp Building, Barrington, New Jersey 08007

Ed-U-Cards Mfg. Corporation, 60 Austin Boulevard, Commack, New York 11725

General Learning Corporation, 250 James Street, Morristown, New Jersey 07960

J. L. Hammett Company, Hammett Place, Braintree, Massachusetts 02184

Ideal School Supply Company, 11000 South Laverne Avenue, Oaklawn, Illinois 60453

Instructo, 1635 North 55th Street, Philadelphia, Pennsylvania 19131

LaPine Scientific Company, 375 Chestnut Street, Norwood, New Jersey 07648

Lyndoncraft Educational Equipment, P.O. Box 12, Rosemead, California 91770

Milton Bradley, 74 Park Street, Springfield, Massachusetts 01101

NOVO Educational Toy and Equipment Corporation, 585 Sixth Avenue, New York, New York 10011

Playskool, Inc., 3720 North Ketzi Avenue, Chicago, Illinois 60618

Preschool Press, Inc., 159 West 53rd Street, New York, New York 10003

School Days Equipment Company, 973 North Main Street, Los Angeles, California 90012

Science Research Associates, 259 East Erie Street, Chicago, Illinois 60611

SIFO Educational Materials, General Learning Corporation, Mafex Associates, 111 Barren Avenue, Johnstown, Pennsylvania 15906

Society for Visual Education, Inc., 1345 Diversey Parkway, Chicago, Illinois 60614

R. H. Stone Products, Box 414, Detroit, Michigan 48231

Zia School and Office Supply, Second Street, Albuquerque, New Mexico 87105

7. Guidelines for job-hunting

Even though you may be just at the start of "becoming a teacher of young children," it is not too early to plan for landing a job. The first factor in job-hunting, especially in a tight job market, is your own competence. You can tackle that right now, using the contents of this text as a guide. Use Nancy, described in Chapter 2, as your model for active involvement in seeking new experiences, risking, trying, and trying again. Build up your competence so that you feel good about taking on tough tasks of teaching. The teacher preparation program provided by your college probably will not supply you with sufficient depth or breadth of experiences to give you the extra confidence you will need to be out in front in job-hunting. The experiences that will make the difference are likely to be those that you arrange for yourself—above and beyond those set out for you as minimal requirements for graduation and certification.

Try to enter the job market with realistic expectations. Getting the job you want may be very difficult, despite your preparation. Be prepared to mail scores of inquiries and applications and to be selected for interviews in only a few situations. Set up a file for carbons of letters of inquiry and application forms and a record-keeping sheet to keep track of paper work. On the record sheet you can record the name and address of each organization contacted, the job title, and the date(s) you sent a letter of inquiry and your resume; the date you receive a reply or application forms; the date the application form is submitted; the date you arranged for your credentials to be sent; the date you are invited for an interview. Once you have reached this stage, set up a separate folder within which you file all information relevant to the particular opening, such as job description, salary, local facts, funding sources, and benefits.

Spend a good deal of time and effort in preparing your resume. Have it neatly typed and in an attractive format. Make sure it provides succinctly all of the basic information on your qualifications, and be sure to place your name, address, and telephone number in a prominent position. Carefully select those academic and relevant nonacademic experiences (travel, work experience, community service, etc.) that will present you in the most favorable light and will indicate your potential worth to a prospective employer. You may want to consider what range of work, travel, educational, and recreational experiences you would *now* be able to cite on a resume. You can then set out to gain the kinds of experiences that could be presented to your advantage in seeking employment. Seasoned employers know that an acceptable academic record may not be enough to qualify you for teaching. On the other hand a range of rich experiences can provide insights that are very useful in professional efforts.

Provide readable, coherent, and informative responses to items on forms in your credential folder and for applications to individual school districts or centers. Take time to do this paper work well, double-checking your responses for content and for spelling or grammatical errors. Let the initial impressions from your written materials present your case in a positive fashion, or you may not progress to the point of having the opportunity to make first-hand impressions in an interview. At this point, you may wish to obtain samples of the kinds of forms provided by your college placement agency for your credential folder and the kinds of forms required for applications to school districts and other places of employment. Each is likely to be different, and you can become better prepared by analyzing the types of items to which responses are typically requested. Are you currently prepared to respond to these types of questions with confidence that your answers reflect your thinking and skill?

Think early about who will write recommendations for you to include in your credential file. Who is now aware of your developing abilities and could testify to your competence? Who will be aware that you are committed, sensitive, resourceful, and an able organizer? *Now* is the time to make contacts with professionals from whom you can learn and who can later attest to your promise as a professional.

Most hiring in public schools is done between March and September, with the peak months being May and June. Vacancies are filled at other times, however, in public schools as well as in child-care and other year-round programs. You will probably need to apply for several jobs simultaneously, and you may need to send out applications for several months. There are many formal sources of information about openings. These include your college and university placement bureau, state departments of education, state employment agencies, and private employment agencies (which may require payment of a percentage of your first year's salary). However, these formal sources may not be as helpful as your personal contacts. More people hear about jobs through friends, relatives, or their own professional contacts than in any other way. You will want to make sure that many people know of your availability and the kind of job you are looking for. If some of the people who know about you are persons connected with programs where teaching positions may develop, so much the better!

Chapter 16 asks you to consider the setting within which you would most like to teach. Some of these settings present many more opportunities than others. There are, for example, more jobs available in urban areas than in the suburbs. There are likely to be more openings in states with currently expanding early childhood programs (the Midwest and the South) than in those states with long-established prekindergarten and kindergarten efforts. Investigate the actual status of the job market in the kinds of settings you prefer, and locate a few representative sites for your own reality-testing and learning. Find out *now,* before you are ready to apply for jobs, what specifications are set for employment in terms of training, experiences, personal characteristics, etc. Decide how you can prepare yourself to meet their criteria and increase your employability. Also find out how you can readily learn about the communities in which you are interested. Do not limit yourself to educational concerns—also learn of the political, economic, and recreational activities in these communities. Read the local newspapers. Find out (in advance of having actual job interviews) how you might fit into and contribute to communities representative of those in which you may wish to eventually apply for a job. When you become involved in interviews for positions in given locales and programs, you will be likely to communicate your competence and confidence in more persuasive terms if you are attuned to local needs and concerns and the appropriateness of your own attributes to them.

There may be many more applicants for job openings than there are jobs in the locations in which you wish to work. However, if you are competent and let enough people know that you are, there will likely be teaching jobs for you. But do not wait until you are ready to look for a job to begin your preparation. Start now!

REFERENCES

Alphenfels, E. J. Conformity, censors, sensitivity. *Childhood Education*, 1964, 41, 168–71.

Ames, L. B. The development of a sense of time in the young child. *Journal of Genetic Psychology*, 1946, 68, 97–127.

Ames, L. B., and Learned, J. The development of verbalized space in the young child. *Journal of Genetic Psychology*, 1948, 72, 63–84.

Anderson, M. *et al. Activity methods for children under eight.* London: Evans Brothers, 1962.

Ashton-Warner, S. *Teacher.* New York: Simon and Schuster, 1963.

Ball, S., and Bogatz, G. A. Appendix A. A summary of the major findings in the first year of "Sesame Street": An evaluation. In G. A. Bogatz and S. Ball, *The second year of "Sesame Street": A continuing evaluation.* Vol. I. Princeton, N.J.: Educational Testing Service, 1970.

Barth, R. S. *Open education and the American school.* New York: Agathon Press, 1972.

———. When children enjoy school. *Childhood Education*, 1970, 46, 195–200.

Bayley, N. Some psychological correlates of somatic androgyny. *Child Development*, 1951, 22, 47–60.

Bereiter, C., and Engelmann, S. *Teaching disadvantaged children in the preschool.* Englewood Cliffs, N.J.: Prentice-Hall, 1966.

Bessell, H., and Palomares, U. *Methods in human development.* San Diego, Calif.: Human Development Training Institute, 1967.

Bloom, B. *Stability and change in human characteristics.* New York: John Wiley, 1964.

Brandt, R. M. An observational portrait of a British infant school. In B. Spodek and H. J. Walberg, Eds., *Studies in open education.* New York: Agathon Press, 1975.

Brearly, M., Bott, R., Davies, M. P., *et al. Fundamentals of the First School.* Oxford, England: Basil Blackwell, 1969.

Bronfenbrenner, U. Is early intervention effective? *Teachers College Record*, 1974, 76, 279–303.

Brown, M., and Precious, N. *The integrated day in the primary school.* New York: Agathon Press, 1968.

Brown, P., and Elliott, R. Control of aggression in a nursery school class. *Journal of Experimental Child Psychology*, 1965, 2, 103–7.

Bruce, V. *Dance and dance drama in education.* Oxford: Pergamon Press, 1965.

Bureau of Child Development and Parent Education/The State Education Department. *Equipment for children in kindergarten.* Albany, N.Y.: The University of the State of New York, 1966.

Caldwell, B. M. The importance of beginning early. In J. Jordan and R. F. Dailey, Eds., *Not all little wagons are red: The exceptional child's early years.* Arlington, The Council for Exceptional Children, 1973.

Cazden, C. B. Language programs for young children: Notes from England and Wales. In C. S. Lavatelli, Ed., *Language learning in early childhood education.* Urbana, Ill.: ERIC Clearinghouse on Early Childhood Education, 1971.

Chomsky, C. Stages in language development and reading exposure. *Harvard Education Review*, 1972, 42, 1–33.

Chomsky, N. *Aspects of a theory of syntax.* Cambridge, Mass.: The MIT Press, 1965.

Chow, S., and Elmore, P. *Early childhood information unit: Resource manual and program descriptions.* San Francisco: Far West Laboratory for Educational Research and Development, 1973.

Churchill, E. M. The number concepts of the young child. *Leeds University Research and Studies,* 1958, 17, 34–49.

Cohen, D. H. Continuity from pre-kindergarten to kindergarten. *Young Children,* 1971, 26, 282–86.

————. The effect of literature on vocabulary and reading achievement. *Elementary English,* 45, 1968, 209–13.

————. *The learning child.* New York: Pantheon, 1972.

Combs, A. W. *The professional education of teachers.* Boston: Allyn and Bacon, 1965.

Davidson, M. A., McInnes, R. G., and Parnell, R. W. The distribution of personality traits in seven-year-old children: A combined psychological, psychiatric and somatotype study. *British Journal of Educational Psychology,* 1957, 27, 48–61.

Dean, J. *Room to learn: Working space.* New York: Citation, 1973.

Dennison, G. *The lives of children: The story of the First Street School.* New York: Random House, 1969.

Dewey, J. *My pedagogic creed.* 1897. Reprint. Washington, D.C.: The Progressive Education Association, 1929.

Divoky, D. Education's hard-nosed rebel: Ziggy Engelmann. *Learning,* 1973, 29–31, 68.

Dolch, E. W. *Teaching primary reading.* Champaign, Ill.: Garrard Press, 1941.

Dopyera, J. *Assessing the micro-environments of individual preschool children.* Final Report to the Office of Economic Opportunity, Head Start Evaluation and Research, Contract No. OEO4120. Syracuse, N.Y.: Syracuse University, 1969.

Dopyera, J., and Lay, M. Assessment of openness in program studies. In B. Spodek and H. J. Walberg, Eds., *Studies in open education.* New York: Agathon Press, 1975.

Douglas, J. W. B., Ross, J. M., and Simpson, H. R. The relation between height and measured educational ability in school children of the same social class, family size and stage of sexual development. *Human Biology,* 1965, 37, 178–182.

Downing, J., and Thackray, D. *Reading readiness.* London: University of London Press, 1971.

Durkin, D. *Children who read early: Two longitudinal studies.* New York: Teachers College Press, 1966.

Ebbeck, F. N. Learning from play in other cultures. *Childhood Education,* 1971, 48, 2–3.

Education Commission of the States. *Early childhood programs: A state survey 1974–75.* Denver, Colo.: Education Commission of the States, 1975.

Education Products Information Exchange Institute. *Early childhood education: How to select and evaluate materials.* Education Product Report No. 42. New York: Education Products Information Exchange Institute, 1972.

Elkind, D., and Deblinger, J. A. *Reading achievement in disadvantaged children as a consequence of non-verbal perceptual training.* Rochester University, Rochester, N.Y., 1968. ERIC Document Reproduction Service No. ED 021 704.

Erikson, E. *Childhood and society.* New York: W. W. Norton, 1950.

————. A healthy personality for every child. White House Conference on Children and Youth, 1951. Adapted from the writings of Erik H. Erikson. In J. F. Rosenblith, W. Allinsmith, and J. P. Williams, Eds., *The causes of behavior: Readings in child development and educational psychology.* Boston: Allyn and Bacon, 1972.

Falik, L. H. The effects of special perceptual-motor training in kindergarten on second grade reading. *Journal of Learning Disabilities,* 1969, 2, 325–29.

Featherstone, J. *The primary school revolution in Britain.* A Pitman/New Republic Reprint. New York: Pitman, 1967.

Flavell, J. H. *The developmental psychology of Jean Piaget.* New York: D. Van Nostrand, 1963.

Frostig, M., and Horne, D. *The Frostig program for the development of visual perception.* Chicago: Follett Publishing Co., 1964.

Garn, S. M. Body size and its implications. In L. W. Hoffman, and M. L. Hoffman, Eds. *Review of child development research.* Vol. 3. New York: Russell Sage, 1966.

Getman, G. N., Kane, E. R., Halgren, M. R., and McGee, G. W. *Developing learning readiness.* Manchester, Mo.: McGraw-Hill, Webster Division, 1968.

Gordon, I. J. Developing parent power. In E. H. Grotberg, Ed., *Critical issues in research related to disadvantaged children.* Princeton, N.J.: Educational Testing Service, 1969.

Gray, S. W., Klaus, R. A., Miller, J. O., and Forrester, B. J. *Before first grade.* New York: Teachers College Press, 1966.

Grotberg, E. H. Institutional responsibilities for early childhood education. In I. J. Gordon, Ed., *The seventy-first yearbook of National Society for Study of Education.* Part II. *Early childhood education.* Chicago: University of Chicago Press, 1972.

Hale, C. J. Physiological maturity of Little League baseball players. *Research Quarterly American Association of Health, Physical Education and Recreation,* 1956, 27, 276–84.

Halverson, L. E. A real look at the young child. In *Motor activity for early childhood.* Washington, D.C.: American Association for Health, Physical Education and Recreation, 1971. ERIC Document Reproduction Service No. ED 069 331.

Hess, R. D., Bloch, M., Costello, J., Knowles, R. T., and Largay, D. Parent involvement in early education. In E. H. Grotberg, Ed., *Day care: Resources for decisions.* Reprint by Day Care and Child Development Council of America, Inc. Office of Economic Opportunity, no date.

Hess, R. D., and Shipman, V. C. Early experience and the socialization of cognitive modes in children. *Child Development,* 1965, 36, 869–86.

———. *Parents as teachers: How lower class and middle class mothers teach.* Chicago: University of Chicago, 1967. ERIC Document Reproduction Service No. ED 025 301.

Hildebrand, V. *Introduction to early childhood education.* New York: Macmillan, 1971.

Hildreth, G. The development and training of hand dominance. *Journal of Genetic Psychology,* 1950, 76, 39–100, 101–44.

Horney, K. *Neurosis and human growth.* New York: W. W. Norton, 1950.

Hughes, M. M. *et al. The assessment of the quality of teaching: A research report.* U.S. Office of Education Research Project No. 353. Salt Lake City: University of Utah, 1959.

Hunt, J. McV. *Intelligence and experience.* New York: The Ronald Press, 1961.

Hurlock, E. B. *Child development,* 4th ed. New York: McGraw-Hill, 1964.

Hymes, J. L., Jr. *Behavior and misbehavior.* Englewood Cliffs, N.J.: Prentice-Hall, 1955.

———. *A child development point of view.* Englewood Cliffs, N.J.: Prentice-Hall, 1955.

Ilg, F. L., and Ames, L. B. *School readiness.* New York: Harper & Row, 1964.

Jackson, P. *Life in classrooms.* New York: Holt, Rinehart and Winston, 1968.

Jacobs, J. N., Wirthlin, L. D., and Miller, C. B. A follow-up evaluation of the Frostig visual-perceptual training program. *Educational Leadership Research Supplement,* 1968, 4, 169–75.

Karnes, M. B., and Zehrback, R. R. Flexibility in getting parents involved in the school. *Teaching exceptional children,* 1972, 5, 6–19.

Kephart, N. C. *The slow learner in the classroom,* 2nd ed. Columbus, Ohio: Charles E. Merrill, 1971.

Kohlberg, L. Early education: A cognitive-developmental view. *Child Development,* 1968, 39, 1013–62.

Langer, J. *Theories of development.* New York: Holt, Rinehart and Winston, 1969.

Larsen, S., and Hammill, D. D. The relationship of selected visual perceptual skills to academic abilities. *Journal of Special Education,* 1975, 281–91.

Lay, M. Z. *The responsive care model: A program manual and report of implementation.* Syracuse, N.Y.: Syracuse University Early Childhood Education Center, 1972.

Lee, L. C. Social encounters of infants: The social strategies of two individual infants. *Cornell Journal of Social Relations,* 1973, 8, 243–55.

Leeper, S. H., Dales, R. J., Skipper, D. S., and Witherspoon, R. L. *Good schools for young children,* 3rd ed. New York: Macmillan, 1974.

Lenneberg, E. H. *Biological foundation of language.* New York: John Wiley, 1967.

Lichtenberg, P., and Norton, D. G. *Cognitive and mental development in the first five years: A review of recent research.* Washington, D.C.: Department of Health, Education, and Welfare Publications No. (HSM) 72-9102, 1972.

McNeill, D. *The acquisition of language: The study of developmental psycholinguistics.* New York: Harper & Row, 1970.

Medley, D. M., Schluck, C. G., and Ames, N. P. *Recording individual pupil experiences in the classroom: A manual for PROSE recorders.* Princeton, N.J.: Educational Testing Service, 1968.

Merrow, J. G. G., II. *The politics of competence: A review of competency-based teacher education.* Washington, D.C.: National Institute of Education, 1975.

Moffett, J. *A student-centered language arts curriculum, grades K-6: A handbook for teachers.* Boston: Houghton Mifflin, 1968.

Montessori, M. *Reconstruction in education.* Wheaton, Ill.: Theosophical Press, 1964.

————. *The secret of childhood.* Calcutta: Orient Longmans, 1963.

Moore, R. S., and Moore, D. R. How early should they go to school? *Childhood Education,* 1973, 50, 14–20.

Murphy, L. B., and Leeper, E. M. *Away from bedlam.* Washington, D.C.: Department of Health, Education, and Welfare Publication No. (OCD) 73-1029, 1970.

Myer, J. W. An informal survey of child care workers. *Child Care Quarterly,* 1975, 4, 120.

National School Public Relations Association. *Education U.S.A.* Washington, D.C.: National School Public Relations Association, May 26, 1975.

NEA Research Division. *Status of the American public school teacher, 1970–71.* Washington, D.C.: National Education Association, 1972.

Needels, M., and Stallings, J. *Classroom processes related to absence rate.* Menlo Park, Calif.: Stanford Research Institute, 1975. ERIC Document Reproduction Service No. ED 110 199.

Office of Economic Opportunity. *Project Head Start: Daily program I.* Washington, D.C.: Office of Economic Opportunity, 1967.

Pflaum, S. W. *The development of language and reading in the young child.* Columbus, Ohio: Charles E. Merrill, 1974.

Piaget, J. *The origins of intelligence.* New York: Norton, 1952.

Piaget, J., and Inhelder, B. *The psychology of the child.* New York: Basic Books, 1969.

Plessas, G. P., and Oakes, C. R. Prereading experiences of selected early readers. *Reading Teacher,* 1964, 17, 241–45.

Premack, D. Reinforcement theory. In D. Levine, Ed., *Nebraska symposium on motivation.* Lincoln: University of Nebraska Press, 1965, 123–180.

————. Toward empirical behavior laws: I. Positive reinforcement. *Psychological Review,* 1959, 66, 219–33.

Prescott, E. *Who thrives in group day care?* Pasadena, Calif.: Pacific Oaks College, 1972.

Prescott, E., and Jones, E., with Kritchevsky, S. Group day care as a child-rearing environment. Report to Children's Bureau, U.S. Department of Health, Education, and Welfare. Pasadena, Calif.: Pacific Oaks College, 1967. ERIC Document Reproduction Service No. ED 024 453.

Rambusch, N. McC. *Learning how to learn: An American approach to Montessori.* Baltimore, Md.: Helicon Press, 1962.

Richardson, S. A., Goodman, N., *et al.* Cultural uniformity in reaction to physical disabilities. *American Sociological Review,* 1961, 261, 241–47.

Robinson, H. Perceptual training: Does it result in reading improvement? In R. C. Auckerman, Ed. *Some persistent questions on beginning reading.* Newark, Del.: International Reading Association, 1972.

Rosenshine, B., and Furst, N. F. The use of direct observation to study teaching. In M. W. Travers, Ed., *Second handbook of research on teaching.* Chicago: Rand McNally, 1973.

Rousseau, J. J. The evils of education. Reprint. In R. Gross, Ed., *The teacher and the taught.* New York: Dell, 1963.

Science Research Associates. *DISTAR.* Chicago: Science Research Associates, 1969.

Sheldon, W. H. *The varieties of temperament: A psychology of constitutional differences.* New York: Harper, 1942.

Sheldon, W. H., Dupertuis, C. W., and McDermott, E. *Atlas of man: A guide for somatotyping the adult male at all ages.* New York: Harper & Row, 1954.

Skinner, B. F. *Beyond freedom and dignity.* New York: Alfred A. Knopf, 1971.

Smilansky, S. *The effects of sociodramatic play on disadvantaged preschool children.* New York: John Wiley, 1968.

Smith, M. E. *An investigation of the development of the sentence and the extent of vocabulary in young children.* Ames, Iowa: State University of Iowa, 1926.

Smith, M. S. Evaluation findings in Head Start Planned Variation. In A. M. Rivlin and T. M. Timpane, Eds., *Planned variation in education.* Washington, D.C.: Brookings Institution, 1975.

Soar, R. *Follow Through classroom process measurement and pupil growth.* Gainesville, Fla.: Institute for Development of Human Resources, 1973. ERIC Document Reproduction Service No. ED 106 297.

Spivack, G., and Shure, M. B. *Social adjustment of young children: A cognitive approach to solving problems.* San Francisco: Jossey-Bass, 1974.

Stallings, J. *Relationships between classroom instructional practices and child development.* Menlo Park, Calif.: Stanford Research Institute, 1975. ERIC Document Reproduction Service No. ED 110 200.

Standard Education Almanac 1975–76, 8th ed. Chicago: Marquis Academic Media, 1975.

Valett, R. E. *The remediation of learning disabilities: A handbook of psychoeducational resource programs.* Palo Alto, Calif.: Fearon Publishers, 1974.

Walker, R. N. *Body build and behavior in young children. 1. Body build and nursery school teachers' ratings*. Monograph Society for Research on Child Development, 1962, p. 27.

Weikart, D. P., Rogers, L., and Adcock, C. *The cognitively oriented curriculum: A framework for preschool teachers*. ERIC/NAEYC Publication. Urbana, Ill.: University of Illinois, 1971.

Whitehurst, K. Motor activities for early childhood. In American Association for Health, Physical Education and Recreation, *Report of NAEYC and AAHPER conference on the young child: The significance of motor development*. ERIC Document Reproduction Service No. ED 069 331. Washington, D.C.: American Association for Health, Physical Education, and Recreation, 1971.

Whiting, J. W., Child, I. L., and Lambert, W. W. *Child training and personality*. New Haven: Yale University Press, 1953.

Wiederholt, J. L., and Hammill, D. D. Use of the Frostig-Horne perception program in the urban school. *Psychology in the Schools*, 1971, 8, 268–74.

Yardley, A. *The teacher of young children*. New York: Citation Press, 1973.

Young, H. B., and Knapp, R. Personality characteristics of converted left-handers. In R. C. Smart and M. S. Smart, Eds., *Readings in child development and relationships*. New York: Macmillan, 1972.

GLOSSARY

accommodation the process, according to the Piagetian view, whereby an internal mental organization is altered to incorporate certain aspects of new experiences that previously could not be assimilated (see **assimilation**); or, as more broadly used, the process whereby existing patterns of behavior are modified to cope with new situations

achievement levels accomplishment or performance in a skill or knowledge area, stated normatively; that is, by age or grade (see **norm**)

adaptation the process of change whereby the individual is better fitted to cope with his or her environment; consists, according to Piagetian theory, of the dual processes of assimilation and accommodation

affective behavior behavior related to the feeling function or functions; includes motivations, interests, and values

age score equivalents a derived score for a learner that indicates the age level at which his or her achievement is typically attained

agility the ability to move flexibly—to stretch, bend, spin, arch, leap, turn, throw, run, jump, etc.

aide a person (typically with little or no professional training) employed to perform specified tasks under the direct supervision of professional personnel

analytic approach (reading) a method of teaching reading in which whole words are presented initially and then are broken into subelements for phonic analysis

assimilation the process whereby new experiences (objects, events, etc.) are incorporated into existing mental structures

associate degree the degree typically conferred at the completion of a two-year junior college, community college, or technical training program

associative play play involving two or more children in which there is some sharing of materials but little other interaction

attachment a bond of affection that binds two or more individuals together; implies a relationship that endures across time

attending actively focusing on only certain aspects of a complex situation or experience

auditory discrimination the act of differentiating between sounds, including those sounds that comprise words

balance the effective alignment of body parts to maintain the vertical center of gravity to allow movement without falling

behavioral assessments a description of an individual's current status in various areas of functioning that fully supports with reports of observed behavior any inferences and evaluative statements

behavior management the application of systematic principles (especially reinforcement technology) to influence and control the behavior of an individual

behavior modification a change in an accustomed mode of behavior resulting from external encounters; in more specific current usage, the application of systematic principles (especially reinforcement technology) to change behavior

behaviorists persons who analyze the conditions or events that can be shown to have an effect on overt behavior; modern behaviorists often use their findings to manipulate conditions and events to control (manage or modify) behavior (see **environmentalist**)

biological maturation changes in the characteristics of an individual that result from anatomical, physiological, and neurological development; different than changes due to experience or learning

CDA see **Child Development Associate**

certification the issuing of a license to teach by an agency legally authorized by the state to grant such a license

Child Development Associate person awarded an associate degree as a child care specialist; the degree, based on demonstrated competency, is awarded by the Child Development Associate Consortium, a private, nonprofit corporation initiated by the Office of Child Development, a federal agency

classification the act of systematically grouping objects or events according to identifiable common characteristics

cognitive behavior behavior related to thought processes or perceptions (such as classifying, recalling, anticipating, imagining, and discriminating)

cognitive structure the coherent and integrated cognitive system by which an individual organizes experience and relates to the environment

compensatory education educational programs, often sponsored by federal or state governments, intended to lessen or eliminate those differences considered to be disadvantageous for members of various subcultural and/or economically deprived groups

commitment the act of pledging or engaging oneself; the specific usage in this text refers to personal identification with the occupational role of teaching

concept the common element or feature of cognition, which functions to identify groups or classes; a concept is usually given a name, but the word itself is not the concept, only the symbol of the concept

concrete operations mental activities concerned with actual objects, including ordering, seriation, classification, and mathematical processes, all of which are reversible (see **reversibility**); characterizes the thinking of children from age seven or eight to approximately age eleven or twelve; problem-solving is limited to events that can be visualized in concrete terms (see **operations/operating**)

conservation refers to the awareness that number or other quantitative attributes (weight, volume, etc.) remain the same (despite changes in appearance) unless there are additions or deletions; term used by Piaget

contingent the degree to which one thing depends on another; for example, the degree to which reinforcement is aligned with the occurrence of a given behavior (see **contingency management**)

contingency management the control of rein-

forcements to affect the frequency of desirable or undesirable behaviors

continuous reinforcement a schedule of reinforcement in which every instance of a given target behavior is reinforced

cooperative a type of early childhood program organized by parents who employ a professional teacher but who may also directly assist in staffing and maintenance on a regular basis

cooperative play play in which a group is working together toward a common purpose such as making some material product, dramatizing a situation, or playing formal games

curriculum guides statements suggesting an overall plan for the content and/or specific materials of instruction to be offered in a program; may include goals, a variety of suggestions for instructional techniques and materials, and evaluation approaches

decentering being aware of the secondary aspects of a phenomenon beyond its most compelling features; incorporation of secondary aspects of stimulus into the total perception

decoding the process of obtaining meaning from written symbols; reading

deductive thinking the derivation of specific conclusions from general propositions

departmentalized an organizational arrangement whereby each teacher is responsible for teaching only one or two specialized subjects; the teacher moves either from class to class or classes move from room to room during different segments of the day

developmental crises as proposed by Erikson, the succession of eight stages universally encountered in psychosocial development, each of which presents polar possibilities that require resolution

differentiation the progressive series of changes in an individual's development whereby generalized movements and relatively simple conceptualizations become more precise; results in increased abilities

disadvantaged lacking normal or usual advantages such as safe and healthful living conditions, opportunities to learn facilitating skills and attitudes, etc.

discussion/action group a small group of three to seven persons pursuing similar goals who regularly exchange experiences, explore ideas and issues, and cooperatively undertake relevant projects and efforts

dominance the preference for the use of either the right or left hand, foot, or eye

dramatic play the "acting out" or dramatization of a direct, vicarious, or imagined experience through personal identification with the characters involved

ectomorph an individual with a thin, tall physique, likely deficient in strength

egocentric lack of discrimination between what is self and what is not self; lack of awareness of anything outside one's own immediate experiencing

encoding the process of recording ideas in written symbols; writing

endomorph an individual with a tendency to soft roundness and fatness in body physique

endurance the extent to which movement(s) can be continued without need for rest

evaluating the process of determining the meaning of behavior (or other phenomena) in terms of a standard

environmentalists persons primarily concerned with determining how environmental forces shape particular kinds of behavior in individuals and/or characteristics of species (see **behaviorist**)

event sampling obtaining a record of observed behavior only during certain preselected types of incidents, such as play time, conflicts, or interaction with peers

field experiences direct opportunities for practice within school or other group settings in providing for children's care and/or education

fixed interval schedule a reinforcement of behavior according to the amount of time elapsed since the last reinforcement of that behavior

fixed ratio schedule the reinforcement of behavior on a schedule set according to the number of occurrences of the behavior required for reinforcement

flexible grouping instructional arrangements within a given classroom whereby children are asked to come together only for short-term purposes (a specific interest or activity), in contrast to relatively permanent grouping according to achievement level

flexible scheduling a schedule that permits program periods to be lengthened, shortened, combined, or otherwise shifted to meet the varying time demands of specific activities

Follow Through evaluation project initiated in 1968 as part of a federal compensatory education effort; variations in types of programing in kindergarten and primary grades were studied with the goal of sustaining the advantages of participation in Head Start programs

formal operations mental activities concerned with abstract thought, such as hypotheses and logical propositions (see **operations/operating**)

formal sharing an exchange of ideas or information within a group situation structured by a leader (typically, the teacher) for that purpose

grade-score equivalents a derived score that indicates the achievement of a student in terms of the grade level at which the score is typically attained by the "average" student

gross movement the use of the large muscles of the body, principally the arms and the legs

handedness preference for use of the right or left hand either in tasks requiring the use of one hand or in the more difficult aspects of tasks in which both hands are used

Head Start a federally funded program designed to provide experiences for low-income children that would allow them to enter public school with the attitudes and skills necessary for their successful participation

Head Start Planned Variation a study of the implementation and effects of differing program approaches to compensatory education

image memories of past experience; centrally aroused internal experience based upon prior perceptions of external experience

index (level of representation) the aspect (part) of an object that provides a signal or cue as to its identity; for example, one infers the presence of a duck upon seeing duck footprints, and the presence of a telephone from the sound of ringing

individualize organizing instructional programs

so that different learners can progress according to their respective abilities and interests

individualized instruction differentiation of instruction according to individual differences among learners

inductive thinking the process of deriving a general conclusion from specific factual evidence; drawing inferences from observations

inferring drawing a tentative conclusion regarding the likely meaning of facts and observations; going beyond the evidence available through logical extensions of what is known

informal sharing a spontaneous exchange of ideas or information without formality or ceremony

instructional packages a set of materials (may include elements such as rationale and background information, directions for use, materials for instruction and/or learner's use, or measures for evaluation of learner status) intended to be useful in the accomplishment of a specific set of objectives

integration the state of having fully incorporated an action, skill, idea, etc., into an overall behavior pattern so there is little need for conscious effort

intellect the capacity to integrate experience via cognitive processes

intellectual behavior aspects of behavior that involve the cognitive integration of experience

intelligence quotient (IQ) score expressing the level of an individual's mental age in relation to his or her chronological age; obtained by dividing mental age (as measured by an intelligence test) by chronological age and multiplying by 100

interactionists persons who are primarily concerned with studying how children attempt to make sense of what they encounter, what means they use in their explorations and thinking, and, especially, how their interactions with their environments help them move to more complex stages of development

intermittent reinforcement a schedule of reinforcement in which the reinforcement is not applied to each instance of the behavior identified for reinforcement, but instead occurs only periodically

intervention the provision of new experiences (such as educational programs) with the goal of modifying the performance or state of the recipient of these experiences; has been especially applied in providing new experiences or programs to change the status of the economically or culturally disadvantaged (see **disadvantaged**)

intuitive thinking a term used by Piaget to describe a nonconceptual and imaginative self-projection in thinking processes; based on immediate perceptions

invariance a term used by Piaget to describe the unchanging aspects of phenomena, such as the constancy of objects (learned by the infant) and the constancy of number, quantity, etc. (learned by the child in performing operations on objects) (see **conservation; reversibility**)

kindergarten a program generally restricted to children under age six for the year prior to entrance to first grade

language experience (reading) an approach to reading instruction that predominantly uses the oral and written expressions of children as the medium for instruction, rather than teacher-prepared or commercially prepared materials

lateral dominance sidedness; preferential use of one hand, foot, or eye rather than the other; a combination of handedness, footedness, and eyedness; assumed dominance of one cerebral hemisphere over the other in respect to motor functions

lesson plan a plan, usually written, for a short period of instruction to be devoted to a specific limited topic, skill, or concept; may include a statement of objectives, materials to be used, procedures, and an evaluation plan

maturationist person who holds the view that the pervasive and important changes in individuals occur primarily as a result of biological development, rather than due to experience and learning

mental age the average mental development for a given chronological age; the level of an individual's mental ability expressed in terms of norms based on the "average" mental age of persons having the same chronological age

mental sets expectations or assumptions that influence what is actually perceived by different individuals in the same situation

mental structure (see **cognitive structure**)

mesomorph an individual with a muscular, strong, athletic physique

mixed dominance a preference for the use of the right hand and the left eye (or the left hand and the right eye)

model (program) a distinctive and coherent organizational and/or procedural pattern that is specific enough to be replicated

motor behavior aspects of behavior related to movement and overt action (see **gross movement; small muscle coordination**)

motor intelligence early modes of thinking that, according to Piaget, consist only of the infant's own actions and the direct sensory qualities of objects encountered; interiorized symbolic representations of reality are lacking (see **sensorimotor**)

motoric competence the facility with which an individual can accomplish various physical acts involving strength, muscular coordination, speed of reaction, etc.

multiage grouping a placement plan whereby pupils are placed within classroom groups to comprise an approximately equal proportion of each of two or more contiguous age groups (for example, five-, six-, and seven-year-olds)

multiple classifications the act of systematically and simultaneously grouping objects or events according to two or more identifiable dimensions; for example, sorting simultaneously according to both color and size

negative reinforcements a circumstance in which behaviors are reinforced through the reduction or removal of events that have been annoying or painful

nongraded plan classroom placement or instruction based on school criteria other than age or year, such as achievement level, interests, etc.; sometimes referred to as the *continuous progress plan* or *continuous growth plan*

norm(s) the expected; average (mean, median, or mode); usual according to age, grade, or other criteria

objectives purposes to be realized directly through instructional and program activity; statements of what behaviors are anticipated as the outcomes of a planned program

operant behaviors any behavior whose frequency of occurrence can be controlled (at least in part) by the consequences that follow its appearance

operant conditioning a type of learning in which the individual learns which behaviors in his or her repertoire will operate on the environment to yield reinforcement

operant psychology the study of human behavior that focuses on determining and utilizing the relationship between the emission of a behavior by an individual, the reinforcement of that behavior, and the subsequent frequency or probability of that behavior recurring

operations/operating terms used by Piaget to refer to interiorized mental actions (see **concrete operations; formal operations**)

organizational ability the ability to form a whole from interdependent or coordinated parts; in this text, specifically refers to the ability to combine elements, such as organization of time, arrangement and use of space, selection and use of equipment and materials, and the establishment of ground rules within a program, all with the goal of enhancing children's development

packaged curricula (see **instructional packages**)

parallel play play in which one child is near another and both are engaged in the same sorts of activities but with no active cooperation or sharing and no attempt to achieve a common goal

paraprofessional (see **aide**)

percentile scores a dividing point based on percentage; for example, the sixty-second percentile is the dividing line in a distribution of test scores between the upper 38 percent of the scores and the bottom 62 percent—a percentile score of sixty-two thus indicates that 38 percent of the scores were higher and 62 percent were the same or lower

perceptual processes neurological processes that lead to the awareness of objects or other data through the medium of the senses

perceptual-motor task any task requiring muscular coordination in responding to perceptual stimuli; for example, the drawing of straight, curved, or angled lines between boundaries, or the copying of forms and patterns

performance items those items within a test battery that require a response by overt action (such as the manipulation of materials) rather than by verbal or written responses

physical characteristics aspects of an individual related to appearance; includes bodily and facial features (size, proportion, etc.)

positive reinforcement a type of reinforcement, after the occurrence of a particular behavior, that increases the probability of that behavior being repeated or strengthened

portfolio a set of accumulated materials related to one's professional development; sometimes used as evidence of one's professional development or competency

preconceptual a term used by Piaget to describe the developmental status in which thinking processes are intuitive (see **intuitive thinking**), concepts (see **concepts**) are only primitively employed, and representatives of a class are confused with the whole class; characteristic of children between the ages of two and four

prekindergarten the age period prior to entrance into kindergarten; programs developed for children of ages three and four prior to kindergarten enrollment

Premack principle the reinforcement principle, proposed by Donald Premack, whereby an individual's high-probability behavior can be used to reinforce and increase his or her low-probability behavior

preoperational the stage of cognitive development, according to Piaget, that precedes the emergence of logical, reversible operations (see **operations/operating; concrete operations; formal operations**); characterized by intuitive and egocentric thinking linked to perception

primary the division of elementary school that includes grades one through three

programed materials prepared instructional materials in which the learner is guided toward making correct responses in a series of carefully sequenced gradients of difficulty and is positively reinforced by being informed of the correctness of the responses

psychoanalysis an approach to the study of human behavior, developed by Sigmund Freud, in which the focus is on both normal and abnormal reactions and unconscious mental processes

psychosexual conflicts the developmental clashes proposed by psychoanalytic theory as inevitable, since socializing events of weaning, toilet training, and sexual control run counter to predominant sources of bodily satisfactions (oral, anal, genital)

punishment an unpleasant experience that is a consequence of specific acts or behaviors; typically administered with the expectation that it will reduce the probability of the behavior recurring

ratio schedule reinforcement schedules whereby reinforcement is made contingent upon the number of times a target behavior has occurred since the previous reinforcement (see **fixed ratio schedule; variable ratio schedule**)

reading readiness the physical, mental, and emotional states prerequisite for benefiting from instruction in reading

realia tangible objects (in contrast to representations such as pictures, models, etc.)

reflexive behavior instinctual behavior patterns and automatic reactions (which may be a combination of both learning and instinct) that occur involuntarily and are not under conscious control

reinforcement anything that increases the likelihood that an act will be repeated at the next opportunity

repertoire the skills, talents, or response patterns that an individual (or animal) possesses and can use in given circumstances

reporting giving an oral or written account of actual happenings that are observed, without inference or evaluation

resourcefulness the ability to deal skillfully and promptly with new situations; in this text, specifically refers to the ability and repertoire for providing children with experiences and instruction that match their needs, interests, and capabilities

reversibility a term used by Piaget to describe the aspect of logical thinking operations in which one's mind reverses its actions and mentally "undoes" the previous action in order to coordinate the present circumstances with what was previously observed. For example, a child without reversible thought measures out an equal volume of water into two tall tumblers and says that both containers have the same amount. Upon pouring the water from one tumbler into a flat bowl, he or she declares there to be more water in the tumbler. The child does not consider the previously recognized equivalence and responds instead to the immediate perceptual cues

rhythm   the ability to pattern movements in a predictable, repetitive sequence

scheduling of reinforcements   the timing and sequencing of reinforcements presented to an individual to increase or strengthen the probability of selected behaviors

schema   a pattern of behavior (at the sensorimotor stage) or the internal general form of a conceptualization (at later stages); a mental structure or cognitive structure for a specific aspect of "knowing"

self-concept   those aspects of the individual's imagery that have been differentiated as relatively stable and characteristic

self-correcting   the attribute of a learning device or learning equipment that allows the user to independently determine whether actions (or responses) are appropriate or inappropriate (without the presence of a teacher or other experienced user); often used to describe Montessori equipment, with which inappropriate alignment of the apparatus is apparent to the user

sensitivity   the state or quality of being sensitive and perceptive; in this text, specifically refers to awareness of variations in individual children's behavior and development

sensorimotor   an initial means whereby the individual comes to "know" and learn of the world through specific sensory input and motoric actions

sensorimotor period   the initial stage of development, as proposed by Piaget; encompasses the years from birth to approximately age two

seriation   the process of ordering or aligning objects or events according to variations in an identifiable characteristic, such as size, weight, or color intensity

sex-appropriate   a designation as to whether behaviors or objects are, according to social consensus, identified with males or females

sex identification   those aspects of the individual's imagery, relative to maleness or femaleness, that are differentiated as relatively stable and are viewed as characteristic of self

shape/shaping   reinforcement of each successive approximate response toward a desired behavioral goal

sign (level of representation)   the use, through social agreement, of abstract configurations to represent real experience, such as the written word

signaling systems   external behaviors whereby the infant consistently communicates inward states; for example, crying indicates discomfort, cooing indicates pleasure

small muscle coordination   the ability to use one's hands to grasp and manipulate objects

social behavior   those aspects of behavior that involve interactions with one or more others

sociodramatic play   dramatic or pretend play involving cooperative effort with one or more others to enact a contrived situation

solitary play   play in which a child plays alone with toys and/or materials that are different from those used by other children

speed   in human movement, the effective alignment of body parts to allow rapid and efficient movement

standardized test   a test for which norms have been established, for which uniform methods of administering and scoring have been developed, and which may be scored with a relatively high degree of objectivity

strength   the effective alignment of body parts to push or release power

structure (program)   the arrangements, provided by a programer, that determine the nature and variety of the behaviors that will be accommodated

symbol (level of representation)   something that stands for or suggests something else, such as pictures, models, and objects used in children's play to represent other objects

synthetic approach   a method of teaching reading based on the mastery of the phonic elements of words, which are then blended together to determine word units

target behaviors the behavior or class of behaviors identified for observation, assessment, or modification

task persistence the ability to sustain effort in a work or problem-solving situation

teacher's manuals a written guide containing suggested or required instructional procedures, references, etc.; usually arranged for use with specific prepared materials such as textbooks, workbooks, or instructional packages

teacher-proof an attribute of commercially prepared materials arranged with such precision and with such detailed directions that teachers are not expected to deviate from the developer's intentions

tenure a system of employment in which the employee, having served a set probationary period, retains the position indefinitely and may be dismissed only according to certain specific procedures

test manual a manual to accompany standardized tests that typically includes descriptions of the standardization process and the norming groups and gives detailed instructions for administering and scoring the test

time sampling obtaining a record of observed behavior for preset time spans at recurring intervals

token reinforcements objects (such as poker chips, marks, or paper slips) awarded for positive behaviors (as perceived by the reinforcing agent) that may later be exchanged for various types of rewards

variable interval schedule a reinforcement schedule whereby reinforcement is made only to the first response to occur after a certain time interval since the previous reinforcement, and the interval is varied at random

variable ratio schedule a reinforcement schedule whereby reinforcement is made according to the number of times a behavior has occurred since the last reinforcement, and the number of responses required is varied at random

verbal items test items that require written or spoken responses

visual discrimination the act of differentiating between phenomena viewed including objects, forms, letters, or words

INDEX

Absenteeism, 392
Academic Preschool. *See* DISTAR
Accommodation, 147–49
Achievement levels
  grouping by, 18
Achievement tests, 205
Activity centers, 413
Adaptation, 147–49, 180
Adelam, Leone, 264
Administration, 23
Affective development, 38, 119, *142*
  and children's literature, 284–87
  and manipulative materials, 226–28
  and match, 138–42
  and pretend play, 306–308
  and sharing, 328–29
  and toilet training, 122
  in infants and toddlers, 119–22
  in three- to five-year-olds, 122–25
  in six- and seven-year-olds, 125–27
  observing, 187, 192–96
  suppression of feelings, 125–26
Aggression, 63, 131–33
Agility, 94
Aide. *See* Paraprofessional aide
Alienation, 66
Alphenfels, E.J., 59
American Association on Mental
    Deficiencies, 170
American Library Association, 284
American Montessori Society, 410
Ames, L.B., 381, 395
Anderson, C.W., 292
Anderson, M., 413
Anger, 119, 132, 135
Animals, 246, *269–70*, 271
  activities with, *271*
  and affective development, 254–56
  and cognitive and intellectual
    development, 257–70
  and motor development, 252–54
  and social development, 256
  and teaching science, 270
Anticipation, 88
Ants, 250–51, *272*
Aquarium, 247–48, *272*
Art activities. *See* Manipulative
    materials; Sand; Water; Clay;
    Blocks
Ashton-Warner, Sylvia, 331
Assimilation, 147–49, 309–10
Attachment bonds, 121
Attractiveness, 93, *114*
Atwater, Florence, 293
Atwater, Richard, 293
Austin, Mary, 282

Authority, 40–42, 51
Autonomy
  development, 121, 328
  observing, 135
  versus shame or doubt, 65, 120–22
Averill, Esther, 269, 295

Backyard groups/mobile preschools,
    15
Balance, 93–94
Bank Street College of Education, 379
Bank Street model, 379–80, 395,
    407–408, 422
Barbara (geologist), 59–60
Barth, Roland, 387, 422
Barton, Byron, 287
Becker, Wesley, 371
Behavior
  and body type, 92
  cognitive base, 383
  components of, 119
  defiant, 40–41
  environmental influence, 61–64,
    66–67
  exploratory, 88, 98, 123, 150
  operant, 367
  reflexive, 88, 113, 148, 150, 367
  repertoire, 107, 119, 289
    and aggression, 133
    and language, 162
    and social development, 141
  sex-appropriate, 124–25
  shaping, 62–65
  shocking, 123
  teacher
    and student growth, 42
    monitoring, 444–47
    with children, 50–52
Behavioral assessments, 79–81, 106,
    189–203
Behavior Analysis model, 14, 372–74,
    392, 395, *398*
  facilities, 412
  parent-teacher relationship, 427
  time schedules, 406–407
Behaviorist orientation. *See* Environ-
    mentalist orientation
Behavior management, 63
Behavior modification, 63, *398*
Bereiter, Carl, 370–71, 412, 418,
    436–37
Berenstain, Jan, 269
Berenstain, Stan, 269
Berkeley, Ethel, 291
Bessell, H., 329
Bike riding, 95–96

Black English, 161–62
Blocks, 224–25, *244*. *See also* Manipu-
    lative materials
Bloom, Benjamin, 13, 456
Body size, 90–92
Body type, 92
Bollenbach, Carolyn Stoke, 340
Bonsall, Crosby, 289
Brandenburg, Aliki, 264, 281
Brandt, R.M., 335, 423
Branley, Franklyn, 258, 292
Brinkloe, Julie, 264
British infant schools, 335–36
British integrated day model, 387–89,
    395, *399–400*, 422–23
Brooks, June. *See* June
Bronfenbrenner, U., 424
Brown, Margaret Wise, 255, 409
Brown, P., 63
Bruce, V., 315
Burton, Virginia Lee, 275, 292
Bushnell, Don, Jr., 372
Butch (three-year-old), 140

Caldecott medal, 284
Caldwell, B.M., 170
Carl (student), 118–19
Caroline (meteorologist), 59–60
Category systems, 78–79
Causality
  and animals, 260–61
  and children's literature, 291
  and manipulative materials, 234–36
  and pretend play, 311–12
  and sharing, 333
  observing, 174
  preoperational stage, 157–58
Cazden, Courtnay, 347
Certification, 8–11, 19–20, 28–29
Child-care centers, 12, 13, 15, 253–54,
    353–54, *358*
Child development, 454
  basic principles, 65–69, 122
  internal influences, 65
  orientations, 55, 61–68
  sensitivity to, 35
  stage theory, 64–65, 67
    Erikson's, 119–120
    Piaget's, 68
CDA consortium, 11
Child Development Associates (CDAs),
    10–11, *29*
Children
  as companions, 24–26
  feelings toward, 48–52
  knowledge of, 51

Figures in italic indicate references.

Choice, 121
Chomsky, Noam, 152
Chow, S., 375
Clarity, 42
Classification, 383
  and animals, 257–58
  and children's literature, 289
  and manipulative materials, 229–32
  and pretend play, 310–11
  and sharing, 332–33
  in preoperational stage, 154–55
  observing, 172
  of action-images, 148
Classroom
  alternatives, 30
  organization, 276, 390
Clay, 221–22, *244. See also* Manipu-
    lative materials
Client groups, 11
Cognitive and intellectual develop-
    ment, 119, 142, *180–81. See
    also* Causality; Classification;
    Conservation of mass; Conser-
    vation of number; Language de-
    velopment; Number concepts;
    Seriation; Space concepts;
    Time concepts; Written lan-
    guage development
  ages three through seven, 153–72
  and animals, 257–70
  and manipulative materials, 229–41
  and pretend play, 309–15
  and sharing, 332–39
  and social repertoire, 133
  in Cognitive Curriculum, 389–90
  in infants and toddlers, 149–53
  interactionist view, 383
  observing, 146–47, 172–79, 188,
    197–99
  peer influence, 147
  Piaget's stages, 148
  sensitivity to, 171
  stimulating, 179–80
Cognitive Curriculum, 14, 389–90,
    395, *400*
  goals, 437
  outcomes, 392
  parent-teacher relations, 426
  time schedules, 407–408
Cohen, Dorothy, 218
Collier, Ethel, 264
Commitment, 1, 7–8, 28, 32, 35–36,
    41–52, 454
Communication for social interaction,
    130–32
Compensatory education, 13. *See also*
    Disadvantaged children
Competence, 140
Competency-based teacher education,
    10–11
Competition, 126, 422
Concrete operations period, 148

Conflict (developmental), 142
Conflict (interpersonal)
  basis, 132
  in two- to three-year-olds, 121–22
  in three- to four-year-olds, 131–32
  resolution, 37–38, 119, 137, 256,
    353
Conservation, 68
Conservation of mass
  and animals, 260
  and manipulative materials, 232–34
  and pretend play, 311
  observing, 173–74
  preoperational, 156–57
Conservation of number, 155–56, 260
Contingency management, 63
Cooperatives, 426
Crying, 119
Cumulative folder, 437–38, 441
Curiosity, 260–62
Curriculum guides, 349
Curriculum specialist, 16
Curtis (four-year-old), 86–87

Daily log, 444–45
Dalgleish, Alice, 293
Dance, 315
Danny (three-year-old), 448
DARCEE (Early Training Program)
    model, 374–75, 395, *399*
  parent-teacher relations, 426–27
  time schedules, 406
Day care. *See* Child-care centers
Death, 255–56
Decision-making, 7, 28, 121–22, 132,
    288, 449
Deductive thinking, 234
Demonstration and Research Center
    for Early Education at George
    Peabody College for Teachers,
    374
Demonstration schools, 15
Dennison, George, 381
Dependency, 135. *See also* Autonomy
de Regnier, Beatrice Schenk, 236
Descriptive narrative, 76–78
Despair, 65, 120
Developmental crises, 65
Dewey, John, 67, 387, 391
Dialect, 161–62
Differentiation, 87, 96–97
Disabilities, *115*
Disadvantaged children, 13, 18, 370–
    72, 374, 379, 393–94, 424
Discipline. *See* Behavior management;
    Ground rules; Punishment;
    Reinforcement
Disease, 103–105
DISTAR (Academic Preschool/
    Engelmann-Becker model), 14,
    370–72, 392, 395, *398*
  facilities, 412

  goals, 436
  ground rules, 418–19
Distress, 119–20, 134
Dominance, 100–101
Donna (five-year-old), 147, 149
Doubt and shame, 65, 120–21
Downing, J., 100, 168
Dramatic play, 96, 131–32. *See also*
    Pretend play
Dressing, 98
Duvoisin, Roger, 275

Early childhood education
  changes, 12–17
  contextual constraints, 432–34
  employment, 8, 15–17, 19–20, 26,
    28
  enrollment figures, 8
  goals, 14
  opportunities, 13
  programs, 14–15
  roles in, 15–16
  structure, 14
Earthworms, 251, *272*
Eastman, P.D., 269, 295
Ectomorph, 92
EDC Open Education model, 387
Educational Products Information
    Exchange Institute, 384
Education Development Center
    (EDC), 387
Egocentrism, 129–31, 209, 334
Elkin, Benjamin, 290
Elliott, R., 63
Elmore, P., 375
Emily (teacher), 39–41
Employment, 8, 15–17, 19–20, 26,
    28. *See also* Appendix 7
Endomorph, 92
Endurance, 94
Energy level, 39
Engelmann, Siegfried, 370–71, 412,
    418, 436–37
Engelmann-Becker model. *See*
    DISTAR
Enthusiasm, 42
Environment
  and British integrated day, 388
  influence on behavior, 61–64, 66–
    67
  influence on sensitivity, 71
  interactions with, 66–67, 354, 383
  resource, 345–49
Environmentalist models, 428. *See
    also* Behavior Analysis; DARCEE;
    DISTAR; Traditional primary
    school
  facilities, 411–12, 439
  goals, 435–37
  ground rules, 418–19, 440
  programing principles, 365–66

teacher role, 375
time schedules, 403–407, 411, 438
Environmentalist orientation, 61–64, *82*
  approach to planning, 210–11
  expectations for development, 67
  view of language acquisition, 152–53
Equipment, 411. *See also* Facilities; Manipulative materials; Appendix 5
Erikson, Erik, 65, 119–22, 142
Evaluating, 73–74, 201–202
Event sampling, 77
Expectations, of six- and seven-year-olds, 125–27
Expressive art. *See* Art activities; Dramatic play; Pretend play

Facilities, 411, 414–15, *429*, 466–69
  and goals, 417, 439
  and pretend play, 301–304
  and time schedules, 439
  arrangement, 439–40
  environmentalist programs, 411–12
  interactionist programs, 413–17
  maturationist programs, 412–13
Family, 203. *See also* Parent-teacher relations
Family day care, 15
Fantasy play. *See* Pretend play
Fatigue, 71, 105
Fear, 119, 134–35, 308
Featherstone, Joseph, 388
Federal programs, 361
  CDA consortium, 11
  competency credentials, 11
  Florida Parent Education Follow Through model, 426
  Follow Through, 15, 361, 392–94, 426–27
    Bank Street model, 379–80
    Behavior Analysis model, 372
    EDC model, 387
    Engelmann-Becker (DISTAR) model, 371–72
  Head Start, 12–15, *30*, 361, 392–93, 424, 457
    Bank Street model, 379–80
    Behavior Analysis model, 372
    EDC model, 387
    Engelmann-Becker (DISTAR) model, 371–72
    goals, 435
    parent roles, 427–28
    parent-teacher relations, 424, 426–27
    Title I, 424
    Title IV-A of Social Security Act, 14
Feelings, 125–28
Fields, Kay. *See* Kay
Fife, Dale, 264

Filing system, 39
Fisher, Aillen, 258
Five-year-olds
  ability range, 51
  affective development, 123–24
  and literature, 276, 277, 281, 291
  cognitive and intellectual development, 154–56, 158, 161, 260, 281, 291
  early childhood education experience, 365
  handedness, 99
  motor development, 95–96, 98, 305
  pretend play, 309, 312
  sharing, 321
  social development, 131
  teacher responsibilities, 355
Flannel board, 263–64, 279
Flavell, J.H., 150
Flexibility, 42
Flexible grouping, 18
Flexible scheduling, 18
Foran, Robert, 255
Formal operations, 148
Four-year-olds
  affective development, 122–23
  aggressiveness, 131
  cognitive and intellectual development, 155, 158–59, 161, 277, 281, 287
  early childhood education experiences, 365
  motor development, 86–87, 95, 98, 305
  social development, 131
  teacher responsibility, 355
  time schedules, 404–405
Fred (seven-year-old), 147, 149
Freedom, 37–38, 42, 381
Free school movement, 381
Freud, Sigmund, 65
Friedenberg, Edgar, 36, 381
Froebel, 387
Frostig, Marianne, 98
Frustration, 119, 132
Fujikawa, Gyo, 275
Furst, N.F., 42

Gag, Wanda, 281
Games, 96–97, 132
Garelik, May, 258, 264
Garm, Stanley, 91
Geisel, Theodore (Dr. Seuss), 269, 281–82, 295
Generativity
  versus stagnation, 65, 120
Geography, 313, 333–34
Gesell, Arnold, 65, 381, 385, 395
Getman, Gerald, 98
Gilkeson, Elizabeth, 379
Goals, 380, 392, 435–38
God, 256

Goldin, Augusta, 280
Goodman, Paul, 381
Gordon (six-year-old), 24–25
Gordon, Judith, 255
Gordon, I.J., 425
Gordon, Sol, 255
Graham, Margaret, 264
Grammar, 152–53
Grasping, 88–89
Gray, Susan, 374
Green, M., 258
Gregor, Arthur, 290
Grotberg, E.H., 425
Ground rules, 34–35, 37–38, 41, 417–24, *429–30*
  and goals, 441
  developing, 440–41
  general guidelines, 423–24
  in environmentalist models, 418–19
  in interactionist models, 422–23
  in maturationist models, 419–22
Group discussion, 132–33, 138
Grouping, 18, 378, 381–82
Grouping (intellectual process), 148
Growth
  and teacher characteristics, 42
  physical, 90
Guilefoile, E., 295
Guilt, 65, 120

Hall, G.S., 376
Halverson, L.E., 98
Handicapped children, 170. *See also* Disabilities; Retardation
Hanover Nursery School at Dartmouth College, 63
Head Start. *See* Federal programs, Head Start
Head teacher, 16
Health, 103–104
Hengesbough, James, 291
Herndon, James, 36, 381
Hess, R.D., 232, 428
High Scope Institute, 389
Hildebrand, V., 407
Hildreth, G., 101
Hoff, S., 295
Holt, John, 36, 381
Home programs, 15
Horney, Karen, 66
Hospital schools, 15
Hughes, K.M., 335–36
Hunt, J. McVicker, 13, 113, 149, 456
Hurlock, E.B., 103
Hymes, James, Jr., 377
Hyperactivity, 40, 282, 305–306

Identity
  sense of, 122
  versus identity diffusion, 65, 120
Identity diffusion, 65, 120
Idiosyncracies, 72–73

Ilg, F.L., 381, 395
Independence. *See* Autonomy
Index, 389
Individuality, *142*
Inductive thinking, 234
Industry
 sense of, 126
 versus inferiority, 65, 120
Infants and toddlers, 88–89, 119–22,
 129, 149–53
Inference, 77
Inferiority, 65, 120
Inferring, 73–76
Initiative
 development, 122–23
 observing, 135
 versus guilt, 65, 120
Insects, 249–50, *272*
Instructional packages, 349, *351*
Integrated day, 409–11. *See also*
 British integrated day model;
 Open education; Syracuse Re-
 sponsive Care model
Integration, 96–97, 112
Integrity
 versus despair, 65, 120
Intellect, 87
Intellectual structures, 67. *See also*
 Schemas
Intelligence, 148. *See also* IQ
Intelligence tests, 204–205, *212*,
 392–94
Interactionist models, 383–94, 428
 activities, 391
 facilities, 439
 goals, 435, 437
 ground rules, 422–23, 440
 programing principles, 384
 time schedules, 438
Interactionist orientation, 66–68, *82*
 expectations for development, 67–68
 match, 149
 planning, 208–209, 211
 view of cognitive development, 149
 view of language acquisition, 152
Ironmonger, Ira, 264
Intimacy
 versus isolation, 65, 120
Intuitive phase. *See* Preoperational
 stage
Ipcar, Dahlov, 258, 291
IQ, 170, 204–205
Isolation, 65, 120, 419, 421

Jackson, Philip, 46
Janey (student), 330
Jeffrey (student), 40–41
Jimmy (student), 327
Jimmy (three-year-old), 367
Jones, E., 48
Jones, Miss (teacher), 330
Julie (student), 327

June (beginning teacher), 36–38,
 42–43, 51

Karnes, M.B., 170
Kay (beginning teacher), 33–38, 42
Keats, Ezra Jack, 275, 289, 290
Ken (seven-year-old), 24
Kephart, Newell, 98
Kim (six-year-old), 127
Kindergarten, 12–14, 18, 355,
 358–59
Kohl, Herbert, 381
Kohlberg, L., 383
Kohn, Bernice, 289, 291
Kozol, Jonathan, 36
Krauss, Ruth, 284
Kritchevsky, S., 48
Kruss, James, 290

Laboratory schools, 15
Langer, J., 383
Language acquisition, 151–53,
 159–63
Language development, *181–82*
 and animals, 263–64
 and children's literature, 292–93
 and manipulative materials, 238–39
 and pretend play, 313–14
 and sharing, 325, 334–36
 observing, 175–77, 188, 199–200
Lasker, Joe, 285–86
Lay, M. Z., 131
Leaf, Munro, 277
Lee, Lee, 129
Leeper, Ethel, 420
Lenneberg, E.H., 152
Lesson plan, 345
Letter-sound relationship, 167–68
Letting go, 89
Lichtenberg, P., 139
Lionni, Leo, 275
Listening-questioning patterns, 335–36
Literature, 274–80, *295–98*
 and affective development, 284–87
 and cognitive and intellectual devel-
 opment, 289–96
 and motor development, 280–84
 and physical development, 280
 and social development, 287–89
 book corner, 275–76
 easy-to-read, *295*
 periodicals about, *298*
 periodicals for children, *298*
 story time, 275, 277–80
Lobel, Arnold, 270
Locke, John, 61
Lofgren, Ulf, 289
Lucy (four-year-old), 77, 189–202,
 209–10
Lynn (student), 330

McCloskey, Robert, 277, 339

McIntier, Alla, 268
McNeil, D., 152
Magic circle, 329
Mainstreaming, 101, 382
Mammals, 248–49, *272*
Manipulative materials
 and affective development, 226–28
 and cognitive and intellectual development, 229–41
 and motor development, 224–26
 and social development, 228–29
 in environmentalist programs, 412
 in Montessori programs, 386
 kinds of, 242–43
 play, *243–44*
 sensitivity to, 223
 unstructured, 218–19
Mason, Miriam, 293
Masturbation, 103
Match
 and affective development, 138–42
 and behavioral assessment, 208
 and cognitive and intellectual development, 129
 and instructional packages, 349–
 51
 and manipulative activities, 242–43
 and social development, 138–42
 based on motor skills, 111–13
Materials, 411. *See also* Facilities;
 Manipulative materials; Appendix 5
Mathematics activities. *See* Classification; Conservation of mass;
 Conservation of number;
 Number concepts; Seriation
Maturationist models, 376–82, *399*,
 428
 facilities, 412–13, 439
 goals, 435, 437
 ground rules, 419–22, 440
 grouping, 395
 preference for home, 376–77
 programing principles, 377–79
 time schedules, 407–409, 411, 438
Maturationist orientation, 64–66, *82*
 approach to planning, 209–11
 expectations for development, 67
 view of language acquisition, 152
Mealworm jar, 251–52
Mental
 age, 204–205
 overload, 70
 set, 344–49, 356
 structures, 88 (*see also* Schemas)
Merriam, Eve, 290
Merrow, John G.G., II, 10
Mesomorph, 92
Mike (four-year-old), 141
Milgram, Harvey, 291
Minarik, Else, 270, 295
Mistrust, 65, 119–21

Mizumura, Kazue, 264
Modeling
  and language acquisition, 160
  for cognitive and intellectual development, 179
  for formal sharing, 324
  for motor activities, 113
  for social development, 141
  importance for five-year-olds, 123
Models, 361, 364–65, 394, *395–98*
Moffett, James, 325
Montessori, Maria, 385–87, 415–16
Montessori program, 14, 385–87, 395, *399*, 428
  facilities, 415–17
  time schedules, 410
Moore, D.R., 376
Moore, R.S., 376
Motor development, 114, *115*
  and animals, 252–54
  and children's literature, 280–84
  and manipulative materials, 224–26
  and pretend play, 304–306, 315
  and sharing, 326–27
  in infants and toddlers, 87–90
  in three-year-olds, 94–95
  in four-year-olds, 95
  in five- and six-year-olds, 95–96
  in seven-year-olds, 96
Motoric competence, 86–87, 98
Motor intelligence, 87
Movement, 86–87, 93–94
Multiage classrooms, 18
Murphy, Lois, 420
Myller, Rolf, 291
Myrick, Mildred, 270

Nancy (beginning teacher), 38–41, 43
Nancy (three-year-old), 448
Neill, A.S., 36, 381
Nicky (five-year-old), 171–72
Nongraded classrooms, 18
Nonreinforcement, 369
Nonthrivers, 392
Norfield, Mr., (British educator), 347
Norms, 65–66
Norton, D.G., 139
Number concepts
  and animals, 258–60
  and children's literature, 289–91
  and manipulative materials, 229–32
  and pretend play, 310–11
  and sharing, 332–33
  observing, 173
  one-to-one correspondence, 155
Numbering of action-images, 148
Nursery school, 14, 352–53, 358

Observation, *83*, 106–107
  behavioral assessment, 79–81, 106, 189–203
  confidentiality, 80

context, 74–76
  evaluation, 201–202
  event sampling, 77
  guidelines, 80
  in classroom, 202–203
  inference, 200–201
  of affective states, 134–35
  of motor development, 108–10
  of physical characteristics, 107, 110–11
  of self-concept, 135–36
  of social development, 136–38
  recording, 76–82, 106, 200–201. *See also* Behavioral assessments; Category systems; Descriptive narrative
  summarizing, 186–89, 211–12
  time sampling, 77
Observational biases, 72–74
Office of Child Development (OCD), 11
"Open" education, 36–37. *See also* British integrated day model
Open time schedules, 409–11
Operant conditioning, 63
Operant psychology, 61–62
Ordering of action-images, 148
Organizational ability, 41–43
Orientation, 454
Oxenbury, Helen, 290

Palomares, U., 329
Paraprofessional aide, 13, 16, 18, 375, 426–27
Parent-child center, 15
Parent educational specialist, 16
Parenting, 119–21, 232
Parent roles, 426–28
Parent-teacher relations, 35, 127–28, *143*, 203, 424–28, *430*
  child-care centers, 354–55
  developing, 441–42
  home visits, 426
  nursery schools, 353
Patterning, 98
Peer pressure
  among five-year-olds, 124
  among six- and seven-year-olds, 126
Perceptions, 59–60, 149–50
Perceptual development, 114, 115
Perske, Robert, 170
Peters, Miss (teacher), 330
Physical condition, 71
Physical development, 114
  and children's literature, 280
  and sharing, 326
  attractiveness, 93, *114*
  body types, 92
  disabilities, 101–103, *115*
  dominance, 99–101
  gross movements, 93–97
  nervous traits, 103

observing, 187, 189–92
  posture, 92–93
  sensitivity to, 105–106
  size and weight, 90–92
  small muscle development, 97–99
Piaget, Jean, 68, 87–88, 114, 130, 147–51, 160, 180, *181*, 315, 383, 387
Piaget, Lucienne, 88, 150–51
Planning
  Behaviorist approach, 210–11
  goals, 361
  guidelines, 208
  in Cognitive Curriculum, 390
  interactionist approach, 208–209, 211
  maturationist approach, 209–211
  need for, 50
Play. *See also* Pretend play
  and facilities, 412
  and manipulative materials, 228
  associative, 129–31
  cooperative, 131, 329
  in Bank Street model, 379–80
  observing, 136–37
  parallel, 129, 131
  sociodramatic, 301, 308, 313
  solitary, 129
Playfulness, 139–40, 179–80
Play groups. *See* Backyard groups/mobile preschools
Pleasure, 134, 140
Posture, 92–93
Potter, Beatrix, 292
Precious, N., 409
Preconceptual phase. *See* Preoperational stage
Prekindergarten, 14, 17–18, 25
Premack, David, 62, 368, 395
Premack principle, 62–63
Preoperational stage, 148, 153–80
Preparation for teaching, 33–35, 39–42
Prepared environment, 415–17
Preprimary settings, 14
Prescott, E., 48, 392
Pretend play, 95–96, 123, *317. See also* Dramatic play
  among six- and seven-year-olds, 126
  and affective development, 306–308
  and motor development, 304–306, 315
  and social development, 308–309
  assimilation in, 309–10
  cultural component, 300–301
  encouragement of, 308–309
  equipment, 301–304
  Montessori program, 416
  sound effects, 315
  value, 301, 308–10, 316
Primary school, 12, 15, 18, 355, *359*
Problem-solving, 132–33, 287–88, 307

Program decisions, 402–403, 428–29
Program director, 16
Programed instruction, 372–73, 375
Program evaluator, 16
Program organization, 454
Project Follow Through. *See* Federal
    programs, Follow Through
Psychoanalysis, 65
Psychosexual conflicts, 65
Punishment, 369, 419
Puppets, 304

Rambusch, Nancy McCormick, 410
Readiness tests, 205
Reading activities, 275–296. *See also*
    Written language development
Reading readiness, 91, 166–69
Reality, 147, 416
"Reality base," 32–33, 42–43, 51
Record-keeping, 442–49. *See also*
    Observation
Reinforcement, 62–63, 210–11,
    367–76, 418–19, 423
Reporting, 73–74
Reproduction, 255
Resourcefulness, 41, 215, 356, *356–57*,
    454
Responsibility, 423
Responsive Environment model, 407–
    408
Retardation, 170, *182–83*
Rewards
    in Behavior Analysis model, 373–74
Rey, H.A., 292
Rhythm, 94
Roberts, Margaret, 347
Rosenshine, B., 42
Rothschild, Alice, 293
Rousseau, Jean Jacques, 64, 376
Routines, 419–20
Rules, 132, 152

Salary, 19
Sand, 219–20, *244. See also* Manipula-
    tive materials
Scarry, Richard, 289
Schemas, 88, 113–14, 150, 153, 383
Schlein, Miriam, 291, 292
Schneider, Herman, 291
Schneider, Nina, 291
Schoenherr, John, 264
Science activities. *See* Animals;
    Causality; Classification; Con-
    servation of mass; Conserva-
    tion of number; Space concepts;
    Time concepts
School records, 203–204
Self, 66, 122
Self-awareness, 328–29
Self-concept, 135–36, 140–41
Selsam, Millicent, 255, 258, 270,
    289

Sendak, Maurice, 275, 291, 292
Sensitivity, 41, 55, 59–61, 70–73,
    454
    to affective development, 128–29,
        138
    to physical development, 105–106
    to social behavior, 138
Sensorimotor period, 88–89, 148,
    150
Sensory organs, 149–50
Seriation
    and animals, 258
    and children's literature, 291
    and manipulative materials, 229–32
    and pretend play, 310
    and sharing, 332
    observing, 173
    preoperational, 156
"Sesame Street," 160
Seuss, Dr. *See* Geisel, Theodore
Seven-year-olds
    ability range, 51
    affective development, 125–27
    and children's literature, 276–77,
        281, 287, 291, 293
    cognitive development, 155–56, 257,
        260, 262, 264
    motor development, 96, 98–99
    physical development, 91
    pretend play, 309, 311–12, 314
    sharing, 331–32
    social development, 132–33
Sexism, 125
Sex-role identification, 124, 136,
    143, 285–86
Shadows, 236
Shame or doubt, 65, 120
Shapp, Charles, 291
Shapp, Martha, 291
Sharing, *341*
    and affective development, 328–29
    and cognitive and intellectual de-
        velopment, 325, 332–39
    and motor development, 326–27
    and physical development, 326
    and social development, 329–32
    formal, 320–21, 323–26, 329–32,
        339–40
    informal, 320–23, 339–40
Sheldon, W.H., 92
Shipman, V.C., 232
Shower, Paul, 280
Shure, M.B., 133, 141, 162, 288
Sign, 389
Signaling systems, 119, 131
Simon, Norma, 288
Simon, Seymour, 291
Sitting, 89
Six-year-olds
    affective development, 125–27
    and children's literature, 276–77,
        287, 291, 293

cognitive development, 155, 158,
    260, 262, 264
motor development, 95–96, 98–99
physical development, 91
pretend play, 309, 311–12, 314
sharing, 321
social development, 132–33
teacher responsibilities, 355
Skinner, B.F., 61–62, 369, 395
Slobodkina, Esphyr, 280
Small muscle development, 97–99
Smilansky, S., 301, 308
Snakes, 250, *272*
Soar, R., 394
Social development, 119, 129–33, 142
    and animals, 256
    and children's literature, 287–89
    and language development, 162
    and manipulative materials, 228–29
    and match, 138–42
    and pretend play, 308–309
    and sharing, 329–32
    observing, 136–38, 188, 196–97
Songs, *298*
Space concepts
    and animals, 262–63
    and children's literature, 291–92
    and manipulative materials, 236–38
    and pretend play, 312–13
    and sharing, 333–34
    observing, 174
    preoperational, 158
Specialists, 207–208
Speed, 94
Spivack, G., 133, 141, 162, 288
Stages. *See* Child development, stage
    theory
Stagnation, 65, 120
Stallings, J., 392, 446
Standardized tests, 204–207, 449
Stevens, Carla, 255
Stevie (student), 327
Stimuli, 62, 149
Strength, 94
Strictness, 36
Student teaching, 33–34, 37, 39–41
Sucking, 88
Supervision, 23–24
Suzanne (botanist), 59–60
Symbol, 389
Symbolic representation, 150–52
Syracuse Responsive Care model,
    390–91, 395, *400*, 410–11, 417
Syracuse University Early Childhood
    Center

Taboos, 72
Tabula rasa, 61
Target behavior, 63
Teacher-child relations, 347, *357–58*,
    422

Teacher, 16
  as authority, 40, 422–23
  characteristics, 41–42
  outside pressure on, 12, 22–23
  responsibility, 355, 361
  role, 51, 128, 140–41
    environmentalist, 375–76
    interactionist, 388
    maturationist, 378–82
    Montessori, 385–88
    Responsive Care program, 390–91
  training, 9–11
Teacher's manuals, 349
Teaching
  advantages, 21–29
  as career, 30
  as profession, 11–12, 18–19
  creativity, 22–23, 27
  cultural constraints, 455–57
  disadvantages, 21–29
  elementary, 8
  incidental, 332, 345
  individualized, 18, 339, 349–52
  men in, 26, 29
  methods, 22–23
  objectives, 350–51, 361
  preparation for, 17, 449–51, 454–
    55, 457–58
  repertoire, 34–35, 215, 356
  tasks, 46–48, 353
Teasing, 121
Teeth, loss of, 126–27
Tension, 127, 226, 282, 306
Tenure, 19
Terrarium, 247, 271
Thackray, D., 100, 168
Thaddeus (four-year-old), 118–19
Thorndike, Edward, 61
Three-year-olds
  ability range, 51
  affective development, 121–22
  and children's literature, 277, 281,
    287

cognitive development, 152–53,
    155, 158–61
early childhood education experience,
    364–65
egocentrism, 129–31
motor development, 94–98, 114
physical development, 91
self-concept, 140
social development, 131
teacher responsibility, 355
Thrivers, 392
Throwing (balls), 95–96, 224
Time
  organization of, 402–11, 438
Time concepts, 159, 175, 292
  and animals, 263
  and manipulative materials, 238
  and pretend play, 312
  and sharing, 334
Time sampling, 77
Tina (four-year-old), 147, 149
Toilet training, 122
Tolstoi, Alexi, 291
Tommy (student), 164–66
Traditional primary school, 366–67,
    405–406, 419
Training specialist, 16
Transactionists. See Interactionist
  orientation
Trust
  development, 119–21
  versus mistrust, 65, 119–20
Two-year-olds
  affective development, 121–22
  motor development, 89, 96–98

Udry, Janice May, 286–89
Ungerer, Tomi, 275, 293

Valett, R.E., 98
Viorst, Judith, 286
Visual discrimination, 166–68
Vocabulary, 152, 159, 313–14, 331

Water, 220–21, 244. See also Manipu-
    lative materials
Weikart, David, 389, 390, 437
Weikart Cognitive Curriculum. See
  Cognitive Curriculum
Whitehurst, Keturah, 94
Whitney, Mr. (teacher), 330
Wildsmith, Brian, 275
Woods, Nancy. See Nancy
Words
  acquisition, 151–52
  as entities, 167–68
  high frequency, 268–69, 293–94
  meanings, 132, 151, 162–63
Written language development, 182
  and animals, 264–69
  and children's literature, 293–96
  and manipulative materials, 239–41
  and pretend play, 314–15
  and sharing, 336–38
  Ashton-Warner's organic approach,
    331
  assessing difficulty of books, 292–93
  case study (Tommy), 164–66
  decoding, 166–69
  encoding, 169–72
  in Bank Street model, 380
  in DISTAR (Academic Preschool)
    model, 405–406
  in five- to seven-year-olds, 98–99
  left-to-right orientation, 164–65, 169
  observing, 178–79, 188, 200

Yardley, A., 423
Yashima, Taro, 275, 339
Yiang, Len, 292
Ylla (pseud.) Koffler, Camille, 258

Zaffo, George, 275, 281, 289
Zehrback, R.R., 170
Zim, Herbert S., 264
Zion, Gene, 270
Zolotow, Charlotte, 286–87